BRISTOL BS8 2LR,
ENGLAND.
Telephone: (0272) 732211

Birds of the Strait of Gibraltar

To my father

Birds of the
Strait of Gibraltar

by CLIVE FINLAYSON

Illustrated by Ian Willis

T. & A. D. POYSER

London

First published in 1992 by T. & A. D. Poyser Ltd
24–28 Oval Road, London NW1 7DX

United States Edition published by
ACADEMIC PRESS INC.
San Diego, CA 92101

Text set in Bembo
Typeset by Paston Press, Loddon, Norfolk
Printed and bound in Great Britain by
Mackays of Chatham PLC, Chatham, Kent

A catalogue record for this book is available from the British Library

ISBN 0–85661–066–6

Contents

List of Photographs

List of Figures

A Chough searches for food on a mountain pasture. This is an abundant species in most mountain areas, often occurring in large flocks.

List of Tables

Two Eagle Owl chicks at the nest

Preface

The massive and spectacular movements of migratory birds, especially raptors and storks, across the Strait of Gibraltar attracted the attention of the Reverend John White in the 18th Century. He wrote to his brother, Gilbert of Selborne, providing him with evidence of 'the fact of migration'. It was only appropriate that the Strait of Gibraltar should play a significant role in confirming to the scientific community of the day that birds did migrate to southerly winter quarters.

Gibraltar, being a British colony since 1704, provided a southerly outpost for ornithologists, botanists and other naturalists, many of whom were officers of the British Army who spent their leisure time exploring the Spanish, and less frequently the Moorish, countryside. The most prominent among these was Howard Irby who wrote *The Ornithology of the Straits of Gibraltar* in 1875, followed by a revised and enlarged edition in 1895, which became the standard reference work for the area. Irby's thorough and systematic works are of great value since they provide an accurate picture of the avifauna of the area before Man's destructive hand started to inflict serious damage in this zone of the globe. Irby's works are well supported by the vivid descriptions of birds and country-side provided by Willoughby Verner (*My Life among the Wild Birds in Spain*, 1910) and Abel Chapman and Walter Buck (*Wild Spain*, 1893, and *Unexplored Spain*, 1910) as well as a series of papers which appeared in journals, principally *The Ibis*.

The early interest in the ornithology of the Strait has persisted, but the early investigations were not followed up in so much detail. Visitors to the area published irregularly, and not always convincingly. In Gibraltar itself, an interesting development took place in the late 1960s when a group of local youngsters took up the systematic recording of bird movements and started to publish annual reports. This group was the precursor of the Gibraltar Ornithological Society which today runs the Strait of Gibraltar Bird Observatory (SGBO). Until 1985, the closed border between Gibraltar and Spain meant that the Society's activities were restricted to the Rock of Gibraltar. The body of information that was accumulated led to the publication of *The Birds of Gibraltar* in 1980. This was published just after the important work on the Tangier Peninsula, *Les oiseaux de la Peninsule Tingitane*, by Pineau and Giraud-Audine in 1979.

My own interest in birds was generated in the late 1960s, chiefly by the amazing movements of hawks and kites over the Rock. The works of Irby and Verner, in particular, triggered my imagination and spurred me towards a disciplined approach to the subject. After working on the comparative biology of the Swift and the Pallid Swift at Gibraltar for my doctoral thesis at Oxford, I returned to the Rock and concentrated my efforts on studying the movements of seabirds past the Strait of Gibraltar. The opening of the border in 1985 allowed me to start a survey of Irby's countryside and these, hitherto largely unpublished, results together with the results of my earlier work on Gibraltar form the basis of this book.

In writing this book I was determined not to produce another systematic list of the birds of an area, which would have been the easy, but to my mind dull, thing to do. I have therefore relegated this aspect to an Appendix and have concentrated on describing aspects of the bird ecology of the Strait, in the first part on the migratory movements of the main groups—soaring birds, other land birds, waterbirds, and seabirds—and in the second part on the breeding and wintering communities and the ornithological importance of the region. The list of references is large but not regionally exhaustive. I have made no attempt to refer to every paper that has made reference, directly or indirectly, to birds and the Strait. I have included only those which I felt were of relevance to the text.

There are many people who deserve acknowledgement since they have all, in some measure, contributed towards this book. I would not be writing these lines today had it not been for the stimulus which my late father provided many years ago when he introduced me to the study of ornithology and the works of Irby. My wife Geraldine has accompanied me regularly in the field and has always been at hand to provide encouragement and good ideas. Her participation in this work has been indispensable. More recently, my son Stewart has accompanied me in the field and convinced me of the enthusiasm and love for nature which young children have when they are exposed to it from an early age.

Of my many colleagues in the Gibraltar Ornithological Society, who have spent countless hours with me in the field, I must highlight Harry Van-Gils, Ernest Pardo and Paul Acolina, who have been friends and tireless field workers, never concerned about the time of day or night or the weather conditions in which we were working. Dr John Cortés, whom I have known since my earliest days in school, has been a committed conservationist with a wide general knowledge of ecology who has always been available to discuss scientific matters. David Price, who worked with me for several years on seabird migration while he was lighthouse keeper at Gibraltar, and Steve Holliday, who was the Strait of Gibraltar's first recorder, have been important contributors to the work presented in this book.

I am extremely grateful to those who have patiently and very professionally commented on the various chapters of this book in draft: Dr Juan Amat, Dr Franz Bairlein, Dr W. R. P. Bourne, Dr Nigel Collar, Richard Porter and Dr Jose Luis Tellería.

Finally, I acknowledge the help and contribution of the following: Betty Allen, Fernando Barrios, Marnie Clark, Brian Etheridge, Joe Fiteni, Andrew Fortuna,

Dr Ernest Garcia, Alfonso Gonzalez Carbonell, Martin Caruana, Dr José María Fernandez-Palacios, Michael Grech, Dean Hashmi, Mario A. J. Mosquera, Jesus Parody, Charles Perez, Colin Pomeroy, Bill Quantrill, Rowena Quantrill, Darrien Ramos, Nigel Ramos, Vincent Robba, Paul Rocca, Roger Rutherford, Jeffrey Saez, Nigel Shennan, Phil Stidwill, Brian Thomas, David Tomlinson, Andrew Upton, Alberto Vega, Andrew Williams, Dr Steve Wratten.

Clive Finlayson

A female Goshawk. One of the typical resident tree-nesting raptors of the oak woods of the Strait.

CHAPTER 1

Introduction

The Strait of Gibraltar is a narrow channel, 14 km wide at its narrowest point between the Spanish coast northeast of Tarifa and the Moroccan coast at Ras Cires. To its north lies the Iberian Peninsula and to its south Morocco. This is the geographical area covered by this book, approximately that covered in Irby's (1875, 1895) *Ornithology of the Straits of Gibraltar*. Place names referred to in the text, and the main topographical and geographical features, are illustrated in Figures 1 and 2. Throughout the book references to 'the Strait' or 'the Strait area' refer to the Strait of Gibraltar as defined in Chapter 1.

On the Iberian side, the Strait area extends from the Marismas del Guadalquivir (including the Coto Doñana) in the north-west, southeastwards across the northern fringe of the Province of Cádiz and south towards the Mediterranean coast of Málaga Province at Marbella. The area is dominated by the Triassic and Jurassic limestone mountain chain of the Serranía de Ronda in the north-east, with the highest peak the Torrecilla (1919 m) in the Sierra de las Nieves. This

1

(a)

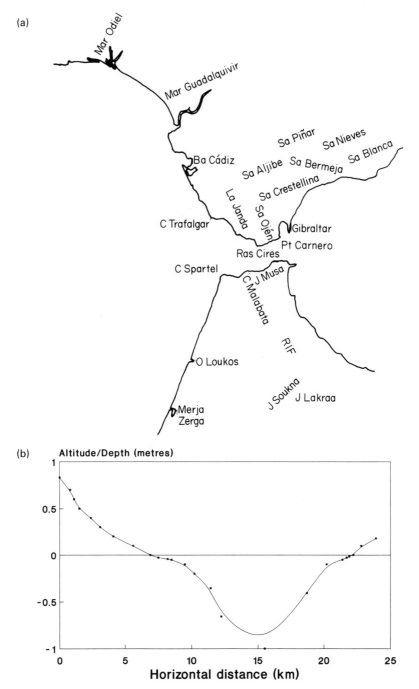

(b)

Figure 1. (a) Main topographical and geographical features of the Strait of Gibraltar. (b) Profile of the Strait of Gibraltar between Guadalmesí and Ras Cires.

Figure 2.   Main place names mentioned in text.

mountain mass includes the Sierra Blanca, close to the coast at Marbella (1270 m), and the peaks of the Sierra del Pinar close to Grazalema (1654 m). Southwest of the Serranía de Ronda lies the impressive coastal Sierra Bermeja (1449 m), composed of red volcanic peridotite rock. West and southwest of this area, gentler mountains stretch down to the shores of the Strait between Tarifa and Punta del Carnero. These are siliceous (Tertiary sandstone) rocks of younger age than the limestone. The sandstone sierras are known as the Aljibe-Ojén complex, and their highest point is the Aljibe itself (1092 m). Isolated outcrops of limestone appear within these sandstones, the most conspicuous being Sierra Crestellina (926 m) and the Rock of Gibraltar (426 m). The acidic sandstone sierras contrast with the alkaline soils of the limestone mountains. This difference is of significance to their vegetation (e.g. Finlayson & Cortes, 1987), including tree species composition (see Chapter 6). To illustrate this, the main physical areas and potential vegetation formations in the province of Cádiz are illustrated in Figures 3 and 4 as an example.

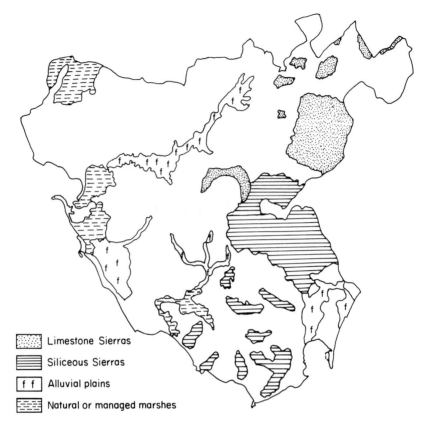

Figure 3.   Main physical characteristics of the Province of Cádiz (after Acosta Bono, 1984).

The profiles of the Strait where the mountains reach the sea are dramatic, and the presence of a gentler shelf on the European side is important in determining the feeding distribution of some seabirds and cetaceans (see Chapter 5).

West of the mountain chains are lowland areas, largely dominated by agricultural landscapes such as the campiñas of Jerez, where vines, sunflowers and beet are grown, and including land drained from marshes, for example La Janda and Trebujena. A number of large rivers flow westwards from the sierras towards the Atlantic, the largest and best-known being the Guadalquivir, which forms the huge marshland complex of the Marismas del Guadalquivir (see Chapter 7). Other important rivers are the Guadalete, opening to the sea at Cádiz Bay, and the Barbate, opening into the Atlantic northwest of the Strait. The rivers running into the Mediterranean are comparatively smaller, the Guadiaro being the largest. Smaller rivers (Palmones, Guadarranque, Guadalmesí) open into Gibraltar Bay or the Strait.

The Moroccan side of the Strait approximates to the area of the Tangier

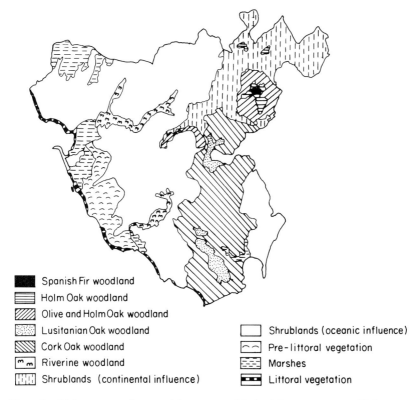

Spanish Fir woodland

Holm Oak woodland

Olive and Holm Oak woodland

Lusitanian Oak woodland

Cork Oak woodland

Riverine woodland

Shrublands (continental influence)

Shrublands (oceanic influence)

Pre-littoral vegetation

Marshes

Littoral vegetation

Figure 4.   Main vegetation features of the Province of Cádiz (after Acosta Bono, 1984).

Peninsula (Pineau & Giraud-Audine, 1979), with a westerly extension south to include the Merdja Zerga (see Chapter 7). In many respects it is a mirror image of the Iberian side, with the limestone mountains of the Rif stretching northwards to reach the sea at the Jebel Musa (841 m), and the highest peak the Jebel Lakraa (2159 m) on the southeastern limit of the Moroccan Strait area. West of this limestone chain are lower hills (maximum 1610 m, at Jebel Soukna) which are separated from it by a long depression associated with the upper reaches of the Laou and Martil rivers. To the west of these hills are the lowland plains, which in places reach the Atlantic as estuarine marshes, the most extensive marshes being those of the Loukos River.

The rivers on the Moroccan side are generally smaller than those of the Spanish side. The Loukos and the smaller Tahadart (and their tributaries) open into the Atlantic, and the Martil and Laou are the main rivers reaching the Mediterranean coast. Only small streams empty into the Strait.

The coastlines of the Strait converge towards it in a southwesterly and southeasterly manner on the Iberian side, reaching an apex at Tarifa, and in a northeasterly and northwesterly manner along the Moroccan coast. The two sides of the Strait therefore roughly resemble two triangles intersecting at the Strait itself, an important feature which influences the movements of migratory birds in the area. The Atlantic coastline along both sides of the Strait is dominated by long stretches of sandy beaches, punctuated by occasional estuaries, marshes and small cliffs along the essentially low-lying coast (e.g. west of Barbáte and south of Larache). In contrast, moving eastwards into the Strait and the Mediterranean, the coast is predominantly rocky as the mountains reach the sea, and sandy beaches (which are smaller than those on the Atlantic coasts) occur scattered in coves and inlets and, less frequently, along longer stretches (e.g. Eastern Beach, Gibraltar, to the Guadiaro Estuary). Natural lagoons are typical of the western lowlands of the Iberian side of the Strait, and artificial reservoirs occur on both sides.

CLIMATE

The Strait has a Mediterranean climate, characterized by long, hot and dry summers and wet and mild winters (Figure 5), though it is tempered by the proximity of the Atlantic. The Spanish side of the Strait lies between the 24 and 25°C July isotherms in the north-east and the 23 and 24°C in the south-west (Escardo, 1970), with mean January temperatures of 11 to 12°C throughout the area. Local conditions modify this general pattern and the higher mountains are generally cooler and sustain snow in the winter.

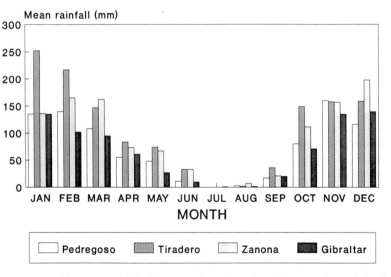

Figure 5.   Monthly mean rainfall for four sites on the northern shore of the Strait (Spanish data from Fernandez-Pasquier, 1982).

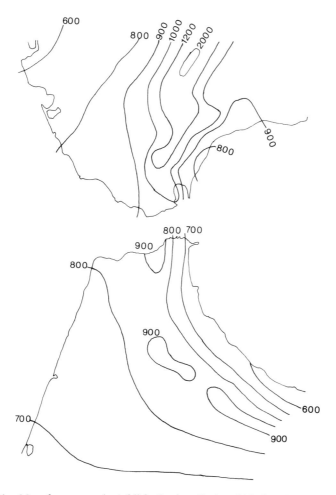

Figure 6. Map of mean annual rainfall for Southern Spain and Northern Morocco.

Most of the rain comes between October and April, and although it can fall even in mid-summer, it is then usually irregular and brief in duration. Because there is considerable variation in the onset of the rains, the drought may end at any stage between late August and November, though mid-September to mid-October is the most usual time. On the Spanish side, the town of Grazalema has the highest annual rainfall in Spain (1200 mm), and the higher peaks on the Moroccan side reach this level, in some cases even attaining 2000 mm per annum (Pineau & Giraud-Audine, 1979). The drier areas, along the Atlantic littoral or in rain shadows, average 600 mm a year (Figure 6).

The most dramatic meteorological feature of the Strait is the predominance of strong winds, mainly easterly and westerly, i.e. lateral winds. These blow over the Strait on 87% of all days in summer and autumn (Bernis, 1980). Tarifa has a mean monthly wind speed of over 22 km/h with gusts of over 109 km/h every month (Bernis, 1980). Winds are not as strong away from the Strait itself, although the effects of high winds over the Strait are often felt right up to the limits of the area covered by this book. Thus Cádiz, 85 km away from Tarifa, has mean monthly wind speeds below 13 km/h (Bernis, 1980).

Easterly, humid winds (locally termed Levante), resulting from eastward extensions of the Azores anticyclone, predominate during the summer months and form dense clouds over mountain peaks, especially near the coast, the most conspicuous and best known being the cloud that forms over the Rock of Gibraltar. Winds can be very strong in summer, affecting the western sectors of the Strait more dramatically than further east. Between October and April, the regular passage of Atlantic depressions causes westerly winds to blow over the Strait, and they often bring with them rain associated with passing cold fronts. At Gibraltar, from 1930 to 1971, westerly winds accounted for 41.8% of the days in spring but for only 30.6% of the days in summer and early autumn, and easterlies were dominant in summer and autumn (53.9% of days) but less so in spring (49.6% of days) (Cortés *et al.*, 1980).

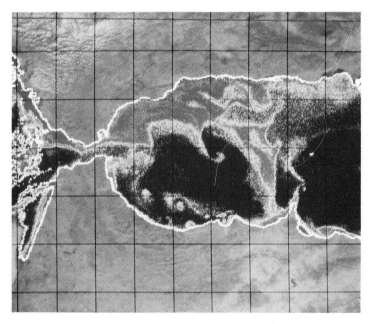

Satellite view of the Strait of Gibraltar, with Gibraltar showing clearly at the north-eastern (top right hand) corner of the narrow Strait. Tarifa is the southern-most point on the European (northern) shore. (Courtesy of Deutsche Luft und Raumfahrtgesellschaft)

Variation in wind strength and direction between years is generally high. For example, in some years easterlies may predominate throughout the summer and, less usually, westerlies may do so for several weeks without interruption.

Fog banks are common in the Strait, especially in the summer, and inland in winter in calm conditions. During the summer, inshore sea breezes with a westerly component often blow over the Strait in the afternoon, in calm or light westerly conditions, and then disperse morning fog patches.

THE STRAIT OF GIBRALTAR AND BIRD MIGRATION

Since Africa and Europe last became separated at the Strait, around five and a half million years ago (Hsu, 1983), and the Mediterranean once more became a sea as the Atlantic filled it via the Strait of Gibraltar, the area of the Strait must have played a prominent role in the movements of birds (and of other animals such as tuna, turtles or cetaceans). With subsequent global climatic changes, the shape of the Strait's coastline varied as sea levels rose and fell, and with these variations so must the width of the channel have varied. There has also been shifting of climatic belts, altering the abundance and distribution of bird species in the Palaearctic (e.g. Moreau, 1972). Consequently, migratory patterns must have evolved several times in different directions in response to these variations. The present

Aerial view of the Rock of Gibraltar from the south-east. This is a view which many Palaearctic migrants will see in the spring as they arrive in Europe from Africa. (Photograph: Sigurd Tesche.)

migratory patterns, which form the basis of the next four chapters of this book, and species distributions (Chapters 6 and 7) must have evolved in the last 10 000 years, since the climatic change at the end of the most recent glaciation. It is fair to assume that, in such a relatively short evolutionary time, the migratory strategies of the different species are unlikely to have been perfected.

In addition to the gradual and progressive evolution of behavioural patterns in response to changing climatic conditions, shorter term variations cause shifts in migratory patterns. The recent changes in wintering areas of Blackcaps (Chapters 3 and 6) illustrate the rapidity of evolutionary responses to changing environmental conditions, through differential selection of individuals wintering in different latitudes.

The present patterns of migration between the Palaearctic and Africa are considered in this book in relation to the specific migratory picture observed from the Strait. These are examined within a wider framework of the significance of the history of the climatic changes of the last 10 000 years in moulding both the present distributions of species and their present migratory tactics. It is my opinion that the constantly changing resources in the Palaearctic and African zones utilized by Palaearctic migrants creates an almost continuous movement of individuals of many species, both land- and seabirds, outside the breeding season. This view, central to the book, is a departure from the traditional view that migratory birds have two homes (breeding and wintering areas), and sees them as being instead in virtually continuous movement in relation to seasonally changing resources, except when nesting requirements demand a greater degree of residency.

From these basic tenets, an interpretation can be made of what is regarded a subsystem of the Palaearctic–African system, between the western Palaearctic and West Africa. Despite comments that the migration of land birds across the Mediterranean is broad-fronted (e.g. Casement, 1966), there is strong evidence in support of migrants following specific routes between breeding grounds and wintering areas. There is overwhelming evidence in favour of southwesterly routes in autumn, by central and western European birds, through Iberia and the Strait area (Moreau, 1961; Bernis, 1962; Finlayson, 1979). Many species are said to exhibit migratory divides, with some populations migrating southwest in autumn and others southeast. It is now generally accepted that areas of the central Mediterranean, the longest crossings, and central Sahara, the most barren sectors, are avoided by the main flows of migrants (Bairlein, in press), so creating this east–west divide. This division applies also to many pre-Saharan migrants

An immature Bonelli's Eagle. A typical cliff-nesting raptor of the region.

that do not have to cross the desert at all but nevertheless migrate southwest to winter in Iberia and northwest Africa. The east–west division is most accentuated in the soaring birds, which are most restricted because of their method of locomotion (Chapter 2). Within this western subsystem, I examine the relationship between Mediterranean areas of Iberia and Morocco and tropical West Africa, and propose that Iberian–Moroccan populations are evolving independently, especially in cases where Iberian–Moroccan populations are isolated from others in western Europe.

There is an analogous situation among marine birds (Chapter 5). Those which breed in the Mediterranean do so mostly in the western sector, which is the richest in plankton. They invariably leave the Mediterranean in summer, when the stratification of the sea reduces primary production. The Strait and adjacent Atlantic areas, the English Channel and Bay of Biscay and, especially, the coasts of West Africa are vital areas for these birds outside the breeding season. Once the Mediterranean's food resources improve with the autumn and winter storms, the western end of the sea regains some value and the Mediterranean breeding seabirds return along with northeast Atlantic and Black Sea birds, which utilize this sea as an extended portion of the proximate Atlantic feeding areas. The continuity of movement in search of resources outside the breeding season is most pronounced in seabirds, which, along with aerial plankton feeders, exploit the most rapidly changing environments.

EVOLUTION OF BIRD MIGRATION

A summary of the way migration is thought to have evolved in birds is essential in a book investigating the movements of birds through an area of such importance as the Strait.

The evolution of bird migration has been considered by several authors (e.g. Salomonsen, 1955; Lack, 1968; von Haartman, 1968; Baker, 1978). In general, it is thought that migratory behaviour evolves in populations in which the advantages of leaving the breeding grounds in autumn outweigh the disadvantages of migration, so that the individuals which migrate are better off than those which remain in the breeding grounds. According to von Haartman (1968), resident species in temperate areas tolerate lower survival in winter in exchange for the increased reproductive effort achieved by being at the breeding grounds at the start of the spring. Migrants might obtain increased winter survival in favourable tropical environments, but would be less successful in breeding because of their late return to the breeding grounds.

In areas of low environmental stability and predictability, if part of a population evolves migratory behaviour due to an absence of site fidelity, and if its productivity is as a result higher than in the remaining population, then natural selection will favour migration (Alerstam & Enckell, 1979). This leads to situations where completely migratory land bird species originate from areas of low environmental stability. Migration is then directed to areas where environmental stability and production during the breeding season are higher than in the non-breeding areas.

Site fidelity is strongly selected for in birds because of its many advantages — knowledge of surroundings improves feeding, shelter and avoidance of predation (Greenwood & Harvey, 1976) — and has been well documented (Greenwood, 1980; Lawn, 1982). It follows that site fidelity is an important factor countering the evolution of migration.

The outcome of competition in the non-breeding grounds is vital in the evolution of migratory behaviour (Alerstam & Enckell, 1979). Residents should be at an advantage because of the advantages of site fidelity, but several factors will eventually decide the outcome of competition: if the non-breeding areas are in a seasonal environment (e.g. pastures of the Strait; Chapter 6), then the migrants may not be at such a great disadvantage since site fidelity among residents will be low; if the non-breeding areas are unpredictable in resource availability from year to year, then residents will be unable to gain significant advantages. The advantages of site fidelity are smaller in structurally simple niches (e.g. the sea or the air or secondary successional habitats), and it is in simple habitats that migrants are expected to be at an advantage. Where the niche of a species is not fully occupied by residents, then migrants may be able to exploit marginal areas.

O'Connor (1985) compared migratory and resident strategies, based on a study of nine British passerines. When under high population pressure, resident species bred earlier and produced more offspring than did migratory species. Residents were able to improve chick survival by delaying laying so that the young were raised in better vegetated habitat or on the richer food supply available later in the season. Nevertheless, O'Connor's analysis suggested that, even with an early start to breeding, resident species did not produce more fledglings than migrants did, and may generally produce fewer. Thus, von Haartman's (1968) prediction has been contradicted, although it could be shown to hold if juvenile survival could be shown to be higher in birds that produce offspring earlier in the season, and there is some evidence for this (Kluyver, 1966). If this were the case, the advantages for residents over migrants would therefore not lie with increased productivity but rather in improved post-fledging or adult survival. Migrants would produce more offspring, with a consequent cost in terms of adult survival. O'Connor suggested that increased adult mortality in migrants could be due to migrants being in poorer condition, as a result of increased reproductive effort, when preparing for the post-nuptial migration. Von Haartman's hypothesis could be considered in terms of advantages open to residents, which could choose the safer habitats by virtue of being present in the breeding grounds early in the season. O'Connor concluded that residents could be regarded as having population levels near their carrying capacities, whereas migrants are more likely to exploit marginal habitats not yet exploited by competitively superior residents.

Several hypotheses have been put forward to explain why some birds migrate further from the breeding areas than others. Pienkowski & Evans (1985) have

Long-eared Owl which breeds in pine woods in the area and whose numbers are augmented in winter with the arrival of small numbers from the north.

summarized these into non–competition and competition models. A classic non-competition hypothesis (which actually is not well supported by evidence) is that larger birds are better able to spend the winter further north, in accordance with Bergman's rule. Greenberg (1980) has suggested that the amount of time spent in the non-breeding area, which is devoted to maximizing survival, is determined by the length of the profitable season devoted to reproduction. Assuming that wintering grounds furthest from the breeding grounds are best for survival, then the longer the migrants spend in the wintering grounds, the greater the overall chances of survival by comparison with a less distant wintering site, once the costs of migration are taken into account. On the other hand, competition models propose that birds try to winter as near to the breeding areas as possible, but that some are displaced further away by competition (Cox, 1968; Gathreaux, 1982). Pienkowski & Evans have argued that the available evidence for waders in the eastern Atlantic suggests that this is indeed the case.

Partial migration occurs when a proportion of the population is resident and a proportion migrant (Lack, 1943, 1944). Laboratory experiments have demonstrated that the resident and migratory behaviours in populations of Blackcaps and Robins are genetically controlled (Berthold & Querner, 1981; Biebach, 1983). This contrasts with the view that behavioural dominance determines which individuals can set up territories and which are forced to move away in the autumn (Kalela, 1954; Gathreaux, 1978). Lundberg (1987) analysed partial migration from the point of view of an evolutionary stable strategy (ESS) (Maynard Smith, 1974), and pointed out that a balanced genetic polymorphism will result only if the fitness of the genotype is related to its frequency (Fisher, 1930). Lundberg suggested that partial migration can be regarded as a conditional strategy, with frequency–dependent choice which may be conditioned by individual asymmetries such as social dominance. Biebach's (1983) suggestion that partial migration has evolved as a 'bet-hedging' strategy, regulated by a genetic dimorphism, with parents producing resident and migrant offspring, could not be easily explained.

Under certain conditions some species will exhibit delayed autumn migration, remaining in the breeding area throughout the winter when conditions remain favourable (Haila *et al.*, 1986). Delayed autumn migration may be viewed as an extreme and more flexible form of partial migration, since all individuals have the potential to move away from the wintering area if conditions become unfavourable. Some species may survive from one breeding season to the next by migrating all the time in search of suitable resources (Haila *et al.*, 1986), a theme which is developed later in this book.

Stop-over areas are important to migrating birds (Rappole & Warner, 1976). Migration has been viewed as occurring in a series of physiological alternations between states of increased feeding and storage of excess lipid (*Zugdisposition*) and sustained migratory activity (*Zugstimmung*) (Groebbels, 1928; Berthold, 1975). Individual birds alternate between the two strategies during the course of migration. Those which stop at intermediate points and are in a state of fattening will attempt to remain and set up feeding territories (Bibby & Green, 1980), although they may be forced to move by other individuals (Mehlum, 1983a,b). Those which are forced to settle but are in a state of migratory activity will resume the journey quickly. These behavioural patterns are evident in migrants pausing in mid-Sahara at oases or in mid-desert (Bairlein, in press), fat migrants resting and continuing the journey quickly and lean ones actively feeding to regain lost weight.

Mechanisms of avoiding interspecific competition in stop-over areas (for example, habitat occupation) are known to occur (Bairlein, 1983), and differences in passage periods between closely related species may have evolved, in part at least, to avoid competition in such areas (Abramsky & Safriel, 1980). There is only a small step between using a series of stop-over areas on the way to or from a more permanent wintering area and using a series of semi–permanent areas in succession outside the breeding season. The use of the same stop-over areas by individual migrants in successive years (Moreau, 1961), and recurrence in winter quarters (Moreau, 1972), are adaptations which may improve individual chances of survival until the next breeding season, for example through knowledge of a site. In certain cases, if not most, there appears to be sufficient flexibility to allow a change of site if conditions are unsuitable in any particular year (Finlayson, 1981). Similarly, physiological strategies associated with migratory behaviour, such as fat deposition, are also utilised over greater periods of the year, an excellent example being that of the Crag Martin at Gibraltar in midwinter (see Chapter 8).

CHAPTER 2

Migration of Soaring Birds

The existing patterns of migration within the Palaearctic and between the Palaearctic and African (Ethiopian) regions, and hence the migratory patterns observed over the Strait of Gibraltar, have evolved since the end of the last glaciation, 10000 years ago. Before this, the Strait probably first became an important barrier between Iberia and North Africa around 5 million years ago, when the waters of the Atlantic broke through to fill the drying Mediterranean (Hsu, 1983), and it has remained so ever since.

Gibraltar, with its many limestone caves rich in deposits, has been the source of a great variety of skeletal remains. Many species of bird have been identified from deposits in Gibraltar's caves (Duckworth, 1911, 1912; Breuil, 1922; Garrod *et al.*, 1928; Eastham, 1968), showing the changing distribution of species associated with the successive phases of the last glaciation. The deposits include such northern species as the White-tailed Eagle, Long-tailed Duck, Red-throated Diver, Velvet Scoter and Little Auk. Post-glacial remains, however, are consistent with current species distributions (Waechter, 1964; Eastham, 1968).

The vegetation of southwest Iberia and northwest Africa changed considerably during the glacial periods. At the height of the last glaciation, 18000 years ago,

17

southwest Iberia was covered in mixed woodland, while much of Europe was covered by tundra (Moreau, 1972). No Mediterranean vegetation as we know it today existed at that time. The recovery concomitant with climatic amelioration appears to have been rapid; much of Europe was covered in woodland by about 7000 years ago, when temperatures were higher than today. Most of Iberia was covered in Mediterranean forest, maquis or garigue by about 5000 years ago (Moreau, 1972).

Changes in vegetation, not only in the immediate vicinity of the Strait but throughout Europe, must have caused changes in the migration patterns and species' abundance. The use of the Strait by birds on migration must have changed accordingly. Changes in sea levels will also have caused modifications, though on a smaller scale. As temperatures rose (to above those of the present day) the sea level rose around Gibraltar; the Rock of Gibraltar was then a small offshore island, and the Strait must have been wider than it is today. During colder periods the sea level dropped, and the Strait must have been considerably narrower and easier to cross.

During periods of low temperatures, when the belt of Mediterranean vegetation was displaced well to the south, species such as the Subalpine Warbler, Bee-eater or Short-toed Eagle would not have featured as migrants across the Strait. Others, such as the Wheatear, must have been much more abundant than at present (Moreau, 1972). The migration of soaring birds would have been particularly affected. A number of species must have been scarcer than after the glaciation, for example, White Stork, Black Stork, Honey Buzzard, Black Kite (all the fossil remains of kites from Gibraltar during the glacial phases are of Red Kite, which is essentially only a winter visitor today), Egyptian Vulture, Short-toed Eagle, Montagu's Harrier, Sparrowhawk, Booted Eagle, Lesser Kestrel and Hobby. Other species may have reached the area as migrants or winter visitors in greater numbers than at any other time. These may have included White-tailed Eagle, Hen Harrier, Rough-legged Buzzard, Merlin and Gyrfalcon. The period following the last glaciation almost certainly marked the heyday of soaring bird migration across the Strait. Subsequently, as Man began to modify habitats, pollute the environment and directly persecute species, numbers have probably declined considerably until the present day.

While the importance of the Strait to migrating soaring birds (essentially storks and raptors) must therefore have changed considerably over time, the existing pattern has probably been relatively unchanged since the end of the last glaciation. The concentration of migrants over the Strait is not exclusive to raptors and storks, although it is probably most pronounced in these species because of their flight strategy. Small birds fly slower than large ones, as a rule, because they are able to remain airborne for longer by flying at minimum-power speed (Pennycuick, 1969). Such endurance may be important in emergencies, especially if a migrant is blown far off course and becomes lost over the sea. In such an event, the best tactic is to slow down to minimum-power speed and remain airborne as long as possible in the hope of being carried towards land by the wind (Pennycuick, 1969). This is a major problem facing large soaring birds since,

Jebel Musa, Morocco from Punta Carnero, Spain. At its narrowest point the Strait of Gibraltar is 14 km wide and it is this gap which most soaring birds aim to cross in light winds.

because of their flight strategy, they are unable to endure emergencies over the sea for long periods. There is no doubt that a short sea-crossing minimizes this risk and, as will be seen later in this chapter, soaring birds are reluctant to make even a short crossing when unfavourable winds increase the risk of being drifted out to sea.

The dependence of soaring birds on the short sea-crossing is most accentuated in the largest species, which rely to a great extent on soaring flight with little flapping (Gibraltar examples include Griffon Vulture, White Stork or Short-toed Eagle). These birds are probably unable to fly over the sea for a long time, and they are often seen to arrive over Gibraltar in spring in poor condition, attempting to land, after crossing the 21 km of sea. Most other (so-called) soaring birds regularly utilize flapping flight and are able to cross longer stretches of sea. Nevertheless, they too congregate over the Strait in large numbers, probably to avoid the unnecessary risks consequent to excessive periods out of sight of land.

The need for large raptors to congregate over narrow sea-crossings is probably necessary for several reasons. It would be impossible for raptors to migrate in successive 'hops' using intermediate stop-over areas for refuelling. A sudden arrival of large numbers at an area for a brief period, all attempting to feed, would create excessive demands on the stop-over area; it would in any case be very difficult for individual raptors to disperse from flocks and defend feeding territories. Yet, there are sound reasons why raptors should migrate in flocks: in the few cases of raptors that do feed on migration (e.g. insectivorous falcons), flocking could improve feeding efficiency (Kerlinger, 1989). Furthermore, travelling in flocks is thought to improve orientation in some species, for example the Honey Buzzard. The concentration of their passage over a brief period increases the chances of individuals coming into contact and forming large flocks (Thake, 1980). Finally, raptors travelling in flocks increase their efficiency at locating and utilizing thermals (Kerlinger, 1989). Of these factors, all of which are probably significant in different species and situations, the location of thermals is likely to be the most important in the case of those species that depend heavily on soaring.

Most raptors fast during the migratory journey, which is performed in a single movement (with rest periods at night when soaring flight is made impossible by the absence of thermals), since large gatherings preclude the utilization of stop-over feeding areas. This in turn means that, as their size imposes constraints on the amount of fat they can carry (Pennycuick, 1969), they must employ less energy-demanding forms of flight, such as soaring and gliding, rather than flapping. Long flights over the sea, with little opportunity to use thermals, must be avoided, with the consequent concentration of individuals at narrow sea-crossings. Some of these soaring birds would probably be quite capable of crossing longer stretches of sea (in fact, stronger fliers such as Honey Buzzards regularly cross from Italy to Tunisia), but the crossing would drain them of so much energy as to seriously reduce the chances of completion of the migration.

There are, therefore, strong selection pressures on large birds to favour routes that avoid long sea-crossings. A large range of raptors and two species of storks migrate regularly between the Palaearctic and Africa, and the Mediterranean Sea presents a formidable barrier to their migration (Moreau, 1972). Their routes have evolved in relation to the locations of the breeding grounds and the wintering areas (both determined by ecological factors) and, rather than being the shortest possible route, have been modified by the need to avoid long sea crossings. Thus, Swiss Black Kites are known to migrate southwest towards the Iberian Peninsula in late summer (Bernis, 1966) so as to cross into North Africa via the Strait, even though a more direct route would be possible over the Mediterranean Sea.

CHARACTERISTICS OF SOARING BIRD FLYWAYS

As a result of the pressures favouring short sea-crossings, specific crossing points (recently termed 'bottleneck areas'; Bijlsma, 1987), have become important for raptors and storks on migration between the Palaearctic and Africa (Figure 7). These are summarized in Porter & Beaman (1985). Three main areas can be recognized:

(a) *The eastern flyway* (Bosphorus and Middle East) utilized by individuals from eastern Europe and the Asiatic Palaearctic wintering in East Africa.

(b) *The central flyway* (southern Italy, Malta, Tunisia) utilized by some individuals of central European origin which are probably aiming for central or

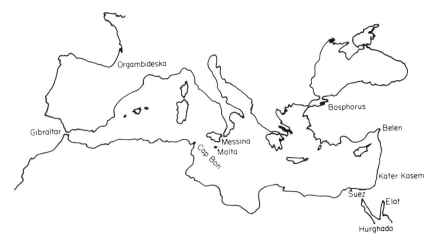

Figure 7.   Location of main soaring bird bottleneck areas in the Mediterranean region.

western areas of tropical Africa. This flyway involves longer sea-crossings than the other two, and species highly-dependent on soaring (e.g. White Storks, Short-toed Eagles) avoid it almost completely (Beaman & Galea, 1974). The scale of migration is considerably lower than over the other two flyways.

(c) *The western flyway* (Strait of Gibraltar) utilized by individuals of West European origin. Central European and western USSR birds are also involved (in an unknown proportion). The scale of migration is large but less than that of the eastern flyway, and there are significant differences in species composition and numbers of particular species.

THE EASTERN FLYWAY

The eastern flyway draws individuals that breed in the Asiatic and eastern European Palaearctic and winter in East and South Africa. Birds using this flyway have a number of options available. In autumn, eastern European birds approach Lebanon and Israel from the north-west via the Belen Pass or the Gulf of Iskenderun in southeast Turkey (Cameron *et al.*, 1967; Sutherland & Brooks, 1981) after crossing the Bosphorus (see Porter & Willis, 1968). Western USSR and some northern and eastern European raptors approach from the east coast of the Black Sea, with conspicuous concentrations at Borcka and Arhavi in northeast Turkey (Andrews *et al.*, 1977; Beaman, 1977). Birds from further east in the USSR, including most Steppe Eagles and Imperial Eagles, approach from the western and eastern coasts of the Caspian Sea, although the precise points of concentration are not known. Major concentrations occur where these migratory streams converge, as observed at Kaffer Kassem in Israel (Dovrat, 1982; Horin &

Dovrat, 1983), Suez in Egypt (Bijlsma, 1983) and over Bab-el-Mandeb at the southern end of the Red Sea (Welch & Welch, 1988). Similar routes are chosen in spring, although the species composition and numbers may differ, as is the case at Eilat in Israel (Yom-Tov, 1984). The essential differences between this flyway and the western flyway are:

(i) A number of alternative focal points are available and are utilized by soaring birds approaching the head of the Red Sea, so that different species concentrate on different points within and between seasons. Variability between spring and autumn passage at any site is therefore high (Table 1). The western flyway is the sole point of convergence for soaring birds breeding in western Europe and wintering in West Africa, and variability between spring and autumn is low (Table 1).

(ii) Because this flyway is utilized by birds from a different geographical area from those using the western flyway, there are significant differences in species composition and abundances (Tables 2–4). The following are practically exclusive to the eastern flyway: Levant Sparrowhawk, Steppe Buzzard, Long-legged Buzzard, Lesser Spotted Eagle, Spotted Eagle, Steppe Eagle and Imperial Eagle.

Table 1   *Variability between spring and autumn raptor passage at three Mediterranean bottleneck areas.*[1]

Genus	Gibraltar	Malta	Suez
Pernis	0.984	0.352	10.977
Milvus	0.947	0.875	33.281
Accipiter	2.787	0.736	2.518
Falco	4.023	1.154	0.319
Circus	1.388	9.730	0.435
Neophron/Gyps	0.731	0.263	0.671
Aquila	—	—	0.348
Circaetus	0.719	—	0.238
Buteo	4.005	0.145	36.389
Pandion	4.278	16.610	1.115
Hieraaëtus	0.675	—	0.412
Standard deviation	1.463	5.722	13.065

[1] Index for each genus is derived from Table 2: Proportion contributed by genus to site's spring passage ÷ proportion contributed by genus to site's autumn passage. The closer the index is to 1, the less the difference between spring and autumn. >1 indicates greater contribution in spring. <1 indicates greater contribution in autumn. Standard deviation measures the overall variation between spring and autumn: i.e. composition of the passage by genera is most similar between spring and autumn in Gibraltar and least so in Suez.

THE CENTRAL FLYWAY

A relatively small proportion of raptors from central Europe and Italy migrate into North Africa via Italy, with a small number passing over Malta (Beaman & Galea, 1974). In spring, many raptors leave North Africa from Cap Bon in Tunisia (Thiollay, 1975, 1977; De Jong, 1974; Dejonghe, 1980), heading towards Sicily, from where they cross the Strait of Messina into Italy (Dimarca & Iapichino, 1984), with a passage over Malta in certain winds (Beaman & Galea, 1974). The main differences between this flyway and the western flyway are as follows.

(i) The greater distances that birds have to travel over the sea, which effectively excludes species heavily dependent on soaring, for example the White Stork.

Table 2   Distribution (%) of raptor groups along three main Mediterranean flyways.

(a) Spring migration

Genus	Gibraltar	Cap Bon	Messina	Malta	Eilat	Suez
Pernis	53.602	57.550	61.996	16.197	27.856	0.483
Milvus	35.278	22.501	7.502	0.888	4.927	2.962
Accipiter	1.402	0.168	0.067	0.184	1.087	0.282
Falco	1.758	6.995	18.737	56.001	0.028	0.103
Circus	1.435	2.855	9.716	25.628	0.030	0.020
Neophron/Gyps	0.828	1.604	0.463	0.031	0.118	1.020
Aquila	0.000	0.318	0.132	0.000	4.700	30.35
Circaetus	1.789	0.835	0.000	0.000	0.040	2.347
Buteo	2.371	6.079	1.322	0.092	45.510	62.08
Pandion	0.154	0.051	0.066	0.980	0.014	0.001
Hieraaëtus	1.383	1.044	0.000	0.000	0.032	0.353

(b) Autumn migration

Genus	Gibraltar	Malta	Bosphorus	Kaffer Kassem	Suez
Pernius	54.489	46.042	33.571	59.348	0.044
Milvus	37.240	1.015	3.582	0.109	0.089
Accipiter	0.503	0.250	10.874	5.772	0.112
Falco	0.437	48.543	0.397	0.354	0.323
Circus	1.034	2.634	0.001	0.185	0.046
Neophron/Gyps	1.133	0.118	0.872	0.082	1.521
Aquila	0.000	0.265	24.005	19.232	87.165
Circaetus	2.487	0.324	3.019	1.597	9.844
Buteo	0.592	0.633	23.083	0.038	1.706
Pandion	0.036	0.059	0.001	0.012	0.001
Hieraaëtus	2.050	0.074	0.585	0.282	0.857

Note: Sources referred to in text.

(ii) The smaller overall number of birds using this flyway.

(iii) The relative importance for raptors with low wing-loadings, for example harriers and falcons (Table 2), and Honey Buzzards.

(iv) The appearance of 'eastern' species, including Pallid Harrier, Red-footed Falcon and a relatively large passage of Eleonora's Falcon.

Table 3   Relative scale of migration in different bottlenecks in autumn.

Species	Site				
	Gibraltar	Malta	Bosphorus	Kaffer Kassem	Suez
Honey Buzzard	+++++	+++	++++	++++++	++
Black Kite	+++++	++	++++	++++	+++
Red Kite	++	+	+	−	+
White-tailed Eagle	−	−	+	+	−
Egyptian Vulture	++++	+	+++	+++	+++
Griffon Vulture	+++	−	++	++	+++
Black Vulture	+	−	+	−	+
Bearded Vulture	−	−	−	−	+
Short-toed Eagle	++++	+	++++	++++	++++
Marsh Harrier	+++	++	+	+++	++
Hen Harrier	++	+	+	+	+
Montagu's Harrier	++++	−	+	++	+
Pallid Harrier	−	+	+	++	+
Goshawk	+	−	+	+	+
Sparrowhawk	+++	+	++	+++	++
Levant Sparrowhawk	−	−	++++	+++++	++
Buzzard	+++	+	+++++	+++	+++
Long-legged Buzzard	−	−	+	++	+++
Lesser Spotted Eagle	−	+	+++++	+++++	+++++
Spotted Eagle	−	−	+	++	++
Steppe Eagle	−	−	−	+++	+++++
Imperial Eagle	+	−	+	++	+++
Golden Eagle	+	−	+	+	+
Booted Eagle	++++	+	+++	+++	+++
Bonelli's Eagle	+	−	−	+	+
Osprey	++	+	+	++	+
Lesser Kestrel	+++	+	+	++	++
Kestrel	+++	++	+	++	++
Red-footed Falcon	−	+++	+	+++	+++
Merlin	+	+	+	−	+
Hobby	++	+	++	++	++
Eleonora's Falcon	+	+++	+	++	++
Sooty Falcon	−	−	−	−	+
Lanner	−	+	+	−	−
Saker	−	+	+	−	−
Peregrine	+	+	+	+	+

Key: +, <10; ++, 11–100; +++, 101–1000; ++++, 1001–10 000; +++++, 10 001–100 000; ++++++, >100 000.

THE WESTERN FLYWAY

The Strait of Gibraltar is the only narrow crossing point for soaring birds from western Europe, including important populations from the Iberian Peninsula. Its main characteristics are as follows.

(i) Species compositions are similar in spring and autumn.

Table 4   Relative scale of migration in different bottlenecks in spring.

Species	Site					
	Gibraltar	C. Bon	Malta	Beit Sh	Eilat	Suez
Honey Buzzard	+++++	++++	++	+++	++++++	+++
Black Kite	+++++	++++	+	+++	+++++	++++
Red Kite	+	+	−	−	−	+
White-tailed Eagle	−	−	−	−	−	−
Egyptian Vulture	++++	+++	+	++	+++	+++
Griffon Vulture	+++	−	−	+	++	++
Black Vulture	+	−	−	−	−	−
Bearded Vulture	−	−	−	−	−	−
Short-toed Eagle	++++	+++	−	+++	+++	++++
Marsh Harrier	+++	+++	++	++	++	++
Hen Harrier	++	+	+	+	+	−
Montagu's Harrier	++++	++	++	+	+	−
Pallid Harrier	−	+	++	+	+	+
Goshawk	+	−	−	+	+	−
Sparrowhawk	+++	++	+	++	++	++
Levant Sparrowhawk	−	+	−	++++	++++	++
Buzzard	+++	+++	+	++++	++++++	+++++
Long-legged Buzzard	−	++	−	++	++	++
Lesser Spotted Eagle	−	++	−	++++	++	++++
Spotted Eagle	−	−	−	+	+	++
Steppe Eagle	−	+	−	++	+++++	+++++
Imperial Eagle	+	−	−	+	++	++
Golden Eagle	−	−	−	−	−	−
Booted Eagle	++++	+++	−	++	++	+++
Bonelli's Eagle	+	+	−	−	+	+
Osprey	++	+	+	+	++	+
Lesser Kestrel	+++	++	++	+	++	+
Kestrel	+++	++	+++	++	++	++
Red-footed Falcon	−	+++	++	+	+	+
Merlin	+	+	+	+	−	+
Hobby	++	++	++	++	+	+
Eleonora's Falcon	+	+	+	+	+	+
Sooty Falcon	−	−	−	−	−	−
Lanner	−	−	−	−	+	+
Saker	−	+	−	−	+	−
Peregrine	+	+	−	+	−	+

(ii)   The migration is dominated by three species, White Stork, Honey Buzzard and Black Kite (Table 2), with important numbers of Egyptian Vulture, Short-toed Eagle, Montagu's Harrier and Booted Eagle, and a significant passage of Griffon Vulture, Marsh Harrier, Sparrowhawk and Buzzard. The migration of harriers is the most conspicuous of any of the flyways.

THE STRAIT OF GIBRALTAR AS A FLYWAY FOR RAPTORS AND STORKS

The migration of raptors and storks over the Strait is concentrated over the narrowest sea-crossing: between Ras Cires on the North African shore and a point on the Spanish coast between Punta del Carnero and the village of Guadalmesí (see Figure 1). In calm weather in spring or autumn, the streams of migrants use this 14 km crossing of the Strait. However, the Strait is rarely calm, and the streams of migrants are deflected depending on the strength and direction of the wind.

Westerly winds are more frequent in spring than in autumn and easterly winds predominate in summer and autumn (see Chapter 1); calm days are infrequent (8.6% in spring and 15.5% in autumn) (Cortés *et al.* 1980). It is therefore very difficult to count visible migration from any one point along the width of the Strait, and a team of observers, regularly spaced from east to west, is essential for this purpose. Even then, weather and relief are significant in determining the altitude of migration to an extent that makes counting unpredictable and very difficult. The only full-scale counts of soaring bird migration across the entire width of the Strait are those of Bernis (1980) for the autumn migration. There are no comparable full counts for the spring migration, although day counts at different times of the spring season are available for Gibraltar. These counts are based on passage over the Rock in very similar conditions (westerly winds of moderate to fresh strength) and, allowing for inter-seasonal differences, permit an approximation of the main periods of passage and give an indication of relative abundances. Nevertheless, each species behaves in a different way from the next, sufficient to make any but the most general comments about their migration inconclusive. The main species migrating over the Strait are therefore considered separately.

WHITE STORK

Based on recoveries of ringed birds, Bernis (1966c, 1980) concluded that White Storks crossing the Strait breed in Spain, Portugal, Holland, Alsace, part of West Germany and Switzerland (recently re-introduced storks). In addition, a small proportion of birds from an intermediate point in the White Stork's east/west migratory divide—from Denmark in the north to Bavaria in the south—also fly southwest in autumn towards Gibraltar. The remainder of the birds from this intermediate zone and those from further east, migrate southeast towards the Bosphorus. Occasionally there are exceptional movements from one side of the divide to the other and individuals from Poland, Czechoslovakia and East Germany have been recovered towards the south-west (Bernis, 1980).

The White Storks that migrate over the Strait winter south of the Sahara, around 15°N, from Senegal in the west to Chad in the east, with occasional birds south to Zambia, Zimbabwe and South Africa (Bernis, 1980). Recent recoveries of Iberian-born White Storks indicate a main wintering area in Mali and smaller numbers in Nigeria, Upper Volta, Ghana and the Central African Republic, with passage through Morocco and Mauretania (Fernandez-Cruz, 1982). Some storks remain on the Moroccan (Pineau & Giraud-Audine, 1979) and Spanish sides of the Strait, although it is difficult to determine to what extent such birds are wintering or are early or late migrants.

The most accurate recent counts of White Storks crossing the Strait are those carried out during the southward migrations of 1976 and 1977 by Bernis (1980) and 1978 by Fernandez-Cruz (in Bernis, 1980). Daily observations were made across the width of the Spanish side of the Strait during the main passage period of the White Stork and the totals counted were 50 281 (1976), 39 162 (1977) and 33 453 (1978).

The White Stork has declined considerably in western Europe since 1900 and the migration must once have involved greater numbers than today (see Irby, 1875, 1895). Bernis (1980) suggested that the western and central European (excluding Iberian) population of White Storks has declined from 5453 pairs in 1934 to 1488 pairs in 1972, having disappeared altogether from Switzerland and dwindled to a very small size in Holland. Iberian populations have also declined. Spanish censuses revealed 14 508 occupied nests in 1948, 12 688 in 1957 and 7340 in 1974. Bernis has estimated that the migration over the Strait in 1957 could have involved around 68 500 storks. This figure could have reached 80 000 in 1948 and may have been in excess of 100 000 before 1939. The majority of White Storks crossing the Strait today are Spanish and Portuguese breeders.

The numbers of White Storks crossing into Africa from Gibraltar is considerably lower (around 16%) than the numbers entering via the Bosphorus, where autumn counts have reached 315 000 birds (Beaman & Jacobsen, 1973). Passage elsewhere across the Mediterranean is virtually non-existent, and the movement of White Storks between Europe and Africa is therefore concentrated over the western and eastern ends of the Mediterranean Sea.

The southward passage over Gibraltar is concentrated over a short period from mid-July to mid-August, with a small number in September (Figure 8). The return, northward migration is extended, with small groups occasionally arriving from the south in October and November; adult birds are regularly seen on nests in the Strait area in December. Passage north is most pronounced between January and March, although, exceptionally, flocks have been observed as late as May.

As young Iberian White Storks fledge between May and July they gather into groups, sometimes large, and disperse away from the nest sites. Flocks of adult

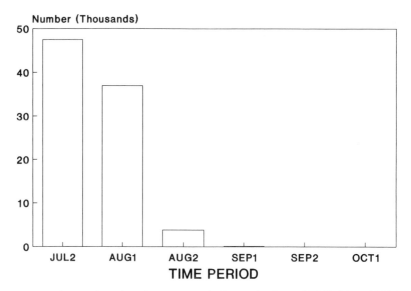

Figure 8.   White Stork southward passage over the Strait, after Bernis (1980). (Years 1976–77.)

and juvenile birds gradually commence moving south towards the Strait. As they approach the Strait, a number of traditional sites are used for feeding and resting. The Marismas del Guadalquivir in Spain (see Figure 1 for locations) attract large numbers of Iberian White Storks as these head south during July and August (some as early as June), initially local birds but later flocks from further north. They stop to rest and feed on fish trapped in pools that are drying up in the summer drought (Bernis, 1980). Further south, White Storks may stop in the marshes around Cádiz Bay or may continue towards the coast of the Strait.

Most Iberian White Storks approach the Strait from the north-west or north-north-west. The site of the former freshwater lagoon, Laguna de La Janda (see Chapter 7), is a major point of congregation. The lagoon was drained during the 1950s, and must have been of greater importance as a stop-over area for migrating White Storks in the past, when they could feed as they do today in the Marismas del Guadalquivir. Nevertheless, the vast, open fields are sufficiently undisturbed to remain important to migrating White Storks, which feed on the numerous large orthopterans (bush crickets, locusts) which abound in the summer. The cork oak woods surrounding the open fields have been tradition-ally used as roosts by White Storks, and large numbers gather at favourite sites in the evenings. From La Janda, White Storks fly directly towards the nearby Strait. A last resting and feeding opportunity is provided by the valley of the Jara River which opens to the sea northwest of Tarifa (see Figure 2).

The lower Jara valley is the site of large accumulations of White Storks when strong easterly winds make a Strait crossing very difficult. In such circumstances several flocks may coalesce in the air or on the ground and, after repeated

A flock of White Storks leaves the parched August fields near Tarifa, about to cross the Strait towards Morocco.

attempts at crossing, will settle on the fields, hunched and facing the wind, for the remainder of the day. The cork oak woods bordering the valley also provide roosts. White Storks cross the Strait in large, compact flocks, preferentially during the morning although flocks may cross until 2 hours before sunset.

The behaviour of White Storks is different in easterlies and westerlies. In July and August easterly winds predominate over the Strait, and White Storks approaching from the north-west meet strong headwinds long before reaching it. They fly slower and higher than in westerlies and are drifted close to the Atlantic coastline (Figure 9); occasionally flocks drift out to sea, but most manage to return inland. With strong easterlies, White Storks run the risk of being drifted out towards the Atlantic Ocean and flocks circle persistently well inland from the coast, sometimes not approaching it at all. Those flocks that do cross in easterlies do so after soaring very high and leave the coast from Tarifa or the area immediately to the east (Figure 9). They drift laterally over the sea and arrive over the Moroccan coastline around Cape Malabata and Tangier Bay. Flocks sometimes change direction once over the sea and return towards the Spanish coast. Bernis (1980) has suggested that White Storks are adapted to crossing the Strait in easterlies since these are the predominant winds.

In westerlies, White Storks approach the Strait with a tail wind and arrive at lower altitude. In circling to gain height they drift eastwards, some flocks reaching as far as Punta Carnero. The birds do not usually cross the Strait from so far east but fly into the wind and cross from the coast east of Tarifa. White Storks rarely land here in westerlies, contradicting somewhat Bernis's conclusions of the

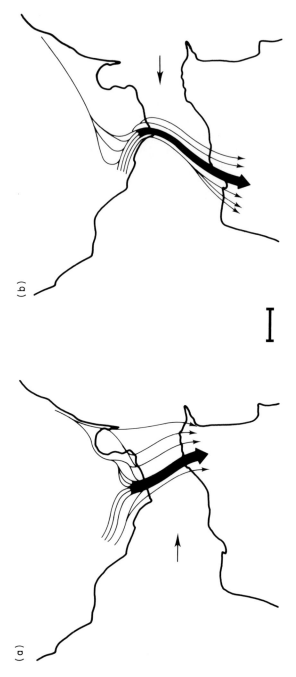

Figure 9. Routes followed by White Storks on autumn passage across the Strait in relation to prevailing winds (scale = 10 km).

preference to cross in easterlies. During the westerly sea-crossing, White Storks drift east, facing the wind, and generally arrive in the area of Ras Cires from where they fly inland or coast into the wind. In calm weather, which is unusual, White Storks do attempt the shortest sea-crossing from east of Tarifa to Ras Cires.

A small proportion of White Storks, mostly continental, approach the Strait from the north-east. In easterlies, tail winds drift them towards Tarifa or beyond, but in westerlies, especially northwesterlies, they drift towards the Rock of Gibraltar from where they may attempt a crossing or, more usually, continue to fly into the wind towards Punta Carnero and then along the Spanish coast towards a shorter crossing point.

The behaviour during the northward migration is similar, although large accumulations prior to crossing are less frequent on the Moroccan side because easterlies are not as persistent as in late summer/early autumn and the passage is not concentrated over so short a period. White Storks approach the Strait from the south-west and aim for the short crossing from Ras Cires to the Spanish coast (Pineau & Giraud-Audine, 1979). With easterlies they encounter headwinds as they turn at Cape Spartel and then coast towards the east into the wind. They may set off over the sea from the stretch west of Ras Cires and, depending on the strength of the wind, will arrive on the opposite shore around Tarifa or to the west, some as far as Cape Trafalgar. In westerlies, departures take place from the Ras Cires area and White Storks then reach the opposite shore west of Punta Carnero. In fresh westerlies and northwesterlies, flocks drift further and reach the Rock of Gibraltar. From here they head northwest, into the wind, towards the breeding areas. Favourable resting and feeding areas, particularly La Janda near the Strait and Cádiz Bay and the Marismas del Guadalquivir, are used by northward migrating White Storks.

BLACK STORK

Black Storks have become scarce in many parts of their range, especially in western Europe, and the numbers entering Africa in winter are far fewer than in earlier times (Moreau, 1972). Most of those crossing the Strait belong to the reduced Portuguese and west Spanish population, although a few from the westernmost parts of the central European range also fly southwest in autumn, as demonstrated by recoveries in Spain of Black Storks ringed in Denmark (where Black Storks no longer breed) and Czechoslovakia (Bernis, 1966a, 1980). Small numbers (but more than White Storks) have been observed crossing the western Pyrenees at Orgambideska in recent years in autumn (Sagot & Tanguy le Gac, 1984), confirming that some birds from north of Pyrenees regularly migrate southwest in autumn. They continue south over Morocco where they have not been recovered, unlike Spanish-born Black Storks (Fernandez-Cruz, 1982). Although some Black Storks are observed in southern and western Spain (Bernis, 1980) and Morocco (Thévenot *et al.*, 1981, 1982) in winter, most probably migrate to south of the Sahara Desert where, in view of the small numbers involved, it is an uncommon winter visitor to West Africa (Serle *et al.*, 1977) in Chad, Nigeria, Ghana, Portuguese Guinea, the Gambia and Senegal (Moreau, 1972; Bernis, 1980).

With no more than 150 pairs in Iberia (Bernis, 1980), the passage over the Strait is small and was of the order of 200–400 individuals during the late seventies. Autumn counts for the entire Strait (summarized by Bernis, 1980), range from 191 in 1977 to 384 in 1976, although the increased incidence of flocks on passage over the Strait in recent years may indicate a recovery. Flocks of 20–50 are a regular occurrence over the Strait, numbers sometimes reaching 70–80 birds in a single flock (*SGBO Reports*). The passage may now be in excess of 600 birds, although detailed counts are not available. This passage, still small, contrasts with the much larger migration over the eastern end of the Mediterranean of Black Storks from eastern Europe and further east to winter in East Africa, probably no further south than the equator (Moreau, 1972). Recent autumn counts at the Bosphorus have ranged from 4300 to 7200 individuals (Beaman, 1973; Beaman & Jacobson, 1973). Small numbers also migrate between Italy and North Africa. A similar number of Black Storks and White Storks are shot over Malta each year (Magnin, 1986), and spring passage has been recorded from Cap Bon, Tunisia, with 47 in 1979 (Dejonghe, 1980) and the Straits of Messina (Dimarca & Iapichino, 1984). The Gibraltar passage is only between 5 and 10% of the Bosphorus passage.

The southward passage across the Strait is later than that of the White Stork, mainly between the middle of September and the middle of October, with a peak at the end of September (Figure 10). The northward passage com-

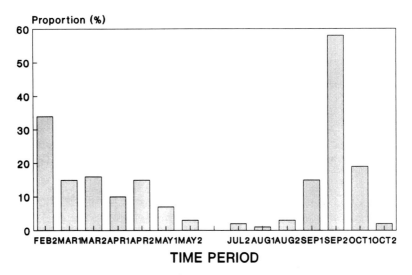

Figure 10.   Black Stork passage periods across the Strait of Gibraltar. Spring, N = 177; autumn, N = 384.

mences in mid-February and is thinly spread, some individuals passing as late as June.

The behaviour of migrating Black Storks over the Strait differs significantly from that of White Storks. A smaller species, the Black Stork employs flapping flight more frequently than the White Stork, which may explain why some migrate via Italy and Tunisia. The approach towards the Strait in autumn varies according to the wind, with groups arriving from the north-east in westerlies, something which rarely happens with White Storks except for those arriving from western Europe. In westerlies, Black Storks fly over the Rock of Gibraltar or over the Bay of Gibraltar, usually on a southwesterly track that takes them towards the central part of the Strait from where they cross into Morocco. Occasionally, they cross directly from the Rock. Birds approaching from the north-east could be non-Iberian in origin or they could have been displaced eastwards by the prevailing winds, an infrequent occurrence with White Storks. It is possible that Black Storks are less restricted than White Storks to flying mainly over the lowland belt of southwestern Spain—they regularly approach the Strait over wooded mountains and valleys—which would explain the difference. In view of the known Pyrenean passage it seems likely, however, that at least a proportion of the Black Storks arriving from the north-east are non-Iberian.

In easterlies, Black Storks arrive from the north-west and spend much time soaring and flying parallel to the coast into the wind. They are reluctant to cross in easterlies, and small flocks aggregate to form groups of over 30, an exceptional flock of 82 birds having been recorded on 16 September 1987 (Holliday, 1990a). Westerlies or calm days are preferred for the Strait crossing.

In spring, the approach from the south is similar to that described for the White Stork. In westerlies, the departures are from Ras Cires, and Black Storks drift eastwards over the sea to arrive over Gibraltar, the Bay or Punta Carnero. In calm conditions the shortest crossing is taken, and in easterlies birds drift westwards over the sea and may arrive west of Tarifa. In strong easterlies or strong southwesterlies migration does not take place.

OSPREY

The number of Ospreys observed at migration bottlenecks does not reflect the numbers migrating because Ospreys are not restricted by flight strategy to such narrow sea-crossings. The majority travelling southwest towards Gibraltar in autumn are Scandinavian, in particular Swedish (Bernis, 1966c). Ospreys from as far east as Finland have been recovered in Iberia, although Finnish birds generally take a more easterly track than Swedish or Norwegian birds (Osterlof, 1977). Scottish and at least some east European Ospreys also migrate via the Iberian Peninsula. Most, if not all, of these cross the Pyrenees; autumn counts at Orgambideska have reached 74 (Sagot & Tanguy le Gac, 1984). Moroccan recoveries fit this pattern, with 1 Scottish, 9 Swedish and 1 Finnish bird (Bergier, 1987).

The wintering area of Scandinavian Ospreys is essentially West Africa, from Senegal to Gabon (Moreau, 1972), where they are widespread winter visitors (Serle *et al.*, 1977). Swedish birds winter further west than Finnish ones, although there is a considerable overlap in West Africa (Osterlof, 1977). Two birds ringed in Senegal were recovered in Morocco on passage (Bergier, 1987). A small number of Ospreys winter north of the Sahara Desert, in Morocco and Spain, including the Atlantic coast of Morocco close to the Strait (Pineau & Giraud-Audine, 1979) and the European shore of the Strait and the adjacent coastline. Wintering birds are sometimes seen inland, in reservoirs or along slow-flowing rivers.

Ospreys are usually solitary on migration, often flying high and fast, making detection difficult. Thus, observations from the Rock of Gibraltar (426 m above the surrounding hinterland) in suitable conditions have produced higher counts than corresponding observations over the Spanish side of the Strait in autumn (see, for example, Bernis, 1980), where they are no doubt overlooked. In 1977, 30 Ospreys were counted over the Rock of Gibraltar between the 17th and the 21st September with westerly winds, including 12 on the 17th; none were recorded over the Spanish side of the Strait. From the 22nd to the 26th in light winds or easterlies (unsuitable for passage over the Rock of Gibraltar) none were counted over the Rock, but only four were seen over the Spanish side where the passage was expected to have shifted to. This suggests that Ospreys are under-counted in autumn over the Strait. Despite this, autumn counts for the entire Strait have been high for a species not supposed to congregate at narrow sea-crossings (Mead, 1983). Autumn counts range from 40 to 61 (Bernis, 1980), comparable to the passage over the Pyrenees. The spring passage is more conspicuous over the European shore, as birds arrive at lower altitude after the sea-crossing. Spring counts over the entire width of the Strait are not available, but day counts over the Rock of Gibraltar in westerly winds have reached 12 and Ospreys are sighted daily in suitable weather. 54 Ospreys were counted over the Rock alone in the spring of 1978 (Mosquera, 1978).

Spring migration over the Strait probably exceeds 100 individuals and is comparable to the spring passage over Eilat, Israel, where 122 Ospreys were counted in spring 1977 (Christensen *et al.*, 1981). Passage over the central Mediterranean is smaller (maximum 10 at Cap Bon—Thiollay, 1975; De Jong, 1974: maximum 10 over Malta—Beaman & Galea, 1974).

The numbers of Ospreys counted over the Strait are similar to Middle Eastern routes. Autumn passage over Kaffer Kassem, Israel, is of the order of 30–50 Ospreys (Dovrat, 1982; Horin & Dovrat, 1983), although counts at the Bosphorus (maximum 10—Beaman, 1973) and Suez (maximum 9—Bijlsma, 1983) are considerably smaller. Presumably many of the Ospreys converging over Kaffer Kassem have approached from the north-east (passage over north-east Turkey has been detected – Andrews *et al.*, 1977) with a smaller number from the Bosphorus. Since many Ospreys from northeast Europe migrate southwest, it is possible that relatively few east European Ospreys migrate towards the Middle East. Numbers of Ospreys over Malta in autumn are small (1–2 birds—Beaman & Galea, 1974).

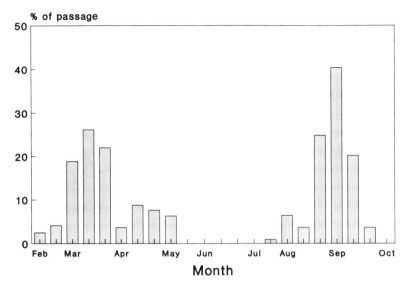

Figure 11.   Osprey passage periods—Strait of Gibraltar. Spring, N = 231; *autumn,* N = 104.

The numbers indicate that there is some concentration of Ospreys over either end of the Mediterranean, with a smaller passage over Tunisia, Malta and Italy. Statements that Ospreys cross the Mediterranean on a broad front (Cramp *et al.*, 1980) are misleading. Reports of land birds at sea for the period 1978–86 (Reports in *Sea Swallow*) only produced one Osprey observation, of an individual sighted in autumn close to Malta.

The southward passage spans the period late July to early October, with a well-defined peak centred on the middle of September. In autumn, 85% of Ospreys pass south during September (Figure 11). In spring, migrants are observed from the middle of February, and exceptionally late individuals have been seen during the first half of June. The main passage, when 67% of the Ospreys are noted, takes place from the middle of March to the first third of April, with a peak at the end of March (Figure 11).

Ospreys usually migrate singly throughout the day with little variation during the day. In autumn the main approach to the Strait is from the north-east because virtually all the Ospreys crossing into Africa are non-Iberian. In westerlies, these birds drift over the Rock of Gibraltar, crossing directly towards Morocco. In fresh westerlies Ospreys may depart from northeast of the Rock and fly south over the sea east of Gibraltar. In lighter westerlies, most Ospreys fly over the Rock and then continue southwest over the Bay of Gibraltar towards the Spanish shore, from where they cross into Morocco. In these conditions, other Ospreys fly along the northern shore of the Bay towards the central part of the Strait (Figure 12). This is the route usually taken in calm or light variable conditions, indicating that Ospreys prefer to take the shortest sea crossing . In easterlies,

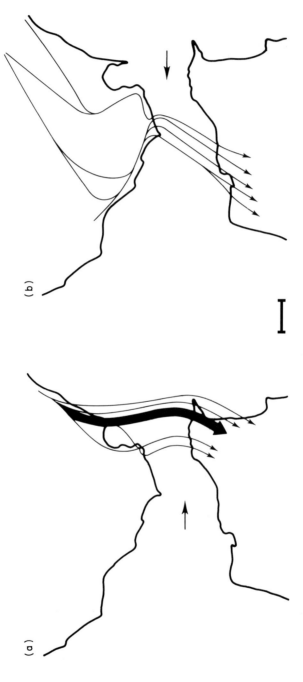

Figure 12. Routes followed by Ospreys on autumn passage across the Strait in relation to prevailing winds (scale = 10 km).

Ospreys drift westwards and will then approach the Strait from the north-west, flying into the wind, to cross from the area east of Tarifa (Figure 12).

In spring, Ospreys departing from the Ras Cires area arrive along the central part of the European shore of the Strait in light winds. In westerlies they arrive over the Rock or the Bay of Gibraltar, and in easterlies drift westwards towards Tarifa or the coastline to the north-west.

It is unlikely that Ospreys regularly depart over the sea to the west or east of the Strait, except when they are drifted out to sea by strong winds. If they did, then birds leaving the Mediterranean European coastline for Africa would be expected to drift westwards towards the Rock of Gibraltar in easterly winds, which none do. The reverse situation would be expected to apply if Ospreys departed from the Atlantic coast, since they should then be seen over the western end of the Strait in westerlies.

The behaviour of Ospreys on passage differs significantly from that of other raptors. They are solitary and are often observed perched near rivers, reservoirs, salt pans or lagoons where they rest and catch fish. They even catch fish from the sea while on active passage over the Strait, and have been observed on several occasions arriving at Gibraltar in spring carrying fish. This suggests that the migratory strategy of the Osprey is one of moving in stages with intermediate resting areas. These could be stop-over areas, as happens with passerines. Alternatively, the pauses in migration may be of an opportunistic nature, depending on the condition of individuals, the state of migratory restlessness, and the availability of hunting opportunities on the way. Clearly, though, this strategy can only be successfully open to a predator that travels singly and feeds on prey likely to be relatively abundant in well-defined patches. Ospreys can probably afford a more leisurely migration than other raptors, which have to fast during the migration and must aim for a rapid passage with little energy expenditure. That, despite this strategy, Ospreys avoid long sea-crossings seems to confirm that the main reason for doing so is to reduce the risk of being blown far out to sea with little chance of recovery, rather than to save energy by reducing the time spent flapping.

HONEY BUZZARD

The majority of Swedish and west European Honey Buzzards travel southwest towards the Strait, the proportion of individuals from further east, including Finland, being unknown (Bernis, 1980). A smaller number of Swedish and central European Honey Buzzards travel south over Italy to cross to Africa via Sicily, Malta and Tunisia (Beaman & Galea, 1974). The proportion of Finnish birds using this route is probably larger, although the majority are likely to migrate southeast towards the Bosphorus. The small number of Honey Buzzards counted over the Bosphorus in autumn (maximum autumn counts of under 26 000; Beaman, 1973) suggests that the tendency to migrate southwest may also be prevalent among east European Honey Buzzards.

The main wintering grounds appear to be in tropical and equatorial West Africa, where the species is associated with evergreen forest although it does not penetrate the interior (Moreau, 1972). Wintering birds have been recorded from West Guinea to the Congo, which appears to be an important wintering area. Honey Buzzards ringed in Scandinavia and central Europe have been recovered in West Guinea, south Mali, Ivory Coast, Ghana, Togo, Nigeria, Cameroon, the Central African Republic, Gabon and Congo (Moreau, 1972; Bernis, 1980). Smaller numbers winter in East and South Africa where suitable habitat is less frequent than further west. Serle *et al.* (1977) record passage in Mali and Chad. Passage over Chad may involve birds from the central Mediterranean route or from the Middle East flying southwest towards the wintering grounds. The apparent tendency of Honey Buzzards to fly southwest in autumn may therefore be linked with location of the main winter quarters in the western parts of Africa. The conspicuous spring passage from Cap Bon, Tunisia, to Sicily (Thiollay, 1977; Dejonghe, 1980) and then over the Strait of Messina (Dimarca & Iapichino, 1984) suggests a direct migration towards north–northeast to central European breeding grounds at that time.

The southward migration of Honey Buzzards over the Strait is spectacular. It is the most numerous raptor to cross the Strait, and counts over the entire season across the width of the Strait have ranged from 57 631 to 115 696 (Bernis, 1980), the variation being due to differences in coverage and detectability of birds in different weather conditions. The highest day count is for the Rock of Gibraltar—11 262 on 31 August, 1976. Spring numbers are also very high, though complete counts are not available; day counts over the Rock have exceeded 9000.

The intense autumn migration over Israel (380 576 at Kaffer Kassem in a season—Dovrat, in Bijlsma, 1987) mainly draws individuals from the north-east where heavy migration has been reported in northeast Turkey (138 000 at Borcka/Arhavi in a season—Andrews *et al.*, 1977), and fewer from the Bosphorus. Passage is surprisingly small over Suez (Bijlsma, 1983), and birds may pass to the north on a southwesterly course bound for West Africa rather than turning south at Suez. Autumn passage over the central Mediterranean is poorly documented, but numbers over Malta do not exceed 1000 (Beaman & Galea, 1974). Spring passage over Cap Bon involves at least 10 000 Honey Buzzards (Thiollay, 1977; Dejonghe, 1980).

On present evidence, it appears that the number of Honey Buzzards entering Africa in winter is in the region of half a million, with around 20–25% doing so over the Strait.

The passage periods of the Honey Buzzard are characterized in both seasons by the concentration of birds within a narrow time frame (Figure 13) which, as we have seen, is thought to increase the probability of large flocks forming, with consequent advantages. In spring, the passage spans the period April to mid-June, with 84% of the birds during the first 20 days of May (Figure 13). A similar picture emerges for the southward migration, which takes place from August to mid-October, with 82% of the birds passing from the last third of August to the first third of September.

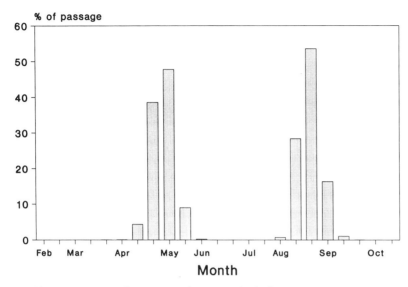

*Figure 13. Honey Buzzard passage periods — Strait of Gibraltar. Spring, N = 68 683; autumn,
N = 161 716.*

Flocks vary in size and are largest (several hundred birds) at the height of the
migration, when passage over an observation point takes the form of a large and
continuous stream that may progressively alter the point over which it is flying so
that the migration front 'sweeps' in one direction only to resume the original
point a few minutes later. Several streams may be in progress at the same time
over the same points. Honey Buzzards usually travel in single-species flocks,
although other raptors may temporarily become attached to flocks. Solitary
Honey Buzzards occasionally join flocks of Black Kites or other raptors.

Despite their ability to fly over the sea, Honey Buzzards aim for the shortest
crossing of the Strait in spring and autumn, and it is lateral displacement by
prevailing winds that modifies the routes which are taken. In autumn, almost the
entire population of Honey Buzzards approaches the Strait from the north-east
(the breeding population in the western half of the Iberian Peninsula is negligible). Honey Buzzards from central and northern Europe fly over the Pyrenees
(Bernis, 1980; Sagot & Tanguy le Gac, 1984) and then approach the Strait in a
southwesterly direction, flying over the central and eastern Spanish mountains.
They approach the Spanish Mediterranean coastline along the east Andalucian
provinces (Málaga, Granada and Almeria) and then follow the coast in a west-
southwest direction towards the Strait (Figure 14).

In calm conditions, Honey Buzzards skirt the Bay of Gibraltar along its
northern edge and approach the coast west of Punta Carnero, from where they
cross directly towards Africa. Westerly winds deflect the streams close to the
Mediterranean coastline, even over the sea, and most Honey Buzzards then fly
over the Rock of Gibraltar. In moderate westerlies, Honey Buzzards approach
from the north-east and many then continue southwestwards over the rock or the

Figure 14.   Honey Buzzard autumn migration routes.

Bay towards Punta Carnero to cross from the Spanish coast of the Strait. In fresh westerlies, many Honey Buzzards approach Gibraltar from the sea to the east and the vast majority cross directly from the Rock. In such conditions the passage is concentrated totally over Gibraltar, with flocks even departing from the Mediterranean coast northeast of the Rock and passing south-southwest over the sea to the east of Gibraltar (Figure 15). The arrivals over the Moroccan coast are then concentrated east of Ras Cires, depending on wind strength, with large flocks passing over Ceuta.

In easterlies, the streams drift inland on approaching the Strait, bypassing the Rock and the Bay. Depending on the strength of the wind, the birds then fly west-southwest over the mountains to the north of the Strait, gradually turning to approach the Strait from the north or north-west. Most Honey Buzzards leave the Spanish coastline along the central portion of the Strait, although many streams depart from further west, some of those that have approached from the north-west setting off from the area of Los Lances Beach, northwest of Tarifa (Figure 15). The streams drift substantially over the sea and the main arrivals on the Moroccan side take place from Tangier Bay eastwards, depending on wind

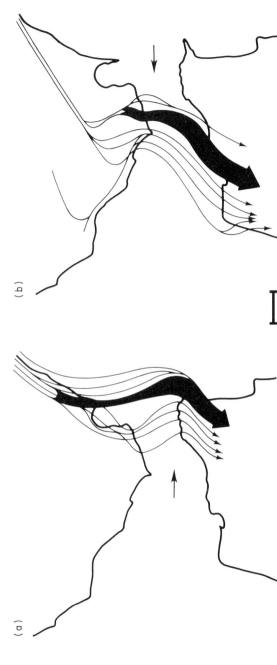

(a)   (b)

Figure 15.   *Routes followed by Honey Buzzards on autumn passage across the Strait in relation to prevailing winds (scale = 10 km).*

strength. In strong easterlies, flocks also arrive between Tangier and Cape Spartel, with some approaching the Moroccan Atlantic coast from the north-west (Pineau & Giraud-Audine, 1979).

In spring, Honey Buzzards depart north from the Ras Cires area in light winds, arriving between Guadalmesí and Punta Carnero, and drifting eastwards with westerlies. In fresh westerlies, passage is concentrated over the Rock of Gibraltar, with flocks regularly drifting over the sea to the east to make the landfall along the Spanish Mediterranean coast. In easterlies, while many Honey Buzzards do set off from Ras Cires, other flocks depart along the coastline to the west. Honey Buzzards arrive along the Spanish coast in the vicinity of Tarifa and the coast to the north-west, some arriving as far west as Cape Trafalgar.

The most striking aspects of Honey Buzzard behaviour on migration over the Strait are the ability to fly in wind conditions unsuitable for other soaring birds and the formation of large flocks that often merge into streams. The Honey Buzzard has a powerful flight and flapping is frequent, particularly in strong winds. Passage over the sea therefore takes place even in easterlies strong enough to ground Black Kites, White Storks and most other soaring birds. Conse-quently, it is unusual to see migrating Honey Buzzards settling during the day. They are able to fly over the sea with relative ease, arriving over the opposite shore higher than other species, rarely attempting to land to rest after having performed the crossing. It follows that Honey Buzzards do not hunt while on passage, and those migrants that have been examined have had empty stomachs and considerable layers of fat in the abdomen (Bernis, 1980). It is possible therefore that, while not reaching the levels of fat accumulation of the smaller migrants, Honey Buzzards are able to deposit some fat, providing additional reserves of energy during passage.

At night Honey Buzzards settle in isolated woods along hillsides and valleys to roost, but the roosts are not used from year to year or by different flocks during the same season as is the case with Black Kites and White Storks. Instead, flocks appear to settle wherever they are at sunset and resume the journey shortly after sunrise. On several occasions Honey Buzzards have been seen starting a crossing of the Strait at first light, and it is possible that some may migrate in the dark. This is not an unreasonable supposition for a species that is not dependent on thermals and is able to combine flapping flight with utilization of updraughts caused by the effect of winds against slopes.

BLACK KITE

The large Spanish and Portuguese breeding population of Black Kites converges on the Strait in spring and autumn. Some birds from the western part of the European breeding range, including France, West Germany and Switzerland, also use the Strait route on migration (Bernis, 1966c) — a Polish-ringed Black Kite has been recovered in Spain (Bernis, 1980), as have East German birds (Cramp,

1980). However, most birds from eastern Europe probably migrate south or southeast. In Morocco, Black Kites ringed in Spain (9), France (16), West Germany (4), East Germany (3) and Switzerland (47) have been recovered on passage (Bergier, 1987). The majority, if not all, of the Black Kites that cross the Strait winter in West Africa, between 10° and 15°N, from Senegal to Nigeria (Moreau, 1972).

After the Honey Buzzard, the Black Kite is the most numerous raptor to cross the Strait: counts during the southward migration have ranged between 24 577 and 63 032 (Bernis, 1980). Passage can be intense on days with weather conditions favourable for a crossing, especially after strong winds have halted migration for several days. On one such day in August 1977, over 8600 Black Kites crossed the Strait (Bernis, 1980). In spring, passage can also be heavy, especially in mid-March when the main contingent arrives in Europe—up to 4000 a day. Despite being less strong fliers than Honey Buzzards (appearing to congregate at narrow sea-crossings to a greater extent), numbers of Black Kites crossing from Cap Bon to Sicily in spring are relatively high (e.g. over 4000 in 1974—De Jong, 1974; Thiollay, 1975), although very few appear over Malta (Beaman & Galea, 1974).

Black Kite migration over the eastern Mediterranean appears to be less spectacular than that of other, more common, soaring raptors. The low figures so far recorded may simply reflect low levels of observation early in the autumn, at a time when most Black Kites migrate. Nevertheless, counts at Eilat and Suez in spring (where there has been detailed observation) have been relatively low (20 000–27 000 at Eilat—Christensen *et al.*, 1981; Swanquist, 1981: under 4000 at Suez—Wimpfheimer *et al.*, 1983). Over the Bosphorus, autumn counts are below 3000 birds (Porter & Willis, 1968; Beaman, 1973; Beaman & Jacobsen, 1973). Data on the number of Black Kites entering Africa in autumn is incomplete but, in comparison with Honey Buzzards, it seems to show that a far larger proportion do so via the western end of the Mediterranean (possibly over 60%). There has been a dramatic decrease in Black Kites in eastern Europe/Turkey in the past 20 years, which may well have some bearing on the difference between eastern and western flyways (R. F. Porter, pers. comm.).

The Black Kite is the earliest raptor to migrate south, many individuals crossing the Strait during the second half of July and most doing so in August, with a peak during the middle 10 days of the month (Figure 16). Very few pass during September and only a few stragglers in October. The northward passage spans a longer period. Passage commences early, during the last third of February, some individuals passing earlier. The mass movement north takes place in March, especially in the middle of the month, and there is then a progressive decline through April and May, with passage continuing during early July. It is likely that the early peaks are of Iberian Black Kites and that, among those passing in April, there is a larger proportion of northern birds. The later movements, from late April onwards, are characterized by the predominance of immature birds. Those passing towards the end of the period are clearly non-breeders. In June, flocks of up to 60 Black Kites have been seen crossing the Strait northwards into Europe, too late for breeding to be possible. Few

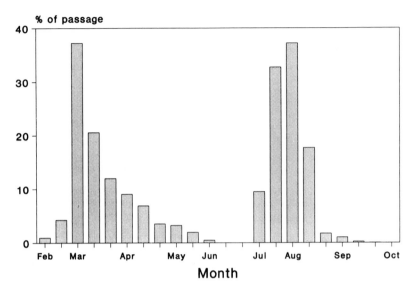

Figure 16.   Black Kite passage periods — Strait of Gibraltar. Spring, N = 29 263; autumn, N = 110 162.

immature Black Kites return to central European breeding areas in spring but instead remain in northwest Africa, Spain and France (Cramp, 1980).

Black Kites on migration differ strikingly from Honey Buzzards in their behaviour. Black Kites have a buoyant, erratic flight which, in light or moderate winds, is interspersed with long periods of gliding or soaring. This flight method is probably economical at relatively slow speeds (Pennycuick, 1969). In stronger winds, frequent over the Strait, Black Kites encounter difficulties and are forced into prolonged spells of flapping flight, with periods when they have to settle on the ground or on trees to rest. During periods of westerlies, wind strength increases through the day, with afternoon inshore breezes often causing a halt in the migration for the day. On many autumn days, spectacular Black Kite movements take place early in the morning as birds which have roosted close to the Strait head off in earnest for the African coast. Bernis (1980) has suggested that this early morning movement may be to permit crossing in favourable light winds. In spring, large early morning movements are regularly recorded; large flocks are also seen in late evening, when westerly breezes subside more quickly than in the hot summer months. Thus, there is considerable day-to-day variation in the timing of both spring and autumn passage, depending on wind conditions.

In calm conditions the spring and autumn flow of Black Kites follows the shortest sea-crossing between Ras Cires and the Spanish coast near Guadalmesí (Figure 17). Considerable lateral drift over the sea occurs in easterlies and westerlies, more pronounced than it is for Honey Buzzards. During the southward migration the Iberian contingent of Black Kites approaches the Strait from the north-west, having followed the coast down from the Marismas del Guadal-

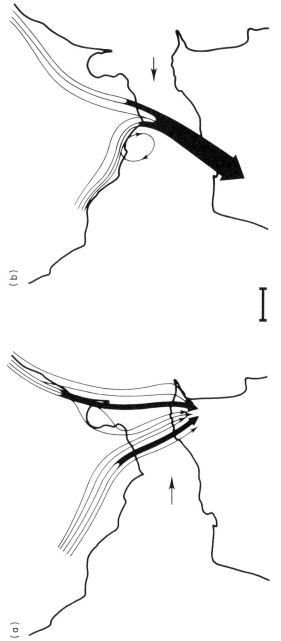

(a)

(b)

Figure 17.   Routes followed by Black Kites on autumn passage across the Strait in relation to prevailing winds (scale = 10 km).

quivir. The European and eastern Iberian Black Kites approach the Strait from the north-east, following close to the Mediterranean coastline to the north-east of Gibraltar.

In fresh westerly winds, even the Iberian birds drift well to the east as they approach the Strait so that the final arrival of Black Kites is almost exclusively from the north-east. In these conditions most pass in a southwesterly direction over the northern end of the Bay of Gibraltar or over the Rock itself, crossing it from north-east to south-west along various points on the ridge. Many continue across the Bay and eventually cross towards Africa from the central Spanish portions of the Strait (Figure 17). Except in the evening, the large number of Black Kites which cross directly into Africa from the Rock in fresh westerlies has been underestimated (Bernis, 1980). At this time of day, Black Kites often return towards land after having started the sea-crossing. In westerlies it is possible to observe groups of Black Kites flying northwards from the sea at various points along the coast, searching for suitable roosts for the night. It is also the case in westerlies that Black Kites that have reached the Tarifa area by coasting into the wind turn inland instead of crossing. Depending on the time of day, these birds may search for a roost or regain height and attempt a Strait crossing later on in the day. Black Kites will often roost wherever they happen to be in the evening, preferring wooded or scrub-covered hillsides. When they have been grounded for several days, as happens in easterlies, they appear more selective in choice of roosts and will repeatedly use the same roosts (also used in successive years), most of which are in woodland in the mountains close to the Strait.

In easterlies the approach is from the north-west, most continental kites having drifted westwards well inland with easterly tail winds. The approach may be along the coast or inland, and in relatively light easterlies there is still considerable passage over the eastern edge of the Sierra del Algarrobo on the western side of Gibraltar Bay (Figure 17). In fresh easterlies most birds drift further west and approach the Strait from the north-west along the coast or over the coastal mountains. Some flocks attempt to cross the Strait from over Tarifa Beach, but these birds usually return inland. Most crossings take place from Tarifa island or the vicinity, especially west of the town. In easterlies the passage is not as continuous as in westerlies, with large flocks passing from time to time and long intervals with no movement.

In very strong easterlies Black Kites appear unable to make progress into the wind and flocks may spend long periods 'hanging' in the wind without advancing. In these conditions, most give up attempts to cross the Strait and settle on fields and woods near the Strait to rest, usually in a hunched posture facing the wind. The fields around Tarifa, especially in the valley of the Vega River, are littered with hundreds or even thousands of Black Kites (often with White Storks, Egyptian Vultures and other raptors) in such weather in August. In spite of these prolonged periods without being able to migrate, Black Kites rarely feed; Bernis (1980) examined the alimentary canals of migratory Black Kites shot in the area of the Strait and found them to be virtually empty. There are instances of opportunistic hunting or scavenging, however.

In spring, Black Kites are equally prone to wind drift, except during the peak movements in March, when the prevailing winds are westerly. The passage is then concentrated over the eastern end of the Strait, the main belt of arrivals being between Punta Carnero and the Rock of Gibraltar, with many individuals being blown even further east, out towards the Mediterranean. Some will continue and reach the Spanish coast around Guadiaro, but many fly into the wind and approach the Rock from the east. Most arrive very low, flapping continuously to avoid the waves, and attempt to land along the coast, apparently exhausted. Easterlies force Black Kites westwards and, depending on the intensity of the wind, some may reach land as far west as Cape Trafalgar.

RED KITE

The Red Kite is a scarce migrant across the Strait. Many central and west European Red Kites winter in the Iberian Peninsula, including the shores of the Strait (Cramp, 1980), but very few go further south and then no further than Morocco. Red Kites are solitary on migration, occasionally travelling in twos or very small groups, making detection difficult. Most individuals are observed during the course of passage of other species.

Because the main passage period in autumn is from mid-September to mid-October, when most other species have passed, it is possible that numbers have been underestimated. Even allowing for this, passage is not large, and complete counts for the southward migration have ranged from 20 to 100 birds (Bernis, 1980). In spring, the passage also involves a few individuals thinly spread out, usually passing singly or in flocks of Black Kites. The migration north spans the period late February to May, with most passing in April; there is one record for

Gibraltar of a bird flying north in June (Cortés *et al.*, 1980). Numbers are also low in the other bottleneck areas.

EGYPTIAN VULTURE

Egyptian Vultures crossing the Strait belong to the Iberian population, although a few pairs may be from the northerly limits of the west European range in the south of France. Most Egyptian Vultures from these areas winter in West Africa just south of the Sahara, but some may remain to winter in the more hospitable areas of the Sahara itself (Bernis, 1980). In general, most wintering Egyptian Vultures do not go further south than 13°N and they are concentrated in countries bordering the Sahara (Moreau, 1972; Serle *et al.*, 1973). Occasional individuals winter in southern Spain and Morocco.

The Egyptian Vulture is one of the regular migrants across the Strait which have probably suffered a considerable decline as a result of human persecution in the breeding areas (Cramp, 1980); it is likely that it featured more predominantly as a migrant over the Strait in the past. Recent counts during the southward passage have ranged between 1300 and 3800 birds (Bernis, 1980). During southward passage large groups may be seen, occasionally up to 50 together, after bad weather has held up the crossing. The passage is concentrated over a brief period, when it is possible to record 30 or 40 birds crossing per day; counts exceeding 100 birds in a day are possible. The return of the adults to the breeding areas in early spring takes place over a brief period, and most appear to migrate singly or in pairs. It is unusual to record large numbers in spring, and the passage takes the form of a trickle of birds across the Strait.

Egyptian Vultures do cross the central Mediterranean in substantial numbers, although they are likely to keep to the shortest crossings. A substantial passage from Cap Bon, Tunisia, has been recorded in May (Thiollay, 1977; Dejonghe, 1980); in view of the late time of year these birds must have been non-breeders. Very few are recorded over Malta in spring or autumn (Beaman & Galea, 1974). There is, then, a polarization of passage, with all west European Vultures crossing the Strait, eastern birds following the Bosphorus and Levant route, and an undetermined proportion following the central flyway. Counts have been made along a number of points along the eastern flyway in spring and autumn (Porter & Willis, 1968; Beaman, 1973; Beaman & Jacobsen, 1973; Christensen *et al.*, 1981; Sutherland & Brooks, 1981; Somsag, 1981; Swanquist, 1981; Dovrat, 1982; Horin & Dovrat, 1983; Bijlsma, 1983; Wimpfheimer *et al.*, 1983). Judging from these counts, which have rarely exceeded 1000 birds, it appears that the numbers of Egyptian Vultures entering and leaving Africa via the western and eastern flyways are approximately the same.

Egyptian Vultures arrive early at their breeding sites in southern Spain, starting in January and February. The northward passage of adults is concentrated during February and March (Figure 18). Birds that pass later must be either non-breeders or adults returning to the northernmost parts of the breeding range. There is a notable northward movement of immature Egyptian Vultures in April and May (Figure 19), and it is likely that any adults crossing at this time are also

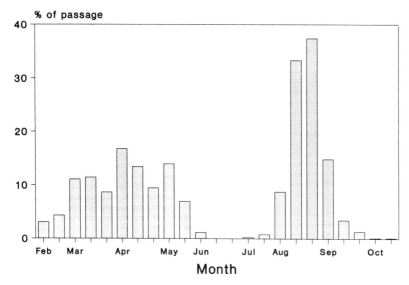

Figure 18. *Egyptian Vulture passage periods—Strait of Gibraltar. Spring, N = 459; autumn, N = 2628.*

non-breeding individuals. The southward passage is more concentrated, between the end of August and the end of September, with most passing early in September (Figure 18). It is possible to observe isolated migrants over the Strait outside this main period, between early August and late October. The average

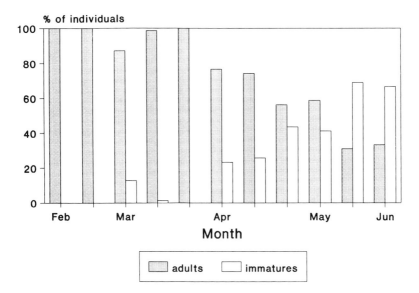

Figure 19. *Egyptian Vulture—differences in spring passage by ages, N = 474.*

stay of an adult Egyptian Vulture in the Iberian Peninsula is therefore around 7 months.

On passage, the Egyptian Vulture behaves like a typical soaring bird, making full use of thermals and updraughts and passing during the warm part of the day. For its size, however, it appears to spend more time flapping than other soaring birds of comparable size (e.g. Short-toed Eagle). It is therefore able to cope with unfavourable winds better than other large soaring birds. In autumn, Egyptian Vultures can fly into the strong easterly wind along the northern shore, in search of a favourable crossing point, and then reach as far east as the Rock of Gibraltar. However, strong autumn easterlies can interrupt migration, and it is possible then to find Egyptian Vultures grounded in many parts of the northern shore of the Strait. At this time Egyptian Vultures migrate singly or in small family parties, but in periods of adverse weather Egyptian Vultures congregate and groups coalesce to produce large aggregations.

During the southward migration, Egyptian Vultures approach the Strait from the north-east in westerly winds and from the north-west in easterly winds, showing that they are subject to drift well before reaching the Strait itself. In calm conditions, many approach the central part of the Strait from the north and cross directly into Morocco. In westerlies, Egyptian Vultures approach the Rock from the north-east and either fly directly towards Morocco or continue southwest across the Bay of Gibraltar towards Punta Carnero to cross from the Spanish coast. Others follow the northern end of the Bay and approach the Strait from the Spanish hills on the western side of the Bay. The tendency is, therefore, towards crossing along the central portions of the Strait, the degree of lateral displacement depending on the wind. In easterlies, crossings may take place from just east of Tarifa.

The return passage in spring follows a similar pattern to the southward migration, although affected by fewer strong easterlies. Large aggregations are very rare. In calm weather, the central route is followed. In westerlies, vultures leaving Ras Cires arrive at Punta Carnero or the Rock; in easterlies arrivals take place around Tarifa, with the Jara Valley forming a flyline to the north.

Egyptian Vultures sometimes mix with other raptors on migration but this appears to be due to chance encounters rather than to active interspecific sociability. In autumn they roost singly or in small groups, and they may associate with Black Kites in particular. Bernis (1980) recorded 32 roosting in 1 ha of oak wood in September 1977.

In the two main years of his study, Bernis (1980) estimated that the proportion of adults to immature birds crossing the Strait in autumn was around 0.7 immatures per 2 adults. His data did not separate the classes of immature (juvenile, second-year) and 'subadults' were included as adults. In fact, Bernis recognized that in the 2 years at least 11.4 and 5.5% of the 'adults' were subadults. Taking this into account, the proportions of adults crossing were 61.3 and 67.7%, against 38.7 and 32.3% immatures. Unfortunately, the proportion of juveniles was unknown. The records of the Gibraltar Ornithological Group for the autumn seasons of 1971–1974 reveal that, of 476 Egyptian Vultures classified by age, 64.3% were adult, 2.7% were fourth-year, 1.3% were third-year, 4.4% were second-year and 27.3% were juvenile. This would give a figure of 0.9 juveniles per two adults. My own observations from Gibraltar in spring show that around 61% of all Egyptian Vultures are adult and up to 39% are immatures, which do not include, at that stage in the year, juveniles. As with other raptors, therefore (e.g. Black Kite and Short-toed Eagle), a large proportion of non-breeding immatures return to the breeding areas in the spring, and these generally arrive some time after the adults (Figure 19).

GRIFFON VULTURE

Iberian Griffon Vultures are partially migratory, juveniles of the more northerly populations apparently being most migratory and adults from the south being essentially resident, although the exact pattern remains unclear. Those that do migrate across the Strait are of Iberian origin. They winter in Morocco, although some are known to cross the Sahara Desert. Bernis (1980) cites recoveries and sightings of Griffon Vultures in the old Spanish Sahara, in Mauretania and Niger, but the proportion of European Griffons reaching south of the Sahara is unknown. It appears that an element of this passage consists of Griffons from northern Spain, judging from recoveries of Griffons ringed in Navarra and subsequently recovered to the south-west, some very close to the Strait (Elosegui & Elosegui, 1977; Bernis, 1980).

The total number of Griffons crossing the Strait is unknown and their passage has not been observed as fully as for other species, in view of the lateness of the movement. However, Bernis (1980) counted over 700 Griffons crossing the Strait in October (November, a month when many Griffons cross the Strait, was not covered). The largest flock of Griffons known to me in the area was one of 260 which flew over the Rock of Gibraltar on 4 November 1973. It is likely that over 1000 Griffon Vultures cross the Strait in autumn but, in a wandering species such as this, it is possible that there are wide inter-annual fluctuations in relation to conditions in Spain in autumn.

The migration of the Griffon Vulture follows two distinct routes, with no passage over the central Mediterranean (Beaman & Galea, 1974; De Jong, 1974; Thiollay, 1975; Thiollay, 1977; Dejonghe, 1980; Dimarca & Iapichino, 1984). Over the eastern flyway small numbers have been recorded at traditional points such as the Bosphorus (Steinfatt, 1932; Porter & Willis, 1968) and the Belen Pass (Cameron *et al.*, 1967). Observations at Suez, which have covered part of November, have revealed a notable movement, with 1284 in 1981 (Bijlsma, 1983). The numbers of Griffon Vultures entering Africa at either end of the Mediterranean are therefore comparable.

The Griffon Vulture is the last raptor to migrate south, doing so in October and November (Figure 20). The return is spread out over a longer period, but the most concentrated passage is between mid-April and mid-May, with a few being recorded in June (Figure 20). Most of these individuals are recognizable as

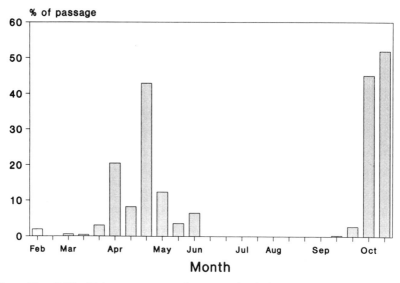

Figure 20.   Griffon Vulture passage periods—Strait of Gibraltar. Spring, N = 297; autumn, N = 734.

A Griffon Vulture on spring passage over the Rock of Gibraltar is mobbed by a resident Yellow-legged Gull. Each spring many of the larger raptors are attacked by local Peregrines and gulls and may be forced to land or may even be driven into the sea where they drown.

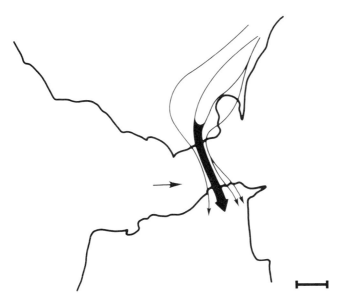

Figure 21.   Routes followed by Griffon Vultures on autumn passage across the Strait in westerly winds (scale = 10 km).

Two exhausted Griffon Vultures rest on the Rock of Gibraltar after having been driven down by gulls.

immature birds, and the late arrival (Griffon Vultures commence breeding in Iberia in January) indicates that they are non-breeders. This supports the view that the majority of Griffon Vultures crossing the Strait south in October and November are juveniles. What proportion returns to the breeding areas the following spring is not known, but there is clearly a substantial passage of many of these over the Strait in late spring.

Griffon Vultures are typical soaring birds, spending much time without flapping and making full use of thermals and other air currents. Their inability to sustain long periods of flapping flight makes them vulnerable to a sea-crossing, and records of Griffon Vultures falling exhausted in the sea and drowning are not infrequent in the Strait. As would be expected, the crossing of the Strait takes a long time—the vultures often appear hesitant and reluctant to fly over the sea even when they have gained considerable altitude. Griffon Vultures cross almost exclusively over the narrowest stretch (Figure 21) and rarely do so in easterlies in either season. In spring, Griffons leaving Ras Cires in fresh westerlies arrive in Europe over Gibraltar. At that time they can be seen arriving off Gibraltar low over the sea, flapping continuously, and they may attempt to settle and rest on reaching the coast.

Griffon Vultures cross mainly during the warm part of the day, from late morning to early afternoon, sometimes in very large flocks. Migratory movements are therefore sporadic; long periods when no birds cross are followed by bursts of passage.

SHORT-TOED EAGLE

The majority of Short-toed Eagles crossing the Strait are of Iberian and French origin; Sagot and Tanguy le Gac (1984) have recorded passage of Short-toed Eagles over Orgambideska Pass in the Pyrenees. Some central European birds may migrate southwest in autumn, but the majority probably fly towards the Bosphorus and thus use the eastern flyway; one Polish Short-toed Eagle has been recovered in France (Bernis, 1966c).

Most, if not all, of the Short-toed Eagles crossing the Strait probably winter along the western part of the wintering range that stretches from the southern edge of the Sahara down to about 10°N (Moreau, 1972). Gibraltar birds probably winter no further east than Chad.

Bernis's (1980) counts across the width of the Strait in late summer and autumn ranged from 3200 birds in 1977 to just under 8800 in 1972, although he admitted that the latter figure probably included a high element of duplication. It seems from his counts that the average number crossing the Strait is around 4000 individuals. Passage can be intense during the peak migration in both seasons: Bernis (1980) recorded 521 on 23 September 1976, while the records of the Gibraltar Ornithological Group give a count of 302 on 13 March 1973, and those of the Strait of Gibraltar Bird Observatory 507 on 13 March, 1990 (*SGBO Reports*).

Short-toed Eagles rely heavily on soaring flight and are therefore unlikely to cross the Mediterranean in any numbers. Passage across the Strait of Messina and the Sicilian Channel is not notable, although Thiollay (1977) counted 239 over Cap Bon, Tunisia, during 2 to 18 May 1975. The late dates suggest the passage of non-breeding individuals. Passage over Malta is negligible in spring and autumn (Beaman & Galea, 1974).

The numbers entering Africa via the eastern flyway are considerable, with seasonal counts exceeding 12 000 individuals over Suez (Bijlsma, 1987). This figure indicates that the proportion of Short-toed Eagles entering Africa via the western and eastern flyways is in the ratio of 1:3. Birds using the eastern flyway must include a number of east European birds (the maximum count over the Bosphorus is 2331, in 1971 — Beaman, 1973) and a large contingent of Russian birds.

The southward passage takes place in September and early October, with the majority passing during the second half of September. Some individuals are noted crossing as early as the first week of August, but these are few. There is then a progressive build-up towards September. Very few pass south after the first half of October. Modifications to the pattern may occur in different winds as migration across the Strait may be delayed by strong winds.

The return to Europe is early. The Short-toed Eagle is among the first raptors to arrive from the south, with good passages taking place in the second half of February. Most pass north in March, with a definite peak during the middle of the month (Figure 22). Numbers then tail off but there is a smaller peak in May of immature birds arriving too late to breed. These birds are all pale-plumaged, in

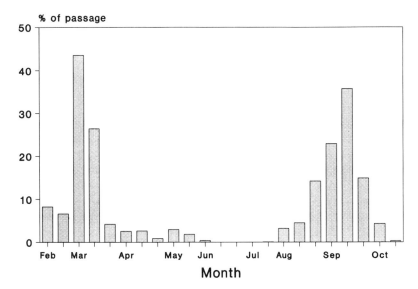

Figure 22.   Short-toed Eagle passage periods—Strait of Gibraltar. Spring, N = 1576; autumn, N = 7392.

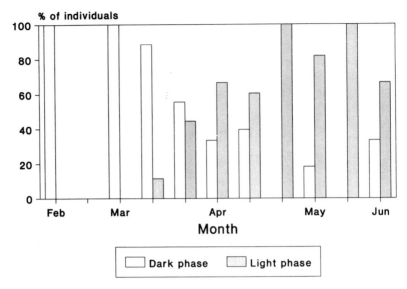

Figure 23.   Short-toed Eagle spring passage by colour phases, N = 163.

moult, as opposed to those which pass in March, which have dark heads and throats (Figure 23). The difference in passage of dark and light birds supports the view that dark birds are adult and light ones young. Immature Short-toed Eagles continue to pass north during the first half of June.

Short-toed Eagles cross at the narrowest point in light winds but they are easily deflected by lateral winds, especially when over the sea (Figure 24). In spring, Short-toed Eagles departing from Ras Cires in light westerlies will reach the European shore at Punta Carnero, and with moderate westerlies will arrive over the Rock of Gibraltar. In fresh westerlies many are blown east of the Rock and then have to fly west into the wind to reach land, often over the eastern side of Gibraltar. In easterlies, arrivals occur west of Tarifa.

In autumn there is considerable overland deflection, depending on the wind. With westerlies the approach to the Strait is from the north-east and north, but most keep inland and very few fly over the Rock. Those which do appear reluctant to cross directly to Morocco instead continue southwestwards to cross from the Spanish coast west of Punta Carnero. The majority follow the hills to the north of the Bay of Gibraltar and then continue towards the central Strait over the sierras of the northern shore. The bulk of the departures in westerlies are from the western half of the Spanish shore of the Strait, but east of Tarifa itself (Figure 24). The pattern is much more complicated in easterlies. In moderate winds many of the birds that arrive from the north-west cross the Strait, mostly from the eastern half of the Spanish shore. Deflection over the sea is considerable, with many arriving in the vicinity of Tangier and Cape Malabata (Figure 24).

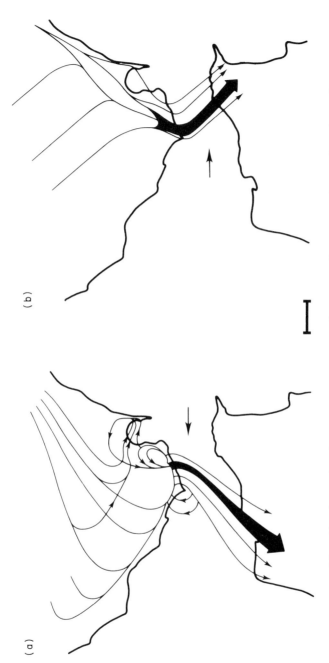

(b)

(a)

Figure 24.   Routes followed by Short-toed Eagles on autumn passage across the Strait in relation to prevailing winds (scale = 10 km).

Many Short-toed Eagles do not cross south when easterlies increase in strength. Unlike other raptors, these eagles do not settle on the ground for long but instead spend prolonged periods flying slowly into the wind, following the coast or inland valleys. Groups may be seen 'hanging' in the wind making little or no progress. If the easterlies persist for several days, Short-toed Eagles will continue flying into the wind and may then reach as far east as the Rock of Gibraltar, where they can be seen approaching from the west and north-west. They may spend some time soaring over the Rock but do not cross towards Morocco, instead returning towards Spain (although in moderate easterlies some do attempt to cross). Similar returns inland occur in other parts of the Strait.

During the afternoon most of these eagles return inland in search of roosts, usually in cork oak woodland. Although Short-toed Eagles are usually solitary, small groups may gather to roost while on passage. Loose groups form during the peak movement, and larger flocks develop after strong winds have held up migration. Cases of up to 100 Short-toed Eagles flying together have been recorded. It is not unusual at this time to see Short-toed Eagles associating with Booted Eagles, which migrate at the same time and behave in a similar fashion.

Short-toed Eagles have been known to hunt while on migration, and from time to time they are observed carrying snakes while moving with other migrants. Bernis (1980) has suggested that the diurnal nature of the Short-toed Eagle's prey makes it possible for them to feed during migration, albeit in an occasional manner.

MARSH HARRIER

Although a few Iberian birds are probably included, the Marsh Harriers that cross the Strait are essentially of west and central European and Scandinavian origin (Bernis, 1980; Cramp, 1980; Bergier, 1987). Marsh Harriers winter in the Iberian Peninsula and Morocco, although many crossing the Strait probably continue across the Sahara Desert to winter in tropical West Africa, where they are '... abundant in winter in the marshes and rice fields in Senegal and Gambia' (Serle *et al.*, 1977). In fact, Marsh Harriers appear widely distributed in West Africa in winter and, in view of the southwesterly orientation of European Marsh Harriers in autumn, most of these birds have probably crossed the Strait (Moreau, 1972). No doubt others will have crossed the Mediterranean on a broad front.

The numbers of Marsh Harriers counted crossing the Strait have been low, usually under 200 in a season (Bernis, 1980). The tendency of harriers to fly over the open sea must reduce the concentration of birds at narrow sea-crossings, but there is no doubt that counts over the Strait have underestimated the total number of Marsh Harriers crossing there. Marsh Harriers usually migrate singly and often fly high. They frequently cross wider stretches of the Strait, which exacerbates the underestimation. Counts from Gibraltar in spring, when birds arrive at lower altitude after having crossed the sea, suggest that the total

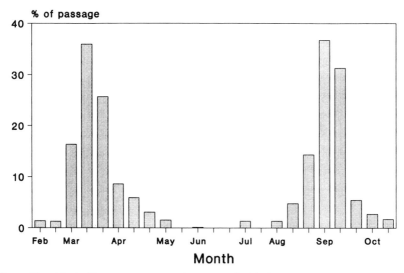

Figure 25. Marsh Harrier passage periods—Strait of Gibraltar. Spring, N = 261; *autumn,* N = 294.

numbers are indeed higher than recorded as day counts of 40–50 Marsh Harriers have been made in suitable weather during the peak passage period in March.

Passage from Tunisia to Italy is comparable to that over the Strait. In spring, counts over Cap Bon, Tunisia, have reached 318 (Thiollay, 1975) in a brief period between the end of March and mid-April. Passage over Malta (Beaman & Galea, 1974) and the Strait of Messina (Dimarca & Iapichino, 1984) is also substantial.

In the east, Marsh Harrier passage is virtually non-existent over the Bosphorus in either season (Porter & Willis, 1968; Beaman, 1973; Beaman & Jacobsen, 1973; Somsag, 1981; Collman & Croxall, 1967; Ritzel, 1980). There is passage on a scale comparable to Gibraltar and Cap Bon over Israel (398 in autumn at Kaffer Kassem—Horin & Dovrat, 1983), suggesting that the numbers of Marsh Harriers entering Africa in autumn via the western, central and eastern flyways is of the same order of magnitude. To these must be added an unknown number of birds that use routes involving longer sea crossing (e.g. Greek islands—Vagliano, 1985).

Marsh Harriers may be seen at any stage in the raptor migration seasons, although there are two well-defined peaks: one of birds passing north between mid-March and early April, and another of birds passing south in the second two-thirds of September (Figure 25). In spring, males precede females (Figure 26).

Marsh Harriers cross the Strait along its entire width and regularly do so away from the narrowest parts. Despite this ability to fly over the sea, they often behave in a similar way to other soaring birds. For example, in spring Marsh Harriers that have drifted east of the Rock of Gibraltar in fresh westerlies will struggle into the wind to reach the Rock instead of continuing north over the sea

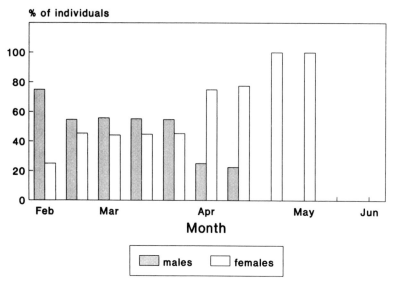

Figure 26.   Marsh Harrier spring passage by sexes. N = 550.

to reach the Spanish Mediterranean coastline. Marsh Harriers drift with lateral winds so that passage is concentrated over the eastern sectors of the Strait in westerlies and over western sectors in easterlies. In spring passage of Marsh Harriers is concentrated over the Rock in westerlies as the birds arrive with other raptors from the south-west. In autumn, many approach the Rock from the north-east in westerlies, having followed the Spanish coastline; from here they may cross the Bay towards the Spanish coast of the Strait or cross directly to Morocco. In easterlies many will approach the Strait from the north-west. As with other harriers, Marsh Harriers are solitary on migration, although some-times presumed family parties are recorded in autumn and small groups of three or four birds in spring.

HEN HARRIER

It is probable that all the Hen Harriers that cross the Strait come from the north-western part of their European range (Cramp, 1980), including some from the northern Iberian Peninsula. Very few cross the Strait, and those that do go no further than Morocco. Many winter in Spain, including lowland areas in the region of the Strait.

The Hen Harrier is the scarcest of the three harriers that regularly cross the Strait, this being a reflection of its more northerly wintering area. Autumn counts across the width of the Strait ranged between 5 and 114 (Bernis, 1980), although November, a month when Hen Harriers may continue to arrive from the north, has not been surveyed. There are no full counts available for spring, but day totals of 4–6 Hen Harriers are not unusual over the Rock itself.

Even though Hen Harriers are scarce over Gibraltar, numbers are considerably higher than over the central flyway (Beaman & Galea, 1974; Thiollay, 1975; Dimarca & Iapichino, 1984) or over the eastern flyway (Somsag, 1981; Christensen *et al.*, 1981; Dovrat, 1982; Horin & Dovrat, 1983; Bijlsma, 1983), where seasonal counts are well below 10 individuals. Passage along mountain passes to the north is conspicuously higher, indicating that many winter within the northern shores of the Mediterranean. Sagot & Tanguy le Gac (1984) recorded up to 127 over Orgambideska in the French Pyrenees in one autumn, and Beaman (1977) recorded 41 in 2 weeks in October over Northeast Turkey.

Precise details of the passage periods of the Hen Harrier are difficult to determine in view of the few records available. The passage appears to be well spread in both seasons, from February to early May and throughout September and October (Figure 27). In spring there is a progressive build-up towards a peak in the first third of April, but the pattern is less clear in autumn. Although there is a peak in September, it seems more probable that the main influx takes place in October—by then it becomes difficult to distinguish migrants on passage from those that have arrived for the winter.

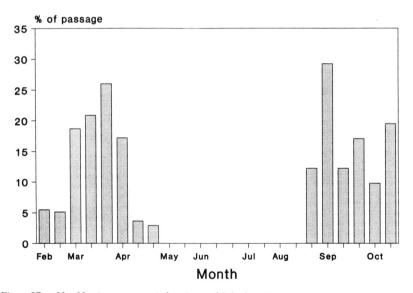

Figure 27.   Hen Harrier passage periods—Strait of Gibraltar. Spring, N = 64; *autumn,* N = 41.

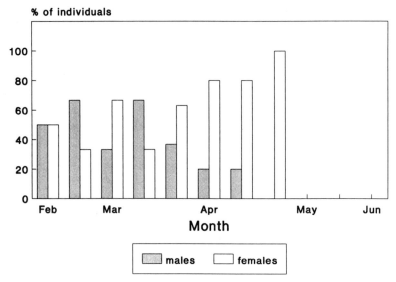

Figure 28.   Hen Harrier spring passage by sexes. N = 72.

In spring, males precede females (Figure 28), as is the case for the other harriers, but in autumn both sexes and young birds arrive together (Bernis, 1980).

Hen Harriers are solitary on passage and behave in a similar fashion to the other two harriers, crossing over the wider stretches of the Strait and drifting with the prevailing wind.

MONTAGU'S HARRIER

West and central European Montagu's Harriers migrate over the Strait alongside Iberian birds (Bernis, 1980; Cramp, 1980; Bergier, 1987). As with other harriers some no doubt cross directly over the Mediterranean but, even so, those reaching the proximity of the Strait react to the coastline in a similar manner to other soaring birds.

Montagu's Harriers winter across tropical Africa within a narrow belt of savanna around 13°N to 16°N and are said to be abundant in the rice fields of the Senegal River (Moreau, 1972). Elsewhere in West Africa they occur from The Gambia to the Central African Republic (Serle *et al.*, 1977). The Montagu's Harriers that cross the Strait probably all go to tropical West Africa, with those wintering in central Africa crossing from Italy to Tunisia. Cramp (1980) record a Dutch bird recovered in Chad and a Swedish bird recovered in Nigeria.

Counting is difficult because Montagu's Harriers cross from any point along either coast of the Strait and are often solitary; a further difficulty is that they often fly high. In fact, autumn counts from the top of the Rock of Gibraltar (where harriers are seen flying at over 500 m above sea level) give a proportionately high count, which suggests that many are missed from lower observatories along other points on the Strait. Bernis (1980) gives autumn counts ranging between 800 and 1700, with maximum day counts of around 100 birds (128 on 18 August 1977). Counts are also high in spring, with a maximum number of 61 over the Rock in a day.

The concentration of Montagu's Harriers over the Strait has been underestimated. Nowhere is passage as pronounced. Over the central flyway numbers are not high, despite comments that harriers fly over the sea without difficulty. In autumn they are rare over Malta and in spring passage is small (maximum 34 birds—Beaman & Galea, 1974). Relatively few pass over Cap Bon, Tunisia, where Thiollay (1975) counted 89 in spring. Passage is also thin over the eastern observatories, with no conspicuous concentration anywhere and seasonal counts failing to reach 20 birds (Collman & Croxall, 1967; Beaman & Jacobsen, 1973; Ritzel, 1980; Christensen *et al.*, 1981; Sutherland & Brooks, 1981; Dovrat, 1982; Bijlsma, 1983). Montagu's Harriers from the eastern parts of the range winter in India, and those that winter in East Africa probably cross Arabia and the Red Sea. The recovery of an East German Montagu's Harrier in Spain in autumn (Bernis, 1966c) suggests that there may well be a tendency for east European Montagu's Harriers to migrate in a southwesterly direction towards the Strait in autumn. The passage of Montagu's Harriers over the Strait is at least 10 times as intense as it is over the central or eastern flyways.

The pattern of passage is that of a typical trans-saharan migrant, with a major arrival in April and departure in late August and early September (Figure 29). In spring passage is detected from mid-March, when the southern Spanish birds

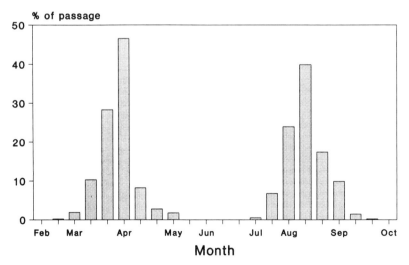

Figure 29. Montagu's Harrier passage periods — Strait of Gibraltar. Spring, N = 472; autumn, N = 2745.

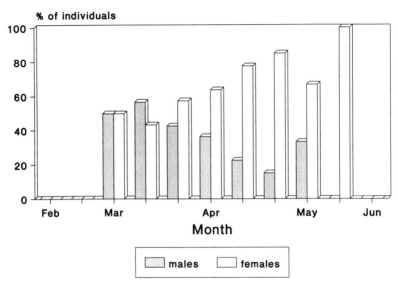

Figure 30.   Montagu's Harrier spring passage by sexes. N = 375.

arrive. Passage continues into mid–May. The return passage commences in late
July and continues into early October.

In autumn, both sexes and juveniles pass at the same time but, in spring, as
with the other harriers, males pass ahead of females (Figure 30). Melanistic
individuals occur in small proportions during both passages, between 3 and 5%
in autumn (Bernis, 1980) and around 2% in spring (sample of 378 birds over the
Rock).

Montagu's Harriers attempt to cross the Strait along the narrowest parts, as
typical soaring birds do, even though they are able to cope with flying over
longer stretches with apparent ease. Unlike their usual low-level flight, Montagu's Harriers fly at all altitudes on passage, often very high (see above).

Montagu's Harriers drift with lateral winds and, in both seasons, passage is
concentrated over the western end of the Strait in easterlies and over the eastern
end in westerlies. In autumn easterlies Montagu's Harriers approach the Strait
from the northwest coast, following the low ground towards La Janda and then
following the coast of the Strait. In strong easterlies they appear unable to cross
and settle for long periods on the ground. In westerlies they either approach from
the Mediterranean coast and follow the hills to the north of the Bay of Gibraltar
and then south towards the Strait, or approach the Rock itself from where they
cross directly to Morocco. Some follow the east side of Gibraltar and others cross
the ridge and continue southwest over the Bay to eventually cross from the
Spanish coast.

Montagu's Harriers migrate singly or in twos, but during the southward
passage in particular they also travel in small, loose flocks. The composition of

some of these groups suggests families migrating together. Montagu's Harriers appear to gather to roost in traditional sites. Bernis (1980) described several such sites in the lowland areas around La Janda, northwest of the Strait, where he recorded between 300 and 400 Montagu's Harriers roosting together during the August passage.

SPARROWHAWK

Bernis (1966c) cited recoveries of central and north European Sparrowhawks in Spain and Portugal but added that many north European birds winter in central Europe. Juveniles show a greater migratory tendency than adults, and males move further and more often than females (Cramp, 1980). In either case, most of the Sparrowhawks crossing the Strait go no further than Morocco, where one Swiss and two German birds have been recovered (Bergier, 1987), although some birds probably reach West Africa (Moreau, 1972). Others winter along the northern shore of the Strait, augmenting the resident population of Sparrow-hawks.

Autumn counts across the width of the Strait in the 1970s ranged between 559 and 907 Sparrowhawks (Bernis, 1980), which no doubt underestimated the passage substantially in view of the small size of this raptor, its ability to fly very high and to flap across the wider stretches of the Strait. During the 1980s Sparrowhawks became increasingly abundant on passage (Finlayson & Cortés, 1987) although full counts are not available. Recent counts over the Rock of Gibraltar in spring have produced regular day counts of the order of 20–40 Sparrowhawks, with up to 80 on 6 April 1988 (*SGBO Report*—April 1988). It would seem realistic to estimate the total passage of Sparrowhawks across the Strait to be at least of the order of 2000 individuals.

In comparison with the Strait, the numbers of Sparrowhawks entering and leaving Africa via the other flyways are small. Thus, maximum counts at Cap Bon, Tunisia, in spring have been under 40 birds (Thiollay, 1975; de Jong, 1974), and passage over Malta is negligible in either season (Beaman & Galea, 1974). Over the eastern flyway, maximum numbers over Kaffer Kassem, Israel, in autumn have been 813 (Dovrat, in Bijlsma, 1987) and spring passage over Eilat, Israel, is small (155 in 1977—Christensen *et al.*, 1981) although many arrive in the area from Northeast Turkey (1057 over Borca/Arhavi in 1977—Beaman, 1977). The volume of Sparrowhawks using the three flyways could be in the ratio of 2:0.05:1, west:central:east, although numbers crossing the Bosphorus have also increased since the last published counts, so the proportions using eastern and western flyways may be similar (R. F. Porter, pers. comm.).

Sparrowhawks are recorded on passage from mid-February to May, with most in late March and early April, and from mid-August to November, with most in September and early October (Figure 31). Although data are not available, it appears that males may precede females in the spring, as is the case for other species.

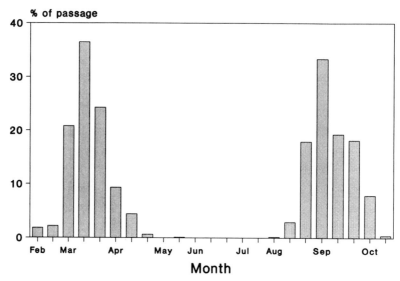

Figure 31.   Sparrowhawk passage periods—Strait of Gibraltar. Spring, N = 1237; *autumn,* N = 1452.

Sparrowhawks utilize flapping flight regularly on migration, although they make use of thermals to soar as larger raptors do. They appear better able to cope with strong winds and are less prone to becoming grounded. Nevertheless, in easterlies in autumn, many Sparrowhawks arrive at Gibraltar from the west alongside Short-toed Eagles and Booted Eagles and remain in wooded areas for several days. In such circumstances, Sparrowhawks appear reluctant to cross the Strait. Unlike other raptors, Sparrowhawks regularly hunt on passage, not just when migration is halted by bad weather but even while actively migrating. In spring Sparrowhawks arriving at Gibraltar often fly low between trees chasing small migrants resting and feeding in the undergrowth. The solitary nature of Sparrowhawks even on migration, and the type of food they consume must be what makes hunting on passage possible.

Despite the ability to flap and cross over relatively wide stretches of sea, Sparrowhawk crossings take place mainly over the narrower points of the Strait. Sparrowhawks drift with prevailing winds. With westerlies the migration is concentrated over the eastern end of the Strait, and with easterlies over the western Strait.

BUZZARD

The Buzzards that cross the Strait belong to the nominate race. Although Buzzards of rufous appearance are seen from time to time (Cortés *et al.*, 1980), there is insufficient evidence to ascribe most of these to the eastern subspecies *vulpinus* (Bernis, 1980). Bergier (1987), however, reported a *vulpinus* Buzzard ringed in Lapland and recovered in Morocco, and another of this subspecies which was ringed on spring passage in Cap Bon, Tunisia, and recovered a subsequent autumn in Morocco. Swedish, Finnish and Norwegian Buzzards have been recovered wintering in Spain and Morocco, and no doubt Scandinavian Buzzards are an important element of those crossing the Strait, but central and even Iberian Buzzards may also be involved (Bernis, 1966c, 1980; Cramp, 1980; Bergier, 1987). A Buzzard ringed in June in the Coto Doñana was recovered the following January in Mauretania, 2100 km to the south-west (Fernandez-Cruz, 1982). The majority of Buzzards crossing the Strait must winter in Morocco, although some migrate further south. Serle *et al.* (1977) consider the Buzzard (*B.b. vulpinus*) to be a rare Palaearctic migrant to West Africa but do not mention *B.b. buteo*.

Bernis's (1980) counts for the Strait in autumn ranged from 792 to 2889. There are no spring counts but day counts over the Rock of Gibraltar have reached 177 in April, with regular day counts of 30–100. In 1987–90, however, spring day counts over the Rock only once exceeded 20 Buzzards suggesting a dramatic decrease in numbers crossing the Strait. In a partially migratory species such as the Buzzard, the possibility exists that the total number of individuals reaching the southernmost parts of the winter range may vary considerably from one year to the next, depending on ecological conditions closer to the breeding grounds.

The highly migratory *B.b. vulpinus* migrates over the eastern flyway to winter in east Africa down to South Africa. There is a large east European contingent, which has produced autumn counts exceeding 18 000 over the Bosphorus in autumn (Beaman, 1973), which merges with an even larger number of Asiatic birds. Counts over Borca/Arhavi in Northeast Turkey in autumn 1976 exceeded 210 000 (Andrews *et al.*, 1977; Beaman, 1977). In spring, Christensen *et al.* (1981) counted 315 767 over Eilat, Israel, in 1977. Passage over the central flyway is small in comparison, though over 850 were counted departing from Cap Bon, Tunisia, in the spring of 1974 (Thiollay, 1975; de Jong, 1974). The number of Buzzards (albeit of a separate race) entering Africa via the eastern flyway exceeds that of the western flyway by 100 to 1.

The southward passage of Buzzards over the Strait is late, with a peak in the middle of October. Early migrants are recorded from mid-August in small numbers, and some may be seen crossing the Strait as late as November. In spring, passage starts during the latter half of February, with a peak at the end of March and early April. The last Buzzards pass north towards the end of May (Figure 32).

The behaviour of migrating Buzzards over the Strait in relation to prevailing winds is similar to that of Honey Buzzards except that, in autumn, the approach to the Strait in either wind is from more inland routes; Honey Buzzards appear to follow the Mediterranean coastline more strictly. As a result, comparatively fewer Buzzards than Honey Buzzards fly over the Rock in autumn westerlies. In easterlies, Buzzards may approach the Rock from the west in a similar manner to Booted Eagles and Short-toed Eagles, and concentrations over the Rock,

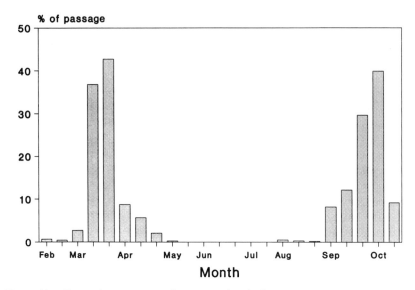

Figure 32. Buzzard passage periods—Strait of Gibraltar. Spring, N = 2175; autumn, N = 1650.

including birds remaining to hunt and roost for brief intervals, have been recorded. In autumn, most Buzzards cross to Africa from the central parts of the Strait; which end of the Spanish sector they concentrate at depends on the prevailing wind. In spring, lateral deflections over the sea in westerlies concentrates the migration over the Ras Cires–Rock of Gibraltar stretch. Buzzards may travel in small groups, but they are usually solitary.

BOOTED EAGLE

The origin of the Booted Eagles that cross the Strait is essentially Iberian; these birds are joined by the smaller south French population. Booted Eagles crossing the Strait are probably those which winter in tropical West Africa, where they appear to be thinly distributed and under-recorded (Moreau, 1972). Small numbers winter in Iberia and Morocco, and Booted Eagles are regular, though scarce, wintering birds within the Strait area.

Bernis's (1980) autumn counts over the Strait ranged from 2772 to 14 492 birds, although the higher counts included a high element of duplication. The average number crossing the Strait is probably around 4000. Spring movements over the Rock of Gibraltar have produced day totals of up to 96 Booted Eagles, with regular day counts of 20–60.

There appears to be less passage over the eastern end of the Mediterranean than

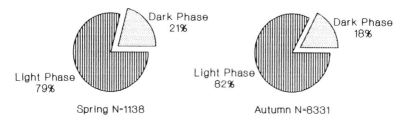

Figure 33.   Booted Eagle phases in spring and autumn passage.

over Gibraltar. 1176 were counted over Kaffer Kassem, Israel, in the autumn of 1982 (Horin & Dovrat, 1983), and the highest count for the Bosphorus is 523 in the autumn of 1971 (Beaman 1973). Over the central Mediterranean, counts have been insignificant (except for a spring count of 299 over Cap Bon in 1975 — Thiollay, 1977), which is not unexpected in view of the scarcity of this eagle as a breeding species in the central Mediterranean countries of Europe. Booted Eagle passage over the Strait is therefore greater than that over the eastern flyway by between 3 and 4 to 1.

Booted Eagles occur in two colour phases. The light phase at all times outnumbers the dark, but there is no indication of significant differences in frequency of each phase during either passage period. Bernis (1980) found that light-phase Booted Eagles accounted for 81–84% of all individuals in autumn ($n = 8331$). In spring over the Rock, 79% of all Booted Eagles were light phase ($n = 1138$) (Figure 33).

During the spring migration Booted Eagles are occasionally recorded as early as mid-February; these are probably wintering birds wandering rather than migrants, as steady passage does not commence until mid-March. Numbers build up to a peak during the first third of April, with a gradual decline towards June. In autumn, very small numbers cross the Strait from the beginning of August, with large-scale migration taking place during September. Substantial numbers continue to pass early in October with very few remaining by the end of the month (Figure 34).

On passage, Booted Eagles behave in a similar manner to Short-toed Eagles, having a tendency to crossing over the narrow stretches of the Strait in calm conditions, with lateral drift towards either end of the Strait in easterlies and westerlies. In easterlies in autumn, they accumulate over the Spanish shore of the Strait and progressively fly eastwards into the wind.

After several days of autumn easterlies large numbers arrive over the Rock from the west and most return north towards Spain and do not cross the Strait, behaviour essentially like that of the Short-toed Eagles. Booted Eagles often then rest and attempt to hunt rabbits and birds over suitable habitat, including the Rock. In such weather large concentrations of Booted Eagles form over the Strait

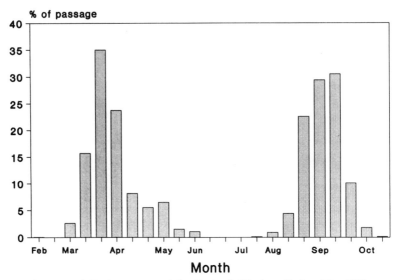

*Figure 34.   Booted Eagle passage periods—Strait of Gibraltar. Spring, N = 1100; autumn,
N = 6108.*

and loose flocks form. Even in such conditions, Booted Eagles are usually
solitary, they appear to disperse in the evenings to roost separately. Large Booted
Eagle roosts are unknown in the Strait, in contrast with Honey Buzzards and
Black Kites.

KESTREL

Kestrels, like other falcons, probably cross the Mediterranean on a wide front,
although there appears to be some concentration of birds over the Strait. These
Kestrels include north European birds with some central European and probably
also Iberian Kestrels. While most Kestrels probably go no further than Morocco,
many cross the Sahara to winter in West Africa and these are not all north
European birds but also include central European Kestrels (Moreau, 1972).

   Bernis's (1980) autumn counts showed great annual variation (160–1195), no
doubt due to the difficulty of locating and therefore counting these relatively
small falcons. It is not always possible to distinguish female and immature
Kestrels from Lesser Kestrels, so each season a large proportion of undetermined
kestrels is recorded. Despite the low seasonal counts there is a well-defined
passage in spring and autumn which, considering that the species is probably
under-recorded, points to some degree of concentration of Kestrels over the
Strait. This appears to be greater than in the other flyways where seasonal totals
have rarely exceeded 100 Kestrels (Porter & Willis, 1968; Beaman & Galea, 1974;
Horin & Dovrat, 1983; Bijlsma, 1987).

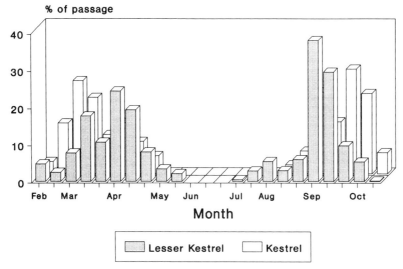

Figure 35. Kestrel/Lesser Kestrel passage periods—Strait of Gibraltar. Lesser Kestrel: spring, N = 302; autumn, N = 778. Kestrel: spring, N = 133; autumn, N = 458.

The passage of Kestrels is spread over a relatively long period of time and is, on average, earlier in spring and later in autumn than that of the Lesser Kestrel (Figure 35). The resident Kestrel population is augmented in winter by migrants from further north, which makes identification of passage birds difficult in early spring and late autumn. Northward passage commences in mid-February and continues until early May with a peak in mid to late March. Southward passage starts at the end of August and steadily builds up to a peak between mid-September and early October, continuing into November.

Kestrels frequently use flapping flight while migrating and regularly cross the wider parts of the Strait. Nevertheless, the majority converge towards the narrow stretches alongside other raptors and react to winds in a similar way. In westerlies, passage is concentrated over the eastern end of the Strait; in autumn, the approach to the Strait is from the Costa del Sol, many then crossing from the Rock of Gibraltar. In easterlies, the approach is from the north-west; in strong autumn easterlies Kestrels arrive on the Rock and usually return north and do not cross the sea.

Bernis's (1980) observations suggested that there was a greater passage of Kestrels than Lesser Kestrels over the eastern Strait; the latter crossed in larger numbers from the western sectors. This was attributed to the continental origins of many of the Kestrels which cross the Strait. Continental Kestrels, like Honey Buzzards for example, would probably approach the Strait down the east coast of Spain, whereas many of the Lesser Kestrels (which would be of Iberian origin) would arrive from the breeding colonies in western Iberia.

Kestrels are usually solitary on passage although small groups have been recorded (Bernis, 1980). They are opportunistic and will hunt when the opportunity arises. If held up by bad weather, they disperse over the hills close to the Strait and spend much time hunting.

LESSER KESTREL

The Lesser Kestrels crossing the Strait are Iberian. Lesser Kestrels from colonies in south France may also be involved, judging from the recovery of a French Lesser Kestrel in Morocco in September (Cramp, 1980). Presumably, these Lesser Kestrels winter in tropical West Africa, where they have been widely but not consistently recorded (Moreau, 1972). Lesser Kestrels are found in winter in southern Iberia, but it is not clear whether these birds are wintering there or are early arrivals back from Africa (Bernis, 1980). The early departure of Lesser Kestrels from southern Iberian colonies (at a similar time to White Storks, which are known to return early to the breeding grounds) suggests that those seen in midwinter are indeed early arrivals from the south. At Gibraltar, Lesser Kestrels regularly come to roost at breeding colonies from December, and the adults are seen displaying from the end of January.

Autumn counts across the Strait are low and variable for the same reasons as for the Kestrel (see above). Bernis's (1980) autumn counts ranged from 266 to 514. No spring counts are available; passage in spring is not conspicuous, Lesser Kestrels passing scattered among other migrating raptors. Passage also appears to be diffuse at both seasons over other bottleneck areas (Bijlsma 1987). Although this may in part reflect broad-front migration, other factors may account for the absence. Moreau (1961) concluded that Lesser Kestrels made a single non-stop flight from the breeding grounds to tropical Africa in autumn, flying high and escaping detection. In spring, the return was more leisurely and in large flocks which, due to their concentration in time, could also be overlooked.

The observed spring passage over Gibraltar — diffuse and commencing in February — is later than that of the Kestrel, peaking in mid-April. Lesser Kestrels continue to pass north until the end of May. This late passage may be of birds from the more northerly colonies, as the southern colonies are occupied by the end of February. Moreau (1961) noted that spring passage in Morocco was obscured by the early arrival of Lesser Kestrels in breeding colonies at the end of January. The southward passage, commencing late in July with a distinct peak in mid-September, may also indicate birds from northerly populations, since the more southerly colonies are abandoned by mid-August (Figure 35).

Lesser Kestrels behave in a similar manner to Kestrels when migrating over the Strait, reacting similarly to wind conditions. They are more sociable than Kestrels; flocks of up to 60 have been recorded on passage over the Strait (Bernis, 1980), although such gatherings are relatively scarce. The main migratory line across the Strait, modified by wind direction, is on average further west than that of the Kestrel.

HOBBY

Some northern and central European birds may cross the Strait, since Hobbies ringed in Sweden, Finland, West and East Germany have been recovered in a number of Mediterranean countries, including Portugal and Spain (Cramp, 1980). However, most are probably Iberian and West European (Bernis, 1966c). Most Hobbies winter in southern Africa, and those which cross the Strait may well continue to these wintering grounds (Moreau, 1972). There is evidence, however, of wintering in tropical West Africa, from Cameroon and Niger in the east to Senegal and The Gambia in the west (Moreau, 1972; Cramp, 1980) and these birds must be from the western part of the breeding range, including at least some birds which have crossed the Strait.

The total number of Hobbies crossing the Strait is low. Bernis's (1980) autumn counts ranged between 32 and 219, which must reflect the ability of Hobbies to cross broad stretches of sea (Cramp, 1980) and to undertake long unbroken flights (Moreau, 1961). Numbers are also low at other bottlenecks (e.g. maximum Middle Eastern seasonal count of 42—Dovrat, in Bijlsma, 1987) and the highest count over the Bosphorus was 168 (Beaman & Jacobsen, 1973). Numbers over the central Mediterranean appear to be similar. In Malta spring counts (17–131) are higher than autumn counts, when Hobbies are scarce (Beaman & Galea, 1974); in Tunisia 45 were recorded over Cap Bon in 17 days in May (Thiollay, 1977); and 82 were counted over the Straits of Messina from 20 April to 19 May (Dimarca & Iapichino, 1984). This pattern suggests an evenly distributed

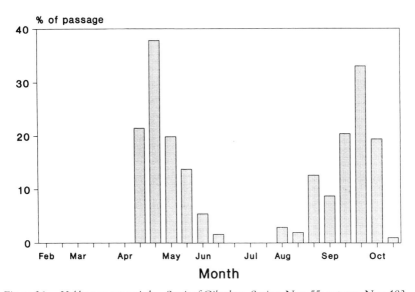

Figure 36.   Hobby passage periods—Strait of Gibraltar. Spring, N = 55; *autumn,* N = 103.

migration across the width of the Mediterranean and a passage over the eastern Mediterranean that is not, as suggested by Moreau (1961), more pronounced.

Together with the Honey Buzzard, the Hobby (Figure 36) is the last species to migrate north in spring, commencing its passage abruptly in mid-April, with a sharp peak at the end of the month followed by a gradual decline towards early June. In autumn, Hobbies begin to move south in mid-August in small numbers, and the peak passage does not take place until late September and early October, most having passed by the end of the month.

Hobbies behave like other falcons on migration, flapping more frequently than the kestrels and crossing the Strait at any point, irrespective of the distance of the sea crossing. They must be affected by wind conditions to some degree, however, as they are only recorded over the Rock of Gibraltar (in either season) in westerly winds. Hobbies are solitary on passage.

OTHER SPECIES

A number of other raptors occur infrequently within the Strait. Several are residents in Morocco and stray northwards, even reaching the Iberian side of the Strait: Black-shouldered Kite, Long-legged Buzzard, Tawny Eagle, Lanner and Dark Chanting Goshawk (Pineau & Giraud-Audine, 1979; Cortés *et al.*, 1980; Bernis, 1980; Finlayson & Cortés, 1987). Others are residents in the area and disperse after the breeding season, then appearing irregularly in unusual sites and sometimes crossing the Strait itself. These include Lammergeier, Black Vulture, Goshawk, Imperial Eagle, Golden Eagle and Bonelli's Eagle (Pineau & Giraud-Audine, 1979; Cortés *et al.*, 1980; Bernis, 1980; Finlayson & Cortés, 1987). Fewer species reach the area very rarely, usually from the east or north-east: Pallid Harrier, Spotted Eagle and Red-footed Falcon (Pineau & Giraud-Audine, 1979;

Cortés *et al.*, 1980; Bernis, 1980; Finlayson & Cortés, 1987). The Merlin is a regular winter visitor in small numbers, the Strait being at the southern edge of its wintering range. Finally, the Eleonora's Falcon is a regular migrant in spring and autumn which is also recorded during the summer (breeding season) months even though the nearest nesting colonies are in southwestern Morocco (e.g. Walter, 1979). Finlayson & Holliday (1990) give 32 reports of this species for the Rock of Gibraltar alone between 1981 and 1987, during the period March to October (main months of observation August and September).

CHAPTER 3

Migration of Other Land Birds

CHARACTERISTICS OF SPRING AND AUTUMN MIGRATION PATTERNS

ROUTES AND PASSAGE PERIODS IN RELATION TO THE STRAIT

Trans-saharan migrants

Many trans–saharan migrants fly southwest in autumn towards the western half of the Iberian Peninsula, where some fatten in advance of the journey across the Sahara (see, for example, Hope Jones *et al.*, 1977). Bernis (1962) suggested that somewhere along the Atlantic coast of Iberia these migrants changed heading, to south or southeast, to enable them to reach the Moroccan coast rather than drowning in the Atlantic. On the other hand, Moreau (1961) considered it probable that many migrants perished annually by continuing in a southwesterly heading. Walter (1979), analysing the arrival of migrants over Eleonora's Falcon colonies on the coast of northwest Morocco, agreed with Moreau's view, accepting that the short time span since the end of the last glaciation (10 000 years) was insufficient to have refined the migratory tactics of the trans-saharan migrants. Hilgerloh (1987), examining radar observations in autumn in southern Portugal, found that passerine night migrants continued in a south-southwest heading after leaving the Portuguese coast, and she calculated that the track would lead them to the northwest Moroccan coast. The change to a southeasterly heading, which is under endogenous control (Gwinner & Wiltschko, 1978), occurs once the birds reach Africa (Hilgerloh, 1987).

Even though Casement (1966) found migration of passerines and other land birds across the width of the Mediterranean, there is very strong evidence to suggest that most populations do not migrate across a broad front but instead utilize specific flyways (Moreau, 1961, 1972; Hope Jones *et al.*, 1977; Bibby & Green, 1981) and so avoid the central Mediterranean and Sahara (Bairlein, in press). It is the sum of all the flyways used by different populations which creates the effect of a broad-fronted movement. Different species clearly adopt significantly distinct routes and strategies. Although many passerines migrate southwest in autumn, others, for example Red-backed Shrike and Lesser Whitethroat, move in a different direction, southeast (Moreau, 1961, 1972; Mead, 1983). The choice of routes has evolved, and continues to evolve, as an eco-evolutionary compromise under distinct selection pressures, the main ones being the ecology of the winter areas and breeding grounds, the need to stop-over at intermediate points of the journey (Rappole & Warner, 1976) and the availability of stop-over sites, natural physical obstacles such as the sea and the desert (Moreau, 1961, 1972) and competition from other species or other populations of the same species (Abramsky & Safriel, 1980).

There is no doubt that the northern tropical areas of West Africa are among the most important reception areas for Palaearctic migrants (Moreau, 1972; Morel, 1973; Serle *et al.*, 1977; Curry & Sayer, 1979), so the choice of routes to these wintering grounds must have a strong southwesterly component, especially so for populations from well east (e.g. Pied Flycatchers from northeastern Europe). The alternative would be a long diagonal (NE–SW) crossing of the Sahara.

The southward passage of trans-saharan migrants, which takes place mainly between late July and early October, coincides with the drought in the Mediterranean and a general scarcity of food resources (Moreau, 1972; Finlayson, 1981). The wetter Atlantic areas of the Iberian Peninsula offer a respite for many migrants which then avoid the eastern Iberian Peninsula (Bernis, 1962). South of the Iberian Peninsula these migrants have to fly over the Sahara Desert which offers little opportunity for refuelling (Moreau, 1961). Within this barren waste, the 500 km wide belt bordering the Atlantic offers some vegetation and opportunities for resting and feeding (Valverde, 1957), so that many migrants are able to benefit from following this coastal route. Those leaving the Portuguese coast in autumn have a high probability of reaching the Moroccan coast just north of this belt, and the journey south from there is likely to be less demanding than the crossing of other sectors of the Sahara. Once south of the Sahara, these migrants presumably follow the coast towards the eventual wintering areas (Hilgerloh, 1987), passage as far south as Senegal being regular in many cases (Moreau, 1972; Morel, 1973).

Henty (1961) thought that there was no concentration of night migrants in the Strait area, but his data were very limited. The Strait appears to receive unusually high night concentrations of trans-saharan migrants during both passages (Nisbet *et al.*, 1961; Bernis, 1962). On the basis of a small number of radar observations, Casement (1966) doubted that there was any such concentration, but Houghton's (1973) radar analysis from Gibraltar clearly indicated major

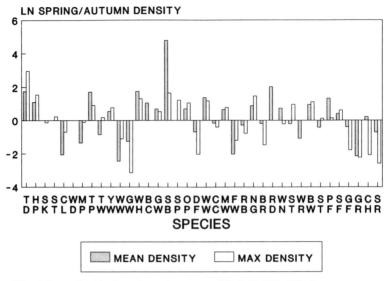

Figure 37.   Migrant densities in spring and autumn at Windmill Hill, Gibraltar.

movements across the Strait at night in the spring. The Strait is situated sufficiently to the west to receive part of the flow of migrants that follow the Atlantic Iberian coast in the autumn. Despite this, overall autumn numbers of trans-saharan migrants are much lower than in the spring (Figure 37). The Strait must be overflown then by many migrants travelling directly to the wintering areas from further north. The avoidance of the area is most pronounced in the case of Iberian-breeding species (e.g. Subalpine Warbler, Bonelli's Warbler), which presumably fatten in the breeding grounds and make a direct flight over the Sahara (Moreau, 1961). On the other hand, ground-foraging insectivores (e.g. Wheatears), are apparently able to find sufficient food on the ground, and the difference in numbers between spring and autumn is less pronounced (Finlayson, 1979). In tropical Africa, ground-foraging trans-saharan migrants are those which remain throughout the whole of the dry season (Morel, 1968).

In spring the Strait area is much more attractive to trans-saharan migrants: food resources are much more diverse and plentiful than in autumn, and there are then corresponding increases in species diversity (Figure 38) (Finlayson 1979, 1981). At this time, many of the migrants are making a landfall after having crossed the Sahara and Morocco and they arrive with low fat reserves (Finlayson, 1981). The return route to Europe is often more direct than in autumn, in many cases in a northeasterly heading (Moreau, 1961). While accepting a broad-front movement over Morocco in spring, Blondel (1969) pointed out that there were concentrations of migrants in the west. The coast then acted as a leading line (Geyr von Schweppenberg, 1963). This effect could explain the high concentrations of migrants in the Strait area in the spring (Nisbet *et al.*, 1961; Bernis,

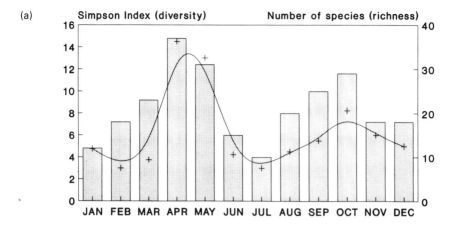

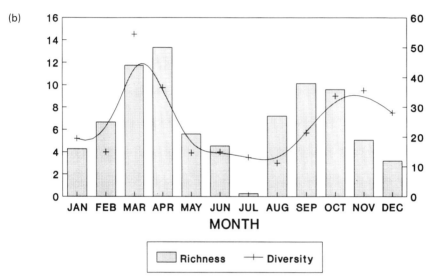

Figure 38. *(a) Species diversity and richness in low maquis, Gibraltar. (b) Species diversity and richness in garigue, Gibraltar. After Finlayson (1979).*

1962). In most cases, the passage takes place between mid–March and late May, at a time when food resources are becoming increasingly available to insectivorous birds (Finlayson, 1981).

Pre-saharan migrants

The situation varies considerably for pre–saharan migrants, species that will not cross the Sahara Desert. These birds also show a southwesterly heading in

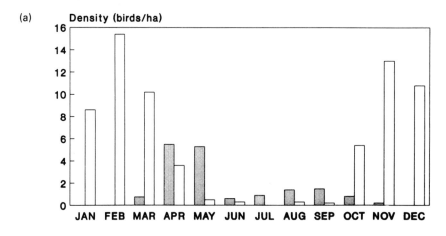

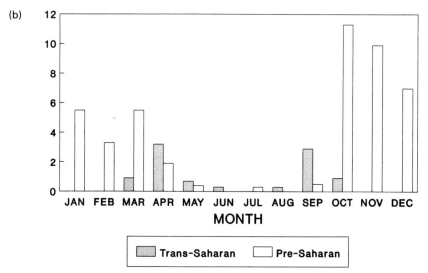

Figure 39.   (a) Densities of main migrant groups in low maquis, Gibraltar. (b) Migrant densities in garigue, Gibraltar. After Finlayson (1979).

autumn (Telleria *et al.*, 1988), but they tend to arrive later than trans–saharan species. The first pre-saharan species are usually noted in mid-September, and the main arrivals take place during October and November (Figure 39). The arrivals thus coincide with the increase in food resources associated with the autumn rains which succeed the drought (Finlayson, 1981). Many of these birds then concentrate along the eastern and southern coasts of Iberia, more so than earlier in autumn, when trans-saharan species show a reverse pattern (Bernis, 1962; Telleria *et al.*, 1988). The high density of pre-saharan migrants in October–

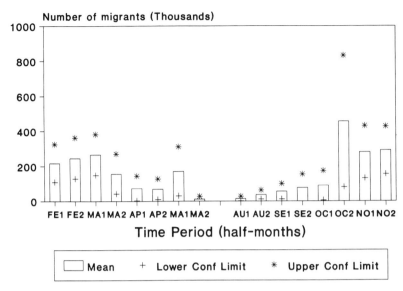

Figure 40.   Estimated number of migrants occupying a 10-km × 30-km belt of the Strait.

November is carried over to a large degree into the winter when some of the highest passerine winter densities of the Iberian Peninsula are recorded (Arroyo & Telleria, 1984; Telleria *et al.*, 1988).

In Figure 40 estimates are given of the total numbers of migrants stopping each day along a 10 km wide, 30 km long belt of Strait, based on the results of censuses carried out on Windmill Hill (Gibraltar). The regular censuses conducted in this 13 ha low scrub site form the basis of the density estimates in the species descriptions given later in this chapter. The estimates have to be treated with caution as it has been assumed that the belt is uniform in habitat (which it is not); therefore it underestimates species that occupy taller vegetation and overestimates those of the open ground. It nevertheless shows the virtual absence of migrants during the summer drought, and the greatest numbers of migrants in late autumn and early spring. From these estimates, the total number of migrants settling in the belt in a season can be calculated to be of the order of 1.2 million.

The winter distributions are characterized by their transitory nature. Some species, such as Robins, set up territories in autumn and remain in these until the following spring when they leave towards the north. Others appear to move around within the wintering area in response to fluctuating food resources (Finlayson, 1980). This is particularly conspicuous in the case of fruit-consuming birds (e.g. Blackcaps) that change location in response to fluctuating supplies of fruit. The result is that specific sites within the wintering area show wide density fluctuations for certain species within and between years. My own observations for the Maquis of the Rock of Gibraltar show that although most species

Table 5   Recurrence of passerines wintering in Gibraltar (after Finlayson, 1980).

Species	No. ringed	No. retrapped	% Returning
Dunnock	2	1	50
Blackcap	237	21	9
Chiffchaff	45	5	11
Firecrest	7	0	0
Robin	101	5	5
Black Redstart	38	1	3
Chaffinch	6	1	17
Serin	10	0	0

wintering there included individuals that returned to the same site in consecutive years, there was considerable variation in recurrence rates (Table 5) which could be linked to inter-annual differences in the success of fruit crops (Finlayson, 1980). Individuals that had been ringed on Gibraltar in good years were retrapped in other sites in southern Spain or Morocco in subsequent years when fruits were scarcer on the Rock. Movement between areas and habitats in winter is not a peculiarity of the migrants wintering in the Strait area. It probably applies to other areas of the Mediterranean Basin, as it does to tropical Africa where migrants often adopt transient strategies within the winter quarters while others return in successive years to the same sites (Moreau, 1972; Pearson, 1972; Aidley & Wilkinson, 1987).

The spring migration of pre-saharan migrants is very conspicuous in some species (e.g. Meadow Pipit, Stonechat), assumed to be those that have substantial wintering populations to the south of the Strait. In other cases, the spring migration takes the form of a gradual reduction of individuals as the spring advances. The general pattern is of a passage which is ahead of that of the trans-saharan migrants, commencing in early February and ending in early April (Finlayson, 1979, 1981).

MIGRATORY STRATEGIES

In a study of trans–saharan species caught at Gibraltar in spring I found that the average weight and fat levels of most were lower than for the same species in autumn (Tables 6 and 7; Finlayson, 1981). These results are consistent with the interpretation that birds passing south in the autumn are ready to cross the desert and have a longer journey ahead of them than in the spring, and that they are likely to be birds which have been forced to land, possibly by bad weather or by daylight (e.g. Bairlein, in press). This pattern of avoidance of the Mediterranean drought is general (Moreau, 1969; Moreau & Dolp, 1970). The trans–saharan migrants stay for only a short while, presumably resuming the journey at the first opportunity (Finlayson, 1981). It has been suggested that Pied Flycatchers might

Table 6   Weights (g) of trans-saharan and pre-saharan migrants trapped at Gibraltar in spring and autumn (after Finlayson, 1981).

Species	Spring Mean	S.D.	n	Autumn Mean	S.D.	n
Trans-saharan						
Melodious Warbler	11.0	0.95	54	11.5	1.85	20
Whitethroat	14.0	2.24	26	16.5	2.43	6
Garden Warbler	16.5	1.60	48	20.0	3.27	45
Reed Warbler	11.0	1.47	7	13.5	1.88	11
Willow Warbler	8.0	0.96	82	9.5	1.47	61
Bonelli's Warbler	7.0	0.63	34	8.5	1.36	3
Nightingale	20.0	2.11	55	24.0	2.17	18
Pied Flycatcher	11.5	0.92	28	14.0	0.28	21
Spotted Flycatcher	14.0	1.32	20	17.5	1.56	6
Redstart	14.0	1.38	24	15.0	0.35	13
Whinchat	16.0	1.94	10	18.5	1.98	2
Woodchat Shrike	29.0	3.26	17	36.0	2.75	3
Pre-saharan						
Blackcap[1]	18.0	1.67	40	18.5	1.25	40
Chiffchaff[1]	7.0	1.07	88	7.0	0.88	76
Black Redstart	17.0	1.43	16	15.5	0.15	30
Robin	16.5	1.44	28	15.5	0.15	62
Stonechat	15.0	0.71	2	16.5	1.94	31
Song Thrush	70.5	5.97	14	74.0	1.32	18

[1] Blackcap and Chiffchaff are included as pre-saharan, though some populations cross the Sahara.

Table 7   Fat levels of migrants trapped at Gibraltar in spring and autumn (after Finlayson, 1981).

Season/Group	Fat level 0	1	2	3	4	Total
Trans-saharan						
Spring	4	25	32	29	23	113
Autumn	2	3	8	21	49	83
Pre-saharan						
Spring	4	14	10	10	10	48
Autumn	41	73	55	50	17	236

$\chi^2 = 129.83$, $P < 0.001$.

even be able to reach the southern edge of the Sahara in good condition in autumn, enabling them to continue further south before making a landfall, but such strategies may not be open to all populations (Moreau & Dolp, 1970). Blondel (1969) calculated that Redstarts leaving the Camargue in autumn would have to re-fatten in southern Spain or North Africa before crossing the Sahara. This is a species that concentrates in the Strait in autumn (Bernis, 1962), so some of the trans-saharan migrants settling in the Strait in autumn might therefore do so through choice. These could belong to populations which regularly fatten in the area. This situation also seems to apply to areas on the northern fringe of the Sahara, which are used as refuelling sites by trans-saharan migrants in autumn (Bairlein, 1987).

Neighbouring breeding populations of a species might, as a result of natural selection, tend to standardize different levels of migratory fat (Moreau & Dolp, 1970). This would imply that different populations of the same species might travel different distances, possibly to avoid competition in transit. Investigating the migratory strategies of Robins at two stop-over sites in southern Sweden, Karlsson *et al.* (1988) found that Robins committed to long-distance and short-distance flights were indeed using different migratory strategies. These types of difference between populations are probably common in nature.

Dowsett & Fry (1971) suggested that migrants deposited even more fat in autumn than they did in spring because the desiccated state of the North African coast in autumn precluded 'refuelling'. In contrast, Moreau & Dolp (1970), considering migration in northwest Egypt, concluded that more fat might be needed for the spring migration when headwinds not present in autumn would be met. Fogden (1972) suggested that water was more likely to limit migratory range than was fat in migratory conditions unfavourable to the water budget. Migrants crossing the Sahara may reduce water loss by flying at high altitude and resting in the shade during the day (e.g. Bairlein, in press), and such a strategy could well apply to the dry areas of the Mediterranean.

In spring, trans-saharan migrants reaching the Gibraltar area have undertaken a long flight during which their fat reserves have been used up. For example, Yellow Wagtails and Wheatears put on 30–40% of their body weight in fat before the desert crossing (Ward, 1963), and Sedge and Reed Warblers in Nigeria put on weight in March–May at the rate of around 0.3 g/day (Aidley & Wilkinson, 1987). Migrants such as these regain fat while in the Strait area and stay for longer periods than in autumn (Finlayson, 1981).

Migrants may have to fatten in inhospitable conditions before crossing the Sahara in spring. Dowsett & Fry (1971) noted that in spring some species arrived at Lake Chad from the south with good fat levels, which indicated that they were slowly moving north; here they had to deposit fat at the most inhospitable time of year (Fry *et al.*, 1970), then feeding on midges and fruits of *Salvadora persica*. In autumn, these migrants arrived south of the Sahara at the end of the wet season when food was plentiful, but the food supply soon diminished after September with the onset of African drought. Morel (1973) has argued that Palaearctic migrants are able to winter in the dry Sahel savannah by capitalizing on the short, rainy season when they arrive in autumn and that, because few native species are able to exploit this short season, the Palaearctic species are at an advantage. A similar situation has been reported for the semi-arid belt in the Sudan (Hogg *et al.*, 1984).

The importance of wild fruit to fattening migrants appears to be a widespread phenomenon, applying to either side of the Sahara at either season (Fry *et al.*, 1970; Blondel, 1969; Morel, 1973; Finlayson, 1979, 1981; Herrera, 1977, 1981a,b, 1984a,b; Jordano, 1983, 1985, 1987; Debussche & Isenmann, 1983; Tejero *et al.*, 1984 — see also Chapter 8). Garden Warblers feeding on figs during the autumn migration in Portugal were heavier than those which were not using this source of food (Thomas, 1979). Jordano (1983) suggested that migrants that do not regularly consume fruits do so in small quantities (*Rubus* and *Ficus*) during the autumn passage in southern Spain as a way of maintaining a positive water balance in the absence of fresh water. The consumption of fruit is an alternative to insects (which have more protein and fat than fruit) at a time when insects are scarce (Jordano, 1981).

Despite the apparently poor conditions at Lake Chad in spring, some migrants lay down fat to such an extent that they had difficulty in flying when released (Fry *et al.*, 1970). The high weights of these migrants may enable them to cross the Sahara and the Mediterranean in one long, 60 hour, flight (Fry *et al.*, 1970). In contrast, Aidley & Wilkinson (1987) found that, for their study site in Nigeria, Sedge Warblers probably departed northwards, as soon as they reached a 'safe' weight which guaranteed a high probability of a successful non–stop 2000 km flight over the Sahara. Excessively heavy birds would presumably have reduced flight performance and would be vulnerable to predators.

If all migrants made for the same landfall zone north of the Sahara, there could be excessive depletion of resources in certain areas. The avoidance by some migrants of areas likely to be used in transit by other migrants may be a way of avoiding competition, just as differences in passage periods might achieve similar results within the same area (Abramsky & Safriel, 1980). Thus, some migrants leaving the southern edge of the Sahara in spring might well aim to just cross to the other side, others may aim to reach beyond the Mediterranean, as suggested by Fry *et al.* (1970), yet others might adopt a 'hopping' strategy with pauses in mid-desert (Smith, 1968; Bairlein *et al.*, 1983; Biebach *et al.*, 1986; Bairlein, 1987). The different trajectories and landfalls could be achieved utilizing air currents at optimal flight altitudes (Elkins, 1988). The different fat deposition strategies of some migrants in oases in the Sahara (Bairlein, 1985) support the view that distinct populations are adopting significantly different migratory tactics and that variations in migratory behaviour of populations are likely to be under genetic control (Berthold & Querner, 1981). Such differences may be related to the existence of superabundant food supplies exploitable by species with particular feeding methods (e.g. Bibby & Green, 1981). On the other hand, choice of such optimal feeding areas may be limited in the case of lean migrants when they have completed a desert crossing; they may have to settle for a less optimal stopping area closer to the desert edge rather than for a better one further away.

Temporary alterations to the 'programmed' flight path may occur, for example when bad weather produces falls. As such migrants are probably in a state of migratory restlessness, they may simply rest and await an improvement in the weather and not feed (Rappole & Warner, 1976), although it seems likely that at least some grounded migrants would forage if opportunities are available.

Trans-saharan migrants arriving in the Strait area in the spring could be making their first landfall after crossing the desert, even though they could presumably have landed further south, in Morocco. There is no doubt that many migrants do indeed descend along the northern edge of the Sahara in spring, often with little fat and with low weights (Smith, 1968; Ash, 1969). Competition in transit areas is therefore likely to be a significant factor moulding the choice of stop-over area by migrants and, within specific areas, one or more characteristics—habitat selection (Bairlein, 1983), dissimilarity in passage periods (Abramsky & Safriel, 1980) or choice of food (Thomas, 1979)—appear to play important roles in avoiding or minimizing competition.

Studying migrating Robins on the island of Store Faerder in Norway, Mehlum (1983a) found that many Robins only stayed on the island for a brief period, even when they were lean. Most Robins lost weight after arrival and were only able to regain weight if they remained longer. This was attributed to the need to establish territories before being able to feed at a rate that would allow fat deposition and to the state of migratory restlessness (*Zugstimmung*) of the individuals (Mehlum, 1983b). Robins that were able to establish feeding territories remained longer and gained weight, and Mehlum concluded that individuals unable to secure a territory would be better off if they moved on. If they remained on the island, they would use up the few reserves they had left and would in all probability perish. If they continued the journey, there was a high risk of death, but there was a chance of finding a new site offering refuelling possibilities. Petterson & Hasselquist (1985) concluded that Robins remaining for several days at a stop-over site at Ottenby, Sweden, were able to deposit sufficient fat to enable them to migrate for several consecutive nights, when they could instead have proceeded earlier with less fat. They attributed this behaviour to the length of time required to deposit fat at stop-over sites: it is better to deposit sufficient fat for several night flights at a single site than to have to use a different stop-over site for refuelling each day. Furthermore, fat deposition strategies may depend on the time left for migration. In particular, spring migrants seem to resume migration at lower fat levels late in the season compared to earlier in the passage (Safriel & Lavee, 1988; experimental data on spring trans-Gulf migrants at coastal Louisiana—F. Bairlein, pers. comm.).

At a stop-over site in southern Texas, Rappole & Warner (1976) found that birds in a state of migratory restlessness (*Zugstimmung*) remained in the site only for a brief period and, even in normally solitary species, were gregarious. Since these birds were not feeding, they had broad habitat occupation patterns. Birds not in this physiological state (i.e. in *Zugdisposition*) were more selective of habitat, remained in the site for longer periods and actively defended feeding territories, steadily building up fat reserves. Not all birds in *Zugdisposition* found territories at the same time. Those which did not had to remain in marginal areas, attempting to establish territories, or move on.

Territoriality in the stop-over area is therefore a response which maximizes the chances of survival of individual migrants (Rappole & Warner, 1976; Bibby & Green, 1980; Mehlum, 1983a). Within the Palaearctic–African system, it is probably widespread judging from accounts of intra- and interspecific aggression between migrants and between residents and migrants, being more prevalent in some groups (chats, flycatchers, shrikes) than others (finches, buntings), presumably in response to the characteristics of the resources being defended (Hartley, 1950; Simmons, 1951; Finlayson, 1979; Bibby & Green, 1980; Mehlum, 1983a; Tye, 1984).

In a relatively new migration system such as the Palaearctic–African system, which has evolved in the last 10 000 years (Moreau, 1972), patterns are still likely to be evolving and the genetic mechanisms determining the actions of individuals from different populations are not likely to have been perfected. The high probability that natural selection is not necessarily moulding different populations in the same way has been largely overlooked. Trans-saharan migrants may adopt single flights over the Sahara (Moreau, 1972; Wood, 1982, 1989) or migrate in stages within the desert (Bairlein, 1987), but these strategies need not be mutually exclusive. Broad-front and narrow-front migratory tactics (Moreau, 1961; Bernis, 1962; Casement, 1966; Finlayson, 1979; Bairlein, in press) are both probably to be found in nature.

There is a polarization of migrants, not just soaring birds, at either end of the Mediterranean with very strong ecological reasons for doing so. The Sahara is a very definite obstacle and the significant southwest movement of migrants towards western Iberia (Henty, 1961; Moreau, 1961; Bernis, 1962), with the subsequent exit via southern Portugal and southwest Spain (Hilgerloh, 1987), leading to mass arrivals in northwest Morocco (Walter, 1979) can be tied in with the passage of these birds to important wintering grounds in West Africa (Moreau, 1972; Morel, 1973; Curry & Sayer, 1979) via the coastal belt of the western Sahara (Valverde, 1967). The passage of trans-saharan migrants in autumn through Senegal (Morel, 1973) contrasts with the virtual absence of such movement inland in the Inundation Zone of the Niger in Mali (Curry & Sayer, 1979). At the other end of the Sahara Desert, the Nile Valley is no doubt an important passage route for many migrants (Fry *et al.*, 1974; Hogg *et al.*, 1984) that winter in eastern and southern Africa. In extreme cases in which the wintering areas are entirely in East or West Africa, entire populations follow routes which avoid large areas of the Mediterranean and the Sahara (e.g. Pied Flycatcher, Melodious Warbler, Subalpine Warbler, west; Lesser Whitethroat, Marsh Warbler, Red-backed Shrike, east). This may not necessarily be a specific avoidance of these areas. It might be that they are just not within the shortest possible route between breeding and wintering grounds.

As a general strategy it would be expected that migrants should choose the energetically least demanding routes between the two areas, which should be the shortest route. By using specific air-streams, migrants may be able to obtain a better energetic package than a straightforward direct-line migration. In those cases where the flight from breeding to wintering grounds cannot be performed in a single flight, modifications to the route will take place to take into account utilization of suitable intermediate feeding grounds (Bernis, 1962; Mead, 1968; Hope Jones *et al.*, 1977; Bibby & Green, 1981, 1983). The most extreme examples of departure from the most direct routes are provided by soaring birds that circumvent large bodies of water (Porter & Willis, 1968; Finlayson *et al.*, 1976) and seabirds which avoid migrating over land (Telleria, 1981; Finlayson & Cortés, 1984; Finlayson & Price, unpubl. obs.).

That many migrants cross the Mediterranean (Casement, 1966) and the Sahara (Moreau, 1961, 1972) along central areas is not in doubt. What remains to be established satisfactorily is the proportion of Palaearctic–African migration systems that preferentially follow such routes. Of those that do, there must be many cases of populations crossing the desert in a direct flight. Some may even continue further, on reaching the southern edge of the desert, as suggested by Moreau (1972). Other populations may well select strategies of short flights with refuelling at intermediate points along the desert; Bairlein's observations (1985) clearly illustrate that not all species (or even individuals of the same species) behave in the same manner while at oases.

Such behaviour is endogenously controlled (Berthold, 1984). If it were possible to distinguish between populations of the same species, differences would no doubt also be found. The final pattern, as observed from the ground, is compounded by fortuitous events which have nothing to do with the basic genetic programming of individual migrants. In the desert, as along coastal areas, inclement weather forces migrants down and can produce large falls (Smith, 1968). Such effects may be subtle and could be the result of migrants meeting unfavourable air-streams (Wood, 1989). This could explain the occurrence of fat migrants in mid-desert, although the very regular occurrence of fat migrants in the desert irrespective of weather conditions (Bairlein *et al.*, 1983, Biebach *et al.*, 1986; Bairlein, 1987; Safriel & Lavee, 1988) suggests that weather may only force birds down in specific sites and then only irregularly and briefly.

In considering the different tactics employed by separate populations of the same species it seems that the southern Iberian/Maghreb populations are evolving along separate lines from continental populations of the same species. Thus in a number of cases (Cuckoo, Nightjar, Yellow Wagtail, etc.) the migratory routes and winter quarters are distinct from those of other populations. The seasonal timing of the migration is also quite distinct, with a generalized pattern of early arrival (late October to early March) coinciding with the rains in southern Iberia and Morocco after the summer drought, and an early departure in July and August in avoidance of the drought. The behaviour of the southern populations appears to be in direct response to the wet and dry seasons, similar to the behaviour of many migrants south of the Sahara but quite distinct from the behaviour of conspecifics in more northerly latitudes.

The migratory patterns of a number of species continue to change in response to changing environmental factors.

In mid-latitudes, the migratory behaviour of certain populations, which is genetically controlled (Berthold & Querner, 1981; Biebach, 1983; Berthold, 1984; Schwabl *et al.*, 1984; Lundberg, 1987), appears to change with climatic conditions. Dhont (1983) found that the number of overwintering Stonechats in Belgium and Holland was significantly correlated with the temperature of the previous winter, which suggested differential survival of overwintering and migratory individuals. Berthold & Terrill (1988) considered the possible selective advantages to the increasing numbers of Blackcaps wintering in the British Isles (Leach, 1981) over those wintering in the traditional Mediterranean wintering areas. Mortality in populations of trans-saharan migrants wintering in the Sahel is greatest in years with lowest rainfall (Morel, 1973; Winstanley *et al.*, 1974; Mead, 1979; Peach & Baillie, 1990) so that, were such conditions to persist for a number of years, individuals wintering in zones least affected would be at an advantage.

The southern Iberian–north Moroccan area is climatically more stable and predictable than central or northern Europe. There is a long summer drought lasting from July to September, sometimes later. During this period the area is avoided by passage migrants and by breeding species which, except for a few residents, leave for south of the Sahara. The arrival of the rainy season is less predictable, usually commencing in October. It (October–April) is characterized by the arrival of birds from the north (pre-saharan migrants in October and November) and from the south (trans-saharan migrants from late October onwards). Pre-saharan migrants abandon the area in March and April at the end of the rains, but trans-saharan migrants make use of the long days and rich insect food supplies (Finlayson, 1979) to breed before the drought. The southern Iberian–north Moroccan rainy season coincides with the sub-saharan drought that commences in September and ends in March (Moreau, 1972), so it is logical that some trans-saharan migrants should leave the area in July and August to avoid the Mediterranean drought, making the most of the sub-saharan rains in West Africa and returning in 'midwinter' to make use of the Mediterranean rains. There are many examples of apparent overwintering of trans-saharan migrants in southern Iberia and northern Morocco (Smith, 1965; Herrera & Hidalgo, 1974; Andrada & Franco, 1975; de Juana, 1977; Cortés *et al.*, 1980; Telleria, 1981; Pineau & Giraud-Audine, 1976) which may be due to regular arrivals from the south. Others arrive in February and March, earlier than more northerly populations of the same species. It may not be possible for these to arrive sooner because of the presence of ecologically similar pre-saharan species. Thus, Redstarts would meet Black Redstarts, Tree Pipits would meet Meadow Pipits, and so on. Others which breed at high altitude, such as Subalpine Warblers, would be unable to reach the high mountains in December and January and would not be able to compete with the larger wintering *Sylvia* species (especially Sardinian Warbler).

THE GIBRALTAR MATORRAL

The matorral or scrub habitats of the Rock of Gibraltar in which the vegetation has remained unaltered by Man for at least 80 years, hold very few resident species (Finlayson, 1979). These habitats present a unique opportunity for the study of seasonal patterns of species diversity and use of the habitats by migratory birds. I have studied two sites in detail at Gibraltar, representing different forms of scrub, the maquis at Jews' Gate and the garigue at Windmill Hill (Finlayson, 1979, 1980, 1981). Censuses in these two sites form the basis of the species accounts later in this chapter.

A peculiar feature of the Gibraltar habitats, presumably related to their geographical location, is the high turnover of individuals within the habitat from one day to the next within the passage periods. Figure 41 illustrates the daily changes in species diversity in the garigue at Windmill Hill during the spring of

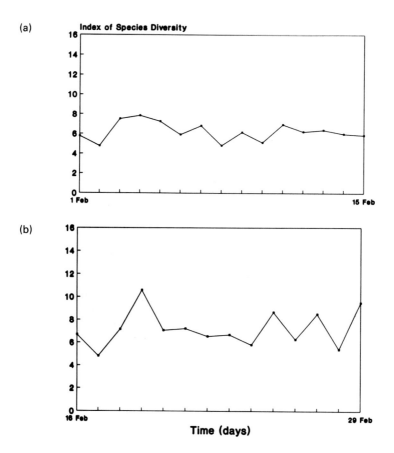

Figure 41.   Daily changes in species diversity at Windmill Hill, Gibraltar.
(a) 1–15 February, (b) 16–29 February.

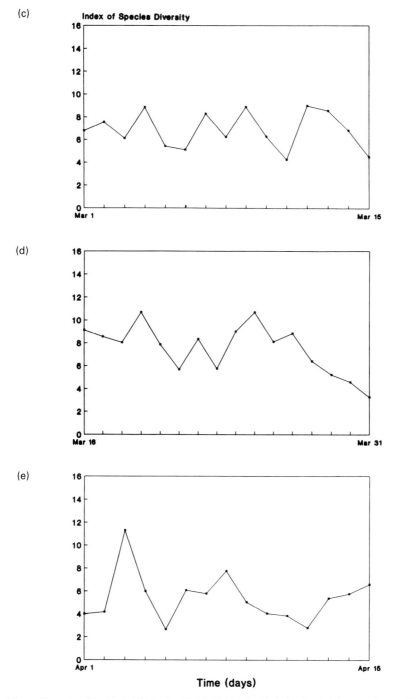

Figure 41 continued. (c) 1–15 March, (d) 16–31 March, (e) 1–30 April. *(Continued on p. 92.)*

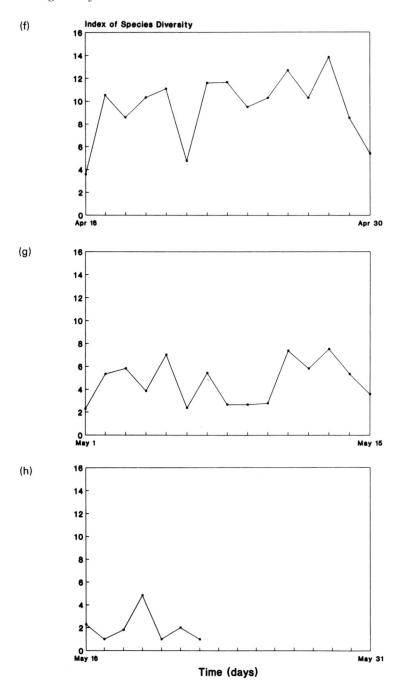

Figure 41 continued.   (f) 16–30 April, (g) 1–15 May, (h) 16–22 May.

1984, and Figure 42 gives three examples of how species abundance curves can change from one day to the next with the arrival and departure of migrants. During the 1984 spring, the community structure varied little in February when most of the migrants were winter residents and not yet moving. At the end of March, when diversity took a sharp drop (Figure 41) there was considerable variation in community structure between days, with some days having a wide

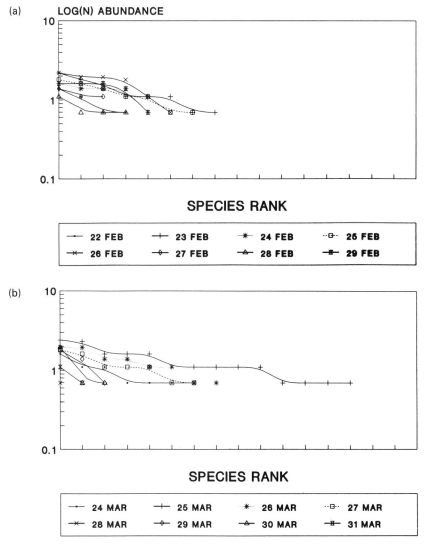

Figure 42.   Species-abundance curves—Windmill Hill, 1984: (a) 22–29 February, (b) 24–31 March. (Continued.)

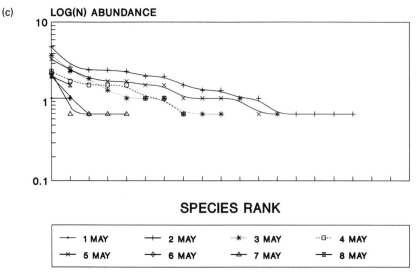

Figure 42 continued.   (c) 1–8 May.

range of species, most of them at similar density, and others having few (numerically dominant) species. During a fall in early May there were once again significant variations in diversity, some days having many species present but dominated by a few species. This explains why during this large fall diversity was lower than at other times during the spring. It is a feature of falls that a small number of species, presumably those dominating the passage the previous night, are much more numerous than the rest.

MAQUIS

Finlayson (1979), studying the maquis community at Jews' Gate, recorded 46 passerine species and a small number of non-passerines (the most frequent being migrants—Turtle Dove, Scops Owl, Hoopoe and Wryneck). The months with highest species diversity were April and May (see Figure 38) with a second, lower, peak in October. In winter, diversity was lower than during the passage periods but it was higher than in summer. The sharp rise in diversity in spring was due to the influxes of many species passing northwards over the Strait area. Very few of these birds remained to breed. Although the number of species in the habitat in August and September was high, diversity was low because most species were only represented by a small number of individuals. Most migrants passing the area during the drought avoid stopping over. Many more migrants stopped and utilized the site after the rains in October, but by then most trans-saharan migrants had moved south and it was the pre-saharan species which

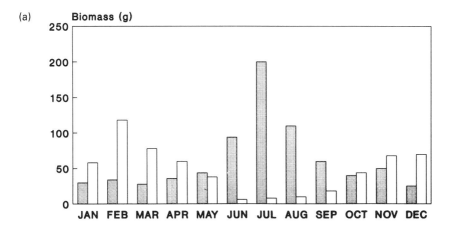

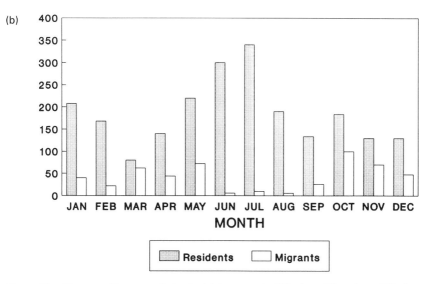

Figure 43. Consumer biomass variation in (a) low maquis, Gibraltar, (b) garigue, Gibraltar. After Finlayson (1979).

dominated (see Figure 39). Even though the number of species at the site increased from January to February, diversity in the latter month was low since the site was then dominated by large numbers of migrating Blackcaps.

Pre-saharan migrants are most abundant in the maquis in early spring and late autumn (see Figure 39). The main species are the Blackcap, Chiffchaff, Black Redstart, Robin and Song Thrush. They are absent during the summer but abundant in winter. Trans-saharan migrants rarely reach the densities of the pre-saharan migrants (see Figure 39), and pass later in spring and earlier in autumn.

The spring peak coincides with the maximum diversity in the community, but in autumn trans-saharan migrants are scarce and contribute little to the total diversity. The main species are the Reed Warbler, Melodious Warbler, Orphean Warbler, Garden Warbler, Whitethroat, Subalpine Warbler, Willow Warbler, Bonelli's Warbler, Pied Flycatcher, Spotted Flycatcher, Redstart, Nightingale and Ortolan Bunting.

There are three biomass peaks in the maquis (Figure 43). The main peak is in July and is related to the emergence of many young birds of the resident species, particularly the Blackbird, Sardinian Warbler and Blackcap. The other peaks, in February and November, are caused by the large numbers of pre-saharan migrants during these months. Biomass is high in winter but is at its lowest in September at the height of the drought when there are few migrants and residents, in the latter case possibly as a result of juvenile mortality. The other low, in May, is related to the small numbers of residents during the breeding season and the low number of trans-saharan migrants stopping at the site.

Use of the habitat

Ground Insectivores. Diversity is generally low except in May and October (Figure 44). In May the main ground insectivores are trans-saharan migrants such as the Woodchat Shrike and the Tree Pipit, but in October pre-saharan migrants such as the Black Redstart and the Dunnock dominate numerically and by biomass. Ground insectivores are never abundant in maquis.

Ground Granivores. Diversity is high outside the period June–August but biomass is low at all times (Figure 44).

Ground Omnivores. Diversity and biomass are high (Figure 44). In summer, the most important contribution is from residents (e.g. Blackbird and the Blue Rock Thrush), but others (e.g. Song Thrush) contribute substantially to the increases in the period November–February.

Foliage Insectivores. This is the dominant group numerically and by biomass. The April–May diversity peak is due to trans-saharan migrants, as is the lower one in September (Figure 44). These contribute little to total biomass, which peaks in February (due to passage Blackcaps) and July (due to juvenile Blackcaps and Sardinian Warblers).

Foliage Granivores. Diversity and biomass are low at all times (Figure 44).

Foliage Omnivores. Diversity and biomass are low, though there is a small rise in biomass in summer (Figure 44).

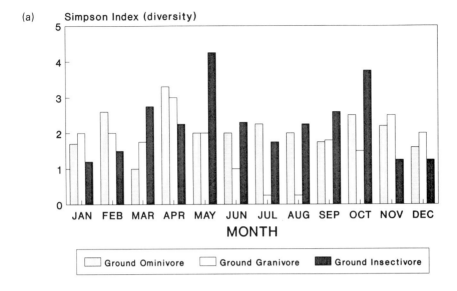

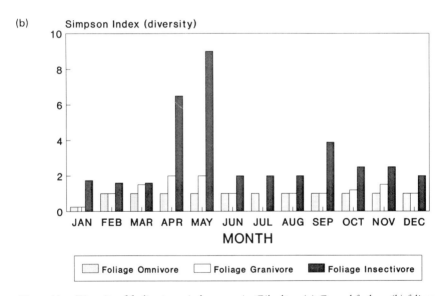

Figure 44. Diversity of feeding types in low maquis, Gibraltar. (a) Ground feeders, (b) foliage feeders. After Finlayson (1979).

General

Five species are resident in the maquis. Two are abundant foliage insectivores, the Blackcap and the Sardinian Warbler, and are able to change diet to other sources (e.g. fruit) in times of insect shortage (Finlayson, 1979; Chapter 8). A third foliage insectivore, the Blue Tit, is scarcer and only utilizes the habitat for foraging. The other two species, the Blackbird and the House Sparrow, are omnivorous ground foragers. Few other species breed in the maquis and those that do are uncommon, the Wren and the Nightingale being regular. Several species enter in winter: two are abundant, the Chiffchaff, a foliage insectivore which takes nectar at the height of the winter (Finlayson, 1979), and the Robin, which is a ground omnivore. Several species occur in smaller numbers: Dunnock, Firecrest, Black Redstart and Song Thrush. The Blackcap population is augmented by many continental migrants. All other species occur only in transit.

The dominant species, numerically and by biomass, are foliage insectivores (which can be almost wholly frugivorous in winter) and ground omnivores. The few residents appear to have catholic tastes (Morse, 1971), the ground feeders coping with the summer drought and the foliage insectivores with the winter low in arthropods. It appears that summer visitors that could utilize the maquis fail to breed in this habitat because of the numerical (McNaughton & Wolf, 1970) and social (Morse, 1974) dominance of the residents. Examples of potential migrant colonizers are the Subalpine Warbler and the Melodious Warbler.

GARIGUE

Annually, 56 passerine species are regular in this habitat. In addition, there are several important non-passerines, notably the Barbary Partridge, Little Owl, Hoopoe and Wryneck. The months with highest species diversity are March, April, October and November (see Figure 38). The spring peak is higher than the autumn peak, as in the maquis, although the difference is not as pronounced. The community is diverse in winter but is impoverished in summer, with a minimum in diversity in August at the height of the drought (see Figure 38).

Pre-saharan migrants are most abundant in October (see Figure 39) and there is a gradual decline in density through the winter, with a slight recovery in March. Winter density is high. Between April and September the density of pre-saharan migrants is negligible. Trans-saharan migrants peak in spring and autumn (see Figure 39), in April and September. Densities are lower than those of pre-saharan migrants. The main pre-saharan species are the Skylark, Crested/Thekla Lark, Song Thrush, Black Redstart, Stonechat, Dartford Warbler, Meadow Pipit, Goldfinch, Greenfinch, Serin, Linnet and Corn Bunting. The main trans-saharan species are the Hoopoe, Short-toed Lark, Wheatear, Black-eared Wheatear, Redstart, Whinchat, Whitethroat, Spectacled Warbler, Rufous Bush Chat, Willow Warbler, Melodious Warbler, Tree Pipit, Tawny Pipit, Woodchat Shrike and Ortolan Bunting.

The main biomass peak is in July and is related to the emergence of juvenile birds, especially Spotless Starlings and Blackbirds (see Figure 43). Peaks in October and January are due to pre-saharan migrants.

Use of habitat

Ground Insectivores. Diversity is low in midsummer when the ground is dry and in midwinter when few insects are active. There are fewer fruiting plants in the garigue than in the maquis in autumn and winter. The two main diversity peaks, in May and September, are due to trans-saharan migrants. The September increase is as a result of some species (e.g. the Wheatear and the Redstart) which do not seem to overfly the area in late summer as much as other trans-saharan migrants do. As ground arthropods are not as scarce as foliage arthropods at this time (Finlayson, 1979, 1981), there may be sufficient food to permit these birds to use the site for fattening.

Ground Granivores. The seasonal changes in this group are similar to those of the ground insectivores except that the spring peak is earlier and higher than the autumn peak, which is in November (Figure 45). Peaks are due to migrant finches and buntings, especially the Linnet, Serin, Goldfinch and Corn Bunting. The summer biomass peak is due to the hatching of young Barbary Partridges and the autumn peak is due to the large numbers of migrating finches.

Ground Omnivores. The community of ground-dwelling polyphagous species is diverse, especially in winter and early spring, but low in numbers in August (Figure 45). The biomass pattern is the reverse, with a summer peak provided by young Spotless Starlings, Blackbirds and House Sparrows.

Foliage Insectivores. This community is diverse and less variable between seasons than the ground insectivore community (Figure 45). The April peak is associated with the passage of trans-saharan warblers. After the summer drought, there is a progressive build-up towards a more diverse winter community, but there is no autumn peak. Juvenile Sardinian Warblers are the main cause of the July biomass peak.

Foliage Granivores. There are very few foliage granivores, and the slight October peak is caused by passage finches (Figure 45).

General

Six species are resident in the garigue. Four are ground omnivores, the Spotless Starling, Blackbird, Blue Rock Thrush and House Sparrow. They all have catholic diets and at least two species move between habitats to forage. The only

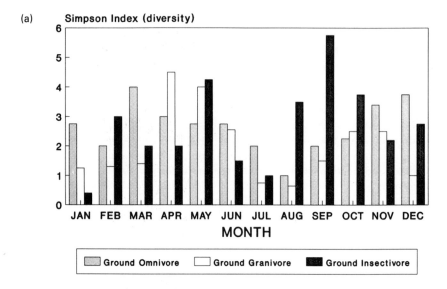

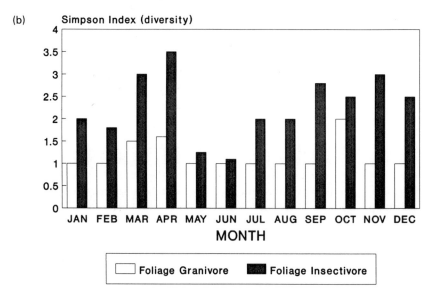

Figure 45.   Diversity of feeding types in garigue, Gibraltar. (a) Ground feeders, (b) foliage feeders. After Finlayson (1979).

resident foliage insectivore is the Sardinian Warbler; the Barbary Partridge is the resident ground granivore (which could be classed as omnivorous because it is not restricted to eating seeds). No other species breed in garigue, although some, like the Fan-tailed Warbler, Spectacled Warbler and Corn Bunting, do so some years. Some of the species entering the community in winter can be numerically important. These are the Skylark, Meadow Pipit, Stonechat, Black Redstart, Robin, Song Thrush, Corn Bunting, Crested Lark, Fan-tailed Warbler and Chiffchaff.

COMPARISON OF MATORRAL COMMUNITIES

The overall pattern of seasonal changes in species diversity is similar for the maquis and garigue (see Figure 38). There is nevertheless a greater species turnover in the garigue. If the species utilization of the garigue and maquis are compared, differences related to the habitat requirements of the migrants can be seen. These habitat differences, which appear to be a feature of regularly utilized stop-over sites (Bairlein, 1983), reflect the use being made of the site by migrants, since those in a state of migratory restlessness (which would not feed) would not be expected to show narrow habitat–occupation patterns (Rappole & Warner, 1976).

A third habitat, i.e. high maquis (a well-developed maquis resembling wood-land), has the least turnover (Figure 46). The more open habitats are likely to be

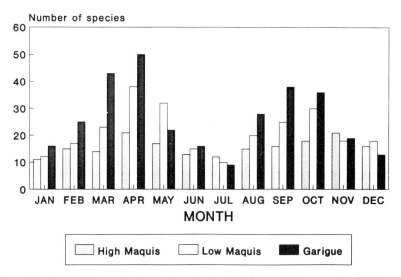

Figure 46.   Seasonal changes in the number of species in high maquis, low maquis and garigue at Gibraltar, after Finlayson (1979).

more seasonal than the structurally more complex habitats, and they are less able to support as many resident species (Cody, 1974; Karr, 1976; Alerstam & Enckell, 1979). The summer low in diversity extends for a greater period than in the maquis (see Figure 38), supporting the view that this habitat is more seasonal than the maquis. The garigue, with the simplest vegetation structure, has a 42 species difference between the month with highest species richness and that with lowest. The equivalent for the maquis is 27 species, and for the high maquis it is only 9.

Winter diversity is similar in the garigue and the maquis even though the maquis has a greater species richness. The diversity peaks during the passage periods are similar, although the garigue has a higher species richness. The diversity peaks do not coincide precisely in the two habitats and are earlier in spring and later in autumn in the garigue than in the maquis, in keeping with the longer, harsher drought period in the garigue.

Pre-saharan migrants always reach higher densities than trans-saharan migrants in the two habitats (see Figure 39). In the maquis, pre-saharan migrants reach a density peak in February and in November; in the garigue, the peaks are in March and October. Pre-saharan migrants are absent from both habitats for a similar period. The trans-saharan density peak is more pronounced in spring than autumn in the maquis, as would be expected, because many more migrants are then seeking refuelling sites after the desert crossing. There is little difference in the seasonal peaks in the garigue. Many of the trans-saharan migrants that use the maquis on passage are foliage insectivores with restricted Mediterranean breeding ranges, and many are known to overfly the Mediterranean in autumn (Moreau, 1972). Many of the trans-saharan migrants that use the garigue are ground insectivores which extend further north into Europe to breed; they probably have to stage the migration in several flights and may not be in good condition to overfly the Mediterranean shores (Blondel, 1969; Smith, 1969; Langslow, 1976). Ground-dwelling insects remain abundant during the summer in these habitats (Finlayson, 1979). This could explain why many of the trans-saharan migrants in the garigue (e.g. Whinchat, Redstart, Wheatear) are as common in autumn as they are in spring.

Consumer biomass (Salt, 1957) is higher in the garigue than the maquis due to the presence of numerically dominant large species (e.g. the Spotless Starling and the Blackbird). The pattern is otherwise similar in the two habitats, with a July peak coinciding with the emergence of the young of the resident species. In the garigue migrant biomass never exceeds resident biomass, but in the maquis migrant biomass exceeds resident biomass from October to April (see Figure 43). In the two habitats, migrant biomass is lowest in summer.

The environment at Gibraltar is highly seasonal and its bird communities reflect this, usually being poor in summer and richer in winter. The communities are most diverse in the spring and the autumn, due to the wide range of migrants which pass through the area. Species with an unrestricted diet (Morse, 1971) are numerically dominant and it is these which are resident (Cody, 1974; Herrera, 1978a,b). In the maquis foliage foragers are more important than in the garigue, which is dominated by ground foragers. Granivores are generally unimportant except for the Barbary Partidge in the garigue and finches and buntings in the garigue in autumn. Insectivores are important in spring and summer, but in winter it is those species which can switch to alternative foods (e.g. fruit) that utilize the habitats. Of the species dominant numerically or by biomass (i.e. those which contribute over 5% to the community) in the maquis, six are warblers which feed mainly on foliage insects, two are ground insectivores and three are ground omnivores. In the garigue only two insectivorous warblers are dominant, but there are six species of ground omnivores, four ground insectivores, three ground granivores and two foliage granivores.

MAIN GROUPS OF NON-SOARING MIGRANTS

PIGEONS AND DOVES

The main species in the vicinity of the Strait is the Turtle Dove, which is a regular migrant, more common in spring than autumn. Woodpigeons cross the Strait in small numbers to winter on the Moroccan side (Pineau & Giraud-Audine, 1979) and are locally abundant in winter on the Spanish side, especially in the cork oak woods around La Janda, where flocks of up to 6500 have been recorded in winter (Telleria, 1981). The wintering population of La Janda has been estimated at 10 000–15 000 (Purroy, 1988). Southwest Spain and Portugal are the main wintering grounds of north European Woodpigeons, especially those from Scandinavia and the Soviet Union, and the total Iberian wintering population is estimated at 5–7 million (Purroy, 1988). The only other migratory species in this group is the Stock Dove, which crosses the Strait in small numbers (Pineau & Giraud-Audine, 1979; Cortés *et al.*, 1980; Telleria, 1981; Finlayson & Cortés, 1987). The recovery of a Swiss bird suggests that the few Stock Doves that reach the Strait may come from outside the Iberian Peninsula (Telleria, 1981). Although Rock Doves breed on both sides of the Strait and may sometimes cross the Strait, there is no evidence to point to a regular passage; the sightings are likely to be of local birds.

Turtle Dove

The Turtle Doves that cross Iberia are western European, including Belgian, Dutch, French, British, German and Czechoslovak birds, and they join Iberian birds to cross into Africa in autumn (Bernis, 1967; Telleria, 1981). These Turtle Doves winter in West Africa where they are numerous in Senegal between September and May (Serle *et al.*, 1977). Isolated individuals winter in Morocco (Smith, 1965; Thevenot *et al.*, 1981, 1982). Recoveries in Senegal and Mali are of western European birds (Cramp, 1985) and include two ringed in Spain and recovered in Senegal (Bernis, 1967).

Although Turtle Doves cross the Mediterranean and the Sahara on a broad front (Moreau, 1961, 1972), there appears to be a concentration in the western

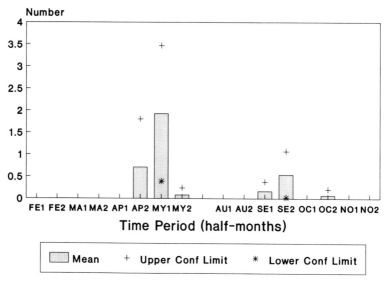

Figure 47. Turtle Dove passage at Windmill Hill, Gibraltar, 1987. For all figures in this chapter, days watched per period are: FE1 (14); FE2 (14); MA1 (12); MA2 (14); AP1 (13); AP2 (14); MY1 (14); MY2 (12); AU1 (15); AU2 (13); SE1 (12); SE2 (11); OC1 (9); OC2 (14); NO1 (11); NO2 (10).

end of the Mediterranean, most pronounced during the southward passage (Moreau, 1961; Smith, 1965; Bernis, 1967) with a major movement through southwest France, Portugal and Atlantic Morocco followed by southwestward coasting (Smith, 1965; Cramp, 1985). The spring migration follows a more easterly route (Bernis, 1967). In the Strait, there is a greater concentration in spring than autumn (Pineau & Giraud-Audine, 1979; Figure 47). During the peak spring migration, mean counts at Windmill Hill are of the order of 2–3 birds/day (0.15–0.23/ha) whereas in autumn mean counts do not exceed 0.5 birds/day (0.04/ha). Spring falls are the most spectacular. The highest spring count at Windmill Hill is 31 (2.39 birds/ha).

The Turtle Dove is a typical trans-saharan migrant with a late spring passage and an early return south. In spring, the passage is concentrated during the second half of April and the first half of May (Figure 47). The first birds arrive during the first half of April, some occasionally in late March (Cortés *et al.*, 1980) and the last birds pass in early June. The southward movement commences in August, sometimes late July, and builds slowly towards a peak in mid-September (Figure 47; Telleria, 1981). Very few pass south in October.

CUCKOOS

The arrival of the Cuckoo to the shores of the Strait in late March and early April is spectacular. Large numbers then stay, in the cork oak woods of the area. The return movement, which is early, in July and August (Telleria, 1981; Finlayson & Cortés, 1987), is inconspicuous. Moreau (1961) suggested that Cuckoos probably fly over the Mediterranean in autumn, and the migratory trend in most European populations is south to southeast, avoiding the Iberian Peninsula (Seel, 1977). Bernis (1970) only gives two British Cuckoo recoveries in Iberia as well as a Belgian one in December, suggesting only occasional wintering. Most European Cuckoos winter in eastern and southern Africa south of 10°S. In contrast, the small Iberian and Moroccan subspecies *bangsi* migrates towards West Africa (Moreau, 1972) although some may then continue southeast (Cramp, 1985). The observations from the Strait are consistent with this pattern. The large spring arrival probably involves mostly Iberian and Moroccan birds, as evidenced by the early arrival dates, and later migrants may be bound for northwestern parts of the breeding range. The early passage in autumn is consistent with the departure of many Iberian breeding trans-saharan migrants, and the absence of passage later in autumn is likely to be due to avoidance of Iberia by continental Cuckoos.

Great Spotted Cuckoos are less conspicuous than Cuckoos and arrive earlier to the breeding grounds. There is a progressive build-up in southern Iberia from December, which leads to a peak in March (Herrera & Hidalgo, 1974; Finlayson & Cortés, 1987). Occasional birds arrive in late November, especially in Morocco (Thevenot *et al.*, 1981, 1982; Mayaud, 1983). Telleria (1981) saw two Great Spotted Cuckoos at Tarifa on 15 October 1977, which may have arrived from Morocco. Great Spotted Cuckoos return early to Iberia, as do other migrants, and autumn and winter records are probably of birds that have arrived from the south. The early departure of Iberian Great Spotted Cuckoos, in July and August with very few left by early September, supports this view. Great Spotted Cuckoos have been seen in large numbers in West Africa in mid-August (Moreau, 1972); presumably these are birds from the western part of the breeding range, i.e. Iberia and southern France.

OWLS

The Scops Owl is the main migratory owl in the area. The first spring arrivals are usually in late March, presumably Iberian birds, and the main passage takes place in April. The southward passage is less conspicuous (Cortés *et al.*, 1980; Telleria, 1981) and takes place between mid-August and mid-October. Moreau (1972) concluded that Scops Owls overflew the western edge of the Sahara in autumn, which is in agreement with these observations. The birds that cross the Strait must be mainly Iberian and French, presumably wintering in tropical West Africa (Moreau, 1972).

Short-eared Owls winter in the Strait in small numbers in marshy habitats (see also Chapter 7). The numbers are nowhere high, but wintering is regular. Pineau & Giraud-Audine (1979) cite the recovery of a Finnish Short-eared Owl on the Moroccan side in winter and Bernis (1967) gives Iberian recoveries of Dutch, northwest German and south Swedish Short-eared Owls. Short-eared Owls are known to cross the Sahara to winter in tropical West Africa (Moreau, 1972) and some of the birds which cross the Strait could conceivably be trans-saharan migrants. Movements of Little and Long-eared Owls are also likely on a small scale (Cortés *et al.*, 1980; Telleria, 1981) and may involve central and north-western European populations (Bernis, 1967): Bernis (1967) gives the recovery in Cádiz Province in winter of a Barn Owl ringed in Switzerland.

NIGHTJARS

There is insufficient information on this group and it requires further study. The Nightjar and the Red-necked Nightjar are migrants across the Strait (Pineau & Giraud-Audine, 1979; Cortés *et al.*, 1980; Telleria, 1981; Finlayson & Cortés, 1987) and appear to be more abundant during the spring passage than the autumn, although the seasonal differences may not be as great as in other trans-saharan migrants.

The Nightjar, which has a wider geographical distribution, is the commoner species in spring, although less noticeably than is actually the case because of the conspicuousness of breeding Red-necked Nightjars within the Strait. These two species are apparently less abundant in the Strait now than they were in the past (Telleria, 1981).

The passage periods are mid-April to early June and September to early November. Although the differences in passage of the two species have not been

A Red-necked Nightjar, a trans-saharan migrant, sleeps on the ground by day before resuming its migration at dusk.

precisely determined, it does appear that Red-necked Nightjars may move south first, in September, and Nightjars later, in October and early November. Nevertheless, Pineau & Giraud-Audine (1979) recorded the passage of Nightjars (subspecies *europaeus*) as being from mid-August to November, and that of Red-necked Nightjars as October and November. The subspecies *meridionalis* of the Nightjar breeds on the Moroccan and Spanish (Moreau, 1972) sides of the Strait, and these presumably join the nominate subspecies on passage. Since most *europaeus* Nightjars winter in eastern and southern Africa (Moreau, 1972), it has to be assumed that the main movements of Nightjars across the Strait in autumn are of the native *meridionalis* which winter in West Africa (Moreau, 1972). There is one recovery of a British-ringed Nightjar in Spain, and another of a Czechoslovak bird in southern Spain (Cramp, 1985), indicating that at least a few *europaeus* (including some from well east) migrate through Iberia. The Red-necked Nightjars of Iberia and Morocco winter in West Africa, in the Inundation Zone in Mali, Ivory Coast and Ghana, but not in Senegal where they are migrants (Morel & Roux, 1966; Moreau, 1972; Lamarche, 1980).

SWIFTS

Five species are found within the Strait (see Chapter 8), with the exception of Little Swift which only breeds on the Moroccan side and appears to be mainly sedentary (Pineau & Giraud-Audine, 1979) only crossing the Strait to the La Janda area sporadically (Wratten, *in litt.*; Parody, pers. comm.). This subspecies (*galilejensis*) winters just south of the Sahara in small numbers (Moreau, 1972), so some Moroccan birds may migrate south in autumn.

The White-rumped Swift, which colonized the Spanish side of the Strait during the 1960s (Brudenell-Bruce, 1969), is widespread. These swifts, which utilize the nests of Red-rumped Swallows, arrive late. The first birds are observed in May, and the majority reach the area in June, breeding during the summer and early autumn, and departing in October, with some remaining into November and December (Telleria, 1981). Passage across the Strait is imperceptible.

Pallid Swifts arrive in February and remain until October (Finlayson, 1979). Their breeding season is described in Chapter 8. The reduced breeding range of this species, and difficulty separating it from the Swift, makes any attempt to describe the migration very difficult. The western Mediterranean subspecies *brehmorum* appears to be thinly spread in tropical and equatorial Africa in winter, reaching Cape Province (Moreau, 1972), although the majority are probably in West Africa, north of the equator.

Swift

The nominate subspecies of the Swift breeds from the Atlantic east to Transcaucasia. Western and central European populations are involved in the Strait crossing. Bernis (1970) gives Iberian recoveries of Swifts ringed in France, England, Holland, Germany, Czechoslovakia, southern Finland and Switzerland. Mayaud (1983) gives Finnish, Dutch, English, Swiss and French recoveries in Morocco. These birds may winter in the southern tropics, where Dutch and British Swifts have been recovered in southwest Congo (Zaïre), Malawi and Zimbabwe, though some must remain to winter in the northern tropical West Africa (Moreau, 1972). British-ringed Swifts have been predominantly recovered in Spain and Morocco in autumn and in France in spring, suggesting a more easterly return to the breeding grounds (Cramp, 1985).

The Swift is the most numerous of the diurnal migrants crossing the Strait; it is estimated that a total of 350 000–400 000 cross in autumn (Telleria, 1981), and this figure may be low. I calculate the total passage to be of the order of 800 000 Swifts per 1 km front of the Strait in autumn, and I have recorded rates of passage of 10 000 birds/hour (Finlayson, 1979). Garcia Rua (1975) counted 100 000 Swifts during the first hour of daylight in a single day, giving an indication of the intensity of the migration. On the basis of passage rates, I consider that the scale of the spring movement is around 40% of the autumn migration, lending support to the hypothesis of a more easterly route being followed in spring (Finlayson, 1979).

The southward passage is concentrated during the second half of July and the first half of August, with a reduced passage continuing into October (Telleria, 1981; Figure 48). The return from Africa commences in early April and continues into early June. Most Swifts pass during the latter half of April and in May (Finlayson, 1979; Figure 48).

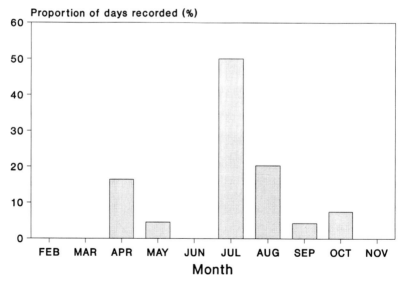

Figure 48.   Swift passage periods over Gibraltar, 1987. For all figures in this chapter, days watched are: FEB (13); MAR (31); APR (30); MAY (31); JUN (13); JUL (12); AUG (31); SEP (30); OCT (17); NOV (5).

Alpine Swift

Western and central European Alpine Swifts migrate towards the Strait in autumn where they join Iberian ones. Swiss-ringed birds have been recovered in France, Mediterranean Spain and Morocco (as well as Italy and Algeria), indicating southwest movement (Bernis, 1970; Mayaud, 1983; Cramp, 1985), which is likely to take them to the Strait. The arrival of Alpine Swifts in the Strait in autumn is predominantly from the north-east, which is a typical approach by many continental migrants. The winter quarters of these nominate birds are imprecisely known, as are those of the subspecies *tuneti*, which breeds in Morocco (Moreau, 1972). Presumably the birds that cross the Strait winter in tropical West Africa (Moreau, 1972).

The passage of Alpine Swifts is not on the same scale as that of the Swift; only 161 were recorded in the autumn of 1977 (Telleria, 1981). This paucity may be related to the fact that many Alpine Swifts fly high—large flocks of over 50 birds on migration are recorded sporadically from the top of the Rock of Gibraltar.

Spring arrivals are concentrated in April, with some arriving in mid-March and others passing into May (Finlayson & Cortés, 1987; Figure 49). Some Alpine Swifts are seen passing with Swifts in late July and August, but the majority migrate south in September after partial completion of the wing moult (see Chapter 8). The last birds pass south in mid-October (Telleria, 1981).

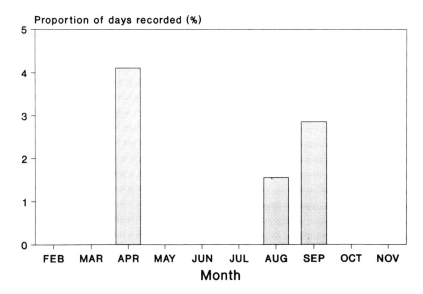

Figure 49.   Alpine Swift passage periods at Gibraltar, 1987.

KINGFISHERS

The precise origins of the Kingfishers that reach the Strait are unknown, but there is no doubt that western European individuals are involved. Telleria (1981) cites the recovery of a Belgian Kingfisher in Jerez in December, and German Kingfishers have been recovered in Spain (Cramp, 1985). French Kingfishers also winter in Spain, and those from further north and east, as far as Czechoslovakia, perform long-distance movements towards the Mediterranean, though probably not as far as the Strait (Morgan & Glue, 1977).

Kingfishers appear in unusual places, including the coast, from the end of June, and there is a notable increase during July and August. Some of these birds may be local, but the majority are probably migrants. Some cross the Strait and winter in Morocco (Pineau & Giraud-Audine, 1976). There is no precise definition of the northward migration; most wintering sites have been abandoned by March (Cortés *et al.*, 1980).

BEE-EATERS

The main species is the European Bee-eater which is a trans-saharan migrant. The Blue-cheeked Bee-eater (sub-species *chrysocercus*) breeds in southern Morocco, wintering in tropical West Africa where it is isolated from eastern populations. Occasionally, Blue-cheeked Bee-eaters stray north towards the Strait, as shown by the sighting of one over Gibraltar on 9 September 1973 (Cortés *et al.*, 1980).

Bee-eater

Essentially, the Bee-eaters that cross the Strait are Iberian, though southern French birds are also involved (Cramp, 1985). These birds, together with those from Morocco, move south in late summer to winter in tropical West Africa, in The Gambia, Senegal and Ivory Coast (Moreau, 1972; Serle *et al.*, 1977). Smith (1965) did not record Bee-eaters crossing the west coast of Morocco in autumn but found them common in the Strait area and east of it, suggesting a concentration there.

The migration of Bee-eaters over the Strait is a spectacular phenomenon which had been noticed by the Reverend John White, brother of Gilbert White, in 1772 (White, 1789). The most complete description of the southward passage is that of Telleria (1979), who estimated that the 1977 migration was of the order of 35 000; earlier counts exceeded 36 000 (Lopez Gordo, 1975). Although the extent to which Bee-eaters concentrate at narrow sea-crossings is unknown, it is probable that many migrate directly over the open sea, at least in areas adjacent to the Strait; Bee-eaters have been recorded on passage in all sectors of the Mediterranean (Moreau, 1961). Bearing in mind the ability of Bee-eaters to fly high and the likelihood of flocks passing unnoticed despite their characteristic flight calls, estimates must be accepted as minimum figures and the total Bee-eater passage, which probably varies between years in relation to weather conditions, could be of the order of 40 000–50 000.

The southward passage commences during the first half of August and builds to a sharp peak during the first half of September when large flocks, usually numbering 60–100 birds, pass south. The estimated mean flock size during the peak period is 36.3 birds/flock (Telleria, 1981). The passage then tails off, with very few, small and isolated, groups in October. The spring migration starts in mid-March, most Bee-eaters passing north during the second half of April and the first half of May. A small passage continues after this, isolated groups passing north as late as early June (Figure 50). The spring movements are spectacular and day counts during the peak passage have been high.

The Bee-eater is a diurnal migrant, though there are instances when they have been heard over Gibraltar at night (e.g. Irby, 1895; Mosquera & Cortés, 1978; Telleria, 1981). Peak migratory activity is concentrated in the morning, passage continuing on a smaller scale throughout the day, with a slight increase in the evening (Telleria, 1981).

Weather conditions over the Strait affect Bee-eaters, and they show a tendency to drift. In autumn westerlies, Bee-eaters approaching the Strait from the north-east cross over Gibraltar in a southwesterly direction. From the Rock they fly directly towards Morocco or across the Bay of Gibraltar towards the Spanish coast. Very few Bee-eaters pass over the Rock in easterlies. Those that do are disorientated in the cloud that forms over Gibraltar and often settle in the vegetation. These birds invariably return inland. In easterlies, most Bee-eater

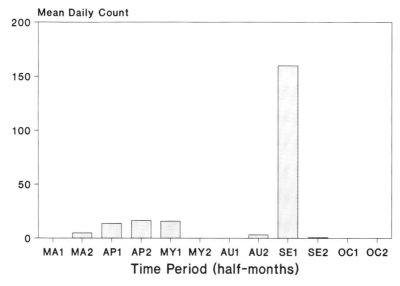

Figure 50.   Bee-eater passage periods over Gibraltar, 1987.

migration takes place over the western end of the Strait, but in very strong winds passage may stop. In spring, most Bee-eaters pass over the Rock in westerly winds.

ROLLER

The Roller is a regular migrant across the Strait but, taking into account its abundance in parts of Iberia during the breeding season, is relatively scarce. During the passage across the Strait, Rollers predominate in open areas in the western half. It is possible that Rollers are making a direct flight from West Africa to the western Iberian breeding grounds in the spring. While the main wintering areas are in eastern and southern Africa, Moreau (1972) considered that wintering of Iberian Rollers in West Africa had been overlooked—they have been found in several West African countries in the winter (Cramp, 1985). The departure from winter quarters appears to take place *en masse* over a short period (Feare, 1983), which may explain the scarcity on passage. The Iberian population probably arrives over a short period. The northward passage commences in mid–April and is over by the end of May. The southward passage starts in July and finishes in the first week of September (Cortés *et al.*, 1980; Telleria, 1981; Finlayson & Cortés, 1987).

HOOPOE

The Hoopoes that cross the Strait belong to the Iberian and western and central European populations (Bernis, 1970; Cramp, 1985). A Swiss-ringed Hoopoe was recovered in San Fernando, Cádiz (Telleria, 1981), and another on passage in Morocco in April was recovered 3 months later in Czechoslovakia (Cramp, 1985). Recoveries have been made in Morocco of birds ringed in Belgium, France, Spain and Switzerland (Mayaud, 1983). A Moroccan-ringed bird was recovered in Senegal. Bernis (1970) gives Iberian recoveries of one southeast German and three Swiss Hoopoes; these confirm a southwesterly heading in autumn, not the direct north to south migration suggested by Moreau (1961).

In Africa, Hoopoes winter in acacia steppe in a belt stretching from Senegal eastwards (Moreau, 1972), where they are present, especially in the drier northern areas, from August to April (Serle *et al.*, 1977). It is probable that Hoopoes that cross the Strait winter in this area of West Africa, though a small number remain in southern Iberia and Morocco (Bernis, 1967; de Juana, 1977; Mayaud, 1983).

At Windmill Hill, mean daily numbers recorded during the peak passage in spring vary between 1 and 1.5 birds (0.08–0.12/ha) and in summer and autumn they are lower at around 0.5 birds (0.04/ha). The significantly lower numbers during the southward passage may reflect overflying, especially by birds which have bred close to the Strait, in order to avoid the drought. During falls caused by

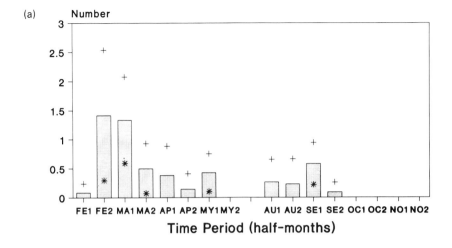

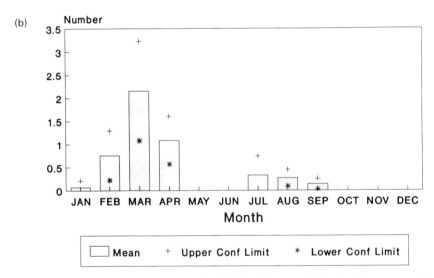

Figure 51.   (a) Hoopoe passage at Windmill Hill, Gibraltar, 1987. (b) Hoopoe seasonal distribution at Windmill Hill, Gibraltar, 1971–89.

poor weather, the density can be substantially greater. The highest spring day count on Windmill Hill is 14 (1.08/ha).

The passage periods resemble those of other species with Iberian populations (e.g. White Stork; see Chapter 2). The arrival is early, especially so for a trans-saharan species, in February, with a rapid increase at the end of the month and early in March, and a gradual reduction towards mid-May when the northward migration ends (Figure 51). Hoopoes are occasionally observed between

November and January and such sightings have been attributed to overwintering (Smith, 1965; Pineau & Giraud-Audine, 1979; Telleria, 1981) or early passage (Cortés *et al.*, 1980; Thevenot *et al.*, 1981, 1982). The southward departure of Hoopoes is early, with migrants passing in July (Cortés *et al.*, 1980; Finlayson & Cortés, 1987), and the main passage taking place in August and early September with only a few left by October. In view of this, it is probable that there is an early return of migrants to southerly breeding areas, starting November, with the main arrival in February and March. Hoopoes passing north after this time probably belong to more northerly populations as they pass at a time when local Hoopoes have already commenced breeding.

WOODPECKERS

The Wryneck is the only migratory woodpecker in the area. It is a regular migrant in spring and autumn and occurs in small numbers in winter (Smith, 1965; Cortés *et al.*, 1980; Thevenot *et al.*, 1981, 1982). Its occurrence within the main passage periods, from September to October and from late February to May (Cortés *et al.*, 1980; Telleria 1981; Finlayson & Cortés, 1987), is erratic. Trans-saharan birds may be included; they are known to winter in northern tropical Africa, west to Senegal. The rest probably winter in Morocco (Pineau & Giraud-Audine, 1979). They may originate well to the north-east since a southwest heading of migrants is the rule in autumn (Moreau, 1961). There is an indication of a migratory divide, with eastern birds flying southeast to the Balkans and northwestern European ones southwest to Iberia (Cramp, 1985). Iberian recoveries include German, south Swedish, south Finnish and Swiss birds (Bernis, 1970); Moroccan recoveries include German and Swedish birds (Mayaud, 1983).

MIGRATION OF PASSERINES

LARKS

Seven species migrate across the Strait, of which only the Short-toed Lark is a trans-saharan migrant. The Skylark is the most abundant migrant and wintering lark. Skylarks, Woodlarks and Crested or Thekla Larks perform regular migratory movements across the Strait. The Calandra Lark performs nomadic movements, and crosses the Strait in small numbers in the autumn (Telleria, 1981). The Lesser Short-toed Lark is considered sedentary by Bernis (1971), but isolated sightings along both shores of the Strait away from traditional sites suggest a small seasonal dispersal (Bruhn & Jeffrey, 1958; Pineau & Giraud-Audine, 1979; Cortés *et al.*, 1980; Finlayson & Cortés, 1987).

Skylark

The Skylark breeds in the area only on open ground at high altitude (above 1400 m; see Chapter 6) but it is an abundant migrant and winter visitor from western Europe: recoveries of birds ringed on passage or breeding in France, Belgium, Holland, Germany, Denmark, Sweden, Finland, Switzerland and Czechoslovakia have been made (Bernis, 1971; Telleria, 1981). The species is a

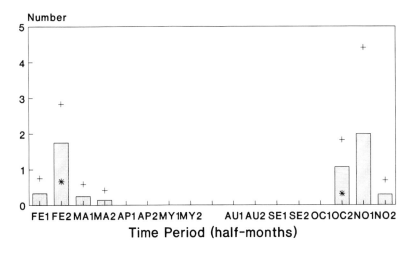

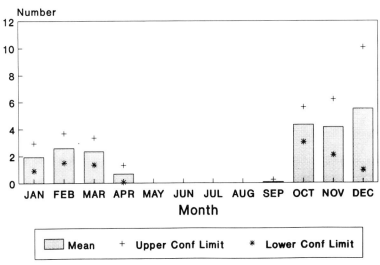

Figure 52. (a) Skylark passage at Windmill Hill, Gibraltar, 1987. (b) Skylark seasonal distribution on Windmill Hill, Gibraltar, 1971–89.

pre-saharan migrant that winters on both shores of the Strait. Wintering on the North African side is irregular (Pineau & Giraud-Audine, 1976): although in some years it is scarce, flocks of 100 birds or more are widespread in cultivated land and wet pastures other years (Pineau & Giraud-Audine, 1979). On the Spanish side, the Skylark is the third most important wintering passerine in pastures, with a density of 41.17 birds per 10 ha (Arroyo & Telleria, 1984). This variable distribution between winters probably depends on conditions within the area and further north. The irregularity of wintering on the Moroccan side suggests that the passage south across the Strait is likely to be intense some years but thin in others.

Telleria (1981) counted 2400 Skylarks migrating south over the Strait by day in the autumn of 1977. Considering that Skylarks also migrate by night, the magnitude of the passage can, in some years at least, be much higher than the movements across the Baltic (Telleria, 1981). At Windmill Hill the mean daily number of grounded birds during the main passage periods varied between 1 and 2 birds in spring and autumn (0.08–0.16 birds/ha). The highest spring count is 15 (1.15 birds/ha) and the highest autumn count is 17 (1.31 birds/ha).

The passage south, which commences in the last days of September, reaches its peak during the second half of October and the first half of November, after which wintering birds settle. The movement north starts early in February and peaks at the end of the month, though this can be later in some years (Figure 52). Most Skylarks have left Gibraltar by early April, although stragglers pass right up to the end of the month.

Short-toed Lark

The Short-toed Larks that cross the Strait come from the western part of the breeding range, in the Iberian Peninsula and southern and western France. These populations, together with the Moroccan ones, winter in the arid belt south of the Sahara, between 14°N and 17°N (Moreau, 1972). Pineau & Giraud-Audine (1979) did not find this lark on the Moroccan side of the Strait in winter, and it seems clear that all the Short-toed Larks migrate across the Sahara in autumn.

Telleria (1981), who saw only 87 Short-toed Larks in active migration across the Strait in the autumn of 1987, commented on the relative scarcity of this species on passage. This is in contrast with other authors' observations in the area (Irby, 1895; Smith, 1965), including Cortés et al. (1980), who recorded flocks of up to 200 Short-toed Larks during the southward migration over Gibraltar. There may in fact be inter-annual differences in passage, since it is not clear whether the species is experiencing a decline. At Windmill Hill, Short-toed Larks appear equally abundant in spring and autumn, although there may be years when they are commoner in one season (Figure 53). Mean daily counts during the main migration periods are of 1 bird (0.08 birds/ha). The highest spring count is 30 (2.31 birds/ha), and the highest autumn count 24 (1.85 birds/ha).

Although some Short-toed Larks arrive at the end of March (Pineau & Giraud-

(a)

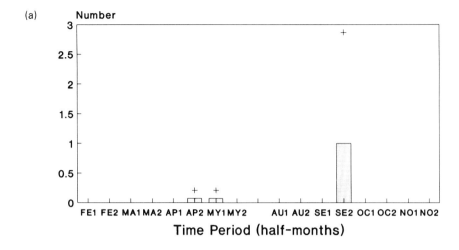

(b)

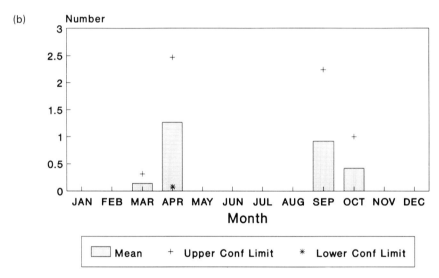

Figure 53. *(a) Short-toed Lark passage at Windmill Hill, Gibraltar, 1987. (b) Short-toed Lark seasonal distribution at Windmill Hill, Gibraltar, 1971–89.*

Audine, 1979; Finlayson & Cortés, 1987), the majority pass north during April and early May, isolated birds being seen in early June (Finlayson & Cortés, 1987). The return movement commences during August (Telleria, 1981) and reaches a peak in mid-September, very few passing south in early October. The pattern, therefore, is one of relatively late arrival (though not as late as other trans–saharan species) and early departure (Figure 53).

Crested and Thekla Lark

These two species are considered together because their close resemblance does not always permit certain identification, especially in the case of migrating birds. The traditional view (Irby, 1875; Cortés *et al.*, 1980) that the majority of those on passage are Crested Larks has been questioned by Telleria (1981), who suggests that most are Thekla Larks. The problem requires further study, and the origins

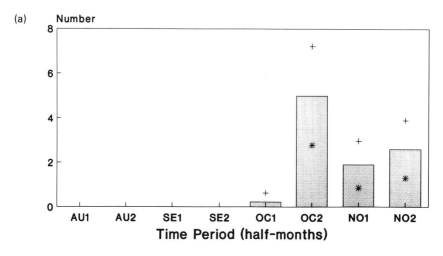

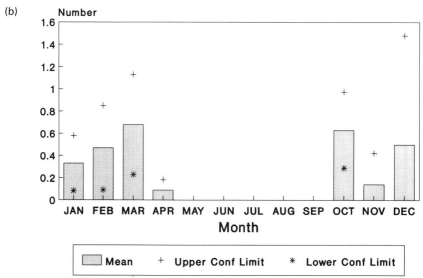

Figure 54.   (a) Crested Lark passage at Windmill Hill, Gibraltar, 1987. No birds were recorded in spring. (b) Crested Lark seasonal distribution at Windmill Hill, Gibraltar, 1971–89.

of the Crested and Thekla Larks crossing the Strait are unknown. Since Thekla Larks only breed in southern and eastern Spain, Portugal and Morocco, any passage must involve birds from nearby regions. On the other hand, Crested Larks breed in western Europe and are known to perform strong movements, a West German bird having been recovered in Portugal (Bernis, 1971). Arroyo & Telleria (1984) recorded only Thekla Larks in pastures on the Spanish side of the Strait in winter (this may have been an artifact of their habitat sampling, since Crested Larks are widespread at that time of year). In the case of either species, autumn movements do not take them further south than Morocco.

Crested/Thekla Larks cross the Strait by day. The volume of migrants is low relative to other migratory species, and it is possible that there are nocturnal movements. Cortés *et al.* (1980) record flocks of up to 50 birds over Gibraltar, but Telleria (1981) only saw 18 in active passage during the 1977 autumn. At Windmill Hill, mean daily numbers during the main passage periods are about 0.7 birds in spring (0.05 birds/ha) and between 0.6 and 5 birds in autumn (0.05–0.39 birds/ha), with maximum daily counts of 6 in spring (0.46 birds/ha) and 12 in autumn (0.92 birds/ha). Spring movements are inconspicuous in some years (Figure 54), suggesting that the increases in numbers in autumn could be due to post-breeding dispersal and redistribution, including movement across the Strait.

The main southward movement of Crested/Thekla Larks takes place in October and November (Figure 54). Smaller numbers are recorded in August and September (Cortés *et al.*, 1980; Telleria, 1981). In spring, a slight increase above winter numbers is detectable in February and March, the last birds passing in early April.

Woodlark

Little is known of the origin of the Woodlarks that cross the Strait other than the three Iberian recoveries of Belgian, Swiss and Czechoslovak birds (Bernis, 1971). Information of passage on the Moroccan side, where the Woodlarks that cross must winter, is meagre (Pineau & Giraud-Audine, 1979).

Telleria (1981) counted 133 Woodlarks in visible migration in the 1977 autumn, which made the Woodlark numerically the second most important lark. Comparing his results with those of other European migration points, Telleria (1981) concluded that the numbers were relatively high and testified to a substantial wintering in North Africa. At Windmill Hill, Woodlarks are irregular and have records almost completely confined to the southward migration. The mean daily count is around 0.75 birds (0.06 birds/ha) and the maximum recorded has been 6 (0.46 birds/ha).

According to Telleria (1981), the passage of Woodlarks commences in the second half of October and continues into November. At Windmill Hill the first Woodlarks have been detected during the first half of October, with an increase during the second half (Figure 55) and scattered observations in November

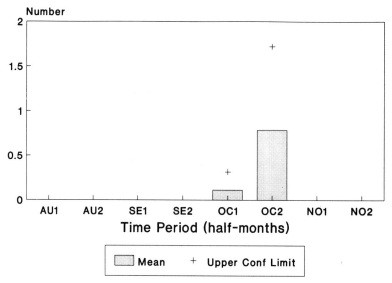

Figure 55.   Woodlark passage at Windmill Hill, Gibraltar, 1987. No birds were recorded in spring.

(Cortés *et al.*, 1980). There is a record of a sighting at Gibraltar in March (Cortés *et al.*, 1980), which is presumably the main month for the northward passage.

HIRUNDINES

The five European hirundines are regular and abundant migrants across the Strait. With the exception of Telleria's (1981) autumn counts of diurnal hirundine passage across the Strait, there are no reliable data available. The observations from Gibraltar (*SGBO Reports*) are inconsistent and do not permit a detailed analysis. Thus, instead of constructing passage periods based on abundances, the histograms given for these species have been based on frequency of occurrence in diurnal passage in each of the main months.

Swallow

The Swallows that cross the Strait, in addition to the large Iberian population, probably come from a wide area of western Europe. Telleria (1981) cited recoveries of French, Belgian and English Swallows; Iberian recoveries are summarized in Figure 56.

In Africa, a minority of Swallows winter north of the equator; they are uncommon in Senegal and The Gambia in winter, though regular on passage

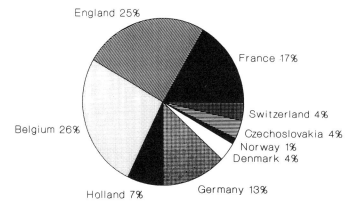

Figure 56. Swallow recoveries in Iberia, after Bernis (1971); N = 83.

(Moreau, 1972). Two Nigerian birds have been recovered in Andalucia (Bernis, 1971). The Swallows which cross the Strait probably winter in the westernmost parts of the wintering range although some must continue further, as British Swallows have been recovered in South Africa (Moreau, 1972). Whatever the case, the pattern of wintering of the different Palaearctic populations of Swallows is complicated; those that cross the Strait, though probably derived from the western parts of the breeding range, do not all necessarily winter in the same part of Africa. Small numbers regularly winter within the Strait.

There is a scarcity of migrating Swallows over western Iberia. In autumn, very few migrate over southwest Iberia even though great numbers crossed the Strait (Moreau, 1961). Ringing recoveries have shown passage to be concentrated over the eastern and southern coasts of Iberia (Bernis, 1971). This scarcity in western Iberia is paralleled over the Atlantic coast of Morocco (e.g. Smith, 1965), the Strait Swallows apparently continuing directly south from the Strait to make a crossing of the Sahara Desert. A similar paucity has been observed in eastern Morocco, and Moreau (1961) concluded that there was a concentration of Swallows within the Strait in autumn. Telleria (1981) found the Swallow to be the second most numerous diurnal non-soaring migrant, and estimated the total passage at over 76 000 in the 1977 autumn, undoubtedly an underestimate. The passage of 10 000 Swallows over the Rock of Gibraltar on 1 October 1988 (*SGBO Reports*) illustrates the magnitude of the migration. In spring there is also a concentration of Swallows in the Strait, after they have followed the Moroccan Atlantic coast (Smith, 1965), although large arrivals can also take place away from the Strait in spring (Nisbet *et al.*, 1961). In both seasons, the concentrations within the Strait appear attributable to the Swallow's habit of following coastlines.

The passage periods are broadly spread throughout the spring and autumn (Figure 57), as expected for a species with a large, widely distributed population.

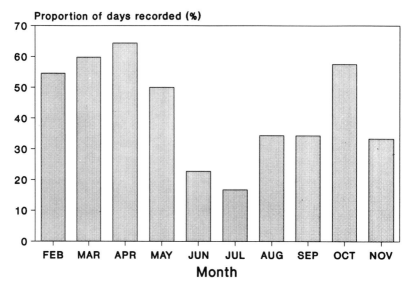

Figure 57.   Swallow passage periods at Gibraltar, 1987.

If to these are added the regular sightings of Swallows in December and January, including the northward passage in January, then the Swallow is present in the Strait all year. Iberian Swallows are the first to arrive, in January and February; the movements in March, April and May must be of continental Swallows, since the Iberian birds breed early. Although Swallows migrate south in July across Europe, those which migrate past the Strait in July and August are presumably mostly Iberian as the breeding sites are abandoned at this time. The main autumn movement, in late September and early October (Telleria, 1981) probably involves continental Swallows.

Red-rumped Swallow

It is the isolated Iberian population of Red-rumped Swallows that crosses the Strait; in autumn, they join those from Morocco on the way to the tropical West African wintering areas. Red-rumped Swallows probably winter across northern tropical Africa in country that is not too dry (Moreau, 1972). It is assumed that those which cross the Strait winter at the western end of this range, although regular passage of Red-rumped Swallows in southeast Morocco (Smith, 1968) suggests that some Iberian and Moroccan birds may winter further east.

Red-rumped Swallows are regular and common migrants in spring and autumn, often passing in mixed flocks with other hirundines. Over 2000 were counted crossing the Strait in the 1977 autumn (Telleria, 1981), which made it the

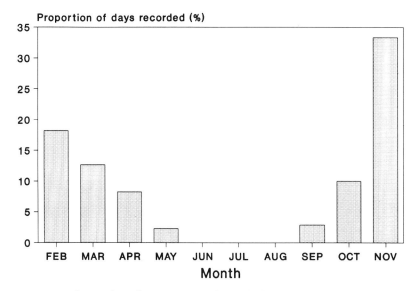

Figure 58.   Red-rumped Swallow passage periods at Gibraltar, 1987.

third most abundant hirundine after the Swallow and the House Martin. The total number crossing is no doubt higher than this figure: Thiollay & Perthuis (1975) counted over 5000 during the first 20 days of October 1974.

Telleria (1981) centred the main passage of Red-rumped Swallows in October, which coincides with the pattern over Gibraltar (Figure 58) (the high frequency in November is probably an artifact of the few observations that month). The southward passage is late, commencing in September and continuing into November with occasional sightings in December (Cortés *et al.*, 1980). Late movement may be a result of the laying of second clutches. As with other Iberian hirundines, the spring arrival is early, with a large influx in February and March, and smaller numbers in April and May (Figure 58).

House Martin

House Martins breed from the Atlantic to 95°E (Moreau, 1972), and the large numbers which cross the Strait are probably derived from much of the western European part of the range (see, for example, Bernis, 1971) and presumably winter in the westernmost areas of tropical and equatorial Africa. Small numbers of House Martins are regularly recorded within the Strait in midwinter. As with the Swallow and Red-rumped Swallow, these birds could be early Iberian arrivals from the south and not birds that have remained resident.

The House Martin was the second most abundant hirundine recorded by Telleria (1981) in autumn, with over 13 500 in 1977. Its numbers are probably

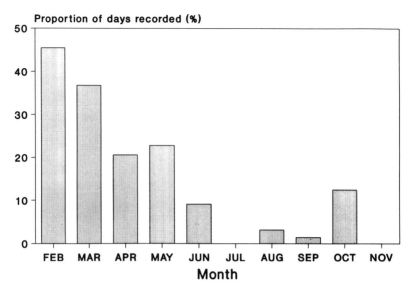

Figure 59.   House Martin passage periods at Gibraltar, 1987.

underestimated in relation to the Swallow as it generally flies higher on migration (Moreau, 1961). The concentration of coasting Swallows is not paralleled by the House Martins, although Bernis (1971) recorded an accumulation of House Martin recoveries in the southeastern half of Iberia. In spring, the House Martin is also the second most numerous hirundine.

The southward migration of House Martins starts in mid–September and builds to a peak at the end of October, followed by a rapid decline in numbers (Telleria, 1981). The pattern illustrated in Figure 59 is typical, with early birds passing south in August. The spring passage appears more conspicuous— perhaps at this time birds which have crossed the sea have lost height—and there is a substantial passage of Iberian House Martins in February and March. The passage extends into June.

Crag Martin

At the large winter roost at Gibraltar (Elkins & Etheridge, 1974; see also Chapter 8) many thousands of Crag Martins have been ringed and have produced breeding-season recoveries in eastern Spain (including the Balearic Islands), the French Atlantic Pyrenees and the Italian Alps, indicating that birds from most of the western part of the range fly southwest to winter in southern Iberia and Morocco, with a minority crossing the Sahara to winter in West Africa (Moreau, 1972).

Counts of this species on passage can be misleading in view of the large roosting movements which take place from October onwards, when the bulk of the wintering birds arrive. Even so, there is evidence of birds crossing the Strait in flocks during October and November, though the scale of the passage is unclear. Thus, Telleria (1981) only counted 600 crossing the Strait in autumn, which is a very low figure considering that flocks of 50–100 birds have been seen crossing the Strait from Gibraltar. It may be that Crag Martins follow the eastern approaches to the Strait in autumn and are thus missed from Tarifa (where Telleria made most of his observations). In winter it is the most abundant hirundine, with the main Gibraltar roost holding between 2000 and 3000 birds. Crag Martins roost in caves; both shores of the eastern end of the Strait, with their limestone formations, offer the greatest opportunities for large roosts. Swallow, Red-rumped Swallow and House Martin have been found in Crag Martin roosts in winter.

The first autumn arrivals take place at the end of September, with large influxes in October and new birds continuing to arrive until mid-November. The departure commences at the end of February, and most leave in March, very few remaining by early April.

Sand Martin

Nominate Sand Martins breed from the Atlantic to 100°E and winter north of the Equator. In parts of West Africa they form large roosts in winter, in Senegal and around Lake Chad (Moreau, 1972). Although those which winter in West Africa have to migrate southwest in autumn, ringing indicates in other cases a north to south movement (Moreau, 1972). The majority of Iberian Sand Martin recoveries are of British-ringed birds (Bernis, 1971; Telleria, 1981) conforming with other analyses of (Mead & Harrison, 1979). Recoveries of birds ringed in France, Belgium, Germany and central USSR have also been made (Bernis, 1971). The westernmost populations appear to winter in the western parts of the wintering range, in Senegal (Mead & Harrison, 1979).

Sand Martins are the scarcest of the hirundines in the Strait, and the recent population changes and eastward shift of migratory routes associated with the Sahel droughts may account for this (Mead & Harrison, 1979). Only 571 were counted in the whole of the 1977 autumn (Telleria, 1981) which, even taking into account the Sand Martin's relative scarcity in autumn compared with spring (Moreau, 1961), is very low. Smith (1965) found them scarce in Morocco in autumn even though passage along the west coast in spring was heavy. It seems clear, therefore, that most Sand Martins, with the exception of the British populations, may migrate east of the Strait. Favier (in Irby, 1875, 1895) considered the Sand Martin to be the scarcest of the swallows on passage, and the recent droughts may have accentuated this scarcity so that observations of flights of thousands of Sand Martins over marshes near Vejer (Irby, 1875, 1895) are no longer observed.

As is the case for the three other trans–saharan hirundines, Sand Martins arrive

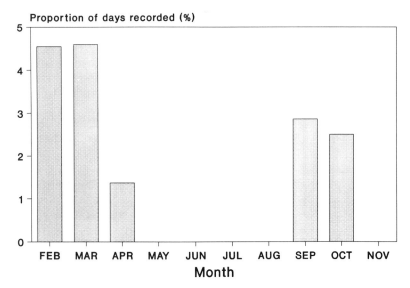

Figure 60.   Sand Martin passage periods at Gibraltar, 1987.

early in spring, in February and March, and most have passed north by May. Although Sand Martins only breed in isolated sites in the Strait (usually in the north-west), they breed elsewhere in Iberia and the early arrivals are presumably of these populations (Figure 60). The southward migration commences in early September and peaks at the end of the month and early in October with most having gone by the end of the month (Telleria, 1981).

Pipits and Wagtails

Three pipits (Tree, Meadow and Tawny) and three wagtails (Yellow, White and Grey) are regular migrants across the Strait. The Water Pipit is a regular winter visitor (see Chapter 7) to coastal wetlands and can be regarded a migrant in small numbers. The Red-throated Pipit, which breeds in the northern tundra, migrates southwest to winter in northern tropical Africa, including West Africa, where they can be locally abundant (Moreau, 1972). Red-throated Pipits also winter regularly in Morocco (Smith, 1965; Pineau & Giraud-Audine, 1976). Garcia Rua (1975) and Telleria (1981) give a series of sightings for the Spanish shore of the Strait in October, and the return is probably in March and early April (Irby, 1875, 1895; Cortés *et al.*, 1980). The Asiatic Richard's Pipit, though scarce, has been reported within the Strait and adjacent areas regularly (Saunders, 1871; Irby, 1875, 1895; Nisbet, 1960; Pineau & Giraud-Audine, 1979; Telleria, 1981; Alba Pallida & Garrido Sanchez, 1983). Telleria (1981) additionally cites a record in January in Cádiz Bay.

Meadow Pipit

The large numbers of Meadow Pipits arriving in autumn to winter in the Strait (Pineau & Giraud-Audine, 1979; Arroyo & Telleria, 1984; Finlayson & Cortés, 1987) and further south in Morocco (Smith, 1965) are essentially northwestern, western and central European in origin (Figure 61). Telleria (1981) states that the main recoveries in southern Andalucia are of Belgian, Dutch and English Meadow Pipits, and Pineau & Giraud-Audine (1979) record an English and a Swedish bird on the Moroccan shore in winter. Meadow Pipits are pre-saharan migrants, and those that cross the Strait in autumn do not move much further south.

The Meadow Pipit is one of the most abundant migrants over the Strait. It is a diurnal migrant (although it is capable of migrating by night) crossing the Strait in flocks, especially during the early hours of the morning. Telleria (1981) counted over 3500 in the 1977 autumn, which made it the eleventh most numerous active diurnal migrant. At Windmill Hill, mean daily numbers of grounded Meadow Pipits vary between 4 and 7 during the main spring passage (0.31–0.54 birds/ha) and between 10 and 27 in autumn (0.77–2.08 birds/ha). Maximum counts illustrate the massive increases caused by waves of Meadow Pipits: maximum daily counts on Windmill Hill are 50 (3.85 birds/ha) in spring and 56 (4.31 birds/ha) in autumn. In winter, Arroyo & Telleria (1984) found it to be the second most important species in pastures, with a mean density of 5.7 birds/ha.

The Meadow Pipit arrives late in the autumn, passage south commencing at the end of September and progressively building towards a peak at the end of October and November, with a suggestion of further increases in December (Figure 62). This pattern contrasts with Telleria's (1981) observations, which pointed to a decrease in numbers after an October peak. In spring, the northward passage is pronounced during February and March (especially in late February and early March), with the last individuals passing north during early April.

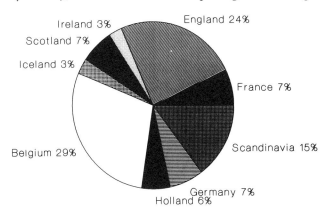

Figure 61.   Meadow Pipit recoveries, after Bernis (1971); N = *337.*

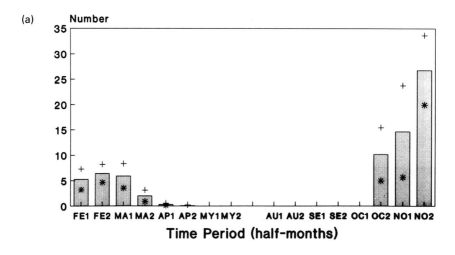

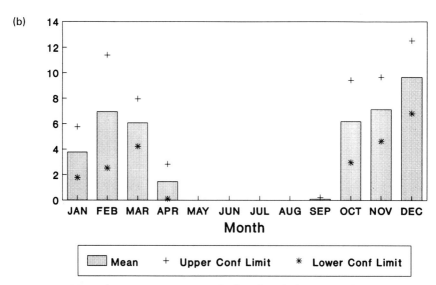

Figure 62. (a) Meadow Pipit passage at Windmill Hill, Gibraltar, 1987. (b) Meadow Pipit seasonal distribution at Windmill Hill, Gibraltar, 1971–89.

Tree Pipit

Tree Pipits breed over much of western and northern Europe, south to northern Spain, and those which migrate over the Strait must belong mainly to these western populations (Bernis, 1971). Spaepen (1953) concluded that British,

Danish and Belgian Tree Pipits flew southwest in autumn with German and Baltic birds following a more direct line south. Telleria (1981) gives autumn recoveries of a German and a Dutch bird. Most of these birds probably cross the Sahara to winter in West Africa where they are common and widespread from September to April, especially in the moist savannas of the south (Serle *et al.*, 1977).

Telleria (1981) recorded very few Tree Pipits in active autumn migration over the Strait. He considered that passage of small groups was probably, as suggested by Moreau (1961), diffuse over the width of the Mediterranean. Tree Pipits are not as uncommon as suggested by Telleria (1981), although they appear to be more abundant in spring than autumn (Figure 63). At Windmill Hill average daily counts vary between 2 and 10 birds (0.15–0.77 birds/ha) in spring, and between 0.75 and 1.75 (0.06–0.14 birds/ha) in autumn. Maximum counts are 37 (2.85 birds/ha) in spring and 15 (1.15 birds/ha) in autumn. The trans-saharan Tree Pipits therefore contrast with the pre-saharan Meadow Pipits, the latter being more abundant in autumn than spring, but in spring the two species reach similar densities.

In the spring, Tree Pipits pass from late March to late May with a clear peak in late April, over a month after the main Meadow Pipit movements (Figure 63). Autumn passage starts during September, reaching a peak during the first half of October, and the last birds pass south early in November. The majority migrate ahead of the main Meadow Pipit arrivals, although there is an overlap in passage in spring and autumn.

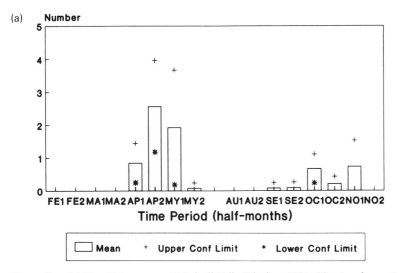

Figure 63. (a) *Tree Pipit passage at Windmill Hill, Gibraltar, 1987. (Continued on p. 130.)*

(b)

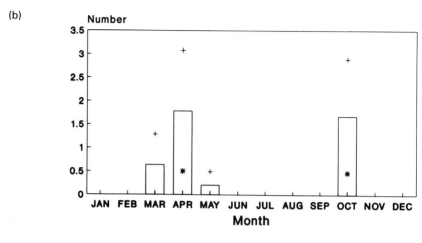

(c)

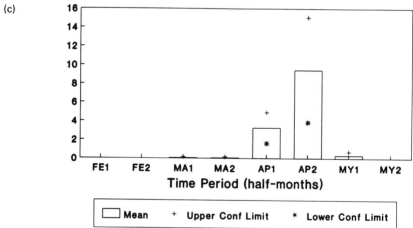

| | Mean   + Upper Conf Limit   * Lower Conf Limit |

Figure 63 continued.   (b) Tree Pipit seasonal distribution at Windmill Hill, Gibraltar, 1971–89. (c) Large Tree Pipit passage at Windmill Hill, Gibraltar, spring 1984.

Tawny Pipit

The Tawny Pipits that cross the Strait are of Iberian, French and Swiss origin (Bernis, 1971; Telleria, 1981). They cross the Sahara to winter in West Africa, where they are considered to be passage migrants and winter visitors from October to May (Serle *et al.*, 1977), being widely distributed in areas bordering the Sahara (Moreau, 1972).

Telleria (1981) found Tawny Pipits to be scarce passage migrants but recognized that his observations contrasted with earlier references for the Strait (Smith, 1965; Garcia, 1977). It is the scarcest of the three most common pipits in the area

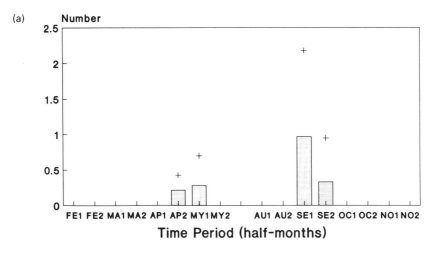

(a)

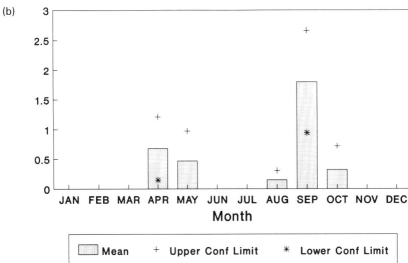

(b)

Figure 64.   (a) Tawny Pipit passage at Windmill Hill, Gibraltar, 1987. (b) Tawny Pipit seasonal distribution at Windmill Hill, Gibraltar, 1971–89.

and appears to be more abundant in autumn than spring. At Windmill Hill, mean spring daily counts vary between 0.5 and 0.8 birds (0.04–0.06 birds/ha), and mean autumn counts between 0.9 and 1.75 (0.07–0.14 birds/ha). Maximum recorded daily counts are 12 birds in spring (0.92 birds/ha) and 10 in autumn (0.77 birds/ha).

Tawny Pipits arrive among the later migrants in spring, with a rapid build up of numbers during the second half of April. The main passage takes place between late April and early May, with a few passing in early June. The southward migration takes place between August and October with a pronounced peak in September (Figure 64).

Yellow Wagtail

Yellow Wagtails breed over much of western and northern Europe, and four subspecies have been recorded over the Strait (Cortés *et al.*, 1980; Finlayson & Cortés, 1987). The main subspecies is *flava*, which breeds from southern Scandinavia to southern France and east to the Urals and winters south of the Sahara, being common in Senegal and Nigeria (Moreau, 1972). On the basis of ringing recoveries, Telleria (1981) gives the main countries of origin of Yellow Wagtails crossing the Strait as Germany, Belgium, Britain, Sweden, Switzerland and France (similar to that given for Iberia by Bernis, 1970; Figure 65), supporting the view that western European birds migrate southwest towards Iberia (Spaepen, 1957).

The British birds belong to the subspecies *flavissima*, which is less abundant than *flava* but is regular over the Strait; *flavissima* breeds in the Britain, Holland and the Atlantic coast of France and the bulk of this small population winters in the westernmost corner of West Africa, being common in Senegal and The Gambia (Moreau, 1972). The race *iberiae* is also a regular migrant across the Strait. It breeds from southern France to the Maghreb, including the Iberian Peninsula, wintering in Senegal (where it is common) and locally in other parts of West Africa (Moreau, 1972). This subspecies retains an element of the population north of the Sahara. Iberian Yellow Wagtails have been found wintering along the Atlantic coast of Morocco (Smith, 1965), as have *flava* (Thevenot & Thuoy, 1974). The two latter subspecies occur in most wet areas along the Moroccan side of the Strait in winter (Pineau & Giraud-Audine, 1979). The least abundant subspecies in the Strait is *thunbergi*, which breeds further north than any other, in the tundra from Scandinavia to 80°E, wintering across the entire width of tropical

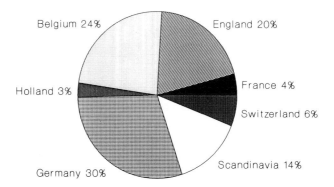

Figure 65.   Yellow Wagtail recoveries in Iberia, after Bernis (1971); N = 217.

Africa (Moreau, 1972). The strong passage of this subspecies over Morocco and over Senegal in spring (Moreau, 1972) suggests that those which cross the Strait winter in West Africa.

The diurnal migration of Yellow Wagtails is not conspicuous and contrasts with the large movements over northern European observatories (Telleria, 1981). In spring and autumn, however, large numbers can be grounded during unfavourable weather, indicating that many may be either migrating at night or too high to be observed. Yellow Wagtails are more abundant in spring than autumn (Figure 66). At Windmill Hill mean spring daily counts vary between 3

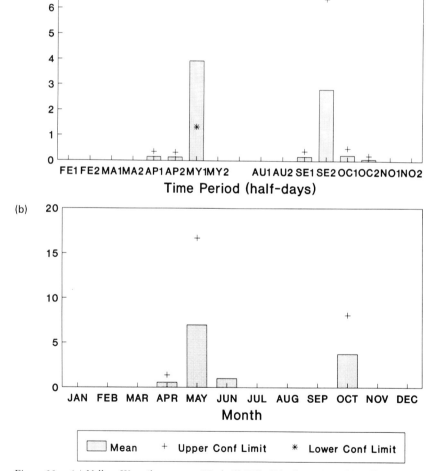

Figure 66.   (a) Yellow Wagtail passage at Windmill Hill, Gibraltar, 1987. (b) Yellow Wagtail seasonal distribution at Windmill Hill, Gibraltar, 1971–89.

and 7 birds (0.23–0.54 birds/ha) and mean autumn counts between 2.5 and 4 birds (0.19–0.31 birds/ha). Maximum daily counts have been higher in autumn when up to 46 Yellow Wagtails have been recorded on Windmill Hill (3.54 birds/ha). The highest spring count is 21 (1.62 birds/ha).

Yellow Wagtails are essentially trans-saharan migrants and this is reflected in the passage periods; late in spring, most passing in late April and May, and earlier than the main pre-saharan waves in autumn, i.e. late September and October (Figure 66). Many *iberiae* individuals return to breeding sites from the middle of February, however, and most early passage Yellow Wagtails belong to this race. Although detailed passage periods cannot be constructed for each subspecies, *thunbergi* appears to pass last, in May, suggesting that there is a progressive passage north, starting with southern populations and ending with the most northerly populations.

White Wagtail

The White Wagtail breeds throughout Europe and a large part of Morocco, although it is a very scarce breeding species in the immediate area of the Strait. Nevertheless, the Strait is within the main wintering area of this species which penetrates south of the Sahara into tropical Africa, probably in relatively small numbers (Moreau, 1972). White Wagtails crossing the Strait in autumn probably go no further than Morocco, where they are abundant in winter (Pineau & Giraud-Audine, 1976, 1979); some, at least, may continue towards West Africa.

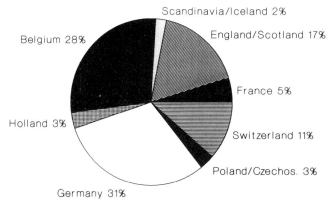

Figure 67. White Wagtail recoveries in Iberia, after Bernis (1971); N = 333.

The subspecies *alba* is the most abundant in winter, though the British *yarrellii* has been recorded (Ingram, 1960; Pineau & Giraud-Audine, 1979; Cortés *et al.*, 1980).

Most *yarrellii* winter in western Iberia (many in Portugal) (Bernis, 1971). Cádiz and Seville were the two most important provinces for White Wagtail re-traps out of a large range of Iberian recoveries (Figure 67). Pineau & Giraud-Audine (1979) controlled a bird ringed in Heligoland in July 1973 in Tangier the following January, and Moreau (1972) cites a record of an Icelandic White Wagtail recovered in Senegal.

Over 2000 White Wagtails were recorded in active southward migration over the Strait in the 1977 autumn (Telleria, 1981). They are most numerous of the wagtails on passage, and large numbers winter within the Strait. Winter censuses (e.g. Arroyo & Telleria, 1984) have underestimated the importance of this species which is found in a variety of habitats, along roadsides, near rivers and in similar habitats not surveyed. At Gibraltar, for example, there is a roost that holds up to 500 White Wagtails in winter (Cortés *et al.*, 1980).

At Windmill Hill spring passage densities are low, not exceeding 0.3 birds daily (0.02 birds/ha) but autumn daily counts are higher, ranging between 1 and 3 (0.08–0.23 birds/ha). Maximum daily counts are 3 in spring (0.23 birds/ha) and 9 in autumn (0.69 birds/ha). The movements on this site are not very obvious and take the form of a peak in October followed by a gradual decline in numbers during November (Figure 68). The arrival is sudden, with little build-up of numbers, a feature also noted by Telleria (1981). The spring migration is small; presumably most wintering birds gradually leave the area in a direct flight to the breeding grounds. Grounded birds must be wagtails coming from further south. The small northward movement takes place from late February to early April (Figure 68).

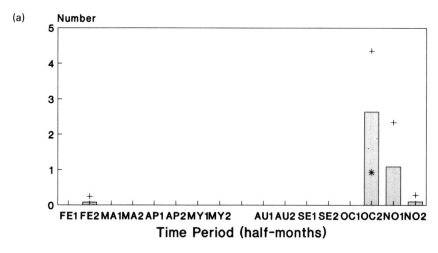

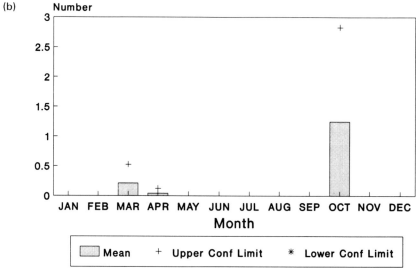

Figure 68.   (a) White Wagtail passage at Windmill Hill, Gibraltar, 1987. (b) White Wagtail seasonal distribution at Windmill Hill, Gibraltar, 1971–89.

Grey Wagtail

Grey Wagtails breed over much of western Europe including the Moroccan side of the Strait (Pineau & Giraud-Audine, 1979). Those that pass and winter in the area must be mostly from the northwestern parts of the breeding range; Bernis (1971) gives Iberian recoveries of French, Belgian, German, Czechoslovak, Swiss and north Italian Grey Wagtails. Most European Grey Wagtails move

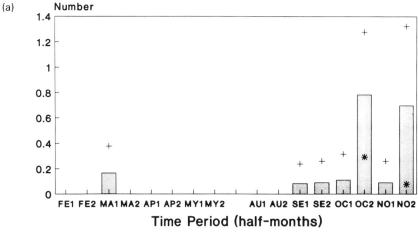

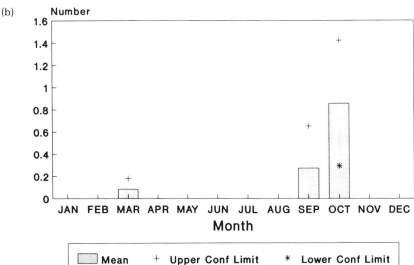

Figure 69. (a) Grey Wagtail passage at Windmill Hill, Gibraltar, 1987. (b) Grey Wagtail seasonal distribution at Windmill Hill, Gibraltar, 1971–89.

southwest in autumn (Jorgensen, 1976), although one ringed near Tarifa in October 1972 was recovered in the Camargue in November 1975 (Garcia Rua, 1975). Although some Grey Wagtails cross the Sahara to winter in tropical Africa (Moreau, 1972), including Senegal and The Gambia (Serle *et al.*, 1977), these are presumably relatively few in comparison to those that winter north of the desert. Most of the migrants crossing the Strait probably go no further than Morocco.

Although it is not a rare bird, the Grey Wagtail is the scarcest of the three wagtails that cross the Strait (Cortés *et al.*, 1980; Telleria, 1981). As happens with the White Wagtail, the passage and arrival of wintering birds in autumn is more pronounced than in spring. At Windmill Hill, mean spring day counts fall below 0.2 birds (0.02 birds/ha); mean autumn counts range from 0.6 to 0.9 birds (0.05–0.07 birds/ha). Grey Wagtails appear singly at this site in spring whereas, in autumn, a maximum of 6 have been recorded (0.46 birds/ha).

Grey Wagtails commence the southward movement during September, with most passing in October (Figure 69) and, fewer, in November. These results coincide with observations by Cortés *et al.* (1980) and Telleria (1981), who noted the first birds at the end of August. The spring passage takes place in March, although some may pass in late February and early April (Cortés *et al.*, 1980).

Wren

Telleria (1981) suggested that there is an arrival of Wrens from northern Europe from the end of September through October, and Bernis (1971) recorded the recovery of a Swedish-ringed Wren in Granada. There may therefore be a passage of this species across the Strait.

ACCENTORS

The Strait is within the southern limits of the wintering range of the Dunnock, and those reaching the Iberian Peninsula are of western, central and northern European origin (Bernis, 1971; Telleria, 1981). Passage is small and concentrated in November, though early birds have been recorded in mid-September (Telleria, 1981). Those which appear in the Gibraltar maquis in autumn must move on since they do not winter on the Rock. Pineau & Giraud-Audine (1976) recorded passage on the Moroccan shore and Arroyo & Telleria (1984) found them on the Spanish side in winter. Cortés *et al.* (1980) recorded March as the main month for the spring migration.

Alpine Accentors are winter visitors to the area, where they appear to occupy traditional wintering sites such as the Rock of Gibraltar (Irby, 1875, 1895; Cortés *et al.*, 1980) and other mountains of the area, including Jebel Musa on the Moroccan shore (Pineau & Giraud-Audine, 1979). The wintering period commences in late October and ends in early April.

CHATS AND THRUSHES

Nine species are regular and abundant migrants and each is discussed in detail in a separate section. Nine other species are regular migrants in smaller numbers and data are insufficient to permit full discussion; current knowledge is summarized below.

The Rufous Bush Chat breeds in southern Iberia and the Maghreb; it is assumed that birds from both areas winter in the dry acacia belt in Senegal, Mali and Niger (Moreau, 1972). The species appears to have become scarce in recent times, possibly for similar reasons to those causing the decline of other Sahel-wintering birds. The northward passage is marked in late April and May, with occasional individuals in early June. The southward passage is thinly spread from mid-July to mid-October (Cortés *et al.*, 1980; Telleria, 1981).

The Bluethroat is a migrant and winter visitor to the area. The continental subspecies *cyanecula* migrates southwest in autumn, wintering in many marshy localities of the Strait. Bluethroats also winter north of 10°N in West Africa in similar habitats (Moreau, 1972). Their incidence on passage is sporadic and the species is yet another one that appears to have been more frequently recorded in the 1960s than subsequently. The northward passage takes place from March to mid-May (Cortés *et al.*, 1980) with a return from late September to November, with most sightings in October. According to Telleria (1981), Belgian and German Bluethroats dominate in Iberian recoveries.

The Rock Thrush breeds at high altitude on both shores of the Strait (Pineau & Giraud-Audine, 1979; Finlayson & Cortés, 1987) and is a scarce migrant. The proximity of the Iberian breeding grounds to the Strait probably means that the arrival is direct from the winter quarters, excluding a stop-over in the area. The departure is probably also direct, overflying the Strait. Pineau & Giraud-Audine (1976) found two in January in the Jebel Musa where the species breeds. The principal wintering grounds are in tropical Africa, but scarcity west of 12°W may reflect a passage route east of the Strait. The passage periods are mid-March to early June, and mid-August to mid-October (Cortés *et al.*, 1980). Small numbers of Blue Rock Thrushes winter in tropical West Africa (Moreau, 1972), but the evidence of passage across the Strait is limited to increases in numbers censused by Telleria (1981) during late September and October.

Ring Ouzels from central, northern and western Europe winter in Morocco (Heim de Balsac & Mayaud, 1962) and in some mountains on the Spanish side. They are recorded on passage between March and April and between September and November (Pineau & Giraud-Audine, 1979; Cortés *et al.*, 1980; Telleria, 1981), sometimes in small flocks. Scandinavian and British birds occur on passage mainly along the eastern half of the Iberian Peninsula, the Scandinavian ones being generally east of the British ones (Durman, 1976).

There is circumstantial evidence pointing to a passage of Blackbirds in February, March, October and November (Cortés *et al.*, 1980), and Telleria (1981) has cited recoveries in southern Andalucia of birds ringed in Germany, France, England and Switzerland. Some of these Blackbirds may winter in Morocco.

Fieldfares are scarce migrants, the Strait being at the southern limit of their wintering range. Telleria (1981) gives the recovery of a Finnish Fieldfare in Sanlucar de Barrameda in December. The main months of passage are October (Garcia Rua, 1975) and February and March (Pineau & Giraud-Audine, 1979; *SGBO Reports*).

Redwings are regular migrants though nowhere abundant. Morocco is the southern limit of the wintering range (Smith, 1965).The passage, which is concentrated in February, March, late October and early November (Cortés *et al.*, 1980; Telleria, 1981), reflects its pre-saharan status. Small numbers winter on both shores of the Strait (Pineau & Giraud-Audine, 1976; Telleria, 1981). Iberian recoveries have been made of birds ringed in Finland, Great Britain, Germany and Sweden (Telleria, 1981).

Mistle Thrushes, which typically breed in broadleaved woodland, are scarce migrants across the Strait, passing mainly in February, March, October and November (Pineau & Giraud-Audine, 1979; Cortés *et al.*, 1980; Telleria, 1981), reaching the southern limit of the wintering range in Morocco. The origins of these Mistle Thrushes are unknown.

Two wheatears, White-crowned Black (Soriguer, 1978) and Desert (pers. obs.), are vagrants to the area from southern Morocco.

Robin

Robins breed over much of western and northern Europe where the birds which migrate past the Strait are thought to originate. The main Iberian recoveries have been from Germany, Poland, Finland, Holland and Switzerland (Telleria, 1981). Summarized Scandinavian ringing data indicate the main wintering area of these Robins to be Italy, France and Iberia (Petterson & Hasselquist, 1985). Gibraltar-ringed Robins have been recovered in France and Germany, and Pineau & Giraud-Audine (1979) gave two cases, of a Scandinavian and of a Finnish Robin, wintering on the Moroccan side.

The migrants are distinct from the resident woodland Robins which breed in southern Iberia and northern Morocco (Pineau & Giraud-Audine, 1979) and, on arrival, occupy habitats not taken up by the residents. They are particularly conspicuous in open woodland and maquis. Robins winter in large numbers in the Mediterranean Basin, and the two sides of the Strait receive many Robins on passage and in winter. Those that continue south go no further than Morocco, since this species does not cross the Sahara (Moreau, 1972).

The southward migration is more conspicuous than the northward passage, which takes the form of a progressive departure from winter quarters (Figure 70). Mean autumn densities are of the order of 4–5 birds/ha in maquis and lower in the shorter vegetation at Windmill Hill, where mean daily counts are of the order of 4 birds (0.31 birds/ha) and maximum counts have reached 35 birds (2.69 birds/ha). Spring densities during the main passage are around 2 birds/ha in maquis, with lower counts at Windmill Hill where mean daily counts are of the order of 3 birds (0.23 birds/ha). Maximum spring counts at Windmill Hill have reached 16 birds (1.23 birds/ha). Mean winter densities in maquis are 2–3 birds/ha, higher than estimates for scrub (1.46 birds/ha) and cork oak wood (1.69 birds/ha) (Arroyo & Telleria, 1984). The differences may be due to the sampling method, mist-netting in the first case and observation in the second.

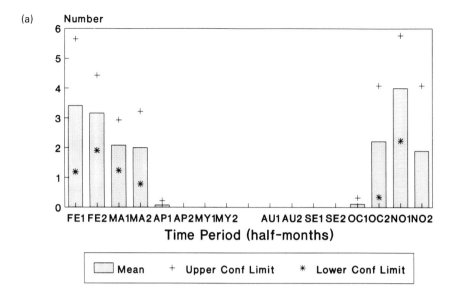

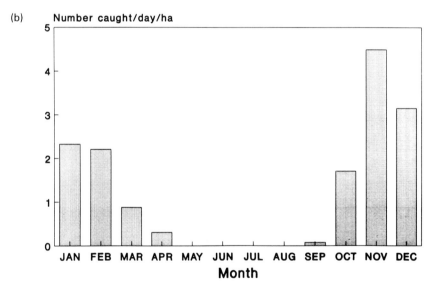

Figure 70. (a) Robin passage at Windmill Hill, Gibraltar, 1987. (b) Number of Robins caught in mist nets at Jews' Gate, Gibraltar, 1973–79.

The Robin arrives late and departs early, the first birds arriving in mid-September (early September in Doñana according to Murillo & Sanch, 1969), with a rapid build-up during October and November and a gradual stabilization of winter numbers as territories are set up (Figure 70). Although many of the birds that arrive in October and November continue south (in other cases they redistribute in other directions, as evidenced by a Robin which arrived in Gibraltar in October and was recovered later the same winter in Córdoba), a number remain in the Strait. The spring passage takes the form of a gradual departure without obvious peaks, the last Robins leaving during the second half of April.

Nightingale

Nightingales breed over much of western Europe and winter in tropical Africa, generally north of the equatorial forests (Moreau, 1972). They are common in Senegal and Nigeria, and a Gibraltar-ringed Nightingale was recovered wintering in Sierra Leone. Few have been recovered in the Iberian Peninsula, but Telleria (1981) highlighted two German and two French birds. In general, therefore, it seems that western European Nightingales are involved in the Strait crossing and that these are bound for tropical West Africa. The extent to which more eastern populations migrate southwest in autumn is undetermined, although there appears to be a significant autumn accumulation in western Iberia of birds from as far as central Germany, with subsequent overflying of Morocco (Moreau, 1961). The spring passage is much more conspicuous along the North African coast (Moreau, 1961).

The migration of Nightingales north over the Strait in spring is generally much more conspicuous than the southward migration (Figure 71), though there are years when both passages are equally strong, possibly as a result of poor weather conditions grounding birds in autumn. This pattern is consistent with the observed behaviour of Nightingales in spring and autumn, with considerable overflying of Mediterranean areas during the southward passage (Moreau, 1961; Heim de Balsac & Mayaud, 1962). At Windmill Hill, mean spring counts during the main passage vary between 0.7 and 1.6 birds (0.05–0.12 birds/ha), and autumn counts between 0.4 and 0.7 birds (0.03–0.05 birds/ha). Densities are greater in the maquis, reaching 1.2 birds/ha in April and 0.2 birds/ha in September. Maximum counts at Windmill Hill support the view that many more Nightingales utilize the Strait in spring than in autumn, up to 22 in spring (1.69 birds/ha) against only 5 in autumn (0.39 birds/ha).

The first Nightingales pass north at the end of March and there is then a rapid build-up of numbers in April, with peak passage during the second half of the month and a reduced passage in early May (Figure 71). A few Nightingales pass north as late as June. The return migration starts in mid-August (earlier observations are likely to be of local birds dispersing after breeding), with peak passage during the first half of September and a decrease towards the end of October. Telleria (1981) remarked on the late (20 October) recovery of a continental Nightingale in Iberia, which suggests that the more northerly populations may move south after the Iberian Nightingales. The latter probably leave in August and early September, judging from their inconspicuousness in the area, in contrast with their massive presence in the spring.

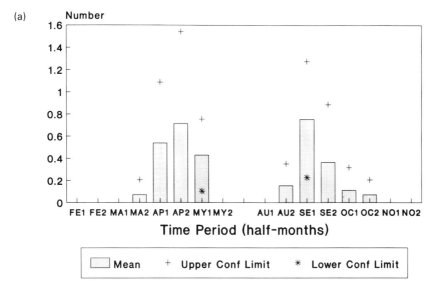

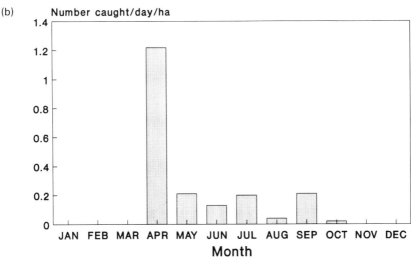

Figure 71. (a) Nightingale passage at Windmill Hill, Gibraltar, 1987. (b) Number of Nightingales caught in mist nets at Jews' Gate, Gibraltar, 1973–79.

Black Redstart

German, Belgian, Swiss and French Black Redstarts have been the main recoveries in Spain (Telleria, 1981), and there have also been British recoveries in southern Spain (Langslow, 1977), indicating that birds from most of the western part of the breeding range move southwest in autumn (Verheyen, 1970; Langs-

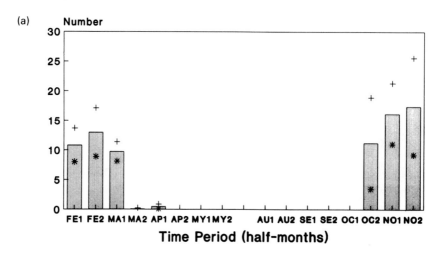

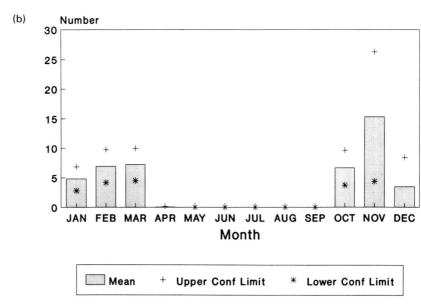

Figure 72.   (a) Black Redstart passage at Windmill Hill, Gibraltar, 1987. (b) Black Redstart seasonal distribution at Windmill Hill, Gibraltar, 1971–89.

low, 1977). Black Redstarts do not cross the Sahara, though they may reach its edge (Moreau, 1972). Those that cross the Strait must winter in Morocco, with the Strait itself being important as a wintering area (Pineau & Giraud-Audine, 1979).

Black Redstarts reach high densities during the passage periods and in winter

(Arroyo & Telleria, 1984). In the open-ground habitat of Windmill Hill, Black Redstarts reach high mean densities. In spring, mean counts at this site vary between 6 and 13 (0.46–1.0 birds/ha) and in autumn between 15 and 16 birds (1.15–1.23 birds/ha). Maximum counts, during spectacular falls, are very high, 34 birds in spring (2.62 birds/ha) and 150 in autumn (11.54 birds/ha). Winter levels remain high, at around 5 birds (0.39 birds/ha) at Windmill Hill, but lower in matorral (0.12 birds/ha) or pastures (0.01 birds/ha), according to Arroyo & Telleria (1984).

The autumn arrival of Black Redstarts is late, and they leave early in spring (Figure 72). The autumn passage commences during the last days of September or early October, with a major increase during the latter half of October leading to peak arrivals in November. The spring passage is more pronounced than in other pre-saharan migrants, with a distinct peak during early March and a very sharp drop after that; hardly any pass in April.

Redstart

The Redstarts that migrate through the area are of western and northern European origin, German and Scandinavian birds predominating (Telleria, 1981). Redstarts may perform a loop migration (Moreau, 1961), birds from as far east as Finland crossing the Iberian Peninsula in autumn, with a more easterly return route in spring. British-ringed birds probably migrate in autumn through southwest France and Iberia (except northwest, east and southeast Iberia) returning slightly to the east (Hope Jones, 1975). Continental birds (Scandinavian, German and Dutch) also pass Iberia and North Africa, apparently east of the British Redstarts. Although occasional birds may winter in the area of the Strait (Pineau & Giraud-Audine, 1976; Telleria, 1981), such cases are isolated and the majority cross the Sahara to winter in northern tropical Africa. There they winter in dry country as far west as Senegal, where there is evidence that eastern European birds winter alongside western European ones (Moreau, 1972).

Redstarts are more abundant in the Strait in spring than autumn, in keeping with the pattern exhibited by other trans-saharan migrants that appear to concentrate along the western coasts of Iberia in autumn (Bernis, 1962). At Windmill Hill, mean spring counts during the main passage of between 1.5 and 2 birds (0.12–0.15 birds/ha) contrast with mean autumn counts of around 0.3 birds (0.02 birds/ha). Mist-netting results in the maquis support this observation, with spring densities of around 0.3–0.35 birds/ha and autumn densities of around 0.1 birds/ha (Figure 73). Maximum counts at Windmill Hill are nevertheless the same for autumn and spring, 15 birds (1.15 birds/ha).

The spring migration commences at the end of March, the main passage taking place during the second half of April and the first half of May (Figure 73). The autumn passage, commencing in late August (Cortés *et al.*, 1980; Telleria, 1981), reaches a maximum during the first half of October with smaller numbers passing until the end of the month (Figure 73).

(a)

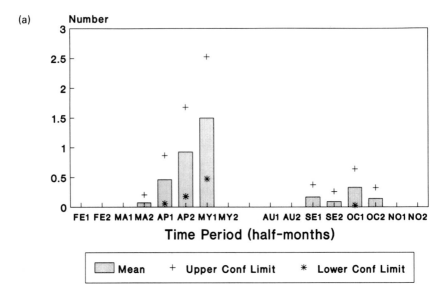

(b)

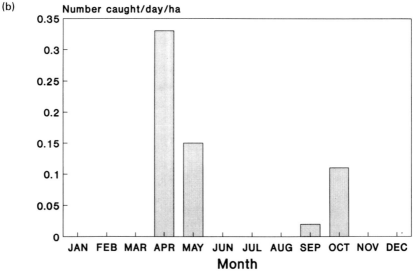

Figure 73.   (a) Redstart passage at Windmill Hill, Gibraltar, 1987. (b) Numbers of Redstarts caught in mist nets at Jews' Gate, Gibraltar, 1973–79.

Whinchat

Whinchats breed over much of central and northern Europe, south to northern Spain. Eastern birds may loop far to the west, over Iberia in autumn, returning to the breeding grounds by a more direct route (Moreau, 1961). Whinchats winter

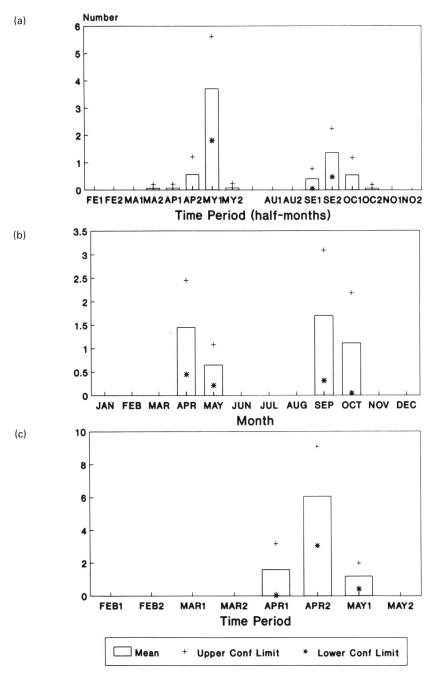

Figure 74. (a) Whinchat passage at Windmill Hill, Gibraltar, 1987. (b) Whinchat seasonal distribution at Windmill Hill, Gibraltar, 1971–89. (c) Large Whinchat passage at Windmill Hill, Gibraltar, in late April 1984.

south of the Sahara in tropical Africa, where they are abundant and widespread in savanna, being found between 5 and 15°N in the west (Moreau, 1972; Serle *et al.*, 1977). Telleria (1981) cited a winter record for the Spanish side of the Strait, of a German Whinchat recovered in December.

The difference between spring and autumn passage is not as marked as in other trans-saharan migrants, though during individual years the difference can be high (Figure 74). Mean spring counts at Windmill Hill during the main passage period vary between 1.5 and 4 birds (0.12–0.31 birds/ha), and mean autumn counts between 1.5 and 2 birds (0.12–0.15 birds/ha). Maximum counts at this site are 20 in spring (1.54 birds/ha) and 25 in autumn (1.92 birds/ha).

Whinchats are among the latest spring arrivals, the first individuals appearing during the first half of April and most passing in late April and early May. Late migrants are recorded in early June (Cortés *et al.*, 1980). The southward passage, which according to Cortés *et al.* (1980) and Telleria (1981) commences in late

Thousands of migrants are ringed by the Strait of Gibraltar Bird Observatory. Here, a Whinchat on spring passage north from tropical West Africa towards north-western Europe, is ringed and examined by scientists before release.

August, has its maximum during the second half of September, the last birds passing at the end of October or, on the Moroccan side, early November (Pineau & Giraud-Audine, 1979).

Stonechat

Stonechats are common nesting birds on both shores of the Strait, but there is a distinct passage and winter arrival of birds from northern and western Europe,

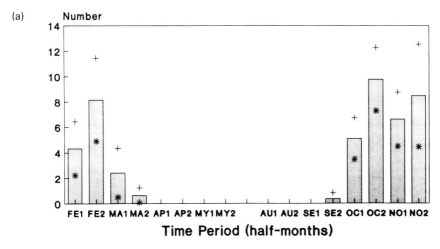

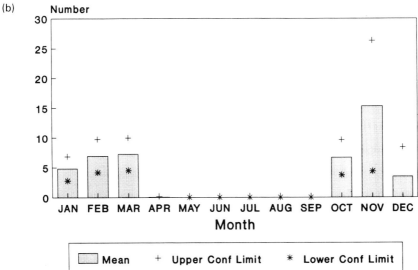

Figure 75. (a) Stonechat passage at Windmill Hill, Gibraltar, 1987. (b) Stonechat seasonal distribution at Windmill Hill, Gibraltar, 1971–89.

which add to the local, apparently resident, population: Telleria (1981) gave recoveries of Belgian, French and English Stonechats. This passage and wintering of Stonechats has been recorded by several authors (Pineau & Giraud-Audine, 1979; Cortés *et al.*, 1980; Telleria, 1981; Finlayson & Cortés, 1987). There is no evidence of trans-saharan migration into West Africa.

The clearest evidence of migration and wintering of Stonechats comes from Gibraltar, where there are no resident Stonechats. At Windmill Hill, pronounced movements occur in spring and autumn. In spring, mean counts during the main passage period are of the order of 6–8 birds (0.46–0.62 birds/ha); in autumn, mean counts range from 8 to 10 birds (0.62–0.77 birds/ha). Maximum counts at this site are considerably higher in spring, however, illustrating the high densities that can be reached during falls. The highest spring count is 65 (5 birds/ha) and the highest autumn count is 25 (1.92 birds/ha). During the winter, mean counts at Windmill Hill fall to between 2 and 3 birds (0.15–0.23 birds/ha). On the Spanish side of the Strait, higher wintering densities have been recorded (Arroyo & Telleria, 1984), 0.34 birds/ha in pastures and 0.59 birds/ha in the matorral. In these Spanish habitats, resident Stonechats could not be distinguished from migrants.

Stonechat passage periods are similar to those of other pre-saharan migrants, with a main arrival in October and November and departure in February and March (Figure 75). Within this broad scheme there are slight differences in detail. Stonechats arrive from mid-September onwards, and the main passage is in October with fewer birds in November. In spring there is a peak during late February and early March, with the last birds passing in early April.

Wheatear

The main catchment area of the Wheatears that cross the Strait is western and northern Europe as indicated by recoveries summarized by Telleria (1981); these include British, German, Finnish, French and Icelandic Wheatears. Moreau (1961) noted that there was a great tendency for Wheatears to migrate southwest in autumn, so the recovery of a Finnish Wheatear is not surprising. Furthermore, the regular occurrence of Wheatears of the Greenland subspecies *leucorrhoa* shows that birds from the northwesternmost parts of the breeding range also pass through the Strait. These Wheatears must winter in the westernmost areas of the northern tropical African wintering range, where they avoid the driest zones just south of the desert (Moreau, 1972). Greenland Wheatears winter furthest west, having been recorded from Senegal to Sierra Leone (Moreau, 1972), where they occur alongside the nominate subspecies and *seebohmi* from Morocco.

Moreau (1961) noted that there was little difference in the abundance of this species along the Mediterranean in spring and autumn; he attributed this to the suitability of semi-desert for this species, which would be able to exploit dry areas that other migrants would avoid. The pattern at Gibraltar is consistent with this interpretation, and contrasts with the pattern for most other trans-saharan migrants. Thus, passage is approximately the same in spring and autumn (Figure

(a)

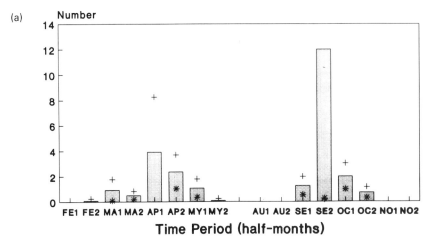

Time Period (half-months)

(b)

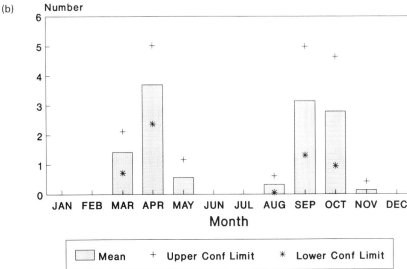

Month

☐ Mean   + Upper Conf Limit   ✳ Lower Conf Limit

Figure 76. (a) Wheatear passage at Windmill Hill, Gibraltar, 1987. (b) Wheatear seasonal distribution at Windmill Hill, Gibraltar, 1971–89.

76), and during specific years may be even greater in autumn than spring. Mean spring densities at Windmill Hill during the main passage are consistently around 4 birds (0.31 birds/ha), and mean autumn densities range from 3 to 12 birds (0.23–0.92 birds/ha). Maximum counts are of 30 birds in each season (2.31 birds/ha).

As noted by Moreau (1961), spring passage is early, individuals sometimes arriving as early as the end of February. Peak passage takes place during April and the May passage is dominated by *leucorrhoa*. The return commences in mid-

August and is prolonged into early November, the October–November passage being of *leucorrhoa*. Peak autumn passage takes place in late September (Figure 76).

Black-eared Wheatear

The Black-eared Wheatears that cross the Strait must belong to the western Mediterranean populations, probably Iberian and some south French. Together

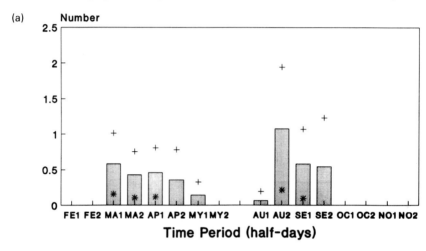

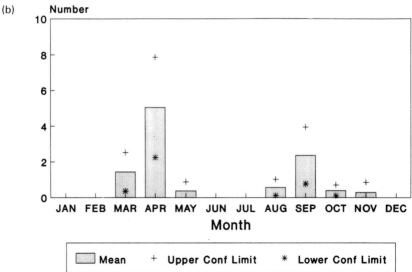

Figure 77.   (a) Black-eared Wheatear passage at Windmill Hill, Gibraltar, 1987. (b) Black-eared Wheatear seasonal distribution at Windmill Hill, Gibraltar, 1971–89.

with others that breed on the Moroccan side of the Strait, they are assumed to winter in the western parts of the winter range, which stretches as a belt across the width of Africa between 14 and 17°N (Moreau, 1972).

The general pattern of observations on Windmill Hill suggests that the spring passage is on average more conspicuous than the autumn passage (Figure 77), though the pattern can be substantially modified, even reversed, in some years. Mean spring counts at Windmill Hill during the main passage vary between 0.5 and 5 birds (0.04–0.39 birds/ha) and autumn counts between 1 and 2 birds (0.08–0.15 birds/ha). Maximum counts are much higher in spring, with up to 60 birds (4.62 birds/ha), than in autumn when the maximum count has been 20 (1.54 birds/ha). The proximity of the breeding grounds to the edge of the Sahara may explain the gradual reduction in numbers in autumn, when birds may fly direct to the wintering areas.

The migratory periods of the Black-eared Wheatear indicate an early arrival in spring, during the first half of March, with a strong passage in April and a very small movement in early May (Figure 77). The southward passage begins in early August, with the main passage taking place during September and a progressive reduction in numbers with isolated birds passing in early November.

Song Thrush

The catchment area of the Song Thrushes that reach the Strait and cross it extends into northern and eastern Europe. The main areas from which Spanish recoveries originate are Scandinavia, Germany, Holland and the Baltic (Telleria, 1981). To these can be added a Soviet Baltic bird which was recovered on autumn passage at Gibraltar. Song Thrushes winter in large numbers in the Strait, on the Moroccan side especially in matorral (Pinea & Giraud-Audine, 1979), and rarely wander south of the Sahara, though Moreau (1972) records one in Senegal in November.

Song Thrushes can be numerous migrants within the Strait. Mean spring counts during the main passage at Windmill Hill vary between 1 and 2 birds (0.08–0.15 birds/ha) and in autumn between 2 and 3 birds (0.15–0.23 birds/ha). Mist-netting in maquis at Gibraltar gives average densities during the main passage of around 0.3 birds/ha in spring and 0.2 birds/ha in autumn. Maximum counts at Windmill Hill show a similar pattern, 18 in spring (1.39 birds/ha) and 16 in autumn (1.23 birds/ha).

The passage of Song Thrushes is typically that of pre-saharan migrants (Figure 78). Arrivals from the north commence at the end of September (Cortés *et al.*, 1980) and are important during late October and early November. In spring there is a regular passage in February and March, with very few passing in April. The February passage can be particularly spectacular, especially in open cork oak woods and olive groves where large flocks of Song Thrushes gather alongside Blackcaps and Chaffinches. Winter densities in the Gibraltar maquis are of the order of 0.1–0.15 birds/ha, which is significantly lower than the 0.99 birds/ha recorded in matorral on the Spanish side of the Strait by Arroyo & Telleria (1984).

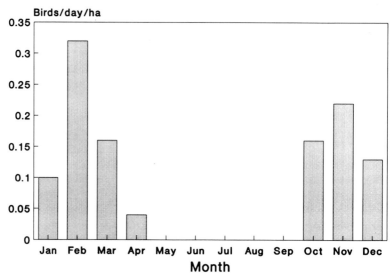

Figure 78.   Seasonal distribution of Song Thrush at Jews' Gate, Gibraltar. Birds ringed, 1973–79.

WARBLERS

A number of species that occur regularly on passage but, because of skulking habits or choice of specialized habitat for example, have not been recorded with sufficient frequency to allow a detailed analysis of their migration across the Strait are dealt with briefly below. The 13 well-documented species are each discussed in a separate section.

Cetti's Warbler is probably a passage migrant overlooked on account of its shy habits and the substantial local resident population. Birds caught at Defilia Oasis in southeast Morocco were considered to be migrants (Smith, 1965, 1968). Occasionally some Cetti's Warblers must cross the Sahara as it has been recorded in Nigeria (Elgood *et al.*, 1966). Current evidence of passage is not entirely satisfactory (Lathbury, 1970; Pineau & Giraud-Audine, 1979; Cortés *et al.*, 1980; Telleria, 1981).

The Grasshopper Warbler is a regular migrant which is very rarely observed but is caught in mist nets during the main passage periods. Its autumn passage down the Moroccan Atlantic coast must be substantial, judging from the numbers caught by Eleonora's Falcons (Vaughan, 1961; Walter, 1979) and observed by Smith (1965). Grasshopper Warblers winter in tropical West Africa, in Senegal (Moreau, 1961, 1972; Serle *et al.*, 1977) and probably in more humid areas to the south (Moreau, 1972). They do not winter in the Strait. The warblers that occur on passage are presumably from western and central Europe, and the recovery of a German-ringed bird in October in Jerez (Telleria, 1981) is in agreement with this pattern. The spring passage, when Grasshopper Warblers appear most frequently, takes place from mid-March to May (Pineau & Giraud-Audine, 1979; Cortés *et al.*, 1980; Finlayson & Cortés, 1987) and the autumn passage from late August to mid-October (Cortés *et al.*, 1980; Telleria, 1981; Finlayson & Cortés, 1987).

The River Warbler, which breeds from Germany east to about 75°E and is thought to winter in East Africa (Moreau, 1972), may stray west on passage. Smith (1968) recorded it at Defilia Oasis (1°15′W) in southeast Morocco in spring, so it may wander west towards the Strait, although there are no records.

Savi's Warbler, which breeds in southern Iberia and parts of western and central Europe and winters in the westernmost parts of tropical West Africa (Moreau, 1972), is a scarce passage migrant across the Strait; it is probably often overlooked on account of its skulking habits. A bird ringed in olive maquis at Gibraltar in September was undoubtedly a migrant (pers. obs.), and Irby (1875) considered that local breeding birds arrived in March and left by September.

Some Moustached Warblers that breed in the Mediterranean Basin migrate to south of the Sahara where they have been reported in winter from Lake Chad (Moreau, 1972). Some winter in Morocco, close to the Strait (Thevenot & Thuoy, 1974), and there have been occasional sightings on both shores of the Strait, in localities where they are not resident (Pineau & Giraud-Audine, 1979; Finlayson & Cortés, 1987), indicating a passage in April and from mid-September to early November.

The precise winter quarters of the eastern European and western Asiatic populations of Aquatic Warbler are not precisely known; they have been recorded in winter in the Inundation Zone of the Niger in Mali (Moreau, 1972; Serle *et al.*, 1977). Passage birds have also been reported through Iberia, western Morocco and the Canary Islands (Moreau, 1961), so there may be other wintering areas in West Africa (Moreau, 1972). Pineau & Giraud-Audine (1979) recorded a small passage from mid-March to mid-April and a fall of exhausted Aquatic Warblers near Tangier on 23 March 1972. They only saw this species once in autumn, in October.

Sedge Warblers from the northwest European part of the breeding range are thought to migrate southwest to winter in tropical West Africa, judging from the recoveries of English, and one Danish, Sedge Warblers in southwest Spain in autumn (Telleria, 1981). A Sedge Warbler ringed on spring passage near Tangier has been recovered on Lundy Island in May of the same season (Pineau & Giraud-Audine, 1979). In West Africa they are known from Senegal (Moreau, 1972) and are very common on passage in the lower Senegal River (Serle *et al.*, 1977). Sedge Warblers are regular migrants in the Strait area in spring, as early as 18 February (Pineau & Giraud-Audine, 1979) but mainly between early March and early May, though nowhere numerous. They are very rare in autumn (Pineau & Giraud-Audine, 1979; Telleria, 1981; Finlayson & Cortés, 1987), when they seem to overfly the Mediterranean (Moreau, 1972), but are more common from mid-September to mid-October further south, in southwest Morocco (Smith, 1965).

Blyth's Reed Warbler breeds from the Baltic eastwards and winters in India.

There is one record for the Strait, of a bird ringed on the Rock of Gibraltar on the 24 September, 1973 (Cortés *et al.*, 1980).

Marsh Warblers winter in eastern and southern Africa and migrate south and southeast from the European and Asiatic breeding grounds (Moreau, 1972). Nevertheless, Telleria (1981) cites the recovery in Chipiona (Cádiz Province) in September of a Marsh Warbler ringed the same year in Luxembourg. There are no other records for the area, and the species must be regarded as a rare visitor from the main migratory routes.

The Great Reed Warbler breeds over much of western Europe, including the Iberian Peninsula and in the Maghreb, and winters over much of tropical Africa (Moreau, 1972). Western populations are thought to winter in West Africa and show a southwesterly migration in autumn (Erard & Yeatman, 1966). As with other swamp warblers, evidence of passage is fragmented, and long flights between refuelling grounds are probably the rule (Moreau, 1961). There is little evidence of passage in the Strait area. In spring, the arrival of local breeding birds is sudden and probably masks any subsequent passage. Allowing for this problem, the spring migration probably spans the period late March to early May (Pineau & Giraud-Audine, 1979); a few Great Reed Warblers have been recorded on passage at Defilia, southeastern Morocco, in mid-April (Smith, 1968). In autumn, Telleria (1981) recorded a small passage in August and September and Garcia Rua (1975) ringed a few near Tarifa in early October. They are nevertheless uncommon, and there is little evidence of passage of birds from the north (Pineau & Giraud-Audine, 1979); overflying at this time seems likely to be the rule.

The subspecies *opaca* of the Olivaceous Warbler breeds in Iberia and the Maghreb and winters in tropical West Africa from Senegal to Nigeria (Moreau, 1972). Olivaceous Warblers occur regularly on passage within the Strait, though they are never common. The spring passage commences in late March and may continue into early June (Finlayson & Cortés, 1987), judging from late sightings on the Rock of Gibraltar where the species does not breed. This is an unusually long passage for a population that breeds no further north than Iberia, and the later birds may be non-breeders. Olivaceous Warblers are scarcer in autumn when a direct flight to the wintering grounds seems likely. The passage then commences in mid-July and is over by mid-September, with most records in August (Finlayson & Cortés, 1987).

Icterine Warblers migrate southeast to winter quarters in eastern and southern Africa in autumn and may return via a more westerly route (Moreau, 1972). In any case, the Strait lies well west of the migratory lines; consequently, there is only one record for the area, of a bird ringed on the Rock of Gibraltar on 25 August 1973 (Cortés *et al.*, 1980).

Marmora's Warbler is a very scarce visitor to the Strait from western Mediterranean islands; many sightings appear to be due to confusion with juvenile Dartford Warblers (Finlayson & Cortés, 1987). Tristram's Warbler from the Moroccan desert has recently been reported from Gibraltar (*SGBO Reports*).

Sardinian Warblers are known to winter in tropical West Africa in small numbers (Moreau, 1972), so there may be a small passage of western populations from France and Iberia via the Strait. If such passage exists it is masked by the large resident population (Pineau & Giraud-Audine, 1979; Cortés *et al.*, 1980; Telleria, 1981; Finlayson & Cortés, 1987).

Barred Warblers breed from the Baltic and France to Mongolia, wintering in eastern Africa (Moreau, 1972). Despite their occurrence west of the breeding range in autumn (Williamson, 1964), they have not been recorded from the Strait, which is well west of the passage routes. Lesser Whitethroats breed across Europe west to the British Isles and winter in the eastern northern tropics west to northern Nigeria, migrating southeast in autumn (Moreau, 1972). There are no records for the Strait which is well west of the main migratory routes.

Four northeastern *Phylloscopus* species, Arctic, Yellow-browed, Radde's and Dusky Warblers, have been recorded in the Strait in autumn and winter and can only be considered rare, off-course, migrants (Valverde, 1967; Finlayson & Cortés, 1987). Of these, the Yellow-browed Warbler has been the most frequently recorded (Rait-Kerr, 1934–35; Valverde, 1967; Finlayson & Cortés, 1987), in keeping with its status as the most frequent of the Siberian *Phylloscopus* vagrants in western Europe.

The Wood Warbler breeds from the British Isles in the west to about 60°E, and winters between 9°N and the Gulf of Guinea or the equator, and between 10°W and 35°E (Moreau, 1972). In autumn, Wood Warblers overfly the Mediterranean and are generally scarce throughout (Moreau, 1961, 1972). There is only one autumn record for the Strait (Garcia Rua, 1975); Telleria (1981) cited the recovery of a German bird in autumn in Almonte near the Guadalquivir. They are commoner in spring. The Strait lies at the western edge of a line leading from the western side of the winter quarters to the western side of the breeding grounds; consequently Wood Warblers are regular passage migrants from late March to May but are the scarcest of the four European *Phylloscopus*, the main passage being to the east. Wood Warblers have been recorded regularly, sometimes in groups, at Defilia Oasis in southeast Morocco between late March and early May (Smith, 1968).

The Firecrest is a regular migrant across the Strait, being most conspicuous in autumn when they pass south from late September to November (Cortés *et al.*, 1980; Telleria, 1981; Finlayson & Cortés, 1987). Firecrests winter in the Strait (Pineau & Giraud-Audine, 1979; Arroyo & Telleria, 1984), adding to the resident population, but the origins of these migrants are unknown. The return movement, which is less pronounced, takes place from February to April (Finlayson & Cortés, 1987) and, as with other pre-saharan species, probably takes the form of a gradual departure from the wintering areas. The Goldcrest is a rare migrant and winter visitor to the Strait (Pineau & Giraud-Audine, 1979; Cortés *et al.*, 1980), and there has been a Spanish recovery of a Danish-ringed Goldcrest (Telleria, 1981).

Whitethroat

Whitethroats are summer visitors to most of Europe except the far north. European Whitethroat populations exhibit a migratory divide which is, however, not as pronounced as in the Blackcap or the Garden Warbler (Williamson, 1964). There is a clear tendency for Whitethroats from the British Isles, north-

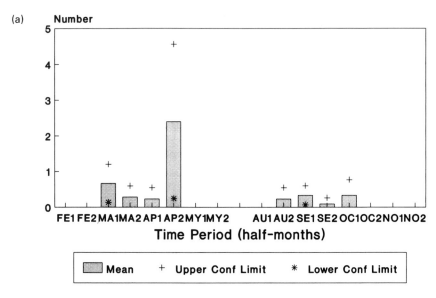

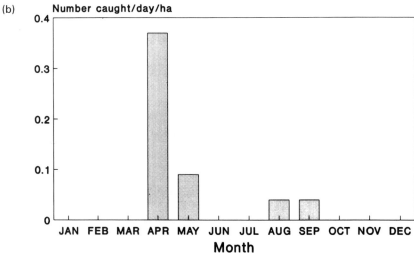

Figure 79.   (a) Whitethroat passage at Windmill Hill, Gibraltar, 1987. (b) Number of White-throats caught in mist nets at Jews' Gate, Gibraltar, 1973–79.

eastern France and Belgium to migrate towards the Iberian Peninsula in autumn, and German birds west of 10°E also showed a tendency to fly southwest at this time. A Swiss bird has been recovered in Portugal (Erard & Yeatman, 1966). Da Prato & da Prato (1983) suggested that British Whitethroats utilize western Iberia as a feeding area before the final flight to tropical Africa, with a more direct return route in spring. British-ringed birds have also been recovered in Morocco and Senegal, indicating that they are wintering south of the Sahara in the western-most part of the wintering range, west of continental European Whitethroats (Zink, 1975). In general, Whitethroats do not winter north of the Sahara (Telleria, 1981; da Prato & da Prato, 1983) but occupy a belt across Africa between 10 and 18°N, and further south in eastern Africa, in acacia steppe and savanna (Moreau, 1972). The Whitethroats that cross the Strait are therefore derived from western Europe and winter in tropical West Africa.

Cortés *et al.* (1980) have suggested that Whitethroats were more common in Gibraltar prior to the population crash of 1969 (Winstanley *et al.*, 1974) and that there was evidence of a recovery after 1976. This recovery appears to have continued, and Whitethroats are once again regular and common migrants in the area of the Strait. They are more abundant in spring than in autumn, concordant with the hypothesis that they follow a more direct spring route from the winter quarters than the westerly orientated passage in autumn, which may include overflying southern Iberia. At Windmill Hill, mean spring counts during the main movement range from 2 to 3 birds (0.15–0.23 birds/ha); mean autumn counts fall below 0.5 birds (0.04 birds/ha). Mist-netting in taller maquis confirms this pattern, though recorded densities are lower. Maximum counts at Windmill Hill are also higher in spring (15 birds; 1.15 birds/ha) than autumn (4 birds; 0.31 birds/ha)

Occasionally, Whitethroats are recorded as early as the end of February, but the main spring movement does not usually commence until March, with a peak at the end of April followed by a decrease in numbers in May (Figure 79). Males precede females, as is the case for other *Sylvia* warblers, and the early arrivals are probably southern Spanish breeding birds. The southward passage starts during the second half of August and continues until early October, without a well-defined peak. However, Herrera (1974) recorded a peak in September in Doñana, with the first birds passing in early August. Pineau & Giraud-Audine (1979) and Telleria (1981) noted late birds in early November.

Blackcap

The Blackcap is a widespread breeding species throughout Europe, except in the far north, and in Morocco. The northern populations are migratory, showing a *Zugscheide* (migratory divide) at about 10–11°E (Brickenstein-Stockhammer & Drost, 1956). Birds east of the divide migrate southeast, and those from west of the divide migrate southwest towards the Iberian Peninsula. The pattern of recoveries for the Iberian Peninsula and Morocco reflects this, with German,

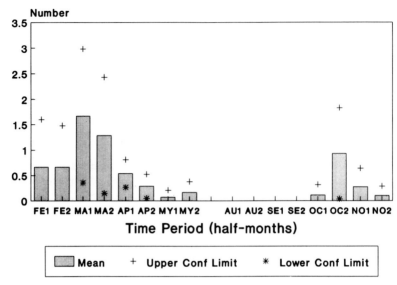

Figure 80.   Blackcap passage at Windmill Hill, Gibraltar, 1987.

Belgian, French and English Blackcaps predominating (Erard & Yeatman, 1966; Telleria, 1981). Recoveries at Gibraltar include Dutch, Belgian, French and German Blackcaps. Many Blackcaps winter within the Mediterranean Basin, so a large proportion of those arriving in the Strait area remain there or move south only a short distance into Morocco. An unknown proportion cross the Sahara and winter in tropical West Africa. Moreau (1972) concluded that most Blackcaps wintered in tropical Africa, not the Mediterranean Basin, but Serle *et al.* (1977) judged the species to be a sparse, locally common, winter visitor to West Africa. In the west, Blackcaps winter in the acacia steppe belt in Volta, Mali and Senegal, and in the wetter areas to the south; numbers fluctuated in relation to the crop of wild fruit (Moreau, 1972). A similar relationship occurs in the Mediterranean, and the numbers crossing the Sahara Desert might be dependent on feeding opportunities north of the desert (see also Chapter 8).

Blackcaps are very abundant migrants, reaching high densities in some habitats. At Windmill Hill, where Blackcaps only occur in transit, preferring taller and denser scrub, mean spring counts vary between 1.5 and 3 birds (0.12–0.23 birds/ha) and mean autumn counts are lower, around 1 bird (0.08 birds/ha) (Figure 80). Maximum spring and autumn counts are 6 birds (0.46 birds/ha). In the taller olive scrub in Gibraltar, Blackcaps reach much higher densities. Based on mist-netting results, I estimated mean spring densities to be between 6 and 10 birds/ha and mean autumn densities between 4 and 5 birds/ha, with even higher numbers during falls (Finlayson, 1979). These densities were much higher than those reached by resident Blackcaps (Figure 81), which could be identified from the migrants in the hand (Finlayson, 1980).

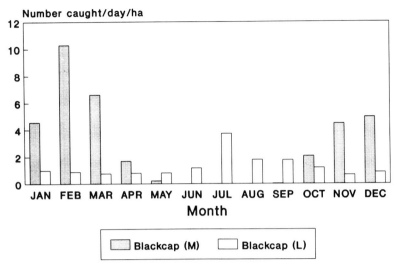

Figure 81.   Number of local and migrant Blackcaps caught in mist nets at Jews' Gate, Gibraltar, 1973–79.

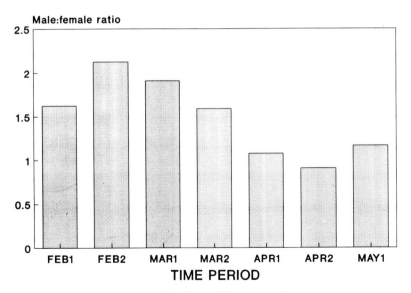

Figure 82.   Blackcap spring passage—distribution of sexes, N = 497.

Blackcaps arrive from the north during the last week of September, and successive waves of migrants pass the area in October and November (Figure 80). Peak passage takes place during the second half of October and the first half of November. Although many of the early migrants continue south into Morocco, ringing in Gibraltar has shown that some of these Blackcaps remain in the area for the winter. The spring passage is spread out over a long period. Numbers build up in the area from the end of January and there is a large northward movement during February and early March; presumably the majority are birds that have wintered north of the Sahara; males precede females (Figure 82). Passage continues into May, and these latter migrants may be mainly trans-saharan. A Blackcap ringed on passage at Gibraltar in May was recovered in Belgium a month later. There is strong evidence to support the view that Blackcaps move around in response to changing food sources during the winter (see Chapter 8) so that passage can take place even in December and January. The main departure in February may reflect the reduced fruit crops which have been depleted over the winter.

Garden Warbler

The Garden Warbler breeds throughout western Europe south to northern Spain. It does not breed within the area of the Strait. There is a migratory divide around 10–11°E but Scandinavian birds, including Finnish Garden Warblers, migrate southwest towards the Iberian Peninsula in autumn, unlike Blackcaps, which move southeast (Williamson, 1964; Erard & Yeatman, 1966). The migrants that pass the Strait therefore come from western and northern Europe, with recoveries of German, French, Danish and English birds predominating in the Iberian Peninsula and Morocco (Erard & Yeatman, 1966; Telleria, 1981). Garden Warblers are trans-saharan migrants, although there are isolated cases of winter-ing in the Strait (Telleria, 1981). Ringing recoveries of Garden Warblers show trends towards southerly and southwestly passage, so it seems that those passing the Strait must winter in West Africa south of the acacia belt in which Blackcaps winter, in Guinea, Sierra Leone and Ivory Coast (Moreau, 1972). A bird ringed near Tarifa in September was recovered in Sierra Leone (Garcia Rua, 1975).

Garden Warblers are skulking birds on passage and are easily overlooked. Mist-netting has demonstrated that they are common migrants (Garcia Rua, 1975; Finlayson, 1979). Mean spring counts at Windmill Hill vary between 0.6 and 1.5 birds (0.05–0.12 birds/ha) and mean autumn counts between 0.6 and 0.8 birds (0.05–0.06 birds/ha). Maximum counts are 5 in spring (0.39 birds/ha) and 3 in autumn (0.23 birds/ha). Mist-netting gives higher estimates, up to 0.98 birds/ha in spring and 0.23 birds/ha in autumn (Finlayson, 1979).

Spring passage of Garden Warblers is late, commencing in mid-April, with many passing during the second half of the month and in May (Figure 83). The return, which commences in August, is centred in September and early October, with a few passing as late as early November some years. The passage is, on average, later in spring and earlier in autumn than that of the Blackcap.

(a)

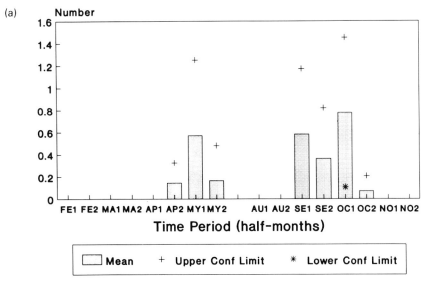

(b)

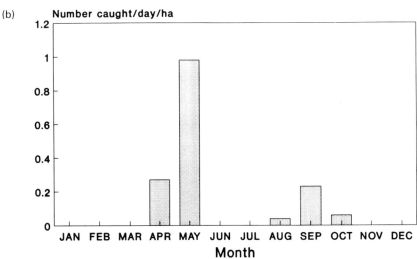

Figure 83. (a) Garden Warbler passage at Windmill Hill, Gibraltar, 1987. (b) Number of Garden Warblers caught in mist nets at Jews' Gate, Gibraltar, 1973–79.

Subalpine Warbler

The Subalpine Warbler breeds in the Iberian Peninsula and the south of France, eastwards along the Mediterranean, and on the North African side from Morocco eastwards across the Maghreb. The Subalpine Warblers that cross the Strait must therefore be mostly Spanish with a few French and Portuguese birds.

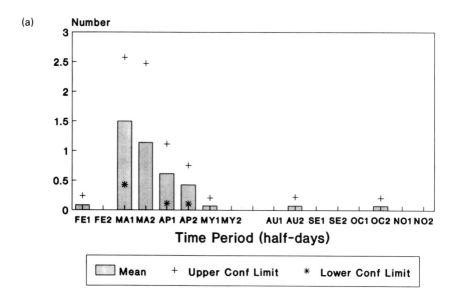

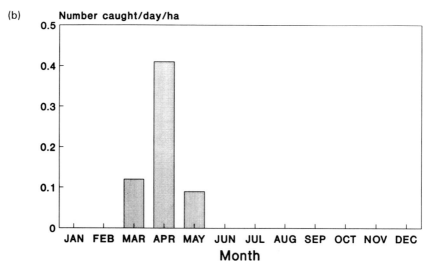

Figure 84.   (a) Subalpine Warbler passage at Windmill Hill, Gibraltar, 1987. (b) Number of Subalpine Warblers caught in mist nets at Jews' Gate, Gibraltar, 1973–79.

Subalpine Warblers winter in tropical Africa, generally west of the breeding range (Moreau, 1961), and those that pass the Strait are thought to winter in West Africa where they are widespread in the thorn scrub belt bordering the desert (Serle *et al.*, 1977).

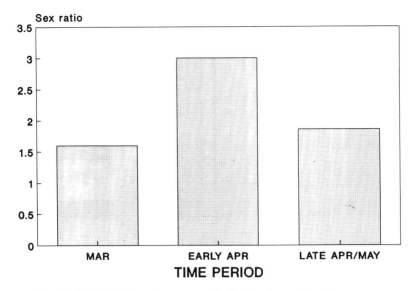

Figure 85.   Subalpine Warbler spring passage—distribution of sexes, N = 42.

Subalpine Warblers are very scarce during the southward migration, presumably as a result of the proximity of the breeding range to the Sahara and the wintering area—they may fly directly to the winter quarters. Telleria (1981) only recorded one bird in autumn, and autumn counts at Windmill Hill have been very low (Figure 84), very few birds having been mist-netted. This contrasts with the spring, when Subalpine Warblers are regular, at times abundant, migrants. Mean spring counts at Windmill Hill vary between 1 and 1.5 birds (0.08–0.12 birds/ha) and, in the taller scrub, mist-netting results give densities of up to 0.4 birds/ha (Finlayson, 1979). Maximum counts at Windmill Hill are 10 in spring (0.78 birds/ha) and 2 in autumn (0.15 birds/ha).

Spring passage commences early, in March, with isolated individuals in February (Figure 84). Passage continues into early May and most late birds are females since males pass earlier. The main passage is in March (males) and April (females) (Figure 85). The southward passage is difficult to determine, but migrants have been observed from August to October.

Spectacled Warbler

The movements of Spectacled Warblers are not well understood. They breed along both shores of the Mediterranean, from Italy and Tunisia westwards (see Chapter 8). It is thought to be a partial migrant which winters in the Saharan oases (Williamson, 1964), and it does not appear to reach much further south than

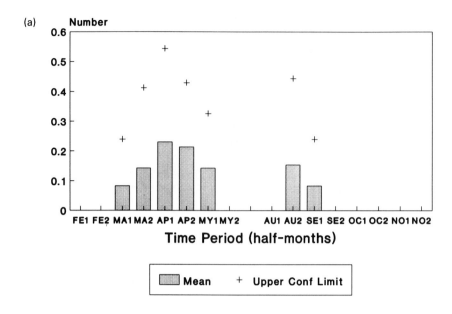

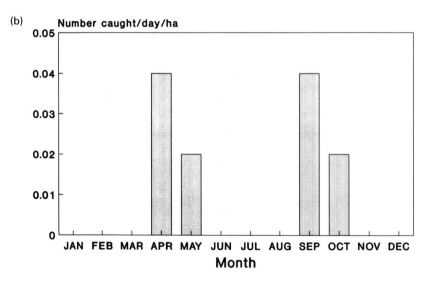

Figure 86.   (a) Spectacled Warbler passage at Windmill Hill, Gibraltar, 1987. (b) Number of Spectacled Warblers caught in mist nets at Jews' Gate, Gibraltar, 1973–79.

this (Moreau, 1972). Further north its status is uncertain. Pineau & Giraud-Audine (1979) recorded an individual on the Moroccan shore in February but found no other evidence of wintering. Although some Spectacled Warblers may be resident, there is a regular passage over the Strait of birds which must belong to the northernmost, Spanish and French, populations.

The Spectacled Warbler is a regular, though not numerous, migrant. At Windmill Hill it is a regular species, with mean spring counts of between 0.2 and 0.3 birds during the main movement (0.02 birds/ha), and mean autumn counts of between 0.1 and 0.2 birds (0.01–0.02 birds/ha). Maximum counts can be considerably higher, especially in spring when up to 10 have been recorded at this site (0.78 birds/ha). The highest number in autumn has been 3 (0.23 birds/ha). In the taller maquis, mist-netting produces fewer Spectacled Warblers.

The main spring movement is centred in April, especially the first half of the month, with the first birds passing in early March and the last ones in early May. The southward migration, which is less conspicuous, commences at the end of August and continues into October without a well-defined peak (Figure 86). The pattern of passage resembles that of trans-saharan migrants, and the birds involved, which breed in the northern parts of the range, may be wintering in the southernmost limits of the wintering areas.

Orphean Warbler

The Orphean Warbler populations that cross the Strait must belong to the westernmost parts of the circum-Mediterranean range of this species. Spain, Portugal, south and central France and southwest Switzerland could be sources of birds migrating over the Strait. These birds winter in the arid belt south of the Sahara, between 14 and 17°N (Moreau, 1972), in Senegal, Mali and Niger (Serle et al., 1977).

Orphean Warblers are more common in spring migration than autumn (Cortés et al., 1980; Telleria, 1981; Finlayson & Cortés, 1987). Moreau (1961) attributed the scarcity in the Mediterranean during the southward passage to the performance of a single, unbroken flight from the breeding grounds to the winter quarters. During the spring migration, mean counts at Windmill Hill vary from 0.05 to 0.2 birds (0.01–0.02 birds/ha), and mean autumn counts are lower, around 0.08 birds (0.01 birds/ha). The maximum number recorded at this site in spring is three (0.23 birds/ha), whereas in autumn Orphean Warblers have always been recorded singly. In the taller maquis a similar pattern is evident from ringing results.

The spring passage commences in early April and continues into June, most birds passing during late April and early May. The autumn passage appears to take place in late August and September (Figure 87), with the last birds early in October (Cortés et al., 1980).

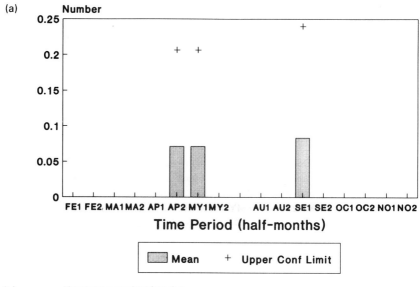

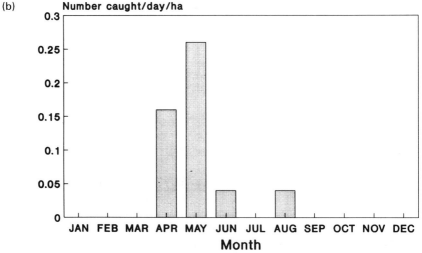

Figure 87.   (a) Orphean Warbler passage at Windmill Hill, Gibraltar, 1987. (b) Number of Orphean Warblers caught in mist nets at Jews' Gate, Gibraltar, 1973–79.

Dartford Warbler

Dartford Warblers breed on either side of the Strait and north to the French Atlantic and the southern English coasts. They are regarded as essentially sedentary, but the regular appearance of Dartford Warblers in unusual locations

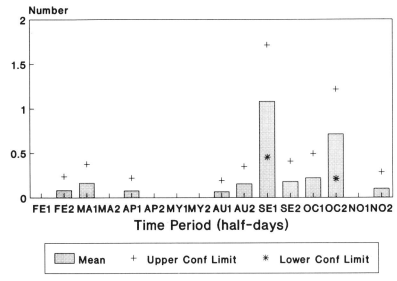

Figure 88.   Dartford Warbler passage at Windmill Hill, Gibraltar, 1987.

and habitats within the Strait indicates that there is an influx, varying in magnitude from year to year (Finlayson, 1978), into North Africa in autumn (Heim de Balsac & Mayaud, 1962; Pineau & Giraud-Audine, 1979; Cortés *et al.*, 1980; Telleria, 1981; Finlayson & Cortés, 1987). The origin of these birds is not known, though it seems likely that continental birds from the northern areas of the breeding range may be involved. I have found that Dartford Warblers caught at Gibraltar in autumn had low fat reserves and weights (Finlayson, 1978), which indicates that they are unlikely to travel much further south.

Dartford Warblers are more abundant in autumn than in spring: mean autumn counts at Windmill Hill are around 1 bird (0.08 birds/ha) and maximum counts of 15 birds (1.15 birds/ha). In spring, mean counts during the main passage are of the order of 0.5 birds (0.04 birds/ha), and never more than 2 birds have been recorded on the same day (0.15 birds/ha).

The southbound movement commences early in August, with an increase in numbers in September and October and smaller numbers in November. The spring passage starts at the end of February and continues into early April, with a slight increase during March (Figure 88).

Willow Warbler

Willow Warblers breed across the Palaearctic, east to 145°E in Siberia (Williamson, 1962; Moreau, 1972). The wintering range is mainly in Africa, south of the Sahara, from about 10°N south to southeast Africa (Moreau, 1972). Within these

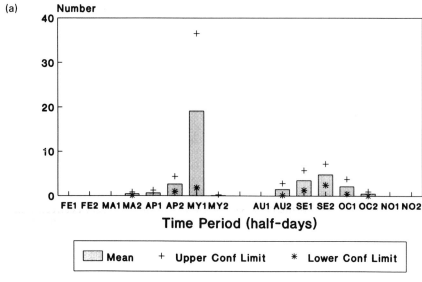

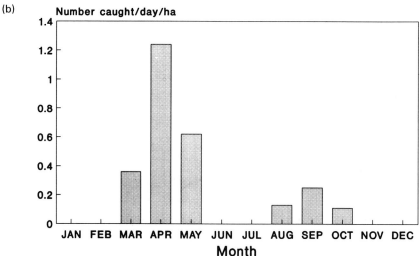

Figure 89.   (a) Willow Warbler passage at Windmill Hill, Gibraltar, 1987. (b) Number of Willow Warblers caught in mist nets at Jews' Gate, Gibraltar, 1973–79.

vast breeding and wintering ranges the western populations winter in the westernmost parts. Moreau (1961) considered that the nominate, western, subspecies migrated between south and southwest in autumn. This tendency is supported by ringing evidence (e.g. Erard & Yeatman, 1966). There have been Spanish recoveries of Willow Warblers from Sweden, England, Belgium and

Poland (Telleria, 1981). Examination of the migration path followed by British Willow Warblers in autumn indicates that there is a concentration of birds in western France, northwestern Spain and Portugal, with very few recoveries south of 37°N (Norman & Norman, 1985). It therefore appears that this population, at least, fattens in northwest Iberia and then performs a direct flight to tropical Africa. The main wintering area of the British population seems to be around the Gulf of Guinea, west of the wintering areas of the Scandinavian and northern populations (Zink, 1973). In contrast with the autumn passage, there is not a concentration of British Willow Warblers in northwest Iberia (Norman & Norman, 1986), and it has concluded that a more direct, easterly, route to the breeding grounds is followed in spring.

Willow Warblers are more numerous in the Strait in spring than autumn (Figure 89), supporting the hypothesis that many overfly the area in autumn. At Windmill Hill, mean spring counts during the main passage vary between 7 and 20 birds (0.54–1.54 birds/ha), whereas mean autumn counts always fall below 5 birds (0.39 birds/ha). Maximum counts conform with this pattern. Up to 130 Willow Warblers have been counted on Windmill Hill in a single day in spring (10 birds/ha), whereas the maximum autumn count is 40 (3.08 birds/ha). Mist-netting in maquis follows the same pattern.

In spring, the first Willow Warblers arrive at the beginning of March, and migration continues well into May, reflecting the passage of different populations. The main passage takes place in the second half of April, though large falls may occur in early May (Figure 89). The autumn passage takes place between August and October, most passing in September (Figure 89).

Chiffchaff

Chiffchaffs breed over much of the Palaearctic, east to 150°E (Moreau, 1972). The western, nominate, and the eastern *abietinus* subspecies winter in the Mediterranean Basin and the Saharan oases, a small proportion wintering in tropical Africa (Moreau, 1972). In West Africa, Chiffchaffs are common in winter in the lower Senegal and are recorded from The Gambia, Mali, Nigeria and Chad (Serle *et al.*, 1977). There appears to be a southwesterly tendency in autumn (Erard & Yeatman, 1966), with Dutch, French and British Chiffchaffs predominating among Spanish recoveries (Telleria, 1981). Erard & Yeatman (1966) state that most German, Dutch, Belgian and British as well as large numbers of Swiss Chiffchaffs winter in Iberia and Morocco. They cite the recovery of a Madrid-ringed Chiffchaff 12 days later in Vienna. Pineau & Giraud-Audine (1979) cite winter recoveries of a Belgian and a Dutch Chiffchaff on the Moroccan side of the Strait. The wintering Chiffchaffs of the Strait belong almost exclusively to the subspecies *collybita* (Finlayson, 1977; Telleria, 1981), with isolated individuals of *abietinus* and the Russian *tristis* (Cortés *et al.*, 1980; *SGBO Reports*). The race *ibericus*, which breeds on both sides of the Strait, appears to be sedentary.

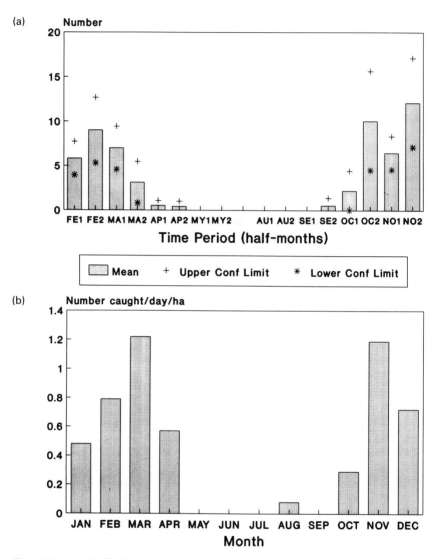

Figure 90.   (a) Chiffchaff passage at Windmill Hill, Gibraltar, 1987. (b) Number of Chiffchaffs caught in mist nets at Jews' Gate, Gibraltar, 1973–79.

Chiffchaffs are common migrants and winter visitors to the Strait. Spring and autumn numbers are approximately the same, though autumn counts can be higher. Mean spring counts at Windmill Hill during the main passage vary between 6 and 10 birds (0.46–0.77 birds/ha) and mean autumn counts range from 10 to 12 birds (0.77–0.92 birds/ha). Mist-netting results in tall maquis confirm this pattern. Maximum counts at Windmill Hill are higher in autumn than spring. The maximum spring count is 28 birds (2.15 birds/ha), and the maximum autumn count is 42 birds (3.23 birds/ha). The overall pattern of numbers contrasts with that of the Willow Warbler, which is conspicuously more abundant in spring than in autumn. In winter, Chiffchaffs are common in oak woodland, scrub and open vegetation (Cortés *et al.*, 1980; Arroyo & Telleria, 1984), although their localization close to food resources may make them appear more abundant in certain habitats. Arroyo & Telleria (1984) recorded densities, varying according to habitat, from 0.09–0.7 birds/ha. In the Gibraltar maquis, mean winter densities, estimated from ringing, average 0.5–0.8 birds/ha (Finlayson, 1979).

The passage of the Chiffchaff is typically that of a pre-saharan migrant, with trans–saharan elements. Thus, the main spring passage is earlier than that of the Willow Warbler, in late February and early March (Figure 90), the first birds passing early in February and the last in late April. The southbound passage starts in August and builds to a peak in late October and November, with the progressive arrival of wintering birds (Figure 90).

Bonelli's Warbler

The nominate subspecies breeds from Portugal in the west to Czechoslovakia in the east and in the Maghreb (Williamson, 1962). It winters in tropical West Africa, generally between 11 and 17°N (Moreau, 1972), being common in dry areas in Senegal, The Gambia, Mali, Niger, Nigeria, Cameroon and Chad (Serle *et al.*, 1977). The birds that migrate across the Strait are assumed to belong to the westernmost populations.

Moreau (1961, 1972) suggested that the southward migration of the Bonelli's Warbler consisted of a long, unbroken, flight from the breeding grounds to the winter quarters, which would account for its scarcity in the Mediterranean in late summer and autumn. The spring passage over the Strait is more pronounced than the southward movement. Counts at Windmill Hill do not portray the pattern, because this woodland species avoids open habitats even on passage: maximum counts at this site are 4 birds in spring (0.31 birds/ha) and 2 in autumn (0.15 birds/ha). It is frequent in the taller maquis, where mean spring densities are of the order of 0.3–0.4 birds/ha. Densities during the southward migration are considerably lower (below 0.05 birds/ha), supporting Moreau's view.

In spring Bonelli's Warblers arrive late, especially considering that they breed in the south of the Iberian Peninsula. Although some arrive at the end of March, the main passage takes place in April and, to a lesser extent, May (Figure 91). The southward passage takes place in August and September (occasional birds as from mid-July; Cortés *et al.*, 1980) without any discernible peak. The disappearance of Bonelli's Warblers from woodland breeding sites in the Strait during August (Telleria, 1981) suggests an early departure of the southern populations.

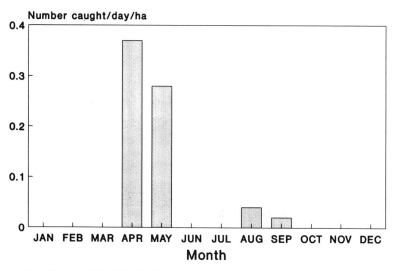

Figure 91.   Number of Bonelli's Warblers caught in mist nets at Jews' Gate, Gibraltar, 1973–79.

Melodious Warbler

Melodious Warblers breed in the Iberian Peninsula, much of France, Italy and North Africa, wintering in West Africa from Senegal to Cameroon (Williamson, 1960). They therefore have a western distribution within the Mediterranean region, and the winter quarters are, similarly, western and limited to West Africa (Moreau, 1972). The Melodious Warblers that cross the Strait must belong to the westernmost, Iberian and French, populations. Moreau (1961) cites a bird ringed in the Camargue which was recovered in Córdoba, indicating a southwesterly tendency in autumn. He went on to suggest that even north Italian birds might move southwest at this time, since very few were reported on passage from Tunisia where they were greatly outnumbered by Icterine Warblers.

Melodious Warblers are more numerous in the Strait area in spring than autumn (Figure 92). At Windmill Hill, mean spring counts during the main passage range from 1.5 to 3 birds (0.12–0.23 birds/ha) and mean autumn counts between 1 and 1.5 birds (0.08–0.12 birds/ha). The pattern in maquis is similar although average densities are higher, 1.1 birds/ha in spring and 0.4–0.6 birds/ha in autumn. Maximum counts at Windmill Hill are considerably higher in spring (11 birds; 0.85 birds/ha) than in autumn (5 birds; 0.39 birds/ha).

Spring passage is late, the first birds arriving in the area in early April (exceptionally late March) and passage building to a peak early in May (Figure 92). Migrants continue to pass into early June. The southward movement commences early, with a regular passage in July, and continues until the end of September or middle of October (Telleria, 1981).

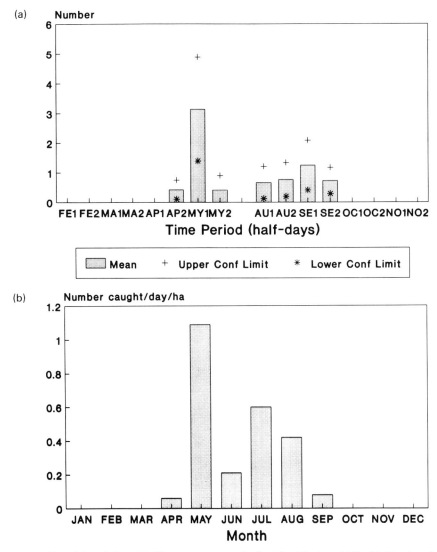

Figure 92.   (a) Melodious Warbler passage at Windmill Hill, Gibraltar, 1987. (b) Number of Melodious Warblers caught in mist nets at Jews' Gate, Gibraltar, 1973–79.

Reed Warbler

Reed Warblers breed over most of Europe and areas of North Africa (Williamson, 1960) and winter in tropical Africa (Moreau, 1972). In West Africa, where the birds that cross the Strait are assumed to winter, they have been recorded in

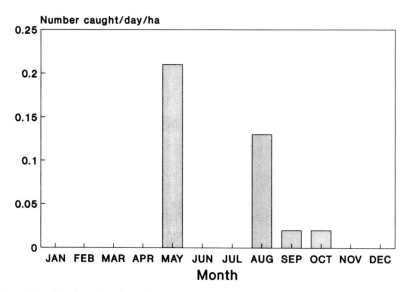

Figure 93.   Number of Reed Warblers caught in mist nets at Jews' Gate, Gibraltar, 1973–79.

many countries (Serle *et al.*, 1977), although their status is not well defined; presumably they winter in humid areas south of the dry, sub-saharan, belt (Moreau, 1972). This species shows a very clear southwesterly migration trend in autumn, with French-ringed birds recovered in Ivory Coast, Portugal, southern Spain and USSR, and French recoveries of birds ringed in Scandinavia, Germany, Switzerland, Holland, Belgium and Britain (Erard & Yeatman, 1966). Telleria (1981) summarizes Spanish recoveries in which German, Swedish and Dutch birds predominate; he also cites an interesting record, of a Dutch-ringed Reed Warbler recovered in December near Rota in Cádiz Province.

Within the Strait, the Reed Warbler is a regular migrant which is not confined to aquatic habitats; for example, it is regularly recorded in the dry maquis at Gibraltar. As the species has also been recorded in dry habitats in tropical Africa in winter (Moreau, 1972), the confinement to aquatic habitats appears to apply only to the breeding season. Because of their shy habits, Reed Warblers are often overlooked on passage, and their appearance is more readily detected when mist-netting. Reed Warblers are more abundant in the maquis in spring than autumn. In spring, densities are around 0.2 birds/ha and in autumn around 0.13 birds/ha.

Reed Warblers pass the Strait late in the spring, almost exclusively in May (Figure 93), with a few in late April and early June (Cortés *et al.*, 1980). The autumn passage is more spread out, with the first birds passing as from mid-August and the last in October or even early November (Finlayson & Cortés, 1987).

Fan-tailed Warbler

The Fan-tailed Warbler breeds in the Iberian Peninsula, north to France and east across the Mediterranean. It also breeds along the North African shore where numbers increase in winter as a result of influxes of European Fan-tailed Warblers from across the Strait in July and August (Elkins, 1976; Finlayson, 1979b). The species is sedentary in West Africa (Serle *et al.*, 1977), and there is no evidence of a

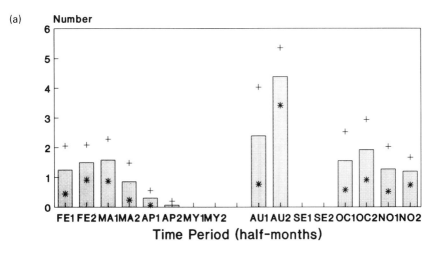

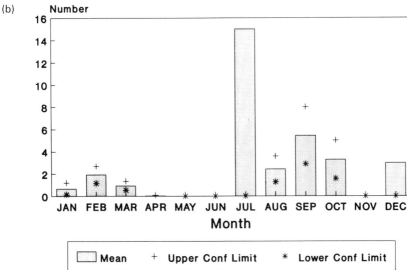

Figure 94. *(a) Fan-tailed Warbler passage at Windmill Hill, Gibraltar, 1987. (b) Fan-tailed Warbler seasonal distribution at Windmill Hill, Gibraltar, 1971–89.*

desert crossing by Palaearctic birds (Moreau, 1972). The weak flight of this species makes it unlikely that passage should take place across the Mediterranean except at narrow sea crossings. The origins of the Fan-tailed Warblers that cross the Strait are unknown.

Fan-tailed Warblers can be numerous during the southward passage but are generally less conspicuous during the return movement (Finlayson, 1979b). They migrate actively by day, when up to 70 have been recorded over the Rock of Gibraltar in 2 hours (Elkins, 1976). There is considerable variation between years (Elkins, 1976; Finlayson, 1979b), and mean counts at Windmill Hill during the main passage periods vary from 5–15 during the southward passage (0.39–1.15 birds/ha) to 1–2 birds in spring (0.08–0.15 birds/ha) (Figure 94). Maximum counts at this site are higher, 20 in autumn (1.54 birds/ha) and possibly slightly higher than that (Elkins, 1976), and 6 in spring (0.46 birds/ha).

The main southward movement, which commences as early as June (Elkins, 1976), is most intense in July and August (Figure 94), with smaller numbers later, which appear to remain in the area to moult and winter (Finlayson, 1979b). The return movement appears to take place in late February and early March, the last birds having passed by the middle of April (occasionally late April). Passage birds carry large fat deposits (Finlayson, 1979b). The suggestion is, therefore, of an early departure followed by an early return, very similar to the behaviour of other aquatic or semi-aquatic birds breeding in the south of the Iberian Peninsula (e.g. White Stork, Black Kite), departing in the summer drought and returning with the rains.

FLYCATCHERS

The Collared Flycatcher, which breeds from the Baltic to the Balkans eastward, winters in the Congo and East Africa (Moreau, 1972) with a few wintering further west, in Niger, Chad, Ghana, Nigeria and Central African Republic (Serle *et al.*, 1977). Collared Flycatchers overfly the Mediterranean during the autumn passage and, in spring, the western limit of the migratory route lies to the east of the Strait (Moreau, 1961), with a small spring passage probably occurring regularly in eastern Morocco (Smith, 1968). Saunders (1871) recorded one in spring from Seville. The eastern Red-breasted Flycatcher has been recorded once on autumn passage within the Strait (Telleria, 1981).

Pied Flycatcher

Pied Flycatchers from Britain, western, central and northern Europe east to the Soviet Union are known to fly southwest towards the Iberian Peninsula in autumn (Moreau, 1961), concentrating in the west (Bernis, 1962) where they fatten and may migrate directly to the winter quarters (Hope Jones *et al.*, 1977). The main countries of origin are, from ringing results, Finland, Sweden, Germany and France (Telleria, 1981). The return in spring is not so concentrated

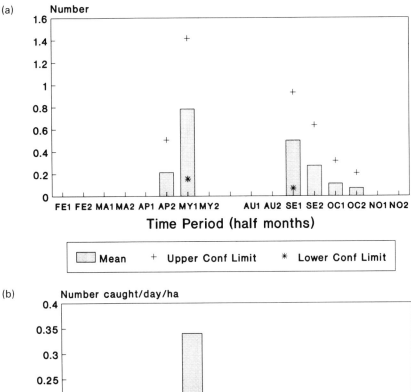

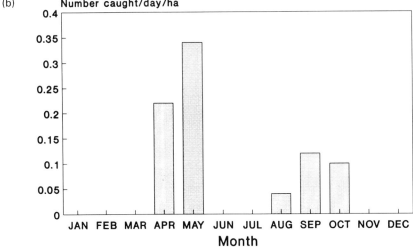

Figure 95. (a) Pied Flycatcher passage at Windmill Hill, Gibraltar, 1987. (b) Number of Pied Flycatchers caught in mist nets at Jews' Gate, Gibraltar, 1973–79.

to the west, some returning via the same route but others returning to the breeding grounds via more eastern routes (Moreau, 1961). In Africa, Pied Flycatchers winter west of 20°E (Moreau, 1961), and those that cross the Iberian Peninsula and the Strait presumably winter in the western part of this wintering range, where they are widespread in the gallery forest north of the main forests but south of the dry country (Serle *et al.*, 1977).

Pied Flycatchers are more abundant in spring than autumn over the Strait, lending support to the view that those which fatten in northwestern Iberia subsequently overfly arid areas to the south. Mean spring counts at Windmill Hill during the main passage vary between 0.8 and 2 birds (0.06–0.15 birds/ha), and mean autumn counts vary between 0.3 and 0.5 birds (0.02–0.04 birds/ha). Maximum counts at Windmill Hill have been similar for both seasons, 8 (0.62 birds/ha) in spring and 7 (0.54 birds/ha) in autumn. In the maquis, which they prefer, densities are higher, but the seasonal pattern remains: mean densities are around 0.35 birds/ha in spring and 0.1 birds/ha in autumn.

Pied Flycatchers pass north late and return south ahead of the pre-saharan migrants. The northward passage is rapid, commencing in mid-April (end of March according to Pineau & Giraud-Audine, 1979) with a peak in May and very few in June (Figure 95). The return passage, which starts in mid-August, reaches a maximum in September with a declining passage throughout October.

Spotted Flycatcher

Spotted Flycatchers breed throughout Europe (except the far north), and east to 100°E (Moreau, 1972). Only a few winter in the northern tropics and avoid the drier zones, the majority wintering further south (Moreau, 1972). North European birds show a migratory divide (Creutz, 1940), those west of the longitude of Copenhagen flying southwest in autumn and those to the east flying south-southeast. Moreau (1961) felt that this divide did not apply to more southerly populations, as passage was uniformly distributed across the Mediterranean. Telleria (1981) cited the main Iberian recoveries from England, France, Germany, Denmark and Belgium, confirming a southwest trend in autumn. Additionally, Telleria (1981) noted a wintering Spotted Flycatcher in Jerez which was ringed in England; the species winters sporadically in the Strait (Pineau & Giraud-Audine, 1979; Telleria, 1981). Although the wintering grounds of the Spotted Flycatchers that cross the Strait are not known, it can be assumed that they are towards the west of the wintering range. Serle *et al.* (1977) record this species as locally common in West Africa in winter in forest clearings and the savanna near the forest. Spotted Flycatchers of the *balearica* subspecies have been identified in Ivory Coast, Cameroon and southwest Africa (Moreau, 1972).

Unlike the Pied Flycatcher, which is distinctly absent from the Mediterranean areas in autumn but common in spring, the Spotted Flycatcher is common in both seasons (Moreau, 1961). Within the Strait, Spotted Flycatchers are much more abundant in spring than autumn, and the difference in its two passages is at least as great as it is in the Pied Flycatcher. At Windmill Hill, mean spring counts during the main passage are around 1.5 birds (0.12 birds/ha) and mean autumn counts reach 1 bird (0.08 birds/ha). Maximum counts at this site are greater in spring (15 birds; 1.15 birds/ha) than autumn (8 birds; 0.62 birds/ha). In the maquis, mist-netting reveals an even more pronounced difference, with spring densities of 0.4–0.5 birds/ha and autumn densities of 0.05 birds/ha. These differences suggest that, to a large degree, Spotted Flycatchers overfly the

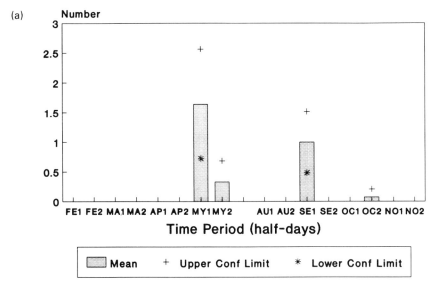

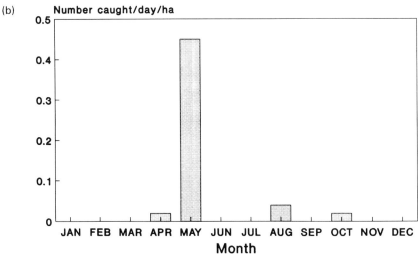

Figure 96. (a) Spotted Flycatcher passage at Windmill Hill, Gibraltar, 1987. (b) Number of Spotted Flycatchers caught in mist nets at Jews' Gate, Gibraltar, 1973–79.

western end of the Mediterranean in autumn in a similar manner to Pied Flycatchers.

Spotted Flycatchers arrive later than Pied Flycatchers, in mid-April, with a short, well-defined, peak in May and a few in early June (Figure 96). The return passage commences in mid-August and continues into October without a clearly defined peak. Telleria (1981) recorded a gradual increase in Spotted Flycatchers until mid-September with a gradual decline towards the end of October.

TITS

There is very little evidence of migration of tits across the Strait with the exception of the Blue Tit, which is considered to be a migrant in small numbers, as some have been observed departing from Tarifa in autumn (Telleria, 1981). On the basis of slight autumnal increases in numbers in census sites, some Great Tits may also be migrants (Telleria, 1981). Sightings of Crested Tits and Long-tailed Tits away from typical sites in autumn also suggest dispersal on a small scale. The Penduline Tit is perhaps the most conspicuous migrant, wintering in many reedbeds in the area and disappearing in the spring. It must therefore be regarded a regular winter visitor (Finlayson & Cortés, 1987).

SHORT-TOED TREE CREEPER

This is a typical resident which appears to migrate in small numbers across the Strait, from September to November and in February and March (Cortés *et al.*, 1980; Telleria, 1981; Finlayson & Cortés, 1987).

GOLDEN ORIOLE

Golden Orioles from western and central Europe migrate southeast in autumn (Stresemann, 1948; Moreau, 1961, 1972) to winter in eastern and southern Africa. Moreau (1972) considered that there was probably a migratory divide in this species, with Iberian and Maghreb birds flying southwest in autumn to winter in West Africa, where it has been recorded from most countries on passage (Serle *et al.*, 1977). Within the Strait, the Golden Oriole is a scarce autumn migrant (Telleria, 1981), being more noticeable in spring. As with the Roller, Red-necked Nightjar, Nightjar and Cuckoo, the spring conspicuousness may be due to the arrival of the Iberian breeding population; the absence of prolonged passage and the scarcity of sightings in non-breeding sites point to a rapid arrival of birds in Iberia and support the view that more northerly populations migrate east of the Strait. The scarcity of autumn sightings indicates a rapid departure of Iberian birds with no subsequent passage of northern birds (Telleria, 1981). The spring passage is late, the first orioles arriving in mid-April, most passing by the middle of May and the last ones passing in mid-June. The southward passage takes place early, in August and September (Pineau & Giraud-Audine, 1979; Cortés *et al.*, 1980; Telleria, 1981; Finlayson & Cortés, 1987).

SHRIKES

The Great Grey Shrike, which breeds in the area, is a migrant and winter visitor in small numbers in March (occasionally April–June), August, September and

October (Pineau & Giraud-Audine, 1979; Cortés *et al.*, 1980; Telleria, 1981; Finlayson & Cortés, 1987). Lesser Grey and Red-backed Shrikes perform loop migrations in a southeasterly direction in autumn, completely avoiding the Strait and the western Mediterranean. There are no records of Lesser Grey Shrike and very few (all autumn) of Red-backed Shrike (Telleria, 1981; Finlayson & Cortés, 1987; *SGBO Reports*). The eastern Masked Shrike is a vagrant (Saunders, 1871; Mountfort & Ferguson-Lees, 1961).

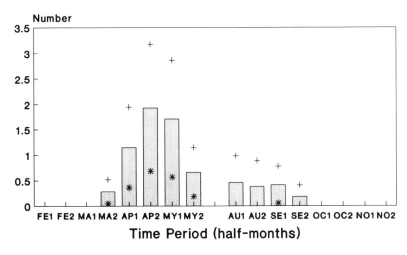

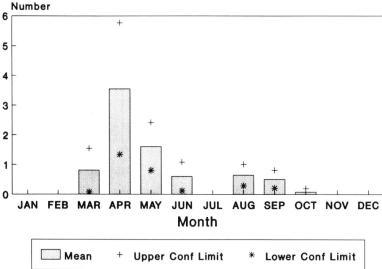

Figure 97.   (a) Woodchat Shrike passage at Windmill Hill, Gibraltar, 1987. (b) Woodchat Shrike seasonal distribution at Windmill Hill, Gibraltar, 1971–89.

Woodchat Shrike

Woodchat Shrikes breed throughout central and western Europe, Iberia and the Maghreb, but not in the north. The wintering grounds of the Woodchats that pass the Strait are probably in tropical West Africa where the nominate subspecies winters in a belt from Senegal to Darfur and south to the northeast Congo (Moreau, 1972). There is evidence of southwest movement in autumn, German and Swiss Woodchats having been recovered in the Iberian Peninsula, with a more easterly return in spring (Moreau, 1961). Telleria (1981) additionally gives a recovery of a bird ringed in the Camargue.

The Woodchat Shrike is the most abundant shrike and a regular migrant over the Strait, being more abundant in spring than in autumn (Figure 97). Mean spring counts at Windmill Hill vary between 1.5 and 4 birds (0.12–0.31 birds/ha), whereas autumn counts vary between 0.05 and 1 bird (0.04–0.08 birds/ha). The maximum spring count at this site is 60 (4.62 birds/ha), contrasting with only 5 in autumn (0.39 birds/ha). The differences between spring and autumn are consistent with the behaviour of this species elsewhere along the Mediterranean, which is apparently overflown in autumn (Moreau, 1961, 1972). In this context it is interesting that at Mogador, northwestern Morocco, Woodchat Shrikes are the commonest prey of Eleonora's Falcons (Walter, 1979).

Passage of Woodchat Shrikes in spring commences during the middle of March, building to a peak during the second half of April and continuing into June (Figure 97). The southward passage starts in late July (Cortés *et al.*, 1980) with most passing in August and the last birds in October. Telleria (1981) observed a Woodchat Shrike near Tarifa in January 1978.

CROWS

There is no regular migration of any corvid across the Strait, although Jackdaw and Carrion Crow appear to winter on the Moroccan side in small numbers and are seen crossing the Strait occasionally in spring and autumn. Magpie, Chough and Alpine Chough have also been recorded crossing the Strait at very irregular intervals (Pineau & Giraud-Audine, 1979; Cortés *et al.*, 1980; Telleria, 1981; Finlayson & Cortés, 1987; *SGBO Reports*).

STARLINGS

The Spotless Starling crosses the Strait in small numbers, and the European Starling is a regular migrant and winter visitor, being very abundant some winters (Pineau & Giraud-Audine, 1976, 1979; Finlayson & Cortés, 1987), arriving in October and leaving in March. Arroyo & Telleria (1984) found the Spotless Starling to be more common than the Starling in winter, outnumbering the latter by 5:1. In years when high numbers of Starlings arrive, the proportion is reversed (Pineau & Giraud–Audine, 1976, 1979; Finlayson & Cortés, 1987). Commenting on the variability of wintering numbers, Pineau & Giraud–Audine (1979) concluded that whereas some years they arrived in small numbers, other years over a million Starlings wintered on the Moroccan shore of the Strait. The Rose-coloured Starling is a vagrant from the east (Irby, 1895).

SPARROWS

Telleria (1981) drew attention to the substantial passage of House Sparrows south across the Strait in autumn, from mid-September to mid-November. His diurnal passage counts made the House Sparrow the fourth most abundant diurnal migrant, the total autumn count for 1977 exceeding 23 000 birds. The origin of these birds is unknown, and the time at which they return to Europe is not clear either. The Spanish Sparrow and the Tree Sparrow are regular migrants in small numbers, the latter being more abundant (Telleria, 1981). Spring passage is in March and April for the two species. In autumn, Spanish Sparrows pass from mid-July to October, the early birds probably being local. Most Tree Sparrows pass south between September and mid-November. There is one record of the Rock Sparrow for the Rock of Gibraltar, in September, where it is not usually found (Cortés *et al.*, 1980), suggesting the occasional dispersal of local birds away from breeding sites.

FINCHES

Six species have been recorded in small numbers or irregularly on passage or as rare visitors: Brambling, Siskin, Crossbill, Trumpeter Finch, Bullfinch and Hawfinch.

The Brambling reaches the southern limit of its wintering range in the Strait and is regularly recorded on passage in very small numbers, often mixed with Chaffinches, in March, April, October and early November (Finlayson & Cortés, 1987). It is known to arrive in large waves in Iberia some winters (Lope *et al.*, 1983). Cortés *et al.* (1980) recorded an exceptional sighting on the Rock of Gibraltar in August, and Telleria (1981) noted the recovery of a Swedish Brambling in Cádiz Province in January.

The Siskin is a regular migrant which, as is the case for other species (e.g. Lapwing, Starling), can be numerous some years and scarcer others. Conspicuous invasion years have been 1949–50, 1959–60, 1961–62, 1965–66, 1966–67, 1972–73 (Asensio, 1985c) and 1988–89 (*SGBO Reports*). They were plentiful wherever there were alder trees in the winter of 1870–71 (Irby, 1875). The main passage months are February to early April, October and November (Finlayson & Cortés, 1987). Asensio (1985c) analysed Iberian recoveries and found that they indicated a wider catchment area than for most other finches. There was considerable westward displacement, which included Russian, Yugoslav and

Italian Siskins. The number of recoveries within the Strait was conspicuously higher than for other finches.

The Crossbill, which breeds in the mountains of the area, occurs irregularly on passage, being most frequent in years of eruption (Cortés *et al.*, 1980; Finlayson & Cortés, 1987). The Trumpeter Finch is an irregular visitor, breeding to the south in Morocco and to the east in Spain, being most frequently observed in spring (Finlayson & Cortés, 1987). The Strait is within the southerly limit of the wintering range of the Bullfinch, which has been recorded on several occasions on both shores (Pineau & Giraud-Audine, 1979; Finlayson & Cortés, 1987). The Hawfinch, which breeds in the Strait, is a regular migrant in March, early April, October and early November (Telleria, 1981; Finlayson & Cortés, 1987). The origin of these migrants is unknown.

Goldfinch

Goldfinches show clear evidence of migration in a southwest direction in autumn, the main Iberian recoveries being of birds ringed in France, England, Germany, Switzerland and Belgium, with smaller numbers from further east (USSR, Czechoslovakia, Austria, Yugoslavia, Italy) (Figure 98; Asensio, 1986). European Goldfinches follow a passage route via the western Pyrenees which eventually takes them towards the Strait and Morocco; Spanish birds joined them and crossed the Strait (Asensio, 1984). The more northerly populations migrate after the southern ones, and females predominate in the southern wintering grounds whereas males do further north (Asensio, 1986). Goldfinches are pre-saharan migrants and those that reach the Strait in autumn either remain there all winter or continue to winter in Morocco but go no further. The movement into Morocco is more pronounced than for other finches, which mainly winter in Iberia (Telleria, 1981; Asensio, 1986).

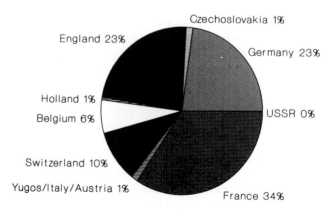

Figure 98.   Goldfinch recoveries in Iberia, after Asensio (1986); N = 753.

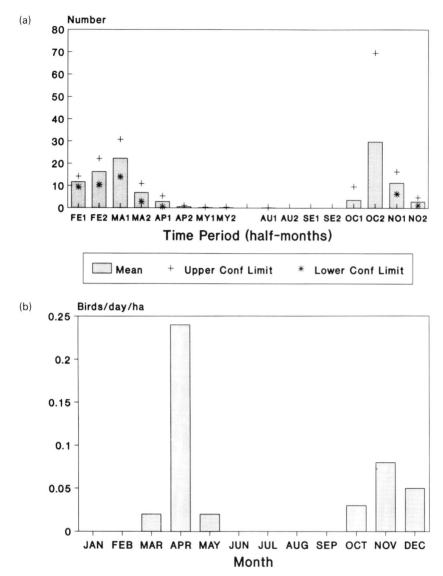

Figure 99.   (a) Goldfinch passage at Windmill Hill, Gibraltar, 1987. (b) Number of Goldfinches caught in mist nets at Jews' Gate, Gibraltar, 1973–79.

Telleria (1981) considered the Goldfinch to be the most numerous migrant finch and the third most abundant non-soaring diurnal migrant after the Swift and the Swallow. His counts for the 1977 autumn exceeded 58 000 which, even allowing for the possible range of errors in such counts, testify to the scale of the passage. The Goldfinch is the most abundant wintering species in pastures on the northern shore of the Strait (mean density of 6.49 birds/ha) with a lower, but significant, number in the matorral (mean density 0.7 birds/ha) (Arroyo & Telleria, 1984). Accurate diurnal counts are not available for the spring passage, but some of the counts for Gibraltar at this time indicate that the passage can also be strong at that time (*SGBO Reports*). The pattern of grounded Goldfinches in autumn follows the pattern of active migration closely (Telleria, 1981). At Windmill Hill, mean spring counts vary between 2 and 20 birds (0.15–1.54 birds/ ha) and in autumn is of the order of 30 birds (2.31 birds/ha). Maximum counts at Windmill Hill clearly illustrate the massiveness of the movements: 300 in autumn (23.02 birds/ha) and 50 in spring (3.85 birds/ha). The pattern from ringing in the less-favoured maquis suggests more birds grounded in spring. Mean spring density is around 0.2 birds/ha, mean autumn density around 0.1 bird/ha, but these differences are probably not significant.

The arrival of the main waves of Goldfinches is late in the autumn, as is the case for most other pre-saharan migrants (Figure 99). Although isolated groups of, presumably local, Goldfinches may be observed as from August, the first migrants probably arrive around the middle of September (Cortés *et al.*, 1980; Telleria, 1981), the main passage taking place during the second half of October and the first half of November. Small numbers continue to move south during December (Garcia Rua, 1975; Asensio, 1986) and north in January so that, as Telleria (1981) recognized, there is virtually continuous movement during the winter months. The main spring passage north takes place in March and early April with very few passing as late as May (Figure 99).

Greenfinch

The origins of the Greenfinches that cross the Strait are similar to those of the Goldfinches, Iberian recoveries being essentially of western European birds, for example Belgian, French, Norwegian and Danish (Telleria, 1981). Nevertheless, it has been argued that most Greenfinches that cross the Strait are Iberian in origin (Asensio, 1984). Greenfinches winter in the Strait and in Morocco; birds crossing the Strait thus have little further to migrate in autumn.

The Greenfinch is considered to be the fifth most important diurnal migrant across the Strait (Telleria, 1981), with over 20 000 birds passing. On the basis of counts of grounded migrants at Windmill Hill, it is clear that, even though they are common in spring, Greenfinches are more abundant in autumn. The massive autumn passage produces mean counts of around 8–9 birds (0.62–0.69 birds/ha) and the spring passage produces counts that vary little from 1 bird (0.08 birds/ ha). In the taller maquis, autumn densities from ringing give a figure of 0.5 birds/ ha, which contrasts with the 0.2 birds/ha in the spring. Maximum counts at Windmill Hill confirm the greater magnitude of the autumn passage: 150 in autumn (11.54 birds/ha) and 16 in spring (1.23 birds/ha). Many Greenfinches must continue south into Morocco, since the numbers wintering in the Strait are low in comparison with the passage numbers: with densities in different habitats

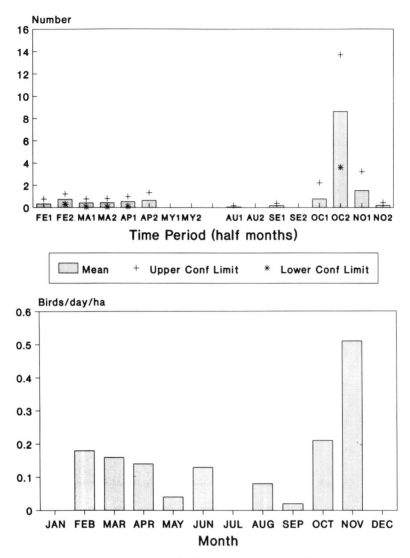

Figure 100.　(a) Greenfinch passage at Windmill Hill, Gibraltar, 1987. (b) Number of Green-finches caught in mist nets at Jews' Gate, Gibraltar, 1973–79.

ranging between 0.03 and 0.14 birds/ha, they are relatively scarce (Arroyo & Telleria, 1984).

The first autumn Greenfinches arrive during the second half of September. Earlier movements probably relate to dispersal of local Greenfinches. The main thrust of the passage is at the end of October and early November, with a reduced number during the second half of November (Figure 100). This pattern clearly indicates a continued passage south. The return migration commences in early February and continues into early May, the main movement taking place in the first half of March (Figure 100).

Chaffinch

The origins of the Chaffinches that migrate past the Strait are western and northern European. Analysis of the spectrum of Iberian recoveries shows that a greater proportion of northerly populations is involved than is the case with other finches (Asensio, 1985a; Figure 101). Two separate fronts reached Iberia (Asensio, 1985a): Finnish and Baltic birds following the Atlantic coasts of Europe to winter in western Iberia, and central European birds wintering in eastern Spain. The latter go no further than Morocco and many remain to winter in the Strait. Small flocks of the North African subspecies *africana* have recently been observed alongside nominate birds in spring at Gibraltar (*SGBO Reports*).

The Chaffinch is the ninth most abundant active diurnal non-soaring migrant over the Strait, with over 11 000 individuals in the autumn of 1977 (Telleria, 1981). There is less difference between autumn and spring passages in this species than in other finches. Mean spring counts at Windmill Hill vary considerably, between 2 and 10 birds (0.15–0.77 birds/ha); autumn counts are around 8 birds (0.62 birds/ha). In the taller maquis, Chaffinches are more numerous in autumn (0.3 birds/ha) than spring (0.08 birds/ha). Maximum counts at Windmill Hill are also greater in autumn (250 birds; 19.23 birds/ha) than in spring (31 birds; 2.39 birds/ha). Autumn passage is therefore of a higher magnitude than spring but, in certain cases, the position may be reversed. The Chaffinch is an important winter visitor to most habitats in the area—the second most important species in oak woods, at a density 1.27 birds/ha, and even higher densities (1.37 birds/ha) in pastures (Arroyo & Telleria, 1984).

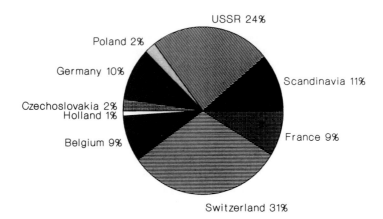

Figure 101.   Chaffinch recoveries in Iberia, after Asensio (1985); N = 622.

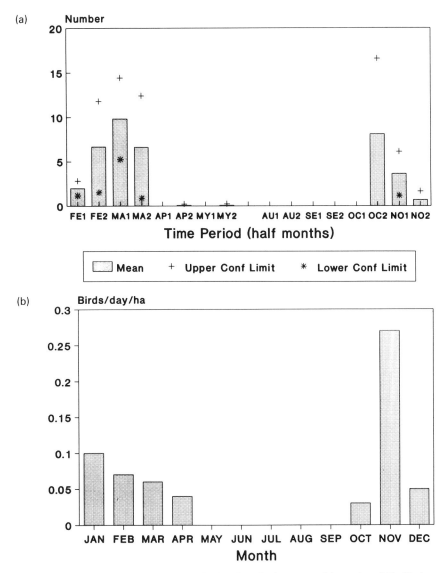

Figure 102. (a) Chaffinch passage at Windmill Hill, Gibraltar, 1987. (b) Number of Chaffinches caught in mist nets at Jews' Gate, Gibraltar, 1973–79.

Although Chaffinch passage may commence in mid–September, the main movements do not start until the second half of October, with a peak between the end of the month and the first half of November (Figure 102). The passage continues into early December. The return movement is earlier than that of other finches, commencing early in February with a maximum during the first half of March and the last birds passing in early April.

Serin

Serins from western and central Europe winter in the Iberian Peninsula (Asensio, 1985b; Telleria *et al.*, 1988). Telleria (1981) gives a recovery near Coín, Málaga, of a French-ringed Serin. According to Asensio (1985b) most recoveries are in Spanish Mediterranean coastal provinces, relatively few recoveries being made in

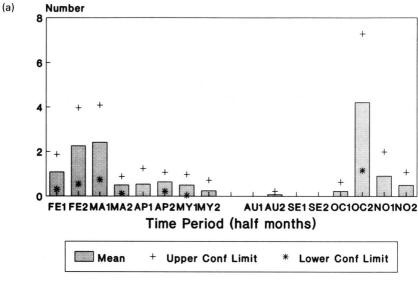

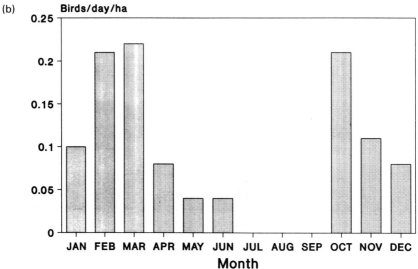

Figure 103.   (a) Serin passage at Windmill Hill, Gibraltar, 1987. (b) Number of Serins caught in mist nets at Jews' Gate, Gibraltar, 1973–79.

the Strait; he suggested that few Serins crossed into Morocco, most wintering in Iberia. Those crossing the Strait are likely to be mainly Iberian in origin (Asensio, 1984). Like other finches, Serins do not migrate beyond Morocco.

The Serin is the sixth most abundant diurnal non-soaring migrant, over 15 000 birds crossing the Strait in the autumn of 1977 (Telleria, 1981). At Windmill Hill, mean numbers of grounded birds were higher in autumn than spring. Mean autumn counts were of the order of 4 birds (0.31 birds/ha), and mean spring counts between 0.75 and 2 birds (0.06 birds/ha). Mist-netting in maquis gave a mean density of 0.25 birds/ha in spring and 0.12 birds/ha in autumn (these differences may not have been significant). Maximum counts at Windmill Hill were substantially higher in autumn than in spring: 200 in autumn (15.39 birds/ha) and 15 in spring (1.15 birds/ha). Wintering densities on the northern shore of the Strait ranged from 0.02 birds/ha in matorral to 0.06 birds/ha in pastures, so that its presence appears widely scattered at low densities (Arroyo & Telleria, 1984). In the Gibraltar maquis, winter densities calculated from mist-netting results were of the order of 0.08 birds/ha.

The autumn passage, preceded by sporadic flocks of local birds, commences in early October and peaks during the second half of the month and in the first days of November. There is a reduction in numbers towards the end of November (Figure 103). In spring, passage starts early in February and peaks during the first half of March, with a reduced movement which reaches the end of May or June. These latter birds may be local non-breeding individuals.

Linnet

The main Iberian recoveries are of western and central European Linnets, especially French, Belgian and English (Telleria, 1981); 37 of 46 European Linnets recovered in the Strait were Belgian or French (Asensio, 1984). This abundance of Linnets from middle latitudes is typical of most finch species that migrate through the Iberian Peninsula, with the exception of the Chaffinch (Telleria *et al.*, 1988). As are other finches, Linnets are pre-saharan migrants, and those that cross the Strait winter within Morocco. Many Iberian Linnets cross and, of the German and French populations that reach Iberia, more French than German Linnets reach Morocco (Asensio, 1984).

Linnets were the sixth most abundant non-soaring diurnal migrants across the Strait in the autumn of 1977, with just under 20 000 individuals counted (Telleria, 1981). They are more abundant at Windmill Hill in autumn than in spring, with mean autumn counts of between 2 and 3 birds (0.15–0.23 birds/ha) and mean spring counts of 1–2 birds (0.08–0.15 birds/ha). Maximum counts conform with this pattern: 50 in autumn (3.85 birds/ha) and 12 in spring (0.92 birds/ha).

Linnets are the first finches to migrate south over the Strait (Cortés *et al.*, 1980; Telleria, 1981), passage commencing during the second half of September and reaching a peak in mid-October which can continue into November (Figure 104). In spring, passage starts early in February and peaks during the second half of March. The last birds pass north in late April.

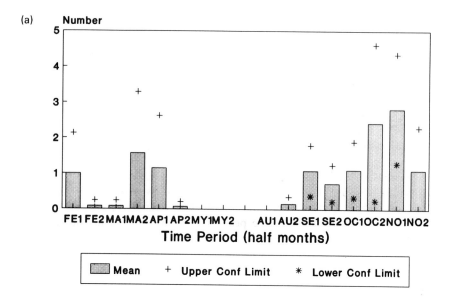

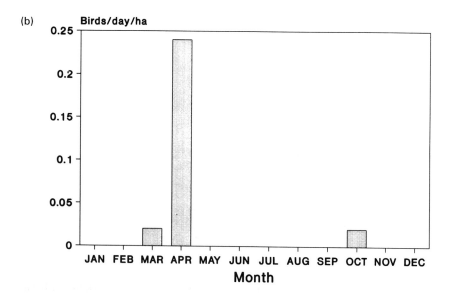

Figure 104.   (a) Linnet passage at Windmill Hill, Gibraltar, 1987. (b) Number of Linnets caught in mist nets at Jews' Gate, Gibraltar, 1973–79.

BUNTINGS

The Cirl Bunting, the Rock Bunting and the Reed Bunting are regular migrants and winter visitors, augmenting the sizes of the resident populations (Cortés *et al.*, 1980; Telleria, 1981; Finlayson & Cortés, 1987). The origins of the Cirl and Rock Buntings are unknown. German, Belgian, Swedish, French and Swiss Reed Buntings have been recovered in the Iberian Peninsula in autumn (Telleria, 1981). The Reed Bunting is a scarce breeding bird in the Strait (Thevenot & Thuoy, 1974; Pineau & Giraud-Audine, 1979), but is regular and, in places common, in many reedbeds in the winter. According to Telleria (1981) the main autumn passage of the Cirl Bunting takes place in late September and early October, and that of the Rock Bunting is later, reaching a peak during the second half of October. Reed Buntings appear to arrive during October and early November, without a discernible peak. The spring movements of the three buntings take the form of gradual departures of wintering birds during February, March and early April, but the relatively small numbers involved and the presence of local birds masks any passage.

Buntings feature prominently as vagrants to the area, no doubt because of the likelihood of capture by finch trappers. Species recorded in the Strait are White-throated Sparrow, Snow Bunting, Yellowhammer, Little Bunting, House Bunting, Yellow-breasted Bunting and Red-headed Bunting (Irby, 1895; Smith, 1965; Hidalgo, 1971; Giraud-Audine & Pineau, 1973; Dubois & Duhautois, 1977; Telleria, 1981; Finlayson & Cortés, 1987).

Ortolan Bunting

Ortolan Buntings breed from Iberia to Scandinavia in the west to 90°E (Moreau, 1972), and the westernmost populations winter in tropical West Africa where they have been reported in Nigeria, The Gambia, Chad (Serle *et al.*, 1977) and Senegal, where they also occur as migrants (Moreau, 1972). Three autumn recoveries, of Italian, Swiss and Belgian birds (Telleria, 1981), suggest a south-westerly orientation at this time.

Generally, Ortolan Buntings are scarce migrants, though they do occasionally occur in flocks during falls. Mean spring counts at Windmill Hill vary between 0.1 and 1.5 birds (0.001–0.12 birds/ha) and autumn counts between 0.2 and 0.4 birds (0.02–0.03 birds/ha), indicating that they can be more common in spring than autumn. This is supported by maximum counts at this site: 12 in spring (0.92 birds/ha) and 6 in autumn (0.46 birds/ha). These results are consistent with the pattern across the Mediterranean, Ortolans being nowhere common but decidedly rarer in autumn than spring (Moreau, 1961).

The species is a late spring migrant, the first individuals passing in early April, with peak numbers in late April and early May and only a few passing in late May. The passage is therefore concentrated over a short period (Figure 105). Autumn passage occurs mainly in September and early October.

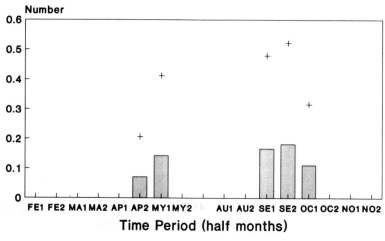

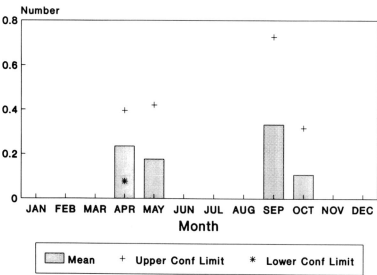

Figure 105.   (a) Ortolan Bunting passage at Windmill Hill, Gibraltar, 1987. (b) Ortolan Bunting seasonal distribution at Windmill Hill, Gibraltar, 1971–89.

Corn Bunting

Corn Buntings breed over much of central and western Europe, Iberia and the Maghreb. They winter within this geographical area; birds recorded on passage across the Strait go no further than Morocco in winter, where they reach the south of the country and are scarcer in the north (Pineau & Giraud-Audine, 1977, 1979).

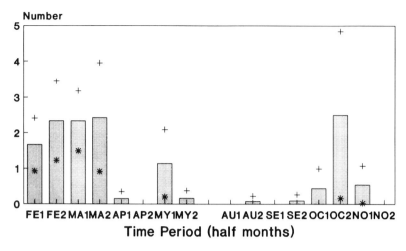

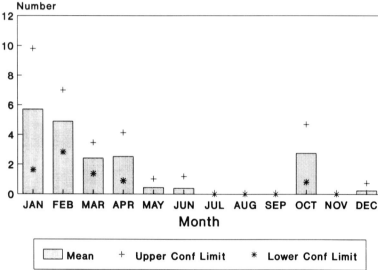

Figure 106. *(a) Corn Bunting passage at Windmill Hill, Gibraltar, 1987. (b) Corn Bunting seasonal distribution at Windmill Hill, Gibraltar, 1971–89.*

Numbers of passage Corn Buntings are very similar in spring and autumn, with mean counts at Windmill Hill averaging 2–3 birds (0.15–0.23 birds/ha). Maximum counts at this site are 40 in spring (3.08 birds/ha) and 30 in autumn (2.31 birds/ha). In winter, Arroyo & Telleria (1984) recorded densities of 1 bird/ ha in pastures and reduced densities in matorral (0.01 birds/ha). At Windmill Hill, mid–winter densities are of the order of 0.46 birds/ha, predictably in a low matorral with open ground.

Corn Buntings behave as most pre-saharan migrants, showing a build-up of numbers during October, maintaining a high density during the winter months, with a slow reduction through the spring (Figure 106). The appearance of late birds, in May and June, may be related to birds trying to breed at this site or indicative of first brood young dispersing.

CHAPTER 4

Migration and Wintering of Waterbirds

In this chapter the main waterbird species that migrate through the Strait or which visit it in winter are described. The wetlands of the Strait area and its breeding and wintering communities are described in Chapter 7.

The most important wetlands of the Strait are concentrated along the Atlantic coastal belt, with the marshes of the Odiel and Guadalquivir in the north-west and the Merja Zerga in the south-west marking its limits. These wetlands are part of a chain that runs from the British and western continental sites to the southern Moroccan, Mauretanian and West African wetlands. Utilization of the various wetland sites varies from year to year depending on climate. Numbers of ducks and geese wintering in Morocco are greater in years when drought, flooding or cold force birds south from Iberia. And Iberia itself receives additional populations of waterbirds in mid-winter, especially when lakes freeze in continental Europe in harsh winters. Winter influxes to Iberian wetlands are often spectacular, like the winter invasion of Lapwings in the 1965–66 winter.

This chapter treats herons and related groups, ducks and geese, waders and a few other species (e.g. Greater Flamingo and Crane), as 'waterbirds'. Species of lesser importance in the area, or for which current information is superficial, are discussed in the introductory text for the respective group. Some of the other migrant groups utilizing wetlands (e.g. storks and terns) are dealt with in other chapters.

199

Little Bittern. A nocturnal trans-Saharan migrant, resting in unusual surroundings — a lentisc bush in the scrub-covered hillsides of the Rock of Gibraltar.

A Whiskered Tern arrives from West Africa in spring to its breeding site in the vast marshes (Marismas) of the Guadalquivir.

DIVERS

The Strait lies at the southern limit of the winter range of divers, which are scarce winter visitors, mainly to Atlantic areas. According to Irby (1895) the Red-throated Diver was common in the Strait in winter. He considered the Black-throated Diver and the Great Northern Diver to be occasional in the Strait in winter.

The Red-throated Diver can no longer be described as common, but it is the most frequently recorded of the three divers, being scarce and irregular to coastal waters from October to March (Finlayson & Cortés, 1987). Red-throated Divers from Scandinavia, Iceland and Greenland disperse towards British waters in winter and some Scottish birds move south into French waters. Small numbers continue south down the Atlantic coast of Iberia to reach the Strait. Very few continue along the Moroccan coast (Pineau & Giraud-Audine, 1979), and some may reach areas south of the Strait—a probable sighting has been reported near Casablanca (Thevenot *et al.*, 1981). Others winter in the western Mediterranean (e.g. see Paterson, 1987) and may do so via the Strait or along continental inland routes.

Black-throated Divers are scarce in Iberia (Bernis, 1966a); they occur in certain areas of the Mediterranean (Heim de Balsac & Mayaud, 1962; Cramp & Simmons, 1977). These birds, which are presumably from Scandinavia and western USSR may follow continental routes into the Mediterranean rather than passing via the Strait. Two were observed, however, off the coast of Doñana in January 1987 (de Juana, 1988).

Great Northern Divers breed in the Nearctic and those that winter in the eastern Atlantic presumably derive from Iceland and Greenland. Very small numbers winter along the Atlantic coast of Iberia, reaching the Strait, and they have recently been found wintering regularly in Cádiz Bay, where up to five have been recorded together (de Juana, 1984b). Occasionally, they reach the Strait (*SGBO Reports*) and enter the Mediterranean (Paterson, 1987).

It is unlikely that either the Black-throated Diver or the Great Northern Diver reach south of the Strait (Pineau & Giraud-Audine, 1979). The White-billed Diver (*Gavia immer*) of northeastern Scandinavia and the USSR has never been recorded in the Strait, and the first Iberian record was of two birds off northwest Spain in December 1985 (de Juana, 1987).

GREBES

Five species have been reported from the Strait area. Three, Great Crested, Little and Black-necked, are regular and are considered separately.

The Slavonian Grebe, which breeds from Iceland and Scotland east to Kamchatka, winters south over much of Europe in coastal and inland waters, reaching parts of the Mediterranean. It very rarely reaches the Strait of Gibraltar (one was recently observed on 19 December, 1989—*SGBO Reports*) and nearby Mediterranean coastal areas (de Juana, 1987). Irby (1875, 1895) obtained a specimen from the Strait in October 1867.

The Red-necked Grebe, which breeds from Denmark to the USSR, winters west and south, reaching the Baltic, the North Sea and inland areas of western Europe, but not Iberia. The statement by Irby (1875, 1895) that they were likely to breed in Ras-el-Doura seems improbable as do the sightings there of 'many' in April. This species, which has recently been reported from northern Spain in winter (de Juana, 1988), is probably accidental to the Strait, but there are no firm records.

LITTLE GREBE

The Little Grebe breeds across the central and southern Palaearctic from the Atlantic to the Pacific. In autumn, northern and central European Little Grebes migrate west/southwest (Prater, 1981), and some birds may then reach Iberia to augment the local population. There may be a passage into Morocco. The record of a Little Grebe which flew into the Europa Point lighthouse at Gibraltar, away from any suitable habitat, on 16 August 1952 (Tuke, 1953) supports this view.

This species is the most abundant of the grebes and occurs in many freshwater habitats, including slow-flowing rivers and canals. The passage and wintering population is likely to be very high. Large concentrations occur during September in the Cádiz lagoons, especially Medina, where 436 were counted on 17 August 1988 (*SGBO Report*).

Judging from increases in numbers at sites normally frequented by Little Grebes, the main passage periods appear to be February to April and September to November (Pineau & Giraud-Audine, 1979; Finlayson & Cortés, 1987).

GREAT CRESTED GREBE

The Great Crested Grebe breeds over much of the temperate Palaearctic, from Ireland, Iberia and Morocco east to the Pacific. Western, central and some northern European populations migrate southwest/west while eastern and other northern populations migrate southeast (Bernis, 1966a). The Strait's local breeding population is substantially augmented in autumn by wintering birds arriving from the north. These migrants do not winter further south than Morocco.

Great Crested Grebes are widely distributed in winter in lagoons and on the coast, in bays and estuaries. In some sites they gather in large concentrations: Telleria (1981) counted 200 in Cádiz Bay in January 1978. On the Moroccan side they are not abundant but are regular in suitable sites (Pineau & Giraud-Audine, 1979), although they can be numerous in other localities away from the Strait; for example, 523 were counted on 10 January 1980, at Sebkha bou Areg on the Mediterranean coast (Thevenot *et al.*, 1981). On passage, increases are detected in regular sites, or groups may appear in unusual ones. At the Laguna de Medina, up to 50 have been counted in September, and 60 were seen on the Castellar Reservoir (a site not used regularly by this species) on 26 September 1976 (Telleria, 1981).

Passage is not well-defined, but increases during September suggest a passage at that time. In spring, there appears to be a small peak in some lagoons during March, which is reduced by April.

BLACK-NECKED GREBE

The Black-necked Grebe breeds in mid and southerly latitudes from Iberia and the British Isles (few) to the central USSR. The continental populations migrate south or southwest in autumn. Bernis (1966a) cited a record of a Black-necked Grebe ringed in Lake Constance and recovered in northern Spain, and comments that Danish birds have been recovered in France and Italy. Black-necked Grebes winter on the Moroccan side of the Strait, usually in small numbers (Pineau & Giraud-Audine, 1979).

Concentrations of 40–60 birds are regular in December and January at the Laguna de Medina. Larger numbers are found in late March, suggesting passage, with 76 at Laguna de Medina and 64 at Laguna Salada on 30 March 1987 (Holliday, 1990a). Individuals and small groups are regular along the coast in winter. Irby (1895) considered this grebe to be plentiful in Gibraltar Bay in winter. This is not the case today, though the Black-necked Grebe does occur there regularly in winter.

The main spring increases are from February to May, with a similar pattern from September to November (Pineau & Giraud-Audine, 1979; Finlayson & Cortés, 1987).

HERONS

The Bittern breeds across middle latitudes of the Palaearctic from North Africa and Iberia to the Pacific coast. Northern and eastern European Bitterns migrate west and south to winter in western Europe and the Mediterranean (Bernis, 1966a). It has become virtually extinct as a breeding species within the Strait, no longer breeding in the Marismas del Guadalquivir and probably not in the Loukos marshes either (Pineau & Giraud-Audine, 1979). Irby (1895) said that Bitterns bred in the Laguna de la Janda and surrounding areas (e.g. Laguna del Torero near Vejer), as well as the Rocio marshes near the Coto Doñana and, in Morocco, south to Rabat. They were more abundant in winter, arriving in October, and were at times quite numerous in some places. This status has changed dramatically since Irby's day and Bitterns are rare, but probably regular, migrants. There have been three sightings for the Moroccan side of the Strait (Tangier, Loukos and Smir) in March and April, suggesting passage (Pineau & Giraud-Audine, 1979). The Bitterns that pass the area are likely to be north

European and may winter south to Morocco but no further, since they are rare in West Africa (Moreau, 1972). Bernis (1966a) gives three Iberian recoveries: one bird from Germany and two from Sweden.

The Little Bittern breeds across the middle Palaearctic from North Africa and Iberia to about 90°E, most Palaearctic birds wintering in Africa (Moreau, 1972). Within the Strait they breed in marshes and along the edges of many lagoons in Spain and Morocco (Pineau & Giraud-Audine, 1979; Finlayson & Cortés, 1987). According to Bernis (1966a) the Little Bittern shows a south to southeast migration pattern in autumn, which may explain its scarcity in the Strait at this time. He gave a Swiss and a Czech recovery in the Congo, and one Belgian and two Dutch birds on passage in northeastern Spain. Spring records for the Strait are more numerous, but the shy habits of this species makes it an inconspicuous migrant. Irby (1895), who considered that Little Bitterns arrived in April, also remarked that he had no evidence of autumn passage although all (i.e. the local breeding population) were gone by October. Finlayson & Cortés (1987) recorded the arrival of some birds by the end of February.

The Night Heron breeds across southerly latitudes of the Palaearctic from North Africa and Iberia to the Pacific. Most birds from the western Palaearctic winter in tropical Africa, very few remaining in Iberia and Morocco in winter (Pineau & Giraud-Audine, 1979; Telleria, 1981). Night Herons breed in the Marismas del Guadalquivir (Fernandez-Cruz, 1975), northern Cádiz province (del Junco & Dominguez, 1975) and at Emsa on the Moroccan Mediterranean coast of the Strait (Pineau & Giraud-Audine, 1979), having disappeared from other sites due to habitat destruction (Irby, 1895; Fernandez-Cruz, 1975; Pineau & Giraud-Audine, 1979).

According to Moreau (1972), Night Herons from Iberia and France winter in West Africa, recoveries having been made in Senegal, The Gambia, Sierra Leone and western Mali. Birds from further east winter to the east of these populations. Autumn passage over Iberia is mainly along the east coast with some along the south (Bernis, 1966a). Iberian recoveries (Bernis, 1966a) illustrate the passage of west European Night Herons with occasional ones from further east: southeast France (11), northeast France (4), southwest France (1), northwest France (1), Holland (1), Hungary (1). Spanish birds, which disperse northwards and eastwards in summer, migrate south through Morocco (Pineau & Giraud-Audine, 1979), presumably alongside birds from further north. The passage periods are March to May and August to November (Finlayson & Cortés, 1987), when groups of 15–20 occur at unusual sites, along riversides or even in dry scrub as on the Rock of Gibraltar (Cortés *et al.*, 1980).

Squacco Herons breed in southerly latitudes of the Palaearctic, from Morocco and Iberia to east of the Aral Sea, and winter in northern tropical Africa (Moreau, 1972), though some winter in Morocco (Smith, 1965). Within the Strait the Squacco Heron now only breeds in the Marismas del Guadalquivir (Fernandez-Cruz, 1975) and the Loukos marshes (Pineau & Giraud-Audine, 1979). It was more widespread and abundant in the past: Irby (1895), for example, found it in great numbers at Ras-el-Doura in April, where it was the commonest heron.

Passage is not conspicuous across the Strait and must have been more marked when the local breeding population was larger. The birds that do cross the area are presumably Spanish (and possibly French) and winter in tropical West Africa. March to May and August to October are the passage periods (Finlayson & Cortés, 1987). There are records of a recovery of a bird ringed in eastern Spain in Sierra Leone and of another ringed near Seville in Ghana (Fernandez-Cruz, 1975). Some Spanish birds may follow a more easterly route. A Squacco ringed as a chick in eastern Spain was recovered several years later on spring passage through Tunisia (Fernandez-Cruz, 1975). Eastern birds winter further east and probably do not reach the Strait on migration. Yugoslav and Hungarian birds have been recovered in Nigeria and Cameroon (Bernis, 1966a; Moreau, 1972).

In western Europe, Cattle Egrets breed in Iberia, the south of France and in Morocco. In the Strait there are colonies in Emsa and Larache (Pineau & Giraud-Audine, 1979) and at Barbate (on sea cliffs), Medina Sidonia, the Bornos Reservoir and the Marismas del Guadalquivir (Fernandez-Cruz, 1975). Other colonies have disappeared (see Chapter 7). Telleria (1981) noted cross-Strait movements and highlights August as the principal month. These movements involve Spanish birds crossing into Morocco and Moroccan birds moving north into Spain.

Little Egrets breed across the southern Palaearctic from Morocco and Iberia to the Pacific. Within the Strait, Little Egrets breed at Emsa and Sidi Embarek (near Larache) (Pineau & Giraud-Audine, 1979) and at Barbate, Medina Sidonia, Bornos and the Marismas del Guadalquivir (Fernandez-Cruz, 1975; del Junco & Dominguez, 1975; Holliday, 1990a), having disappeared from sites where they used to breed (Irby, 1895; Yeates, 1945). Western birds winter within the Mediterranean and in tropical Africa. The autumn migration follows a southwest orientation, westernmost populations wintering west of those from further east (Moreau, 1972). Passage over Iberia includes birds from southeast France that follow the eastern and southern coasts of Spain (Bernis, 1966a). French birds have been recovered in Senegal, The Gambia and Mali and a Spanish bird in Guinea (Moreau, 1972), and there have also been recoveries of birds from eastern Spain in Senegal and in the Banc d'Arguin, Mauretania (Fernandez-Cruz, 1982). Within the Strait, Little Egrets occur in flocks on passage, and at many sites (inland and coastal) on passage and in winter. In late summer, flocks are regularly seen approaching Europa Point, Gibraltar, from the Mediterranean coast and continuing towards the west. The passage periods are March to May and late July to early November (Finlayson & Cortés, 1987). The autumn peak is in September (Telleria, 1981). In late summer and autumn, concentrations of up to 250 have been recorded at the Bonanza saltpans (Holliday, 1990a).

The Great White Egrets of eastern Europe and the USSR disperse south towards the eastern Mediterranean and some, at least, cross the Sahara Desert to winter in central tropical Africa (Moreau, 1972). The Strait area therefore lies well to the west of their normal range. It is a species reported from both sides of the Strait, mainly in spring (Irby, 1895; Gonzalez Diez, 1965; Allen, 1971; Pineau & Giraud-Audine, 1979), suggesting an irregular wandering or overshooting

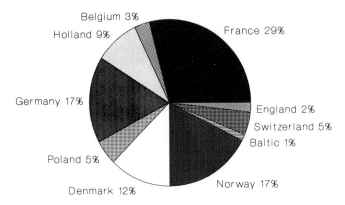

Figure 107.   Grey Heron recoveries in Iberia, after Bernis (1966a). N = 33.

westwards. The species is becoming increasingly regular in western Europe, including Spain (de Juana, 1985).

The Grey Heron breeds across much of the central and southern Palaearctic from Britain, Iberia and North Africa to the Pacific. In the Strait it breeds in the Marismas del Guadalquivir (Fernandez-Cruz, 1975). Northern and eastern populations migrate southwest to winter in western Europe, the Mediterranean and tropical Africa. Iberian recoveries (Figure 107) clearly indicate this movement which continues into Morocco (Bernis, 1966a), with many remaining to winter in the Strait. Moroccan recoveries all fall within the pattern of Iberian recoveries (Pineau & Giraud-Audine, 1979). Other Grey Herons must continue towards tropical West Africa where the location of wintering populations from west to east reflects a similar breeding distribution (Moreau, 1972). Birds ringed in France and Sweden have been recovered in Senegal, Portuguese Guinea and Sierra Leone (Moreau, 1972). It is these western birds that are most likely to pass the Strait. Grey Herons are numerous on passage and in winter, occurring in estuaries, salt pans, canals, rivers and other aquatic habitats. Over 700 were counted in Cádiz Bay in January 1990 (AMA, Cádiz). The total wintering population is probably several thousand and was probably greater in the past, when the Laguna de La Janda must have held a large population (e.g. see Telleria, 1981). The passage, which is well marked, lasts from late February to May and late July to November (Pineau & Giraud-Audine, 1979; Telleria, 1981; Finlayson & Cortés, 1987).

The Purple Heron breeds from Iberia and North Africa, east over parts of southern and western Europe to central USSR. Other populations breed further east. Within the Strait area, Purple Herons breed in the Loukos, the Marismas del Guadalquivir and occasionally in some of the Cádiz lagoons (Fernandez-Cruz, 1975; Pineau & Giraud-Audine, 1979). They were more widespread in the past (Irby, 1895; Yeates, 1945; Pineau & Giraud-Audine, 1979; Telleria, 1981).

Palaearctic Purple Herons winter in tropical Africa (Moreau, 1972). Birds from the western populations migrate southwest in autumn to join Iberian and Moroccan birds, and continue south towards tropical West Africa. Birds ringed in France (6), Holland (24) and Switzerland (4) have been recovered in Iberia (Bernis, 1966a). Some of these birds may return by a more easterly route, judging from the recovery of a Seville bird in spring in Algeria and of a Doñana bird in spring in Tunisia (Fernandez-Cruz, 1982). In general, Purple Herons wintering in West Africa are Iberian, French and Dutch (Moreau, 1972; Fernandez-Cruz, 1982). Purple Herons usually migrate singly or in small groups and are nowhere as abundant as Grey Herons, although they do occur in many suitable sites on passage. The passage periods are March to May and late July to October (Pineau & Giraud-Audine, 1979; Telleria, 1981; Finlayson & Cortés, 1987).

IBISES AND SPOONBILLS

The Glossy Ibis, which breeds in eastern Europe eastwards, was formerly a common bird in the Strait, breeding in the Moroccan side and in the Laguna del Torero and the Marismas del Guadalquivir on the European side (Irby, 1895). According to Irby, it was then a regular migrant across the Strait, passing northwards in April and May, when he saw great flocks at Ras-el-Doura. The Glossy Ibis is today a scarce visitor to the area, usually from May to October (Pineau & Giraud-Audine, 1979; Cortés *et al.*, 1980; Telleria, 1981; Finlayson & Cortés, 1987; Holliday, 1990a), which may attempt to breed certain years, especially in the Marismas del Guadalquivir. The occurrences may reflect wandering or overshooting of eastern birds that winter in West Africa where the species is numerous in the Inundation Zone of the Niger (Curry & Sayer, 1979) and present in other countries, including Senegal, Niger, northern Nigeria, Ghana and Chad (Serle *et al.*, 1977). Moreau (1972) records the recovery of a bird ringed on the coast of the Sea of Azov in Niger, suggesting a southwesterly movement of birds from eastern Europe and USSR.

The Bald Ibis had a wider distribution in the past. It may have been a regular migrant or may have wandered into the area; Favier's (in Irby, 1895) observation from Tangier and Valverde's (1959) from Doñana are the only known records. Its present scarcity makes it a very unlikely visitor.

The Spoonbill has a fragmented distribution across the middle and southern Palaearctic, from Iberia to the Pacific. The isolated southern Iberian population is probably mainly resident, although some may cross the Strait to winter in Morocco together with Dutch birds, which have been recovered along the western coast of Iberia (Bernis, 1966a). Although some of these birds may reach Senegal, the majority wintering there probably belong to the Mauretanian breeding population (Moreau, 1972). The Spoonbill may never have bred in Morocco (Pineau & Giraud-Audine, 1979), but it once had a wider distribution on the Spanish side of the Strait, breeding in the Laguna del Torero and the Soto de Malabrigo close to the Laguna de La Janda (Irby, 1875, 1895; Yeates, 1945) in addition to the present colonies in the Marismas del Guadalquivir and Odiel.

The Spoonbill currently occurs in a variety of inland and coastal wetland sites irregularly on passage, and as a winter visitor, in groups of up to 50 birds (and larger, close to Doñana). This passage must have been larger, when the species was more widespread, and more numerous as suggested by Irby's (1875, 1895) observation of many, apparently on passage in April, near Larache. The passage periods are March to May and late July to early November (Pineau & Giraud-Audine, 1979; Telleria, 1981; Finlayson & Cortés, 1987).

FLAMINGOES

The Lesser Flamingo of East Africa is uncommon in West Africa, including Senegal and Mauretania (Serle *et al.*, 1977). Occasional birds wander northwards along the coast of northwest Africa and reach Morocco, including the Merja Zerga (Thevenot *et al.*, 1981, 1982; Mayaud, 1982) and could conceivably reach the Spanish side of the Strait.

GREATER FLAMINGO

The populations involved in movements within the Strait are those from the western Mediterranean breeding colonies, specifically those from the Camargue, of which there are numerous recoveries in southern Spain (Bernis, 1966a; Telleria, 1981) and Morocco (Pineau & Giraud-Audine, 1979), and those from Fuente de Piedra. Other breeding nuclei in this area are in Tunisia and southern Morocco, but it seems unlikely that these birds reach the Strait. The extent of interchange between these western Mediterranean flamingoes and those of the eastern Mediterranean or of western Africa is unknown but, even if there is any, it is not likely to be great (Fernandez-Cruz, 1988).

The movements of Greater Flamingoes are determined largely by the state of the water in the preferred sites. Many Camargue birds winter in Tunisia, and smaller numbers do so in southwest Spain and northern Morocco. During cold spells in midwinter many Camargue flamingoes move southwest along the Spanish Mediterranean coast towards the Strait; in an exceptional year when the waters of the Marismas del Guadalquivir froze, many moved south of this towards Morocco (Fernandez-Cruz, 1988). Otherwise, the general trend is for the main wintering nucleus to be concentrated in the Marismas del Guadalquivir and the nearby Bonanza saltpans, with smaller numbers in adjacent areas (e.g. Cádiz Bay). These birds depart in early spring for the main breeding site of the Laguna de Fuente de Piedra, just northeast of the Strait, and others towards the Camargue (Fernandez-Cruz, 1988).

There is therefore an irregular movement of flocks of Greater Flamingoes within the Strait, which reaches its peak between the end of one breeding season

Part of a flock of Greater Flamingoes, feeding in salt pans on the Atlantic side of the Strait. Large flocks roam the Strait after breeding and salt pans are favoured sites for resting and feeding.

and the start of the next, in response to changing water levels and mid-winter freezing.

The western Mediterranean wintering population has been estimated at just under 60000, with Spain the third most important country after Tunisia and France, holding 15% of the wintering total (Fernandez-Cruz, 1988). The wintering population is estimated at 9000 along the Mediterranean and southwest Spanish coasts (reaching close to 16000 in November 1986, including over 13000 in the Guadalquivir zone, reflecting an increase in the area since 1982) with an additional 1300 in Atlantic Morocco (Fernandez-Cruz, 1988). The Moroccan wintering population is probably higher than estimated by Fernandez-Cruz (1988) and may reflect the increase in Spain since 1982: over 2000 were counted in Merja Zerga in winter and over 6000 at this site in April (Thevenot *et al.*, 1981, 1982), suggesting passage from the south. There have been a number of Moroccan recoveries of Camargue birds.

Within the Strait, in addition to the large concentrations in the Guadalquivir and the Merja Zerga, flocks ranging from a few birds to 800 or more occur in estuaries, saltpans and lagoons (Pineau & Giraud-Audine, 1979; Finlayson & Cortés, 1987; Holliday, 1990a).

Passage periods are difficult to determine as the species is present throughout the year, breeding in the Marismas del Guadalquivir and the Laguna de Fuente de Piedra and summering in other sites. There are strong movements in late July and August, presumably birds that have finished breeding, and from February through to May (Pineau & Giraud-Audine, 1979; Cortés *et al.*, 1980; Telleria, 1981; Finlayson & Cortés, 1987).

SWANS, GEESE AND DUCKS

The range of wildfowl recorded in the area is large. A number of species only visit the area sporadically, with the Marismas del Guadalquivir and the Cádiz lagoons (both reasonably well watched areas) accounting for the majority of sightings. Among these are accidentals, birds which have strayed significantly from their normal migration routes (Table 8). The Strait lies at the southern limit, or beyond the southern limit, of the wintering range of many wildfowl species and for these there are isolated records for the area or its vicinity (Table 8). Several other species are regular on migration and in winter.

The Iberian wintering population of Shelducks, estimated at an average of 2000 (Dolz & Gomez, 1988), is very small in relation to the 120 000–130 000 estimated to winter in western Europe (Atkinson-Willes, 1976). Wintering numbers within the Strait are usually small, and include around 300 in the saltpans at Bonanza, 200 in Cádiz Bay (Finlayson & Cortés, 1987) and over 100 in Merja Zerga (Thevenot *et al.*, 1981). Numbers wintering in the area may be considerably higher some years (Pineau & Giraud-Audine, 1979; Telleria, 1981). Thevenot *et al.* (1982) recorded 3300 in the Merja Zerga in January 1981, and Ena & Purroy (1982) recorded over 2000 in the Marismas del Guadalquivir in January 1979.

Table 8   *Swans, geese and ducks: accidentals and rare winter visitors.*

Accidentals[1]	Rare winter visitors[2]
Red-breasted Goose	Whooper Swan
Bar-headed Goose	Bean Goose
Lesser White-fronted Goose	Pink-footed Goose
Canada Goose	White-fronted Goose
Snow Goose	Barnacle Goose
American Wigeon	Brent Goose
Blue-winged Teal	Scaup
Ring-necked Duck	Eider
Ruddy Duck	Long-tailed Duck
	Velvet Scoter
	Goldeneye
	Smew
	Goosander

[1] Irby (1875, 1895), Ybarra (1966), Castroviejo (1971), Hildago & Rodriguez (1972), Cano & Ybarra (1973), Ree (1973), Hildago & Rubio (1974), Martin (1977), de Juana (1982, 1988a).

[2] Irby (1875, 1895), Duclos (1955), Bernis (1963, 1966a), Dominguez (1971), Ree (1973), Cortés *et al.* (1980), Muntaner & Ferrer (1981), Thevenot *et al.* (1982), Padilla & Garrido Sanchez (1983), de Juana (1982, 1988b, 1989), *SGBO Reports*.

The Tufted Duck is a regular winter visitor in small numbers between November and March (Finlayson & Cortés, 1987). Relatively few of the 500 000 wintering in western Europe (Prater, 1981) do so in Iberia, averaging over 2000 (Dolz & Gomez, 1988). Within the Strait the population is very small, probably under 300 birds, although larger numbers may arrive some years (e.g. 1000 in Merja Zerga in January 1981 — Thevenot *et al.*, 1982). Bernis (1966a) gives Iberian recoveries of birds ringed in England, Ireland, Iceland, Germany, Denmark and Finland, and Fernandez-Cruz (1982) reports a bird ringed in Doñana in February 1965 recovered in Poland in October 1968.

The Common Scoter winters along the Atlantic coasts of the Strait where it is fairly numerous, but very few enter the Mediterranean via the Strait (Cortés *et al.*, 1980; Finlayson & Cortés, 1987). Over 3000 were counted off the coast of southwest Spain between Sanlúcar de Barrameda and Ayamonte on the Portuguese border in January 1983 (Ena & Purroy, 1984), and gatherings of over 7000 have been recorded along coastal Morocco, south of the Strait (Mayaud, 1982; Thevenot *et al.*, 1982). Smith (1965) counted 3900 flying south in 56 flocks past Cap Cantin (north of Mogador) in 5 hours in October 1962, and passage occurred at this point on other days in September 1963, with return passage in February. These numbers are nevertheless a small fraction of the 400 000–500 000 that winter off the coasts of western Europe (Atkinson-Willes, 1978). There have been three Iberian recoveries of Icelandic-ringed birds (Bernis, 1966a). The main arrivals are in October and November, although early birds do arrive in August. Spring movements start in February, with isolated birds remaining into May, occasionally June (Cortés *et al.*, 1980; Finlayson & Cortés, 1987).

The Red-breasted Merganser is another winter visitor, from November to March, in relatively small numbers and is scarcer than the Common Scoter (Finlayson & Cortés, 1987). The average size of the Iberian wintering population is estimated at around 300 (Dolz & Gomez, 1988) but is probably larger as offshore birds are easily overlooked. The Odiel Estuary, northwest of the Guadalquivir, held 120 in 1986. Small flocks are also recorded from other coastal sites (e.g. Cádiz Bay, Tarifa Beach—Telleria, 1981; Ena & Purroy, 1982; Holliday, 1990a), including the Mediterranean coast where small groups winter (Pineau & Giraud-Audine, 1979; Thevenot *et al.*, 1982). The wintering population is clearly very small in relation to the 40 000 that winter in northwest Europe (Prater, 1981). Although there are no ringing recoveries, the Red-breasted Mergansers that reach the area are likely to be of north Russian, Fenno-Scandinavian or Icelandic origin (Bernis, 1966a).

Four species were more common in the area in the past than they are today and all bred: Ruddy Shelduck, Marbled Duck, Ferruginous Duck and White-headed Duck. Of these, the Ruddy Shelduck and Ferruginous Duck no longer breed (the Ferruginous Duck may do so in the Loukos—Chapter 7), and the other two are scarce, though the White-headed Duck has recovered substantially in the late eighties (Amat & Raya, 1989). These ducks would have performed movements of limited extent (except possibly Ferruginous Duck, which is migratory in other parts of its range).

The Ruddy Shelduck may have bred in the Marismas del Guadalquivir (including the saltpans at Bonanza) and the Laguna de Fuente de Piedra but was commoner on the Moroccan side of the Strait (Irby, 1875, 1895). Although they still breed in parts of Morocco (Mayaud, 1982), they no longer do so within the Strait area, where they appear irregularly and rarely outside the breeding season (Trigo de Yarto, 1960; Pineau & Giraud-Audine, 1979; Amat, 1981; Alberto Vega, pers. comm.). Hidalgo (1989) has summarized the movements of this species in the Marismas del Guadalquivir, where they arrive (presumably from Morocco) during August and remain until February or March, occupying the saltier lakes and saltpans, where up to 500 gathered in 1962. In Morocco, Smith (1965) found it a common duck in inland waters, with smaller numbers on the coast in 1963–64. Since then the species has become scarce.

The Marbled Duck has declined dramatically since the days of Irby (1875, 1895) when they were exceedingly abundant in Morocco, with flocks numbering many hundreds at Ras-el-Doura in April 1871. They were also very numerous in the Marismas del Guadalquivir. There was a clear passage with birds appearing in many water habitats; they were essentially summer visitors between late February and September (Irby, 1895). Today Marbled Ducks are scarcer (see Chapter 7). Movements are difficult to interpret and appear related to fluctuating water levels so that it is possible to find them even in mid-winter and in unusual sites (e.g. wintering in the Palmones marsh in the 1988–89 and 1989–90 winters). 110 were recorded at the Laguna de Medina in August 1986 (Finlayson & Cortés, 1987), 500 in the Lucio del Cangrejo in the Marismas del Guadalquivir in October 1985 (de Juana, 1988a), 500 at Merja Zerga in October 1980 (Thevenot *et al.*, 1981) and 790 at Sidi bou Rhaba in November 1981 (Thevenot *et al.*, 1982). A Marbled Duck ringed near Seville in August 1975 was recovered in Algeria in February 1977 (Fernandez-Cruz, 1982).

The Ferruginous Duck, like the Marbled Duck, was an abundant breeding species, especially on the Moroccan side where Irby (1875, 1895) recorded many hundreds in large flocks as late as the end of April at Ras-el-Doura. They were also numerous in certain parts of the Marismas del Guadalquivir, where Valverde (1960) estimated a breeding population of 500 pairs, may have bred in the Smir, and they bred in the Laguna del Torero near La Janda (Yeates, 1945). It was essentially a summer visitor with isolated winter records. Presumably these birds migrated south to winter in West Africa, where they still occur in small numbers in Senegal and the Niger Inundation Zone (Moreau, 1972; Curry and Sayer, 1979). Ferruginous Ducks are scarce and irregular migrants and winter visitors, occurring mainly in deep water lagoons. The only known breeding site is the Loukos near Larache (Pineau & Giraud-Audine, 1979).

During the 1980s the White-headed Ducks from Córdoba re-established as a breeding species in the Cádiz lagoons. It no longer breeds in Morocco (Pineau & Giraud-Audine, 1979), nor is it a regular migrant, though it does gather in flocks in late summer in the Cádiz lagoons if water levels are suitable. In December 1988, 358 were recorded in the Laguna de Medina (de Juana, 1989), where gatherings of over one hundred are regular (*SGBO Reports*) and there are isolated records from other sites (e.g. Laguna de La Janda—Holliday, 1990a).

Greylag Goose

Greylag Geese wintering in southwest Spain and Morocco are mostly from the northwestern European breeding populations, and do not include Icelandic birds (which winter in Britain) (Bernis, 1963, 1966b; Amat 1986). Of over 200 recoveries made in the Marismas del Guadalquivir, 130 were Danish, 48 Swedish and 15 German, with the remainder from other central and northern European countries (Telleria, 1981). The Greylags that arrive in the area in autumn spend the winter in the Marismas, with smaller numbers scattered in other suitable localities on the Spanish and Moroccan shores. Those which cross the Strait are therefore northwest European and winter no further south than Morocco.

The numbers wintering in the Marismas del Guadalquivir rose from 15 000–20 000 in the early 1970s to 60 000–75 000 from the 1978–79 winter onwards (Amat, 1986). Numbers wintering elsewhere vary substantially. During the drought winters of 1980–81 and 1981–82 more Greylags were counted in Morocco than normal (Thevenot *et al.*, 1982), and this was related to birds from the Marismas moving south (Amat, 1986). During the very wet 1989–90 winter, many Greylags moved away from heavily flooded zones in the Marismas and flocks were regularly observed on the Moroccan side of the Strait and crossing the Strait between Europe and North Africa. At most, a few hundred Greylags winter in Morocco, mostly in the northwest (Pineau & Giraud-Audine, 1979; Thevenot *et al.*, 1982; Beaubrun & Thevenot, 1983). The numbers wintering in areas of the Strait that have been drained, particularly La Janda where thousands wintered once, were very high until at least the turn of the century (Irby, 1875, 1895; Verner, 1910).

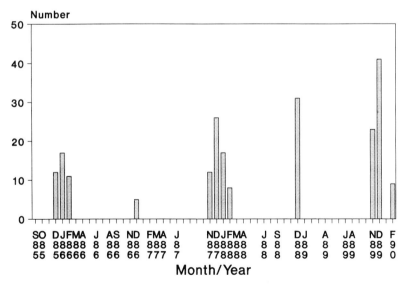

Figure 108.   Greylag Goose counts at Laguna de Medina, 1985–90. In this and other figures in this chapter, months when counts were made are indicated.

Passage across the Strait is irregular and includes crossings in mid-winter (Pineau & Giraud-Audine, 1979; Telleria, 1981; Finlayson & Cortés, 1987). In the Marismas, Greylags arrive at the end of September and the beginning of October, being most abundant in December and January; they depart during February and March and very few are left in April (Amat, 1986). A similar pattern is observed in the Cádiz lagoons (Figure 108).

WIGEON

Wigeon breed from Iceland and the British Isles eastwards across Scandinavia and the Soviet Union to the Pacific. The western populations winter in western Europe, the Mediterranean Basin and North Africa (Prater, 1981), very few reaching tropical West Africa (Moreau, 1972). Iberian recoveries illustrate the southwest autumn migration: England (1), Iceland (2), Holland (13), Denmark (2), Finland (1), Russia (4) (Bernis, 1966b). Bernis (1966b) cited the recovery of a bird in Jaén (Andalucia) in winter which was ringed in Kazakhstan (USSR) 2 months earlier having travelled 5600 km west/west-southwest. A Wigeon ringed in Murmansk (USSR) was recovered in Merja Zerga (Pineau & Giraud-Audine, 1979). The Wigeon that reach the Strait area and cross it to winter in Morocco are essentially northwest European and from the Soviet Union (Figure 109).

The Marismas del Guadalquivir is the most important Iberian site for wintering Wigeon, with a total varying from 30 000 to 115 000 between years (Ena & Purroy, 1982; Dolz & Gomez, 1988). Other coastal sites in the area are also

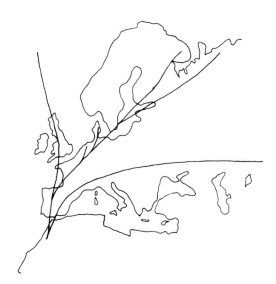

Figure 109.   Southward migratory routes followed by Wigeons passing the Strait.

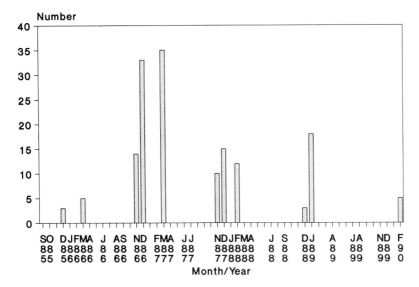

Figure 110.   Wigeon counts at Laguna de Medina, 1985–90.

important. Cádiz Bay holds on average over 5000 Wigeon (Ena & Purroy, 1982; Grimmett & Jones, 1989). Up to 30 000 winter in Morocco, mostly in the north-west (Beaubrun & Thevenot, 1983), where 25 000 were present in Merja Zerga in January 1981 (Thevenot *et al.*, 1982) and over 1000 at Oualad Khallouf in December 1975 (Pineau & Giraud-Audine, 1979). As with other wintering waterbirds, there is substantial variation in numbers crossing the Strait to winter in Morocco, depending on conditions on the European side of the Strait. It was the commonest duck, in thousands, in La Janda during the 19th Century (Irby, 1895).

Passage is not well defined. First arrivals take place in October and the last birds leave in April, very few remaining in May (Figure 110; Amat, 1984; Finlayson & Cortés, 1987). Pineau & Giraud-Audine (1979) record migratory movements in November (8000 at Larache) and February (4500 at Oualad Khallouf).

GADWALL

In the Palaearctic, the Gadwall breeds from Iceland, the British Isles and Iberia in the west, eastwards across mid-latitudes to the Pacific coast. It is not an abundant species and the total wintering population in Europe has been estimated at 55 000 (Prater, 1981). Relatively small numbers winter in Iberia in comparison to further north. The mean wintering numbers are *c.* 8000, with the Marismas del Guadalquivir being the main site (Dolz & Gomez, 1988), where winter numbers

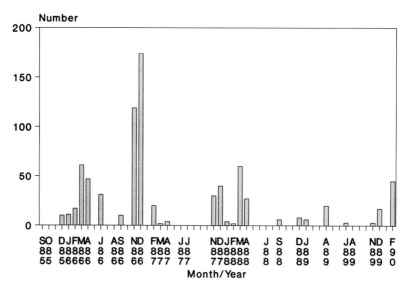

Figure 111.   Gadwall counts at Laguna de Medina, 1985–90.

have ranged between 1300 and 2800 in recent years (Ena & Purroy, 1982; Dolz & Gomez, 1988). Smaller numbers reach Morocco, which constitutes the southern limit of the winter range in the western Palaearctic, with 677 counted in January 1983 (Beaubrun & Thevenot, 1983). In Morocco, most Gadwalls winter in the north-west, near the Strait, and the Middle Atlas. It is very rare in tropical West Africa (Moreau, 1972).

According to Moreau (1972) the northern populations of Gadwall are migratory. Recoveries have been as follows: Iberian recoveries of two birds ringed in southeast France and of another ringed in Belgium (Bernis, 1966b); two native English, one Russian and one Dutch in Doñana (Telleria, 1981); and one Andalucian Gadwall in Merja Zerga (Pineau & Giraud-Audine, 1979). The Gadwall that cross the Strait and winter in the area are probably a combination of western European and the more migratory northern populations.

In addition to the concentrations in the Marismas, the Cádiz lagoons and other wetlands of the area hold small populations of Gadwall throughout the year with increases in winter (Figure 111). The Laguna de Medina holds between 100 and 200 some winters, and 100 have been recorded at Larache (Pineau & Giraud-Audine, 1979). In general, though, the movements of this species are inconspicuous (Pineau & Giraud-Audine, 1979; Telleria, 1981; Finlayson & Cortés, 1987).

The arrival of birds from the north takes place in October and the departures occur during March and April, by which time the smaller breeding population is established (Amat, 1984; Finlayson & Cortés, 1987).

T E A L

In the Palaearctic, the Teal breeds from Iceland, Britain and Iberia in the west, eastwards across central Europe and southern Scandinavia to the Kamchatka Peninsula. The breeding range is, on the whole, south of the Wigeon though overlapping considerably with it. The nominate subspecies breeds and winters in Europe, having an estimated breeding population of 90 000, the greatest proportion in Finland (Prater, 1981). 150 000 Teal winter in Europe, mostly in Britain, The Netherlands and western France, with smaller numbers down to North Africa (Prater, 1981). The Iberian Peninsula is, however, more important than is usually realized. Mean wintering numbers in recent years have been of the order of 79 000 but over 145 000 have wintered some years (Dolz & Gomez, 1988), suggesting that Iberia may gain in significance when harsh conditions in central and western Europe force wintering birds further south. The Marismas del Guadalquivir is the main Iberian site, with winter counts ranging from 50 000 to 127 000 (Ena & Purroy, 1982; Dolz & Gomez, 1988). Smaller numbers reach Morocco although there are significant inter-annual differences, which may be related to conditions in Europe: in January 1983, the wintering population was estimated to be 2862 (Beabrun & Thevenot, 1983), whereas in

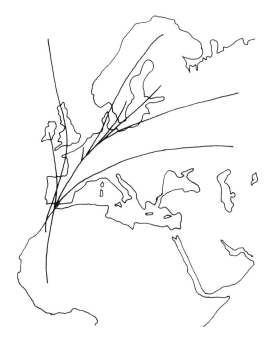

Figure 112. Southward migratory routes followed by Teal passing the Strait.

November 1981 it was 10834 (Thevenot *et al.*, 1982). Very few Teal reach tropical West Africa, where they are regular in some localities in Ghana, northern Nigeria and Chad (Serle *et al.*, 1977), but a Dutch-ringed Teal has been recovered in the Inundation Zone of the Niger in Mali (Moreau, 1972).

Teal reaching the Strait either winter there or continue into Morocco, some reaching West Africa. They come from western and central Europe and the Soviet Union. Birds recovered in Iberia had the following countries of origin (Bernis, 1966b): France (254—all ringed on passage in Camargue), Ireland (1), Scotland (1), Iceland (2), Belgium (24), Denmark (14), south Sweden (5), northern Scandinavia (4), south Finland (1), central Russia (1), southern Russia (2), Switzerland (3). Telleria (1981) noted 22 Dutch recoveries (Figure 112).

In addition to the large concentrations in the Marismas, Teal also gather in large numbers in the Merja Zerga where Thevenot *et al.* (1982) estimated up to 10000 in November 1981. Smaller numbers are found scattered in lagoons and marshes in the area. 100–200 have been recorded in the Smir, Larache and Oualad Khallouf (Pineau & Giraud-Audine, 1979). In winter, 80–100 are regular in the Laguna de Medina and other Cádiz lagoons, and over 200 have been recorded in the old Laguna de La Janda (where they were once very numerous—Irby, 1895) after winter flooding (Holliday, 1990a).

Although some Teal do occur in the area in summer, the first main winter arrivals take place in September with numbers building up through the autumn (Figure 113). Birds start to leave, northwards in February; all have left by early April (Pineau & Giraud-Audine, 1979; Amat, 1984; Finlayson & Cortés, 1987).

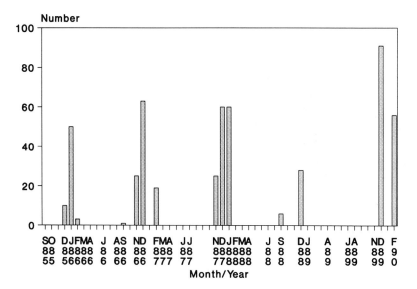

Figure 113.   Teal counts at Laguna de Medina, 1985–90.

MALLARD

The Mallard breeds widely throughout the Palaearctic, from Greenland, Iceland, Britain and Morocco to the Pacific. The western European wintering population has been estimated at 1.5 million (Prater, 1981), residents being augmented by birds from Scandinavia, Iceland and the western USSR. These birds winter south to Iberia and North Africa. The mean number wintering in Iberia in recent years has been estimated at 80 000, reaching over 131 000 some years (Dolz & Gomez, 1988). The Marismas del Guadalquivir, with a wintering population of between 10 000–22 000, is the most important Spanish nucleus. Smaller numbers winter in Morocco where over 12 000 were recorded in December 1980 (Thevenot *et al.*, 1981). The Mallard is almost unknown in West Africa (Moreau, 1972).

This is a species with complicated movements. Bernis (1966b) considers that the most regular populations wintering in Iberia are likely to be those from central and eastern Europe. This is backed to a certain extent by the spectrum of Iberian recoveries, which include French, English, Belgian, Dutch, Danish, south Swedish and Czechoslovak ringed birds (Bernis, 1966b). These birds enter Iberia, some continuing towards the Marismas, others south into Morocco. The numbers reaching Morocco vary between years. Pineau & Giraud-Audine (1979) cite five recoveries in Morocco of Mallard ringed in Andalucia. After moulting local Mallard's movements are strongly affected by water levels (J. Amat, pers. comm.).

After the concentration in the Marismas, the Merja Zerga probably holds the largest wintering population of Mallard, with up to 10 000 (Thevenot *et al.*,

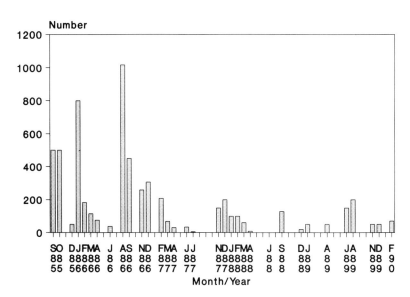

Figure 114.   Mallard counts at Laguna de Medina, 1985–90.

1981). The old Laguna de La Janda was another stronghold of this duck (Irby, 1895; Verner, 1910) and up to 2500 have recently been counted at this site after flooding in winter (Holliday, 1990a). During the moult in late summer, up to 6000 have been counted in La Janda (Telleria, 1981). In other lagoons, e.g. Medina, numbers may in some years reach 1000 in late summer, stabilizing to around 800 in midwinter, being lower other years.

Mallards are present the year round (Figure 114), but there is an indication of movement in August to November and March to May (Finlayson & Cortés, 1987). The main winter influxes take place in October and November, and the main departures during March and April.

PINTAIL

The Pintail breeds across the Palaearctic, from Iceland, Britain and Iberia to Kamchatka, generally in northerly latitudes. Prater (1981) identified four main wintering areas of the European and Russian populations, northwestern Europe (50 000) and West Africa (over 100 000) being the two areas which may involve birds that pass the Strait. The northwest European wintering population is concentrated in Britain and The Netherlands, with smaller numbers in France and Iberia. The mean number wintering in Iberia in recent years has been estimated at over 17 000, *c.* 45 000 in 1985 (Dolz & Gomez, 1988). The small Moroccan wintering element is an offshoot of this wintering population.

These Pintail come from northern Europe and the USSR, as borne out by Iberian recoveries: England (4), Belgium (1), Holland (37), Denmark (11), south Sweden (1) and south Russia (11) (Bernis, 1966b). Of 38 recoveries made in southwest Andalucia, 34 were of Dutch-ringed Pintail (Telleria, 1981); a Danish-ringed bird has been recorded at Merja Zerga (Pineau & Giraud-Audine, 1979).

South of Morocco, there are large wintering concentrations in Senegal (80 000 in January 1971—Cramp & Simmons, 1977), and the Niger Inundation Zone in Mali (over 100 000—Curry & Sayer, 1979). These birds may reach the wintering grounds via the Strait or they may pursue more direct routes from the north-east. Their origin is unknown (Prater, 1981) although, as Moreau (1972) states that several rings from the Volga have been recovered from the Inundation Zone, they may come from the USSR.

The Marismas del Guadalquivir hold the largest Spanish wintering number, 6000–20 000 (Ena & Purroy, 1982; Dolz & Gomez, 1988). Most of the 2000 or so wintering in Morocco do so in the north-west, close to the Strait. Merja Zerga held 2177 Pintail in January 1983 (Beaubrun & Thevenot, 1983). Smaller flocks (usually up to 150 birds) are found in lagoons on either side of the Strait (e.g. Smir, Cádiz lagoons).

The Pintail is a winter visitor between October and May (Figure 115; Finlayson & Cortés, 1987). October, November and February are the main passage months (Pineau & Giraud-Audine, 1979). Counts in Andalucian lagoons show a sudden arrival in October with a steep decline in March and very few remaining by April (Amat, 1984).

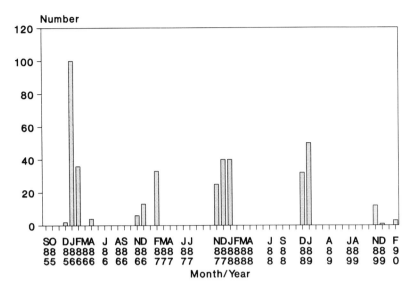

Figure 115. Pintail counts at Laguna de Medina, 1985–90.

GARGANEY

Garganeys breed across the mid-Palaearctic from Britain and France in the west to the Pacific in the east; they occasionally breed in the Marismas del Guadalquivir (J. Amat, pers. comm.). The majority of western Garganeys winter in tropical Africa. Large numbers winter in West Africa, but they are very scarce in winter in Iberia or Morocco (Pineau & Giraud-Audine, 1979; Beaubrun & Thevenot, 1983; Dolz & Gomez, 1988). In contrast, Moreau (1972) estimated at least 100 000 wintering in Senegal, and over a million do so in the Niger Inundation Zone in Mali (Curry & Sayer, 1979). The numbers wintering in West Africa are thought to be well in excess of those raised in western Europe, so Garganeys from further east must travel to these winter quarters (Moreau, 1972). Garganeys ringed in the moulting grounds on the Volga have later been recovered west to Holland, Italy and France, with others further east (Moreau, 1972); a Volga-ringed bird was recovered in Nigeria, and others ringed in western Europe (which could have come from the USSR) were recovered in Senegal, the Niger and Lake Chad.

Evidence for the migratory routes followed is sketchy. Birds that migrate towards western Europe in autumn presumably continue into West Africa via Iberia and Morocco, although the small numbers recorded on passage in autumn indicate that more easterly routes must be followed or birds must overfly these areas in autumn. Bernis (1966b) gives Iberian recoveries of Garganeys ringed in southeast France (4), England (1), Belgium (3), Holland (4), Czechoslovakia (1) and Byelorussia (USSR) (1).

Although Garganeys are not abundant passage migrants across the Strait,

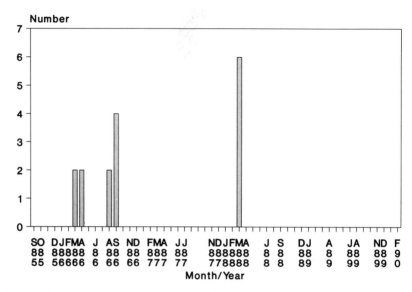

Figure 116.   Garganey counts at Laguna de Medina, 1985–90.

thousands are recorded some years in the Guadalquivir (e.g. 1985) during the spring migration (J. Amat, pers. comm.). They are generally more frequent and numerous in spring than in autumn (Pineau & Giraud-Audine, 1979; Finlayson & Cortés, 1987) and pass in small groups, but occasionally occur in larger concentrations, of up to 300, in autumn (see, for example, Pineau & Giraud-Audine, 1979). They are not confined to permanent water, also occurring in temporarily flooded fields and in sheltered bays.

The migration appears to be rapid (Figure 116). In spring, passage takes place in late February, March and April—usually the latter half of March and early April. The return movement is centred principally in August and early September, with occasional birds in October (Pineau & Giraud-Audine, 1979; Finlayson & Cortés, 1987). Further south in Morocco, passage is from early February, with occasional individuals in January (Thevenot *et al.*, 1982).

SHOVELER

In the Palaearctic, the Shoveler breeds over a wide belt from Ireland, France and the Guadalquivir to the Pacific coast. Western populations winter in Europe and North Africa, some reaching tropical Africa. According to Prater (1981), about 20 000 winter in western Europe, but this must be an underestimate as Dolz & Gomez (1988) calculated a mean wintering number of over 60 000 in Iberia, reaching almost 120 000 some winters. The Marismas del Guadalquivir are the Iberian stronghold, with a winter population that has varied from 22 000 to

Figure 117. Southward migratory routes followed by Shovelers passing the Strait.

33 000 in recent years (Ena & Purroy, 1982; Dolz & Gomez, 1988). Other lagoons in the area also support large wintering populations, notably the Laguna de Medina with over 1500 in some winters. Numbers wintering in Morocco, mostly in the north-west close to the Strait, are lower and vary between winters, but over 15 000 have been censused, with 10 000 in Merja Zerga (Thevenot *et al.*, 1981). Concentrations of 500 to 1000 occur in other lagoons of the area (e.g. the Smir, Oualad Khallouf). The Strait is therefore within a major wintering area of this duck. Further south, Shovelers reach tropical West Africa in smaller numbers, wintering in hundreds in Senegal but scarcer in the Niger Inundation Zone (Moreau, 1972; Curry & Sayer, 1979).

Iberian and Moroccan recoveries indicate the substantial westward movement of some Shovelers reaching the area. Bernis (1966b) gives the following Iberian recoveries: southeast France (6), Britain (6), Holland (42), Belgium (1), north-west Germany (1), Denmark (5), south Sweden (2), south Finland (4), Baltic (1) and Hungary (2). Fernandez-Cruz (1982) records a Shoveler ringed in November 1970 near Seville, recovered in October 1975 in Volgograd, USSR, 4250 km east/northeast. Telleria (1981) cites among Spanish recoveries three Russian Shovelers. Pineau & Giraud-Audine (1979) add three Moroccan recoveries at Merja Zerga of birds ringed in Denmark, Estonia (USSR) and Novgorod (USSR). The Shovelers that reach and cross the Strait area therefore come from a wide area of western and northern Europe and the western USSR (Figure 117).

Large concentrations occur within the Strait in winter, particularly in the major wetland areas. In peak years, the wintering population may be in excess of 50 000.

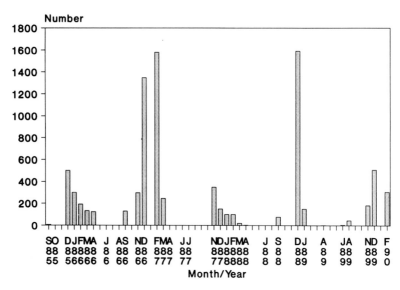

Figure 118.   Shoveler counts at Laguna de Medina, 1985–90.

Shovelers arrive from the north from August onwards with peak movements during October, stabilizing to winter levels after this (Figure 118). In spring, northward passage commences in February and peaks during March, last birds usually leaving the area in April (Pineau & Giraud-Audine, 1979; Amat, 1981, 1984; Holliday, 1990a).

RED-CRESTED POCHARD

The Red-crested Pochard breeds from Iberia eastwards, in parts of central and western Europe, north to Denmark, in the Mediterranean and in middle to lower latitudes to the east. Small numbers may breed in northwest Morocco (Pineau & Giraud-Audine, 1979) where very few winter. The Iberian wintering population is augmented by birds from the north: there have been Iberian recoveries of Red-crested Pochards ringed in southeast France (4), southwest Germany (8) and Denmark (2) (Bernis, 1966b). Iberian birds perform post-breeding dispersal movements in a number of directions: for example, a bird ringed in Seville in July 1975 was recovered in Ireland in January 1977 (Fernandez-Cruz, 1982).

Dolz & Gomez (1988) estimated an average wintering population of 23 000 Red-crested Pochards in Iberia in recent years, with a maximum of over 44 000 in 1979. The largest concentrations are in eastern and northern Spain, up to 20 000 in the Albufera, Valencia (Gomez *et al.*, 1983), and up to 36 000 in Gallocanta lagoon (J. Amat, pers. comm.). The wintering Andalucian population in the late 1970s was 1000–2000 (Ena & Purroy, 1982), the majority in the Marismas del Guadal-

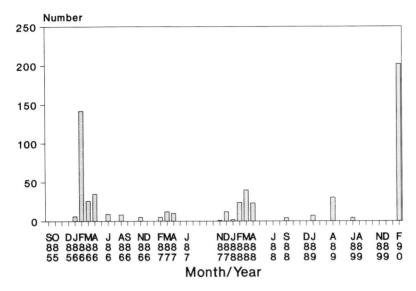

Figure 119.   Red-crested Pochard counts at Laguna de Medina, 1985–90.

quivir and significant concentrations in the Laguna de Medina (775 in January 1983—Ena & Purroy, 1984; 1120 in March 1980—Amat, 1984).

Wintering birds begin to arrive in October and the last migrants leave in early May (Finlayson & Cortés, 1987). Others remain to breed. Midwinter influxes from the north occur, resulting in peak counts in January and February in some years (Figure 119). There is no passage as such, since very few move south of the Strait area.

POCHARD

The Pochard breeds across middle latitudes of the Palaearctic from Ireland eastwards to central USSR (110°E). There is an isolated breeding population in southern Spain: 1000 pairs in the Marismas del Guadalquivir (Amat, 1982) and smaller numbers in the Cádiz lagoons. Pochards winter south of the breeding range, large numbers entering Iberia and North Africa, and a few reaching tropical West Africa (Moreau, 1972). According to Moreau, Pochards have only been recorded in West Africa in Senegal and northern Nigeria, but Curry & Sayer (1979) found them in winter in the Niger Inundation Zone, though in much smaller numbers than Garganey and Pintail.

Pochards from western and central Europe migrate west/southwest to winter in Iberia and, presumably, Morocco. These, alongside Spanish birds, form the main contingent of birds involved in movements and wintering in the Strait. Iberian recoveries include Pochards ringed in southeast France, England, Den-

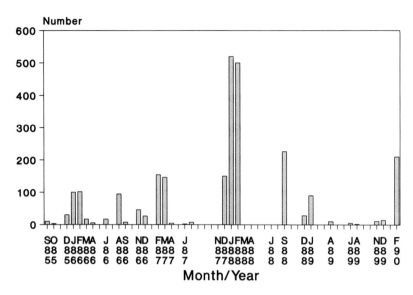

Figure 120.   Pochard counts at Laguna de Medina, 1985–90.

mark, the Baltic, Czechoslovakia and Hungary (Bernis, 1966b). A Pochard ringed in Guadiamar (Seville) in April 1975 was recovered in May of the following year in Finland, and another ringed at the same site in July 1975 was recovered in August of the following year in Poland (Fernandez-Cruz, 1982). Spanish-bred Pochard disperse widely, into Morocco, France, Portugal, Switzerland and Italy (Fernandez-Cruz, 1982).

On average, just under 49 000 Pochards have wintered in Iberia in recent years, with over 95 000 in 1979 (Dolz & Gomez, 1988). The Marismas del Guadalquivir are a major Iberian wintering site, with between 4000 and 6500 birds (Ena & Purroy, 1982; Dolz & Gomez, 1988). Inland lagoons are also favoured sites when water levels are high, with counts of up to 500 at the Laguna de Medina alone. Numbers wintering in Morocco average 4000–6000, but there is substantial variation between years (Thevenot *et al.*, 1981, 1982; Beaubrun & Thevenot, 1983). Groups of 100–500 are regular in some sites (e.g. the Merja Zerga, Smir) (Pineau & Giraud-Audine, 1979; Beaubrun & Thevenot, 1983).

Wintering birds arrive from late September onwards. Some remain until early April (Pineau & Giraud-Audine, 1979; Finlayson & Cortés, 1987), and others breed in spring. Main arrivals take place in October and November (Figure 120).

RAILS, CRAKES AND COOTS

The shy and skulking habits of most rails, crakes and coots make them difficult to observe; consequently the status of most species is known less precisely than is the case for other waterbirds. They are among the species that have suffered most drastically from loss of marshland and swamp habitat.

The Water Rail is probably the most widespread and abundant species, and was described by Irby (1875, 1895) as very common in all suitable localities, being most common in winter. They still breed on both sides of the Strait (Smith, 1965; Pineau & Giraud-Audine, 1979; pers. obs.), and local numbers are augmented in winter (Mayaud, 1982c; Finlayson & Cortés, 1987). Passage takes place in March, April, September and October (Thevenot *et al.*, 1982).

Irby (1875, 1895) considered the Spotted Crake to be extremely abundant on the Spanish side of the Strait, where it was more numerous than the Water Rail or the Moorhen. On the Moroccan side, Favier (in Irby, 1875, 1895) considered it to be the most common of these species, though not in great numbers near Tangier. The status of this species has changed dramatically; sightings are now few, though regular, in March, April, September and November (Pineau & Giraud-Audine, 1979; Thevenot *et al.*, 1981, 1982; Holliday, 1990a). Telleria (1981) cited the recovery of a Dutch bird in Sanlúcar de Barrameda in September 1963. Bernis (1966a) recorded a northwest German bird recovered in Iberia.

The Little Crake has probably always been scarce, as neither Irby (1875, 1895) nor Favier (in Irby) ever recorded it, though the former had seen Andalucian specimens. Most recent records are for the Moroccan side, and then usually south of the Strait, where they occur on passage in March and April but have not been seen in autumn (Thevenot *et al.*, 1981, 1982; Mayaud, 1982c). Pineau & Giraud-Audine (1979) only recorded it once, on 11 March 1971, and Thevenot *et al.* (1981) saw another in the Loukos on 3 March 1970. It probably occurs on the Spanish side in the Marismas del Guadalquivir.

Baillon's Crake was described as very common in the swamps of Casas Viejas and at La Janda from October to March with some remaining to breed in summer (Irby, 1875, 1895). Favier (in Irby, 1875, 1895) considered it rare in Morocco and it may have been overlooked; according to Pineau & Giraud-Audine (1979) it used to nest, and probably still does, in the Loukos and the Smir as well as in the dry Foret du Sahel. On the Spanish side of the Strait it breeds in the Marismas del Guadalquivir and probably in the Cádiz lagoons (Holliday, 1990a). Most passage sightings are in March and April with an autumn observation in November (Pineau & Giraud-Audine, 1979; Thevenot *et al.*, 1982; Holliday, 1990a).

The Corncrake, never described as abundant, was probably once an over-looked but regular migrant (Irby, 1875, 1895) that has become increasingly rare as a result of the declining European breeding population. It is still a regular migrant, between August and October and March to April (Pineau & Giraud-Audine, 1979). A Scottish Corncrake has been recovered in northeast Spain (Bernis, 1966a).

The Moorhen is a common breeding species, numbers increasing during passage and in winter. Its status has probably changed little in recent times. The migratory movements take place mainly in late February and March and in late September to early November but are not conspicuous (Pineau & Giraud-Audine, 1979; Finlayson & Cortés, 1987). Two records for the Rock of Gibraltar

(Cortés *et al.*, 1980), where there is no suitable habitat, confirm the existence of movements within the Strait. Estimates of passage or wintering populations are not available, but gatherings of 30 or more birds are regular at many sites (e.g. Holliday, 1990a). Iberian recoveries include birds ringed in southeast France, Belgium, Holland, Germany and Denmark (Bernis, 1966a).

The Purple Gallinule, which must have declined through loss of habitat, appears to have recovered in numbers in recent years. Irby (1875, 1895) found Purple Gallinules irregular in appearance (in both time and location) but, because he saw them in unusual sites near Gibraltar in January and February, thought that they performed migratory movements. In wet seasons they used to nest in the Soto Malabrigo near La Janda and in the Marismas del Guadalquivir. Today they continue to breed in the Marismas and in the Cádiz lagoons. On the Moroccan side they used to breed in the Smir and near Tangier, and still do in the Loukos where there is a stable population (Pineau & Giraud-Audine, 1979; Thevenot *et al.*, 1981). Some Andalucian birds may cross the Strait to winter in Morocco (Pineau & Giraud-Audine, 1979). The appearance of a Purple Gallinule in a small lagoon near the Guadiaro River in two consecutive winters, and in the Guadal-horce Estuary (de Juana, 1982) (well away from the usual breeding sites), and the spread of the species in recent years indicates that there is considerable dispersal of birds in autumn.

Although the precise origins (probably West African) of the Allen's Gallinule are unknown, this species has been recorded in the Strait and adjacent areas on several occasions. There have been two records (one of a bird caught by a dog) in the Guadalhorce Estuary (east of the Strait) in December 1975 and December 1977 (Padilla & Garrido Sanchez, 1983) and a Moroccan record early in 1976 (Mayaud, 1982c). The species may visit southern Europe regularly or during years of population expansion.

The Coot is a numerous bird on both shores of the Strait. Coots nested in large numbers in the Laguna de La Janda until it was drained (Irby, 1875, 1895), and they still do so in the Marismas del Guadalquivir and adjacent Cádiz lagoons, the Oueds Smir and Negro, and at Larache (Pineau & Giraud-Audine, 1979) and Merja Zerga (Thevenot *et al.*, 1982). In summer and autumn, birds from the Marismas del Guadalquivir disperse and large gatherings form on either side of the Strait (Figure 121). In the Cádiz lagoons up to 10 000 have been counted in the Laguna de Medina in October (Finlayson & Cortés, 1987), 1000 in the Smir in August (Pineau & Giraud-Audine, 1979), 30 000–50 000 in Merja Zerga in September and October (Smith, 1965; Pineau & Giraud-Audine, 1979) and 60 000 at this site in January 1981 (Thevenot *et al.*, 1982). Ringing recoveries of Andalucian birds in Morocco (Pineau & Giraud-Audine, 1979; Thevenot *et al.*, 1982) confirm the movement of Spanish birds across the Strait in autumn. Coots from western and central Europe visit Iberia and probably also contribute to the large numbers present in autumn. This is particularly likely for Coots from southeast France which dominate the spectrum of Iberian recoveries (Bernis, 1966a). Other countries of origin of Iberian recoveries are England, Holland, Germany, Czechoslovakia, Denmark, Sweden and the Baltic.

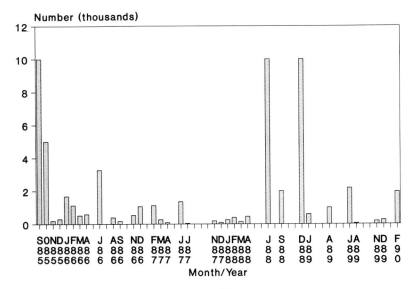

Figure 121. Coot counts at Laguna de Medina, 1985–90.

The Crested Coot, which has seriously declined in numbers this century, bred in numbers in Ras-el-Doura and had been obtained from La Janda (Irby, 1875, 1895). Yeates (1945) found it during the breeding season in the Laguna del Torero near Vejer. Although not specifically noted by Irby, Crested Coots probably bred in the Marismas del Guadalquivir, where a small population still survives today. Isolated pairs also breed in many of the Cádiz lagoons, depending on water levels. In Morocco they breed in the Loukos and southwards towards Rabat, being commonest in Sidi bou Rhaba where Thevenot *et al.* (1981) recorded 30 pairs. They also breed in the Middle Atlas range (Mayaud, 1982c). According to Pineau & Giraud-Audine (1979) they formerly bred in the Smir and near Tangier. There is little evidence of major movements by this species, except for their appearance and disappearance from lagoons in response to fluctuating water levels.

CRANES

The Demoiselle Crane may have once bred in the Marismas del Guadalquivir and even close to La Janda (Irby, 1875, 1895). It may then have been a regular migrant in the Strait. The species was formerly reported from Larache (Reid, 1885), the Oued Martil (Drake, 1867) and near Tangier (Favier, in Irby, 1895). It has now become rarified as a breeding species in the Middle Atlas (Mayaud, 1982c) and must be considered a very rare visitor to the Strait area.

CRANE

The Cranes of Scandinavia and the Baltic migrate southwest in autumn to winter principally in the Iberian Peninsula and Morocco (Bernis, 1966a; Alonso & Alonso, 1988). It is now accepted that the majority winter in southwestern Iberia, the greater proportion in Extremadura and the southernmost Iberian populations in La Janda (Fernandez-Cruz, 1981; Alonso & Alonso, 1988). Recent counts at this site have revealed maxima of 500 birds in winter and over 1000 during the peak autumn passage in November. The size of the Moroccan wintering population has been the subject of debate, but it appears to be small in comparison to the Iberian population (Smith, 1965; Bernis, 1966a; Dubois & Duhautois, 1977; Alonso & Alonso, 1988).

The Crane is a regular winter visitor to the Moroccan side of the Strait occurring in groups of 250–300 birds (Pineau & Giraud-Audine, 1979). Groups on the northwest corner of Morocco vary in size between 250 and 500 (Mayaud, 1982c). Up to 400 were counted at Briech, south of Tangier, in December 1980, with smaller groups further south (Thevenot *et al.*, 1981). Cranes winter south of the Strait, and numbers on the Moroccan side of the Strait are augmented during passage periods by birds from the south (Pineau & Giraud-Audine, 1979). Thus, although it has to be accepted that perhaps under 2000 Cranes winter in Morocco (a low number in comparison with the 40 000–50 000 wintering in Iberia— Alonso & Alonso, 1988), the size of the wintering population has perhaps been underestimated in the past. The wintering nucleus, which includes birds in northwest Morocco and at La Janda, is probably fairly homogeneous, and the levels wintering on either shore of the Strait may be determined by local environmental conditions. Midwinter movements across the Strait in either direction have been noted by several authors (Smith, 1965; Pineau & Giraud-Audine, 1979).

Cranes must have been more abundant in the past. They nested in the Laguna de La Janda, where Irby (1875, 1895) estimated 30–40 pairs (see also Chapter 7), as well as in the Marismas del Guadalquivir, but they may not have done so in Morocco. The Laguna de La Janda must have been of great significance for Cranes as a resting place for migrants as well as a wintering ground. The wintering population on both shores of the Strait must once have been higher, as evidenced by Irby's (1875, 1895) comments on passage of flocks numbering 200–300 birds, with smaller groups of 30–40 in the autumn, and his description of a spectacular movement from Morocco to Europe in the morning of 11 March 1874, when 4000 were counted migrating northwards.

The Strait therefore forms the southern limit of the wintering range of northwestern European Cranes. The total wintering population is probably of the order of 3000 birds, the largest wintering concentrations nowadays being to the north-west of the Strait.

The first Cranes begin to arrive in mid-October and the main passage takes place in November. The departures to the north commence in mid-February and the peak northward movement is in March (Pineau & Giraud-Audine, 1979; Telleria, 1981; Finlayson & Cortés, 1987).

WADERS

The main species which migrate or winter in the Strait are each discussed in a separate section below. There are in addition a number of scarcer but regular migrants. These include species with winter quarters southwest of the breeding grounds but with normal migratory routes east of the Strait (Table 9). Their scarce but regular appearance in the area indicates regular deflections west of the main migratory routes. Vagrants are also listed in Table 9. Several further species probably migrate regularly and even winter in the area but are observed irregularly and never in large numbers. The most striking case is that of the Dotterel, for which there are very few records (Irby, 1895; Pineau & Giraud-Audine, 1974). Woodcock and Jack Snipe are probably largely overlooked because of their secretive habits (Irby, 1895; Smith, 1965; Pineau & Giraud-Audine, 1976; Cortés *et al.*, 1980; Telleria, 1981; Arroyo & Telleria, 1984).

The Stone Curlew, which breeds in the grasslands of the area (Pineau & Giraud-Audine, 1979; Finlayson & Cortés, 1987), is irregularly recorded on passage and in winter in flocks, for example 78 together near Jeli Lagoon in Cádiz Province (Telleria, 1981), up to 40 near Larache in December (Smith, 1965), and wintering groups of 50–80 on the Moroccan side of the Strait, with a flock of 130 at Sidi Kacem in November 1979 (Pineau & Giraud-Audine, 1979). These observations are in accord with those of Irby (1895), who said that Stone Curlews migrated through the area in lots of 5–50 birds, occurring mainly in ploughed fields. The main passage periods are March, April, October and November (Irby, 1895; Pineau & Giraud-Audine, 1979; Finlayson & Cortés, 1987). The

Table 9   Waders: scarce migrants and vagrants.

Migrants[1]	Vagrants[2]	
Temminck's Stint	Sociable Plover	
Great Snipe	Spur-winged Plover	} from the east
Marsh Sandpiper	Broad-billed Sandpiper	
Terek Sandpiper		
(less frequent)	Cream-coloured Courser	} from the south
	American Golden Plover	
	Buff-breasted Sandpiper	
	Short-billed Dowitcher	
	Pectoral Sandpiper	} from America
	Lesser Yellowlegs	
	Wilson's Phalarope	

[1]Irby (1895), Smith (1965), Hiraldo (1971), Pineau & Giraud-Audine (1974, 1976), Dubois & Duhautois (1977), Melcher (1977), de Juana *et al.* (1981, 1982, 1987), Padilla & Garrido Sanchez (1983).

[2]Saunders (1871), Irby (1895), Tuke (1953), Edge (1956), Petzer (1965), Junco (1966), Alden *et al.* (1973), Franco *et al.* (1973), Giraud-Audine & Pineau (1973), Ree (1973), Pineau & Giraud-Audine (1974), Fernandez & Mellado (1977), de Juana *et al.* (1981, 1982, 1987), Padilla & Garrido Sanchez (1983).

passage and wintering birds probably originate from western Europe, Bernis (1966b) recording Iberian recoveries of birds ringed in southwest France, England and Holland.

The Grey Phalarope is probably a regular migrant along the Atlantic coast towards its winter quarters in West Africa (Taning, 1933; Stanford, 1953). It is scarce along the coast except when Atlantic gales coincide with the migratory movements. This happened in November 1983 when wrecked birds were found along the Atlantic coast, within the Strait and adjacent Mediterranean coastline (Finlayson & Cortés, 1987). The Red-necked Phalarope is rarer but nevertheless regular in suitable sites on the Atlantic coast (e.g. the Bonanza saltpans) especially in spring (de Juana, 1989; *SGBO Reports*; Holliday, 1990a). It seems probable that a few winter off the coast of West Africa as reported by Taning (1933).

The Purple Sandpiper winters regularly in small numbers along several stretches of Atlantic and Strait coastline, including Morocco (Irby, 1895; Solís, 1977; Finlayson & Cortés, 1987; de Juana, 1988b). The wintering range of this species reaches its southerly limit in this area, although a recent sighting in the Canary Islands (de Juana, 1989) suggests that some may winter even further south.

The rare Slender-billed Curlew winters exclusively along the Moroccan coasts of the Strait especially on the Merja Zerga (van den Berg, 1990). The extreme rarity of this species makes it a very rare migrant and winter visitor. In the past it must have been more common though probably not numerous. Chapman & Buck (1910) stated that it appeared on the Spanish side of the Strait in February and at no other time, and then in limited areas and for brief periods. Reid (1885), however, found numerous flights at Meshree el Haddar, and it was abundant in the Loukos valley in the winter of 1884–85 in flocks of 20–100. More recently, Valverde (1955, 1956) saw 50 at Larache in July 1953 and Blondel & Blondel (1964) found groups of 10–100 along the Moroccan Atlantic coast, with 500–800 in Puerto Cansado in southern Morocco. Other authors have recorded small groups and singles, mostly in northwest Morocco near the Strait (Larache, Merja Zerga, Tahadart), and the species must be regarded a very rare winter visitor (Smith, 1965; Dubois & Duhautois, 1977; Pineau & Giraud-Audine, 1979; Mayaud, 1982c).

OYSTERCATCHER

Oystercatchers breed across a wide belt from Iceland and the British Isles to the Pacific coasts of Eurasia including Kamchatka. The western populations winter in large numbers in central and western Europe. Smaller numbers winter in Iberia, where Alberto & Velasco (1988) estimated 1800 (0.2% of the western European wintering population). Relatively few of these winter on the Atlantic coasts of the Strait (Pineau & Giraud-Audine, 1979; Telleria, 1981; Finlayson & Cortés, 1987) but larger wintering populations are found in southern Morocco (1500 — Kersten & Smit, 1984) and Banc d'Arguin, Mauretania (up to 9200 – Engelmoer *et al.*, 1984). Nevertheless, these are small in comparison with European wintering numbers. The Oystercatchers that occur on passage must therefore winter in Morocco and Mauretania, some reaching the coasts of tropical West Africa where they are uncommon from Senegal to the Niger Delta (Serle *et al.*, 1977). Essentially, these birds are derived from west and north European breeding populations. Iberian recoveries include birds ringed in the following countries: England, Ireland, Scotland, Holland, northwest Germany, south Norway and south Sweden (Bernis, 1966b).

Oystercatchers are relatively scarce migrants, frequenting coastal areas singly or in small groups. The total passage may not involve more than a few hundred birds. Passage takes place between mid-February and early June, and late July to early November (Pineau & Giraud-Audine, 1979; Telleria, 1981; Finlayson & Cortés, 1987).

BLACK-WINGED STILT

Black-winged Stilts from Iberian populations must be the main ones migrating across the Strait, although individuals from France and the low countries probably also migrate via the Iberian Peninsula (one recovery of a Dutch Black-winged Stilt in France — Bernis, 1966d). It seems likely that the majority cross the

Sahara to winter in tropical West Africa (Moreau, 1972) where they occur from Senegal and The Gambia east to Chad, and south to Gabon and Congo (Serle *et al.*, 1977). Black-winged Stilts do not appear to winter in the Banc d'Arguin, Mauretania (Knight & Dick, 1975; Engelmoer *et al.*, 1984). Wintering within the Strait is regular, with larger numbers on the Moroccan side than the Spanish (Telleria, 1981; Finlayson & Cortés, 1987): around 70 winter regularly at Larache (Pineau & Giraud-Audine, 1979), and up to 150 at this site and at Merja Zerga (Kersten & Smit, 1984). Wintering on the Spanish side may be greater than previously thought, however, since Alberto & Velasco (1988) estimated the Spanish wintering population at around 1200 (85.7% of the stilts wintering in western Europe), with the main concentrations in the Marismas del Guadalquivir and Cádiz Bay. The total wintering population along the European and African Atlantic coasts has been estimated at 10 700 (Engelmoer *et al.*, 1984).

The number of Black-winged Stilts crossing the Strait cannot be quantified on present data. Maximum counts at typical passage localities may exceed 200 stilts in autumn and concentrations in favoured locations (e.g. Cádiz Bay) are probably much higher.

The first migrants in spring are observed in February and the main arrivals take place in March and April, with smaller numbers arriving in May (Figure 122). The departure at the end of the breeding season appears to start early, in July (Finlayson & Cortés, 1987), reaching a peak during August with a reduced passage in September and October, and resulting in the lower winter levels (Figure 122).

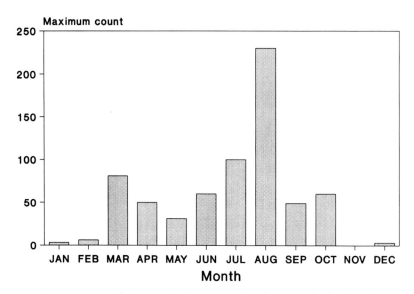

Figure 122.   Maximum Black-winged Stilt counts in selected Strait wetlands, 1985–90.

AVOCET

In addition to Iberian Avocets, it is probable that west European birds may also cross the Strait or arrive there for the winter. Bernis (1966d), summarized Iberian recoveries of European Avocets which included 42 Danish, 30 Dutch, 19 northwest German, and smaller numbers of Swedish, Belgian and French birds. Most recoveries were concentrated along the Atlantic coasts including the south-west of the Iberian Peninsula. Some English Avocets also migrate towards Iberia in autumn (Prater, 1981). Very few Avocets winter south of the Sahara, where they reach Senegal, The Gambia, Mali and Nigeria (Moreau, 1972). It is not a wintering wader in the Banc d'Arguin, Mauretania, either (Knight & Dick, 1975; Engelmoer *et al.*, 1984). The main wintering grounds of west European Avocets are therefore further north, and include Morocco and Iberia, with the Strait at the core. The Moroccan wintering population has been estimated at around 3000, including up to 400 at Larache and 2000 at Merja Zerga (Kersten and Smit, 1984). The numbers wintering in Morocco vary considerably between years (Pineau & Giraud-Audine, 1979). For Iberia, the estimate (Alberto & Velasco, 1988) is 7200 Avocets (21.8% of the west European wintering population) with the Marismas del Guadalquivir, the Odiel Estuary and Cádiz Bay as important wintering nuclei. 700 Avocets were counted along the Cádiz Atlantic coast in January 1978 (Telleria, 1981).

Accurate estimates of Avocet passage are not available, but concentrations at favoured localities (e.g. the Bonanza saltpans) can be spectacular. Gatherings during the migratory periods at these sites fluctuate between 1000 and 3000. In

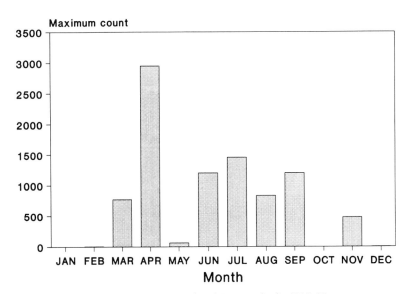

Figure 123. Maximum Avocet counts in selected Strait wetlands, 1985–90.

other sites, their appearance is erratic and usually in the form of small parties. Groups varying from 2 to 30 birds have been recorded passing the Rock of Gibraltar (Holliday, 1990a).

The spring movement of Avocets starts in March and reaches a peak during April, very few migrants remaining by May (Figure 123). Concentrations of Avocets become increasingly evident during June, but these are probably local birds that have finished breeding. The main movement seems to be in August and September, passage continuing into November (Figure 123). This extended autumn passage period may reflect migration of different Avocet populations within the area.

COLLARED PRATINCOLE

Spanish and Portuguese Collared Pratincoles cross the Strait southwards in autumn and join Moroccan ones to winter south of the Sahara, where the species is widely distributed in the dry northern areas of West Africa (Serle *et al.*, 1977). It is unlikely that birds other than Spanish and Portuguese cross the Strait north-wards in spring.

The migration of the Collared Pratincole appears to be concentrated over a brief period, consisting of arrival *en masse* of large flocks that appear to each belong to single colonies. It is very difficult to assess the numbers crossing an area on migration as the appearance of flocks is sporadic. Colonies vary in size from a few to several hundred pairs, and flocks exceeding 100 birds have been reported

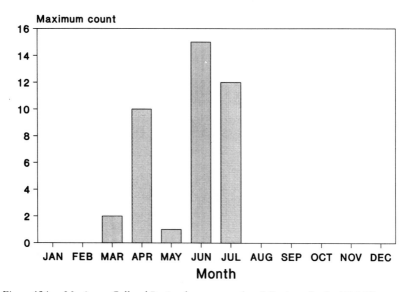

Figure 124.   Maximum Collared Pratincole counts at selected Strait wetlands, 1985–90.

in the Strait on passage (Telleria, 1981) and in excess of 200 at breeding colonies (Holliday, 1990a).

The first Collared Pratincoles arrive during March and the main movement takes place in April (Figure 124). There is then a stabilizing of numbers during the breeding season. The departure for Africa is very early (Bernis, 1966d) and takes the form of a rapid exodus from the breeding colonies during July, very few remaining by August (Figure 124), though passage in the area has been noted in late August and early September (Garcia Rua, 1975).

LITTLE RINGED PLOVER

During the breeding season Little Ringed Plovers are widely distributed in central and western Europe, including the Iberian Peninsula. They winter in tropical Africa, in the west in inland waters in Senegal, the Niger Inundation Zone in Mali and in Nigeria (Moreau, 1972). A Belgian-ringed bird was recovered in Senegal in October (Bernis, 1966b). Small numbers winter in Spain (Alberto & Velasco, 1988) including the area of the Strait (Finlayson & Cortés, 1987) and on the Moroccan side (Pineau & Giraud-Audine, 1979), but the majority must winter south of the Sahara Desert. West European birds occur on passage in the Iberian Peninsula with recoveries of English, Belgian, Dutch, south Finnish (Bernis, 1966d) and French birds (Telleria, 1981). Recoveries of English Little Ringed Plovers in France, Iberia and Morocco indicate the migration route of this population (Bernis, 1966d).

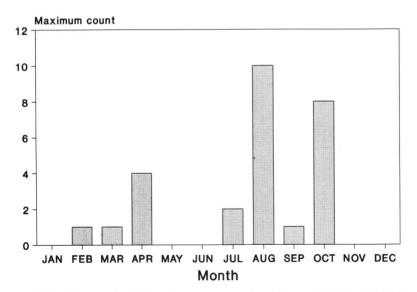

Figure 125. Maximum Little Ringed Plover counts at selected Strait wetland sites, 1985–90.

Little Ringed Plovers occur singly or in small parties on migration and counts at specific sites rarely exceed 10 birds. Telleria (1981) recorded a maximum of 13 at Tarifa Beach on 12 September 1976.

The first spring arrivals are recorded in February and the main passage appears to take place during April (Figure 125). Local birds are established at breeding sites in March, so the later movement is presumably of birds which will continue northwards. The southward passage commences in late July and continues into October (Figure 125). Telleria (1981) considers that the peak movement is in September with the last birds passing in mid-October although Pineau & Giraud-Audine (1979) and Finlayson & Cortés (1987) consider that passage continues into early November.

RINGED PLOVER

Finnish, Swedish, Norwegian, Baltic and Danish Ringed Plovers migrate south-west in autumn towards the Iberian Peninsula, where they concentrate mostly along the Atlantic coastal areas (Bernis, 1966d). To these should be added Ringed Plovers from Iceland and Greenland [Bernis (1966b) gives two Iberian recoveries of Iceland-ringed birds]. The Ringed Plover is regarded as a species that undertakes a 'leap-frog' migration (Salomonsen, 1955), with populations derived from secondary hybridization tending to migrate shorter distances than non-hybrid populations breeding further north (Hale, 1980). The birds that winter along the coasts (as well as inland) of West Africa are derived from northern populations, Ringed Plovers from Greenland and north Germany having been recovered in Senegal (Moreau, 1972). According to Moreau (1972) most Ringed Plovers wintering in West Africa belong to the nominate subspecies, although the dominant subspecies wintering in Africa is *tundrae*, which breeds from Russia eastwards.

Birds occurring on passage in the Strait are therefore from the northwestern parts of the breeding range and may winter south to West Africa. There is a major concentration in the Banc d'Arguin, Mauretania, where up to 136 500 (55% of the east Atlantic wintering population) are thought to winter (Engelmoer *et al.*, 1984). Smaller numbers winter in the Strait. Alberto & Velasco (1988) estimated the Iberian wintering population at 4500 (14.1% of the west European wintering population) with 1700 in Cádiz Bay (Grimmett & Jones, 1989). In Morocco, *c.* 5000 winter in the Merja Zerga (Kersten & Smit, 1984); Zwarts (1972) estimated 20 000 wintering at this site. Smaller numbers winter in suitable locations in northern Morocco.

Apart from the wintering concentrations, Ringed Plovers also occur in many estuaries, beaches, saltpans and lagoons on passage, usually in groups ranging between 10 and 150 birds. Telleria (1981) estimated around 2 birds per kilometre of Cádiz coast in winter.

Ringed Plovers are present in the area most months of the year with the main passage periods being March–May (many in March) and late July–October (Figure 126). The autumn peak appears to occur in September (Telleria, 1981).

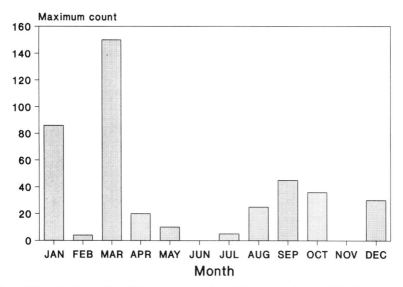

Figure 126.   Maximum Ringed Plover counts at selected Strait wetland sites, 1985–90.

KENTISH PLOVER

To those that breed along the coasts of the Strait must be added, in winter, Kentish Plovers from the coastal areas of northwestern Europe. Danish, north German, Dutch and Belgian Kentish Plovers have been recovered in France and 2 Dutch and 11 northwestern German were recovered along the Atlantic coasts of Iberia (Bernis, 1966d). An unknown proportion of these cross the Strait into Morocco in autumn and reach the other side of the Sahara, where Serle *et al.* (1977) considered it a rather scarce winter visitor and passage migrant to the west African coast as far east as Nigeria (see also Moreau, 1967). The majority must therefore winter north of Morocco. Up to 18 000 Kentish Plovers (18% of the east Atlantic wintering population) wintered in the Banc d'Arguin in Mauretania (Engelmoer *et al.*, 1984) and an additional 3000 along the Atlantic coast of Morocco, with between 2000 and 3000 in the Merja Zerga alone (Kersten & Smit, 1984). The Iberian wintering population is estimated as 6800 (85% of the west European wintering population) (Alberto & Velasco, 1988), Cádiz Bay being an important nucleus with a wintering population of over 1800 (Grimmett & Jones, 1989). There were an estimated 1000 along specific points on the Cádiz coast in the 1978 winter, with an additional density of 5–6 birds per kilometre of beach (Telleria, 1981). It seems likely, therefore, that the wintering population of Kentish Plovers along the Atlantic coasts of the Strait may be of the order of 4000–5000 birds (*c.* 9% of the east Atlantic wintering population).

   There are no specific counts giving an indication of the volume of migration although, if it is assumed that most of the birds that winter along the West African coasts follow the Atlantic coasts of the Strait, the total movement must be large.

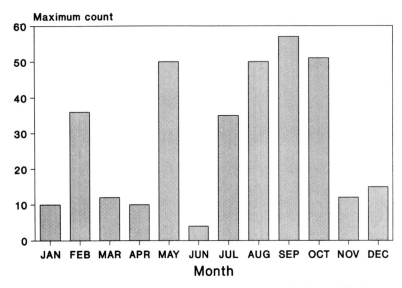

Figure 127.   Maximum Kentish Plover counts at selected Strait wetland sites, 1985–90.

Several authors (Irby, 1895; Pienkowski & Knight, 1977; Telleria, 1981) have commented on the concentrations of migrants which take place in autumn. Figure 127 illustrates this increase in autumn numbers, with counts of 50–60 at specific sites. 150 were recorded at Tarifa Beach on 9 March 1987 (Holliday, 1990a).

The southward passage is centred around September, though birds do occur in unusual locations as from the end of July. Passage continues into October (Figure 127). This pattern is agreed with by other authors (Irby, 1895; Pineau & Giraud-Audine, 1979; Telleria, 1981; Finlayson & Cortés, 1987). The spring passage lasts from March to May (Pineau & Giraud-Audine, 1979; Finlayson & Cortés, 1987), and whereas some have placed the peak in April, passage in substantial numbers continues into May (see Figure 127).

GOLDEN PLOVER

The majority of Golden Plovers reaching Iberia and Morocco in autumn belong to the northern subspecies *albifrons* (Bernis, 1966d), which breeds in Iceland, northern Scandinavia and east to the central USSR (Prater, 1981). A few *albifrons* winter in Britain and western Europe, but most breed in the central and western Mediterranean. Iberian recoveries, mostly in the western half (Portugal, Extremadura and Andalucia), confirm this area of origin, with 23 Icelandic recoveries

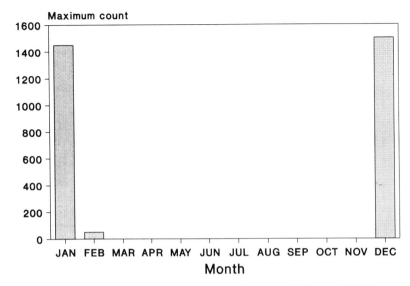

Figure 128. Maximum Golden Plover counts at selected Strait wetland sites, 1985–90.

as well as others from the Faeroes, Scandinavia and western Europe (probably passage and not native birds). Golden Plovers cross the Strait to winter in Morocco (Pineau & Giraud-Audine, 1979) but do not continue further south.

Several authors have remarked on the variability in wintering (and hence also passage) numbers in the Strait between years (Irby, 1875, 1895; Pineau & Giraud-Audine, 1979; Telleria, 1981). A number of sites are well known for this species. The old Laguna de La Janda attracts large numbers of Golden Plovers in winter with flocks of up to 5000 some winters (Holliday, 1990a), and appears to be a traditional wintering site (Irby, 1895). On the Moroccan side of the Strait a similar number have been recorded in the plaine de Bougdour in January (Pineau & Giraud-Audine, 1979). Blondel & Blondel (1964) estimated up to 17 000 wintering in northwest Morocco, up to 10 000 in the Merja Zerga. Given these estimates a wintering population of 20 000–25 000 on the two shores of the Strait would not seem unduly unrealistic for those winters when there are influxes of Golden Plovers, although the size of the wintering population is probably lower most years. The Strait could therefore account for up to 2.5% of the western European wintering population of Golden Plovers (Prater, 1981).

Golden Plovers arrive at the end of October and the last birds leave in early April (Finlayson & Cortés, 1987). The majority, however, do not arrive until November and have departed by February (Figure 128). This pattern of late arrival and early departure had also been noted by Irby (1895) and Pineau & Giraud-Audine (1979).

GREY PLOVER

The Grey Plover is essentially a breeding species of the Siberian tundra and migrates southwest or west/southwest in autumn, passing over much of northern and western Europe to winter on the Atlantic coasts of Europe and Africa. This southwest migration is well illustrated by birds ringed on passage in Norway and subsequently recovered in Denmark, France, Morocco and Senegal (Bernis, 1966d). Bernis (1966d) also cites the case of a bird ringed on passage in central Sweden and recovered in Ghana and of another ringed on passage in Denmark and recovered in Togo. There are four recoveries for southern Spain, of birds ringed on passage in Denmark, Finland, Holland and Britain (Telleria, 1981).

The wintering area of the Grey Plover stretches over much of the eastern Atlantic seaboard, from Scotland to South Africa (Prater, 1981). It is a fairly common winter visitor to coastal West Africa, from the Cape Verde Islands and Senegal to Congo (Serle *et al.*, 1977). Further north, up to 24 000 winter in the Banc d'Arguin, constituting 13% of the eastern Atlantic wintering population (Engelmoer *et al.*, 1984). Around 6000 winter in Morocco (Kersten & Smit, 1984); counts at Merja Zerga alone have been close to 10 000 (Blondel & Blondel, 1984), though 2000 is likely to be an average figure at this site (Kersten & Smit, 1984). Alberto & Velasco (1988) have estimated the Spanish wintering population at 5800 (10.7% of the European wintering element), with concentrations in Cádiz Bay and the Marismas del Guadalquivir. The Strait is therefore an important area for passage Grey Plovers wintering in West Africa and Morocco and retains a proportion of these birds in winter.

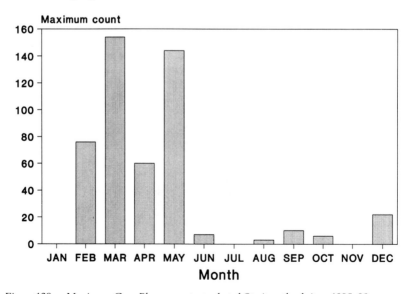

Figure 129.   Maximum Grey Plover counts at selected Strait wetland sites, 1985–90.

Concentrations of up to 150 Grey Plovers are regular during the spring migration, but autumn counts are usually lower (Figure 129). Flocks in Cádiz Bay and the Guadalquivir can be higher. Holliday (1990a) reported 1000 in the Bonanza saltpans on 26 April 1987, and I saw a very large roosting movement in the Trebujena marsh at dusk on 5 May 1990, a movement that involved at least 2000 Grey Plovers, passing in flocks of 30–40 and settling in the open fields inland. Grey Plovers are also widely distributed on the Moroccan coast, with groups of up to 400 birds at favoured sites (e.g. the Loukos Estuary) (Pineau & Giraud-Audine, 1979).

The spring passage commences in March and peaks during the second half of April and early May, continuing into early June (Pineau & Giraud-Audine, 1979; Finlayson & Cortés, 1987). The southward migration begins in mid-August and ends in early November, most birds passing during October (Pineau & Giraud-Audine, 1979; Telleria, 1981; Finlayson & Cortés, 1987).

LAPWING

The Iberian Peninsula is one of the main wintering areas of the Lapwing in the Palaearctic, and northwest Africa receives an overspill from this population (Bernis, 1966d). The general autumn migratory trend appears to be southwest with the exception of British Birds which move south/southeast, and this is borne out by recoveries. Bernis (1966d) stated that Iberian wintering Lapwings included many Russian birds and probably some from Siberia. He found that Scandinavian Lapwings also migrated southwest to winter in Iberia and north-west Africa, this trend being more pronounced in Finnish Lapwings than in Norwegian or Swedish ones, which also wintered in Ireland, Britain and France. The general spectrum of recoveries for Iberia (Figure 130) bears out this trend,

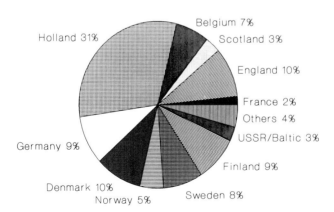

Figure 130. Lapwing recoveries in Iberia. Others: Poland, Czechoslovakia, Switzerland, Italy and Hungary. After Bernis (1966d). N = 956.

and Cádiz province was the third highest Spanish province for recoveries, which derived from a variety of countries including Britain, Holland, Belgium and the Scandinavian nations. North Africa marks the southern limit of the Lapwing's winter range, and it does not cross the Sahara Desert. Moroccan recoveries conform with the pattern described (Pineau & Giraud-Audine, 1979).

Lapwings are abundant winter visitors to the area but, like the Golden Plovers, vary greatly in number between years. In some years, large influxes (which appear related to cold weather in central Europe) occur in winter, when heavy passage takes place into Morocco. Blondel & Blondel's (1964) counts of 40 000–50 000 Lapwings in the Merja Zerga in January 1964 are an example of this, the usual wintering population at this site being under 5000 (Kersten & Smit, 1984). Junco (1966) reported such an influx in November 1965, when he recorded a quarter of a million Lapwings between the Marismas del Guadalquivir and Jerez; 15 000 were counted over the Rock of Gibraltar (not a usual site for this species) in a week in December of the same year (Cortés *et al.*, 1980). On such occasions flocks of Lapwings cross the Strait, usually flying low over the waves, throughout the day.

The first Lapwings arrive during October, the main arrivals in November. In harsh winters birds continue to arrive from the north during December and January. The departure north commences in February, and very few birds remain into mid-April (Pineau & Giraud-Audine, 1979; Finlayson & Cortés, 1987).

It can be seen, then, that the total number of Lapwings crossing the Strait varies substantially between years; migration as such is never conspicuous. As with the Golden Plover, the movements take the form of arrivals for the winter and departures at the end of the winter.

KNOT

The majority of Knots that migrate via the Iberian Peninsula and Morocco are Siberian, following a great circle route to wintering grounds in West Africa (Dick *et al.*, 1976; Hale, 1980). Those from Greenland and northeast Canada winter in Britain (Prater, 1981), some reaching the Iberian Peninsula (Bernis, 1966d). The main wintering areas of Knot are Britain (which supports 65% of the wintering European and northwest African population), Holland, France and Mauretania (Prater, 1976, 1981). Estimates of the wintering Knot population in the Banc d'Arguin, Mauretania, vary from 130 000 (Knight & Dick, 1975) to 367 000 (Kersten & Smit, 1984), which would account for up to 47% of the Knot wintering in the eastern Atlantic. The Iberian Peninsula holds only around 0.1% of the western European wintering Knot population (Alberto & Velasco, 1988).

Knot are scarce migrants in the Strait, rarely occurring in the large flocks that characterize the species elsewhere. Small groups, rarely exceeding 5 birds, are the rule. Telleria (1981) found them in small groups on autumn passage at Tarifa Beach where they were regular, with the largest number being 20 birds. On the Moroccan side, Pineau & Giraud-Audine (1979) found them on passage in small groups, although flocks of up to 200 were recorded in spring. This relative scarcity in a species that winters in large numbers to the southwest of the Strait is difficult to explain. Since the birds are essentially Siberian in origin, it may well be that they miss the Strait by following a great circle route or that they overfly it, having fattened to the north in autumn and to the south in spring. This is borne out by the paucity of ringing recoveries in Iberia: Bernis (1966d) cited only eight recoveries, of birds ringed on passage in south Norway (5), south Sweden (1), Iceland (1) and England (1).

Very few winter in the Strait. Telleria (1981) only found a group of 8 along the Cádiz coast in January 1978. The species is not regarded as wintering in northern Morocco (Pineau & Giraud-Audine, 1979), and the wintering population in the Merja Zerga is small, under 100 birds (Kersten & Smit, 1984).

Knots are late migrants in spring, mostly in May, with the first birds moving north in mid–March and the last in early June (Pineau & Giraud-Audine, 1979; Finlayson & Cortés, 1987). The southward passage lasts from mid–August to November, mostly in September (Pineau & Giraud-Audine, 1979; Finlayson & Cortés, 1987).

SANDERLING

The Sanderlings of the Siberian tundra migrate southwest in autumn, following the Atlantic coasts of Europe (where some remain to winter) down to northwest, west and southern Africa. Birds from the Greenland populations have been recovered in Britain, so that some at least winter along the European Atlantic coast. In West Africa, Sanderlings are fairly common winter visitors and passage migrants from Senegal to Gabon and Congo and the Cape Verde Islands (Serle *et al.*, 1977). Further north, up to 34 000 winter in the Banc d'Arguin, Mauretania, (11% of the east Atlantic wintering population). The number wintering in Morocco is estimated at 1500 (Kersten & Smit, 1984), but, as indicated by this figure may be an underestimate (Pienkowski & Knight, 1977) due to the inadequate sampling that arises from Sanderlings being widely distributed in small flocks along many kilometres of sandy beach. Pineau & Giraud-Audine (1979) found flocks of up to 60 birds well distributed along the northwest Moroccan coast. The pattern is similar along the Spanish Atlantic coast of the Strait, where Telleria (1981) found Sanderlings to be the most abundant waders on sandy beaches, with an average density of 7 birds per kilometre of beach and an additional 600 in favoured localities in January 1978. Tarifa Beach is an important wintering site with up to 400 Sanderlings in midwinter (Finlayson & Cortés, 1987), over 1.5% of the west European wintering population (Alberto & Velasco, 1988). These are rather high figures in view of the estimated Iberian wintering population of 2100 Sanderlings (8.8% of the west European wintering population) (Alberto & Velasco, 1988).

Most of the Sanderlings that pass or winter in the Strait must be Siberian. Sanderlings ringed on passage in Norway have been subsequently recovered in

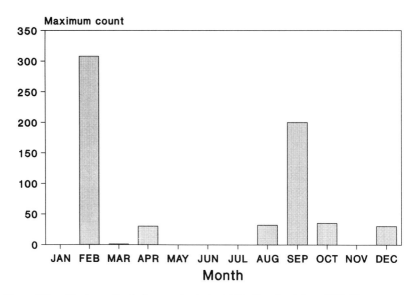

Figure 131.   Maximum Sanderling counts at selected Strait wetland sites, 1985–90.

western Europe, Morocco and (one) Senegal (Bernis, 1966d). Two winter recoveries of Sanderlings ringed on passage in Britain (Telleria, 1981) indicate that it is possible that a few Greenland Sanderlings may also be involved.

The scale of the migration of Sanderlings is difficult to determine as passage birds may be overlooked in wintering sites and flocks are likely to be more widely distributed along beaches than is the case for other waders, which have more restricted habitat preferences. Flocks of 200–300 Sanderlings occur on passage at many coastal and inland sites, suggesting a large and widely spread migration.

The northward passage starts in March and continues into May, with the return migration starting in August, with a peak in September, and continuing into early November (Pineau & Giraud-Audine, 1979; Telleria, 1981; Finlayson & Cortés, 1987; Figure 131).

LITTLE STINT

Little Stints breed in the High Arctic Tundra from 20 to 130°E. In winter they are widely distributed in Africa and southwest Asia. The western populations migrate southwest in autumn, passing regularly along the western European coasts, with small numbers remaining to winter in Britain and France (Prater, 1981). Little Stints ringed in England (2), northwest Germany (1), south Norway (2) and south Finland (2) have been recovered during autumn passage and winter and Swedish brids have been recovered in France (Bernis, 1966d).

1400 Little Stints winter in Iberia, constituting 70% of the west European

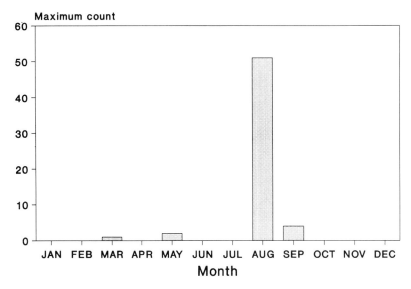

Figure 132.   Maximum Little Stint counts at selected Strait wetland sites, 1985–90.

wintering population (Alberto & Velasco, 1988), a relatively small number in comparison with the larger numbers that winter in Africa. The Little Stints which pass the Iberian Peninsula continue southwest towards Morocco and Mauretania via the Atlantic coastal areas of the Strait. Relatively few winter in Morocco (wintering population estimated at 1000 birds), being more abundant in the south (Kersten & Smit, 1984) than closer to the Strait (Pineau & Giraud-Audine, 1979). The majority winter in the Banc d'Arguin, Mauretania, where the population has been estimated as up to 44 000 in winter (21% of the Little Stints wintering along the east Atlantic seaboard) (Engelmoer *et al.*, 1984). Others continue further down the Atlantic coasts of Africa (an estimated 150 000 wintering along the Atlantic African coast—Engelmoer *et al.*, 1984), being a common and widespread passage migrant and winter visitor from The Gambia and Senegal east to Chad and south to Gabon and Congo (Serle *et al.*, 1977).

Little Stints are not abundant on passage in the Strait, although they are regularly found in many coastal and inland sites. They are more abundant in autumn than spring, occurring in concentrations of up to 50 birds. Very few winter on the Spanish side of the Strait, but they appear more abundant on the Moroccan side where wintering flocks of up to 60 birds have been found around Larache and Oualad Khallouf (Pineau & Giraud-Audine, 1979).

Spring passage commences in March and continues into mid-June, peaking in April. The southward passage, which is more conspicuous, commences during late July and continues into October, peak passage occurring in late August and early September (Pineau & Giraud-Audine, 1979; Telleria, 1981; Finlayson & Cortés, 1987; Figure 132).

CURLEW SANDPIPER

Curlew Sandpipers breed in the Siberian High Arctic and winter in Africa, India and Australasia. The westernmost populations migrate southwest via western Europe in autumn towards major wintering grounds along the Atlantic coasts of Africa. Those wintering in South Africa probably avoid western Europe by flying a great circle route (Hale, 1980). The Curlew Sandpipers that migrate across the Strait therefore most probably originate from the western Siberian breeding populations and winter in West Africa. Bernis (1966d) gives two south Swedish and one Danish Curlew Sandpiper, ringed on passage, recovered in Iberia and another Swedish bird recovered in Morocco.

Curlew Sandpipers do not winter on either shore of the Strait (Pineau & Giraud-Audine, 1979; Finlayson & Cortés, 1987). Further south, small numbers winter in favoured localities (e.g. Merja Zerga), but the Moroccan wintering population is very small (Kersten & Smit, 1984). Major concentrations occur in the Banc d'Arguin, Mauretania, where the total wintering population is up to 174 000 (39% of the east Atlantic wintering population) of the 400 000 wintering along the Atlantic coasts of Africa (Engelmoer et al., 1984). To the south of Mauretania, the Curlew Sandpiper is a well distributed species along the coast from Senegal to Gabon (Serle et al., 1977).

Curlew Sandpipers on passage along the Moroccan side of the Strait are usually recorded in small groups of 10 or 15, exceptionally 30 (Pineau & Giraud-Audine, 1979). On the European shore, they are more abundant, with concentrations of 200 or 300 birds being regular and, occasionally, gatherings of up to 1000 birds in the Cádiz saltpans. Although generally regarded as more common in autumn

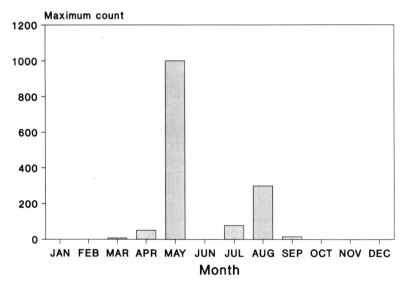

Figure 133.   Maximum Curlew Sandpiper counts at selected Strait wetland sites, 1985–90.

than in spring in western Europe, very large concentrations along the Spanish Atlantic coast in May indicate that West African birds may use this area for refuelling before continuing their migration northeast to the breeding grounds.

The Curlew Sandpiper is strictly a passage migrant with a short, well-defined, passage. In spring, the migration commences in mid-April and continues until early June, with a sharp peak in May. In autumn the passage starts in July and ends in October (exceptionally November), most passing south in August and September (Pineau & Giraud-Audine, 1979; Finlayson & Cortés, 1987; Figure 133).

DUNLIN

Three subspecies are likely to be involved in migratory movements in the area of the Strait. The nominate *alpina*, which breeds in northern Scandinavia and the USSR, winters in the British Isles and as far south as Morocco. Morocco and Mauretania hold the main wintering grounds of two other subspecies, *arctica* from northeastern Greenland and *schinzii* from Britain, southeast Greenland, Iceland, The Netherlands and the Baltic (e.g. see Prater, 1981). These origins and the areas covered on passage are confirmed by Spanish and Moroccan recoveries, which include birds ringed in Sweden, Norway, Denmark, Finland, Iceland, Great Britain, Ireland and Switzerland (Bernis, 1966d). Scottish and Swedish Dunlins have been recovered in Mauretania and an English Dunlin in the former Spanish Sahara (Bernis, 1966d). Most recoveries are coastal, with relatively few along the Mediterranean coasts compared with the Atlantic coasts.

Many Dunlins migrate past Iberia into Africa via the Strait. Wintering numbers in Iberia are relatively small, around 28 000 (2.4% of the west European wintering population), Cádiz Bay being an important nucleus (Alberto & Velasco, 1988). 5600 were counted along the Atlantic coast of Cádiz in January 1978 (Telleria, 1981). Larger numbers winter along the Atlantic coast of Morocco, estimated at 40 000 by Kersten & Smit (1984) with around 20 000 in Merja Zerga. Numbers at this site may be far higher however: Blondel & Blondel (1964) estimated between 130 000 and 150 000 Dunlin in Merja Zerga in January 1964. The largest concentrations, presumably where most of the Dunlins which cross the Strait winter, are in Banc d'Arguin, Mauretania (over 800 000, 31% of the east Atlantic wintering population—Engelmoer *et al.*, 1984). Further south, the Dunlin is regarded as an uncommon winter visitor and passage migrant to West Africa (Serle *et al.*, 1977).

The Dunlin is the most abundant passage wader, and migration through the Strait probably involves tens of thousands of birds. During passage periods, concentrations of 200–500 birds are regular in favoured localities, with smaller groups in many other sites (e.g. small estuaries, beaches, etc.).

The spring passage lasts from mid-March to early June with a peak during April, and the southward migration commences in August and ends in early November with a peak in September (Pineau & Giraud-Audine, 1979; Telleria, 1981; Finlayson & Cortés, 1987; Figure 134).

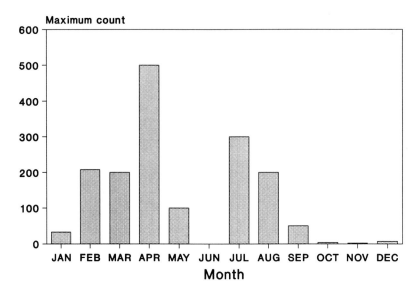

Figure 134.   Maximum Dunlin counts at selected Strait wetland sites, 1985–90.

RUFF

Ruffs breed over much of northern Europe and east across the USSR, with small populations in Britain, France and Holland. Although some Ruffs winter in Asia, the majority winter in Africa and many birds from the eastern USSR probably migrate west of south across western Europe before entering Africa. Moreau (1972) considered that the numbers of Ruffs wintering in West Africa were too great to be derived only from breeding populations due north and northeast, concluding that many Ruffs from the Asiatic USSR wintered in West Africa, birds from as far east as 145°E having been recovered on passage in Holland. Ruffs ringed in Sweden, Denmark, Holland, Germany and Finland have also been recovered in Mauretania, Senegal, Mali and Niger (Bernis, 1966d; Moreau, 1972).

It is likely, then, that Ruffs migrating across the Strait may be derived from northern and eastern populations. Iberian recoveries include Ruffs ringed in Scotland, Belgium, Holland, Germany, Denmark, Sweden and Finland (Bernis, 1966d). The majority winter in tropical West Africa where they are very common in the flooded plains, marshes and rice fields in Senegal, Mali, Niger, northern Nigeria and Chad (Moreau, 1972; Serle *et al.*, 1977). In comparison to these large numbers (estimated at over one million) (Prater, 1976), only 2500 are thought to winter in western Europe, 1300 (52%) of these in Iberia (Alberto & Velasco, 1988). To these can be added around 500 wintering in Morocco (Kersten & Smit, 1984), mostly south of the Strait. Only small numbers winter on the

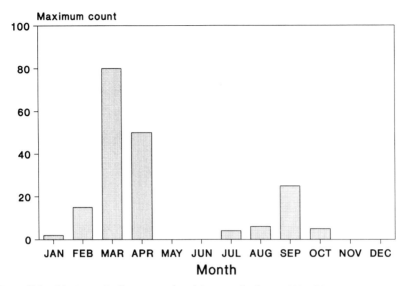

Figure 135.   Maximum Ruff counts at selected Strait wetland sites, 1985–90.

Moroccan side of the Strait, with the exception of 300–350 in the Larache saltpans in December 1974 (Pineau & Giraud-Audine, 1979).

Ruffs occur on passage in the Strait in small parties. Usually the largest passage concentrations are of 50–80 birds at any specific site. Some authors (Smith, 1965; Pineau & Giraud-Audine, 1979; Telleria, 1981) have suggested that, in autumn, many Ruffs may overfly the Strait direct into the African wintering grounds. The return route in spring is further east (e.g. see Mead, 1983).

The spring migration commences in February and continues until May, and the return passage south starts in July and ends in November (Finlayson & Cortés, 1987). The main passage months are March, April and September (Figure 135).

Snipe

The Snipe breeds over large areas of the central and northern Holarctic. The wintering grounds of Palaearctic Snipes include western Europe and northern tropical Africa. Palaearctic Snipes migrate southwest and west/southwest in autumn, birds from eastern parts of the breeding range wintering well to the west. Bernis (1966d) and Pineau & Giraud-Audine (1979) list Iberian and Moroccan recoveries of Snipe, which confirm this movement (Figure 136). Subsequently, Fernandez-Cruz (1982) reported a Snipe ringed near Madrid (40°18′N, 03°44′W) in winter and recovered a subsequent summer at Lake Ilmen,

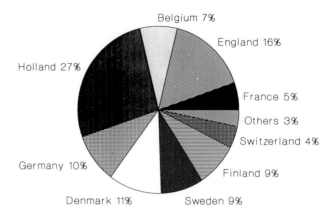

Figure 136.   Snipe recoveries in Iberia. Others: Iceland, Czechoslovakia and Poland. After Bernis (1966d). N = 94.

USSR (58°49'N, 31°27'E), 3150 km to the northeast, and two other recoveries of birds from the USSR, including one from Smolensk recovered near Ronda in midwinter.

This species does not frequent the open coastal areas utilized by other waders but instead prefers marshes. For this reason it does not feature in coastal wader counts, and its numbers are more difficult to census. The Iberian Peninsula and Morocco are nevertheless important wintering grounds, and many Snipe occur

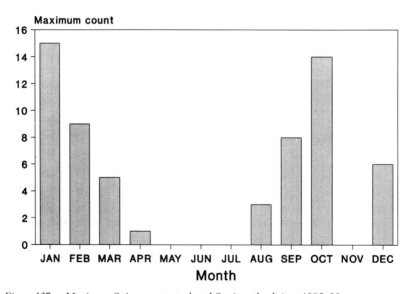

Figure 137.   Maximum Snipe counts at selected Strait wetland sites, 1985–90.

on passage in the Strait. These probably winter mainly in Morocco, where they are abundant in winter (Pineau & Giraud-Audine, 1979). The northern shore of the Strait was probably of greater importance to wintering Snipe in the past, before suitable marshlands were drained. It was an extremely abundant species in the area of La Janda in the western Strait in the late 19th and early 20th Centuries (Irby, 1875, 1895; Verner, 1910). Smaller numbers still winter in the flooded fields around the old lagoon. The Snipe is also a winter visitor to tropical West Africa, where it is widely but unevenly distributed from Senegal and The Gambia in the west to Chad and Cameroon in the east (Moreau, 1972; Serle *et al.*, 1977).

It is even more difficult to give precise information on Snipe numbers than it is for other waders. Generally, they occur in small groups, 10–15 birds being the rule in most sites and occasionally up to 30 (Holliday, 1990a). These numbers reflect the substantial reduction during the 20th Century.

The northward migration commences in mid–February and ends towards the end of April, with a peak in March; the return passage lasts from late August to early November with a peak in October (Pineau & Giraud-Audine, 1979; Finlayson & Cortés, 1987; Figure 137).

BLACK-TAILED GODWIT

Black-tailed Godwits breed in Iceland (subspecies *islandica*) and in western and central Europe, eastwards almost to Lake Baikal (subspecies *limosa*). The Icelandic subspecies winters in Atlantic Europe and northwest Africa (Prater, 1975), and the nominate subspecies winters south of the Sahara (Moreau, 1972). The precise boundaries of the wintering ranges of the two subspecies are uncertain. Thus, Pineau & Giraud-Audine (1979) concluded that recoveries of ringed birds indicate the Moroccan wintering population to be dominated by Dutch birds, so that perhaps only a minority *islandica* reach North Africa. If this is so, then the wintering population on the northern shore of the Strait may include an element of *limosa* (at the northern end of their wintering range) and another of *islandica* (at the southern end of their wintering range). The dominant passage birds across the Strait must be of the nominate subspecies on their way to and from the African wintering areas (Figure 138), and the timing of their passage supports this view. Spanish recoveries are essentially of Dutch birds with a few Belgian, German, Danish and south Swedish (Bernis, 1966d; Telleria, 1981). Most of these recoveries are of passage birds, but do also include some in winter, confirming the presence of *limosa* wintering in southern Spain.

Black-tailed Godwits winter in Morocco, where the wintering population is estimated at 15 000 (Kersten & Smit, 1984), although, as with some other waders, numbers can be much higher (probably in relation to weather conditions in Europe). An example of this is the estimate of 80 000–120 000 in the Merja Zerga alone in January 1964 (Blondel & Blondel, 1964), whereas this site holds 4000–10 000 at other times in winter (Kersten & Smit, 1984). In West Africa, the Black-tailed Godwit is a common winter visitor from Senegal, through Mali, Niger and

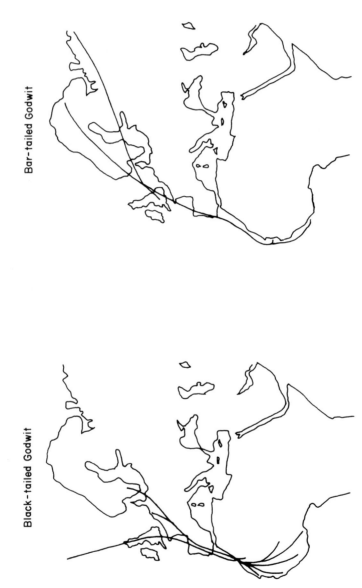

Black-tailed Godwit

Bar-tailed Godwit

Figure 138. Southward migratory routes followed by Black-tailed and Bar-tailed Godwits passing the Strait, 1985–90.

northern Nigeria, being more common along inundated areas inland than on the coast (Serle *et al.*, 1977). 11 000 winter in Senegal and around 100 000 in the Niger Inundation Zone (Roux, 1973). These large numbers in western and north-western Africa indicate that many Black-tailed Godwits from east of the Baltic must migrate southwest to winter there alongside European ones. Dutch and Danish birds have been recovered in Senegal (Moreau, 1972).

On the Spanish side of the Strait, the Black-tailed Godwit is more abundant in winter than previously recognized, and this may be due in part to the expansion of the Icelandic population (Prater, 1975). About 21 600 winter in Iberia (38.6% of the west European wintering population) with major wintering sites in Cádiz Bay and the Marismas del Guadalquivir (Alberto & Velasco, 1988). Along the coast of Cádiz, 6000 Black-tailed Godwits were counted in January 1978 and over 4000 in Cádiz Bay (Telleria, 1981).

Black-tailed Godwits occur in large concentrations during the southward passage in favoured sites, for example the Bonanza saltpans where up to 4000 have been counted. The autumn migration is more pronounced with smaller groups appearing in spring.

The southward passage commences early, with large numbers in late June and July and passage continuing in August and September, very few birds passing in October. This early movement coincides with the departure from continental breeding sites (e.g. see Prater, 1981). The northward passage commences during February, with the main passage in March continuing into mid-April and occasionally May (Pineau & Giraud-Audine, 1979; Finlayson & Cortés, 1987; Figure 139). Small numbers summer in the area.

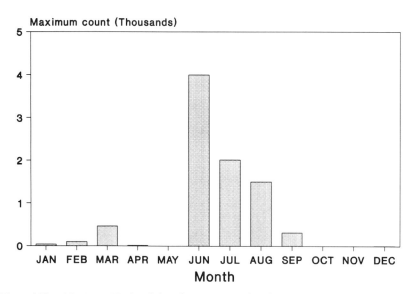

Figure 139. Maximum Black-tailed Godwit counts at selected Strait wetland sites.

Bar-tailed Godwit

The Bar-tailed Godwit breeds north of the Black-tailed Godwit, from Scandinavia in the west, across the USSR to northwest Alaska. The nominate subspecies breeds in Scandinavia and the western USSR and migrates across Europe. Bar-tailed Godwits winter along the Atlantic coasts of Europe and Africa. There are two main wintering nuclei (Prater, 1976, 1981), the British Isles with a population in excess of 58 000 and the Banc d'Arguin, Mauretania, with a population of 210 000. A more recent estimate of the wintering population in the Banc d'Arguin (based on new counts) is up to 543 000, or 77% of the east Atlantic wintering population (Engelmoer *et al.*, 1984).

To the north, a smaller population winters in Morocco and Spain. The Spanish wintering population is of the order of 1700 (1.4% of the west European wintering population) and the Moroccan population was estimated at over 5000 by Prater (1981) and at 3000 by Kersten & Smit (1984). The numbers wintering on either side of the Strait are relatively small in comparison to numbers in Mauretania. Bar-tailed Godwits winter on the Moroccan side of the Strait in small groups not exceeding 30 birds (Pineau & Giraud-Audine, 1979) and only 160 were counted along the entire Cádiz coast in January 1978 (Telleria, 1981). To the south of the Banc d'Arguin, Bar-tailed Godwits occur in winter on the coast from Senegal to Nigeria but are uncommon (Serle *et al.*, 1977).

Bar-tailed Godwits passing the Strait therefore come from breeding grounds in Scandinavia and the western USSR, and most continue south to winter in the Banc d'Arguin, smaller numbers continuing to West Africa or remaining in Morocco (Figure 140). This is borne out by ringing recoveries. Bernis (1966d)

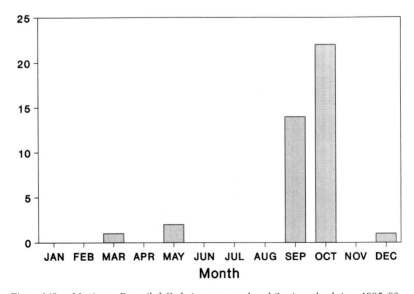

Figure 140.   Maximum Bar-tailed Godwit counts at selected Strait wetland sites, 1985–90.

commented that Scandinavian Bar-tailed Godwits show a marked southwesterly movement in autumn, following the coasts of Great Britain, Atlantic France and Iberia. This author cited the recovery of a Norwegian bird in Senegal, of a Swedish and a Norwegian bird in Morocco and of two Norwegian birds in Iberia. Since Scandinavian-ringed birds have been recovered in Russia and southwest Siberia, it seems more than likely that birds from the Soviet Union reach Iberia and cross the Strait.

Telleria (1981) considered this bird to be more numerous than the Black-tailed Godwit on passage through the Strait, but this may have been a reflection of the sites regularly censused by him. Although a regular migrant, the Bar-tailed Godwit does not form the large concentrations of the Black-tailed Godwit, groups of 20 being typical of the autumn passage.

The spring migration lasts from February to early June, with peak passage in March, and the return migration lasts from August to October, peaking in September and early October (Pineau & Giraud-Audine, 1979; Telleria, 1981; Finlayson & Cortés, 1987; Figure 140).

WHIMBREL

The Whimbrel has a circumpolar breeding distribution. The nominate subspecies breeds in Iceland and east to the western USSR. From there eastwards it is replaced by the subspecies *variegatus* and by *hudsonicus* in Canada. The subspecies *phaeopus* migrates southwest across western Europe in autumn to the main wintering grounds in West Africa (Prater, 1981): ringing recoveries include a Scottish bird in Ghana, a bird ringed on passage in England in Nigeria, two Icelandic birds in Senegal, a Dutch passage bird in Sierra Leone and a Danish passage bird in Togo (Bernis, 1966d). Birds from well east migrate through western Europe. Prater (1981) gave recoveries of Whimbrels ringed on passage in Britain in Finland and USSR. Icelandic Whimbrels migrate south via Britain, the French Atlantic coast and the Iberian Peninsula (Bernis, 1966d): Iberian recoveries of two Icelandic and one Lapp Whimbrel has been made (Bernis, 1966d).

Very few Whimbrels winter in western Europe, virtually all of those that do in the Iberian Peninsula, where the estimated total population is *c.* 300 (Alberto & Velasco, 1988). Only eight were counted along the entire Cádiz coast in January 1978 (Telleria, 1981). Small numbers also winter along the Moroccan coast, for example up to 20 in the Merja Zerga (Kersten & Smit, 1984). The number wintering in the Strait is therefore small and the majority occurring on passage must proceed further south in autumn. According to Engelmoer *et al.* (1984), 50 000 Whimbrel winter along the Atlantic African coasts of which up to 15 600 do so in the Banc d'Arguin, Mauretania. The remainder winter down to the Cape, with many along the West African coast, widely distributed along coastal areas from Senegal to Congo (Serle *et al.*, 1977).

Whimbrels occur on both rocky and sandy shores and along estuaries and saltpans on passage through the Strait. Counting is therefore very difficult,

A migrant Whimbrel actively searching for food while on passage on the rocky shores of the Strait near Europa Point.

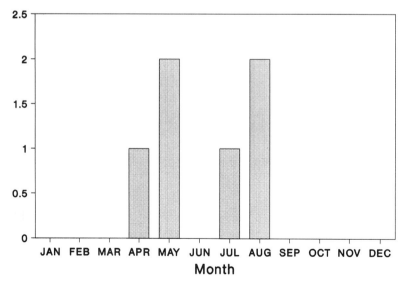

Figure 141.   Maximum Whimbrel counts at selected Strait wetland sites, 1985–90.

especially as the species travels singly or in small groups. Consequently, it is not possible to estimate the size of the passage population, which must nevertheless be large because the Whimbrel is one of the most common and widely distributed waders in the Strait, especially in autumn, and because the Strait is within the passage route from breeding grounds to wintering grounds.

The northward passage takes place during March, April and May (occasionally early June) and is not very pronounced, the main migration lines probably being to the east of the Strait at this time. The autumn passage commences early, in July, with peak movements in August and a continued passage into early November (Pineau & Giraud-Audine, 1979; Telleria, 1981; Finlayson & Cortés, 1987; Figure 141). Summering birds are regular in the Strait.

CURLEW

The Curlew breeds across the Palaearctic, generally south of the Whimbrel, from Ireland in the west to the eastern USSR. The nominate subspecies, which breeds west of the Urals, winters in western Europe, with smaller numbers down to Morocco and Mauretania (Prater, 1976). Curlews crossing the Strait or reaching it for the winter come from the greater part of the continental range, but British Curlews only reach the north of Iberia (Bainbridge & Minton, 1978). The following are the recoveries for Iberia: England (3), Belgium (10), Holland (12), Germany (10), Denmark (1), Sweden (1), Finland (12) and Austria (1) (Bernis, 1966d). This Austrian bird was ringed as young in May and recovered in Cádiz in October. Telleria (1981) illustrated the early movement southwest: a Curlew ringed as a chick in Germany in late June was recovered in San Fernando, Cádiz, at the end of August of the same year. Most of these recoveries were of passage or wintering birds along the west coast of Iberia. Birds from the USSR are likely to reach Iberia and the Strait. Bernis (1966d) gave the case of a Belgian-ringed Curlew recovered in northwest Russia and of a French ringed bird recovered in Estonia. Bainbridge & Minton (1978) gave an Irish recovery of a Russian-ringed Curlew.

Up to 125 000 Curlews of the estimated 200 000 in western Europe winter in Britain (Prater, 1981). More recently, the wintering western European population has been estimated at 317 000 of which only 3200 (1%) winter in Iberia, concentrating mainly in Cádiz Bay and the Huelva marshes (Alberto & Velasco, 1988). Kersten & Smit (1984) estimated 1500 wintering in Morocco with up to 300 in the Merja Zerga. The Banc d'Arguin holds a further concentration, up to 14 200, which is relatively small (3% of the east Atlantic wintering population) in comparison with wintering numbers in western Europe (Engelmoer *et al.*, 1984). Other Curlews reach tropical West Africa, where they are found in coastal areas from Senegal to the Congo but are outnumbered by Whimbrels (Serle *et al.*, 1977).

Curlews generally occur singly or in small flocks and are not confined to coastal areas, being found in flooded meadows and pastures in winter. Concen-

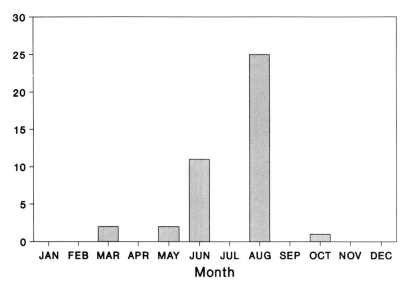

Figure 142.   Maximum Curlew counts at selected Strait wetland sites, 1985–90.

trations of 20–30 birds have been recorded on passage on the northern shore, with up to 150 in July at Larache, Morocco (Pineau & Giraud-Audine, 1979).

The spring passage takes place in March and April, with an early return movement south commencing in late July and continuing until October (Pineau & Giraud-Audine, 1979; Finlayson & Cortés, 1987; Figure 142). Summering birds are regular on both sides of the Strait.

SPOTTED REDSHANK

Spotted Redshanks breed from northern Scandinavia east across the USSR in the boreal belt. They winter in the northern tropics of Africa, with major concentrations off West Africa, some reaching the Cape (Prater, 1981). Small numbers winter in western Europe and North Africa. The wintering population in Iberia is insignificant, and only isolated individuals occur within the Strait area in winter. 25 000 of the 27 200 Spotted Redshanks wintering along the eastern Atlantic coasts do so in Africa. Only 400 winter in Morocco on average (Kersten & Smit, 1984) although up to 500 may do so in the Merja Zerga alone (Zwarts, 1972). Around 200 winter in Larache (Kersten & Smit, 1984), with maximum winter counts sometimes reaching 400 (Pineau & Giraud-Audine, 1979). Scattered birds winter in other sites along the Moroccan shore of the Strait. The bulk of the wintering population is, therefore, in West Africa, where it is found from Senegal to the Congo (Serle *et al.*, 1977), with a concentration in Ghana (Grimes, 1969).

The Spotted Redshanks that cross the Strait are probably mostly bound for

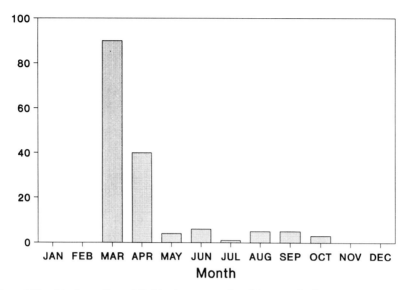

Figure 143. Maximum Spotted Redshank counts at selected Strait wetland sites, 1985–90.

these West African wintering grounds and come from the westernmost parts of the breeding range, in Scandinavia and the western USSR. Bernis (1966d) pointed to a general southwest migration in autumn, some moving through Scandinavia and down the Atlantic coast of France, Iberia and Morocco, with others following a more eastern route via Italy and Tunisia. This author gave two Iberian recoveries, of birds ringed on passage in Belgium and Denmark.

Spotted Redshanks are common and, in certain sites, abundant passage migrants occurring in flocks of up to 150 birds (Pineau & Giraud-Audine, 1979). Atlantic coastal sites (e.g. Larache and Bonanza) are favoured, and the spring passage appears to be more pronounced than the autumn passage (Figure 143). It is likely that many West African wintering birds follow the Atlantic coasts of Morocco and Iberia on passage.

The spring passage starts in March and continues into May, with the return starting in July and continuing until October (Finlayson & Cortés, 1987; Figure 143). Groups recorded in late June (Holliday, 1990a) may be summering or, alternatively, early southbound migrants.

REDSHANK

Redshanks breed from Iceland, Ireland and Iberia in the west, across much of the central Palaearctic east to the Pacific coast. The nominate subspecies breeds in western Europe and is replaced by the larger *robusta* in Iceland and Faeroes. In Europe there are many intermediate, hybrid, populations (Hale, 1971). Different populations of Redshank have distinct winter quarters and those most likely to be involved in movements within the Strait are those from western and northern Europe (Hale, 1973). Redshanks from Denmark, Germany, Holland and Belgium winter southwestwards, reaching the Iberian Peninsula and northern Morocco. Swedish and Norwegian birds exhibit a leap-frog migration, wintering further south, reaching tropical West Africa. British Redshanks reach the Atlantic coasts of Iberia but are unlikely to go as far south as the Strait. However, Redshanks with characteristics of the Icelandic subspecies have been observed on several occasions in Morocco (Pineau & Giraud-Audine, 1979). Analysis of Iberian ringing recoveries confirms this pattern (Bernis, 1966d).

Around 125 000–150 000 Redshanks winter along the coasts of western Europe (Prater, 1976, 1981), of which only 5700 (3.9%) winter in the Iberian Peninsula (Alberto & Velasco, 1988). The province of Cádiz is a major wintering area within Iberia (Bernis, 1966d). An additional 7000 winter in Morocco, between 3000 and 6000 in Merja Zerga (Kersten & Smit, 1984). Redshanks are widely distributed along the shores of the Strait in winter, with concentrations in Cádiz Bay, Barbate and Larache, in addition to Merja Zerga and the Odiel Estuary on the southern and northern fringes of the Strait.

Many of the Redshanks that migrate past the Strait must continue south of Morocco to winter in West Africa. The Banc d'Arguin, Mauretania, holds up to 100 000 of the 200 000 wintering in Atlantic coastal Africa (14% of all the Redshanks wintering in the eastern Atlantic coasts) (Engelmoer *et al.*, 1984). To the south, Redshanks occur on the coast between Senegal and Cameroon as well as inland, and they are local but not uncommon (Serle *et al.*, 1977). Judging from

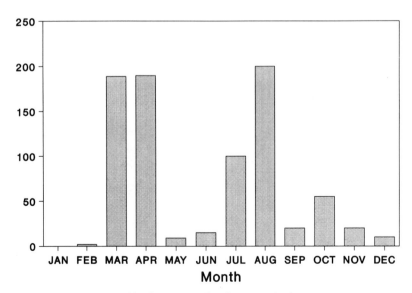

Figure 144.   Maximum Redshank counts at selected Strait wetland sites, 1985–90.

the total number of Redshanks wintering in West Africa, it is likely that birds from east of Scandinavia may also be involved.

The Redshank is one of the most abundant passage waders in the Strait and is found regularly in flocks of up to 200 birds in estuaries and saltpans in particular. The total migratory movement probably involves tens of thousands of birds.

The spring passage starts in March and continues into early May, with an early southward return as from mid-July. The main autumn movements take place in August and September, with significant reductions in numbers by October (Pineau & Giraud-Audine, 1979; Telleria, 1981; Finlayson & Cortés, 1987; Figure 144). Summering birds are regular.

GREENSHANK

The Greenshank breeds from Ireland and northern Scotland in the west, eastwards over the Scandinavian Peninsula and much of the USSR to the Kamchatka Peninsula, occupying a latitudinal belt roughly intermediate between that of the Spotted Redshank to the north and the Redshank to the south, but overlapping widely with both. The wintering range of the western populations covers much of Africa as well as the Mediterranean, Atlantic Iberia and France and Britain.

The main wintering grounds are in Africa, where 45 000 of the 46 600 wintering along the eastern Atlantic coasts are found (Engelmoer *et al.*, 1984). To these must be added an unknown number wintering inland, which is likely to be greater than on the coasts (Moreau, 1972). Only 1500 winter on the Banc d'Arguin, Mauretania, and around 100 in Atlantic Morocco (Kersten & Smit, 1984). Isolated individuals and small groups, not usually exceeding a dozen birds, winter on both shores of the Strait (Pineau & Giraud-Audine, 1979; Finlayson & Cortés, 1987).

The Greenshanks that pass the Strait on migration are therefore bound for the main West African wintering grounds, a small proportion remaining to winter between West Africa and the Strait itself. These birds presumably come from the Scandinavian and, possibly, the western USSR breeding populations. Bernis (1966d) gave three Iberian recoveries of birds ringed on passage in Denmark, two of which were wintering birds (Telleria, 1981), and cited recoveries of Danish-ringed Greenshanks in Mali and northern Congo.

Greenshanks migrate singly or in small groups so that large concentrations are not the rule. Groups of up to 12 birds occur in spring and autumn. The total numbers migrating past the Strait are not as high as for some other *Tringa* species (e.g. the Redshank and Spotted Redshank), and the regular use of inland sites on passage and winter may permit this species to enter West Africa on a relatively broad front. Greenshanks are, nevertheless, not uncommon passage migrants in the Strait.

Greenshanks migrate north from mid-March to early May, and south from late July to October, the peak periods being April, August and early September (Pineau & Giraud-Audine, 1979; Finlayson & Cortés, 1987; Figure 145).

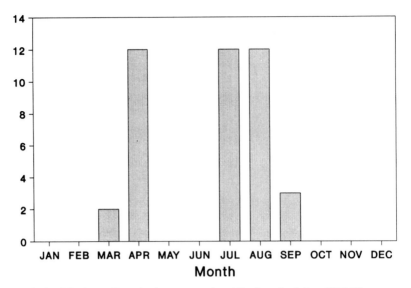

Figure 145.   Maximum Greenshank counts at selected Strait wetland sites, 1985–90.

GREEN SANDPIPER

The Green Sandpiper breeds in a belt from Scandinavia eastwards across the USSR to the Pacific coast, being sympatric with the Greenshank over much of its range. Very few breed in Britain. The wintering grounds are mainly in tropical Africa, some reaching the Cape (Moreau, 1972), with relatively few wintering in the Mediterranean Basin, France and Britain (e.g. Prater, 1981). The solitary habits and inland distribution of this species makes population estimates very difficult. In West Africa, it is common and widespread inland but rare on the coast (Serle *et al.*, 1977).

The Green Sandpipers that migrate through the Strait are probably Scandinavian in origin. Scandinavian birds occur on autumn passage in southern and eastern England (Prater, 1981), and these presumably continue, alongside others migrating over France, towards the Iberian Peninsula. Bernis (1966d) noted a southwest/south-southwest autumn trend in this species and Iberian recoveries support this view: France (2), England (4), Belgium (1), northwest Germany (2), Denmark (2), south Norway (1), south Sweden (3). It is possible that some western USSR birds may also cross Iberia, although the majority probably follow more direct inland routes to Africa.

The difficulty in estimating numbers of inland migrating waders makes it very hard to quantify the volume of Green Sandpiper migration through the Strait. Its frequent and widespread occurrence along streams and canals, however, indicates that substantial numbers pass the area. These migrants are usually solitary

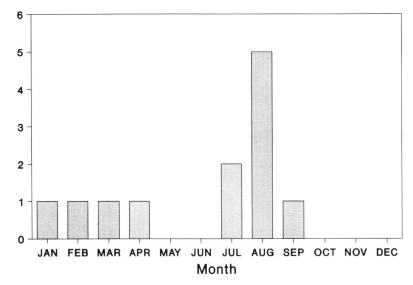

Figure 146.   Maximum Green Sandpiper counts at selected Strait wetland sites, 1985–90.

or in small parties of 4 or 5 birds. Holliday (1990a) recorded 9 at the Laguna de Medina on 29 August 1987.

The northward migration spans the period March to May, and the southward passage commences in mid-July and continues into early November (Finlayson & Cortés, 1987). Late August–early September is the main passage period in autumn (Figure 146).

WOOD SANDPIPER

Wood Sandpipers breed from Scotland and Scandinavia eastwards across the USSR to the Kamchatka Peninsula, occupying a similar geographical area to the Green Sandpiper but extending further north. The western populations winter in tropical Africa, some reaching the Cape. Wood Sandpipers do not winter in Europe. In West Africa it is common on the coast and inland from Senegal and The Gambia to Chad and Gabon (Serle *et al.*, 1977). Moreau (1972) recorded a count of 65 along 500 m of bank along a swamp in Senegal, indicating the abundance of this species.

In the Strait, the Wood Sandpiper is a regular migrant which appears to have been largely overlooked in the past. There is no doubt that many follow inland routes east of the Strait, from the French Camargue through eastern Morocco (Telleria, 1981), but passage to the west of this is regular in spring and autumn. Presumably the Wood Sandpipers passing the Strait come from the westernmost

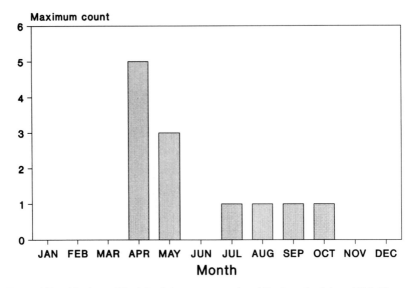

Figure 147.   Maximum Wood Sandpiper counts at selected Strait wetland sites, 1985–90.

parts of the breeding range and winter in the extreme west of Africa. This inland movement over Europe was noted by Bernis (1966d), who reported a variable autumn movement between south/southwest and south/southeast. This author calculated that a third of the birds passing Sweden and Denmark in spring followed a route via Morocco, Iberia and France, and the remainder followed a route via Italy. The Po marshes and the Camargue are known fattening areas, and a Camargue ringed bird has been recovered in Senegal and a Senegal-ringed bird in northern Italy. Iberian recoveries of birds ringed on passage in Belgium (2), southwest Germany (3), Denmark (3) and southern Sweden (3) (Bernis, 1966d) confirm the western route.

Wood Sandpipers occur in the Strait singly or in small parties of 5–10 birds in spring and autumn, usually inland but occasionally on the coast. The scale of the migration appears greater in spring than in autumn although it is the scarcest of the (regular) *Tringa* species migrating through the Strait.

The spring passage takes place in April and May, and the return migration lasts from late July to October (Finlayson & Cortés, 1987; Figure 147).

COMMON SANDPIPER

The Common Sandpiper has a widespread breeding distribution throughout the Palaearctic, from Iberia and Britain in the west to the Kamchatka Peninsula in the east. Western populations winter in tropical and southern Africa, with some remaining in Europe, in Iberia, Atlantic France and southwest Britain. Scandinavian and west European birds migrate southwest towards Iberia, most presum-

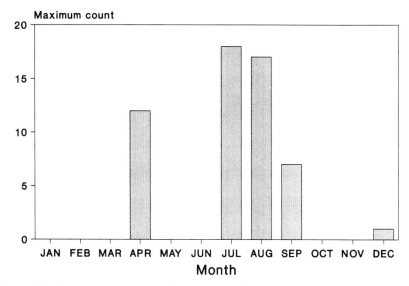

Figure 148.   Maximum Common Sandpiper counts at selected Strait wetland sites, 1985–90.

ably continuing into Africa. Bernis (1966d) and Fernandez-Cruz (1982), summarizing Iberian recoveries, confirmed this movement with French, English, Scottish, Belgian, German, Danish, Norwegian and Swedish recoveries.

Small numbers winter on either shore of the Strait, inland and on the coast (Pineau & Giraud-Audine, 1979; Telleria, 1981; Finlayson & Cortés, 1987). They are more abundant in tropical West Africa, which is where the Strait passage birds must continue to. It is considered to be the most abundant *Tringa* species in Africa (Moreau, 1972), being widely distributed wherever there was open water (Serle *et al.*, 1977).

Common Sandpipers are common passage migrants, more abundant in autumn than in spring. They occur inland as well as on the coast, frequenting sandy and rocky habitats in flocks of up to 40 birds (Finlayson & Cortés, 1987). This is one of the commonest passage waders, and the total migration must be of the order of thousands of individuals.

The spring passage, which lasts from March to May, peaks during April; the return migration is early, starting in late July, with a distinct peak in August and a continuation into early November (Pineau & Giraud-Audine, 1979; Telleria, 1981; Finlayson & Cortés, 1987; Figure 148).

TURNSTONE

The nominate subspecies breeds in coastal areas from Ellesmere Island in Canada, east through Greenland and Spitsbergen, and along the Scandinavian and USSR coasts to Kamchatka. The Nearctic subspecies *morinella* is a vagrant to Europe.

The nominate subspecies winter on the coasts of Europe, Africa and southern Asia. Turnstones from Greenland and northeast Canada winter along the European Atlantic coasts, while Scandinavian birds migrate across Europe to winter in Africa (Branson *et al.*, 1978). The two populations overlap on passage and in winter: Greenland and Canadian Turnstones have been recovered along the Atlantic coasts of Iberia on passage and in winter, and along the Moroccan Atlantic coast in winter, with the majority remaining in Europe. North European Turnstones, on the other hand, winter mainly in Africa, with only a small proportion remaining in Europe in winter (Branson *et al.*, 1978).

It appears that few Turnstones winter along the Iberian coasts, which may be a consequence of the main wintering quarters being to the north (Canadian/Greenland birds) and south (north European birds). The Iberian wintering population is *c.* 900 birds (2.1% of the west European wintering population— Alberto & Velasco, 1988), and these winter mainly on the Atlantic coasts, including the Strait area (Bernis, 1966d). The Moroccan population is also small, estimated at 400 (Kersten & Smit, 1984), and spread out south from the Strait (Pineau & Giraud-Audine, 1979). It is likely that these wintering populations may be larger since Turnstones occur widely scattered along rocky coasts and are difficult to census accurately. Numbers are substantially higher further south, up to 17 000 of the estimated African wintering population of 50 000 in the Banc d'Arguin, Mauretania, constituting 14% of the east Atlantic wintering population (Engelmoer *et al.*, 1984). The remainder winter from Senegal to the Cape (Moreau, 1972; Serle *et al.*, 1977). Most Turnstones migrating past the Strait

must therefore be of Scandinavian and Soviet (e.g. see Telleria, 1981) origin, with a smaller proportion of birds from northeastern Canada and Greenland.

Turnstones are among the difficult waders to census. They are regular and widespread on the Strait's rocky coasts on passage in groups of up to 30 birds (Pineau & Giraud-Audine, 1979). The coastal habits of this species suggest that many birds wintering in West Africa follow the Iberian and Moroccan Atlantic coasts, including the Strait, though they are also known to occur inland (e.g. see Moreau, 1972), which may make the total number occurring on passage higher than is apparent.

The spring passage takes place from February to May, and the return movement south is from late July to early November (Pineau & Giraud-Audine, 1979; Finlayson & Cortés, 1987). The period late September to mid-October is thought to be the peak for the autumn migration (Telleria, 1981). Summering birds are regular on both sides of the Strait.

CHAPTER 5

Migration of Seabirds

Seabirds adjust and respond to fluctuating resources between years, between seasons and within seasons, by performing regular movements. These frequent changes of location are the product of the relatively simple environment which they exploit (e.g. Bourne, 1963). Seabird movements between the Mediterranean and the Atlantic via the Strait of Gibraltar provide a particularly good opportunity for the study of seabirds' responses to changing resources.

The Mediterranean Sea is highly saline as a result of an excess of evaporation over precipitation. Atlantic water enters the Mediterranean via the Strait (at a rate of about one million cubic metres per second, above the depth of 100 m) and overcompensates for evaporation losses. Although low in nutrients, the Atlantic water is relatively richer than the adjacent Mediterranean surface water. Deep water, rich in nutrients, flows out of the Mediterranean and is raised towards the euphotic zone in the Strait itself as a result of intense turbulence (Lacombe & Richez, 1982). This mixing of different waters makes the Strait a highly fertile area, with a highly diverse zooplankton community. Primary production exceeds even that of the Gulf of Cadiz in the Atlantic (Estrada *et al.*, 1985). The richness and influence of Atlantic species is continued to some extent by the main Atlantic current (the North Atlantic Water Mass) which flows into the Alborán Sea and continues along the North African coast (Hopkins, 1985).

In the Mediterranean there is a decline in primary production in summer, associated with the development of a thermocline which restricts the transfer of nutrients from deep water to the euphotic zone (Estrada *et al.*, 1985; Flos, 1985). At this time, the richest feeding areas are associated with estuaries (e.g. the Ebro Delta) or with local upwellings or turbulence usually connected with the inflowing Atlantic water via the Strait. One example of this is the zone of cold water along the North African coast, supplied by Atlantic water, which is recirculated towards the coast by the Alborán anticyclonic gyre (Hopkins, 1985). Because of the mixing of Atlantic water with the nutrient-rich deep outflowing Mediterranean water (Minas *et al.*, 1982), the Strait is rich throughout the year, and is therefore an important feeding area for seabirds for most of the year.

Production increases in the Mediterranean with the arrival of the autumn storms, which mix the stratified water layers. The autumn (November) peak in primary production is followed by a second peak in late winter and spring (January–March), once nutrients have been brought to the surface by turbulence or upwelling and the water column has become sufficiently stable to permit growth of phytoplankton populations. The high midwinter turbulence, which prevents such growth, and the reduced light intensity prevent an earlier peak in primary production (Margalef & Castelví, 1967; Estrada *et al.*, 1985).

These seasonal changes in the Mediterranean's productivity must be seen in relation to neighbouring sea areas utilized by seabirds. An important zone of upwelling off West Africa (part of a larger area of upwelling stretching from Portugal to Guinea) is associated with cold water that reaches the surface after offshore winds blow surface water away from the coast. North of Cap Blanc (Mauretania, 21°N) this water (Canary upwelling) is rich, but less so than that to the south (Senegal upwelling), which has a higher phosphate content (Cushing, 1971; Brown, 1979). The Senegal upwelling reaches its highest production between December and March and is poorest in July and August. One of the zones rich in summer is that associated with a marine front off the west coast of France (Bourne *et al.*, 1988).

The pattern of movements in response to seasonally fluctuating resources is similar for all Mediterranean breeding seabirds. Balearic Shearwaters (Yesou, 1985; Le Mao & Yesou, in press), Yellow-legged Gulls (Yesou, 1985; Carrera *et al.*, in press) and, occasionally, Cory's Shearwaters (Yesou, 1982) migrate to rich feeding areas off the Atlantic coast of France in summer and early autumn, when the Mediterranean is least productive and West African water is at a production low, and return to the Mediterranean from October once production begins to increase there. Some, like the Balearic Shearwater, may continue southwards past the Strait at this time, towards the northwest African coast (Bourne *et al.*, 1988). The gulls migrate overland and the shearwaters via the Strait.

The western populations of the Levantine Shearwater leave the Mediterranean during the summer months (July–September) and feed and moult in the Strait and adjacent waters. The Strait's relatively high summer production is also utilized by Cory's Shearwaters and migrating species leaving the Mediterranean (e.g. Audouin's Gull).

The other important feeding area for Mediterranean seabirds from late summer to winter is the area of upwelling off the West African coast (Morocco–Senegal), associated with the cold Canary and Senegal currents (see above). Several species leave the Mediterranean in summer for this area, where they join

North Atlantic species (Bourne, 1963; Brown, 1979). These include Audouin's Gull, Lesser Crested Tern, Sandwich Tern, Common Tern and Little Tern. Other species pass the Strait area towards these feeding grounds, for example Wilson's Storm Petrel, Gannet, Pomarine Skua, Lesser Black-backed Gull, Caspian Tern, other populations of Sandwich Tern, Common Tern and Little Tern, Roseate Tern, Arctic Tern, Black Tern and Grey Phalarope (see Chapter 4).

As production increases in the western Mediterranean after October, breeding Mediterranean species (e.g. Balearic Shearwaters) start the return to their colonies. Most species return early to exploit these resources, and the increasing daylength, to breed. Mediterranean breeding species return to the nesting colonies in February and early March. The rich period from October to April is also exploited by species from the northeast Atlantic (e.g. Gannet, Sandwich Tern, Great Skua, Lesser Black-backed Gull, Razorbill and Puffin), from the Black Sea (Mediterranean Gull, Sandwich Tern) and from the USSR (Black-headed Gull, Little Gull).

The movements of seabirds in the Strait must therefore be interpreted in relation to these seasonally changing resources in the western Mediterranean, West Africa, the northeast Atlantic and the eastern Mediterranean/Black Sea area. On a local scale, movements may be modified by patches of food, where birds may temporarily gather, and by the eastward passage of Atlantic depressions over the Strait or the strong southeasterly gales associated with eastward extensions of the Azores anticyclone. Such movements in relation to

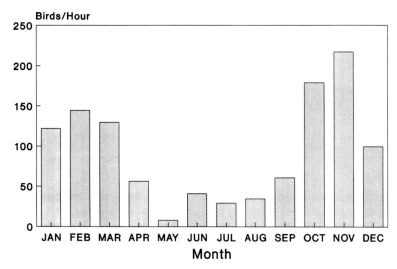

Figure 149.   Total seabird density (birds passing Europa Point/hour): July 1982–June 1983. Excludes Yellow-legged Gull. For all figures in this chapter, the number of days of observation are: JAN (26); FEB (21); MAR (26); APR (29); MAY (11); JUN (22); JUL (28); AUG (26); SEP (23); OCT (26); NOV (20); DEC (22).

wind circulation are well known in seabirds (e.g. Blomqvist & Peterz, 1984). Examples of the effects of local feeding conditions and of winds on seabird distributions in the Strait will be found in the species descriptions which follow.

The total number of seabirds within the Strait is highest in the period October–March (Figure 149), and this is related to the high arrival of Atlantic species and the return of Mediterranean breeding species. The November peak is also due, in part, to the migration of Cory's Shearwaters into the Atlantic at the end of the breeding season. The Strait has fewest seabirds in the period May–August, when most northeastern Atlantic seabirds have left the area; it has least in May, when the Mediterranean breeding species are near their colonies, but there is a small peak in June, due to the exodus of Balearic Shearwaters. The increase towards September is related to the exit of Mediterranean breeding species (e.g. Audouin's Gull) and other migrants (e.g. Black Tern) and to the increased use of the Strait by species still breeding in the western Mediterranean at that time (especially Cory's Shearwater).

The number of seabird species present in the Strait (Figure 150) follows a similar pattern, with the period May–July being poorest and numbers being higher at other times. The number of species in December is also low, this being the winter month with fewest Mediterranean species. The seabird communities in the Strait are lowest in diversity and equitability in the period November–February, when the Strait is occupied by a small number of species reaching high density (Balearic Shearwater, Gannet, Black-headed Gull and Lesser Black-backed Gull). June is another month of low diversity and equitability (the latter not as low as in the winter), due to the dominance of Balearic Shearwaters at that

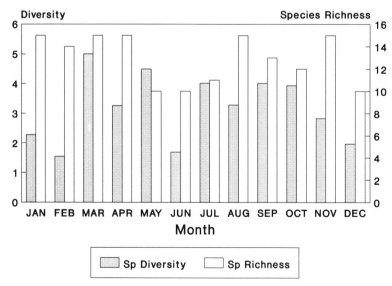

Figure 150.   Seabird species richness and diversity off Europa Point, Gibraltar, July 1982–June 1983.

time. The remaining periods (March–May, July–October) the higher species diversity and equitability seems to be related to the greater spread of species during the main migration periods.

Between October and March, the Strait therefore supports a large number of seabirds belonging to a few northeastern Atlantic and several Mediterranean species. This high density coincides with the autumn and late winter/spring periods of high primary production in the western Mediterranean. It is interesting that there is a low in seabird density, species richness, diversity and equitability in December when primary production is expected to be lower than immediately before and after. The species present are large, and the total biomass is likely to be very high. The period April to September supports fewer seabirds and the community is more diverse. Towards the summer, as conditions in the Mediterranean deteriorate, an increasing number of Mediterranean seabirds (Cory's Shearwater, Balearic Shearwater, Audouin's Gull) move into the Strait (and the Atlantic beyond), which then becomes an important focus for seabirds that breed in the western Mediterranean.

SHEARWATERS

Cory's and Balearic Shearwaters are the main species in the Strait and are found in large numbers at certain times of year. Levantine Shearwaters reach the Strait from the east in summer (Garcia, 1973; Cortés *et al.*, 1980; Finlayson & Cortés, 1987) in varying numbers, abundant in some years but less so in others. Large rafts of up to 6000 were regular in the Bay of Gibraltar during the 1960s (Bourne & Norris, 1966) and the early 1970s, and rafts of up to 1000 still moult there in some years; presumably these originate from the western and central Mediterranean populations. The Manx Shearwater enters the Mediterranean infrequently (Finlayson & Cortés, 1987; Hashmi, pers. comm.). Great and Sooty Shearwaters are regular in small numbers during their southward autumn passage along the eastern Atlantic coasts (Smith, 1965; Bourne & Norris, 1966; Garcia, 1973; Pineau & Giraud-Audine, 1974; Dubois & Duhautois, 1977; Cortés *et al.*, 1980; Finlayson & Cortés, 1987; Hashmi, pers. comm.). Little Shearwaters are very scarce visitors, usually in late summer (de Juana & Paterson, 1986; Finlayson & Cortés, 1987; Holliday, 1990a,b; Hashmi, pers. comm.).

CORY'S SHEARWATER

Cory's Shearwaters are widely distributed within the Mediterranean, breeding on islands and remote stretches of rocky coastline. The nearest breeding colonies are in Chafarinas off Mediterranean Morocco (de Juana & Paterson, 1986), where up to 1000 pairs may breed (Paterson, 1990), and the Habibas Islands off western Algeria (Jacob & Courbet, 1980), but they may also breed on the Mediterranean Moroccan coast closer to the Strait (Berthon & Berthon, 1984). They may have

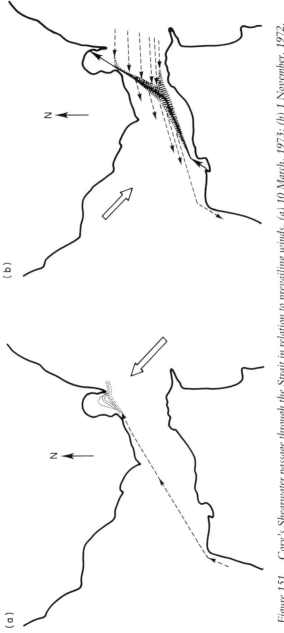

Figure 151.   Cory's Shearwater passage through the Strait in relation to prevailing winds. (a) 10 March, 1973; (b) 1 November, 1972.

bred on the Rock of Gibraltar in the past (Irby, 1895), and they do feature in sub-fossil remains (Breuil, 1922; Garrod *et al.*, 1928). Cory's Shearwaters winter in the Southern Hemisphere, notably off South Africa (Bourne, 1955) and few are seen then in the Strait.

Cory's Shearwaters perform spectacular movements during the annual migrations between breeding and wintering grounds. These movements, which may include nocturnal passage, often go by undetected from the shore as the birds fly down the centre of the Strait. With onshore winds, especially in gales, Cory's Shearwaters hug the coastline, and the main streams are then close to the shore. For example, they pass close to Europa Point (Gibraltar) during the spring passage in southeasterlies. They are then flying into the wind; this slows their progress, and its lateral component drives them into the Bay of Gibraltar (Figure 151).

During their departure from the Mediterranean in October and November, it is southwesterly gales which force Cory's Shearwaters close to the northern shore of the Strait. Counts of passage during these conditions give a good indication of the magnitude of the passage at peak times. Thus, on 10 March 1973, a massive movement commenced during the morning in a southeasterly gale, when the rate of passage past Europa Point was 480 per hour; during the afternoon the passage intensified to a rate of 3600/hour. While carrying out a transect of the Strait by ship on 1 November 1972, I observed the westward movement of Cory's Shearwaters in fresh northwesterly winds. In these conditions very few shearwaters passed close to Gibraltar, and the movement was concentrated along the Moroccan coast (Figure 151). A stream of 1200 Cory's Shearwaters crossed in 10 min, and the apparent steadiness of the flow indicated a very large movement. Ten Great Shearwaters were observed with the Cory's Shearwaters (presumably having drifted into the Strait with the northwesterlies).

Telleria (1980), counting the autumn migration from Tarifa, calculated that the total exodus in October and November exceeded 100 000 birds, and this was a minimum estimate since he was not including shearwaters passing along the Moroccan shore and any passing at night. Recent evidence suggests that the passage may be substantially higher along the Moroccan coast (Hashmi, pers. comm.): 20 460 Cory's Shearwaters were counted passing Ceuta in 185 min (6636 per hour) on 25 October 1987, and the impression was of passage forming an 'endless chain' along the Moroccan side of the Strait.

From the end of May until the migration in October, Cory's Shearwaters regularly feed in areas of turbulence within the Strait. These are presumably breeding birds from colonies in the western Mediterranean close to the Strait; non-breeding birds may also be involved (Mougin *et al.*, 1987). The numbers off Europa Point during this period vary according to weather conditions and, presumably, availability of food (Figure 152). There are also differences between seasons. In September 1989, groups of 200–300 birds were regular occurrences off Europa Point, apparently feeding on flying fish (*SGBO Report*) and on 20 September 1988, 1200 passed this point in an easterly direction in 1 hour. During the summer, Paterson (1987) recorded Cory's Shearwaters in Málaga Bay,

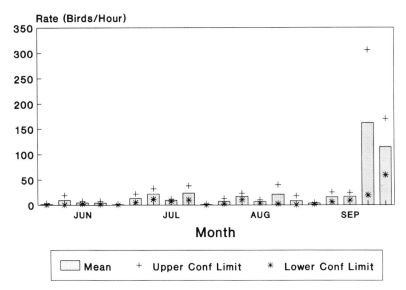

Figure 152. Cory's Shearwater numbers off Europa Point, Gibraltar in summer, 1982–83.

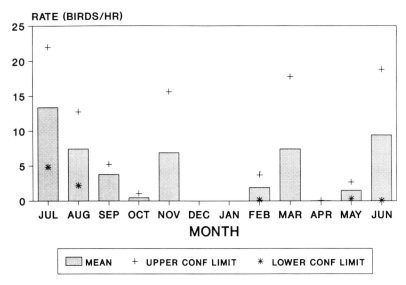

Figure 153. Cory's Shearwater seasonal distribution off Europa Point, Gibraltar, July 1982–June 1983.

approximately 100 km northeast of Europa Point, although the overall numbers recorded were lower than for the Strait. It is likely that the Strait, with its turbulent waters and upwellings, is particularly favoured as a feeding ground, especially as the summer advances and the Mediterranean becomes increasingly sterile. Paterson did not detect the migration of Cory's Shearwaters at Málaga Bay, which indicates that migration takes place well away from the coast except when passing the narrow Strait.

There are two well-defined passages. The departure from the Mediterranean takes place between mid-October and mid-November (Telleria, 1980; Figure 153) and the return is from mid-February to late March. Because the full passage is observed only close to the shore in certain wind conditions, the precise peaks as observed from the shore may vary from year to year. The main passages take the form of mass movements, often comprising flocks of several hundred birds, and the entire migration appears to be concentrated over a short period.

BALEARIC SHEARWATER

Balearic Shearwaters breed in the Balearic Islands (de Juana, 1984) and may do so in other sites in the western Mediterranean (Michelot & Laurent, 1988), without apparent overlap with the Levantine Shearwaters of the western, central and eastern Mediterranean (Bourne et al., 1988). No colonies are known in the Alboran Sea or the Strait (de Juana & Paterson, 1986), although Balearic Shearwaters have been detected around Chafarinas Islands during the breeding season (Paterson, 1990). The species has been identified in excavations of the Gibraltar Pleistocene caves (Breuil, 1922; Garrod et al., 1928; Waechter, 1964; Eastham, 1968).

De Juana (1984) estimated the Balearic Island breeding population at 1000–5000 pairs, and Capella & Muntaner (in Paterson, 1990) estimated 2930–3430 pairs in 1988. These birds abandon the colonies at the end of the breeding season and move out into the Atlantic, northwards to the Bay of Biscay where 10 000–15 000 gather to feed off rich upwellings in late summer and to moult. A few reach the English Channel and the North Sea (Yesou, 1985a, 1986). These birds return south along the Atlantic coast of Iberia towards the Strait between September and February.

Balearic Shearwaters also occur off the Moroccan Atlantic coast in autumn and winter, but it is not certain whether these are individuals returning from the north or different birds altogether.

There are no estimates of the numbers of Balearic Shearwaters crossing the Strait. Throughout the year, mean passage rates usually fall between 5 and 10 birds/hour, with a significant increase during June when the exodus of the breeding population into the Atlantic takes place (Figure 154), and passage rates can be very high on some days. Thus, during the 1983 passage, 1079 Balearic Shearwaters were counted in just over 2 hours off Europa Point (8.99 birds/minute) on 24 June, and 1044 in 2.3 hours (7.57/min) from the same point on 26

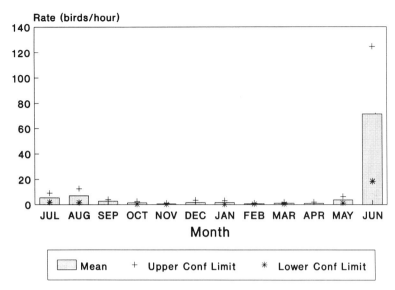

Figure 154.   Balearic Shearwater seasonal distribution off Europa Point, Gibraltar, July 1982–June 1983.

June. This density is not reached at any other time, although concentrations of several hundred birds can occur where there is food. The return towards the Mediterranean appears to commence in October, and passage east can be large between November and January: 449 were recorded passing Europa Point in 3 hours (2.49 birds/minute) on 5 November 1988, 317 in 2 hours (2.64/min) on 29 November 1988, and 176 in one hour (2.93/min) on 25 January 1987 (*SGBO Reports*). At this time, 'bursts' of passage appear to alternate with periods of little movement. The very large numbers observed in passage in the Strait suggest that there may be other colonies in addition to those in the Balearic Islands. It has been suggested (Jacob & Courbet, 1980) that they may breed along the western Algerian coastline, an area which holds high concentrations of this species in late summer (Michelot & Laurent, 1988).

The westward passage towards the Atlantic commences towards the end of May, with a rapid build-up of numbers in June. The main movements take place at the end of June. Passage west continues throughout July and into August, but in smaller numbers. During August and September, the birds found within the Strait may be feeding rather than being late migrants. Between May and March, Balearic Shearwaters are present in the Strait at all times, and it becomes difficult to separate migrants from feeding birds. It seems that an eastbound movement commences in October, which would coincide with completion of moult by birds on the French Atlantic coast (Yesou, 1985a), and large movements are then recorded until January at least, sometimes even in February and March. Very few are observed within the Strait during the breeding season, in contrast with Cory's Shearwater which breeds later and regularly visits the Strait while breeding. This may reflect (1) a greater feeding range in Cory's Shearwater, (2) proximity of the Strait to breeding colonies of Cory's but not Balearic Shearwater, (3) the reduced feeding opportunities in the western Mediterranean during the Cory's Shearwater breeding season at a time when Balearic Shearwaters have already left the Mediterranean, or (4) a combination of these factors.

STORM PETRELS

The Storm Petrel is the most regular of the storm petrels, occurring away from the shore between April and September (Finlayson & Cortés, 1987); this is the main period of occurrence, although they have been recorded in most months of the year (Cortés *et al.*, 1980; Finlayson, 1983). The closest known colonies are off Cabo de Palos (Murcia) (de Juana & Paterson, 1986) although they may nest closer to the Strait, as suggested by Irby (1875, 1895). Close to the island of Alborán 120 were seen in July 1986 (Michelot & Laurent, 1988). These birds presumably belonged to the Mediterranean subspecies *melitensis*, which is thought to be partially migratory (Brizhetti, 1980) and may join the Atlantic populations wintering off South Africa (Mainwood, 1976). Hashmi (pers. comm.), studying passage in mid-Strait, considered that most Storm Petrels seen between September and November are Atlantic birds entering the Mediterranean, since most were seen flying east at this time, even in calm weather. Very few are seen in August. However, this is the time when the Mediterranean population would be expected to migrate west past the Strait, so the question of what the Mediterranean Storm Petrels do after the breeding season remains unresolved.

Leach's Storm Petrel winters in the Atlantic approaches of the Strait and is driven onshore during westerly gales when many may be wrecked or enter the Mediterranean (see, for example, Irby, 1895; Pineau & Giraud-Audine, 1979; de Juana & Paterson, 1986). These birds are derived from breeding populations in the north Atlantic; a bird ringed in August in Newfoundland was recovered dead in Huelva after gales in the winter of 1963 (Bernis, 1966a).

Wilson's Storm Petrel is a regular migrant in groups of up to 50 in the Atlantic, west of the Strait, from June to September (Bourne & Norris, 1966). The species rarely approaches the Strait itself (de Juana & Paterson, 1986) but may enter the Mediterranean (Irby, 1895; Cramp & Simmons, 1977), although it is less likely than Leach's Storm Petrel to be drifted ashore by gales (which in any case are fewer and less severe than in winter).

GANNET

The northeastern Atlantic Gannets, breeding mainly in the British Isles but also in northwestern France, Norway and Iceland, migrate south along the eastern

Atlantic coast in autumn, reaching equatorial West Africa (Nelson, 1978). The tendency to migrate is strongest in the first year of life and, while the adults disperse in home waters after breeding, these birds do not return for several years (Thomson, 1939). The Strait is used as a transit area by Gannets entering the Mediterranean (Nelson, 1978; Finlayson & Cortés, 1984) although it is probable that some Gannets following the Atlantic seaboard between Europe and Africa also enter the Strait and the Mediterranean, especially in the lee of Atlantic depressions. Thus, even during the entry into the Mediterranean in autumn, Gannets are also observed passing westwards. Others remain within the Strait in winter, and immatures are regular throughout the summer.

Estimates of the number of Gannets passing the Strait vary. In the spring of 1980, using counts of birds leaving the Strait, Finlayson & Cortés (1984) estimated that the mean number of Gannets passing the Strait after wintering in the Mediterranean was of the order of 7500, which represented 4% of the northeastern Atlantic population. More recently, Hashmi (in press) has suggested that 20 000–24 000 Gannets may enter (based on line transects between Algeciras and Ceuta). This figure is not unreasonable as it is an absolute number (7500 was a mean), and the entire width of the Strait was covered; the Gannet

One of thousands of Gannets which pass the Strait in spring and autumn, some remaining all winter and fewer throughout the summer.

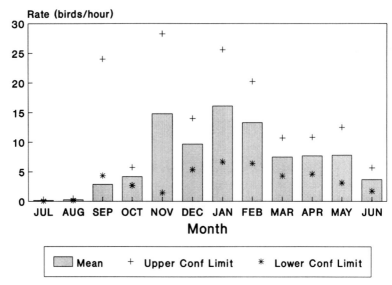

Figure 155.   Gannet seasonal distribution off Europa Point, Gibraltar, July 1982–June 1983.

population appears to have increased since the earlier study. Mean rates of passage in the study by Finlayson & Cortés (1984) varied: around 6–14 birds/hour in February and March, falling to 2–6 birds/hour in May. The passage rates given in Figure 155 are consistent with these results and illustrate the progressive increase in numbers during the autumn and gradual reduction during the spring as birds return towards the breeding colonies. According to Cortés *et al.* (1980) the highest recorded passage rate for the Strait is 14 birds/hour; during intense passage peaks rates can in fact be substantially higher (up to 76 birds/hour in the spring). High rates can also be recorded in midwinter, after Gannets from the Atlantic have been forced to shelter in the Strait by incoming depressions: a flock of 200 Gannets off Europa Point (29 January 1987) coincided with a south-westerly gale and rain (*SGBO Report*).

During the wintering period, high concentrations of Gannets frequently occur within the Strait, often where pilot whales, dolphins and tuna drive fish to the surface. These concentrations may involve anything from a few Gannets to large accumulations of 50 or more. For example, on 30 November 1982, 240 Gannets were observed diving repeatedly near a school of cetaceans off Europa Point (140 on 21 January 1983). Hashmi (pers. comm.) has shown that Gannets entering the Strait on autumn migration avoid the central, deeper areas of the channel. First-winter birds are especially concentrated along the European side of the Strait, but adults are equally divided on both shores. Feeding birds (between Algeciras and Ceuta) are, however, concentrated almost exclusively along the European coast, feeding in large numbers at the entrance to the Bay of Gibraltar. This pattern may reflect concentration in areas of upwelling and may be different in other sectors of

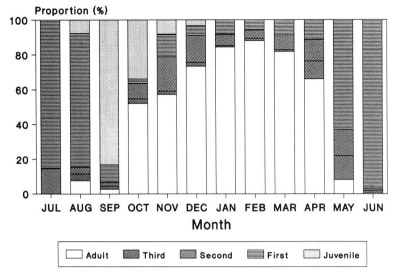

Figure 156. Gannet seasonal distribution by ages—Europa Point, Gibraltar, July 1982–June 1983. N = 1982.

the Strait (e.g. regular Gannet concentrations off the Moroccan Cape Malabata in the western Strait; pers. obs.).

Gannets migrate in groups. Finlayson & Cortés (1984) estimated that only 36% of Gannets migrating in spring did so individually. During the early spring most groups were of adults only, but as the season advanced groups of mixed ages became common.

Although Gannets are present throughout the year, there are two main migratory periods (Figure 155). The main passage in autumn takes place between late August and mid-November, juveniles in late August and September preceding adults, which pass in October (Figure 156). These juveniles must continue the migration since the majority of wintering Gannets are adult. Ninety per cent of Gannets observed in January 1980 were adult, while only 4% were first-winter birds (Finlayson & Cortés, 1984). This situation contrasts with that off Senegal where it has been estimated that only 25% of the Gannets are adults (Brown, 1979).

The spring passage lasts from late January to early June (Finlayson & Cortés, 1984), with a clear dominance of adults until April (Figure 156), the subsequent passage being mainly of immature Gannets. This pattern is consistent with the known migratory behaviour of Gannets of different ages (Nelson, 1978). Adults return early to breeding colonies, but immatures are rare there. As the immatures become older, they return closer to the breeding sites; the return is later in the season as they are not under pressure to breed. The January passage of Gannets in the Strait has been disputed by Paterson (1990) on the basis of observations in Málaga Bay, where Gannets are far less abundant and migratory movements less likely to be detected with accuracy than in the Strait. Whether the January movements of Gannets are early migration or local movements is open to debate, but the distinct increase starting at the end of January and developing in February seems to be related to migration (Finlayson & Cortés, 1984), especially as such movements are not as evident earlier in the winter.

CORMORANTS

The Cormorant is essentially a winter visitor to the Strait between late September and early April (Finlayson & Cortés, 1987), being common along the Atlantic coast (274 in Cádiz Bay in January 1990 — AMA, Cádiz). About six birds winter regularly in Gibraltar Bay. Most individuals appear to belong to the subspecies *sinensis*, ringed birds of which are recovered equally along the Mediterranean and Atlantic coasts of Iberia; nominate birds are only recovered along the Atlantic coast (Bernis, 1966a). De Juana & Paterson (1986) only record *sinensis* in Alborán, as do Finlayson & Cortés (1987) in the Strait.

The Shag, which now breeds only on the Rock of Gibraltar (Cortés *et al.*, 1980; Finlayson & Cortés, 1987), where there are around ten breeding individuals, is sedentary. Formerly it was widespread in the Strait (Irby, 1875, 1895; Verner, 1910).

SKUAS

Three species are regular migrants, the Great, the Arctic and the Pomarine, in order of abundance.

The Long-tailed Skua from the Arctic is a vagrant to the Strait (Irby, 1875, 1895; Hashmi, pers. comm.), presumably on its way to south Atlantic wintering grounds (Bourne & Norris, 1966; Furness, 1987). One bird was recorded in August in Málaga Bay (Paterson, 1987) and singles were seen in mid-Strait on two days in October 1987 (Hashmi, pers. comm.), so it is possible that small numbers may move towards the Atlantic via the Mediterranean or enter the Strait from the Atlantic in autumn.

Pomarine Skuas breed in the high Arctic tundra, and winter off West and southwest Africa (Brown, 1979; Furness, 1987). They are scarce but regular migrants. Presumably, they enter the Strait during the migrations along the Atlantic coasts, where they are more common (Bourne & Norris, 1966) than in the Mediterranean (de Juana & Paterson, 1986), although some may migrate along the Spanish Mediterranean coast (Martinez Vilalta *et al.*, 1984; Paterson, 1987), probably from the central Mediterranean (Iapichino, 1984a). At Gibraltar they are regular between late March and May and from August to October (Garcia, 1973; Pineau & Giraud-Audine, 1979; Finlayson, 1983; Finlayson & Cortés, 1987; Holliday, 1990b).

GREAT SKUA

British Great Skuas migrate into the eastern North Atlantic (including Iberia and Morocco) in autumn, whereas Icelandic ones migrate southwest towards the western Atlantic (Tuck, 1971; Furness, 1978). Bernis (1967) recorded 18 Scottish and one Icelandic recovery along the Iberian Atlantic coast during passage periods and winter. Furness (1978) showed that young Great Skuas displayed a greater migratory tendency and migrated further than adults, some reaching south of the equator. Many of the immature birds, including 3-year-old individuals, remain in southerly latitudes throughout the summer. The Great Skuas that occur in the Strait are in all probability predominantly birds from this population.

Although usually solitary, Great Skuas are regularly observed within the Strait in large numbers after bad weather in the Atlantic has forced them in. At such times up to 50 have been observed passing Europa Point in 1 hour (*SGBO Report*). The mean passage rate between December and March varies between 0.4 and 1.5 birds/hour (Figure 157). It is difficult therefore to estimate the Mediterranean wintering population, as most Great Skuas appear to remain within the Strait and adjacent Atlantic waters, and passage may be related to changing weather rather than reflecting migration. However, some birds certainly spread throughout the Mediterranean (Bourne, in press). It has been speculated that the species has become more common in the area in winter during this century, as a

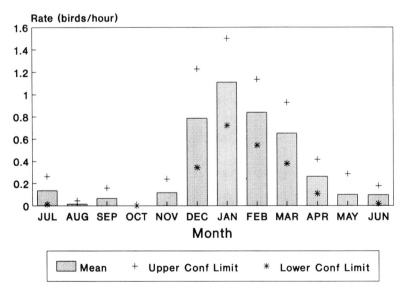

Figure 157.   Great Skua seasonal distribution off Europa Point, Gibraltar, July 1982–June 1983.

result of the increasing breeding population in the Shetlands (de Juana & Paterson, 1986).

The pattern of occurrence of Great Skuas within the Strait is consistent with the pattern reported from ringing recoveries (Furness, 1978). There is a progressive arrival of Great Skuas during the autumn, with a sharp increase during December and January (Figure 157). This is followed by a gradual decrease in numbers during the spring, presumably because adults are returning to the breeding colonies. Smaller numbers are recorded throughout the summer, and these are likely to be immatures that do not return to the breeding sites. It is this local movement of non-breeding birds that was detected by Paterson (1987) from Málaga Bay.

ARCTIC SKUA

The Arctic Skuas of the northern tundra winter principally in the southern hemisphere, with a concentration off southwest Africa (Furness, 1987); Bernis (1967) gives three Iberian recoveries of birds ringed as chicks on Fair Isle. Arctic Skuas are also occasionally recorded in the area in mid-winter (Irby, 1895; Smith, 1965; Pineau & Giraud-Audine, 1973; Cortés *et al.*, 1980; Telleria, 1981; de Juana & Paterson, 1986; Finlayson & Cortés, 1987).

Arctic Skuas are regular migrants in the Strait and are the second most numerous skuas. In observations of skuas in mid-Strait between 18 September and 13 November 1987, Hashmi (pers. comm.) counted 167 Great, 65 Arctic, 32

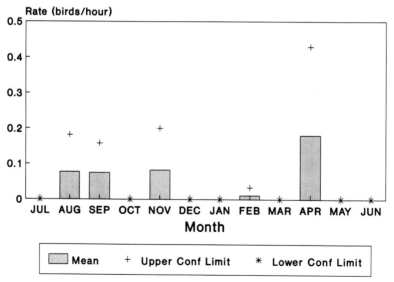

Figure 158.   Arctic Skua seasonal distribution off Europa Point, Gibraltar, July 1982–June 1983.

Pomarine, 15 Arctic/Pomarine and 2 Long-tailed, confirming the observations from the coast. At Gibraltar, mean passage rates in spring and autumn are of 0.1–0.2 birds/hour (Figure 158). Most Arctic Skuas pass singly or in small flocks (usually less than five birds).

The main passage periods are late February to early May (peak in April) and late July to November (peak in September/October) (Pineau & Giraud-Audine, 1979; Cortés *et al.*, 1980; Paterson, 1987; Finlayson & Cortés, 1987; Figure 158).

GULLS

The main gulls of the Strait are Black-headed Gull, Slender-billed Gull, Mediterranean Gull, Audouin's Gull, Herring Gull, Lesser Black-backed Gull, Little Gull and Kittiwake. Common Gulls are sporadic, and Great Black-backed Gulls are very scarce winter visitors (Isenmann, 1976; Finlayson & Cortés, 1987). Sabine's Gulls are rarely observed from the coast, even though they migrate down the edge of the Atlantic continental shelf, close to the area (mainly in September; Bourne & Norris, 1966). They appear in mid-Strait in small numbers (Hashmi, pers. comm.) in October, November and, less commonly, December. A small number may therefore winter in Atlantic areas close to the Strait. The Atlantic Herring Gull visits the area in small numbers in winter, being commonest along the Atlantic coast but also entering the Mediterranean via the Strait. Ring-billed, Laughing, Franklin's, Grey-headed and Iceland Gulls are vagrants to the area (Ree, 1973; Noticiario Ornitologico; Ardeola, 1981; Finlayson & Cortés, 1987; Paterson, 1990).

Mediterranean Gull

The Mediterranean Gulls that pass and winter in the Strait presumably originate mainly from the huge colonies in the Black and Azov Seas. Of birds ringed at colonies on Orlov (Black Sea), Bernis (1967) recorded 41 recoveries on the Mediterranean Iberian coast, with a few in the Atlantic. Recoveries spanned the period August to March, with the majority between December and February. The small population that passes the Strait westwards in late July and early August, and consists almost exclusively of adults, is probably composed of non-breeding birds that have spent the summer in the western Mediterranean (Figure 159), but it may also include breeding birds from the smaller Italian, Camargue and Ebro Delta populations. The main influxes occur later, in autumn, and the gulls that continue west at this time presumably winter off the Atlantic coast of Morocco (Smith, 1965; Isenmann, 1978) and possibly further south. Many winter within the western Mediterranean, and the winter concentrations within the Strait after easterlies are of Mediterranean-wintering gulls.

In winter, the numbers of Mediterranean Gulls in the Strait are variable and dependent on prevailing winds. During peak migration, rates of passage can be

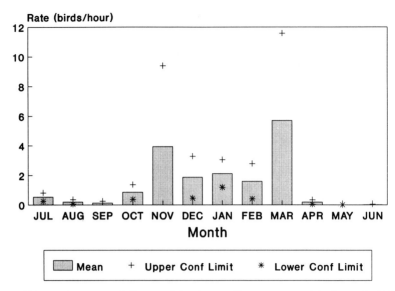

Figure 159.   Mediterranean Gull seasonal distribution off Europa Point, Gibraltar, July 1982–June 1983.

high. At Europa Point, concentrated migratory movements close to the shore occur with strong to gale-force onshore winds, particularly southeasterlies, as is illustrated by the following examples. In 2 hours at Europa Point 199 Mediterranean Gulls passed in a fresh southeasterly on 20 November 1983 (99.5 birds/hour), and 120 passed on 2 November 1988 (60 birds/hour), also in easterlies. There was a marked passage of Mediterranean Gulls from the Atlantic to the Mediterranean during a southeasterly gale on 7–8 March 1983: 168 birds passed in 4 hours (42 birds/hour) on the first day and 86 passed in 1.25 h on the second day (68.8/h). These are not isolated observations; they illustrate the scale of the movements during conditions which drift these gulls close to the shore. At other times during the migratory periods, passage presumably continues offshore, with smaller numbers passing inshore.

The overall number of wintering Mediterranean Gulls in the Strait is probably small in comparison with the major wintering areas along the east coast of Spain (Isenmann, 1976; Carrera *et al.*, 1981) where the population is estimated at over 43 000 (Carrera, 1988). Carrera (1981) considers the Mediterranean coast of Spain to be the main wintering area for this species in the western Mediterranean, although the Mediterranean coast east of Gibraltar is not considered a major wintering area (de Juana & Paterson, 1986; Paterson, 1987, 1990) despite Isenmann (1976) recording large numbers there in December. The western coast of Italy also holds a significant number in winter (Isenmann & Czajkowski, 1978). Within the Strait, winter concentrations of Mediterranean Gulls occur in estuaries (e.g. Guadiaro) and occasionally in inland lagoons (e.g. Laguna de Medina). Inland lagoons receive birds from the nearby Cádiz Bay where Mediterranean Gulls are wintering in increasing numbers (J. M. Fernandez-Palacios, pers. comm.).

The Black Sea and Azov Sea populations of the Mediterranean Gull have increased in the past decade as a result of increased protection of the Soviet Union's colonies (Cramp & Simmons, 1973). In 1988 317 000 pairs bred there (Chernichko, in Paterson, 1990). A comparison of numbers recorded off Europa Point in winter (November–February) shows a corresponding increase in wintering numbers between 1971 and 1989 (Figure 160). The wintering population had a high number of birds in first-winter plumage (78%), which may reflect high productivity as the population expands, a higher migratory tendency in young birds (as is the case with other seabirds) or a greater trend for young birds to feed inshore. The summer movement, which is smaller, reveals a clear absence of juveniles and so contrasts with the winter pattern (Figure 161).

The arrival of Mediterranean Gulls begins during October and November, in large numbers on some days and smaller numbers on others. This pattern coincides with that further east, the main passage in Sicily taking place between mid-October and late November (Iapichino, 1984a). Occasionally, the first birds arrive in late September. The pattern is that of a progressive build-up of individuals for the winter although, no doubt, some continue west towards the Atlantic. In winter their distribution is even (except during bad weather, when

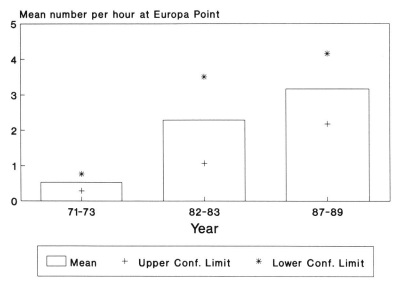

Figure 160. *Mediterranean Gull—increase in wintering numbers 1971–1989. 1971–73, N = 76; 1982–83, N = 86; 1987–89, N = 170.*

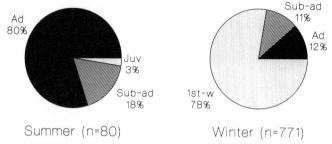

Figure 161.   Age composition of wintering and summer passage Mediterranean Gulls. Summer, June–August 1982 and 1983; Winter, November–March, 1982–83.

there can be local concentrations); following this there is a passage in March and early April of birds returning from the Atlantic (Figure 159). There is then a gap, when no Mediterranean Gulls are found in the Strait, until late June when the first adults move west.

LITTLE GULL

The Mediterranean Sea is considered to be the main wintering ground of Palaearctic Little Gulls (Erard, 1960) and it has been calculated that the east coast of Spain probably holds the largest Mediterranean winter concentrations of Little Gulls (Carrera *et al.*, 1981; Carrera, 1988). The Strait falls within the wintering area of the Little Gulls, but their origins are not precisely known.

Little Gulls are regular in mid-Strait in winter, and the Strait probably holds a sizeable wintering population. Only with strong easterlies do Little Gulls come inshore at Europa Point. It is at such times that the population's magnitude can be judged, and the appearance of such large numbers in easterlies implies that the main concentrations are out at sea to the east of Gibraltar. Large flocks occur within the wintering period, from December to March, with a frequency that is wind-dependent and progressively decreases towards March (Figure 162). Numbers during the migratory periods are lower.

During easterly gales, flocks of up to 200 birds are regular off Europa Point. Although they may remain feeding offshore for some time, their appearance is usually in the form of a movement into the wind, small groups alternating with periods when there are no birds or occasional larger flocks. The largest movement of this type occurred on 31 March 1990, in gale-force southeasterly winds when 881 Little Gulls passed Europa Point in 2 h. Assuming the passage continued at that rate for a period of 10 h, then the numbers passing this point would have been close to 9000. Since the largest concentrations observed by Carrera (1988) off the east coast of Spain were below 1300, it seems that larger concentrations may occur out at sea south of this area, around the Alborán Sea

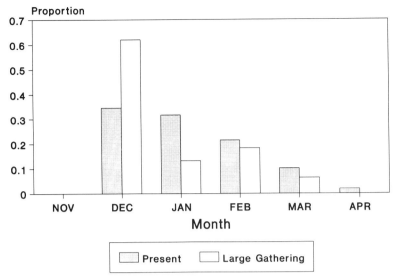

Figure 162.   Little Gull concentrations off Europa Point, Gibraltar, 1972, 1973, 1982, 1983 and 1987–89. Present, proportion of all individuals recorded in specific month; large gathering, proportion of large gatherings (flocks >50) in specified month.

and the Strait, although it is difficult to be precise with a pelagic species such as the Little Gull.

The pattern of wintering numbers suggests a rapid arrival of Little Gulls in December. Small groups and isolated individuals are recorded within the Strait and in surrounding areas from August to October, and in April and May (Finlayson & Cortés, 1987). Birds at either end of the wintering period may also be on passage, and the large numbers recorded off Gibraltar at the end of March may have been passage and not wintering birds, in which case many may winter in the Atlantic, where they have been recorded south to Angola (W. R. P. Bourne, pers. comm.). It has been speculated that the large passage along the Atlantic coast of Europe in autumn and their absence there in spring, together with the reverse pattern in the western Mediterranean, may indicate a loop migration to and from the winter quarters (de Juana & Paterson, 1986). The relatively small wintering numbers in the Atlantic areas of the Strait and the incidence of the species in the Strait in winter after easterlies, support the view that the western Mediterranean is a major wintering area (Erard, 1960; Carrera, 1988). Carrera (1988) recorded 231 wintering in the Tinto and Odiel estuaries in Huelva, and other localized wintering areas may occur on the Moroccan Atlantic coast, which Little Gulls reach in winter (Pineau & Giraud-Audine, 1979).

The pattern observed in the Strait contrasts with that given by Paterson (1987, 1990) for Málaga Bay, northeast of the Strait, where most Little Gulls were observed on passage in spring and very few were seen at other times.

Black-headed Gull

Telleria (1981) recorded about 450 recoveries for southern Andalucía, the main countries of origin being France, Belgium and Holland, with smaller numbers from Scandinavia and eastern Europe. Many of these birds remain within the Strait in winter, and others continue towards the coast of Morocco (Isenmann, 1978), the main autumn arrivals being from the Mediterranean and down the Atlantic coast from the north. Some birds may continue south to winter in tropical or equatorial West Africa (Cramp & Simmons, 1983).

The Black-headed Gull is a very abundant migrant and winter visitor in the Strait, and the combined wintering population on both shores is probably of the order of 8000–10000 birds (Finlayson & Parody, in prep.), with at least another 5000 between Larache and Rabat (Isenmann, 1978). If to this, 16000 are added for the Marismas del Guadalquivir (Bermejo *et al.*, 1986) and at least 2000 for the Bay of Cádiz (Agencia de Medio Ambiente, Cádiz), the total wintering population must be of the order of 30000–35000 Black-headed Gulls, considerably higher than the 20000 estimated for the entire Alborán Sea and the Strait by de Juana & Paterson (1986). Wintering numbers are likely to increase in some winters, after cold weather in central Europe or storms in the Atlantic. Of course, the passage population must be considerably greater than these estimates. At Europa Point, Gibraltar, the mean rate of passage during spring and autumn varies between 40 and 80 birds/hour (Figure 163) reaching 300/hour in peak conditions.

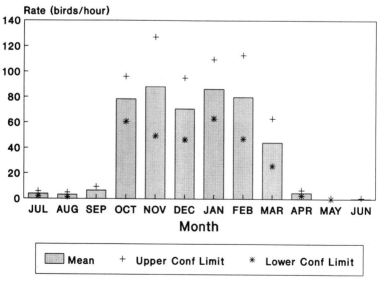

Figure 163.   Black-headed Gull seasonal distribution off Europa Point, Gibraltar, July 1982–June 1983.

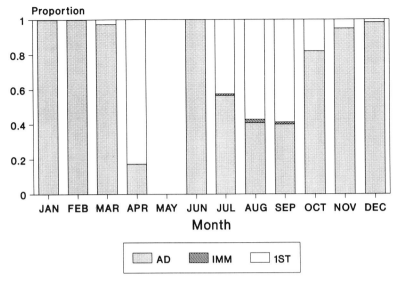

Figure 164. Black-headed Gull seasonal distribution by ages, July 1982–June 1983. N = 9451.

Black-headed Gulls are present in the area throughout the year. A small passage starts at the end of June (Figure 163), characterized by a high proportion of juvenile gulls which continue out of the Strait towards the Atlantic after arriving from the north-east. The main arrivals in October are of adults, which numerically dominate all winter. In spring there is a gradual decrease in numbers, with passage in January and February and smaller numbers in March (Figure 163). The smaller passage in April is of immatures (Figure 164). As is the case for other gulls, young Black-headed Gulls appear to travel further than adults, and their spring migration follows that of the adults.

AUDOUIN'S GULL

The Audouin's Gull breeds in scattered colonies within the Mediterranean Sea (Witt, 1976; Cramp & Simmons, 1982), with over 60% in only two colonies— Chafarinas Islands off the Moroccan Mediterranean coast and the Ebro Delta (Vilalta & Gallissa, 1982) in eastern Spain. The breeding population has recently expanded dramatically (Ferrer & Martinez-Vilalta, 1986; de Juana, 1987) from 600–800 pairs in 1972–74 (Witt, 1976) to over 6000 pairs in 1987 (Hoogendoorn & Mackrill, 1987).

The appearance of individuals and groups of Audouin's Gulls along the northwest African coast between Tangier and Senegal was first noted by Smith (1972). Since then, several authors have remarked on the regular passage of Audouin's Gulls from the Mediterranean Sea into the Atlantic Ocean via the

Mixed flock of Audouin's Gulls of varying ages in flight over the Strait in July on their way towards Atlantic wintering areas.

Strait (Garcia, 1973; Pineau & Giraud-Audine, 1976; Cortés *et al.*, 1980; Telleria, 1981), and in view of the relatively small numbers wintering in the Mediterranean and Atlantic coasts of Morocco (Isenmann, 1978; Beaubrun, 1981, 1983, 1985; Witt *et al.*, 1984) it now appears that most migrate to winter south of Morocco, from Rio de Oro to Senegal (de Juana *et al.*, 1987; Mackrill, 1989). The main wintering area is nevertheless unconfirmed (Hoogendoorn & Mackrill, 1987), though substantial numbers were found in the Delta of the Saloum (Senegal) between September and February, including ringed birds from the Chafarinas colony (Baillon, 1989). The return passage seems less pronounced (Pineau & Giraud-Audine, 1976; Cortés *et al.*, 1980), but in recent years regular passage of adults has taken place off Gibraltar in February and March.

The numbers of Audouin's Gulls passing the Strait between July and October steadily increased during the 1970s and 1980s (Figure 165), and the rise in juvenile numbers was conspicuous (Figure 166). Mean numbers counted passing Europa Point rose from 1.5 birds/hour in 1982 to 18.83/hour in 1989, reflecting the increase in the breeding population during this period (de Juana & Varela, 1980; Witt, 1984; de Juana 1987). Numbers recorded outside the passage periods also increased during the 1970s and 1980s. During the 1982–83 winter (November–January) Audouin's Gulls were recorded off Europa Point on 11.94% of days watched, whereas during the 1988–89 winter they were recorded on 37.26% of the days ($\chi_1^2 = 10.424$, $P < 0.01$).

Audouin's Gulls are present within the Strait throughout the year. There are two periods with notable increases in numbers, coinciding with migratory

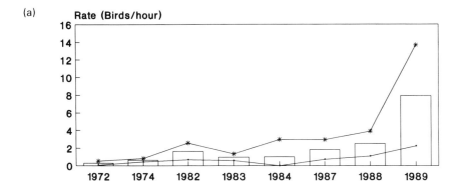

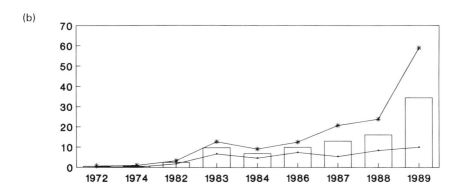

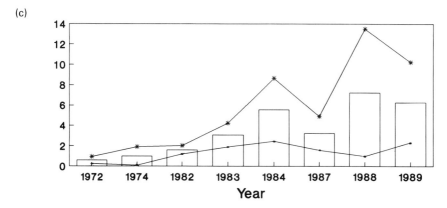

Figure 165.   Audouin's Gull increase in passage during (a) the first phase of the autumn migration, up to 20 July; (b) the second phase of the autumn migration, 21 July–20 August; (c) the third phase of the autumn migration, 21 August onwards. □, Mean;——■——, lower 95% limit; ————, upper 95% limit. 1972–89.*

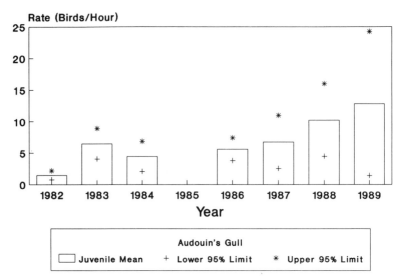

Figure 166.   Audouin's Gull increase in juveniles off Europa Point, Gibraltar. Phase 2: 1982–89.

movements (Figure 167), with passage towards the Atlantic from June to September (some in October) being most conspicuous. There is a well-defined return of adults in February and March, followed by immatures into May. This passage is probably direct along the Moroccan coast (Thevenot *et al.*, 1982) or high overhead, since it was only after prolonged spells of southeasterly winds that Audouin's Gulls were recorded passing Gibraltar eastwards in spring.

The passage into the Atlantic was studied in detail in 1983 (Figure 168). Three phases of passage could be defined and these appear to be fairly constant between years. The first phase (June to 20 July) is dominated by immature birds, mostly first and second summer, but there are no juveniles. The second phase (21 July to 20 August) consists of westward passage of adults and juveniles and is characterized by the highest overall number of gulls; third-summer birds also pass at this time. These early movements are direct and purposeful. The third phase (21 August to October) is dominated by juveniles, with a few adults but very few immatures. The intensity of migration is lower than during the first phase. This is the first time at which individuals start to linger in the area for several days.

Although the westward passage observed in the 1983 study includes immature birds, which had presumably summered in the Mediterranean, the proportion was low. It seems likely that juveniles emigrate from the Mediterranean and remain in the Atlantic during the following summers and that, at first, only a small number of immature birds make the journey back to the Mediterranean in spring. Other seabirds, including gulls, show a more marked migratory tendency in the early years of life when they may summer in the wintering areas

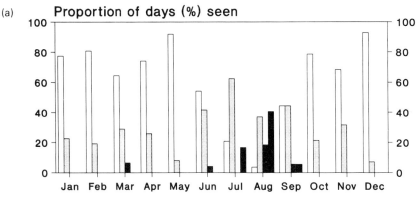

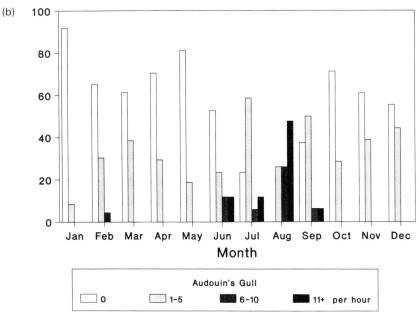

Figure 167. Audouin's Gull seasonal distribution off Europa Point, Gibraltar (a) 1987, (b) 1988.

(Nelson 1980). The proportion of immature birds at the breeding colony at Chafarinas is negligible (E. de Juana, pers. comm.), so that those which do return probably spend their time wandering away from the nesting colonies. For example, Audouin's Gulls do not breed on Sicily or the surrounding islands, but 40–50 (mostly second-year birds) spend the period June to late August along the southeast coast in harbours or salt pans, mixed with large flocks of Yellow-legged Gulls (C. Iapichino, pers. comm.). Immatures were regular in the Ebro Delta in spring, where they were also associated with Yellow-legged Gulls in

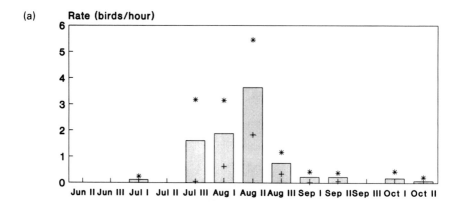

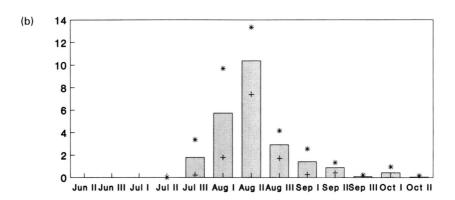

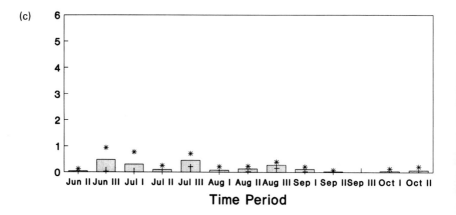

Figure 168.   Audouin's Gull autumn passage—1983 (a) adults, (b) juveniles, (c) first summers. (Continued opposite.)

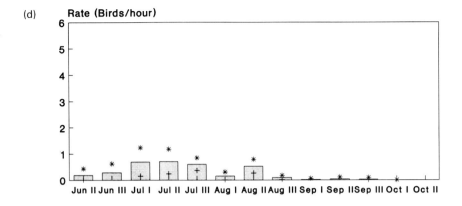

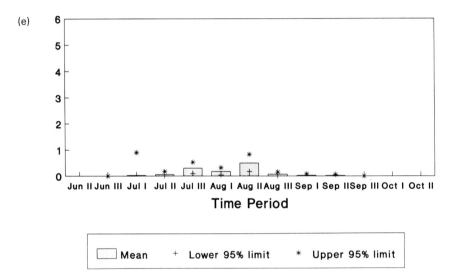

Figure 168 continued. (d) Second summers, (e) third summers.

the years immediately preceding the establishment of the new colony there (Martinez & Motis, 1982).

Many Audouin's Gulls travel in flocks (Figure 169) and the largest flock observed in the 1983 study was of 26 birds. The greatest flocking tendency was noted during the second phase of the migration, when 47.6% of all individuals were in groups. Adults showed the greatest tendency to flock and to form large groups, while first- and second-summer gulls were found in groups in lower frequencies than expected (Figure 169).

In autumn, Audouin's Gulls approach the Strait from the east along the two

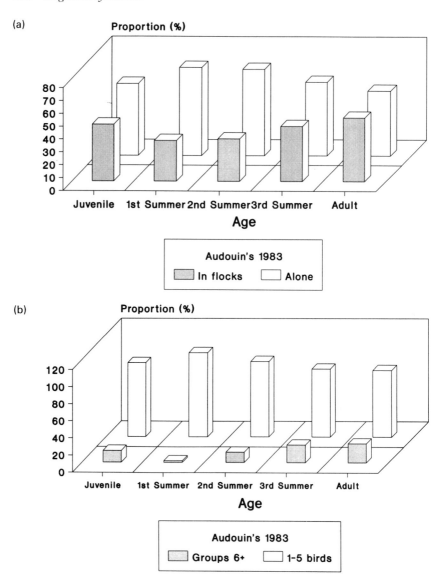

Figure 169.   (a) Audouin's Gull flocking on autumn passage. (b) Audouin's Gull flock size in autumn. 1983.

shores. Those which follow the Moroccan shore continue west towards Cape Spartel and then fly southwest. Those which approach Gibraltar may have rested in the Guadiaro Estuary and include birds from the Chafarinas colony. They cross the Bay of Gibraltar and follow the Spanish coast towards Tarifa, gradually veering southwest to join the Moroccan flow. Punta Carnero and Tarifa Beach are regular roosting sites for large flocks (over 200 birds, compared with up to 12

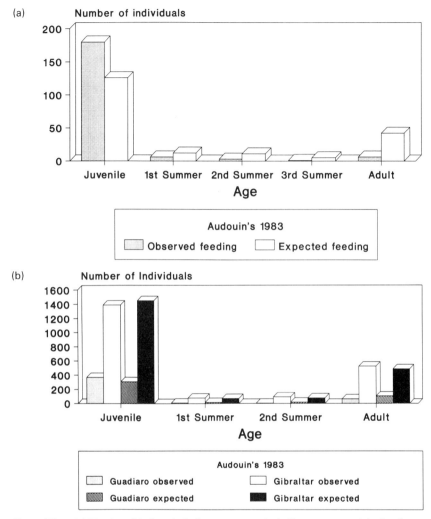

Figure 170. (a) Number of Audouin's Gulls attempting to feed off Europa Point, Gibraltar during autumn passage. (b) Number of Audouin's Gulls stopping at Guadiaro Estuary and Gibraltar on autumn passage. 1983.

in the 1960s). Inshore winds deflect birds towards the coasts, and passage at Gibraltar is strongest in southwesterlies.

On passage, Audouin's Gulls are attracted to river estuaries where they may pause and linger, especially when other gulls are flocking to feed. They have occasionally been seen to pause at Europa Point, Gibraltar, to feed at a sewage outlet alongside Black-headed and Mediterranean Gulls. Most of the Audouin's Gulls found in the Guadiaro Estuary or feeding off Europa Point were juveniles (Figure 170).

LESSER BLACK-BACKED GULL

The majority of Lesser Black-backed Gulls passing or wintering within the Strait and adjacent waters belong to the pale-backed subspecies *graellsii* (and a small proportion of *intermedius*). This has been confirmed by ringing recoveries, which are essentially of British-ringed birds with a few from Denmark, Holland and Norway (Telleria, 1981). Analysis of gulls ringed on Walney Island reveals a similar pattern (Baker, 1980). Most of the gulls seen at Gibraltar enter the Mediterranean in autumn, but it is likely that many of those following the Atlantic coast continue south along the Moroccan coast to winter between the Strait and Senegal, where they are common in winter (Brown, 1979).

Lesser Black-backed Gulls are abundant migrants and winter visitors. Over 4000 adults were counted on the Cádiz coast in the 1978 winter, with an undetermined additional number of immatures (Telleria, 1981), while an esti-mate of close to 2000 was made for Cádiz in January 1984 (Carrera, 1988). This last figure represents 8% of the Iberian wintering population (Carrera, 1988). On the Moroccan side, Beabrun (1985a) recorded 492 Lesser Black-backed Gulls within the Strait, 781 along the Atlantic coast close to the Strait and 214 along the Mediterranean coast close to the Strait, a total of just under 1500. Numbers may be higher, though; Isenmann (1978) recorded over 6500 between Ceuta and Rabat in the winter of 1976. Given these figures, it is possible to estimate the wintering population of Lesser Black-backed Gulls in the Strait at a minimum of 15 000–20 000, higher than the 8000–10 000 estimated for the Strait and Alborán by de Juana & Paterson (1986). Numbers may be even higher in midwinter, when

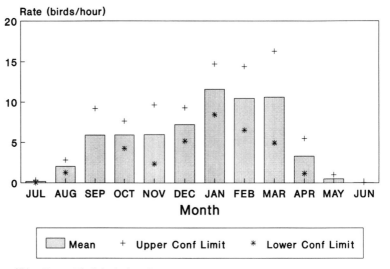

Figure 171.   Lesser Black-backed Gull seasonal distribution off Europa Point, Gibraltar, July 1982–June 1983.

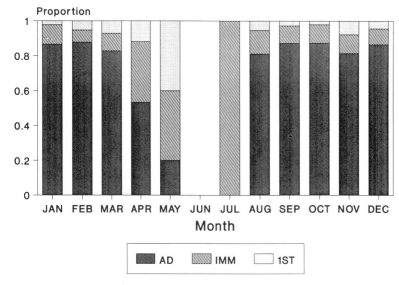

Figure 172. Lesser Black-backed Gull seasonal distribution by ages, July 1982–June 1983. N = 1527.

additional influxes may occur as a result of cold weather to the north (for example, see de Juana & Paterson, 1986).

In autumn and spring, mean numbers on passage off Europa Point vary between 5 and 10 birds/hour (Figure 171), although movements can be of greater intensity, for example 70 in 1 hour on 5 September 1989, and 141 in 2.5 hours (56.4/h) on 4 April 1988 (*SGBO Reports*). During these movements, large flocks gather in suitable localities, for example up to 2000 at Tarifa Beach during the autumn.

Lesser Black-backed Gulls are present in the Strait throughout the year, although in very small numbers between May and July (Figure 171). The entry into the Mediterranean commences during August and reaches its peak early in September. The number then stabilizes until the spring passage in February and March. The later spring migrants, in April and May, are largely immatures (Figure 172) as is the case for other seabird species in which young birds migrate further than adults. Adults predominate in the Strait in winter (Figure 172) as they do in the Alborán Sea (Paterson, 1990).

YELLOW-LEGGED GULL

This abundant species has its largest colony (at least 2500 pairs) on the Rock of Gibraltar. The Strait population has increased during the 1980s (Finlayson & Cortés, 1987; Ruiz Martinez *et al.*, 1990) in similar fashion to those of other areas of the western Mediterranean. The species appears to have been scarce on the

Rock last century (Irby, 1875, 1895) but has now become the dominant breeding seabird of the Strait. Other colonies are situated on the Moroccan coast especially on cliffs along the eastern coast of the Strait, with the largest colony ('several hundred pairs') at Cabo Negro, fewer on the cliffs of Jebel Musa and Leila Island and isolated pairs scattered on Atlantic cliffs between Larache and Tangier (Pineau & Giraud-Audine, 1979). On the Spanish coast Yellow-legged Gulls breed in the Tajo de Barbate (700 pairs; Grimmett & Jones, 1979) and, recently, on the ground in marshes and salt pans in Cádiz Bay, where about 300 pairs nested in 1985 (Ruiz Martinez *et al.*, 1990). A few pairs also breed along the rocky stretch between Punta Carnero and Tarifa, and pairs have recently nested on buildings in Gibraltar and Algeciras. The Strait population of Yellow-legged Gulls, which is in need of detailed censusing, may be of the order of 4000–5000 pairs, of which probably over 60% nest on the Rock of Gibraltar.

The western Mediterranean populations migrate towards temperate Europe at the end of the breeding season to reach nutrient-rich areas in the Alpine lakes and the west European seaboard (Yesou, 1985b; Carrera *et al.*, in press). The Strait population may be sedentary, judging from the large numbers present through-out the year, which may be related to the high productivity of the Strait in comparison to the western Mediterranean. The furthest a Gibraltar-ringed gull has been recovered is Marbella. The gulls resident in Gibraltar are not entirely sedentary; they perform regular movements inland to feed in rubbish tips (e.g. at Manilva and Tarifa), and, during the summer in particular, gather in large flocks off Europa Point, in association with the tuna fishing fleet northeast of the Rock and at the entrance to Gibraltar Bay, to feed on fish brought to the surface by local upwellings and by cetaceans and tuna.

KITTIWAKE

Kittiwakes from the northeast Atlantic colonies winter south to the area of the Strait including the Atlantic, and to a lesser extent, the Mediterranean coasts of Morocco (Pineau & Giraud-Audine, 1979; Beaubrun, 1985a), some as far south as Senegal and as far east as Lebanon (W. R. P. Bourne, pers. comm.). They are regular off the Mediterranean coast of Spain (Carrera *et al.*, 1981). Bernis (1967) gives Iberian recoveries (mostly Atlantic) of birds ringed in England (10), Scotland (1), Denmark (2), Lapland (1) and northern USSR (1); Beaubrun (1985b) gives Moroccan recoveries of Icelandic, English and Scottish Kittiwakes in winter.

The numbers of Kittiwakes wintering in and migrating past the Strait are highly variable. Kittiwakes are pelagic and what numbers are counted from the shore are a reflection of bad weather in the area, although not necessarily just in the Atlantic as suggested by Garcia (1973). The numbers on the Mediterranean coast of Spain have probably been underestimated—sizeable groups have been recorded from boats out at sea (Carrera, 1988). Observations from Europa Point during the 1982–83 winter (a fairly typical year) indicate average passage rates close to the coast of around 0.5–1.0 birds/hour.

In unusual years, conditions further north may force larger numbers of Kittiwakes south into the Mediterranean and along the Atlantic coasts of Morocco, producing large wrecks. The best-documented is the influx of January to March 1984, when 1432 were counted along the Mediterranean coast during the Spanish winter gull census (Carrera, 1988) and many were wrecked along the Moroccan Atlantic coast (Beaubrun, 1985b). This influx was well recorded within the Strait, with several days of heavy movement out of the Mediterranean towards the Atlantic and regular daily sightings off Europa Point. The peak movement took place on 5 March, when 1265 passed in 3 hours 50 minutes (330/hour), with a predominance of adults (Figure 173), a feature also reported by Beaubrun (1985b).

(a)

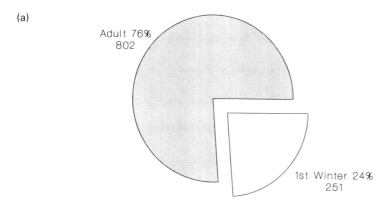

(b)

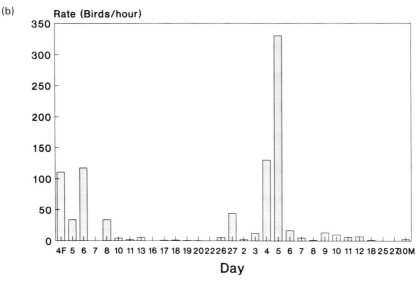

Figure 173. (a) Kittiwake influx 1984—age composition. (b) Kittiwake influx, February—March, 1984.

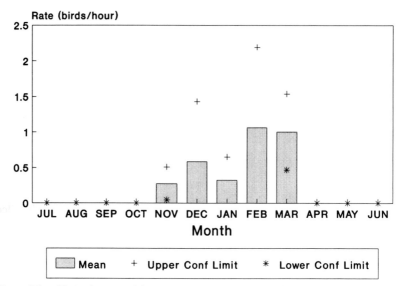

Figure 174.   Kittiwake seasonal distribution off Europa Point, Gibraltar, July 1982–June 1983.

Kittiwakes are essentially winter visitors to the Strait, with little migration through the area. The pattern of seasonal distribution takes the form of a late autumn arrival followed by a variable wintering element and a departure towards March (Figure 174). Smaller numbers occur at either end of this season, in October and April (Finlayson & Cortés, 1987).

SLENDER-BILLED GULL

A small population of Slender-billed Gulls has bred in the Marismas del Guadalquivir at least since 1960 (Weickert, 1960). This colony totals between 16 and 20 pairs (Costa, 1985; Grimmet & Jones, 1989). Small numbers breed irregularly in the Laguna de Fuente de Piedra, northeast of the Strait (Grimmett & Jones, 1989). These birds could be migratory and may winter off the coast of West Africa, in Mauretania and Rio de Oro (Erard, 1958). However, on the basis of winter counts close to breeding colonies (for example by Bermejo *et al.*, 1986), it has been suggested that the Spanish populations may be sedentary (Carrera, 1988). The large Black Sea population migrates southwest in autumn to reach wintering areas in Italy, Sicily and Tunisia, others reaching Egypt and the Persian Gulf (Erard, 1958, 1964). Some Black Sea birds must reach the Strait and beyond, judging from recoveries of birds from the Orlov population in Tenerife and along the coast of Portugal (Bernis, 1967). It is a scarce and irregular bird at sea, and passage down the Atlantic coast is small in relation to the size of the population (Irby, 1895; Garcia-Rua, 1975; Pineau & Giraud-Audine, 1979; Finlayson & Cortés, 1987).

Occasional birds are recorded along the Mediterranean coasts east of the Strait (e.g. de Juana & Paterson, 1986; Holliday, 1990). The incidence there may be expected to increase as a result of the recent increase in numbers in the Ebro Delta, where over 400 pairs bred in 1988 (Martinez Vilalta, 1988).

TERNS

GULL-BILLED TERN

About 1600 pairs of Gull-billed Terns breed in the Marismas del Guadalquivir (Biber, in Paterson, 1990). There is another breeding nucleus at the Laguna de Fuente de Piedra, northeast of the Strait, where the variable population has reached 3500 birds (Vargas *et al.*, 1978). Outside the breeding season Gull-billed Terns become coastal.

The Marismas population follows the Atlantic coast south to winter quarters in Mauretania and Senegal (Moreau, 1972). Fernandez–Cruz (1982) gives recoveries of Spanish-ringed birds in Guinea, Senegal and Mali. Danish birds also follow this route (Bernis, 1967), with some inland passage across Iberia (Cramp, 1985). Birds from the western Mediterranean colonies (Camargue, Ebro, Fuente de Piedra, Cabo de Gata) may follow the coast to the Strait, since small groups pass the Strait westwards in late July and early August. These birds then join the Atlantic flow, although some eastern birds may move directly across the Sahara, to wintering grounds in the Niger Inundation Zone in Mali (Curry & Sayer, 1979), or even southeast via Italy and Greece (Cramp, 1985). There is evidence of spring migration across the Sahara (Moreau, 1967; Smith, 1968) and of a general tendency to follow more easterly routes (Cramp, 1985).

The migratory periods in the Strait are late February to June and late July to October (Finlayson & Cortés, 1987). The species is generally scarce (e.g. 18 past Europa Point on six dates between 15 July and 11 September 1983) and travels singly or in small flocks, usually offshore and rarely pausing, except near estuaries and salt pans.

CASPIAN TERN

Finnish, Swedish and Crimean Caspian Terns have been recovered on passage in the Maghreb and in winter in tropical West Africa (Moreau, 1972), especially in the Niger Inundation Zone and the Gulf of Guinea (Cramp, 1985). Baltic birds have produced a number of passage and winter recoveries in southwestern Iberia (Bernis, 1967), though many migrate southeast and cross the Sahara (Cramp, 1985). A small population (probably around 100 individuals) winters regularly in southern Portugal, northwest Morocco and southwest Spain, including the Strait (Blondel & Blondel, 1964; Smith, 1965; Isenmann, 1978; Pineau & Giraud-Audine, 1979; Thevenot *et al.*, 1982; Bermejo *et al.*, 1986; Carrera, 1988). Presumably these are all Baltic birds (Staav, 1977; Mayaud, 1983).

Passage in the Strait is not well-defined; it involves singles or small groups, usually passing offshore, from March to mid-May and from August to October (Finlayson & Cortés, 1987). These include small numbers that approach the Strait from the Mediterranean coast (de Juana & Paterson, 1986; Paterson, 1987, 1990) and fly west past the Strait in August, September and October, and east in April (Holliday, 1990a,b). The Camargue is a regular stop-over area for this species (Isenmann, 1973).

ROYAL TERN

On completion of the breeding season in June–July (Mayaud, 1983), most Royal Terns from the Banc d'Arguin (Mauretania) migrate south to winter alongside other West African Royal Terns down to equatorial West Africa (Serle *et al.*, 1977). Others migrate northwards along the African Atlantic coast and regularly reach the Strait, where they are locally common between late July and October (Finlayson & Cortés, 1987); there are some records for other months (Irby, 1895; Smith, 1965; Pineau & Giraud-Audine, 1979; Thevenot *et al.*, 1981, 1982). They are most frequent on the Moroccan Atlantic coast but do reach Huelva in the north (Allen *et al.*, 1971, 1972) and the Strait and the Alborán Sea in the east (Martin, 1981; Thevenot *et al.*, 1981, 1982; Alba, 1982; Finlayson & Cortés, 1987; Paterson, 1987; Holliday, 1990a,b). Hashmi (pers. comm.) recorded a total of 16 flying west and four east in mid-Strait between 18 September and 13 November 1987.

LESSER CRESTED TERN

Lesser Crested Terns, assumed to be from the only large population in the Mediterranean in the Gulf of Sirte (Libya), migrate regularly past the Strait between March and May and between late July and early November (Finlayson & Cortés, 1987; Hashmi, pers. comm.) and are more abundant along the north African coast (Smith, 1965; Pineau & Giraud-Audine, 1979) than the European shore (Allen, 1973; Alba, 1981; Callebaut & Sneyders, 1981; Telleria, 1981; Finlayson, 1983; Holliday, 1990a,b). Hashmi (pers. comm.) counted 22 passing Ceuta westwards in 185 minutes on 25 October 1987.

One or two pairs have bred recently in the Ebro Delta (Chokomian, 1981; Ferrer & Martinez Vilalta, 1986; Martinez Vilalta, 1988), and a greater frequency of observations on the European shore would be expected if a colony became established there. The species has also bred recently in the Po Delta in Italy (Brichetti, in Paterson, 1990) and has been reported from Sicily (Iapichino, 1984b), so it may be spreading in a similar manner to other gulls and terns in the western Mediterranean. The Mediterranean population winters in West Africa, being regular on the coast of Gambia (Mayaud, 1983; Cramp, 1985). Occasionally, birds have been recorded in winter along the Moroccan coast close to the Strait (Thevenot *et al.*, 1981).

SANDWICH TERN

The migration of the various populations of Sandwich Terns has been summarized by Bernis (1967). Sandwich Terns from northeastern Atlantic colonies migrate down the coasts of the Atlantic and reach Africa, many wintering from southern Morocco to the Cape. A few winter in the Iberian Peninsula and northwest Morocco and enter the Strait and the western Mediterranean. The Black Sea populations winter in the Mediterranean Sea, with the highest proportion in the west. A few reach the Atlantic coasts of Iberia and Morocco (Isenmann, 1978), occasionally as far as Senegal and Ivory Coast (Cramp, 1985). Camargue and Ebro Delta birds may migrate towards the Atlantic. Iberian recoveries (Figure 175) reflect this pattern (Bernis, 1967).

Sandwich Terns are regular, at times abundant, migrants along all coastal areas of the Strait; mean passage rates are on average around 1.0–1.5 birds/hour, but higher numbers pass close to the coast in strong onshore winds (e.g. 119 flying east past Europa Point in 1 hour in strong southeasterlies on 11 April 1980, and 83 in 1 hour in similar conditions three days later). The main periods of passage are late February to May, with a peak in April, and August to early November with a peak in September (Finlayson & Cortés, 1987; Figure 176).

The total wintering population is small, probably 200–300 birds: Telleria (1981) estimated 200 for the two shores of the Strait in winter and de Juana & Paterson (1986) calculated around 200 in Alborán in winter; Isenmann (1978) counted 129 between Ceuta and Rabat. The western Mediterranean wintering population has been estimated at 3000 (6% of the European breeding population) (Isenmann, 1982).

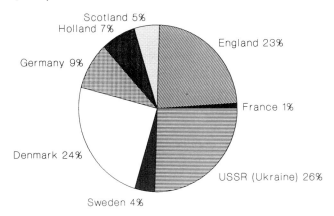

Figure 175. Sandwich Tern recoveries in Iberia, after Bernis (1967). N = 98.

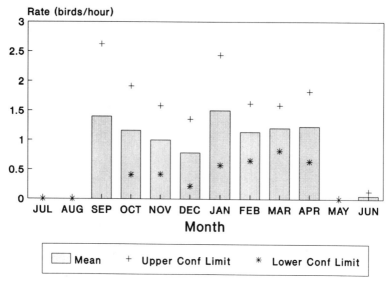

Figure 176.   Sandwich Tern seasonal distribution off Europa Point, Gibraltar, July 1982–June 1983.

ROSEATE TERN

European Roseate Terns migrate down the Atlantic coasts of Iberia and Morocco, including the Strait, to wintering grounds off west and southwest Africa (Bernis, 1967). They are scarce and irregular (Cortés *et al.*, 1980; Tellería, 1981; Finlayson & Cortés, 1987; Hashmi, pers. comm.) and may pass offshore (Bourne & Norris, 1966). They are even more scarce along Mediterranean areas of the Strait and to the east (see, for example, Paterson, 1987, 1990). Tellería (1981) cites recoveries of English birds at Tarifa and Cádiz.

COMMON TERN

The wintering areas of the various populations of Common Terns have been summarized by Bernis (1967) and Muselet (1982). British, Dutch and French birds winter in Atlantic Africa from southern Morocco to the Gulf of Guinea, a few reaching south to Angola. Finnish, northern German, Swedish and Norwegian birds also winter along the west African coast, though in general they winter further south, with a high number in Angola, some in southwest Africa, good numbers in the Cape and some even reaching Natal. Bernis (1967) also cited two Ukrainian birds in the Cape and speculated that Black Sea Common Terns might winter in the Mediterranean. The absence of Iberian and northwest African recoveries of Black Sea birds suggests a diagonal crossing of Africa. Fernandez-

Cruz (1982) gives recoveries of Ebro Delta birds in Mauretania (1), Senegal (2) and Ivory Coast (1). Iberian recoveries reflect the dominance of western and northern European Common Terns on passage (Bernis, 1967).

Within the Strait, Common Terns are regular migrants down the Atlantic coast and through the Strait into the Mediterranean. At times migratory movements may be spectacular when strong winds force birds inshore (e.g. 486 passing Europa Point eastwards in 2 hours on 31 March 1990). The main passage periods are late March to June and July to October (Finlayson & Cortés, 1987). Peak months are April and September. Occasional individuals remain throughout the winter.

ARCTIC TERN

The wintering area of Arctic Terns is not exclusively the Antarctic; for example, wintering is regular along much of the Atlantic African coastline (Cramp, 1985). Essentially, passage along Iberia and Morocco follows the Atlantic coast. Bernis (1967) gives five English, two Scottish and one Finnish recovery. The migration is, in general, inconspicuous in the Strait, presumably because birds normally pass out at sea (see, for example, Bourne & Norris, 1966). Observations away from Atlantic sectors are very few (Garcia, 1973; Cortés *et al.*, 1980; de Juana & Paterson, 1986).

LITTLE TERN

This species breeds abundantly along the Atlantic coasts of the Strait, with around 2000 pairs in the Cádiz–Guadalquivir area (Barcena *et al.*, 1984). The main winter quarters are in West Africa, between Guinea and Cameroon, with some in Mauretania and South Africa (Muselet, 1985), although occasional individuals winter on the Atlantic coast of Morocco (Isenmann 1978). Bernis (1967) gives Iberian recoveries of birds ringed in France, England, Scotland, Holland and Germany, mostly along the Atlantic coast. Western Mediterranean populations approach the Strait from the east to join the Atlantic flow.

Passage is irregular, both along the coast (pers. obs.) and in the middle of the Strait (Hashmi, pers. comm.), usually involving singles or small flocks. The migration is more conspicuous along Atlantic coastal areas where many Little Terns breed (see also Chapter 7). The main migratory periods are April to early June and July to October (Finlayson, 1983; Finlayson & Cortés, 1987).

BLACK TERN

The main wintering grounds of the huge Eurasian populations of Black Terns, which are marine in winter, are in coastal tropical West Africa from Senegambia to Namibia (Mayaud, 1983) with many in the Gulf of Guinea (Cramp, 1985). In autumn, northern and eastern populations follow the western European Atlantic coast via The Netherlands and south along the Iberian and Moroccan Atlantic coasts. Others cross central Europe and reach the Mediterranean to continue towards the Strait. Bernis (1967) gives Iberian recoveries of Czechoslovak, Soviet and Dutch birds, to which Cramp (1985) adds East German birds. Siberian birds probably follow this Mediterranean route (Mayaud, 1983). From the Strait, Black Terns follow the Atlantic coast of Morocco towards West Africa. Occasional birds winter along the Atlantic coast of Morocco (Isenmann, 1978). The passage periods are late March (though Black Terns are occasionally seen in February) to mid-June, and late July to early November, with peaks in late April/ early May and late August/September (Finlayson & Cortés, 1987).

The return passage, which includes diagonal crossings of the Sahara Desert (Smith, 1968), is less marked in the Strait, except when bad weather forces birds close to the shore (e.g. 521 were counted off Europa Point in light winds and rain on 28 April 1990 in 1.5 h of observation). Flocks (100–200 birds) are regular in spring along the Atlantic coast and in salt pans, estuaries and lagoons, and these are probably west and north European birds returning along the Atlantic coast.

The autumn passage at the Strait is heavy and prolonged, the Black Tern being a characteristic migrant in the Strait at this time. Mean passage rates from the coast vary significantly with weather conditions (Figure 177), but flocks of 1000–1500 are not uncommon (see, for example, Finlayson & Cortés, 1987) in autumn in mid-Strait or in estuaries (e.g. the Guadiaro estuary).

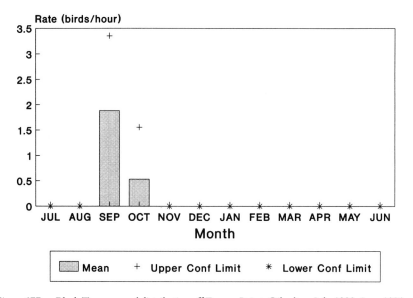

Figure 177.   Black Tern seasonal distribution off Europa Point, Gibraltar, July 1982–June 1983.

WHITE-WINGED BLACK TERN

The White-winged Black Tern is a scarce and irregular, but probably annual, visitor to the Strait in May, September and October (Smith, 1965; Pineau & Giraud-Audine, 1979; Thevenot *et al.*, 1981, 1982; Alba *et al.*, 1983; Finlayson & Cortés, 1987). They are recorded most frequently in lagoons and salt pans and less so on the coast, where they are sometimes seen in large-scale movements of Black Terns. Isenmann (1975) has also reported a regular spring passage in the Camargue. These birds are presumably of western Palaearctic and central Russian origin, wintering inland in tropical West Africa, especially in the Niger Inundation Zone (Moreau, 1972; Curry & Sayer, 1979), the majority following inland cross-desert routes (Morel & Roux, 1966; Moreau, 1967; Smith, 1968; Mayaud, 1983).

WHISKERED TERN

French and Iberian Whiskered Terns winter in tropical West Africa, especially Ghana with smaller numbers south to northern Zaïre (Cramp, 1985). French birds may take inland routes, following rivers, to join Iberian birds. Although coastal routes are probably then followed, inland migration may include crossing the Sahara to reach the Niger Inundation Zone in Mali where, locally, they outnumber White-winged Black Terns (Curry & Sayer, 1979). Small numbers winter irregularly in Spain (Erard & Viellard, 1966; Isenmann, 1972) and Morocco (Thevenot *et al.*, 1981, 1982). Morel & Roux (1966) give a recovery of a Camargue bird in Senegal, and Fernandez-Cruz (1982) gives two Spanish recoveries in Senegal and Ghana, and an unusual one of a bird ringed in June 1973 on the east coast of Spain and recovered in May 1975 in Hungary. Birds cross the Sahara in spring (Smith, 1968), when they may be using direct routes to the breeding grounds.

Passage in the Strait is not conspicuous (Finlayson & Cortés, 1987) and in spring takes the form of a rapid arrival *en masse* at the breeding colonies. They otherwise occur singly or in small parties, mainly in lagoons, estuaries and beaches, usually in the company of Black Terns. Passage periods are March to May and August to October (Finlayson & Cortés, 1987).

PUFFIN AND RAZORBILL

These two species present interesting contrasts in migratory behaviour and wintering. The Guillemot is a scarce visitor to the Strait and the Little Auk is a vagrant (Finlayson & Cortés, 1987).

The western Mediterranean is known to be a wintering area for Razorbills and Puffins (Lloyd, 1974; Mead, 1974; Carboneras, 1988). These birds are derived

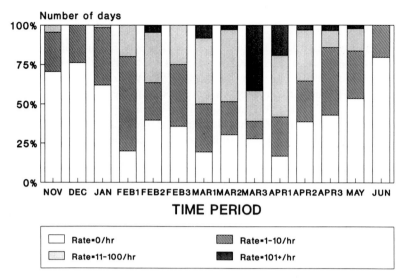

Figure 178.   Auk passage past Europa Point, Gibraltar, N = 479 days.

from the northeastern Atlantic colonies, principally those of the British Isles and France, and reach their southerly limit along the Atlantic coast of Morocco.

Auks are present offshore from November to January. Razorbills progressively increase from October, occasionally gathering in large rafts off estuaries in particular. Passage of Razorbills into the Mediterranean continues in mid–Strait at least until December (Hashmi, pers. comm.). In contrast, Puffins are not detected from Gibraltar at this time, although a small eastward movement is seen from Tarifa (Telleria, 1981). They move southeast towards the open sea and pass well away from the coast. Hashmi (pers. comm.) detected a large entry of Puffins into the Mediterranean in mid–Strait in December 1986, with a peak movement on 17 December when the passage rate was estimated at 5400 birds/hour in the late afternoon, including a stream of 900 in 10 minutes. In 1987, the earliest date Hashmi detected Puffins entering the Mediterranean was 9 November, despite intensive transects from August, which points to a mass migration late in the year.

Most of the auks sighted from the coast in winter are Razorbills, which are often fishing and not moving in any particular direction. They regularly enter the Bay of Gibraltar to fish. Puffins do not come inshore, and the few that are found in the Strait are out at sea. In the Mediterranean, Puffins winter away from the European continental shelf where most wintering Razorbills concentrate, and most Puffin recoveries are from the North African coast where they feed in deep water (Carboneras, 1988). This may account for the view that Razorbills are more abundant in the Mediterranean than Puffins.

In spring, auks move in the opposite direction and appear to commence a

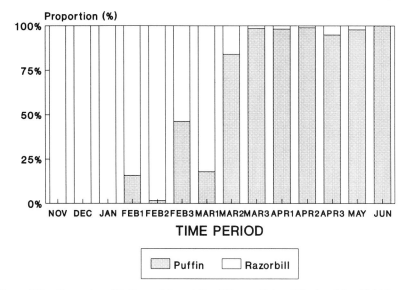

Figure 179. Proportion of Puffins and Razorbills off Europa Point, Gibraltar. N = 30 346.

coastal movement from Gibraltar, where they can be observed easily because the Rock is a prominent headland which they have to fly round. Razorbills probably follow the Spanish Mediterranean coast where they have wintered, and passage is detected in Malaga Bay at this time, where Puffins have hardly ever been detected (Paterson, 1987). During February numbers build up as a westward passage from the Mediterranean to the Atlantic develops (Figure 178). Auk passage builds to a peak at the end of March, followed by a steady decline towards June. The first part of the passage, until the first third of March, is dominated by Razorbills and the second part by Puffins (Figure 179). The late March peak is almost exclusively of Puffins. Passage is often spectacular, with auks passing in large flocks (Table 10). Bimodal passage of Puffins has been suggested by Paterson (1987) on the basis of a very small number of observations, but there is no evidence to support this.

Table 10   Flock sizes of auks passing the Strait of Gibraltar in spring.

	Group size (No. of observations)			
	1	2–10	11–50	Total
Puffin	52	431	215	698
	7.5%	61.7%	30.8%	
Razorbill	32	61	14	107
	29.9%	57.0%	13.1%	

The observed movements of Puffins and Razorbills (Figures 178 and 179) are consistent with the return of the two species to their breeding grounds (Cramp *et al.*, 1974). Razorbills return to their colonies in January and February, with numbers gradually increasing towards March and April. Puffins, on the other hand, return during mid-March in the south, but towards the end of March or early April farther north. The movements can also be linked with passage further north, off Finisterre (Northwest Spain) and Ireland (Sharrock, 1967; Pettit, 1970).

At Gibraltar there is considerable variation in counts within and between years, although the overall pattern is similar. The highest recorded Puffin count off Europa Point is of 13 000 in 5 hours on 28 March 1985. Of 25 936 auks specifically identified during the period 1980–86, 92.6% were Puffins and 7.4% were Razorbills. This suggests that Puffins are more abundant than Razorbills in the Mediterranean in winter but are regularly overlooked because of their very pelagic nature.

CHAPTER 6

Terrestrial Bird Communities

The terrestrial biotopes of the two sides of the Strait are typical of the Mediterranean. The influences of the Atlantic, which makes the Strait's climate more humid than further east in the Mediterranean, and the humid easterlies, which regularly envelop the zone with mists and low cloud, permit the development of rich vegetation zones that are Atlantic in character (Rivas Goday, 1968).

Typical Mediterranean evergreen and semi-evergreen oak forests, belonging to the *Quercion–fagineo–suberis* association (Rivas Martinez, 1975), are found on both shores of the Strait from sea level to altitudes of around 1000 m, depending on exposure and local climatic conditions (Torre, 1955; Pineau & Giraud–Audine, 1979; Finlayson & Cortés, 1987). On the Spanish side (Cádiz & Málaga), they occupy a total surface area of about 262×10^3 ha, of which 169×10^3 ha are in Cádiz Province (de la Rosa & Moreira, 1987). The dominant oaks are cork oak on

317

Vast woods of Cork Oak cover the siliceous hillsides on both sides of the Strait.

the siliceous soils and round–leaved oak (closely related to the holm oak) on the calcareous soils. The kermes oak is a shrub layer component in these woods, and the semi–evergreen *Quercus fruticosa* in dense woods at higher altitudes. In the mountains, oaks characteristic of Mediterranean montane deciduous and semi–evergreen oak woods are found alongside the other oaks, the Lusitanian oak and the Algerian oak in particular on siliceous soils. More than other oaks, the Lusitanian oak forms woods in which it dominates.

Cork oaks are harvested for their bark, which is used in the cork industry, and their economic use has ensured the survival of large tracts of woodland. The least disturbed woods have a rich bush layer (Finlayson & Cortés, 1987) dominated by mastic tree, montpellier broom, gorse, heathers and bramble in damp areas. In areas where the undergrowth has been cleared for grazing, meadows (*dehesa*) give the woods a characteristic appearance, and bracken dominates in the absence of shrubs. Among the trees that grow in between the cork oaks are the strawberry tree, laurel, holly and Laurustinus (Finlayson & Cortés, 1987). In poorer areas, especially on limestone where round–leaved oaks are dominant, degradation of the woodland permits the establishment of mastic trees, dwarf fan palms and olives; these may take over as scrub.

Laurel woodland is virtually non–existent in the Mediterranean, and the species is more typical as a shrub component in the matorral. In the mountains behind Algeciras, laurels grow in mixed stands alongside black poplars, alders, cork oaks and nettle trees (Polunin & Walters, 1985). These sierras have a rich cork oak woodland; their species composition (Fernandez Pasquier, 1982) is given in Appendix 2.

Sweet chestnuts have been planted in stands in mountain areas in the eastern side of the area, with extensive plantations in the Sierra Bermeja and Sierra Blanca. Other introduced species (e.g. walnuts) are found scattered within the sweet chestnut woods. In the lowlands, two eucalypts, the red gum and the Tasmanian blue gum, have been planted extensively and form large woods. Generally, these are unproductive and do not attract many birds.

Mediterranean pine woods are found in coastal and mountain areas of the region, and there has been artificial reforestation in many areas where they once grew naturally. For example, in Cádiz and Málaga Provinces, they occupy a total surface area of 114×10^3 ha, 79×10^3 ha being in Málaga; of this, 59×10^3 and 22×10^3 ha are reforestation in Málaga and Cádiz, respectively (de la Rosa & Moreira, 1987). Aleppo pines are scarce and rarely form woods of any size. Stone pines dominate along large stretches of sandy coastline and maritime pines form large woods on hillsides and mountains (e.g. Sierra del Cabrito, Sierra Bermeja, Sierra de las Nieves) up to 1200 m. Stone pines predominate in the lowland sandy soils. The best-preserved woods have a rich understorey of shrubs, which includes prickly juniper, french lavender, mastic tree, thorny broom, rock roses and holly oak (Finlayson & Cortés, 1987).

The endemic Spanish Fir forms woods on north-facing slopes above 1200 m in the Sierras Bermeja, del Pinar and de las Nieves.

At higher altitudes, the endemic Spanish fir grows in north facing slopes in the Serranía de Ronda above 1200 m, and the closely related Moroccan fir in similar situations in the higher limestone mountains of the Rif. Above the firs, on the Moroccan side, Atlantic cedars grow, forming denser woods to the south, in the high mountains of the Atlas range (Torre, 1955). Fir woods do not have a well-developed shrub layer, although some shrubs and creepers, notably hawthorns, Laurustinus, gorse and ivy, are found in the most open areas. Junipers do not develop into woods within the area, juniper woodland being more typical of higher mountain zones of central Spain (Santos *et al.*, 1981).

Along damp valleys, close to streams, the typical evergreen oak woodland gives way to a sub-Mediterranean wet woodland characterized by the presence of alder, narrow-leaved ash, smooth-leaved elm and white poplar. The term *canuto* is used to define areas where the vegetation is densest and most luxuriant. The shrub layer includes bramble, green heather and rhododendron in the shaded, cooler, locations, and oleander and giant reed in drier areas, especially in the lower reaches of streams. In the lower reaches, the land surrounding streams is devoted to pasture and a belt of oleander and reed marks the position of each stream.

Shrub, Scrub and Open Habitats

Many areas of the region are not covered by woodland—much has been destroyed by Man, and physical conditions in many places do not permit the development of a climax woodland community. Unwooded areas are dominated by the bush communities (matorral) so distinctive of the Mediterranean. Matorral takes up 142×10^3 ha of land in Málaga and Cádiz, and therefore occupies a greater area than pine woodland (de la Rosa & Moreira, 1987). The taller maquis (vegetation over 1 m) communities occur in various stages of development, the mastic tree being the dominant component in many sites. Maquis is best developed in the western Mediterranean as a result of the relatively moist climate, occurring largely on western coasts up to 600 m (Polunin & Walters, 1985). The best-preserved example of maquis is probably that of the Rock of Gibraltar (see Cortés *et al.*, 1980, and Appendix 2). The original vegetation of Gibraltar belonged to the olive–carob zone, a climax community of olive and carob woodland (which may have included the round-leaved oak and nettle tree) characteristic of dry Mediterranean zones up to 600 m. This woodland was removed from Gibraltar in the 18th Century for firewood during the sieges of the Rock. The barren hillsides were grazed by goats until the turn of the century, when much of the area became of restricted access for defence reasons. Unlike other areas of the Strait, therefore, this community has developed untouched for over 80 years. It includes areas of tall olive woodland and a varied shrub community.

In many areas of the Strait, within the evergreen oak zone, different stages of maquis development are to be found, depending on the degree of disturbance to

Typical luxuriant maquis vegetation on the eastern side of the Rock of Gibraltar, dominated in this case by wild olives and dwarf fan palms.

which these communities have been subjected. Typical shrubs of the maquis include mastic and turpentine trees, thorny broom, teline, dwarf fan palm and olive.

At higher altitudes, in the montane and submontane zones, there are large areas (often covering whole hillsides) of maquis where the natural climax vegetation was once montane oak woodland. Here the maquis contains evergreen species (e.g. Lusitanian oak, kermes oak, mastic tree and strawberry tree), heathers and rock roses.

There are many types of garigue community in the Mediterranean, differentiated by species composition (e.g. see Polunin & Walters, 1985) but sharing similar structural characteristics. Garigue is an open community of low shrubs, usually averaging 50 cm in height and rarely exceeding 1 m, with large areas of open, bare ground. Garigue habitats are typical of areas with poor soils or bare rock, and where woodland and maquis has been removed and intense grazing pressure persists. The coastal Mediterranean garigues of the Strait, dominated by spurges and rock roses, cover large areas of hillside. Typical species are French lavender, mastic tree, kermes oak, large Mediterranean spurge, purple Jerusalem sage, Mediterranean mezereon, dwarf fan palm, rock roses and heathers. Garigue is progressively being destroyed by coastal developments, so it is now rare right by the sea on the European shore of the Strait, occurring in the coastal hills a kilometre or more from the coastline itself. In the high mountain zones, above the fir line, where the rigorous climatic conditions do not permit the develop-

Many autumn fruits, such as these figs, are eaten by Palaearctic migrants on their way south. The fruit provide a means of accumulating fat and maintaining a positive water balance in the severe drought conditions.

ment of woodland, there is a belt of garigue with low, usually thorny, shrubs adapted to the high altitude conditions.

Semi-natural grasslands are found where intensive grazing maintains a community dominated by grasses, often including a large element of native species (Appendix 2). Pastures take up 220×10^3 ha in Cádiz and Málaga Provinces, of which 122×10^3 are in Cádiz (de la Rosa & Moreira, 1987). In certain areas, such as the fields surrounding La Janda, a natural steppe vegetation has been largely unmodified by Man. Pastures and land devoted to cultivation are of greatest extent in the low-lying districts of the western side of the Strait: a total of 609.1×10^3 ha are devoted to cultivation in Cádiz and Málaga Provinces. In Cádiz, the principal crops are wheat, beet, sunflowers and some potatoes and beans. Wheat and sunflowers dominate in the Jerez campiñas. In Málaga, avocado and citrus are important in coastal areas, with high cereal production in the Ronda mountains (de la Rosa & Moreira, 1987). Olive plantations cover large areas of land, especially in the northern and western slopes of the Serranía de Ronda, close to the campiñas.

BIRD COMMUNITIES OF THE DIFFERENT HABITATS

Over the last five years, I have censused bird communities in the main habitats of the Spanish side of the Strait. The results are presented in the sections below. Species density records and census methods are given in Appendices 3 and 4.

Non-coniferous Woods

The non-coniferous woods include Mediterranean evergreen and semi-evergreen oak woods, montane deciduous and semi-evergreen oak woods, and wet woods.

The following account is based on my own analysis of the breeding bird communities of four Spanish oak woods close to the Strait. Two sites provided examples of relatively undisturbed woodland, the valley of the Valdeinfierno, a cork oak wood in the siliceous sierras north of the Strait (altitude 200 m), and a round-leaved oak wood in the limestone sierras near the town of Grazalema (altitude 800 m). The other two sites are partly managed and grazed by cattle so that the shrub layer is more disturbed. These sites are a cork oak wood near the town of Benalup (altitude 50 m) and a cork oak wood with scattered introduced trees (e.g. pines and eucalypts) at Almoraima, south of Jimena de la Frontera (altitude 50–100 m). These sites are considered representative of the general pattern of breeding bird communities in oak woods on both sides of the Strait (Pineau & Giraud-Audine, 1979; Finlayson & Cortés, 1987).

Oak woods are rich in passerine breeding bird species, and the sites investigated had between 26 and 42 species. The two most disturbed sites (Benalup and Almoraima) had the greatest number of species, probably as these sites were more heterogeneous than the undisturbed woods (Table 11). Oak woods were dominated numerically by resident species, with a small proportion of trans-saharan migrants (Table 12). The disturbed Benalup site had the greatest number of migrant species in a breeding community, and the mountain site had the greatest proportion of passerine migrants by individuals. Oak woods, dominated by residents, appear to be closed to migrants, only a small number being able to enter the more disturbed areas where there are patches of secondary vegetation (e.g. Black-eared Wheatear, Melodious Warbler and Woodchat Shrike) and some occurring at higher densities there (e.g. Spotted Flycatcher). The mountains, which exhibit the greatest climatic fluctuations between winter and summer, can support a greater density of migrants, which arrive in spring to fill up niches which are vacant. Among these species are the Nightingale, Melodious Warbler, Subalpine Warbler and Bonelli's Warbler.

Some groups of species absent from the undisturbed woods appear where there are clearings in the managed sites. Larks, swallows and martins, and buntings are examples, contrasting with the more 'typical' woodland groups (e.g. tits) which are best represented in the mature woods (Table 13). The numerically dominant species also changed with disturbance (Table 14). The Blackcap, Bonelli's Warbler, Short-toed Tree Creeper and Chaffinch dominated in mature woods but not disturbed woods. The reverse occurred with the Sardinian Warbler, Serin, Greenfinch and Goldfinch. The only dominant species throughout the entire range of woods was the Blue Tit.

By examining habitat breadth and overlap values for each species in a particular site, it is possible to classify species as habitat generalists or specialists. If a species is particularly suited to a site, it should be evenly distributed in the site and should overlap considerably with other species. Such species should reach high densities, above the community mean. Other species may only find discrete patches suitable and will behave as habitat specialists. A species may behave as a specialist in one site and as a generalist in another. The four sites investigated illustrated substantial differences which demonstrated clear differences in community structure within the basic oak woodland habitat (Table 18).

If non-passerines are also included, then the typical, undisturbed, lowland oak wood would be expected to have a range of species from those given in Table 19. In disturbed woods with scrub or open ground in clearings, the species given in Table 20 appear. On higher ground the following additional species are found: residents—Crag Martin, Dartford Warbler, Rock Bunting; migrants—Subalpine Warbler (occasionally breeds at lower altitudes).

Table 11   Species richness in the Strait's terrestrial habitats (breeding species).

Habitat type	Species richness		
and site	Passerine	Non-passerine	Total
Oak			
Almoraima	31	11	42
Benalup	26	15	41
Grazalema	29	9	38
Valdeinfierno	20	6	26
Pine			
Nieves	29	7	36
Piñar del Rey	23	7	30
Blanca	21	6	27
Algaida	11	6	17
Bermeja	14	3	17
Mattoral			
Grazalema	29	10	39
Nieves maquis	27	4	31
Nieves garigue	26	4	30
Jara	21	3	24
Carnero	15	4	19
Manilva	16	3	19
Jimena	11	4	15
Blanca	13	1	14
Gibraltar cliff	8	4	12
Gibraltar maquis	7	2	9
Open			
Janda	24	20	44
Marisma	12	19	31
Ojén	24	7	31
Zahara	10	5	15

Table 12   Proportion of migrants in terrestrial habitats of the Strait (breeding species).

Habitat type and site	Migrants	Residents	% Migrants
BY SPECIES—NON-PASSERINES			
Oak			
Almoraima	5	6	45.5
Benalup	7	8	46.7
Grazalema	3	6	33.3
Valdeinfierno	3	3	50.0
Pine			
Nieves	3	4	42.86
Piñar del Rey	6	1	85.71
Blanca	1	5	16.67
Algaida	4	2	66.67
Bermeja	2	2	50.00
Matorral			
Grazalema	4	6	40.00
Nieves maquis	3	1	75.00
Nieves garigue	1	3	25.00
Jara	2	1	67.67
Carnero	0	4	0.00
Manilva	1	2	33.33
Jimena	2	2	50.00
Blanca	0	1	0.00
Gibraltar cliff	1	4	20.00
Gibraltar maquis	0	2	0.00
Open			
Janda	12	8	60.00
Marisma	8	11	42.11
Ojén	5	2	71.43
Zahara	3	2	60.00
BY SPECIES—PASSERINES			
Oak			
Almoraima	7	24	22.6
Benalup	8	18	30.8
Grazalema	7	22	24.1
Valdeinfierno	5	15	25.0
Pine			
Nieves	8	21	27.59
Piñar del Rey	7	16	30.43
Blanca	3	18	14.29
Algaida	1	10	9.09
Bermeja	0	14	0.00

Continued.

Table 12   Continued

Habitat type and site	Migrants	Residents	% Migrants
BY SPECIES—PASSERINES (*continued*)			
Matorral			
Grazalema	6	23	20.69
Nieves maquis	5	22	18.52
Nieves garigue	7	19	26.92
Jara	7	14	33.33
Carnero	5	10	33.33
Manilva	5	11	31.25
Jimena	1	10	9.09
Blanca	3	10	23.08
Gibraltar cliff	0	8	0.00
Gibraltar maquis	0	7	0.00
Open			
Janda	7	17	29.17
Marisma	5	7	41.67
Ojén	7	17	29.17
Zahara	2	8	20.00
BY DENSITY[1]—PASSERINES			
Oak			
Almoraima	18.7	64.2	22.56
Benalup	36.3	117.9	23.54
Grazalema	39.1	76.4	33.85
Valdeinfierno	25.8	96.6	21.08
Pine			
Nieves	36.5	83.1	30.52
Piñar del Rey	31.7	75.5	29.57
Blanca	10.0	59.5	14.39
Algaida	1.3	99	1.3
Bermeja	0.0	59	0.00
Matorral			
Grazalema	14.6	137.9	9.6
Nieves maquis	25.6	73.1	25.9
Nieves garigue	37	99	27.2
Jara	50	98	33.8
Carnero	16.6	84.8	16.4
Manilva	12.4	101.6	10.9
Jimena	3	67	4.3
Blanca	4.5	40.9	9.9
Gibraltar cliff	0	40	0.00
Gibraltar maquis	0	84	0.00

Continued.

Table 12   Continued

Habitat type and site	Migrants	Residents	% Migrants
BY DENSITY[1] — PASSERINES (*continued*)			
Open			
Janda	96.3	104.9	47.86
Marisma	53.9	60.8	46.99
Ojén	26.7	98	21.41
Zahara	2.5	140.9	1.74

[1] Densities are birds/10 ha.

Table 13   *Representation (%) of passerine groups (by density) in terrestrial bird communities (breeding species).*

Site/habitat	LA	MA	PI	CH	WA	TI	CO	FI	BU	OT
Almoraima (O)	0.8	4.8	0.0	19.4	19.3	13.8	3.3	24.1	4.1	10.4
Benalup (O)	2.3	7.9	0.0	11.1	10.2	11.6	5.1	31.5	2.8	17.6
Grazalema (O)	0.7	0.7	0.0	22.3	28.9	19.5	1.5	20.1	0.7	5.6
Valdeinfierno (O)	0.0	1.4	0.0	8.8	27.9	16.3	2.7	27.2	0.0	15.6
Nieves (P)	6.4	0.0	0.0	12.7	22.0	9.5	8.5	22.1	8.5	10.5
Piñar del Rey (P)	5.1	3.4	0.0	19.5	9.3	15.2	1.7	28.0	11.1	0.0
Blanca (P)	0.0	0.0	0.0	17.1	17.1	10.9	1.9	35.0	0.0	18.0
Algaida (P)	0.0	0.0	0.0	1.3	21.2	16.3	38.7	2.5	0.0	20.0
Bermeja (P)	0.0	0.0	0.0	5.1	28.8	13.6	3.4	17.0	10.2	22.0
Grazalema (M)	0.9	3.9	0.5	20.1	5.6	1.8	42.8	17.0	2.6	4.8
Nieves maquis (M)	4.5	1.1	0.0	20.1	22.5	7.8	7.8	24.8	10.1	1.3
Nieves garigue (M)	5.9	0.0	1.5	39.7	7.4	2.9	8.8	19.9	11.0	3.0
Jara (M)	0.7	6.1	0.0	31.8	31.1	0.0	0.0	9.5	16.2	4.7
Carnero (M)	0.0	7.2	0.0	37.5	32.8	0.7	0.0	14.5	2.0	5.3
Manilva (M)	18.3	4.7	0.0	10.1	37.9	0.0	0.0	17.5	10.1	1.4
Jimena (M)	4.3	5.7	0.0	18.6	51.4	1.4	0.0	2.9	7.1	8.6
Blanca (M)	0.0	0.0	0.0	9.9	56.2	2.0	6.0	16.1	4.0	6.0
Gibraltar cliff (M)	0.0	0.0	0.0	37.5	27.5	0.0	0.0	0.0	2.5	32.5
Gibraltar maquis (M)	0.0	0.0	0.0	21.4	61.9	6.0	0.0	2.4	0.0	8.3
Janda (O)	9.6	36.5	4.3	5.7	13.8	0.0	3.2	16.3	6.8	3.9
Marisma (O)	30.2	18.1	16.7	0.0	16.8	0.0	4.7	13.4	0.0	0.0
Ojén (O)	6.7	4.7	3.4	19.3	8.0	1.4	1.3	22.7	19.3	13.3
Zahara (O)	25.0	0.0	0.6	8.2	7.0	0.0	0.0	10.5	33.7	15.1

O, oak; P, pine; M, matorral; O, open.

Table 14   Presence (%) of numerically dominant[1] passerines in terrestrial habitats of the Strait: oak woods (breeding species).

Species	Almoraima	Benalup	Grazalema	Valdeinfierno
Wren	—	—	5.0	—
Robin	—	—	6.5	—
Nightingale	12.9	6.9	9.4	—
Subalpine Warbler	—	—	10.1	—
Sardinian Warbler	8.8	8.4	—	—
Blackcap	5.7	—	—	7.5
Bonelli's Warbler	—	—	8.7	13.6
Blue Tit	10.5	8.8	7.2	7.5
Short-toed Tree Creeper	—	—	—	6.3
Jackdaw	—	5.1	—	—
House Sparrow	—	6.0	—	—
Chaffinch	—	—	7.2	23.1
Serin	8.1	6.9	5.0	—
Greenfinch	—	6.0	—	—
Goldfinch	8.8	13.0	7.2	—

[1] Species contributing to 5% or more of the community by density.

Table 15   Presence (%) of numerically dominant [1] passerines in terrestrial habitats of the Strait: pine woods (breeding species).

Species	Nieves	Piñar del Rey	Blanca	Algaida	Bermeja
Woodlark	5.3	5.1	0.0	0.0	0.0
Wren	0.0	0.0	11.7	0.0	10.2
Nightingale	0.0	8.5	6.3	0.0	0.0
Blackbird	0.0	9.3	8.1	0.0	5.1
Melodious Warbler	6.3	0.0	0.0	0.0	0.0
Dartford Warbler	0.0	0.0	0.0	0.0	23.7
Subalpine Warbler	10.5	0.0	0.0	0.0	0.0
Sardinian Warbler	0.0	0.0	0.0	21.2	0.0
Blackcap	0.0	0.0	5.5	0.0	0.0
Crested Tit	0.0	0.0	0.0	0.0	5.1
Great Tit	0.0	0.0	0.0	15.0	8.5
Short-toed Tree Creeper	0.0	0.0	0.0	0.0	10.2
Woodchat Shrike	0.0	12.7	0.0	0.0	0.0
Azure-winged Magpie	0.0	0.0	0.0	34.9	0.0
Chough	7.4	0.0	0.0	0.0	0.0
Tree Sparrow	0.0	0.0	0.0	15.0	0.0
Spanish Sparrow	8.4	0.0	0.0	0.0	0.0
Chaffinch	8.4	8.5	13.5	0.0	11.9
Serin	0.0	0.0	18.9	0.0	0.0
Greenfinch	0.0	11.1	0.0	0.0	0.0
Goldfinch	0.0	6.8	0.0	0.0	0.0
Rock Bunting	5.3	0.0	0.0	0.0	10.2
Corn Bunting	0.0	6.8	0.0	0.0	0.0

[1] Species contributing to 5% or more of the community by density.

Table 16   Presence (%) of numerically dominant[1] passerines in terrestrial habitats of the Strait: mattoral (breeding species).

Species	Graz	Nvmq	Nvgr	Jara	Carn	Mani	Jime	Blan	Gbcl	Gbmq
Crested Lark	0.0	0.0	0.0	0.0	0.0	18.3	0.0	0.0	0.0	0.0
Crag Martin	0.0	0.0	0.0	0.0	0.0	0.0	5.7	0.0	0.0	0.0
Swallow	0.0	0.0	0.0	6.1	0.0	0.0	0.0	0.0	0.0	0.0
Wren	0.0	0.0	0.0	0.0	0.0	0.0	8.6	6.0	0.0	8.3
Nightingale	0.0	5.7	0.0	18.9	7.2	0.0	0.0	6.0	0.0	0.0
Black Redstart	0.0	0.0	9.6	0.0	0.0	0.0	0.0	0.0	0.0	0.0
Stonechat	0.0	0.0	0.0	9.5	20.4	8.1	12.9	0.0	0.0	0.0
Wheatear	0.0	0.0	9.6	0.0	0.0	0.0	0.0	0.0	0.0	0.0
Blk-eared Wheatear	0.0	0.0	5.2	0.0	0.0	0.0	0.0	0.0	0.0	0.0
Blue Rock Thrush	6.1	0.0	0.0	0.0	0.0	0.0	0.0	0.0	30.0	0.0
Blackbird	0.0	6.8	0.0	0.0	9.9	0.0	0.0	0.0	0.0	21.4
Fan-tailed Warbler	0.0	0.0	0.0	0.0	0.0	11.5	0.0	0.0	0.0	0.0
Dartford Warbler	0.0	0.0	0.0	0.0	0.0	7.5	22.9	42.1	0.0	0.0
Subalpine Warbler	0.0	7.9	5.9	0.0	0.0	0.0	0.0	0.0	0.0	0.0
Sardinian Warbler	0.0	0.0	0.0	16.2	31.6	14.2	28.6	10.1	25.0	29.8
Blackcap	0.0	0.0	0.0	0.0	0.0	0.0	0.0	0.0	0.0	32.1
Bonelli's Warbler	0.0	9.0	0.0	0.0	0.0	0.0	0.0	0.0	0.0	0.0
Chough	31.5	0.0	8.8	0.0	0.0	0.0	0.0	6.0	0.0	0.0
Jackdaw	11.3	0.0	0.0	0.0	0.0	0.0	0.0	0.0	0.0	0.0
House Sparrow	0.0	0.0	0.0	0.0	0.0	0.0	0.0	0.0	22.5	0.0
Chaffinch	0.0	5.7	5.9	0.0	0.0	0.0	0.0	0.0	0.0	0.0
Goldfinch	6.1	15.8	5.2	6.8	11.1	8.8	0.0	0.0	0.0	0.0
Linnet	6.1	0.0	0.0	0.0	0.0	7.5	0.0	12.1	0.0	0.0
Rock Bunting	0.0	0.0	11.0	0.0	0.0	0.0	7.1	0.0	0.0	0.0
Corn Bunting	0.0	6.8	0.0	16.2	0.0	10.1	0.0	0.0	0.0	0.0

[1] Species contributing to 5% or more of the community by density.

Table 17   Presence (%) of numerically dominant[1] passerines in terrestrial habitats of the Strait: open ground (breeding species).

Species	Janda	Marisma	Ojen	Zahara
Calandra Lark	5.3	12.7	0.0	15.7
Crested Lark	0.0	13.4	0.0	8.2
Swallow	0.0	18.1	0.0	0.0
House Martin	35.5	0.0	0.0	0.0
Yellow Wagtail	0.0	16.7	0.0	0.0
Nightingale	0.0	0.0	5.4	0.0
Stonechat	0.0	0.0	12.7	8.2
Fan-tailed Warbler	7.1	7.4	0.0	6.4
Great Reed Warbler	0.0	9.42	0.0	0.0
Woodchat Shrike	0.0	0.0	5.4	0.0
Spotless Starling	0.0	0.0	6.7	15.1
Goldfinch	10.3	0.0	16.0	10.5
Linnet	0.0	10.0	0.0	0.0
Corn Bunting	6.8	0.0	18.7	33.7

[1] Species contributing to 5% or more of the community by density.

Table 18   Mean community within-habitat breadth and overlap values (breeding species).

Habitat type and site	Breadth[1]	Overlap[2]
Oak		
Almoraima	0.2100	0.1882
Benalup	0.3115	0.3199
Grazalema	0.2324	0.2782
Valdeinfierno	0.3721	0.3807
Pine		
Nieves	0.2430	0.2599
Piñar del Rey	0.2857	0.2745
Blanca	0.2213	0.1977
Algaida	0.2953	0.3287
Bermeja	0.3013	0.2748
Matorral		
Grazalema	0.1848	0.1982
Nieves maquis	0.2754	0.2585
Nieves garigue	0.2663	0.2580
Jara	0.3165	0.3053
Carnero	0.2796	0.2858
Manilva	0.2959	0.3217
Jimena	0.3624	0.3380
Blanca	0.1953	0.1722
Gibraltar cliff	0.2627	0.3827
Gibraltar maquis	0.4468	0.4257
Open		
Janda	0.2637	0.2682
Marisma	0.2292	0.2254
Ojén	0.2612	0.2911
Zahara	0.3589	0.4362

[1]Habitat breadth values calculated for each species using the Simpson index (using proportion of each species found in each plot within the habitat) divided by the number of plots in each site. Mean value for all species in a site was computed to give the mean site within–habitat breadth.

[2]Habitat overlap values were calculated for all possible species pairs in each habitat and the mean within-habitat overlap calculated for each species in each habitat. The mean value for all species in a site was computed to give the mean site within-habitat overlap.

Table 19   Breeding species of undisturbed lowland oak wood.

Residents	Migrants
Goshawk	Booted Eagle
Sparrowhawk	Cuckoo
Buzzard	Bonelli's Warbler
Woodpigeon	Spotted Flycatcher
Green Woodpecker	Golden Oriole
Great Spotted Woodpecker	
Wren	
Robin	
Blackbird	
Mistle Thrush	
Blackcap	
Chiffchaff	
Firecrest	
Crested Tit	
Blue Tit	
Great Tit	
Long-tailed Tit	
Nuthatch	
Short-toed Tree Creeper	
Jay	
Spotless Starling	
Chaffinch	
Hawfinch	

Table 20   Additional breeding species of disturbed woods with scrub and open ground.

Residents	Migrants
Red-legged Partridge	Short-toed Eagle
Woodlark	Turtle Dove
Stonechat	Bee-eater
Sardinian Warbler	Hoopoe
Jackdaw	Swallow
House Sparrow	Red-rumped Swallow
Serin	Nightingale
Greenfinch	Black-eared Wheatear
Goldfinch	Olivaceous Warbler
Cirl Bunting	Melodious Warbler
Corn Bunting	Rufous Bush Chat
	Woodchat Shrike

MEDITERRANEAN AND MEDITERRANEAN MONTANE CONIFEROUS WOODS

Pine woods in the area have a more disjointed distribution than oak woods and in many zones have been extensively replanted. In sandy lowland areas, the dominant species is the stone pine, which covers belts close to the coastline as well as areas further inland. On hillsides and mountain slopes, the maritime pine forms large woods and is the main conifer. A feature of both types of pine wood is the variation in tree height between and within woods, often depending on when the trees were planted. There is also substantial variation in the density of vegetation in the shrub layer, ranging from a few shrubs to a well-developed understorey.

My studies of the breeding communities have included five pine woods representative of the range of woods at different altitudes on the Spanish side of the Strait:

(1) a maritime pine wood on the north-facing slopes of the Sierra Bermeja (altitude 1000 m) north of Estepona;

(2) a stone pine wood at Monte Algaida (altitude 5 m) north of Sanlúcar de Barrameda;

(3) a stone pine wood with small stands of cork oak along its fringes at the Pinar del Rey (altitude 90 m) north of San Roque;

(4) a maritime pine wood with stands of sweet chestnut, eucalypt and olive in the Sierra Blanca (altitude 900 m) north of Marbella;

(5) a plantation of young maritime pines on the northwestern slopes of the Sierra de las Nieves (altitude 1300 m) south of Ronda.

The five woods represent a range from 'pure' stands (Bermeja and Algaida) to mixed stands (Blanca and Pinar del Rey), with a series of ages in the case of maritime pine.

The pine wood passerine communities were not as rich as those of oak woods, and had high dominance values and correspondingly low diversity; the species in the woods were localized and overlapped little with each other. The range of breeding species varied between 17 and 36. The two pure stands had the lowest species richness (17 species in each case), followed by the two mixed woods (27 and 30 species) and the young stand (36 species) (see Table 11). The young wood, which was situated at the highest altitude, had large areas of open, rocky or grassy, ground and patches of low maquis, which created a varied habitat.

The five communities were dominated numerically by resident species (see Table 12). The sites at Sierra de las Nieves and Piñar del Rey had more migrants (by species and density) than the other woods. Habitat heterogeneity and age appear to be key factors in the species diversity of pine woods. The oldest and purest woods were characterized by a small number of species, old mixed woods having a greater number of species, with a greater proportion of migrants in structurally more heterogeneous woods. Young woods had the greatest species-richness and proportion of migrants. Old pine woods had fewer migrants than oak woods, but young pine woods or those with other habitats bordering the

Spectacular mountain scenery in the Serrania de Ronda. The dark band of trees in the distance, sandwiched between the lower woods of Round-leaved Oak and the higher scrub and scree, is of the endemic Spanish Fir.

Sierra Bermeja (1400 m) in mid-winter. The climate of the high mountains of the Strait is harsh in winter and snow cover is not unusual in January. Most birds leave these heights to lower slopes until the spring.

pines had higher proportion of migrants than oak woods. Maritime pine woods had fewer migrants than stone pine woods, probably as the latter formed more open woods with a richer understorey.

In general, pine woods support poorer communities than oak woods and the purest stands are apparently closed to migrant species. Typical breeding migrants in pine woods are the Booted Eagle, Quail, Turtle Dove, Cuckoo, Bee-eater, Hoopoe, Nightingale, Black-eared Wheatear, Olivaceous Warbler, Melodious Warbler, Orphean Warbler, Bonelli's Warbler, Spotted Flycatcher and Wood-chat Shrike. At the higher altitudes, Subalpine Warblers and Redstarts also breed. Woodchat Shrikes reached higher densities at Piñar del Rey than in any other habitat studied. In the majority of cases, however, migrants did not reach the densities achieved in oak woods.

As in the oak woods, some groups absent from the older pine woods appeared in younger, more open ones (e.g. larks and martins; see Table 13). Other groups were represented in proportions similar to those in oak woods. The large contribution made by corvids in Monte Algaida is exceptional, reflecting the abundance of corvids in the Guadalquivir area. Some of the species dominant in the least disturbed oak woods were also dominant in the older pine woods, notably the Wren, Blackcap, Short-toed Tree Creeper and Chaffinch. Bonelli's Warbler was not a dominant species in pine woods. Species dominant in older pine woods but not in oak woods were the Blackbird, Crested Tit and Great Tit.

Table 21   Breeding species of lowland stone pines.

Residents	Migrants
Red Kite (north-west only)	Black Kite (mainly
Wood Pigeon	north-west)
Woodlark	Hobby
Wren	Turtle Dove
Stonechat	Cuckoo
Blackbird	Bee-eater
Sardinian Warbler	Hoopoe
Blackcap	Swallow
Firecrest	House Martin
Blue Tit	Nightingale
Great Tit	Orphean Warbler
Short-toed Tree Creeper	Bonelli's Warbler
Jay	Golden Oriole
Azure-winged Magpie	Woodchat Shrike
(north-west only)	
Magpie (north-west only)	
Raven	
Spotless Starling	
Tree Sparrow	
Chaffinch	

Table 22   Breeding species of maritime pine woods.

Residents	Migrants
Sparrowhawk	Booted Eagle
Wood Pigeon	Nightingale
Green Woodpecker	Subalpine Warbler
Great Spotted Woodpecker	Spotted Flycatcher
Wren	
Robin	
Blackbird	
Dartford Warbler	
Sardinian Warbler	
Blackcap	
Firecrest	
Crested Tit	
Coal Tit	
Blue Tit	
Great Tit	
Short-toed Tree Creeper	
Jay	
Chaffinch	
Serin	
Greenfinch	
Goldfinch	
Linnet	
Crossbill	
Rock Bunting	

Table 23   Additional breeding species of young stands of maritime pine woods.

Residents	Migrants
Red-legged Partridge	Short-toed Eagle
Thekla Lark	Quail
Woodlark	Cuckoo
Stonechat	Redstart
Blue Rock Thrush	Black-eared Wheatear
Great Grey Shrike	Olivaceous Warbler
Spanish Sparrow	Melodious Warbler
Corn Bunting	Orphean Warbler
	Bonelli's Warbler
	Woodchat Shrike

Dartford Warblers and Rock Buntings were dominant at Sierra Bermeja, Sardinian Warblers at Monte Algaida, and Woodlarks, Melodious Warblers, Subalpine Warblers, Chough, Greenfinches, Goldfinches, Corn Buntings and Spanish Sparrows in the more open woods. Of these, the Subalpine Warbler and Chough were essentially high altitude species. Blue Tits were not dominant in pine woods, and the only species that dominated in four out of the five sites was the Chaffinch (see Tables 14–17). Species dominant in at least one pine wood but not dominant in oak woods were the Woodlark, Blackbird, Melodious Warbler, Dartford Warbler, Crested Tit, Great Tit, Woodchat Shrike, Azure-winged Magpie, Chough, Tree Sparrow, Spanish Sparrow, Rock Bunting and Corn Bunting. Species dominant in at least one oak wood but not so in pine woods were the Robin, Bonelli's Warbler, Blue Tit, Jackdaw and House Sparrow.

It can be readily appreciated that it is therefore very difficult to define a typical pine wood community. In lowland stone pines the species given in Table 21 would be expected, and montane maritime pine woods would be expected to have species from the range given in Table 22. In younger stands of maritime pines, additional species (Table 23) would be expected, but some of the species typical of the older woods might not be present.

Mediterranean Bush Communities — Matorral

A wide range of secondary successional scrub habitats are represented in the area. I have had the opportunity to study ten sites, given below.

(1) *Coastal garigue:* a low scrub (under 0.5 m) site near Manilva on the Mediterranean coast, characterized by small bushes (e.g. *Pistacia lentiscus, Daphne gnidium, Lavandula stoechas, Euphorbia characias*) with patches of open ground. Altitude 100 m.

(2) *Montane garigue:* low scrub (under 0.5 m) characterized by low bushes and large open spaces near the summit of Sierra de las Nieves. A small copse of Spanish fir bordered the site. Altitude 1700 m.

(3) *Montane low maquis:* low scrub but taller than garigue, with somes bushes reaching 1 m, in the Sierra Blanca north of Marbella. Shrubs (e.g. *Erica* and *Cistus*) tightly packed with few open spaces. Occasional scattered trees (maritime pine and round-leaved oak). Altitude 1000 m.

(4) *Montane maquis:* tall scrub with many bushes (e.g. strawberry tree, rock roses) over 1 m tall but with patches of shorter scrub (e.g. *Erica*, Gorse), northwest of Jimena de la Frontera. Very few open patches. Altitude 500 m.

(5) *Coastal maquis:* tall scrub with many bushes (e.g. mastic tree, *Teline*) over 1 m tall with patches of shorter scrub (e.g. thorny broom, dwarf fan palm) and very few open spaces near Punta del Carnero. Altitude 50 m.

(6) *Maquis of the olive–carob zone:* unique maquis on the western slopes of the Rock of Gibraltar, undisturbed for at least 80 years, with patches of tall maquis forming olive woodland and shrubs ranging from 1 to 3 m. Dense scrub with

some open patches where the gradient does not permit vegetation development. Species include olive, mastic tree, *Osyris*, buckthorn and dwarf fan palm. Altitude 250 m.

(7) *Riverside maquis:* narrow belt of maquis following the course of the Jara River, west of Tarifa, surrounded by pastureland. Tall maquis reaching 3 m in places and dominated by mastic tree, oleander, bramble, hawthorn. Some alder and cork oak. Altitude 25 m.

(8) *Round-leaved oak maquis:* tall maquis at the base of the Sierra de las Nieves with large areas of small round-leaved oaks forming woodland, mostly under 3–4 m. Some open spaces where trees have been cut. Altitude 1000 m.

(9) *Lowland cliff/scree maquis:* low maquis with large, bare patches of rock where steep gradients do not permit vegetation development along the eastern side of the Rock of Gibraltar with typical maquis shrubs (e.g. olive, mastic tree) growing in pockets where soil has accumulated. Altitude 100 m.

(10) *Montane cliff/scree maquis:* low maquis of similar structure to the previous site but on high ground near Grazalema. Altitude 1200 m.

These sites cover a range of scrub types, from the low, coastal garigue, through coastal maquis to the olive maquis, approaching woodland, of Gibraltar, and from montane garigue, through montane maquis to tall montane maquis approaching woodland. Riverside and cliff scrub completed the sequence, which spanned an altitudinal range from sea level to 1700 m.

In general, matorral habitats were poorer in breeding species than woodland habitats, the number of passerine species ranging from 9 to 39 (see Table 11). Three high-altitude sites were much richer in species than the other sites (30–39 species), followed by the lowland riverside scrub (24 species) and the other sites (lowland and intermediate altitudes: 9–19 species). Of the two sites at 1000 m, the more wooded site had a higher species richness (31 species) than the less developed one (14 species). Resident species dominated all scrub habitats (see Table 12) with the proportion of migrants not exceeding 38% by species or 34% by density (passerines only).

If hirundines and corvids (species that wander between habitats and are likely to appear at specific census sites at irregular intervals) are removed from the census data, then the migrant contribution is altered (see Table 13). There is then a good relationship between altitude and proportion of migrants (Figure 180). For sites at similar altitude, taller scrub supports more migrants than lower scrub (Figure 181). The lowland riverside scrub had a very high migrant density. Being close to a river it attracted migrants that nest in the dense vegetation close to fresh water (Nightingale, Olivaceous Warbler, Melodious Warbler, Orphean Warbler, Woodchat Shrike).

A higher density of breeding migrants was noted for upland oak woods in comparison with oak woods at lower altitudes. A similar trend was found for matorral habitats, the increased proportion of migrants being due to a few species—Black-eared Wheatear, Rock Thrush, Subalpine Warbler and Orphean Warbler—reaching high densities (see Table 13).

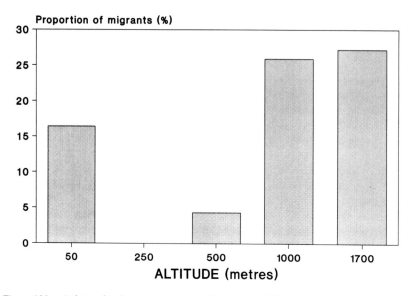

Figure 180.   Relationship between proportion of migrants and altitude in matorral.

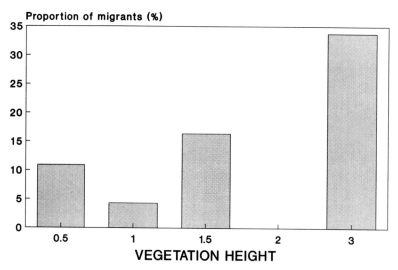

Figure 181.   Relationship between proportion of migrants and vegetation height (m) in matorral at similar altitudes (0–500 m).

The contribution made by different groups of species in matorral habitats differed from woodland (see Tables 14–17). Tits, though represented in most sites, contributed less than in woodland and were best represented in the two sites with best-developed maquis. Larks were better represented in matorral habitats than in oak woods and made a similar contribution to matorral communities as they did to pine wood communities. The exception was the coastal garigue where Crested Larks nested at high density (see Tables 14–17). The most significant increase in matorral was made by warblers (mostly *Sylvia*), which contributed up to 60% of all passerines in the Gibraltar maquis.

Table 24   Breeding species of matorral communities.

Residents	Migrants
Kestrel	Booted Eagle
Red-legged Partridge (Spain)	Cuckoo
Barbary Partridge	Bee-eater
(Gibraltar and Morocco)	Swallow
Little Owl	House Martin
Crested Lark	Rufous Bush Chat
Thekla Lark	Nightingale
Woodlark	Wheatear
Crag Martin	Black-eared Wheatear
Wren	Rock Thrush
Black Redstart	Olivaceous Warbler
Stonechat	Melodious Warbler
Black Wheatear	Spectacled Warbler
Blue Rock Thrush	Subalpine Warbler
Blackbird	Orphean Warbler
Cetti's Warbler	Bonelli's Warbler
Fan-tailed Warbler	Spotted Flycatcher
Dartford Warbler	Woodchat Shrike
Sardinian Warbler	
Blackcap	
Blue Tit	
Great Tit	
Great Grey Shrike	
Chough	
Jackdaw	
Spotless Starling	
House Sparrow	
Chaffinch	
Serin	
Greenfinch	
Goldfinch	
Linnet	
Cirl Bunting	
Rock Bunting	
Corn Bunting	

Nine species not occurring as dominants in woodland were dominant in matorral: i.e. Crested Lark, Crag Martin, Swallow, Black Redstart, Stonechat, Wheatear, Blue Rock Thrush, Fan-tailed Warbler and Linnet (see Tables 14–17). Thirteen species dominant in woodland were not so in matorral: Woodlark, Melodious Warbler, Blue Tit, Crested Tit, Great Tit, Short-toed Tree Creeper, Woodchat Shrike, Azure-winged Magpie, Chough, Serin, Greenfinch, Tree Sparrow and Spanish Sparrow. Species that dominated in some woodland habitats and in some matorral habitats were the Wren, Nightingale, Blackbird, Dartford Warbler, Subalpine Warbler, Sardinian Warbler, Blackcap, Bonelli's Warbler, Jackdaw, House Sparrow, Chaffinch, Goldfinch, Rock Bunting and Corn Bunting. Of these, the Wren, Nightingale, Blackbird, Blackcap and Bonelli's Warbler only occurred in taller, denser matorral. The distribution of matorral specialists and generalists is shown in Table 18.

There is no typical matorral breeding bird community; species composition and representation depend on the successional stage of the vegetation and on altitude. The main species expected in matorral communities are given in Table 24.

OPEN GROUND HABITATS

Areas dominated by open ground, devoted to pasture or cultivation, or naturally existing as steppe, are found in the western, low-lying parts of the area. Some of these have always been covered in steppe vegetation, and others have been created by removal of the original vegetation or through drainage. On higher ground some land has been cleared for pasture, but this generally covers a lower area than lowland pasture. I have studied four areas of open ground habitat in southern Spain:

(1) a mountain pasture grazed by cattle and goats on the northeastern slopes of the Sierra de Ojén (altitude 250 m) surrounded by cork oak woodland;

(2) the drained Laguna de La Janda, northeast of Vejer (altitude 10 m), devoted to cultivation and some cattle ranching and bisected by freshwater drainage canals and natural aquatic vegetation and associated species (e.g. *Phragmites communis, Arundo donax, Tamarix* spp. — see also Chapter 7);

(3) a large area of partly grazed and drained marsh on the southeast bank of the Guadalquivir near the town of Trebujena (altitude 2 m), also bisected by drainage canals which hold aquatic vegetation, and a rich community of dry saltmarsh vegetation (e.g. *Salicornia, Spartina, Limonium, Juncus, Carex, Dactylis*— see also Chapter 7);

(4) an area of pseudo-steppe vegetation east of Sierra de Retín, north of the coastal town of Zahara de los Atunes (altitude 70 m), devoted to cultivation (especially sunflowers) and cattle. Typical plants included thistles, *Scolymus hispanicus, Galactites tomentosa* and *Cynara humilis*, as well as species in genera associated with open ground (e.g. *Convolvulus, Asphodelus, Calendula* and *Vicia*).

Three sites (Ojén, La Janda, Trebujena) had high species richness (31–44 species; see Table 11) although the fourth site (Zahara) had a much lower value (15 species). Zahara had the most homogeneous vegetation, the other sites having a greater range of vegetation variation (including aquatic vegetation and low shrubs) or being surrounded by other vegetation (oak woods) that permitted edge species to penetrate the open ground. In general, open ground breeding communities may be expected to have low species richness except where habitat heterogeneity introduces variety.

The four communities were dominated by residents, though the contribution made by migrants to the open ground communities was above the average for the entire range of communities (see Table 12). The poorest site for migrants was Zahara (passerine migrants 27% by species and 2% by density). La Janda had the highest proportion of migrants by species, and second highest by density.

Table 25   Breeding species of open ground breeding communities.

Residents	Migrants
Cattle Egret	White Stork[1]
Kestrel	Black Kite[1]
Red-legged Partridge	Short-toed Eagle[1]
Little Bustard	Montagu's Harrier[1]
Great Bustard (now rare on both sides of the Strait)	Lesser Kestrel[1]
	Quail
Pin-tailed Sandgrouse (near marshes)	Collared Pratincole
	Turtle Dove
Barn Owl	Cuckoo
Little Owl	Bee-eater
Calandra Lark	Short-toed Lark
Crested Lark	Swallow
Thekla Lark	Red-rumped Swallow
Lesser Short-toed Lark (near marshes)	House Martin
	Tawny Pipit
Stonechat	Yellow Wagtail
Fan-tailed Warbler	Black-eared Wheatear
Sardinian Warbler	
Jackdaw	
Raven	
Spotless Starling	
House Sparrow	
Serin	
Goldfinch	
Linnet	
Corn Bunting	

[1] All subject to availability of nesting sites close to the habitat.

The proportion of the community made up by the main passerine groups was very different from that in other habitats studied. Larks, pipits and wagtails, and hirundines reached high representation, as did buntings, in Zahara; tits and warblers, in contrast, were poorly represented (see Table 13). Five species occurred as dominants in open ground and in no other habitat, i.e. the Calandra Lark, House Martin, Yellow Wagtail, Great Reed Warbler (not truly associated with open ground but with available reedbeds) and Spotless Starling (see Tables 14–17). The other dominant species had also occurred as dominants in matorral. The distribution of habitat generalists and specialists is illustrated in Table 18.

The typical open ground breeding communities may therefore be expected to have a range of the species given in Table 25.

Cliff Nesting Communities

The Strait area is characterized by numerous inland and coastal cliffs. These attract species that breed in the safety of the inaccessible ledges and caverns and often forage in the surrounding countryside. The eastern side of the Strait has large cliff faces, typical of limestone. In the west, especially on the European shore, smaller outcrops of siliceous rocks form sheer faces (locally known as *lajas*) that are also used by breeding birds. The differences between the two rock types are reflected in the breeding abundance and dispersion of certain species. Griffon Vultures, for example, generally form larger colonies on the large, limestone cliff faces than on the smaller siliceous outcrops (Alonso & del Junco, 1981).

Rock outcrops and cliffs surrounded by open countryside are ideal sites for nesting raptors.

The gorge of El Peñou de Zaframagón, a typical raptor cliff with over one hundred pairs of Griffon Vultures, Bonelli's Eagles, Egyptian Vultures, Lesser Kestrels and Eagle Owls.

Several species that bred in cliffs and other rocky areas in the Strait have become extinct in recent times, due to human pressure. These are the Lammergeier, the Osprey and probably Eleonora's Falcon (Irby, 1895; Verner, 1910; Cortés *et al.*, 1980; Finlayson & Cortés, 1987). Other species have been significantly reduced in numbers and their range has contracted; among these are Shag, Egyptian Vulture, Golden Eagle, Bonelli's Eagle, Eagle Owl, Black Wheatear and Raven.

A typical cliff community usually has several species of raptors, which includes a colony of Griffon Vultures, corvids (Jackdaws everywhere and Choughs in the mountains) and a few passerines (e.g. Blue Rock Thrush and Crag Martin). Such communities would be expected to include a number from the breeding species listed in Table 26.

Table 26   Breeding species of cliff communities.

Egyptian Vulture	Alpine Swift
Griffon Vulture	Crag Martin
Long-legged Buzzard	Wren
(Morocco only)	Black Redstart (mountains only)
Golden Eagle (mountains only)	Black Wheatear
Bonelli's Eagle	Blue Rock Thrush
Lesser Kestrel	Rock Thrush (mountains only)
Kestrel	Chough (usually mountains)
Peregrine	Jackdaw
Barn Owl	Raven
Eagle Owl	Spotless Starling
Little Owl	Rock Sparrow
Pallid Swift	Rock Bunting
Additional species on sea cliffs:	
Shag (now only on Gibraltar)	Little Egret
Cattle Egret	Yellow-legged Gull

SPECIES DISTRIBUTIONS ALONG ALTITUDE GRADIENTS

Zamora (1987) has analysed the distribution of breeding passerines along an altitude gradient (800–3100 m) in the Sierra Nevada, northeast of the Strait. In this sierra there is a reduction with altitude (above 1300 m) in species diversity, density and biomass, and an increase in the dominance of a single species. Species richness increases to a peak at 1700 m, then declines steeply. This increase in richness from thermo-Mediterranean to supra-Mediterranean zones has also been noted by Blondel (1970, 1978) and Thevenot (1982), and has been related to the greater structural complexity of the vegetation at these altitudes. The main factor determining the distribution of species in Mediterranean mountains therefore appears to be vegetation structure (see also Able & Noon, 1976) rather than interspecific competition, which is more important in the tropics (Terborgh, 1971, 1977; Terborgh & Weske, 1975; Diamond, 1973). Certainly altitudinal segregation among chats and thrushes in central Spain is the most important factor in the least developed habitats, but the distribution patterns are related to altitudinal physical and biological gradients and not to competitive exclusion (Telleria & Potti, 1984). Exceptions may occur, as with the Rock Thrush/Blue Rock Thrush pair which defend interspecific territories in similar habitats in zones of altitudinal overlap.

Above 1700 m there is an abrupt increase in the number of non-resident breeding species of passerines, all being non-resident above 2900 m. These changes reflect increasing climatic seasonality and reduced vegetation structural complexity (e.g. see Wiens, 1989a). Species abundance curves resemble geo-

Typical mountain habitat in southern Spain: Sierra Crestellina, a limestone outcrop, close to the town of Casares.

metric, rather than log, distributions with increasing altitude, as would be expected for simple communities in harsh environments (May, 1975).

The Sierra Nevada exhibits an impoverished species richness in comparison to other high mountain areas of Europe. This is due to its isolated, southerly, location, which, together with its reduced surface area, may not permit viable populations of the sedentary high-mountain species that have continental distributions (e.g. Snow Finch, Water Pipit), with the exception of the Alpine Accentor (Zamora, 1987, 1988). The absence of such populations may be recent. Saunders (1871) found Wall Creepers, Snow Finches and Alpine Choughs breeding in the Sierra Nevada. It is possible that such species were widely distributed in southern Iberian mountains during the glacial periods but, as the ice receded, were forced up the mountains into reduced areas (Zamora, 1987), with increasing probability of extinctions (MacArthur & Wilson 1967). Few Mediterranean species (e.g. Black Redstart, Red-legged Partridge) are actually able to ascend to the highest peaks.

The higher mountains of the Strait reach the supra-Mediterranean bioclimatic zone. They exhibit the first stages of altitudinal transition in community structure. The communities in the Sierra de las Nieves (maximum altitude 1919 m) are diverse and hold a large number of species (Table 27). These include species which are associated with high altitude in the Sierra Nevada and which do

Table 27   Breeding passerines and near-passerines of Sierra de las Nieves.[1]

Species	Habitat/altitude		
	Oak scrub 1000 m	Young pines 1300 m	Garigue/pinsapo 1700 m
Wood Pigeon	2.5	3.8	0.0
Cuckoo	1.1	1.3	0.0
Bee–eater	4.4	0.0	0.0
Hoopoe	+	0.0	0.0
Green Woodpecker	0.0	6.3	0.0
Greater Spotted Woodpecker	+	0.0	0.0
Thekla Lark	0.0	1.3	2.0
Woodlark	4.4	6.3	1.0
Skylark	0.0	0.0	5.0
Crag Martin	1.1	0.0	0.0
Tawny Pipit	0.0	0.0	2.0
Wren	0.0	0.0	2.0
Nightingale	5.6	0.0	0.0
Black Redstart	0.0	0.0	13.0
Redstart	0.0	1.3	0.0
Stonechat	2.2	5.0	5.0
Wheatear	0.0	0.0	13.0
Black-eared Wheatear	0.0	3.8	7.0
Black Wheatear	2.2	0.0	0.0
Rock Thrush	0.0	0.0	6.0
Blue Rock Thrush	1.1	1.3	4.0
Blackbird	6.7	3.8	2.0
Mistle Thrush	2.2	0.0	4.0
Olivaceous Warbler	0.0	1.3	0.0
Dartford Warbler	1.1	0.0	1.0
Subalpine Warbler	7.8	12.5	8.0
Sardinian Warbler	1.1	0.0	0.0
Orphean Warbler	2.2	2.5	0.0
Bonelli's Warbler	8.9	2.5	1.0
Firecrest	1.1	0.0	0.0
Spotted Flycatcher	1.1	0.0	0.0
Crested Tit	+	5.0	+
Coal Tit	0.0	2.5	4.0
Blue Tit	3.3	2.5	0.0
Great Tit	4.4	1.3	0.0
Short-toed Tree Creeper	+	0.0	0.0
Great Grey Shrike	0.0	1.3	2.0
Woodchat Shrike	0.0	1.3	0.0
Jay	1.1	1.3	0.0
Chough	4.4	8.8	12.0
Jackdaw	2.2	0.0	0.0
Spanish Sparrow	0.0	10.0	0.0

Continued.

Table 27 Continued.

Species	Habitat/altitude		
	Oak scrub 1000 m	Young pines 1300 m	Garigue/pinsapo 1700 m
Rock Sparrow	0.0	+	+
Chaffinch	5.6	10.0	8.0
Serin	2.2	2.5	5.0
Greenfinch	0.0	1.3	0.0
Goldfinch	15.6	5.0	7.0
Linnet	1.1	3.8	5.0
Crossbill	0.0	3.8	2.0
Cirl Bunting	2.2	0.0	0.0
Rock Bunting	1.1	6.3	15.0
Corn Bunting	6.7	3.8	0.0

[1] Mean density (birds/10 ha). +, species present but did not appear in census plots.

not breed at lower levels: Skylark, Wheatear, Rock Thrush, Black Redstart and Ortolan Bunting (Chapman & Buck, 1910; Jourdain, 1936, 1937; Finlayson & Cortés, 1987; Cortés, 1990). A feature of these species is that, while they are restricted in the habitats they occupy, within these habitats they reach high densities and dominance levels in the community and occupy a wide range of situations (see species descriptions in this chapter, and Zamora, 1988). The Alpine Accentor, which is absent from the Sierra de las Nieves but breeds in Sierra Nevada, also exhibits a generalized distribution (Zamora, 1987). Such wide within-habitat dispersion is predicted by island biogeography theory (MacArthur & Wilson, 1967; MacArthur *et al.*, 1972) in 'island-type' impoverished communities such as those of mountain tops (e.g. Terborgh & Weske, 1975).

BREEDING DISTRIBUTION AND ABUNDANCE OF THE MAIN GROUPS OF TERRESTRIAL SPECIES

PASSERINES

The distribution and abundance of the main groups and species that make up the terrestrial bird communities described in the first part of this chapter are discussed below. The patterns of species densities are summarized in Appendix 3.

Larks (Figures 182–190)

Larks are principally open ground species that dominate in steppe and grassland and in some garigue communities, being almost absent from the woodland communities. They have fairly specialized habitat requirements, exhibiting a lower mean between-habitat dispersion than the community mean, though the better dispersed species exceed this mean. Their overall abundance is therefore limited by habitat, although individual species do exceed the mean community abundance.

The most widely dispersed species is the Woodlark, which occupies a range of habitats, including woodland. The Crested Lark exceeds the group dispersion mean but falls below that for the entire community of passerines. The remaining lark species must be considered habitat specialists. The pattern of dispersion of

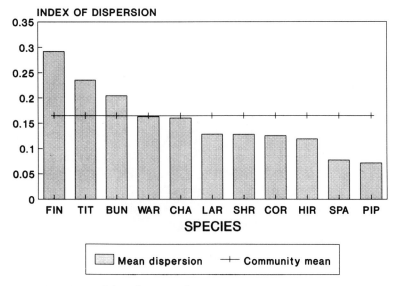

Figure 182.   Between habitat dispersion of main passerine groups.

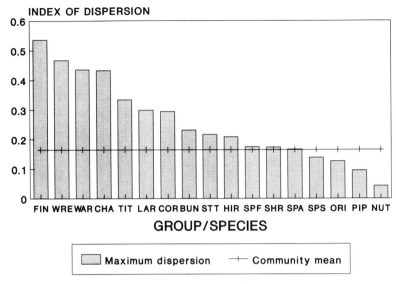

Figure 183.   *Between habitat dispersion of most dispersed species per group.*

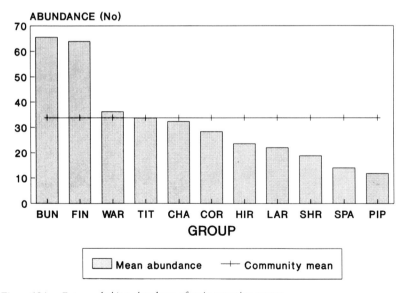

Figure 184.   *Between habitat abundance of main passerine groups.*

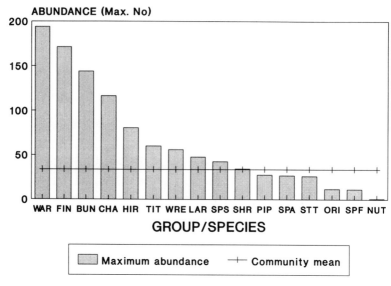

Figure 185.   *Between habitat abundance of most abundant species per group.*

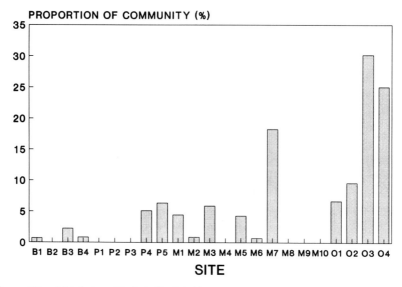

Figure 186.   *Distribution of larks in Strait habitats.*

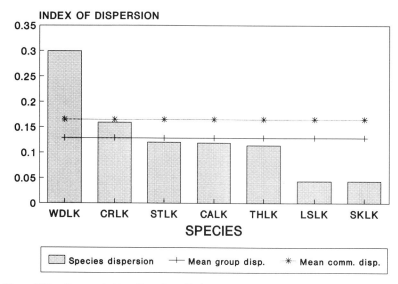

Figure 187. Between habitat dispersion of larks.

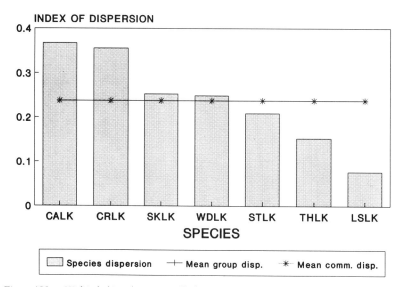

Figure 188. Within habitat dispersion of larks.

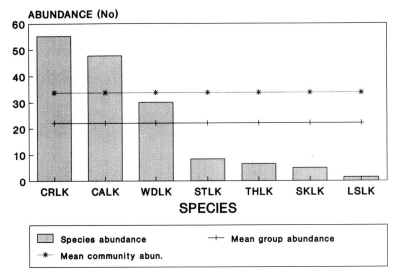

Figure 189.   Between habitat abundance of larks.

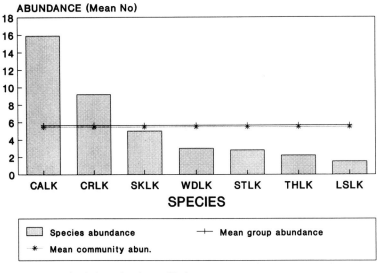

Figure 190.   Within habitat abundance of larks.

larks within habitats is substantially different. Four species, Calandra, Crested, Skylark and Woodlark, behave as within-habitat generalists, occupying a wide range of situations within the preferred habitats. Short-toed, Thekla and Lesser Short-toed Larks are restricted to specific locations within preferred habitats. Mean within-habitat dispersion for larks is similar to the community mean, indicating a mixture of within-habitat generalists and specialists.

Two species, the Crested and Calandra Larks exceed the community mean abundance level, and a third, the Woodlark, exceeds the group mean but falls below the community mean. This pattern is striking, especially for Calandra Larks, in view of the habitat specialization of this species. It is explained largely by the within-habitat abundance, well above the community mean, which shows that it is a species that is very abundant in the few habitats it occupies. The situation is similar for the Crested Lark which exceeds the community abundance means but shows a below mean between-habitat dispersion. The within-habitat abundance mean for the group is similar to the community mean, which indicates a mixture of abundant and scarce species within the habitats occupied.

Hirundines (Figures 182–185, 191–194)

Hirundines are restricted in the habitats they occupy, largely by nest-site availability. They behave as habitat specialists, though some species may exceed the community between-habitat dispersion mean. Although some species are abundant, mean abundance levels fall below the community between-habitat mean. This result may be biased to some extent, since urban environments, where hirundines are extremely numerous, were not sampled.

The Swallow is the most widely dispersed species and the only one exceeding the community between-habitat dispersion mean. The Crag Martin exceeds the group mean, and the Red-rumped Swallow and House Martin show specific habitat restrictions. All species behave as within-habitat specialists (group within-habitat dispersion mean well below the community mean), occurring in specific patches within the habitats occupied, the Red-rumped Swallow showing the widest dispersion and the House Martin the least.

The House Martin and Swallow exceed the community between-habitat abundance mean and the House Martin also exceeds the within-habitat abundance mean. The House Martin is therefore restricted in its distribution but is extremely abundant where it occurs. The Swallow is widely distributed and abundant, less concentrated than the House Martin within habitats. The Crag Martin and the Red-rumped Swallow show complementary patterns. The Crag Martin shows a wider habitat tolerance than the Red-rumped Swallow but is more selective of sites within habitats, being slightly more abundant overall but scarcer within specific habitats. The mean group within-habitat abundance exceeds the community mean, indicating that hirundines are locally abundant.

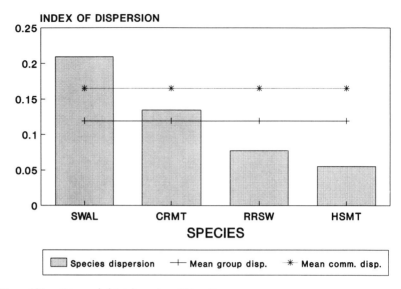

Figure 191.   Between habitat dispersion of hirundines.

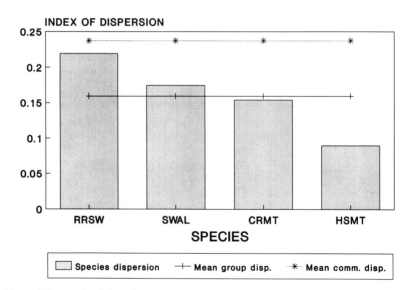

Figure 192.   Within habitat dispersion of hirundines.

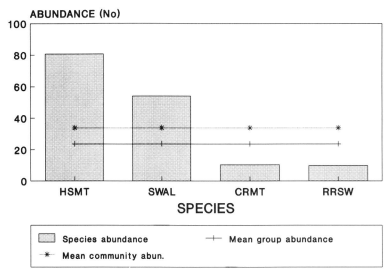

Figure 193.   Between habitat abundance of hirundines.

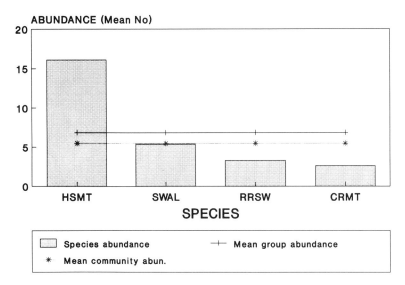

Figure 194.   Within habitat abundance of hirundines.

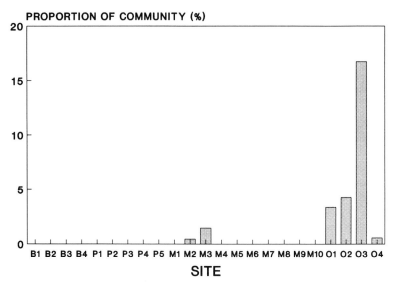

Figure 195.   Distribution of pipits and wagtails in Strait habitats.

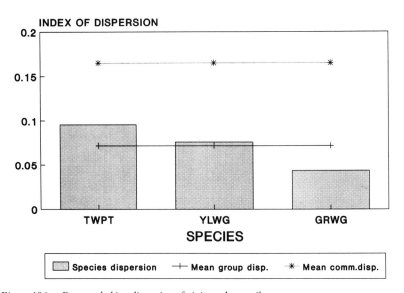

Figure 196.   Between habitat dispersion of pipits and wagtails.

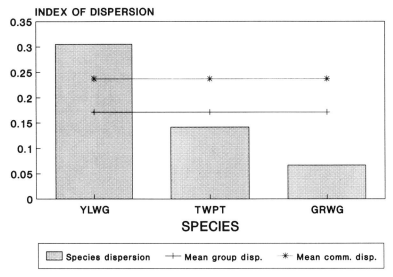

Figure 197.   *Within habitat dispersion of pipits and wagtails.*

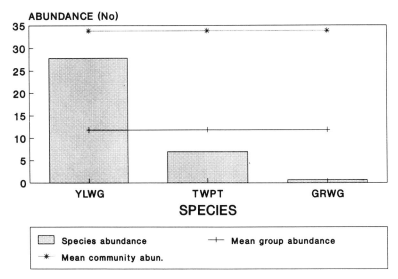

Figure 198.   *Between habitat abundance of pipits and wagtails.*

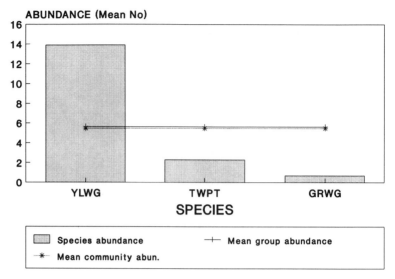

Figure 199.   Within habitat abundance of pipits and wagtails.

Pipits and wagtails (Figures 182–185, 195–199)

Pipits and wagtails are restricted to open habitats and, occasionally, scrub (and woodland) along streams (e.g. Grey Wagtail). The group shows high specialization in distribution patterns between habitats and low overall abundance.

All species are restricted in habitat choice, the Tawny Pipit occupying the greatest range of habitats and the Grey Wagtail the least. The group, as a whole, is also restricted in within-habitat dispersion, only the Yellow Wagtail showing a wide distribution in occupied habitats. The Yellow Wagtail's wide dispersion is reflected in within-habitat and overall abundance levels, the other species being scarce. The group's within-habitat abundance is similar to the community mean, due largely to the concentration of Yellow Wagtails in the few habitats occupied.

Chats and thrushes (Figures 182–185, 200–204)

Because of the large number of species, with well-defined subgroups having distinct ecological requirements, this group is present in all habitat types, being least conspicuous in open ground habitats. Some chats (e.g. Nightingale, Robin) and thrushes are typical of woodland, other chats (e.g. Stonechat) are associated with open matorral and others (e.g. wheatears) with open ground.

Chats have mean between-habitat dispersal values matching the community mean, with some species reaching much higher dispersal values. They are the fifth most generalist group in terms of habitat occupation.

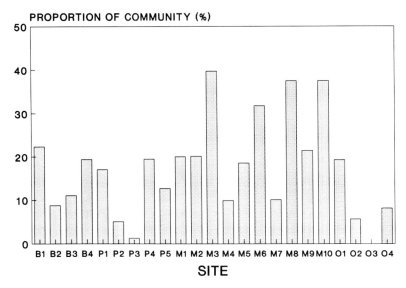

Figure 200.   Distribution of chats and thrushes in Strait habitats.

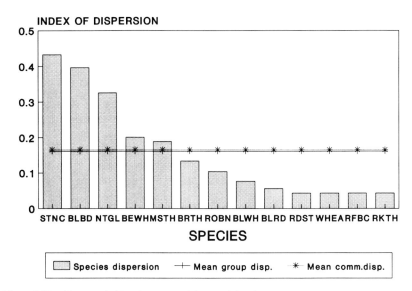

Figure 201.   Between habitat dispersion of chats and thrushes.

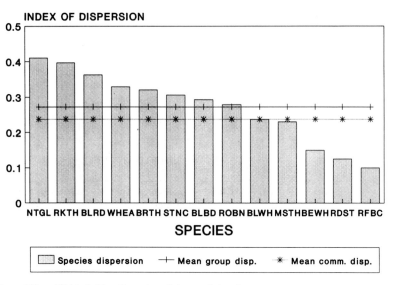

Figure 202.   Within habitat dispersion of chats and thrushes.

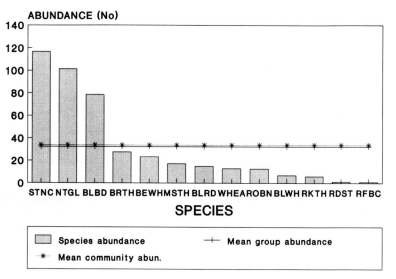

Figure 203.   Between habitat abundance of chats and thrushes.

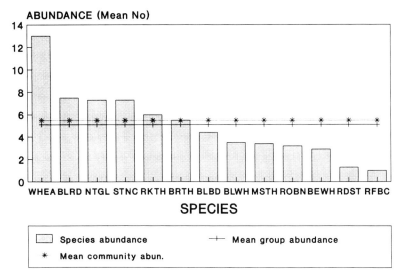

Figure 204. Within habitat abundance of chats and thrushes.

Within the group, five species show above mean between-habitat dispersion values: Stonechat, Blackbird, Nightingale, Black-eared Wheatear and Mistle Thrush. There is also a range of species highly restricted by habitat, in particular the Black Wheatear, Black Redstart, Redstart, Wheatear, Rufous Bush Chat and Rock Thrush. Within-habitat dispersion is remarkably high (the group mean exceeding the community mean) for the majority of species, indicating little specialization in foraging niche utilization and suggesting that ecological separation takes place at habitat or food level. The exceptions are the Black-eared Wheatear, Redstart and Rufous Bush Chat. The most highly dispersed species within preferred habitats are the Nightingale, Rock Thrush, Black Redstart, Wheatear, Blue Rock Thrush, Stonechat, Blackbird and Robin. Some of the strictest habitat specialists therefore behave as generalists within the most frequented habitats.

Chats approach mean between-habitat abundance levels, with some species reaching maxima well above the community mean. This suggests that there is a wide range of abundance levels (as there is for dispersion) in this group. The Stonechat, Nightingale and Blackbird show high, above community mean, between-habitat abundances, and there is then a large range of scarcer species. Within habitats, a few species exceed the community mean and include several habitat specialists. Three of the five highest within-habitat abundances are achieved by habitat specialists (Wheatear, Black Redstart and Rock Thrush), the other two being the Nightingale and Stonechat. The group within-habitat abundance mean is slightly lower than that of the community.

Warblers (Figures 182–185, 205–209

Warblers occupy the entire range of habitats available in the area, and contribute the most to the breeding communities in matorral habitats, where *Sylvia* species are abundant. They make a bigger contribution to woodland communities (*Sylvia*, *Phylloscopus* and *Regulus*) than to open habitat communities (*Cisticola*) and also occupy wetlands (*Acrocephalus*, *Locustella*, etc. —see Chapter 7). This spread of habitat utilization is reflected in the between-habitat dispersion index for the group, which matches the community mean, warblers being the fourth most dispersed group of passerines, some species exceeding the community mean significantly.

The Sardinian Warbler exhibits the widest habitat spread, with a subgroup of species (Fan-tailed Warbler, Firecrest, Dartford Warbler, Subalpine Warbler, Melodious Warbler and Bonelli's Warbler) above the community mean, and several species with narrow habitat occupation (especially Spectacled Warbler, Whitethroat, Chiffchaff, Cetti's Warbler and Great Reed Warbler). The mean group within-habitat dispersion index exceeds the community mean, which indicates that many species occur widely in the habitats occupied.

Warblers are the third most abundant group across all habitats, being above the community mean. The most abundant warbler, the Sardinian Warbler, is also the most abundant passerine in the habitat sequence studied. Apart from this species, five others (Dartford Warbler, Blackcap, Fan-tailed Warbler, Bonelli's Warbler

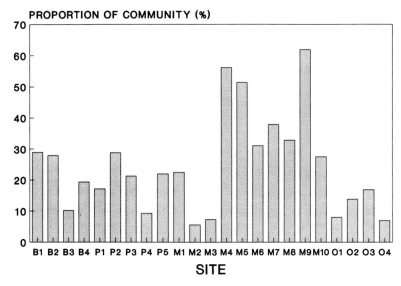

Figure 205.   Distribution of warblers in Strait habitats.

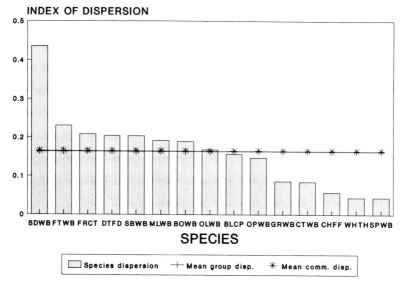

Figure 206.   Between habitat dispersion of warblers.

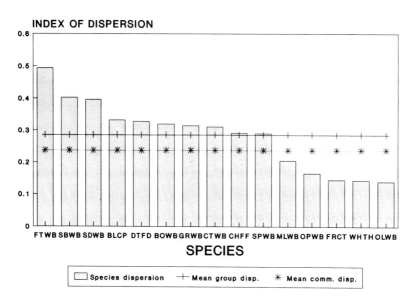

Figure 207.   Within habitat dispersion of warblers.

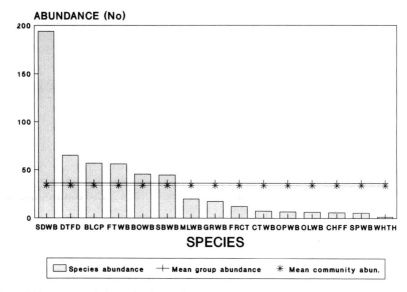

Figure 208.   *Between habitat abundance of warblers.*

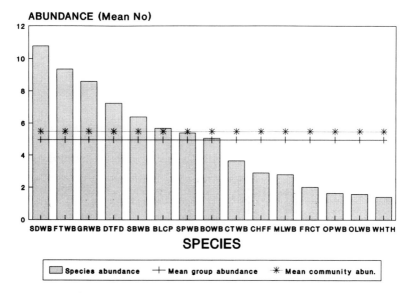

Figure 209.   *Within habitat abundance of warblers.*

and Subalpine Warbler) exceed the community abundance mean but the majority of species fall well below it. The within-habitat abundance mean is slightly higher than the community mean and indicates a spread of within-habitat abundances, with an approximately equal number of species above and below the mean. Warblers are therefore well spread out in most habitats, some species occurring in many habitats and others occupying narrower, complementary, habitat sequences. Most behave as generalists within the preferred habitats, some occurring at high densities and others at low densities.

Tits (Figures 182–185, 210–214)

Tits show very specific habitat requirements for woodland, also contributing in smaller proportions to some matorral communities. As a whole, the group shows a high index of between-habitat dispersion, since the few species are not restricted to one or two habitats (although the Coal Tit is confined to a narrow sequence of habitats—e.g. see Finlayson, 1990). The most widely dispersed species, the Blue Tit, exceeds the community mean considerably.

Blue Tits, Great Tits and Crested Tits exceed the community between-habitat dispersion mean, only the Coal Tit falling below the mean. Within the range of habitats occupied, Blue Tits and Great Tits are well distributed, but Crested Tits and Coal Tits appear to be more restricted to specific locations within the habitats.

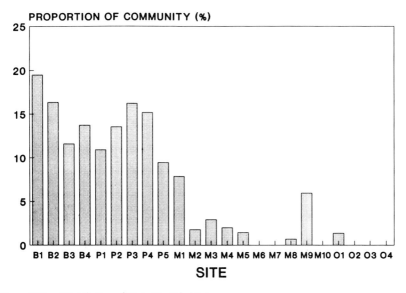

Figure 210.   Distribution of tits in Strait habitats.

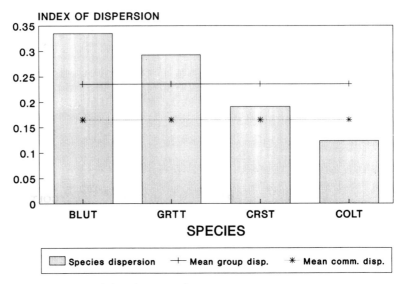

Figure 211.   *Between habitat dispersion of tits.*

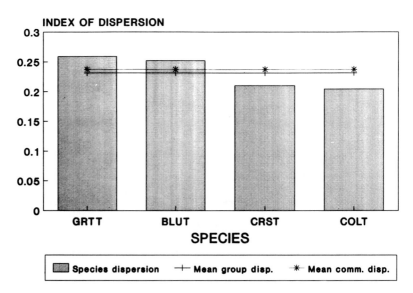

Figure 212.   *Within habitat dispersion of tits.*

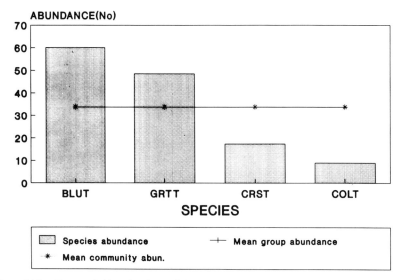

Figure 213.   Between habitat abundance of tits.

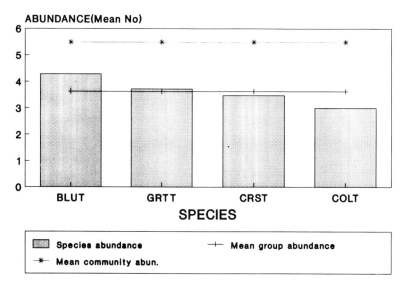

Figure 214.   Within habitat abundance of tits.

The overall abundance level of tits matches the community mean, with the two most abundant species (Blue Tit, Great Tit) exceeding it. Crested Tit and Coal Tit abundances are considerably below the community mean. Within habitats, however, all tits fall below the community mean, i.e. they are nowhere numerous, which is probably related to the high within–habitat dispersion.

Corvids (Figures 182–185, 215–219)

Corvids occur in most habitats but rarely contribute greatly to bird communities, exceptions being Azure-winged Magpies in some pine woods and Choughs and Jackdaws in some habitats close to breeding colonies. It is a group that has a below community mean between-habitat dispersion. Only the Jay, which occupies a wide range of woodland habitats and is not colonial, exceeds the community mean. The other species are all restricted to a narrow range of habitats. Within-habitat dispersion is also narrow, most species except Azure-winged Magpie occurring in discrete patches in the habitats occupied.

Corvids do not exceed the community between-habitat abundance mean, but the Chough and the Jackdaw, which form large breeding colonies, and the Azure-winged Magpie, which breeds in loosely defined colonies, exceed the community mean. Within habitats, these three species exceed the community mean, indicating their occurrence at high density within habitats, the Chough and the Jackdaw at specific locations and Azure-winged Magpie more widely spaced out.

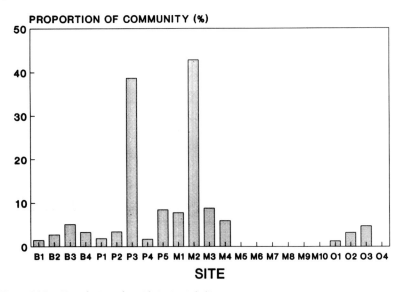

Figure 215.   Distribution of corvids in Strait habitats.

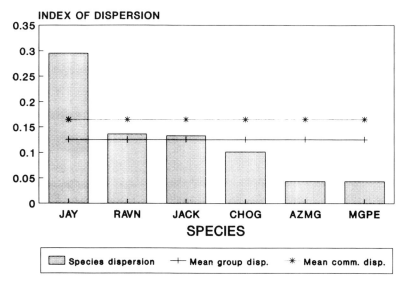

Figure 216.   Between habitat dispersion of corvids.

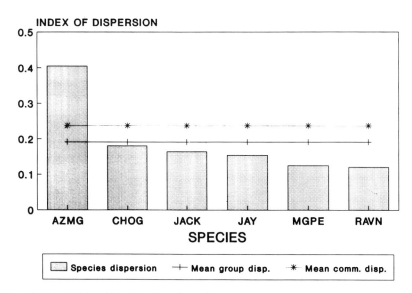

Figure 217.   Within habitat dispersion of corvids.

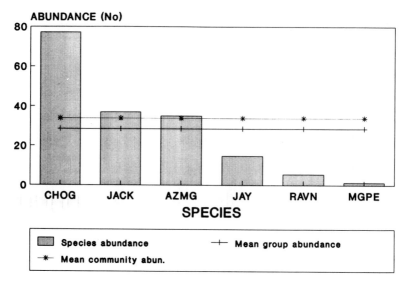

Figure 218.   Between habitat abundance of corvids.

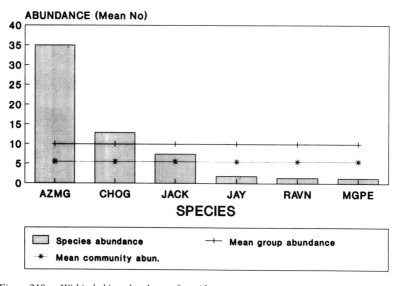

Figure 219.   Within habitat abundance of corvids.

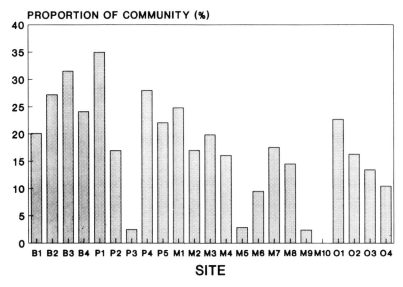

Figure 220.   Distribution of finches in Strait habitats.

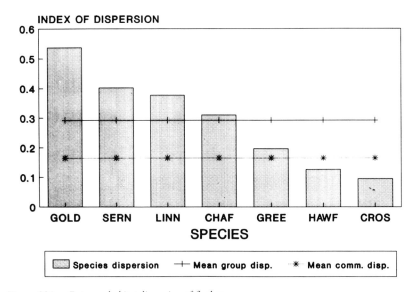

Figure 221.   Between habitat dispersion of finches.

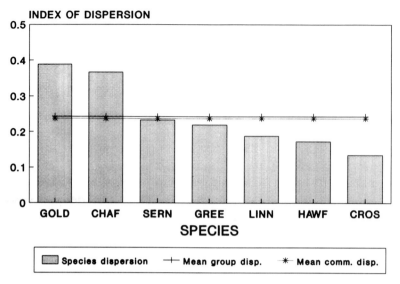

Figure 222.   Within habitat dispersion of finches.

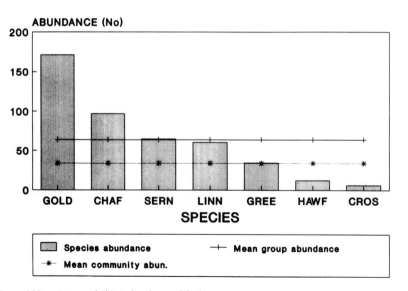

Figure 223.   Between habitat abundance of finches.

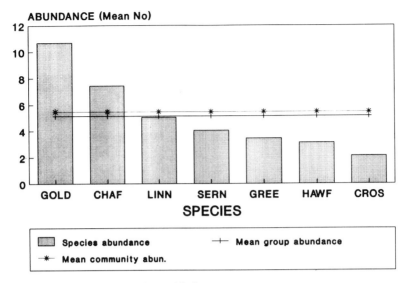

Figure 224.   Within habitat abundance of finches.

Finches (Figures 182–185, 220–224)

Finches occupy a wide range of habitats, from woodland to open ground, and exhibit the highest between-habitat dispersion indices. Only the Hawfinch and Crossbill fall below the community between-habitat dispersion mean; the Goldfinch has the highest between-habitat dispersion index of any passerine. Within habitats, however, many species appear localized, and only the Goldfinch and Chaffinch exceed the community within-habitat dispersion mean.

Finches are also among the most abundant species, being exceeded only by buntings. The Goldfinch, Chaffinch, Serin and Linnet are all above the community mean, and the Goldfinch and Chaffinch are the two most abundant finches within specific habitats, where their within-habitat dispersion indices are high.

Buntings (Figures 182–185, 225–229)

Buntings occur across the entire habitat sequence but dominate in the communities of open ground and, to a lesser degree, matorral. They consequently exhibit high between-habitat dispersion indices, all three species being above the community mean. Within the habitats occupied, however, only the Corn Bunting is widely distributed, Rock and Cirl Buntings being rather more specialized in their requirements.

Buntings are the most abundant group, due in large part to the extremely high density of Corn Buntings in all habitats occupied. The other buntings do not exceed community mean levels.

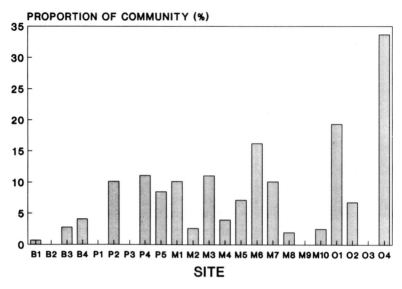

Figure 225.   Distribution of buntings in Strait habitats.

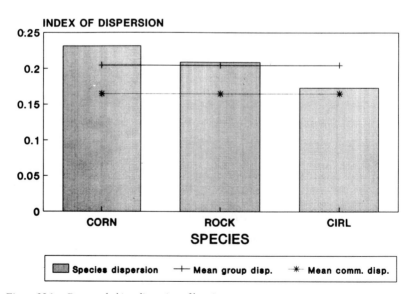

Figure 226.   Between habitat dispersion of buntings.

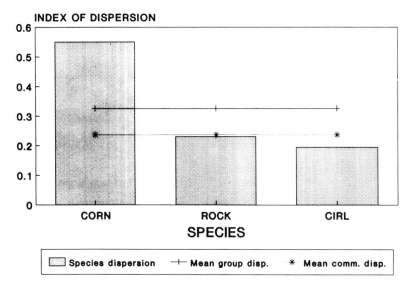

Figure 227. Within habitat dispersion of buntings.

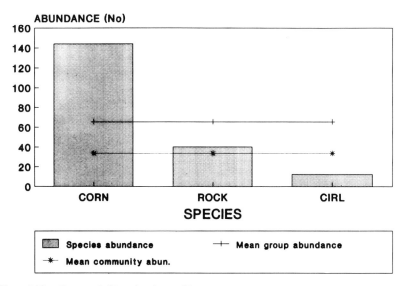

Figure 228. Between habitat abundance of buntings.

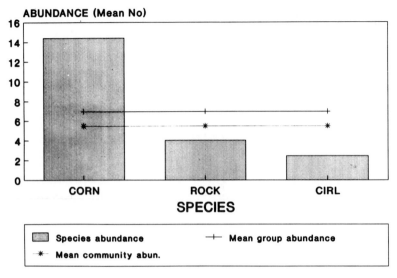

Figure 229.   Within habitat abundance of buntings.

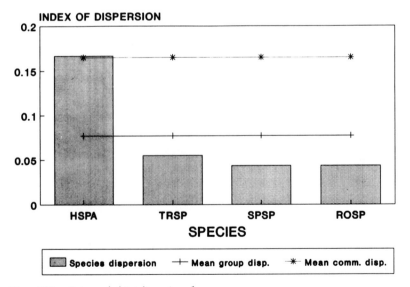

Figure 230.   Between habitat dispersion of sparrows.

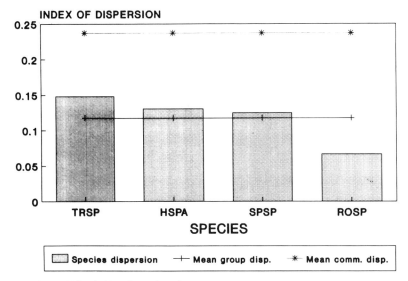

Figure 231.   Within habitat dispersion of sparrows.

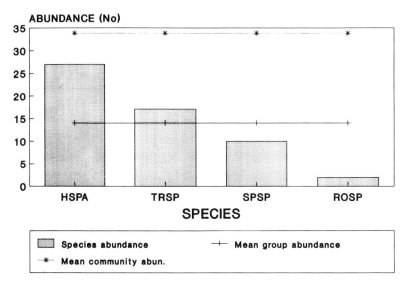

Figure 232.   Between habitat abundance of sparrows.

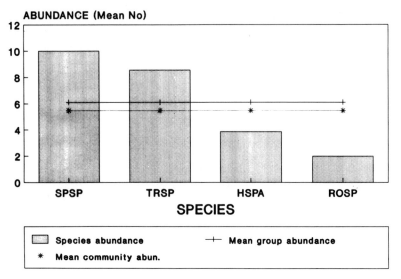

Figure 233.   Within habitat abundance of sparrows.

Sparrows (Figures 182–185, 230–233)

Sparrows, in the habitat range studied, have rather specialized habitat requirements, only the House Sparrow reaching the community between-habitat dispersion mean, and all are localized within the habitats occupied. Abundances are also low, with the House Sparrow the most abundant overall but the Spanish Sparrow and Tree Sparrow the most abundant species within habitats. These results confirm the colonial nature of sparrows, which occur in large numbers in isolated habitat patches. The House Sparrow's abundance in urban environments is not reflected in the range of habitats studied.

Other passerines (Figures 183 and 185)

The Wren is among the most widely dispersed passerines and is well distributed within habitats occupied. It reaches an above-mean overall abundance but its within-habitat abundance falls below the community mean.

The Short-toed Tree Creeper exceeds the community between- and within-habitat dispersion means but is not an abundant species, occurring in most habitats at low densities.

The Spotted Flycatcher only just exceeds the between-community dispersion mean but acts as a specialist within the occupied habitats. It occurs in all habitats at low densities.

Shrike's dispersion means fall below the community between-habitat dispersion mean, although the Woodchat Shrike just exceeds this value. Abundance levels reflect this pattern, shrikes being less abundant than the community mean but the Woodchat just exceeding this value. The Great Grey Shrike is a scarce, localized species and the Woodchat a more widely distributed and abundant species.

The Spotless Starling, which is a typical urban bird, is not widely distributed in natural habitats and is localized in the habitats it utilizes. Within these 'pockets', Spotless Starlings are sufficiently abundant to exceed the community between-habitat mean but the within-habitat mean is not exceeded, the species not being colonial.

The Golden Oriole shows a narrow habitat range and is localized within the habitats it occupies. It is a scarce species throughout.

The Nuthatch is the most restricted and scarcest of passerines.

Non-passerines

Raptors

The distribution of raptors over terrestrial habitats is largely dependent on the availability of nest-sites. In the case of tree-nesting species, hunting usually takes place within the habitat where the species nests (e.g. Goshawk, Sparrowhawk) or in adjacent habitats (e.g. Black Kite, Red Kite). Cliff-nesting species generally wander greater distances from nest sites (e.g. Griffon Vulture).

The habitats over which I have observed some raptors hunting are shown in Figure 234. The two kites, which hunt mainly over marshes and open ground,

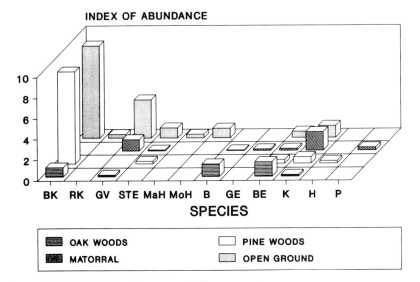

Figure 234.   Distribution of raptors over habitats surveyed.

nest in stone pine woods. The Griffon Vulture (and the Egyptian Vulture) breed on cliffs and roam over large tracts of ground, concentrating over pastureland where the probability of carcasses is greatest. The tree-nesting Short-toed Eagle hunts away from the dense woods where it breeds, and usually in open clearings, over which it hovers for reptiles. The Marsh Harrier is not strictly a species that occupies terrestrial habitats (see Chapter 7), but it does wander into dry areas of marsh and fields close to lagoons to hunt. The Montagu's Harrier breeds in drier situations than the Marsh Harrier, usually in large fields of cereals. The Buzzard and the Booted Eagle are tree-nesting species (especially in oak woods) that hunt over the nesting habitat, and adjacent habitats where these are available. In Morocco, the Buzzard is replaced by the Long-legged Buzzard, which hunts over open ground. The Golden Eagle and Bonelli's Eagle are cliff-nesters that have large hunting territories. They prefer to hunt over open ground or open matorral. The Spanish Imperial Eagle, a tree-nesting species, hunts over open ground in habitats surrounding the nest sites. Of the falcons, the most widely distributed is the mainly tree nesting Kestrel, which hunts over all habitats, preferring open ones. The Lesser Kestrel generally hunts over large open fields but, being a colonial cliff-nesting species, its distribution is considerably patchier than that of the Kestrel, large hunting flocks occurring in some areas and none in others. The Hobby, a tree-nesting species (often in pines), hunts over open ground close to the nest sites, especially over open ground where there are larks and hirundines. The peregrine is a cliff-nesting species with large territories; those that nest on Gibraltar hunt over matorral habitats, urban zones and the sea.

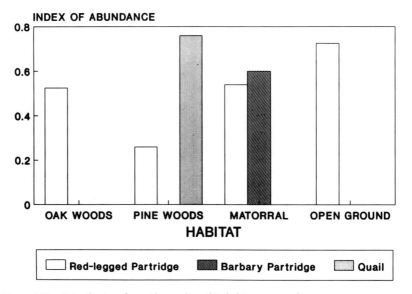

Figure 235.   Distribution of partridges and quail in habitats surveyed.

Partridges

The Red-legged Partridge is found in all the main habitats, preferring the more open woods where it feeds in clearings and, especially, matorral habitats and open ground. It is replaced in Gibraltar and Morocco by the Barbary Partridge, which breeds in matorral habitats and feeds in clearings (Figure 235). Quail breeds in a variety of habitats, typically preferring a tall grass cover. In my survey they were only recorded in the grassy mountain glades within young pine woods, but they also breed in lowland wheatfields (e.g. La Janda) and around lagoons (e.g. Laguna Salada). The Pheasant is an introduced species which breeds in La Janda.

Bustards

Bustards are birds of open ground, requiring large fields in which to breed. The Little Bustard is well distributed in the lowlands of the area but the Great Bustard is now restricted to a few localities and is scarce (see Chapter 8).

Pigeons and doves

Three species breed in the area. The Wood Pigeon breeds in oak woods, with smaller numbers in pine woods and tall matorral habitats (Figure 236). The smaller, migratory, Turtle Dove also nests in woods but appears less confined to the oak woods and regularly feeds in open fields close to nesting sites (Figure 236). The Rock Dove breeds on coastal and inland cliffs and feeds in habitats close to the nest sites, preferring open ground and matorral habitats.

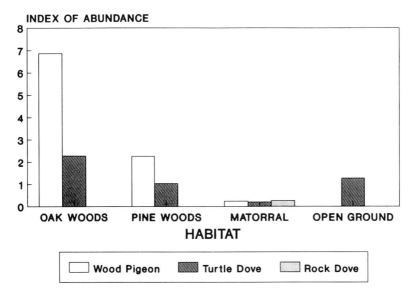

Figure 236.   Distribution of pigeons in habitats surveyed.

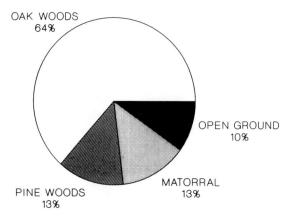

Figure 237.   Distribution of the Cuckoo in habitats surveyed.

Cuckoos

The Great Spotted Cuckoo is confined in its habitat use to areas where the corvids that it parasitizes are abundant. It is therefore most abundant in the pine woods in the north-west of the area. The Cuckoo is widely distributed throughout and occupies all habitats, occurring in highest density in oak woods (Figure 237).

Owls

The Barn Owl nests on cliffs, in old buildings and under bridges in open areas where it is widely distributed. The most widely distributed owl is the Little Owl, which nests on cliffs and in buildings and hunts over open ground and matorral. The Scops Owl nests in woodland, especially open woods with clearings, and hunts close to the nest sites. The Eagle Owl is essentially a cliff-nester, although a few pairs do nest in trees. It hunts over open ground, matorral and rocky areas near the nest sites. The Tawny Owl breeds and hunts in woodland, especially oaks, where it is an abundant species. The Long-eared Owl is a scarce species that breeds in some lowland woods, especially stone pines, and has a patchy distribution in the area. The Marsh Owl is restricted to a few wetland sites in Morocco (see Chapter 7).

Nightjars

The Red-necked Nightjar is a widely distributed and abundant breeding species in pine woods, matorral habitats and near open fields. The difference in habitat utilization between it and the Nightjar, which also breeds but is scarcer, is not clear.

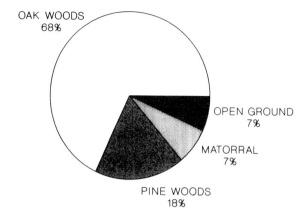

Figure 238.   Distribution of the Bee-eater in habitats surveyed.

Bee-eater

The Bee-eater is abundant and widely distributed and hunts over a variety of habitats. The main factor determining its hunting grounds is the presence of suitable sandbanks for excavating its nest (Figure 238).

Hoopoe

The Hoopoe has a restricted and patchy breeding distribution in the area; it nests exclusively in woodland (generally oak woods) with large clearings (Figure 239). The lowland cork oak woods north of La Janda, the round-leaved oak woods on the Sierra de las Nieves and the stone pine woods around the Marismas del Guadalquivir are regular breeding sites.

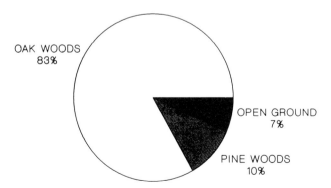

Figure 239.   Distribution of the Hoopoe in habitats surveyed.

Woodpeckers

The Greater Spotted Woodpecker is virtually confined to oak woodland (Figure 240) at all levels where it is a well distributed, but nowhere numerous, species. Green Woodpeckers breed in many oak woods but appear more abundant in pine woods (especially in the mountains), often feeding in open areas close to the woods (Figure 240). The Lesser Spotted Woodpecker probably breeds in some oak woods in the area, where it has been recorded on several occasions; its presence may have been underestimated.

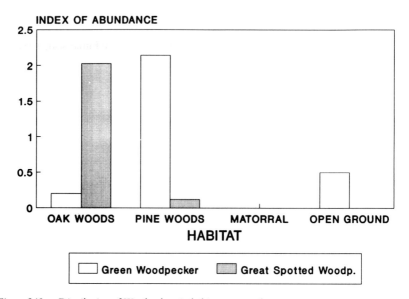

Figure 240.   Distribution of Woodpeckers in habitats surveyed.

SEASONAL VARIATION AND WINTER COMMUNITIES

Seasonal Variation

The composition of bird communities changes seasonally (e.g. see Wiens, 1989), and these changes are pronounced in Mediterranean-type climates (e.g. see Blondel, 1969; Cody, 1974). The typical seasonal pattern for most Mediterranean terrestrial bird communities follows the seasonal climatological and resource regimes (Mooney, 1981; Mooney & Kummerow, 1981; Mooney *et al.*, 1974). The principal seasons of the Palaearctic Mediterranean are as follows:

Summer drought: a predictable period without rain and with very high temperatures. Productivity is lowest at this time.

Autumn/winter rains: a period of regrowth of vegetation and fruiting associated with the termination of the summer drought by the first autumn rains. The mild temperatures permit invertebrate activity (Blondel, 1969; Herrera, 1981). The commencement of these rains varies substantially between years. Once the drought is over, temperature becomes the main factor determining productivity (Mooney, 1981). Structurally simple habitats are most affected by the summer drought and show a greater winter productivity in relation to the summer (Santos & Telleria, 1985).

Spring: the distinction between the winter and spring is not as marked as that between the drought and the first rains. This season is a continuation of the winter but is characterized by increasing daylength and temperatures, and gradual reduction in rains. It is a period of vegetation growth, flowering and increased activity of invertebrates and ectothermic vertebrates (e.g. see Finlayson, 1981).

This pattern is characteristic of thermo–Mediterranean bioclimatic areas (Figure 241) and varies substantially within the Mediterranean (including the mountain tops of the Strait area) with altitude. The pattern in the mountains (oro- and crioro-Mediterranean zones) resembles that of the Euro-Siberian bioclimatic zones (e.g. Santos & Telleria, 1985), low winter temperatures arresting vegetative productivity and invertebrate activity and milder summer conditions permitting an extension of the spring into the summer.

Seasonal variations in Mediterranean bird communities closely follow these climatic and resource variations. Some communities show a summer biomass peak related to the production of young of resident species (Finlayson, 1979; and Chapter 3). But, in general, most communities exhibit a low in species richness, diversity, density and biomass during the summer drought, a gradual increase in

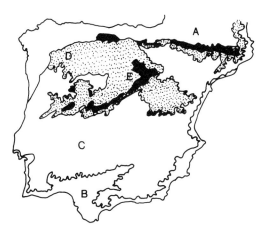

Figure 241.   Main bioclimatic zones of the Iberian Peninsula (after Telleria and Potti, 1984). (a) Euro Siberian, (b) Thermo Mediterranean, (c) Meso Mediterranean, (d) Supra Mediterranean, (e) Oro- and Crioro Mediterranean.

these during the autumn, especially with the arrival of the rains, to a higher winter level and a spring peak (Blondel, 1969; Thuoy, 1976; Herrera, 1980; Abramsky & Safriel, 1980; Finlayson, 1979, 1981; Torres Esquivias & Claveria, 1985). The differences between summer and winter communities are most pronounced in the structurally simpler habitats (Cody, 1974; Finlayson, 1979; Santos & Telleria, 1985). Non-resident species are likely to be better competitors than residents in simple habitats that are more open to environmental fluctuations than the more complex and stable habitats used by residents (Frochot, 1971; Karr, 1976).

Areas close to migration routes experience spring and autumn peaks of community diversity, richness, density and biomass, associated with the passage of migratory species (e.g. Finlayson, 1979, 1981) which may modify the overall seasonal pattern. The seasonal pattern also differs from the typical Mediterranean pattern in the high mountains, where there is usually a peak in density and species richness of bird communities in summer and a low in winter, with diversity varying little between seasons (Zamora & Camacho, 1984a,b).

Telleria *et al.* (1988) have summarized the features that make Iberia favourable as a wintering area for terrestrial birds. These features are equally applicable to northern Morocco:

(1) The latitudinal situation of southwest Europe which is characterized by a mild winter climate with the added mildness provided by the proximity of the Atlantic Ocean and the Mediterranean Sea.

(2) Iberia presents the greatest extension of cold-free area in western Europe in winter.

(3) The Mediterranean region exhibits increased productivity in winter, and probably trophic diversity too, with the arrival of the rains.

This Mediterranean cycle is complementary to that of northern Europe (Telleria *et al.*, 1988) and, as suggested elsewhere in this book, to the alternating rains and drought conditions of northern tropical West Africa. Within Iberia, most species winter within the thermo–Mediterranean bioclimatic zone and achieve highest densities in the south (Telleria *et al.*, 1988). The highest densities are recorded in the habitats of the Strait area (Arroyo & Telleria, 1984).

The proportion of frugivorous species is increased in the thermo-Mediterranean zone in comparison with the Euro-Siberian zone, these species occupying principally the fruit-rich matorral (Finlayson, 1979, 1981). In contrast, seed-eating species prefer open ground to woodland or matorral and, within open ground, select cultivated land (where seeds are more accessible and there is little competition from rodents) in preference to pastures (Telleria *et al.*, 1988).

CHARACTERISTICS OF WINTER COMMUNITIES

Examining pasture, matorral and oak wood communities in the Strait in winter, Arroyo & Telleria (1984) found that pastures supported the highest densities and biomasses of birds, and that their energetic requirements were correspondingly the highest. Species diversity and species richness showed an inverse trend, oak woods being richest and pastures poorest. Pastures supported the highest proportion of migrants (85%), followed by matorral (58%) and oak woods (43%). Pastures received the greatest volume of birds in winter; as they are the simplest habitats, this could be related to the greater inter-seasonal difference in resources in comparison with the more complex woodland and matorral habitats.

In order to compare differences between breeding season (June) and winter (January), I have compared an area of open oak woodland at the northern edge of

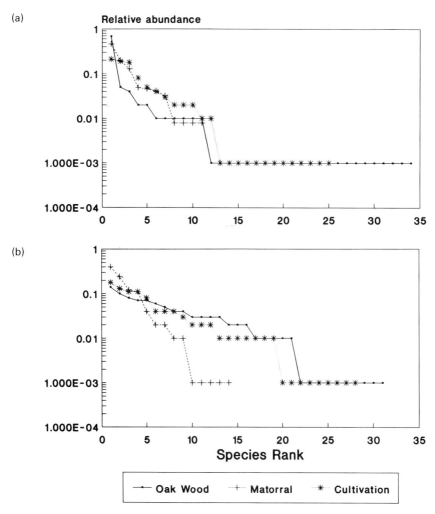

Figure 242.   Species abundance curves for three Strait habitats (a) in January, (b) in June.

(a)

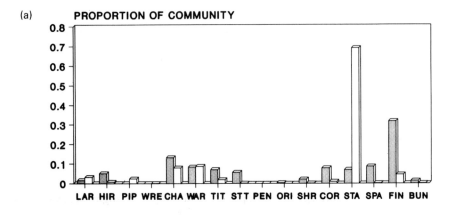

(b)

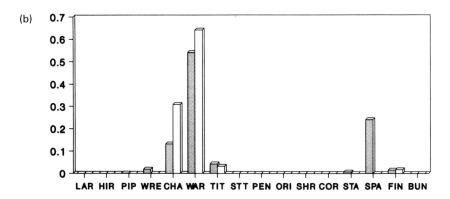

(c)

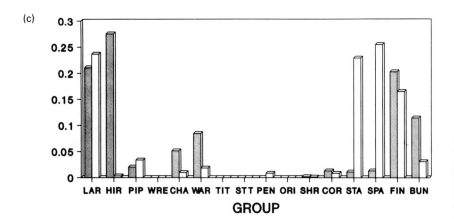

Figure 243.   Contribution of passerine groups to three Strait communities in January (☐) and June (▨), (a) oak wood, (b) matorral, (c) cultivation.

La Janda with an area under cultivation and pasture on the La Janda depression. To these results can be added earlier results from a matorral community on the Rock of Gibraltar (Finlayson, 1979).

The oak wood community differed in several parameters from those studied by Arroyo & Telleria (1984) who examined relatively undisturbed oak woods. The differences may be interpreted in relation to the higher use made of the disturbed oak wood and its large clearings (heterogeneous habitat) by migrants that foraged on acorns and olives also present in the habitat. In general, all communities were poorer in winter than spring (Figures 242 and 243), although the oak wood had a higher species richness in winter, but supported a higher density of passerines. In all cases, the habitats supported more migrant species in winter. The oak wood and the matorral also held higher densities of migrants in winter than in spring, but the open ground showed a slight decrease. The absolute densities achieved in all habitats testify to the importance of the area as a wintering ground.

The conclusions of Arroyo & Telleria (1984) can be modified in the light of these results. Some open ground sites may not hold such high densities as others, and this may be related to the absence of specific food resources (finches were unexpectedly scarce in La Janda the year of my study, which could have been related to fairly extensive flooding). However, pastures generally support high densities of birds in winter. Managed lowland oak woods are structurally more diverse than less disturbed sites and support very high densities of birds in winter. This feature may be enhanced by the presence of fruiting shrubs (e.g. olives) which would be absent from other oak woods. The Gibraltar maquis is an impoverished form of matorral but supports very high densities of a reduced number of species throughout the year (Finlayson, 1979).

WINTERING ABUNDANCE AND DISTRIBUTION OF MAIN GROUPS OF TERRESTRIAL SPECIES

PASSERINES

Larks

Larks make the highest contribution to wintering communities of open ground (Figure 244), with a large increase in density in winter due almost entirely to the arrival of large numbers of Skylarks (Arroyo & Telleria, 1984; see also Chapter 3). The Short-toed Lark is absent from wintering communities.

Hirundines

Only the Crag Martin is widely dispersed in winter, mainly over open habitats close to cave roosts (Elkins & Etheridge 1974). The Swallow, Red-rumped

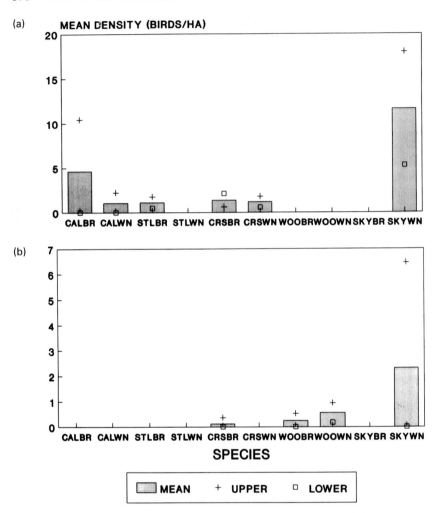

Figure 244.   (a) Lark densities in open cultivation in January and June. (b) Lark densities in open oak woodland in January and June.

Swallow, House Martin and Sand Martin are sporadic during the winter months (Finlayson & Cortés, 1987). The unpredictability of temperatures in winter must make aerial plankton levels insufficient to maintain a diverse aerial insectivore community (see Chapter 8).

Pipits and wagtails

Pipits and wagtails are important only in open habitats. Spectacular winter increases result from massive arrivals of Meadow Pipits and White Wagtails,

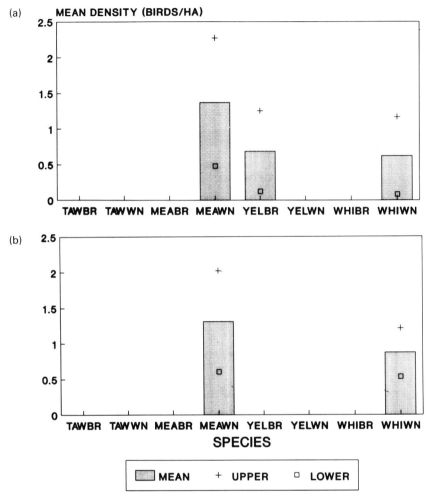

Figure 245.   (a) Wagtail and pipit densities in cultivation in January and June. (b) Wagtail and pipit densities in open oak woodland in January and June.

which dominate open ground communities (Figure 245; Arroyo & Telleria, 1984; see also Chapter 3). Tawny Pipits and Yellow Wagtails are absent in winter (but see Chapters 3 and 7 for Yellow Wagtail wintering).

Chats and thrushes

This group shows spectacular increases in density in winter in matorral and oak woodland but not in pastures (Figure 246). The increases are due mainly to large winter arrivals of Robins, Black Redstarts and Song Thrushes (Finlayson, 1979;

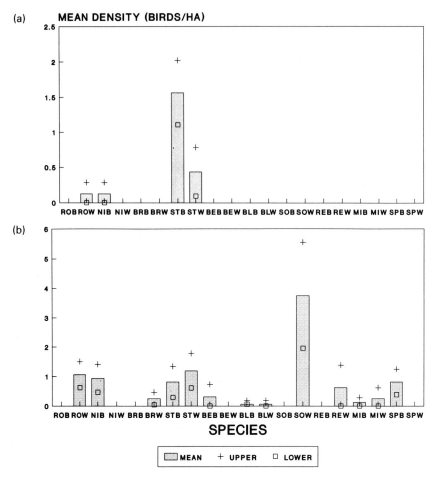

Figure 246.   (a) Chat and thrush densities in cultivation in January and June. (b) Chat and thrush densities in open oak woodland in January and June.

Arroyo & Telleria, 1984; see also Chapter 3), which dominate winter communities. The Black Redstart is most numerous in open matorral alongside cliffs, screes and rocky slopes and is abundant on the Rock of Gibraltar.

Warblers

Warblers are most important in matorral communities (Figure 247). In winter, the main density increases are due to large arrivals of Blackcap and Chiffchaff

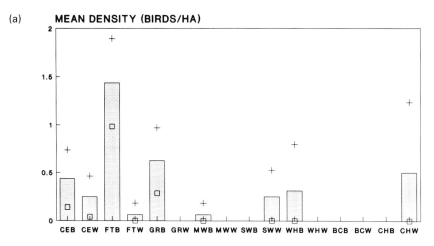

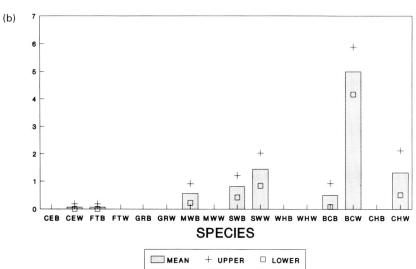

Figure 247. (a) Warbler densities in cultivation in January and June. (b) Warbler densities in oak woodland in January and June.

(Finlayson, 1979, 1981a,b; Arroyo & Telleria, 1984; Chapter 3), which together with the resident Sardinian Warbler, dominate the matorral. A number of breeding warblers disappear from the communities, having migrated south to the tropics (e.g. Melodious Warbler, Whitethroat) or into Morocco (e.g. Fan-tailed Warbler), and the winter warbler community is dominated by fewer species (Figure 247).

Finches

The large influxes of finches in autumn result in important numbers in the Strait in winter, the most notable being Goldfinch, Linnet and Chaffinch (Arroyo & Telleria, 1984), the first two in open ground and the last in open ground and oak woodland (Figure 248). Most winter communities have a high proportion of these finches as well as Serin and Greenfinch and, in irruptive years, Siskin.

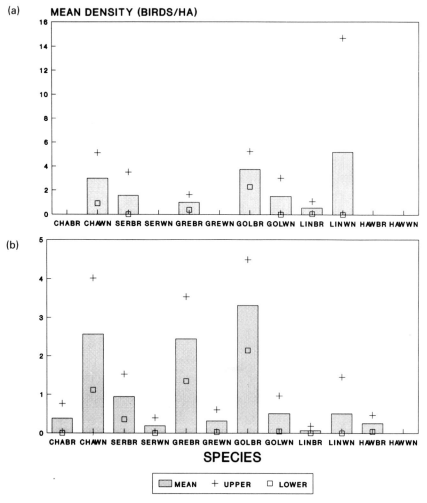

Figure 248.   (a) Finch densities in cultivation in January and June. (b) Finch densities in open oak woodland in January and June.

Other species

The most conspicuous member of the open oak wood community in the year of my study was the Starling, which accounted for 68% of the community. It is a species that arrives from the north in variable numbers, being numerous some years and relatively scarce others (Finlayson & Cortés, 1987), so that its contribution to the wintering communities is likely to be highly variable. Other passerines do not introduce new elements to the wintering passerine communities. Sparrows and buntings are dominant in open ground communities and tits in oak woods.

NON-PASSERINES

The non-passerines are dominated by raptors that winter in the area, the other important group (to flooded fields) being waders (Chapter 4). The lowland woods of the western Strait receive large flocks of Woodpigeons in winter (Chapter 3), and these are important in some communities. The main raptors are Red Kite, Griffon Vulture, Marsh Harrier, Hen Harrier, Goshawk, Sparrowhawk, Buzzard, Golden Eagle, Bonelli's Eagle, Kestrel and Peregrine. In some areas the following are also regular though scarce: Black Vulture, Short-toed Eagle, Long-legged Buzzard, Imperial Eagle, Booted Eagle, Lesser Kestrel and Merlin.

CHAPTER 7

Wetlands

Southern Spain and northern Morocco are situated between the breeding areas and wintering coastal wetlands of waders in northern and western Europe and the major wintering grounds in Mauretania, Senegal and other areas of West Africa (Hale, 1980; Kersten & Smit, 1984). The region functions as a wintering area for large numbers of waders and supports even higher numbers in transit between western Europe and West Africa. In the autumn the Moroccan coast is also a moulting ground for waders (Pienkowski *et al.*, 1976). In the spring, the total number of waders using the Moroccan Atlantic coast on passage may be of the order of 675 000–900 000 (Kersten & Smit, 1984). Southern Spain and Morocco are also important wintering grounds for wildfowl from northern Europe; the Atlantic coast between the Marismas del Guadalquivir in the north and the Merja Zerga in the south, together with important inland lagoons, can hold between 300 000 and 500 000 ducks, geese and coots in winter (Ena & Purroy, 1982; Thevenot *et al.*, 1981, 1982; Beaubrun & Thevenot, 1983; Dolz & Gomez, 1988). In some cases, for example the Greylag Goose, the area holds the main wintering grounds of virtually an entire population (Rooth, 1971; Amat, 1986).

Apart from the importance to passage and wintering wildfowl and waders, the area's wetlands hold breeding populations of very rare species, notably the Marbled Duck, White-headed Duck, Purple Gallinule, Crested Coot and Slender-billed Gull; Ferruginous Ducks, Bitterns and Ruddy Shelducks no longer breed, however. The African Marsh Owl, which was found in La Janda (Irby, 1895), is extinct on the Spanish side of the Strait and its numbers and range in northwest Morocco have been reduced (Mikkola, 1983). The loss of wetland

396

habitats has been the major cause of the decline of these species, with the drainage of the large freshwater Laguna de La Janda and the adjacent Laguna del Torero being the most significant loss in the 20th Century.

In this chapter, the main wetland habitats of the Strait, and its breeding and wintering bird communities, are described. These descriptions are followed by an assessment of the Strait's most important wetland sites and the main water-birds and waders which use them.

COASTAL WETLANDS

Saltmarshes are found in the Atlantic coastal belt, where tidal ranges are sufficiently large to cause regular flooding of areas of coast. East of the Strait,

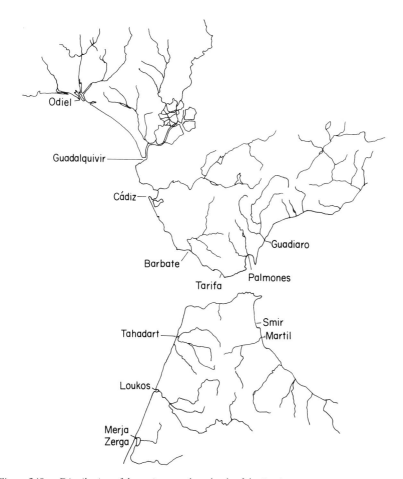

Figure 249.   Distribution of the main coastal wetlands of the Strait.

within the Mediterranean, tidal ranges are very reduced and, in consequence, saltmarshes are of limited extent (Fernandez-Palacios & Figueroa Clemente, 1987). The Atlantic marshes (Figure 249) are discrete patches of marsh habitat from the Portuguese marshes to the north-west to the Moroccan and West African marshes in the south, forming a network of marshlands that occupy the eastern Atlantic coastal areas. The coastal marshes of the Portuguese Algarve, Atlantic southwest Spain and northwest Morocco form a 'Mediterranean–Atlantic' group characterized by an Atlantic tidal regime and a Mediterranean climate (Figueroa *et al.*, 1987) and plant species typical of western European and Mediterranean marshes (Gehu & Rivas Martinez, 1984).

The vegetation of the saltmarshes varies considerably, depending on the relative influence of salt water flooding by regular tides and freshwater flooding caused by rain and rivers. This is often significant in determining the use made of marshes by different species of birds. The basic distribution of vegetation in relation to degree of flooding and salinity is illustrated in Figure 250, which is representative of the area. Of typical saltmarshes along the Atlantic coast, Cádiz Bay, the Odiel Estuary in Huelva and the Loukos in Morocco (Figure 249) are among the most important. The marshes associated with the Guadalquivir Estuary differ from these. They have reached a degree of senescence in which alluvial deposition is progressively filling in areas of marsh upstream and, combined with the gradual blocking of the exit to the sea by the spit that forms

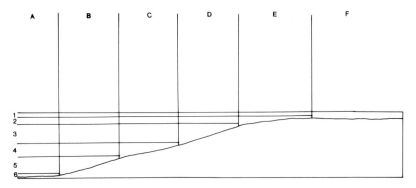

Figure 250.   Distribution of the main vegetation components of Strait coastal wetlands.

Key: (1) freshwater, (2) freshwater/saline, (3) upper marsh, (4) middle marsh, (5) lower marsh, (6) flats. Main species: A, Zostera noltii, Ulva rigida, Enteromorpha spp.; B, Salicornia ramosissima, Puccinellia spp., Spartina maritima; C, Sarcocornia perenne; D, Anthrocnemum macrostachyum, Limoniastrum monopetalum, Sarcocornia fruticosa, Inula crithmoides, Halimione portulacoides, Spartina densiflora, Artemisia caerulescens, Frankenia laevis, Suaeda vera, Juncus acutus, Atriplex halimus, Salsola vermicula; E, Scirpus maritimus; J. subulatus, J. acutus, J. maritimus, Psamolus valerandii, Aster squamatum; F, Phragmites australis, Iris pseudocarus, Tamarix canariensis, Salix spp., Arundo donax, Typha dominguensis.

the sandy area of the Coto Doñana, this has reduced the impact of the tide on the marsh, which is now falling in salinity, especially away from the coast.

An extreme example of freshwater vegetation reaching the very edge of an estuary is found in the Guadiaro, which opens into the Mediterranean Sea (Figure 249). The tidal range in the Mediterranean, generally less than a metre, is considerably less than in the nearby Atlantic. In the Guadiaro, reeds (*Phragmites australis*) grow right by the shore of the estuary.

Saltmarshes have traditionally been exploited as saltpans, in Bonanza, Cádiz, Barbate and Larache in particular. Some of these works date back to the 18th Century (Fernandez-Palacios *et al.*, 1988) and many are now abandoned. Saltpans are attractive to marsh birds, which utilize the vegetated embankments to nest and the pans to feed in. In those in use, the water level changes controlled by Man determine their attractiveness to bird species, with waders feeding in the shallow areas and surface-feeding ducks and flamingoes in the deeper water.

Seasonal variation is very pronounced in the marshes of southern Spain and northern Morocco (e.g. see Amat, 1981). The areas not subjected to regular tidal flooding experience the greatest degree of flooding in winter and spring, as a direct result of rainfall and the increased volume of fresh water brought down by rivers. With the summer drought, large parts of these marshes become totally devoid of water, presenting the appearance of a dry steppe. During this dry period many resident waterbirds congregate in the small lagoons that retain water throughout the summer. Larks, Pin-tailed Sandgrouse and bustards move into the drying marsh from adjacent zones where they breed. In marshes which are being drained by Man, such as the marsh on the east bank of the Guadalquivir near Trebujena, the dry marsh landscape is extended even further.

BREEDING BIRDS

The species that breed in coastal marshes are specialists which are able to live on the edge of a habitat that is prone to regular flooding. A feature of these marshes is the dominance of non-passerine species (Figure 251). The main groups in the breeding season are raptors, wildfowl, gulls, terns and herons.

Among ducks, mainly surface-feeders foraging in shallow water and breeding in dense aquatic vegetation or on nearby banks, the Mallard is the most widespread species; Gadwall, Pochard, Red-crested Pochard are frequent, with smaller numbers of Pintail. Some, such as Teal, Garganey and Shoveler, only breed sporadically in years when water levels are high (Valverde 1960). Some species are now very rare and virtually restricted to the Guadalquivir. The Ruddy Shelduck does not breed in the area, whilst the Ferruginous Duck only breeds in the Loukos marsh (Pineau & Giraud-Audine, 1979). White-headed Ducks are recovering but, being diving ducks, are more frequent in open water lagoons than in marshes. The Marbled Duck breeds in a few marshes, its largest population being in the Guadalquivir (Amat, 1981, 1982) which is highly variable (independently of water levels): hundreds breeding some years and practically

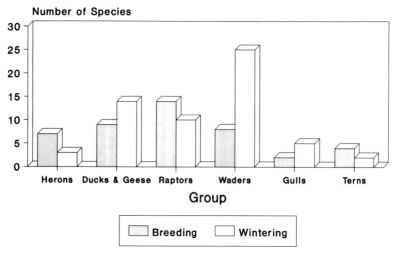

Figure 251.   Number of species breeding and wintering in coastal marshes. Not all groups are represented.

none other years (J. Amat, pers. comm.). Most Ducks breed in the less saline, non-tidal parts, the only species able to nest near or within saltmarsh being the Mallard (Figure 252).

Raptors are well represented, although only the Marsh Harrier breeds within the marshes (Figure 252) (and the Kestrel, where there are human constructions). The Marsh Harrier has seriously declined as a breeding species in the area having once been extremely abundant (Irby, 1895; Verner, 1910). Which species of raptor hunt over coastal marshes during the breeding season depend on the habitats surrounding the marsh. In the Guadalquivir, the surrounding pine and oak woods hold large populations of tree-nesting raptors which hunt almost exclusively in the marshes. The main species are Black Kite, Red Kite, Booted Eagle, Buzzard, Short-toed Eagle, Hobby and Kestrel. The small population of Spanish Imperial Eagles nests in trees around the marshes. Montagu's Harriers are abundant in dry areas of marsh and surrounding fields (Figure 252). Young birds hunt over marshland, as it dries during the summer drought, before departing for Africa. Where cliffs are close, Egyptian and Griffon Vultures, which nest on the ledges, soar over the marshes. Barn, Eagle and Little Owls hunt over marshes where suitable cliffs or buildings are available nearby, but the African Marsh Owl (with a restricted range) is the only true marsh-dwelling owl in the area.

Herons, storks and spoonbills nest in trees adjacent to and feed within the marshes. In the Odiel marshes, the colonies of Spoonbills are established on *Anthrocnemum*, and in the Guadalquivir Purple Herons nest on *Anthrocnemum* and *Scirpus*. Some species, such as the Purple Heron and Little Bittern, nest in dense reedbeds within the marshes. The Guadalquivir holds the most important

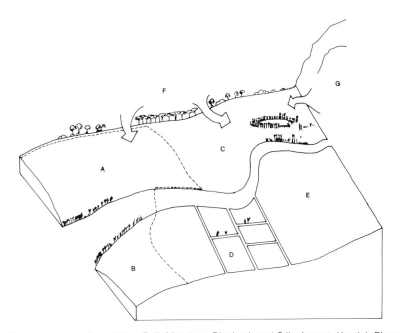

A, B, MAIN MARSH: Mallard, Water Rail, Moorhen, Black-winged Stilt, Avocet, Kentish Plover, Lapwing, Redshank, Slender-billed Gull, Yellow-legged Gull, Gull-billed Tern, Little Tern, Whiskered Tern, Black Tern, Yellow Wagtail, Fan-tailed Warbler, Spectacled Warbler. C, FRESHWATER MARSH/LAGOON: Little Grebe, Black-necked Grebe, Little Bittern, Purple Heron, Gadwall, Marbled Duck, Red-crested Pochard, Pochard, White-headed Duck, Marsh Harrier, Baillon's Crake, Purple Gallinule, Crested Coot, Coot, Little Ringed Plover, Cetti's Warbler, Savi's Warbler, Reed Warbler, Great Reed Warbler. D, DRAINED MARSH: Stone Curlew, Collared Pratincole, Pin-tailed Sandgrouse, Lesser Short-toed Lark, Stonechat, Linnet. E, STEPPE/ PASTURE: Montagu's Harrier, Little Bustard, Calandra Lark, Short-toed Lark, Crested Lark, Black-eared Wheatear, Dartford Warbler, Sardinian Warbler, Goldfinch, Corn Bunting. F, TREES BORDERING MARSH: Night Heron, Squacco Heron, Cattle Egret, Little Egret, Grey Heron, White Stork, Spoonbill, Black Kite, Red Kite, Short-toed Eagle, Buzzard, Imperial Eagle, Booted Eagle, Kestrel, Hobby, Magpie, Jackdaw. G, CLIFFS BORDERING MARSH: Typical species: Egyptian Vulture, Griffon Vulture, Lesser Kestrel, Peregrine, Barn Owl, Little Owl, Swift, Pallid Swift, Swallow, House Martin, Raven.

Figure 252.   Distribution of typical breeding bird species in and around coastal marshes.

populations. Species such as the Squacco Heron are almost exclusively found in these marshes, while Cattle and Little Egrets are more widespread. An unusual breeding colony is that of the Tajo de Barbate where 2600 pairs of Cattle Egrets and 50 pairs of Little Egrets (Grimmett & Jones, 1989) nest in the scrub at the base of a sandstone sea cliff. These birds feed in adjacent fields and the marshes of the Barbate.

The recent history of the heronries on both sides of the Strait illustrates their

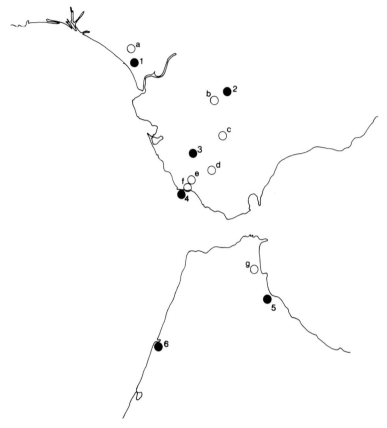

Figure 253.   Distribution of Strait heronries. Abandoned colonies: a, La Rocina; b, Arcos; c, Alcala de los Gazules; d, Celemín; e, La Janda; f, Torero; g, Smir. Existing colonies: 1, Coto Doñana; 2, Bornos; 3, Medina Sidonia; 4, Tajo de Barbate; 5, Emsa; 6, Sidi Embarek.

vulnerability and instability (Figure 253). The Barbate cliff colony, which was discovered in 1952 by Rowan & Bernis (1956), was probably established between 1946 and 1948, and was in all likelihood derived from the large heronry of the Laguna del Torero, near Vejer, which had been drained (Yeates, 1945; Fernandez-Cruz, 1975). In 1966, Gonzalez & del Junco (1968) discovered a heronry in the Celemín Reservoir (north of La Janda). In the first year of colonization, 250 empty Cattle Egret nests were found. The following year there were 800 Cattle Egret and 10 Purple Heron breeding pairs, and in the next 2 years (1968 and 1969) the colony had 600 Cattle Egret pairs and a single Purple Heron pair. All birds (except the Purple Herons) left the site in 1970 (Fernandez-Cruz, 1975). Alonso (1983) has suggested that the Celemín was colonized by surplus birds from the Barbate colony. These birds then apparently moved a short distance northwards to establish a new heronry in a stand of White Poplars and Common Sallows near

Medina Sidonia that same year. This heronry has remained at the same site and holds a minimum of 1000 pairs (Grimmett & Jones, 1989). Other heronries show similar patterns of abandoning (usually due to disturbance and loss of habitat) and colonization of new sites, the general trend being negative (Fernandez-Cruz, 1975; Junco & Dominguez, 1975; Pineau & Giraud-Audine, 1979; Alonso, 1983).

The range of breeding waders is restricted, although those which do nest do so in large numbers and often in colonies. The most characteristic are the Black-winged Stilt, Avocet, Collared Pratincole, Kentish Plover, Redshank and Lapwing. Stone Curlews breed in dry zones such as areas of marsh which are being drained. The Redshank and Little Ringed Plover are more restricted in distribution, the latter being more typical of other habitats. In some of the smaller estuarine marshes, the number of breeding species and the sizes of their populations are considerably reduced.

Gulls are poorly represented in the coastal marshes of the area. A small population of Slender-billed Gulls (about 20 pairs—Grimmett & Jones, 1989) breeds in the Guadalquivir, mixed with Gull-billed Terns, Black-winged Stilts and Avocets (Costa, 1985; Fernandez-Palacios *et al.*, 1988), and forms the only nucleus of the species on either side of the Strait. Yellow-legged Gulls have recently become established in small colonies on the saltmarshes around the Bay of Cádiz (Martinez *et al.*, 1990) but do not breed in any other coastal marsh. Terns are numerous and sometimes form large colonies, although disturbance has meant the loss of some colonies. Whiskered Terns no longer breed on the Moroccan marshes (Pineau & Giraud-Audine, 1979), and Little Terns are absent from some former breeding sites, e.g. the Guadiaro (Irby, 1875). Nevertheless, there is a large Whiskered Tern population in the Guadalquivir, of the order of several thousand pairs (J. Amat, pers. comm.), which is now the core for the species in the area. Little Terns are abundant in Cádiz and the Guadalquivir (see Chapter 5), with smaller numbers in the Loukos and Tahadart estuaries in Morocco (Pineau & Giraud-Audine, 1979). The only Strait breeding site of the Gull-billed Tern is the Guadalquivir (see Chapter 5). Pineau and Giraud-Audine (1979) considered that this species might breed in the Loukos, but their evidence was insufficient to be conclusive.

The dense freshwater marsh vegetation is utilized for breeding by scarce species, the most notable being the Purple Gallinule and the Crested Coot. The Purple Gallinule is well represented in the Guadalquivir where there are several hundred pairs (Grimmett & Jones, 1989) and in the Loukos (Pineau & Giraud-Audine, 1979). The Crested Coot is now very rare and found only in the marshes of the Guadalquivir and the Loukos, and on some inland lagoons. Water Rails, Moorhens, Coots and, probably, Baillon's Crakes are more widespread in the coastal marshes of the region.

Greater Flamingoes breed only in the Guadalquivir marshes and then sporadically, depending on water levels, but they are widespread in the coastal marshes and saltpans of the area throughout the year. Flamingoes from the inland saline lagoon of Fuente de Piedra visit the area's coastal marshes during the breeding season to feed (see Chapter 4).

Marshland within the Coto Doñana, part of the Marismas del Guadalquivir complex. Deer regularly forage where marsh meets drier land.

There are very few passerine species that can be said to be typical nesting birds of coastal marshes (Figure 254). Most are associated with drier areas of marsh, especially the zones that have been drained by Man. This is particularly the case with larks, which are abundant in the steppe-like periphery of coastal marshes (Calandra, Crested, Short-toed and Lesser Short-toed Larks). Other typical breeding species of drained marshes are the Stonechat, Fan-tailed Warbler (also in wetter areas), Dartford Warbler, Spectacled Warbler, Sardinian Warbler, Gold-finch, Linnet and Corn Bunting, which are species associated with steppe and low scrub habitats. Within the marshes, the main breeding passerines are warblers. Fan-tailed Warblers and Spectacled Warblers breed in the least tidal parts of saltmarsh. Cetti's, Fan-tailed and Great Reed Warblers are the most widespread species in vegetation associated with less saline water (e.g. *Phragmites, Typha*), with Reed Warbler, Savi's Warbler and, more rarely, Moustached Warbler (see Thevenot & Thuoy, 1974) breeding in localized patches of swamp-like vege-tation. The Yellow Wagtail (subspecies *iberiae*) is an abundant and widespread breeding species. Very few passerines breed in adjacent habitats and feed within the marshes, contrasting with non-passerines (Figure 254). Only hirundines (usually House Martin and Swallow) and corvids (Magpie, Jackdaw, Raven) do so regularly.

The most complete marsh community left in the region is that of the Marismas del Guadalquivir. Some of the smaller estuaries have a reduced species range, although the precise number of species utilizing the habitat will be greater as species from adjacent habitats utilize it. The number of species using the habitat in

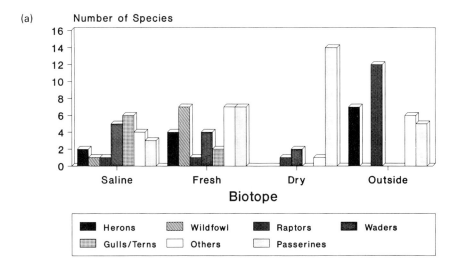

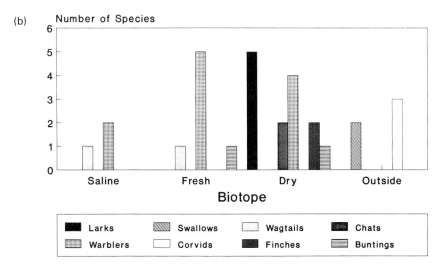

Figure 254. (a) Distribution of main groups feeding in coastal marshes by nesting biotope. (b) Distribution of passerine groups feeding in coastal marshes by nesting biotope.

the breeding season will therefore depend in part on the nature of the adjacent habitats. Generally, the number of species breeding in the saltmarsh is low, species composition varying little between estuaries. The freshwater-dominated Guadiaro Estuary has the species listed in Table 28 (Grupo Ornitologico del Estrecho, 1987). The Palmones Estuary in the Bay of Gibraltar is under greater tidal influence (Table 28).

Table 28   Breeding species on estuarine marshes of the Strait.

Guadiaro Estuary[1] (freshwater-dominated)	Little Grebe, Mallard, Moorhen, Water Rail, Kentish Plover, Little Ringed Plover, Cetti's Warbler, Fan-tailed Warbler, Reed Warbler
Palmones Estuary[2] (more tidal influence)	Mallard, Water Rail, Moorhen, Little Ringed Plover, Kentish Plover, Yellow Wagtail, Cetti's Warbler, Fan-tailed Warbler
Loukos[3] (most tidal influence)	Mallard, Montagu's Harrier, Lapwing, Kentish Plover, Black-winged Stilt, Collared Pratincole, Little Tern, Marsh Owl, Lesser Short-toed Lark, Yellow Wagtail, Cetti's Warbler, Fan-tailed Warbler, Reed Bunting

[1] Grupo Ornitologico del Estrecho (1987).
[2] Vega (1988).
[3] Pineau & Giraud-Audine (1979).

The marsh of the Loukos on the Atlantic is more tidal near the sea than the other two estuaries, although the salinity is lost inland. This difference is seen in the presence of species that do not occur in the other estuaries. (In this respect, the Marsh Owl is a separate case, since its distribution is restricted to Morocco and its presence or absence is not related to the nature of the marsh alone.) The typical breeding species of the Loukos (Pineau & Giraud–Audine, 1979) are given in Table 28.

Part of the freshwater complex of the Marismas del Guadalquivir.

Table 29   Breeding species of saltpans in the region of the Strait.

Mallard	Herring Gull
Gadwall	Little Tern
Marbled Duck (occasional)	Gull-billed Tern
Avocet	Yellow Wagtail
Black-winged Stilt	Fan-tailed Warbler
Kentish Plover	Spectacled Warbler
Redshank	Dartford Warbler
Collarded Pratincole	Sardinian Warbler
Slender-billed Gull	

The breeding communities of saltpans are similar to those of saltmarsh. Some additional species are able to nest in the vegetated embankments which are not covered by the tides. In addition, many birds from adjacent areas visit saltpans to feed. Breeding species of saltpans are listed in Table 29.

WINTERING BIRDS

In winter, the marshes flood after the rains and pools and ponds form. The resident community of birds is augmented by species from further north, especially ducks, geese and waders, the Strait area being within their winter range (see Chapter 4). Birds which have a more restricted habitat choice during the breeding season also utilize the marshes in winter. This is especially the case with raptors, for example the Peregrine, which are attracted to the marshes by the abundance of birds at that time of the year. Coastal marsh wintering communities include a number of the species given in Table 30; not all are present in any one site.

There are striking differences in the species utilizing the marshes in the breeding season and in winter (Figure 255). In winter, wildfowl and waders

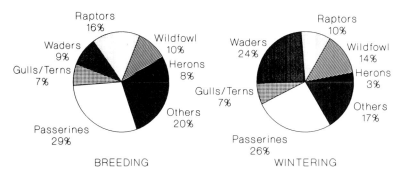

Figure 255.   Composition of coastal marsh bird communities by species. Breeding, 86 species; wintering, 103 species.

Table 30   Wintering species of coastal marshes of the Strait.

Little Grebe	Purple Gallinule	Pin-tailed Sandgrouse
Black-necked Grebe	Coot	Barn Owl
Great Crested Grebe	Crested Coot	Short-eared Owl
Little Egret	Little Bustard (dry marsh)	Kingfisher
Cattle Egret	Oystercatcher	Wryneck
Grey Heron	Black-winged Stilt	Calandra Lark
White Stork	Avocet	Crested Lark
Spoonbill	Stone Curlew	Skylark
Greater Flamingo	Ringed Plover	Crag Martin
Greylag Goose	Kentish Plover	Meadow Pipit
Shelduck	Golden Plover	Water Pipit
Wigeon	Grey Plover	White Wagtail
Gadwall	Lapwing	Yellow Wagtail
Teal	Knot	(Morocco only)
Mallard	Sanderling	Bluethroat
Pintail	Little Stint	Stonechat
Shoveler	Dunlin	Cetti's Warbler
Marbled Duck	Ruff	Fan-tailed Warbler
Red-crested Pochard	Snipe	Moustached Warbler
Pochard	Black-tailed Godwit	Dartford Warbler
Tufted Duck	Bar-tailed Godwit	Sardinian Warbler
Ferruginous Duck	Whimbrel	Chiffchaff
White-headed Duck	Curlew	Penduline Tit
Red Kite	Spotted Redshank	Great Grey Shrike
Griffon Vulture	Greenshank	Jackdaw
Marsh Harrier	Green Sandpiper	Raven
Hen Harrier	Common Sandpiper	Magpie
Buzzard	Turnstone	Starling
Imperial Eagle	Mediterranean Gull	Spotless Starling
Osprey	Little Gull	Tree Sparrow
Kestrel	Yellow-legged Gull	Goldfinch
Merlin	Lesser Black-backed Gull	Linnet
Peregrine	Black-headed Gull	Reed Bunting
Water Rail	Sandwich Tern	Corn Bunting
Moorhen	Caspian Tern	

account for 38% of the species (only 19% in the breeding season) and are usually present in large numbers. For ducks, the Guadalquivir is the most important wintering site in Spain, with about 300 000 depending on conditions (Ena & Purroy, 1984; Grimmett & Jones, 1989). It overshadows all other marshes of the area in terms of diversity and numbers. The wintering population of Greylag Geese, which is the main one of continental Greylags, fluctuates between 60 000 and 75 000 birds (Amat, 1986). Among the most important ducks (maximum figures) are Teal (126 200), Shoveler (86 000) and Pintail (39 900) (Grimmett & Jones, 1989). Figures 256 and 257 indicate the most important species of ducks

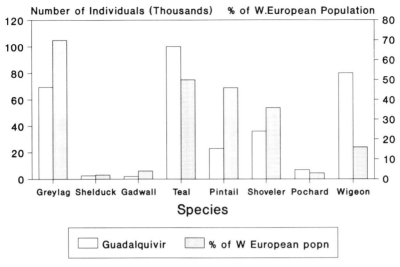

Figure 256. Estimated number of main populations of ducks and geese in winter in the Guadalquivir marshes.

and geese wintering in Andalucía, in particular in the areas covered by the coastal marshes of Huelva, Sevilla and Cádiz, and the inland lagoons (discussed later in this chapter). One species which dominates in coastal areas is the Wigeon, which is an important wintering species: 111 275 Wigeon in the Guadalquivir in January 1979 (Ena & Purroy, 1982); an average of over 5000 in Cádiz Bay in winter (Grimmett & Jones, 1989). On the Moroccan side, the main waterfowl concentrations are in the Merja Zerga, which can hold over 40 000 ducks in winter (Thevenot *et al.*, 1982). Smaller numbers of ducks and geese are dispersed in other coastal marshes of the area in significantly lower numbers.

There is also an increase in species diversity and overall numbers of wintering waders in the coastal marshes of the area. The distribution of species is somewhat different on the European and African shores (Figure 258). The main differences are in the proportions of different species in the community of wintering waders. Noteworthy is the proportion of Black-winged Stilts (which winter in small numbers on the European shore), Avocets, Curlews and Stone Curlews on the African shore, and the overall dominance of Black-tailed Godwits on the European shore. These patterns vary, however, with environmental conditions in Europe. The wintering of Spotted Redshanks on the African shore has no equivalent on the European shore, where the species mainly occurs on passage. On the Moroccan side, there are several important estuaries and marshes for waders. The most important is the Loukos, which has a high diversity of species among which highlight Kentish Plover, Dunlin, Redshank, Black-tailed Godwit, Curlew and Stone Curlew. Other important sites are Oualad Khallouf, Sidi Kacem and Oued Tahadart on the Atlantic coast

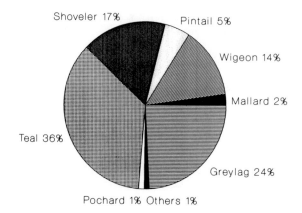

Figure 257.   Distribution of wildfowl in Andalucía in winter (after Ena and Purroy, 1984).
N = 252 203.

and Oued Martil on the Mediterranean shore. In general, the coastal marshes and mudflats of the area have a winter wader community with the composition given in Table 31.

The species range of herons and allied species, and of raptors, decreases in winter, although in some cases replacements are accompanied by numerical increases. Of the herons, the Night Heron, Squacco Heron and Purple Heron are practically absent in winter. Other heron species do not replace these, but the coastal marshes do receive large numbers of Grey Herons (see Chapter 4). Little and Cattle Egrets are more widely dispersed in winter. Greater Flamingoes are regular in most of the coastal marshes in winter, numbers fluctuating considerably with changing water levels. The wintering population of Greater Flamingoes in the area is of the order of 9000–11 000 (Fernandez–Cruz *et al.*, 1988; but see also Chapter 4).

The typical winter raptor community is composed of the Red Kite, Marsh Harrier, Hen Harrier, Buzzard, Osprey and Kestrel. The Hen Harrier and Osprey are wintering species from northern Europe, and the populations of the other species are augmented by north European birds (de Juana *et al.*, 1988).

Table 31   Species present in winter wader communities of the Strait.

Main species throughout	Black-tailed Godwit, Dunlin
Main species in specific sites	Avocet, Redshank, Kentish Plover, Sanderling
Other important species	Ringed Plover, Grey Plover, Bar-tailed Godwit, Spotted Redshank, Black-winged Stilt
Species of minor importance	Oystercatcher, Ruff, Turnstone, Curlew, Whimbrel, Greenshank, Little Stint, Common Sandpiper, Knot

(a)

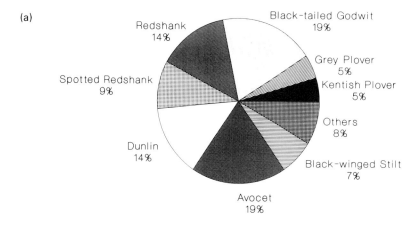

(b)

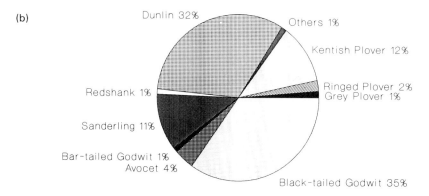

Figure 258.   (a) Distribution of wintering wader species in the Oued Loukos (after Kersten and Smidt, 1984). Others: Oystercatcher, Ringed Plover, Ruff, Turnstone, Curlew, Bar-tailed Godwit, Greenshank, Little Stint and Sanderling. N = 2100. (b) Distribution of wintering wader species on the Cádiz coast (after Telleria, 1981). N = 17 301.

Other raptors occur regularly in coastal marshes but have a patchier distribution: Imperial Eagle, Booted Eagle, Peregrine and Merlin. Imperial Eagles disperse from the nesting areas within Doñana and reach the shores of the Strait and even cross to Morocco. Their scarcity make sightings away from Doñana sporadic. A small population of the migratory Booted Eagle remains within the area and roaming individuals hunt over open country, including coastal habitats. Merlins are scarce visitors from northern Europe, hunting larks and pipits over the marshes. Black Kites, Montagu's Harriers and Hobbies, trans-saharan migrants, are absent in winter. Short-toed Eagles are also absent, though a few sometimes remain in the breeding areas all winter. Short-eared Owls occur in most coastal marshes in winter.

Tidal mud flats on the Atlantic side of the Strait. These habitats are used by migrating waders which winter along Atlantic Morocco, Mauretania and further south in West Africa.

All the breeding terns are summer visitors. There are no truly marsh-dwelling terns in winter, but Sandwich Terns are widespread and abundant in estuaries and beaches. Small numbers of Caspian Terns winter in some estuaries. Gulls are more numerous along the coastal stretches in winter, the main species being the Mediterranean Gull, Black-headed Gull, Lesser Black-backed Gull and Yellow-legged Gull. Flocks of these wander inland regularly.

The passerine community exhibits significant changes from summer to winter (Figure 259), and some species roam the marshes in big groups. Short-toed Larks are absent. Skylarks, which arrive from the north, and the resident Calandra and

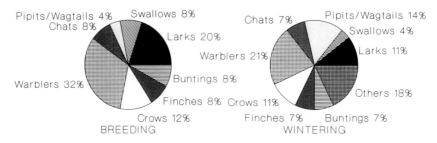

Figure 259. Composition of coastal marsh passerine communities. Breeding, 25 species; wintering, 28 species.

Lesser Short-toed Larks form large flocks that feed in the drier parts of the marshes. Meadow Pipits and White Wagtails are important winter visitors, dominating the marsh communities. Smaller numbers of Water Pipits are present in most marshes, being the main species in the wetter areas. Although most Yellow Wagtails leave for tropical Africa, there is a wintering population of this species in the Loukos marsh and at other points on the Moroccan Atlantic coast. Other passerines typical of coastal marshes in winter but absent during the breeding season are the Bluethroat, Chiffchaff and Penduline Tit.

INLAND WETLANDS

Inland wetlands are found mainly on the Spanish side of the Strait, where they take the form of permanent or semi-permanent lagoons. These are formed where shallow topographical gradients interrupt the drainage flow of surface waters and the underlying rock is impermeable. Some lagoons may have small, often temporary, additional inflows from streams that do not contribute sufficiently to maintain water levels. In some cases, there is additional underground filtration if the surrounding rocks are calcareous.

There is a number of artificial reservoirs on both shores, which, in view of their greatly fluctuating water levels, do not permit the establishment of rich water-bird communities. Their construction has had little positive effect on waterbird communities. The 12 main Cádiz lagoons (Figure 260) and the lagoons in the Guadalquivir marshes, on the other hand, support large numbers of wintering waterfowl and are a refuge to some very rare breeding species. Their importance is accentuated by their proximity to the Guadalquivir marshes, acting as reservoirs of these species, especially in summer, when the marshes become dry (Amat, 1984). There are, additionally, several smaller lagoons with communities that include rare species.

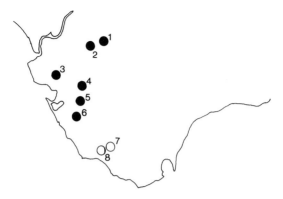

Figure 260.   Distribution of the main Cadiz lagoons. 1, Espera complex; 2, Tollos; 3, Puerto de Santa Maria complex; 4, Medina; 5, Puerto Real complex; 6, Chiclana complex; 7, La Janda (drained); 8, Torero (drained).

   The Cádiz lagoons exhibit the general characteristics of shallow lakes (Burgis & Morris, 1987), which are usually more productive per unit area than deeper lakes. Being shallow, there is little thermal stratification of the waters, and organic matter formed is rapidly recycled. A high proportion of the water is exposed to light conditions which, together with the higher average temperatures of such shallow waters, accelerates the rate of decomposition and production.

   The vegetation of the shallow lagoons varies according to both the profile of the lagoon and its water chemistry (particularly its conductivity). At steeper-sided lagoons, most of the emergent vegetation is concentrated on a narrow band along the shore. Shallower lagoons can be completely covered in aquatic vegetation, with no open water. The typical plant species are reeds, rushes and other plants normally associated with freshwater (*Phragmites*, *Typha*, *Scirpus*, *Juncus*, *Schoenoplectus* and *Tamarix*) and underwater plants, which are especially important as food for waterfowl (e.g. *Chara*, *Zannichellia*, *Ruppia*, *Myriophyllum*, *Potamogeton*). Most lagoons are surrounded by arable land, usually with a belt of scrub (*Chamaerops*, *Olea*, *Pistacia*) separating the fields from the lagoon vegetation.

   Seasonality is very pronounced (Amat & Ferrer, 1988), especially in lagoons that have a very poor supply, or no supply, of water other than through direct rainfall. Such lagoons can dry up completely during the summer, especially after a dry winter. When this happens, waterbirds may abandon the lagoons altogether, moving to reservoirs (Amat & Ferrer, 1988) or further south, and waders may then become more important numerically. In the reverse case, after wet winters, levels may remain high throughout the summer, and a different community of birds is present (Figure 261; Amat, 1984; Amat & Ferrer, 1988). The positive correlation between duck species and numbers and water levels and the negative correlation between wader species and numbers and water levels are general characteristics of Andalucían lagoons (Amat, 1984).

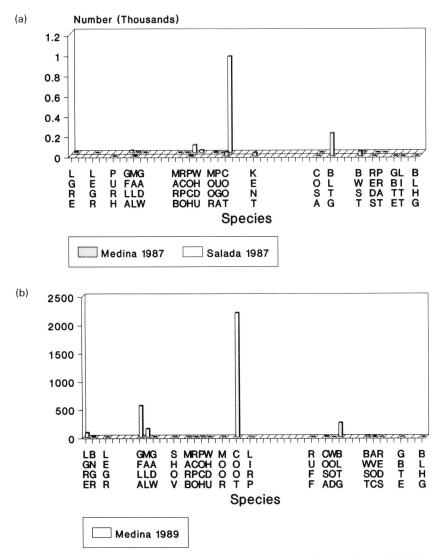

Figure 261. Distribution of waterbirds and waders at Laguna de Medina and Laguna Salada in summer, (a), high water levels, (b), Laguna Salada dry.

Associated with the arrival of birds from the north, there is a considerable increase in species and numbers during the winter (Amat, 1984). The lagoons are then important refuges for ducks. The precise composition of the wintering community depends very much on water levels, with diving ducks being more important in years with high water levels and surface-feeding ducks in years when levels are reduced (Amat & Ferrer, 1988).

BREEDING BIRDS

The composition of the bird communities of the shallow lagoons during the breeding season varies substantially between years and between lagoons, depending on water levels (Figure 262). In years when waters are low, few ducks or grebes breed in the lagoons. In extreme years, when the lagoons dry up completely, there is no duck or grebe breeding at all, but waders (e.g. Black-winged Stilt, Kentish Plover) utilize the extended muddy banks of the lagoon to nest. When water levels rise, there is a richer waterfowl community.

The main non-passerine groups contributing species to inland lagoon communities during the breeding season are wildfowl and raptors. The Mallard is the most widespread and abundant species, contributing up to 50% of all waterfowl in some years at the Laguna de Medina (Figure 262). The other regular duck

(a)

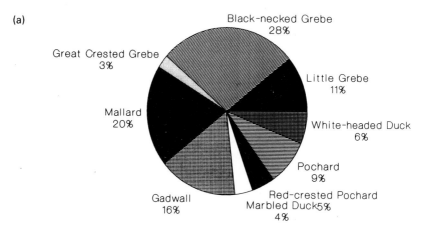

(b)

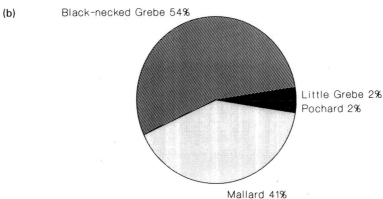

Figure 262.   Duck and grebe numbers at Laguna de Medina during the breeding season, (a) 1986 (count includes all birds seen). N = 3137. (b) 1988 (count includes all birds seen). N = 812. (Continued opposite.)

(c)

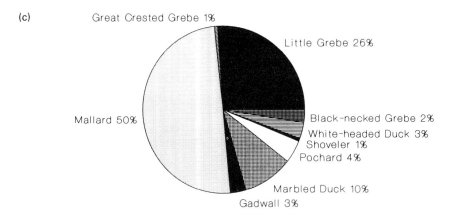

(d)

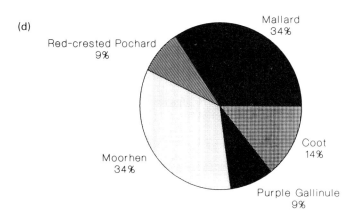

(e)

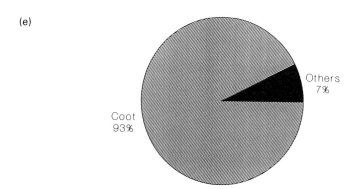

Figure 262 continued. Duck and grebe numbers at Laguna de Medina during the breeding season, (c) 1989 (count includes all birds seen). N = 1034. *(d) Duck and grebe numbers at Laguna de la Pachecas during the breeding season, 1988.* N = 35. *(e) Duck and grebe numbers at Laguna Salada del Puerto during the breeding season, 1988.* N = 686. *(Continued on p. 418.)*

(f)

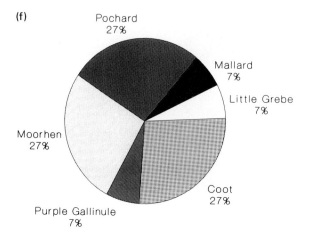

(g)

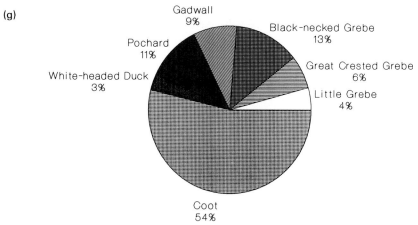

(h)

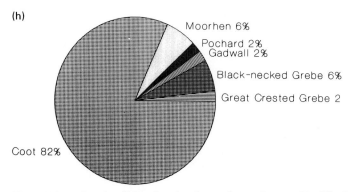

Figure 262 continued.   (f) Duck and grebe numbers at Laguna Hondilla during the breeding season, 1988. N = 16. (g) Duck and grebe numbers at Laguna Salada (Espera) during the breeding season, 1988. N = 93. (h) Duck and grebe numbers at Laguna Dulce during the breeding season, 1988. N = 98.

species are Gadwall, Red-crested Pochard and Pochard. The Shoveler, essentially a winter visitor, nests occasionally when water levels are suitable (Figure 262) but remains a scarce and sporadic breeding species, as it is in the Guadalquivir (Amat, 1981, 1982). During the 1980s the population of White-headed Ducks has increased dramatically in southern Spain as a result of stringent conservation measures. The Cádiz lagoons have provided suitable nesting habitat for the expanding population from the nearby Córdoba lagoons, and the species nests regularly. The Marbled Duck, which is another threatened species, is sporadic in occurrence in the Cádiz lagoons.It is essentially a passage bird (Amat, 1984), which probably does not breed (see Chapter 4). Its movements between its nucleus in the Guadalquivir, the inland lagoons and the wetlands on the Moroccan side of the Strait appear erratic and may be related to fluctuating water levels. Its incidence in the Cádiz lagoons during the breeding season is highly erratic, with a consequent variability in its contribution to the composition of the lagoon duck community (Figure 262).

Other waterbirds also contribute substantially to breeding communities of lagoons. Grebes dominate numerically in some lagoons, especially when water levels are high (Figure 262). On the Spanish side, the Little Grebe is the most widespread, although the Black-necked Grebe is a more numerous species in some lagoons. This situation contrasts with the Moroccan side of the Strait where the Black-necked Grebe does not breed (Pineau & Giraud-Audine 1979). The Great Crested Grebe is the scarcest of the three grebes but occurs regularly in most lagoons (Figure 262). The most numerous species in most lagoons, especially the deeper ones, is the Coot, which can contribute over 80% of all birds. One of the scarcest waterbirds of the area is the Crested Coot, which has a small population within the Marismas del Guadalquivir. Isolated pairs breed in the dense reedbeds in the Cádiz lagoons in most years, especially when water levels are high or when conditions are unsuitable in the Guadalquivir. The dense reedbeds surrounding the lagoons also provide nesting cover for species that feed within the reedbeds or on the edge of the open water. The most spectacular species is the Purple Gallinule, which breeds in most lagoons, especially those with dense aquatic vegetation. Moorhens and Little Bitterns are widespread. The Purple Heron only breeds in a few, well protected, sites. Baillon's Crake breeds in some lagoons, but its status is uncertain in view of its shy habits.

Although, by species, a large proportion of the breeding season community is taken up by raptors, all (with the exception of the Marsh Harrier) breed away from the lagoons and only visit lagoons or adjacent habitats to feed. The Marsh Harrier is now a scarce breeding species in the lagoons and only does so where dense, undisturbed, reedbeds surround the lagoon. Other raptor species that frequently hunt on or around lagoons during the breeding season are the Black Kite, Egyptian Vulture, Griffon Vulture, Short-toed Eagle, Montagu's Harrier, Buzzard, Booted Eagle and Kestrel, each species' presence depending on the proximity of suitable nesting sites.

Only three wader species regularly breed along the muddy shores of lagoons: Black-winged Stilt, Kentish Plover and Collared Pratincole. There is a small Lapwing colony in the Laguna del Comisario (J. Amat, pers. comm.). Waders

Table 32   Breeding species of lagoons in the region of the Strait.

Little Grebe	Red-crested Pochard	Crested Coot
Great Crested Grebe	Pochard	Black-winged Stilt
Black-necked Grebe	White-headed Duck	Collared Pratincole
Little Bittern	Marsh Harrier	Kentish Plover
Purple Heron	Baillon's Crake	Yellow Wagtail
Gadwall	Moorhen	Cetti's Warbler
Mallard	Purple Gallinule	Fan-tailed Warbler
Marbled Duck	Coot	Great Reed Warbler

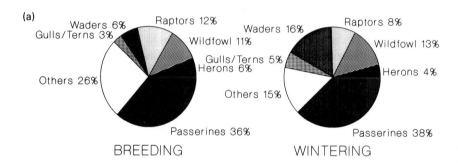

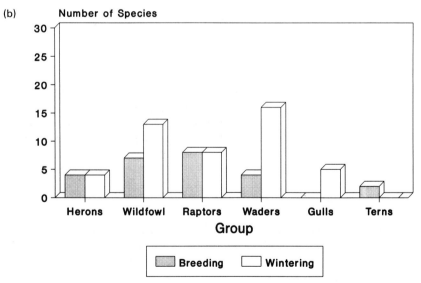

Figure 263.   (a) Composition of lagoon bird communities by species. (b) Number of species breeding and wintering in lagoons.

avoid lagoons with high water levels and no shoreline. Gulls and terns do not breed regularly around lagoons, with the exception of the Whiskered Tern, which breeds sporadically. In general, therefore, freshwater lagoons are mainly utilized by species that can breed within the cover of the reedbeds and feed in the open water or within the reeds. These include species that are very rare and only occur in these habitats, in the Marismas del Guadalquivir and in the marsh of the Loukos. The communities are dominated by non-passerines, and the only passerine species typically associated with the lagoons (as opposed to the adjacent scrub and farmland habitats) are the Yellow Wagtail and Cetti's, Fan-tailed and Great Reed Warblers. Breeding species typical of lagoons are listed in Table 32.

Those lagoons which have scrub surrounding the reedbeds have additional breeding species (e.g. Sardinian Warbler, Melodious Warbler, Woodchat Shrike). Depending on the nature of the countryside surrounding the lagoon, other species may visit the lagoon to hunt. In typical farmland, such species include the White Stork, Montagu's Harrier, Barn Owl and swifts and hirundines.

Taking the Laguna de Medina, the largest of the Cádiz lagoons, as an example the changing composition of the community during the breeding season between years is clear (Figure 263). In the dry summer of 1987, when the lagoon dried completely, waterfowl did not breed in the lagoon at all. In contrast, more species were present in 1986, 1988 and 1989, when water levels were higher. Among the species present in these years were White-headed Duck, Marbled Duck and Crested Coot.

In wet and dry years the lagoons are utilized alternately, depending on water levels. The contrast in numbers of waterfowl at the Laguna de Medina and Laguna Salada in the 1987 spring (when Medina dried but Salada held a good water level) and 1989 (when Medina held some water but Salada dried completely) illustrates the use of alternative sites by lagoon waterbirds (Figure 261; Amat, 1984).

In late summer, after breeding, waterfowl congregate in the available bodies of fresh water. In particular, large numbers of waterfowl from the Marismas may congregate in the few lagoons that retain water, like those of Cádiz. In years when water levels are high in the Cádiz lagoons, there are large gatherings of waterfowl in August and September (Figure 264). In years when water levels are lower and there is a substantial shoreline, passage waders appear in large numbers (Figure 265).

WINTERING BIRDS

The Cádiz lagoons attract large numbers of ducks in winter. Wildfowl and waders then account for 29% of all the species (Figure 263). The use made of the Cádiz lagoons varies according to water levels and conditions further north, large influxes occurring when central European lakes freeze. The Spanish winter census of 1980 revealed a total of 8164 ducks, geese and coots in Cádiz lagoons (Ena & Purroy, 1982), which constituted 30% of all the birds censused in

(a)

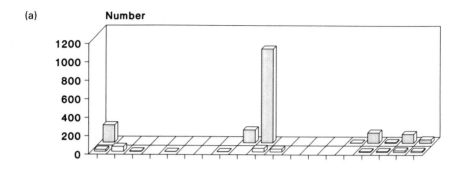

(b)

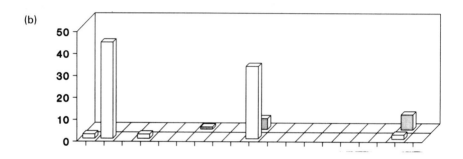

(c)

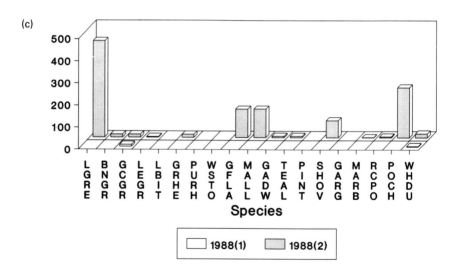

Figure 264.   Changes in waterfowl numbers at Laguna de Medina between June and September, (a) 1986, (b) 1987, (c) 1988, (d) 1989. □, June; ▨, September. (e) Changes in Coot numbers at Laguna de Medina between June and September.

(d)

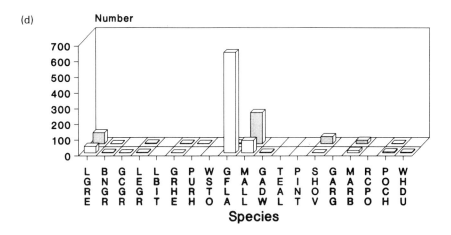

(e)

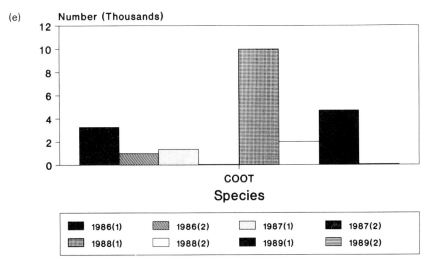

Figure 264. Continued.

Andalucía (excluding the Marismas del Guadalquivir). In years with high water levels diving ducks predominate (Figure 266). Over 300 White-headed Ducks have been counted in the Laguna de Medina in winter, constituting over 60% of the entire Spanish population. The exceptional winter of 1989–90, when water levels at Medina were the highest in recent years, produced a wintering community dominated by the Coot (66%), Shoveler, Red-crested Pochard and Pochard (Figure 266). The relative proportion of Shovelers was substantially lower than in drier years when the lagoon was better suited to this species (Figure 266). Thus, in 1986, 41% of the birds on the lagoon were Shovelers, whereas in 1989 the proportion was reduced to 10%.

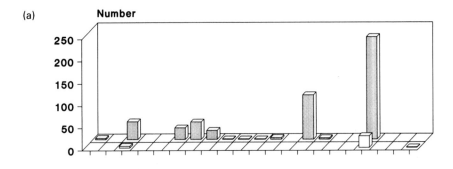

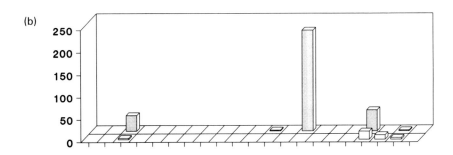

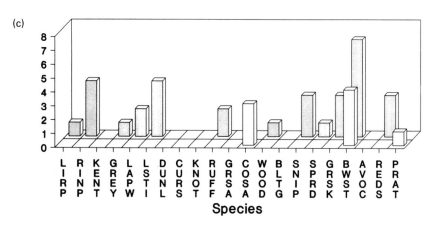

Species

Figure 265.   Changes in wader numbers at Laguna de Medina between June (□) and September (▨) (a) 1986, (b) 1987, (c) 1988, (d) 1989.

(d)

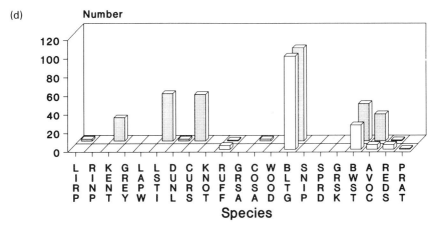

Figure 265. Continued.

When water levels are lower, overall duck numbers are reduced, due, in part, to the reduced area of water available. The community is then more diverse and is dominated by surface-feeding ducks. Immediately following the drought in which Medina dried up completely, the 1987–88 winter water levels were low, and the dominant species in the lagoon waterfowl community were the Mallard, Pochard, Shoveler, Coot, Teal, Gadwall and Pintail (Figure 266). The relative contribution of Coots (12%) was low in contrast with the high proportion in the 1989–90 winter.

The alternating use made of different lagoons by waterbirds within the Cádiz complex is similar to the situation during the breeding season. Figure 267 compares the wintering community at Medina and Salada in the dry 1987–88 winter, when the smaller Laguna Salada had higher water levels than Medina. The number of Pochard in the smaller Salada lagoon was similar to that in Medina, and there was a substantial concentration of White-headed Ducks, which contrasted with the low numbers at Medina. On the other hand, there was a greater range of species at Medina, including surface-feeding ducks, flamingoes and waders.

A striking contrast between breeding season and winter is the total absence of terns in winter and the use made of the lagoons by gulls. The main species are Black-headed, Yellow-legged and Lesser Black-backed Gulls, which appear to visit the lagoons from nearby Atlantic coastal areas. At certain times concentrations of Mediterranean Gulls (over 200 in Medina) and Little Gulls occur; this may be in response to bad weather along the coast.

Among the passerines wintering around the lagoons the most notable is the Penduline Tit, which occurs in flocks along most reed beds throughout the winter.

(a)

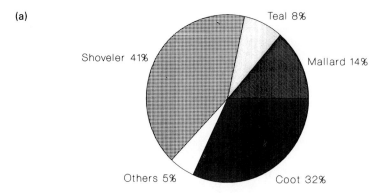

(b)

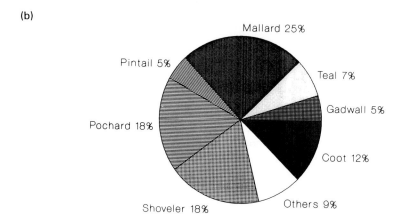

(c)

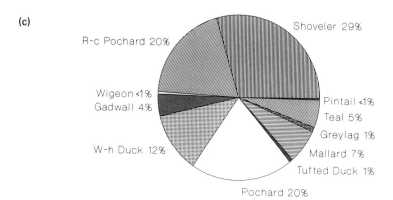

Figure 266. Distribution of ducks and geese at Laguna de Medina (a) December 1986, N = 2137 (b) December 1987, N = 712 (c) January 1990, N = 1034.

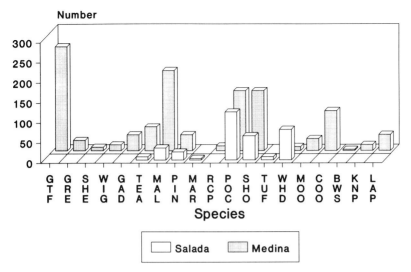

Figure 267. Distribution of ducks, geese, waders and other waterbirds at Laguna de Medina and Salada on 21 December, 1987. Coots were not counted at Laguna Salada.

Having regard to the wide fluctuations in numbers between years, the typical lagoon wintering community (including species from adjacent habitats) would have a number of the species listed in Table 33.

THE LAGUNAS DE LA JANDA AND DEL TORERO

The most tragic and ecologically disastrous loss that the Strait (and arguably the whole of the Iberian Peninsula) has ever sustained has been the drainage of the Laguna de la Janda and its offshoot the Laguna del Torero, north-east of the town of Vejer (Figure 268). These were drained during the 1950s, though some areas had been destroyed even in Verner's (1910) day. Today, the site of the lagoon is farmland, subjected to periodic flooding (sometimes extensive, as in the winter of 1989–90) in winter. The flood waters do not remain for long, as they are rapidly drained by large collecting canals. The canals do retain natural aquatic vegetation, however, and permit the establishment of some aquatic species during the breeding season, on passage or in winter. Reservoirs within the private estate of Las Lomas attract wildfowl, especially in winter. But in essence, although still attractive to some species, the site has been lost.

It is from the descriptions of Irby (1875, 1895), Verner (1890, 1910, 1911), de Quiros (1920) and Yeates (1945) that it is possible to reconstruct the bird community of these lagoons.

La Janda occupied a flat depression, south-west of the Sierras del Niño and Blanquilla (Figure 268), and collected water from the Barbate River (which fed

Table 33   Wintering species of lagoons in the region of the Strait.

Little Grebe	Purple Gallinule	House Martin
Great Crested Grebe	Coot	Meadow Pipit
Black-necked Grebe	Crested Coot	Grey Wagtail
Cattle Egret	Black-winged Stilt	White Wagtail
Little Egret	Avocet	Robin
Grey Heron	Little Ringed Plover	Bluethroat
Greater Flamingo	Ringed Plover	Black Redstart
Greylag Goose	Kentish Plover	Stonechat
Shelduck	Golden Plover	Blackbird
Wigeon	Lapwing	Song Thrush
Gadwall	Dunlin	Cetti's Warbler
Teal	Snipe	Fan-tailed Warbler
Mallard	Black-tailed Godwit	Dartford Warbler
Pintail	Redshank	Sardinian Warbler
Shoveler	Green Sandpiper	Blackcap
Marbled Duck	Common Sandpiper	Chiffchaff
Red-crested Pochard	Mediterranean Gull	Blue Tit
Pochard	Little Gull	Great Tit
Tufted Duck	Black-headed Gull	Penduline Tit
White-headed Duck	Lesser Black-backed Gull	Great Grey Shrike
Red Kite	Yellow-legged Gull	Jackdaw
Griffon Vulture	Barn Owl	Starling
Marsh Harrier	Little Owl	Spotless Starling
Hen Harrier	Short-eared Owl	House Sparrow
Sparrowhawk	Kingfisher	Tree Sparrow
Buzzard	Wryneck	Chaffinch
Kestrel	Calandra Lark	Serin
Peregrine	Crested Lark	Goldfinch
Red-legged Partridge	Skylark	Linnet
Water Rail	Crag Martin	Reed Bunting
Moorhen	Swallow	Corn Bunting

into it from the north) and a series of smaller streams from the sierras. Its main outlet, to the south-west, filled a deeper and smaller lagoon (Laguna del Torero), from which the Barbate continued meandering towards the sea, creating a marsh south of the town of Vejer. As it reached the sea and the tidal influence of the Atlantic, its lower reaches became saline.

La Janda was a large but shallow freshwater lagoon. Its limits extended from Vejer in the south-west to Casas Viejas (now Benalup) in the north-west to the area of Tapatanilla and Tahivilla in the south-east (Figure 268). The Laguna del Torero, part of the La Janda complex, was much smaller (1 km²) and probably similar in size to some of the larger Cádiz lagoons.

Figure 268.   The Laguna de La Janda in 1870 and 1990.

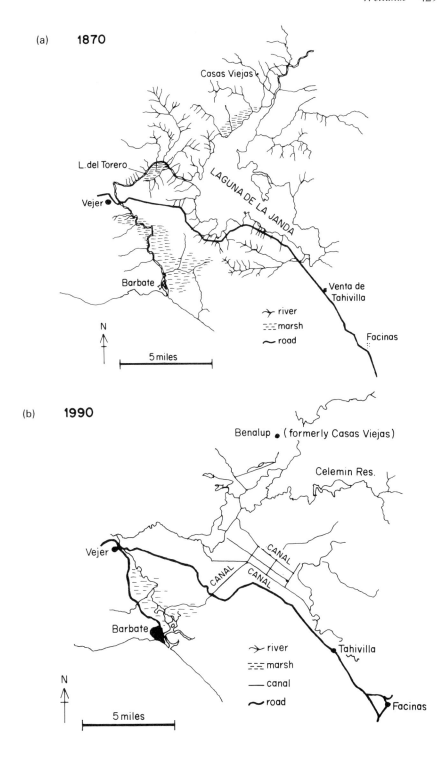

(a) **1870**

Casas Viejas

L. del Torero

Vejer

LAGUNA DE LA JANDA

Barbate

Venta de
Tahivilla

Facinas

N

river
marsh
road

5 miles

(b) **1990**

Benalup (formerly Casas Viejas)

Celemin Res.

Vejer

CANAL

CANAL

CANAL

Barbate

Tahivilla

river
marsh
canal
road

Facinas

N

5 miles

The fields which were once part of the basin of the Laguna de la Janda which was drained during the 1950s.

The Laguna de la Janda was flat-bottomed and the substrate mainly hard. Water levels varied between 80 cm and 1.10 m (depending on rainfall and time of year), so that it was not impossible to wade across large areas of it. In the north-central part of the lagoon the water depth reached 4–6 m in an area known as El Charco de los Ansares (pond of the geese). The subaquatic vegetation was poor but the surface vegetation was luxuriant. In places the vegetation was almost impenetrable, being dominated by club rushes (*Scirpus*) and bulrushes (*Typha*), with reeds (*Phragmites*) in patches. The water was also deeper along channels leading from stream exits into the main lagoon. In the deeper water there were great tracts of bulrushes. Areas of open water were covered in spring by flowering white *Ranunculus*. The northwestern end of La Janda, near Casas Viejas, was less densely reeded. A vast steppe-like grassland (known as *vega*) surrounded the lagoon to the edge of the sierras, where scrubland and cork oak woodland habitats took over.

The adjacent Laguna del Torero had deep waters. In the centre there was a stand of tall rushes that grew to 2 m above the surface. The edge of the lagoon was covered in bulrushes, clubrushes and reeds. Near the shore, at a depth of *c*. 0.7 m, the open water was covered with *Ranunculus*, though at a lesser density than in La Janda.

The lagoons held a highly diverse breeding community of birds and were strongholds for rare species, including some that are now extinct in the area. In winter, La Janda received large influxes of wildfowl and waders in particular, some in very large numbers. These communities contained, at the very least, the

Table 34 Species known to have been present in the Lagunas de la Janda and del Torero before they were drained.

Species	La Janda	Torero
Breeding species		
Great Crested Grebe	++	++
Black-necked Grebe	++	++
Little Grebe	+++	++
Bittern	++	−
Little Bittern	+++	++
Purple Heron	+++	++
Grey Heron	+	−
Cattle Egret	++	+++
White Stork	++	+
Spoonbill	−	++
Glossy Ibis	−	+
Mallard	+++	++
Ferruginous Duck	+	++
White-headed Duck	−	+
Marsh Harrier	+++	++
Stone Curlew	++	−
Collared Pratincole	+++	−
Black-winged Stilt	+++	+
Little Ringed Plover	++	−
Crane	++	−
Crested Coot	+	++
Coot	+++	+
Purple Gallinule	+++	++
Moorhen	++	++
Spotted Crake	+++	++
Baillon's Crake	++	+
Water Rail	++	+
Whiskered Tern	+++	−
Yellow Wagtail	+++	−
Savi's Warbler	++	−
Cetti's Warbler	+++	++
Reed Warbler	++	−
Great Reed Warbler	+++	++
Wintering species		
Little Egret	++	+
Greylag Goose	+++	+
Gadwall	+	++
Shoveler	+++	++
Pintail	+++	++
Teal	+++	++
Wigeon	+++	+
Pochard	+	++

Continued on p. 432.

Table 34   Continued.

Species	La Janda	Torero
Wintering species		
Tufted Duck	+	++
Buzzard	++	++
Hen Harrier	++	++
Merlin	++	−
Golden Plover	+++	−
Lapwing	+++	−
Woodcock	++	−
Snipe	+++	+
Jack Snipe	++	−
Curlew	++	−
Green Sandpiper	+++	+
Black-tailed Godwit	+++	+
Little Gull	+	+
Black-headed Gull	+++	++
Kittiwake	+	−
Reed Bunting	++	+

Key: +++, abundant; ++, present; +, scarce.

species listed in Table 34. This reconstruction is an approximation based on descriptions by several authors. In addition, Black Vulture, Imperial Eagle and Raven bred on or around the lagoons (Irby, 1895; Verner, 1910). Aquatic Warblers and Lesser Short-toed Larks have been cited as breeding and the African Marsh Owl, which was collected at La Janda on several occasions in autumn, was probably resident there. The White-fronted Goose, Bean Goose, Pink-footed Goose and Great Snipe were recorded in winter but were rare. Irby (1895) cited a Great White Egret on 18 May 1875. On passage, the range of wader species was probably higher and must have included all the typical migrants.

The surrounding steppe and low scrub countryside held typical species, which included (as they do to-day) Montagu's Harrier, Great Bustard, Little Bustard, Quail, Stone Curlew, larks and Corn Buntings. The Andalucian Hemipode bred in the fan palm scrub at the northern end of La Janda (Irby, 1895). The cork oak woods and open glades held a rich community of passerines, and birds of prey from the surrounding sierras and woods hunted over the marsh (Bonelli's Eagle, Booted Eagle, Short-toed Eagle, Eagle Owl, Barn Owl).

The value of La Janda was in its unique breeding species (e.g. Crane, Bittern and Glossy Ibis) and a substantial breeding population of other species (e.g. Whiskered Tern, Purple Heron, Purple Gallinule, Crested Coot, Ferruginous Duck), its large wintering populations (e.g. Greylag Goose, Wigeon, Snipe) and its probable importance as a stop-over point for migrants crossing the Strait of Gibraltar.

ORNITHOLOGICAL IMPORTANCE

The wetlands covered in this chapter can be classified according to their importance (Table 35). The two wetlands in Table 35, at either extreme of the area covered by this book, are included because of their importance and proximity and because they form part of a natural sequence of wetlands along the Atlantic coasts of southern Europe and North Africa. These are the Merja Zerga in the south and the Odiel Estuary in the north-west.

In general terms, the Spanish and Moroccan sides of the Strait hold important populations of wildfowl although, bearing in mind that the estimated wintering

Table 35   Importance of wetlands of southern Spain and northern Morocco.[1]

Site	Rank		Rare species[2]
	Waders	Wildfowl	
Marismas del Guadalquivir	A	A	+
Merja Zerga	A	A	
Bahia de Cádiz	A	A	
La Janda	A	C	
Oued Loukos	C	D	+
Marismas del Odiel	C	D	
Oualad Khallouf	C	D	
Laguna de Medina	F	C	+
Lagunas de Espera	F	C	+
Oued Smir	E	C	
Oued Martil	C	E	
Lagunas Pto Sta Maria	F	D	+
Lagunas Pto Real	F	D	+
Lagunas Chiclana	F	D	+
Oued Tahadart	D	D	
Sidi Kacem	D	D	
Barbate Estuary	D	F	
Pantano de Bornos	F	D	
Tangier Bay	E	E	
Los Lances	E	F	
Palmones Estuary	E	F	
Asilah	E	F	
Guadiaro Estuary	F	F	

[1]Categories of wintering numbers: A = 10 000 birds, B = 5000–10 000, C = 1000–5000, D = 500–1000, E = 100–500, F = <100.
[2]Rare species refers to presence of breeding birds.

wildfowl population of the western Palaearctic is 25 million (Scott, 1982), the total numbers are relatively low. The Spanish wintering population, estimated at over 600 000, is about 2.5% of the western Palaearctic wintering population (Dolz & Gomez, 1988) and, of these, about 40% are found along the Andalusian Atlantic coast and associated wetlands. In some cases — White-headed Duck, Greylag Goose, Shelduck, Wigeon, Teal, Common Scoter, Pintail, and Shoveler — the bulk of the Iberian population winters in this area (Dolz & Gomez, 1988). The Guadalquivir marshes support around 93% of the wintering wildfowl population of Spain. The wintering wildfowl population of Morocco is lower, probably under 100 000, of which around 70% are concentrated along the northwest coast close to the Strait (Thevenot *et al.*, 1981, 1982; Beaubrun & Thevenot, 1983). The Merja Zerga is used by around 93% of the wildfowl population wintering in Moroccan wetlands.

Spain is of relatively low importance for wintering waders, with about 240 000 individuals, 3% of the European wintering population (Alberto & Velasco, 1988). It has nevertheless importance for a number of species, in particular the Black-winged Stilt, Avocet, Kentish Plover and Black-tailed Godwit. The most important concentrations of these occur in Cádiz Bay and the Guadalquivir marshes. Cádiz Bay has important populations of the Black-winged Stilt, Avocet, Ringed Plover, Kentish Plover, Grey Plover, Sanderling, Dunlin, Black-tailed Godwit, Whimbrel, Curlew and Redshank, and the Guadalquivir has concentrations of Oystercatcher, Black-winged Stilt, Avocet, Grey Plover, Sanderling, Ruff and Black-tailed Godwit. On a smaller scale, the Odiel is important for Avocet, Bar-tailed Godwit, Curlew and Redshank (Rubio García, 1986; Alberto & Velasco, 1988). Andalucía accounts for around 25–30% of all Spanish wintering waders, and the majority are concentrated in these three sites. The Moroccan wintering wader population is estimated at around 100 000 (Kersten & Smit, 1984), with 45–50% of these in the north-west. The Merja Zerga accounts for around 95% of these (Kersten & Smit, 1984). Thus, although relatively low in relation to areas to the north and south, the wintering population of waders within the Strait is nevertheless around 100 000, and certainly not insignificant.

The wetlands of both sides of the Strait are important also for passage waterbirds and waders, and may hold larger populations during passage periods than in winter (Kersten & Smit, 1984). Their greatest significance lies in the breeding populations of rare species (Amat *et al.*, 1985). The most important wetlands on both shores of the Strait have been classified by numbers of wintering wildfowl and waders, and by the presence of rare breeding species (Table 35). One site, in particular, stands out by having very large wintering populations of wildfowl and waders and rare breeding species, the Marismas del Guadalquivir. Two others have large wintering populations of wildfowl and waterbirds, but not breeding populations, of rare species: Merja Zerga and Cádiz Bay. The site of the former Laguna de La Janda, which floods in winter, holds large numbers of waders, mainly Lapwings and Golden Plovers, and smaller numbers of wildfowl.

The Odiel Estuary, the Loukos Estuary, the Khalouf marshes and the Martil Estuary are important wintering sites for waders. The first three also hold wintering populations of ducks. The freshwater marsh of the Loukos is of particular importance as a breeding site of rare species (Pineau & Giraud-Audine, 1979). The Cádiz lagoons feature as important for wintering wildfowl, especially Medina and the Espera complex, although they hold very small numbers of waders. They are all important breeding sites for rare species.

The remaining listed sites are considered to be important and can hold substantial numbers of some species. The Bornos Reservoir is the only reservoir listed because most others are not of ornithological importance.

Finally, a note of caution. Estimates of wintering numbers, in particular, must be treated with caution and regarded as giving only an approximate average or order of magnitude. Wildfowl and wader populations are subject to wide fluctuations depending on meteorological conditions, and the size of a wintering population in an area can change considerably from one year to the next and even within the same winter. For example, the large wader counts for Morocco during the 1963–64 winter (Blondel & Blondel, 1964) may have been caused by the severe winter in Europe (Pienkowski, 1975). Another example is the effect of varying water levels on the wildfowl in lagoons (discussed earlier). Furthermore, fluctuating water levels can also determine the degree of movement of waterbirds across the Strait of Gibraltar (see Chapter 4).

CHAPTER 8

The Birds of the Strait—Seasonality, Distribution and Biological Importance

In this book I have been concerned with describing a unique area of the world, where the continents of Africa and Europe meet. The book has described the main groups of birds that migrate through the area, as well as its breeding and wintering communities. Its general thesis is one related to the continuous movement of birds in search of resources, to the role of the Strait within a subsystem of the Palaearctic–African system (the western Palaearctic–west African), and, within this, to the unique relationship between the Iberian and Moroccan Mediterranean bioclimatic zones and the northern tropics of West Africa.

This book therefore examines a broad belt covering the northwestern corner of Morocco and the southwestern area of the Iberian Peninsula. The two areas, though separated by the sea, are fairly homogeneous and similar. To the south lie the Atlas mountains and the Sahara Desert. To the north lie the Sierra Morena, the plateau and mountains of central Spain. To the north, bioclimatic zones intergrade more or less continuously, with relatively uniform species replacements. To the south, such a uniform grading is prevented by the presence of the Sahara Desert, which must be regarded as the most formidable natural barrier between western Europe and western Africa.

It is the geographical position of the Strait that has given it its overall ecological richness. The glaciations that ended 10 000 years ago effectively split the Iberian Peninsula and the Balkans into two refuges for Palaearctic migrants. Since that time, the Strait has been central to the movements of birds from the western Palaearctic to western Africa.

West Africa must have been the main winter refuge for Iberian birds at the height of the glaciation. As the ice caps receded, these populations spread northwards to occupy western and northern Europe, while those from the Balkans spread into eastern Europe and western Asia. The period of isolation had, however, been long enough to have permitted speciation in some cases (e.g. Nightingale/Thrush Nightingale).

As species spread north, the Iberian Peninsula itself became an important winter refuge for some migrants, while others continued further into West Africa. The degree of overlap of these populations as they spread northwards must have varied (Figure 269). Some species may have encountered others with sufficiently similar ecological requirements to prevent northwards spread (e.g. Pied Flycatcher/Collared Flycatcher). Some may have met conspecifics and not mixed to any large degree, each population having the competitive edge over the other in its respective area, with a narrow zone of hybridization (e.g. White Stork, Blackcap). Some may have found no competitors, and spread widely (e.g. Honey Buzzard). Others may, equally, have found no competitors, but may have been limited by climate or resources (e.g. Dartford Warbler).

The sources of the migrants that cross the Strait are therefore varied, some species reaching the area from specific regions within the western Palaearctic, others from a wider area. The wintering areas of these migrants are less variable, being as a rule West Africa, Morocco or the Iberian Peninsula. No migrants cross the Strait to winter in East Africa. Even in species which predominantly winter in East Africa (e.g. Roller, Cuckoo), the populations that do cross the Strait winter in isolated nuclei in West Africa.

The observable migratory patterns and strategies continue to evolve, and the Mediterranean areas of Iberia and northwest Africa, with climatic (and therefore resource) patterns quite distinct from more northerly European latitudes, promote a divergence of migratory tactics. The constraint on the separate evolution of the Iberian and northwest African populations is interchange of genetic material with sympatric populations to the north. It is perhaps not surprising that the populations which exhibit the greatest changes are those with no populations in the north. The basic change is related to the three Mediterranean seasons—drought, autumn/winter rains, spring productive season—which contrast with the typical north-temperate seasons of spring, summer, autumn and winter.

The movements of birds, whether local or long-distance, regular or irregular, are related to the exploitation of resources which are, to a greater or lesser degree, patchily distributed in space and/or time. There are two resource peaks in Mediterranean Iberia and northwest Morocco, and a single resource low. The first peak is variable in its commencement and comes with the first post-drought rains. The second peak, which intergrades with the first, comes in the spring and is characterized by a productive season related to increasing daylength and temperatures. There is usually a decrease in precipitation from April onwards, which, together with the constantly rising temperatures, means that the productive breeding season is a short one, ending predictably with the start of the drought in July. The resource peaks are characterized by invasions of bird

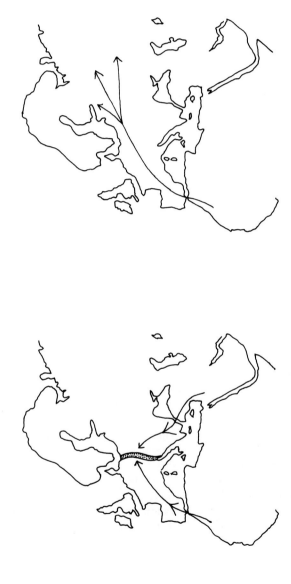

Figure 269. Possible spread of breeding birds to north temperate areas after the last glaciation. Left: Iberian and Balkan species meet in narrow zone of overlap. Right: Iberian species spreads northeastwards throughout Europe, reaching Asia.

populations from the north and south, and the resource low by an avoidance of the region.

Resource Peak 1: this is characterized by a variable start, usually in October, and intergrades with resource peak 2. The boundaries between the two are difficult to define. This period coincides with the harsh climatic conditions of the north and south: much of continental Europe is subjected to cold weather, heavy rains and short days; West Africa commences a drought in September. Movements of birds take place from both directions towards southwest Iberia and northwest Africa. Additional large influxes can occur during severe cold spells in northern Europe.

Resource Peak 2: with increasing daylength, birds that have moved in from the south during resource peak 1 are able to breed. They are joined by others (especially insectivores) that can exploit emerging resources which are related to increasing daylength (photoperiod) and temperatures (e.g. Mooney *et al.*, 1974; Herrera, 1978a). At the same time, conditions to the north are improving, and populations which invaded from the north leave the area. It is a period of intensive migratory activity in the Strait.

Resource Low: with the predictable arrival of the drought, most breeding birds move away, many to south of the Sahara. The movement coincides with the rains in the northern tropics. Aquatic birds (e.g. White Storks) also move south, while others congregate in the reduced bodies of water (e.g. Coots in lagoons) or disperse northwards or eastwards to other zones, usually but not always prior to migration (e.g. egrets). Many migrants from the north avoid the area at this time.

A deviation from this pattern occurs in those populations that breed within the area at high altitude. These behave as north temperate populations would, exploiting a summer resource peak and abandoning the sites in autumn, either as migrants (e.g. Rock Thrush, Wheatear, Subalpine Warbler) or to lower elevations (e.g. Alpine Accentor, Blue Rock Thrush, Black Redstart).

Seabirds also behave differently, since the resource peaks are significantly different (see Chapter 5). The main periods of plankton productivity in the Mediterranean are the autumn and the late winter and spring, when there is substantial mixing of waters in the Mediterranean. Towards late spring a thermal stratification of the sea takes place which effectively makes the Mediterranean Sea a desert in the summer. The movements of seabirds in the Strait are related to these resource fluctuations. Mediterranean-breeding seabirds enter the sea via the Strait in the autumn and winter in order to breed during the period of maximum plankton availability (e.g. Balearic Shearwater, Cory's Shearwater, Audouin's Gull). These species abandon the Mediterranean in summer and autumn and move to richer feeding grounds, off West Africa, northwest Africa or the Bay of Biscay. In the case of the Cory's Shearwater, which has a long breeding season ending in October, much of the feeding activity of adults is concentrated increasingly in the Strait from July onwards. As sea areas around the breeding colonies become more sterile, so the rich waters of the Strait (maintained by regular mixing of inflowing Atlantic water with outflowing colder Mediterranean water) gain in importance.

The autumn renewal of resources within the western Mediterranean also enables Atlantic species to enter via the Strait to exploit these. There is then a period (roughly from late September to mid-April) when Gannets, Razorbills, Puffins, Great Skuas, Sandwich Terns and other species utilize the area as an extension of nearby Atlantic waters. Other populations (from the Black Sea breeding grounds or even from Siberia) approach the Strait from the east and remain there during the same period (e.g. Mediterranean Gull, Little Gull, Sandwich Tern).

The evolution of these seabird movements must be quite separate from those of the land birds. The Mediterranean Sea was land-locked until 5 million years ago. Then the glacial periods must have meant that north Atlantic seabirds must have bred further south than they do today. The regular presence in Gibraltar's fossil record of species that are today extremely rare in winter (e.g. Long-tailed Duck, Velvet Scoter) confirms this. The migration patterns must have been different then, and more difficult to interpret than those of the land birds without an accurate knowledge of movements of water masses. With the climatic amelioration, north Atlantic species would have progressively returned northwards and the present pattern would have evolved.

A juvenile Peregrine Falcon. Species such as this still survive despite intense persecution from farmers and poachers. Increased awareness of nature has improved protection in recent years.

DISTRIBUTION AND ABUNDANCE PATTERNS

BREEDING SEASON

Examining the biogeographical distribution of breeding species within Iberia and Morocco, the Strait appears as the zone of highest species richness. This richness decreases away from the Strait, gradually in Iberia towards a low in the Euro-Siberian zone, and more sharply in Morocco towards the desert region. Richness is also substantially lower on islands (Figure 270). Within the Strait, the European shore supports a greater number of breeding species than the Moroccan shore but the number of species common to both is very high (Figure 271). The Strait does not appear to act as a barrier to the colonization of either shore by breeding species, and the few cases of presence of a species on one side of the Strait and not the other can, in most cases, be attributed to the presence of potential competitors or unsuitable ecological conditions on one shore but not the other (Table 36). Only in very few cases can the cross-Strait distribution pattern be attributed to the action of the Strait as a barrier to dispersal (e.g. Lesser Spotted Woodpecker, Long-tailed Tit, Common Bulbul, Moussier's Redstart and Black-headed Bush Shrike).

Comparing the breeding species of Iberia and Morocco, it is apparent that there is a greater range of species that are not shared than are shared, but in the majority of cases these differences can be related to changing bioclimatic regions (e.g. Telleria, 1987). At the family level, only six are not shared of which three are not represented at all in the Strait fauna (Timaliidae, Tichodromadidae and Remizidae).

The Iberian and Moroccan breeding bird faunas therefore have a high degree of affinity, and the Moroccan land mass largely holds an extension of the West Palaearctic avifauna (Table 36). The seven European families which are absent from Iberia are also absent from Morocco, and of the other six European families which are absent from Morocco but not Iberia, only Aegithalidae occurs on the European side of the Strait. The Sahara Desert, in contrast, presents itself as a greater barrier to the dispersal of species between tropical West Africa and the western Palaearctic, with 25 West African families missing from Morocco and Iberia. The recent interchange of species between Europe and Africa has been very low (Snow, 1978).

At a regional, within-Strait, level the distribution of species is related to the distribution of habitats usually occupied. Many species are widely distributed throughout the area, and those most widely dispersed are species with broad habitat requirements (e.g. Sardinian Warbler and Goldfinch). Others, with more specific habitat requirements, show more localized distribution patterns which may be closely related to specific ecological factors (e.g. Coal Tit in fir wood-land), climatic tolerances (e.g. Skylark and Wheatear in mountain peaks), range restriction as a result of direct competition from con-genetics (probably the case in middle altitudes in certain species pairs, e.g. Blue Rock Thrush/Rock Thrush) or diffuse competition from a community of competitors each having a small

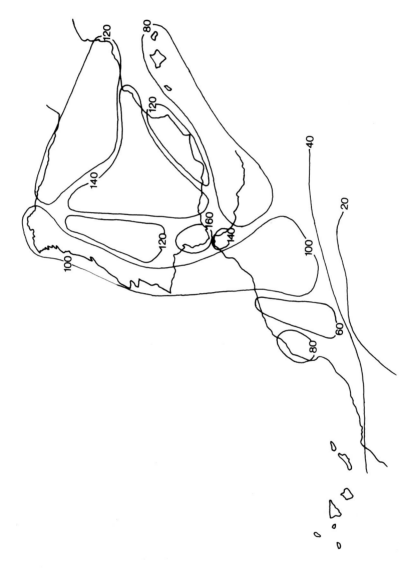

Figure 270.   Approximate distribution of breeding bird species in the Iberian Peninsula and Morocco.

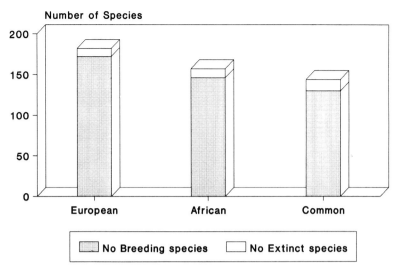

Figure 271. Breeding species on the European and African shores of the Strait.

effect (possibly Redstart). As discussed earlier, the Strait itself may limit the distribution of some species.

Within habitats, dispersion patterns often reflect habitat heterogeneity, the more specialized species being localized to areas where their specific requirements are met. Ideal distributions may be modified as a result of competition (well illustrated in *Sylvia* warblers; see later in this chapter). Within the same patch of habitat, two or more species may show temporal variation in distribution (e.g. Blackcap and Sardinian Warbler at Gibraltar; Finlayson, 1979).

Some patterns of distribution are of recent origin. The best example is the natural colonisation of the Strait by the Red-rumped Swallow during the 20th Century followed (quickly in evolutionary terms) by the White-rumped Swift, which lays its eggs and raises its young in the nests built by the Red-rumped Swallows. Most cases of changing distributions are the result of human activity. This is most dramatic in the reduction in range of many breeding raptors, as a direct result of persecution, habitat destruction and pollution, which has led to the extinction of species from the entire Strait (e.g. Bearded Vulture) or from one side of the Strait (e.g. Spanish Imperial Eagle from Morocco), or reduced the breeding population, and therefore the range, significantly (e.g. Egyptian Vulture). This disruption of the natural distribution and numbers of species has been most evident in wetland species which have been wiped out (e.g. Ruddy Shelduck, Ferruginous Duck and Crane) or reduced sufficiently to bring them to the verge of complete or local extinction (e.g. Crested Coot and White-headed Duck, respectively).

In some cases of change due to human activity, the populations may have been reduced to levels at which they are unable to cope with natural fluctuations (e.g.

Table 36   Breeding species found on the European and Moroccan shores of the Strait of Gibraltar.

Species	Europe	Morocco	Species	Europe	Morocco
Little Grebe	+	+	Golden Eagle	+	+
Great Crested Grebe	+	+	Booted Eagle	+	+
Black-necked Grebe	+	−	Bonelli's Eagle	+	+
Shag	+	E	Osprey	E	E
Bittern	E	E	Lesser Kestrel	+	+
Little Bittern	+	+	Kestrel	+	+
Night Heron	+	+	Hobby	+	+
Squacco Heron	+	+	Lanner	−	+
Cattle Egret	+	+	Peregrine	+	+
Little Egret	+	+	Reg-legged	+	−
Grey Heron	+	−	Partridge		
Purple Heron	+	+	Barbary Partridge	+1	+
White Stork	+	+	Pheasant	+	−
Glossy Ibis	E	E	Quail	+	+
Spoonbill	+	−	Andalucian	E	+
Greater Flamingo	+	−	Hemipode		
Ruddy Shelduck	E	E	Water Rail	+	+
Gadwall	+	−	Baillon's Crake	+	+
Teal	(+)	−	Moorhen	+	+
Mallard	+	+	Purple Gallinule	+	+
Pintail	+	−	Coot	+	+
Garganey	(+)	−	Crested Coot	+	+
Shoveler	(+)	−	Crane	E	−
Marbled Duck	+	+	Little Bustard	+	+
Red-crested Pochard	+	+	Great Bustard	+	+
Pochard	+	−	Black-winged Stilt	+	+
Ferruginous Duck	E	+	Avocet	+	−
White-headed Duck	+	E	Stone Curlew	+	+
Black-shouldered	−	+	Collared Pratincole	+	+
Kite			Little Ringed Plover	+	+
Black Kite	+	+	Kentish Plover	+	+
Red Kite	+	+	Lapwing	+	+
Bearded Vulture	E	E	Redshank	+	−
Egyptian Vulture	+	+	Slender-billed Gull	+	−
Griffon Vulture	+	E	Yellow-legged Gull	+	+
Black Vulture	E	E	Gull-billed Tern	+	(+)
Short-toed Eagle	+	+	Common Tern	+	−
Marsh Harrier	+	+	Little Tern	+	+
Montagu's Harrier	+	+	Whiskered Tern	+	E
Goshawk	+	+	Black Tern	+	−
Sparrowhawk	+	+	Pin-tailed	+	−
Buzzard	+	−	Sandgrouse		
Long-legged			Rock Dove	+	+
Buzzard	−	+	Woodpigeon	+	+
Imperial Eagle	+	E	Turtle Dove	+	+

Continued.

Table 36 Continued.

Species	Europe	Morocco	Species	Europe	Morocco
Great Spotted Cuckoo	+	−	Dipper	+	+
			Wren	+	+
Cuckoo	+	+	Rufous Bush Chat	+	+
Barn Owl	+	+	Robin	+	+
Scops Owl	+	+	Nightingale	+	+
Eagle Owl	+	(+)	Black Redstart	+	+
Little Owl	+	+	Redstart	+	−
Tawny Owl	+	+	Moussier's Redstart	−	+
Long-eared Owl	+	+	Stonechat	+	+
Marsh Owl	E	+	Wheatear	+	−
Nightjar	+	+	Black-eared Wheatear	+	+
Red-necked Nightjar	+	+	Black Wheatear	+	+
Swift	+	+	Rock Thrush	+	+
Pallid Swift	+	+	Blue Rock Thrush	+	+
Alpine Swift	+	+	Blackbird	+	+
White-rumped Swift	+	−	Mistle Thrush	+	+
Little Swift	−	+	Cetti's Warbler	+	+
Kingfisher	+	+	Fan-tailed Warbler	+	+
Bee-eater	+	+	Savi's Warbler	+	+
Roller	−	+	Moustached Warbler	−	+
Hoopoe	+	−	Reed Warbler	+	+
Green Woodpecker	+	−	Great Reed Warbler	+	+
Levaillant's Woodpecker	−	+	Olivaceous Warbler	+	+
			Melodious Warbler	+	+
Great Spotted Woodpecker	+	+	Dartford Warbler	+	+
			Spectacled Warbler	+	+
Lesser Spotted Woodpecker	(+)	−	Subalpine Warbler	+	+
			Sardinian Warbler	+	+
Calandra Lark	+	−	Orphean Warbler	+	−
Short-toed lark	+	+	Whitethroat	+	+
Lesser Short-toed Lark	+	−	Blackcap	+	+
Crested Lark	+	+	Bonelli's Warbler	+	+
Thekla Lark	+	+	Chiffchaff	+	+
Woodlark	+	+	Firecrest	+	+
Skylark	+	−	Spotted Flycatcher	+	+
Crag Martin	+	+	Pied Flycatcher	−	+
Swallow	+	+	Long-tailed Tit	+	−
Red-rumped Swallow	+	+	Crested Tit	+	+
			Coal Tit	+	+
House Martin	+	+	Blue Tit	+	+
Tawny Pipit	+	+	Great Tit	+	+
Yellow Wagtail	+	+	Nuthatch	+	+
Grey Wagtail	+	+	Short-toed Tree Creeper	+	+
Common Bulbul	−	+			

Continued.

Table 36   Continued.

Species	Europe	Morocco	Species	Europe	Morocco
Golden Oriole	+	+	Spanish Sparrow	+	+
Great Grey Shrike	+	+	Tree Sparrow	+	−
Woodchat Shrike	+	+	Rock Sparrow	+	−
Black-headed Bush	−	+	Chaffinch	+	+
Shrike			Serin	+	+
Jay	+	+	Greenfinch	+	+
Azure-winged	+	−	Goldfinch	+	+
Magpie			Linnet	+	+
Magpie	+	−	Crossbill	+	−
Alpine Chough	−	+	Hawfinch	+	+
Chough	+	+	Cirl Bunting	+	+
Jackdaw	+	+	Rock Bunting	+	+
Raven	+	+	Ortolan Bunting	(+)	−
Spotless Starling	+	+	Reed Bunting	+	+
House Sparrow	+	+	Corn Bunting	+	+

[1] Introduced.

Key: +, present; −, absent; E, extinct.

White-headed Duck productivity in relation to annual water levels—Amat, 1989). Such changes are probably frequent, though less severe and conspicuous, throughout the area, and are likely to affect a wide range of species. The extinction of the Swallow as a breeding species on the Rock of Gibraltar during the 1960s has been attributed to the urbanization of the isthmus between Gibraltar and Spain and the resultant loss of areas of mud required for nest construction (Cortés *et al.*, 1980). Alternatively, the loss of these areas may have reduced the Swallow population to such a small size that it later became extinct on the Rock by natural means. The loss of hunting grounds on the isthmus and nearby hills is thought to have also contributed to the significant reduction in the size of the Lesser Kestrel breeding colony on the Rock of Gibraltar (Cortés *et al.*, 1980). The virtual extermination of the Shag from the Strait may have resulted initially from persecution and disturbance on sea-cliffs, which brought the population down to a very low level. Such disturbance drove away the Ospreys from all the breeding sites within the Strait. Subsequent reductions, claimed to be due to shipping, pollution or other factors, could simply be the effect of the small size of the remaining population.

One case of an increase in a population and its range as the result of Man's activities has been the dramatic expansion of the Yellow-legged Gull population in the Strait, with the establishment of a large colony on the Rock of Gibraltar (see Chapter 5), which includes town-nesting gulls, and the expansion into other sites, including low-lying coastal areas (Ruiz Martinez *et al.*, 1990). Such expansions must have occurred in earlier periods as town-dwelling species (e.g. Swift, Spotless Starling and House Sparrow) increased in numbers and distribution with the growth of urban areas. On a smaller, but in some cases significant, scale, the distribution of species has increased as a result of introductions by Man. This effect has been most conspicuous in the case of the Barbary Partridge, which was introduced into Gibraltar from Morocco by the British during the 18th Century (Cortés *et al.*, 1980).

DROUGHT

During the drought, the distribution of birds varies substantially from the earlier, breeding period. Many migratory terrestrial breeding species abandon the Strait at an early stage (July and early August), in a rapid and inconspicuous movement towards tropical West Africa. Many species then show shrinking populations and ranges. This exodus is also shown by migratory waterbirds (e.g. Collared Pratincole, White Stork) and species associated with wetlands (e.g. Black Kite). During the early part of the drought, the composition of the bird communities changes significantly.

Wetlands become severely reduced as the drought progresses, and many waterbirds undertake post-breeding dispersive movements that result in localization of their distribution in the few areas with standing water remaining. The large gatherings of Coots in some lagoons are a good example, but resident (e.g. White-headed Duck) or nomadic (e.g. Greater Flamingo, Marbled Duck) species are also involved.

Very few ducks arrive from the north at this time, but hundreds of thousands of waders migrate southwards towards Atlantic non-breeding areas. The majority follow the Atlantic coast, where there are more, and larger, estuaries, which (being tidal) are not affected by the drought. The extended shorelines of lagoons, caused by the rapidly evaporating waters, provide additional sites for waders migrating inland.

The drought usually continues at least until the middle of September, so that much of the Strait is an inhospitable land for the many trans-saharan migrants crossing Iberia and Morocco on their way south to tropical West Africa (Finlayson, 1981). The geographical distribution of many of these migrants reflects the occurrence of the drought, with vast numbers of insectivorous birds following the western coasts of Iberia and Morocco, which are greener, avoiding the desiccated Mediterranean coastal belt. In many cases the entire area is avoided, as birds fatten north of the Strait and fly over it without pausing. The absence of prolonged spells of bad weather makes heavy falls of trans-saharan migrants rare at this time.

On a local scale, the Strait appears to have a concentrating effect on non-soaring migrants, even at this time (Bernis, 1962), and this may be related to the funnelling of migrants following the Atlantic and Mediterranean coasts. The local easterly winds blowing over the Strait at this time, and the heavy cloud cover which engulfs the Rock in particular, ground many migrants and create a disproportionate distribution pattern of trans-saharan migrants in the immediate coastal fringe of the Strait. This concentration is most pronounced in the case of soaring birds, which congregate upon the Strait for reasons connected with their method of locomotion rather than for reasons of ecology. For a brief period of a few weeks, the zones immediately bordering the Strait have a high diversity and density of raptors.

Apart from the local patchy distributions caused by migratory flows, receding waters and local weather conditions, many species that utilize the Strait's habitats at this time (whether as migrants or as residents) distribute themselves unevenly within habitats in response to changing resources. Water is a critical resource at this time, and many passerines gather near streams and ponds. A few shrubs bear fruit during the drought (e.g. Buckthorn—*Rhamnus alaternus*), and some insectivorous species are attracted by these emerging resources.

RAINY SEASON

Major readjustments occur when the rains arrive, usually in October. Migratory species that breed in the Strait and in summer abandon it (e.g. White Stork, Great Spotted Cuckoo, etc.) commence a return from the south, and there is a progressive readjustment of the breeding season distribution between then and the breeding season itself. During these early stages of arrival, such species concentrate on areas rich in usable resources, which in most cases vary towards the latter part of the rainy season. The distribution and abundance patterns of these species change from absence to progressive increase with substantial spatial redistributions, culminating with choice of nesting sites. Occasionally, even West African birds may venture north across the Sahara and reach the vicinity of the Strait at this time of the year (e.g. Allen's Gallinule, Lesser Flamingo).

The onset of the rains also marks the arrival of other species from the north which disperse within the Strait. In the case of waterbirds, the distribution varies from year to year, depending on water levels. During this season there is a continuation of wader movements in coastal areas, with a gradual settling of species in the estuaries and beaches of the Strait.

Within the season there can be significant readjustments in response to increasing rain or absence of rain; these include considerable movements towards the Moroccan side of the Strait followed by returns to Europe later in the season. Harsh conditions in northern Europe can also bring in waves of birds (e.g. ducks, the Lapwing), which can alter the spatial distribution patterns of these and other species. There can also be changes in the distribution of coastal waders in relation to fluctuating resources.

Among the terrestrial species, changes of a similar nature to those of the waterbirds can take place. The Strait holds important populations of passerines at this time (October–February), including residents (e.g. Sardinian Warbler) and migrants from the north (e.g. Meadow Pipit). The early part of the season (October–November) sees the passage of many migrants that, at this time, are not spatially restricted to the western areas of Iberia but are dispersed more widely (Bernis, 1962). As with other groups of migrants, different populations of the same species may follow different approach routes to the Strait (e.g. Chaffinch and Snipe), which may have an effect on the distribution of the different populations on a local scale. Others will use different routes south and north (e.g. Crane), also causing variations in distribution. These migrants utilize the Strait's habitats in October–November and, as successive waves of migrants pass the area, there are daily changes in local dispersion patterns. These adjustments continue throughout the season, partly because new arrivals continue to reach the area as late as December (e.g. Greylag Goose, Snipe, Meadow Pipit, Goldfinch) partly because changing resources cause the redistribution of individuals. These nomadic movements are a characteristic of many passerines and near-passerines during the rainy season, very few being restricted to territories that are kept throughout the entire season, even though many defend feeding territories of a less permanent nature. In certain cases, such shifts in location occur on a daily basis. At Gibraltar, Black Redstart territories change position in relation to prevailing winds, some individuals leaving exposed sites in harsh weather and returning to them when conditions improve. Two specific cases of fluid spatial distributions during this season (*Sylvia* warblers and Crag Martins) are considered later in this chapter.

Towards the latter part of the rainy season (usually from February) there is a change in distribution as resident species, and migrants which have already arrived, adjust towards a breeding season dispersion. Many of the migrants that arrived from the north leave, and there is a fairly rapid shrinking of these populations and of the areas occupied by them. During the following months, as many species settle to breed, waves of trans-saharan migrants cross the Strait northwards, this time settling for longer periods than in autumn to exploit the surge of resources (especially invertebrates) that follows the rising temperatures. There are then daily changes in the numbers and distribution of migrants, especially close to the Strait itself. During this period, contingents of trans-saharan migrants settle in the Strait and set up breeding distributions. In many cases, such distributions are largely determined by the presence of congeners that are already established; the distribution of many trans-saharan migrants is then restricted to high altitude areas or secondary habitats where residents are not established, as happens in north temperate areas (e.g. Herrera, 1978a) and the tropics (Leck, 1972; Tramer, 1974). Migrants do best in these structurally simpler habitats (Willis, 1966; Alerstam & Enckell, 1979; O'Connor, 1985), since these will not be exploited by residents as successfully as the more stable ones (Frochot, 1971).

Temporal Effects

The patterns so far described can be modified by time. Perhaps the most obvious case is the inter-annual variation in distribution of populations, which results from a number of factors, some external to the Strait. The periodic invasions of birds from the north is often the result of conditions well away from the Strait and, as these vary from year to year, so the distribution and abundance of species vary (e.g. ducks, Kittiwakes, Starlings, Siskins). Absence of site fidelity may be a feature in irruptive species (see, for example, Spaans, 1977; Yunick, 1983). In the case of fruit-eating passerines (e.g. Blackcap, see later) inter-annual variations may be related to the success of the local fruit crop or to the mildness of winters in western Europe (Finlayson, 1980).

The variations in passage periods between species and between populations of the same species can produce regular temporal changes in distribution patterns within the migratory periods. Inter-annual differences in meteorological conditions, with good and bad weather occurring in different time-periods, can nevertheless dramatically alter the appearance, absence or level of presence of some migrants in different years. Such variations may affect populations of the same species, different sexes (males of many species precede females in spring) or different ages (adults of a number of species precede immatures in spring).

Over a longer time-frame, species distributions may also vary in relation to changing climatic conditions, and initially these will most obviously affect species at the edge of their range. Within the Strait area such species could include Purple Sandpiper, divers or certain sea ducks that appear sporadically in winter. Some of these birds were much commoner during the glacial periods (Cortés *et al.*, 1980).

Other changes may be related to population expansions, usually due to increased protection or changing environmental conditions. This has been most dramatically observed in the Strait during the 1980s for the Audouin's Gull, which, from being a scarce migrant, has become an abundant and widely distributed migrant with a year-round presence in the Strait. Recent sightings of Fulmars in the Atlantic coast of the Strait area and in the Canary Islands may be taken to suggest that this species might in time become a regular visitor to the region.

The following three sections describe two insectivorous bird strategies— foliage insectivores (warblers) and aerial insectivores (Crag Martin and swifts)— and how their feeding methods and foods determine their distribution in space and time.

SYLVIA WARBLERS

The warblers of the genus *Sylvia* form a diverse group which is highly represented in the Mediterranean, from where they are thought to have radiated (e.g. see Snow, 1978). The typical Mediterranean species are inhabitants of the matorral, and the few species that range more widely into northern Europe occupy scrub and woodland habitats (Mason, 1976; Cody, 1978; Telleria & Potti, 1984). A number of species pairs or groups appear to have similar ecological requirements and are interspecifically territorial. They are a good example of species limited in their distributions by habitat and climate, having an ability to alternate an essentially summer animal diet by a winter vegetal diet, tracking food resources in spring within breeding territories and outside the breeding season over greater distances.

SYLVIA WARBLER DISTRIBUTIONS IN THE BREEDING SEASON

Sylvia warblers generally segregate along vegetation successional gradients and substantially overlap with each other (Blondel, 1969; Cody & Walter, 1976; Finlayson, 1979; Telleria & Potti, 1984), the main ways of partitioning resources being differences in the diets of species of significantly different size, and differences in habitat utilization and feeding stations (e.g. Lack, 1971). The distribution of *Sylvia* warblers along vegetation gradients is illustrated in Figure 272. Differences along the gradients are not always significantly large, and territories are defended by different species (e.g. Cody & Walter, 1976; Finlayson, 1979; Garcia, 1983). The mechanisms of resource partitioning are greatest in the more southerly communities (Cody, 1985), which have had longer to evolve since the retreat of the ice caps, and least in the northern communities. In structurally similar habitats, individuals seem to differ in choice of patches of vegetation, which may be determined by direct selection of high-quality sites by dominants and by intra- and inter-specific competition forcing subordinates into suboptimal sites (Finlayson, 1979). In situations where superabundant resources may be found, these segregation mechanisms may continue to act in order to reduce interference and prey disturbance, the nature of the foods taken and the method of their collection requiring hunting in isolation.

NON-BREEDING WARBLER DISTRIBUTIONS

Outside the breeding season, warblers respond in different ways to changing resources. The Dartford Warbler, which is a Mediterranean scrub-dwelling species, reaches as far north as the south of England (e.g. see Bibby, 1979). It is mainly a resident, although some populations migrate as evidenced by passage over Gibraltar, and suffers at the northern extremes of its range in hard winters.

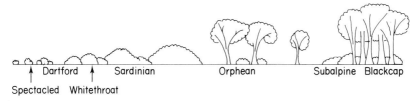

Figure 272. Typical breeding distribution of Sylvia *warblers along a gradient of increasing vegetation complexity.*

The larger Sardinian Warbler also has a Mediterranean distribution but does not extend as far north as the Dartford Warbler; consequently it suffers less in hard winters. Some Sardinian Warbler populations migrate south for the winter (Moreau, 1972), but the majority are resident. In the Strait, the Dartford generally occupies higher ground than the Sardinian Warbler, which coincides with the Dartford's greater latitudinal span, presumably making it better at coping with seasonal climatic fluctuations. The Subalpine Warbler is wholly migratory and, in the Strait, mainly occupies high ground (alongside and above the Dartford Warbler) and is a trans-saharan migrant. Its success presumably lies in occupying habitats that the residents are unable to settle in, hence its occupation of areas of the Mediterranean which have harsher climates (e.g. higher altitudes and latitudes) than those areas supporting the resident Sardinian Warbler.

The distribution of these three species is presumably variable between years, being dependent on the European and tropical African winters. Within the Strait, only Dartford Warblers, Sardinian Warblers and Blackcaps are found between late October and February, the other species wintering in tropical Africa or on the edge of the Sahara.

FRUIT FEEDING

Most *Sylvia* warblers eat fruit at some stage in their life cycle (Schuster, 1930; Turcek, 1961; Diesselhorst, 1973; Ferns, 1975; Gauci & Sultana, 1976; Finlayson, 1979; Herrera, 1981c; Jordano, 1982; Debussche & Isenmann, 1983, 1986). Some, like the Blackcap or Sardinian Warbler, are apparently more dependent on fruit than others (e.g. Dartford Warbler) (Debussche & Isenmann, 1983). *Sylvia* warblers are the most frequent and abundant fruit consumers of all the passerines that use the Mediterranean region (Jordano, 1981, 1983; Tejero *et al.*, 1983; Herrera, 1984a). Their numerical importance in Mediterranean sclerophyllous scrub (the richest fruiting habitats) and their morphological and behavioural characteristics (Herrera, 1981c) have no doubt played a major role in the evolution of the association with these plants which has, in turn, probably enhanced the success of the birds themselves.

Jordano (1981) found that Blackcap, Whitethroat and Garden Warbler on southward migration over the Sierra Morena (south-central Spain) consumed over 90% of their diet (by volume) as fruit. Since these fruits are generally low in fat and protein but high in carbohydrates and water (Herrera, 1981a), migrants have to ingest a small proportion of insects in order to prevent loss of weight (Berthold, 1976; Jordano, 1981). Insects are, however, generally scarce during the summer drought (Herrera, 1978; Finlayson, 1979), and there is an absence of water. This makes fruit an attractive, abundant and easily harvested resource for birds in Mediterranean regions at this time, both migrants and residents (Jordano, 1981, 1983) exploiting fruit to supplement energetic demands and reduce the risk of dehydration, the maintenance of a positive water balance being a limiting factor for many migratory birds (Fogden, 1972). Fruits are therefore of great importance during the drought, especially for migrants that are depositing fat reserves prior to crossing the Sahara Desert (Thomas, 1979).

Warblers wintering in tropical Africa also feed on fruit. The warblers migrating past the Strait during the drought and after the rains, as well as those remaining during the rainy season in the Mediterranean, are heavily dependent on fruit. The Garden Warbler, Subalpine Warbler and Orphean Warbler, for example, eat large amounts of fruit between July and September (Debussche & Isenmann, 1983; Jordano, 1985). An intricate system has resulted through diffuse co-evolution (especially in species consuming fruits after the drought, e.g. Blackcap) between Mediterranean shrubs (see Herrera, 1981b, 1982a,b) and the *Sylvia* warblers (and other passerines) that utilize them (Herrera, 1984a; Jordano, 1985).

The present geographical (and local) distribution of fruit-producing plants and their consumers is likely to be of recent origin, since they probably came into contact about five million years ago (Snow, 1978; Jordano, 1985). It is probable the patterns are even more recent than this, in view of the substantial climatic shifts that took place during the glacial periods. Mediterranean seed dispersing birds show morphological characteristics that may have pre-adapted them to fruit consumption, but they also exhibit physiological adaptations (e.g. having a rapid gut passage time which permits rapid processing of pulp—Herrera, 1984b) and the most efficient seed dispersal patterns (Herrera, 1981c), which must result from their association with fruiting plants. The process of the development of plant–bird distributions may be rapid at local level. The existing dominance of fruit-bearing shrubs in the Gibraltar maquis and the dominance there of *Sylvia* warblers and Blackbirds is likely to be the product of Man's destruction of the native forest two centuries ago. The dominance of fruit-dispersed plants points to an ability of these plants to spearhead the colonization of new areas (e.g. naturally when fires destroy forests, or through the destructive actions of Man).

The dispersion of these birds between October and February is influenced by the success and distribution of fruit in autumn and winter (Jordano, 1985). The increase in density of passerines in the Mediterranean matorral habitats at this time are due mostly to corresponding increases in the number of fruit-feeding birds (Finlayson, 1979, 1981; Jordano, 1985). The *Sylvia* warblers in the Strait exemplify fluidity of 'winter quarters', some individuals remaining for many weeks in a fixed area, others roaming hundreds of kilometres within the wintering range (Finlayson, 1981). It is a feature which, in the Blackcap at least, has been noted in other areas of the wintering range in the Mediterranean (Thevenot, 1973; Benvenutti & Ioale, 1983; Debussche & Isenmann, 1984) and tropical Africa (Morel & Roux, 1966), being related to variation in fruit-crop success. The recent overwintering of Blackcaps in western Europe illustrates how flexible the winter distribution of sylviids is (Leach, 1981; Berthold, 1984). The relationship between the wintering areas of this species in tropical Africa, the Mediterranean and western Europe is apparently a continuously changing one in relation to changing climatic conditions.

The plasticity of the diet of these warblers is evident in the winter at Gibraltar. In January and early February, once most fruit stocks have been consumed, warblers feed extensively on the nectar produced by flowering aloes (introduced from South Africa where they are pollinated by sunbirds). This relatively recent resource is tapped when other resources are low (Finlayson, 1979).

CRAG MARTINS

The Crag Martin is the only aerial insectivore of which a large proportion of the European breeding population remains north of the Sahara Desert during the northern winter. Being an aerial insectivore, it is too specialized to be capable of consuming alternative foods (e.g. the fruit taken by warblers), and its mechanism of resource utilization in winter quarters is therefore significantly different. [The discussion of Crag Martins in this section is largely based on my own (unpublished) data.]

At Gibraltar there is a large wintering population of Crag Martins, in excess of 2000 and occasionally up to 3000 (Elkins & Etheridge, 1974). Elkins & Etheridge (1974, 1977) have indicated that there is a broad relationship between air temperature and Crag Martin body weight, and have hinted that fat deposition may occur during good weather.

During the winter, Crag Martin's weights at a large roost in sea-caves in Gibraltar in the evening varied between 16.0 and 32.5 g. Adults were, on average, 5% heavier than first-year birds (Elkins & Etheridge, 1977), reflecting an overall size difference, adults being longer-winged than first-year birds (difference of 1 mm, $d = 4$, $P < 0.001$). In samples of adults and first-year birds collected the same day, a positive linear relationship existed between wing length and weight in both categories. For adults the relationship was $y = 0.26x - 6.92$ ($t_{39} = 3.25$, $P < 0.01$) and for first-year birds it was $y = 0.2x + 0.94$ ($t_{87} = 2.86$, $P < 0.01$). In adult Crag Martins, weight was linearly related to the average of the

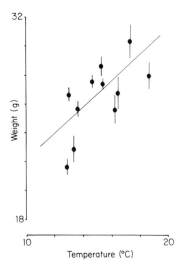

Figure 273. Relationship between adult Crag Martins' weights and the environmental temperature for 3 days prior to the measurement. Note: values are mean with 95% confidence limits. Regression equations are: adult y = 13.2 + 0.9x, P < 0.02; first year y = 14.5 + 0.7x, P > 0.05.

daily mean temperature for the 3 days prior to the measurement (Figure 273). There was no significant trend in first-year birds or between weight and other meteorological factors.

During the winter months Crag Martins deposited more fat in the interclavicular pit than other insectivorous passerines at the same time of year (Table 37). In both adult and first-year Crag Martins, heavier birds carried greater fat deposits than lighter ones (Figure 274) but long-winged birds did not deposit more fat than short-winged ones. First-winter Crag Martins deposited less fat than adults although differences were not significant all days (Table 38).

In first-year Crag Martins the coefficient of variation in body weight (e.g. see Murton et al., 1974) was inversely proportional to fat level, but adults did not

Table 37   Deposition of fat in the interclavicular pit in Crag Martins and in other[1] insectivorous passerines wintering in Gibraltar.[2]

Species	Fat score				
	0	1	2	3	4
Crag Martin	3	49	391	479	264
Others[2]	21	98	73	32	14

[1] $\chi^2 = 399.62$, $P < 0.001$.
[2] Others: Blackcap, Sardinian Warbler, Chiffchaff, Firecrest, Stonechat, Black Redstart and Robin.

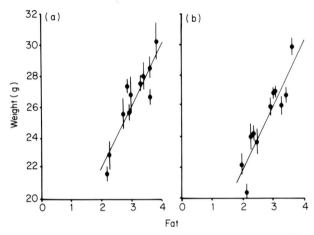

Figure 274. Relationship between fat score and weight in Crag Martins: (a) adult
y = 13.76 + 4.11x, P < 0.02; (b) first year, y = 13.41 + 4.16x, P < 0.05.

Table 38   *Fat deposition in adult and first-winter Crag Martins.*

Date/age	Fat score					(χ^2/P)
	0	1	2	3	4	
28 November 1980						
Adult	0	1	6	12	6	10.317
First-year	0	5	24	14	5	(<0.01)
19 December 1980						
Adult	0	3	19	11	0	0.000
First-year	0	1	11	5	0	(>0.05)
03 January 1981						
Adult	0	0	0	13	23	4.014
First-year	0	0	3	14	12	(<0.05)
17 January 1981						
Adult	0	4	8	10	0	3.214
First-year	1	5	18	7	0	(>0.05)
27 November 1978						
Adult	0	0	7	11	19	6.509
First-year	0	0	11	40	19	(<0.05)
30 November 1978						
Adult	0	1	7	17	6	1.910
First-year	0	1	19	41	28	(>0.05)
07 December 1978						
Adult	0	0	0	5	11	1.794
First-year	0	0	0	11	10	(>0.05)
27 December 1978						
Adult	0	0	4	8	1	2.210
First-year	0	1	8	8	0	(>0.05)

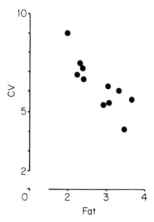

Figure 275. Effect of fat level on the coefficient of body weight variation (CV) in first-year Crag Martins. Note: y = 11.69 − 1.87x, P < 0.05. There is no relationship in adults.

show any trend (Figure 275). The coefficient of variation in body weight was lowest in first-year Crag Martins with the longest wings (Figure 276), but there was no trend in adults. The coefficient of variation of body weight was greater in first-year birds than in adults on seven out of 11 samples.

Crag Martins are extremely variable during the winter (Elkins & Etheridge, 1974), but increases in weight are not connected with specific physiological processes at that time of year (Ward, 1969; Baggot, 1975; Jones & Ward, 1976), since the moult has been completed and there is no migratory or breeding activity (Cortés *et al.*, 1980; Elkins & Etheridge, 1977). Weight increases are therefore apparently in preparation for the maintenance of essential body functions during

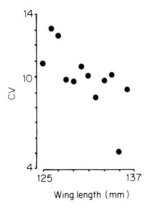

Figure 276. Effect of wing length on the coefficient of body weight variation in first-year Crag Martins. Note: y = 59.24 − 0.38x, P < 0.05. There is no relationship in adults. All birds had a fat score of 3.

times of severe stress, when food may be scarce (Newton & Evans, 1966; Newton, 1969; Pienkowski *et al.*, 1979). There was not the midwinter peak that has been observed in other passerines (Newton, 1968; Evans, 1969). The storage of fat reserves, analogous to that in migratory birds (Fry *et al.*, 1970), is therefore critical in a species that is dependent on a variable food supply. Other wintering insectivorous passerines, which deposited less fat, were able to use alternative (predictable) food sources, i.e. fruit. Excessive deposits of fat can impair flight performance, so large accumulations are avoided if food supplies are predictable (Dick & Pienkowski, 1979; Wood, 1978).

Adult Crag Martins were apparently better able to cope with unpredictable conditions than first-year birds. They responded more efficiently than young birds to warm periods, when presumably more aerial arthropods were active (Taylor, 1963), by increasing body weight (Figure 273). Adults were larger than first-year birds, so their overnight energy requirements to counteract heat loss were probably lower (King, 1972), and they sometimes had greater fat reserves than young birds. In both adults and first-years, body weight reflected size and fat deposition.

Young Crag Martins showed greater weight variability than adults, the variation being greatest in the smallest first-year birds carrying little fat. Of nine freshly dead Crag Martins collected from the floor of a roost after a cold spell, all were first- winter birds with no fat. Eight of these were collected in December and one in January. Those collected in December were in body moult, well after the majority of the population had completed moulting. Seven of the nine birds had wing lengths below the population mean. The weights of these birds ranged from 12.9 to 15.3 g, much lower than the lowest live weights recorded. One had previously been ringed and had lost 7.7 g in 7 days, going from a fat score of 2 to zero. This mortality of young birds through starvation is consistent with the theory that food shortage is important in regulating populations, mainly through changes in density-dependent juvenile mortality (Lack, 1954, 1966).

The Crag Martin's survival strategy is therefore one of depositing fat during spells of warm weather, which enables them to cope with periods when feeding is not possible (e.g. rainy weather) or when food is scarce (e.g. cold weather) (Finlayson, 1978). During long periods of unfavourable weather, it is the young martins, especially the lean individuals that have not completed growth and moult, which perish. In these young birds, body weight is highly variable and reaches low levels from which there is no recovery.

SWIFTS

In spring and summer it is the swifts which dominate as aerial foragers over Gibraltar. This section, based on my earlier work (Finlayson, 1979), describes the ecology of the Swift and the Pallid Swift, which presents parallels and contrasts to that of the Crag Martin at the same locality in the winter.

Five species of *Apus* swifts breed in the Strait. The two most widely distributed and abundant species (Swift and Pallid Swift) are discussed in detail here. The other species are the Alpine Swift, which breeds in colonies in coastal and inland cliffs on both sides of the Strait, the White-rumped Swift, which only breeds on the European side of the Strait, which it colonized during the 1960s (see Chapter 3), and the Little Swift, which breeds in towns on the Moroccan side and occasionally strays northwards across the Strait.

DISTRIBUTION

Numerically, the Swift and the Pallid Swift are the two dominant breeding aerial arthropod foragers at Gibraltar, and this is typical of most towns of the Strait. Neither species is resident, but Pallid Swifts are present in Gibraltar from mid-February to mid-November and Swifts from April to October. The last nesting Swifts leave Gibraltar during the first week of August, those observed after this time being migrants.

The Pallid Swift breeds in the western and central Mediterranean Basin, in the Middle East into Pakistan, and over a wide area of East Africa (Voous, 1960). Recently, it has been found nesting in tropical West Africa (Thiollay, 1974). The western Mediterranean subspecies is *brehmorum* (Hartert). Very little is known about the ecology of this species in the breeding grounds (Heim de Balsac, 1951; Hue, 1951; Hoffmann *et al.*, 1951; Castan, 1955; Affre & Affre, 1967; Bernis, 1970), and the winter quarters are imprecisely known (Lack, 1958; Moreau, 1972). The Swift is common and widespread in the Palaearctic and its life history, both on the breeding grounds (Weitnauer, 1947; Koskimies, 1950; Lack & Lack, 1951; Lack, 1956) and in the winter quarters (Brooke, 1975) are well known. Gibraltar is a zone of sympatry of the two species. Both are abundant nesting species and they often nest in close proximity.

THE BREEDING SEASON

Pallid Swifts regularly fly over breeding colonies from mid-February onwards, but the first eggs are not laid until the second half of April (Figure 277). The peak in egg laying is around the third week in May, and a gradual decline follows until second clutches are started at the end of July (Figure 277). Chicks hatched 3 weeks after the eggs were laid (mean incubation period 21.4 ± 1.4 days; Figure 278). The young took 46.4 ± 2.18 days to fledge, the first young leaving the colony during the third week of June and the majority during the first week of July. Second-brood young left the nests in mid-September, 11th October being the last date when young were found in a nest. The nesting period of the Swift (which arrives much later than the Pallid Swift, in mid-April, and has a shorter pre-breeding period) overlaps with that of Pallid Swift first clutches (Figure 279) but is generally up to 2 weeks behind, laying occasionally commencing in mid-May and young fledging from mid-July to early August.

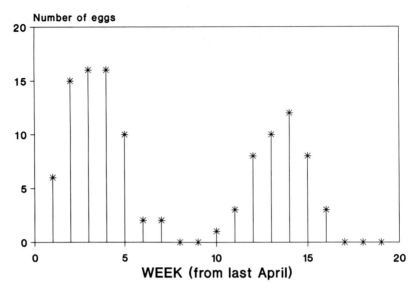

Figure 277.   Pallid Swift egg-laying season at Gibraltar, after Finlayson (1979).

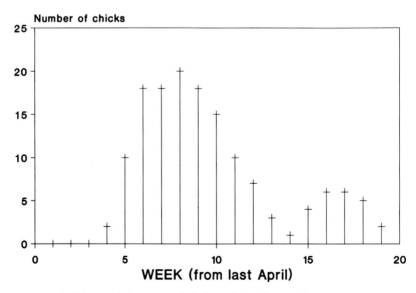

Figure 278.   Pallid Swift chick season at Gibraltar, after Finlayson (1979).

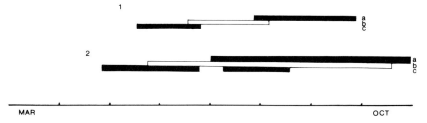

Figure 279.   Swift and Pallid Swift breeding seasons at Gibraltar (after Finlayson, 1979). 1, Swift; 2, Pallid Swift; A, fledglings; B, nestlings; C, eggs.

POPULATION DIFFERENCES

In the more southerly parts of the breeding range the Pallid Swift arrives earlier in spring and leaves earlier in autumn than further north. In Tunisia, Pallid Swifts abandoned colonies by the end of September (Castan, 1955), and they arrive in North Africa in January (Heim de Balsac, 1951). Further south, in the Canary Islands, they commence breeding as early as the first week of January and leave in September (Bannerman, 1963). Occasionally they remain in winter. At Gibraltar, Pallid Swifts arrive later than they do in North Africa (mid-February) but do not breed until April. Daylength or overall aerial insect abundance may be critical factors preventing early breeding. Pallid Swifts leave between mid-October and early November. Further north, in the south of France, the first birds arrive during the first week of April but the majority do so at the end of the month (Hue, 1951). They complete nesting at this latitude in mid-November (Affre & Affre, 1967) and some remain there all winter (Hovette, 1972; Laferrere, 1974). The south of France appears to be the northerly limit of tolerance for the Pallid Swift. If it were somehow able to colonize areas to the north, which would require a later breeding season, it would only be able to raise a single brood, which could place it at a disadvantage over the Swift.

The White-rumped Swift is the last species to arrive in the Strait area in spring, in mid-May. This late arrival means a late breeding season, with young fledging in October. The Strait's aerial environment can clearly support swifts at this time (Pallid swifts regularly have young then), and the late arrival may be related to the habit of this species of taking over nests of Red-rumped Swallows.

THE MOULT

Adult Swifts undertake a single moult in the winter quarters (Niethammer, 1938; de Roo, 1966), and the process starts as soon as they arrive in Africa in mid-August (Herroelen, 1953; de Roo, 1966). The moult is slow and lasts for between

6 and 7 months (de Roo, 1966). Most swifts have long moult periods, which are related to an aerial existence (Naik & Naik, 1965), most species studied taking 6–8 months to fully moult the primaries (Medway, 1962; Naik & Naik, 1965; de Roo, 1966), an exception being the Chimney Swift which takes only 4 months (Johnston, 1958).

Pallid Swifts remained much longer at Gibraltar than Swifts and commenced the primary moult while raising the second brood (Finlayson, 1979). The moult was suspended (Snow, 1967) when breeding was completed, adults migrating south in October and November to complete the moult in winter quarters. The Alpine Swift also commences moulting in the breeding grounds after nesting (in June) and interrupts the moult before migration in September (Stresemann, in Naik & Naik, 1965). The difference between the Pallid Swift and Alpine Swift is that the latter is single-brooded (Bartels, 1931; Arn, 1945). At Gibraltar some Swifts may commence moulting the tenth primary during July and then suspend moulting before migration (Finlayson, 1979). The tenth primary is moulted independently in winter quarters in Africa (de Roo, 1966), and an early moult in some individuals at the breeding grounds may reduce the moulting period in the winter quarters.

RESOURCE PARTITIONING

The Swift and Pallid Swift are morphologically similar and breed alongside in many situations. The nature of their food resources is such that they are likely to use patchily distributed, sometimes superabundant, foods. At Gibraltar, these two species differ in a number of ways (other than the partial temporal separation of breeding) that may assist in permitting co-existence.

During the study, the Swift and Pallid Swift nested in buildings and old walls at Gibraltar, and Pallid (and some Alpine) Swifts also nested in caves and cliffs. A few pairs of Swifts nested in palm trees in the town. A complete survey of the nesting colonies of the town of Gibraltar in 1978 revealed 114 Pallid Swift and 56 Swift breeding colonies, the Pallid Swift having a wider distribution. The breeding populations were estimated at 2030 pairs of Pallid Swifts and 1110 pairs of Swifts (Finlayson, 1979).

Of 82 Pallid Swift colonies in buildings of known age, only 19 (23.17%) were

Table 39　*Occupation of nest sites by Swifts and Pallid Swifts in buildings of different ages at Gibraltar.*

Species	Building age	
	Pre-20th Century	20th Century
Pallid Swift	19	63
Swift	29	7

$\chi^2 = 34.16$, $P < 0.001$.

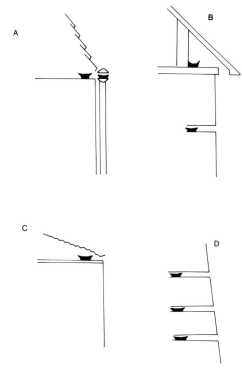

Figure 280. Typical nest sites of Pallid Swifts and Swifts in buildings at Gibraltar (after Finlayson, 1979).

in pre-20th Century constructions, but of 36 Swift colonies in buildings of known age, 29 (80.56%) were in pre-20th Century buildings ($\chi_1^2 = 34.16$, $P < 0.001$). Statistically significant differences were found in the types of nest sites occupied (Figure 280 and Table 39), which may account for the difference, as newer buildings offered different types of nest sites from older ones. Such differences may be related to ancestral, natural nest sites, Swifts being more likely to nest in holes in trees and Pallid Swifts in crevices and overhangs in sea-cliffs.

FORAGING AREAS

The two species foraged in a similar fashion. In the early morning and late evening, most feeding activity was concentrated near the colony. During the middle of the day swifts flew north and west (northeast in the case of cliff-nesting Pallid Swifts on the east side of Gibraltar) into the Spanish hills to feed. Early in the season (February–March) Pallid Swifts formed noisy groups over Gibraltar in the mornings, and these groups gradually moved into Spain during the day. They returned late in the evening. Later in the season, once the young hatched, there was a daily exodus of breeding adults into Spain in mid-morning and a large return in the evening. During the middle of the day, these adults moved to and from the foraging grounds and the colonies as they brought food for the young. On calm mornings feeding activity lasted longer near the colony, and on calm evenings the return was earlier.

As Gibraltar is a small peninsula protruding into an area of sea where strong winds from the east or west prevail, it appears that large concentrations of aerial arthropods are only to be found in calm weather. In strong winds, swifts seek food over ridges along hills inland.

Foraging areas near the colonies

In 1978, I studied an area where Pallid Swifts and Swifts had breeding colonies and foraged close to each other in the mornings and evenings (Finlayson, 1979). The colony density was lower than in the main town of Gibraltar, and swifts from individual colonies could be observed foraging. The swifts from different colonies appeared to have separate foraging ranges which moved with prevailing wind conditions. The separation was made greater still by evident altitudinal differences in the foraging areas of different colonies.

In the centre of Gibraltar, colonies were tightly packed so that it was difficult to observe the foraging ranges of the different colonies. Despite the apparent chaos, however, groups that were followed appeared to remain together and separate from other groups.

Swifts foraged unevenly over any area. Within their foraging area there must have been concentrations of food which they 'latched on' to. From the food consumed by the two species, it was evident that swifts often took swarming insects, especially social Hymenoptera.

Swifts did not remain over one patch all the time, presumably because the disturbance caused by the flock depleted the food supply temporarily. The behaviour of the swift flock was one of moving around an area, allocating time

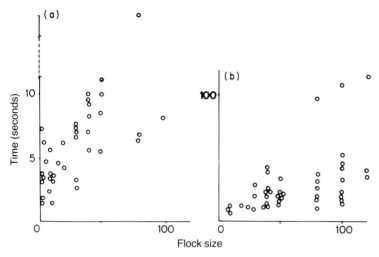

Figure 281. (a) Relationship between flock size and amount of time spent over a 1 ha patch by individuals in a swift flock; y = 3.14 + 0.10x, P < 0.001. (b) Relationship between flock size and amount of time spent over a 1 ha patch by a swift flock; y = 5.33 + 0.38x, P < 0.001. (After Finlayson, 1979.)

spent in patches unevenly (presumably dedicating most time to the most productive patches). The average time taken for a group to return to forage over the same 1 ha patch was estimated at 38.9 ± 18.7 s for Swifts and 27.3 ± 19.0 s for Pallid Swifts. Within the flock, individual swifts were well spaced out, although solitary birds were occasionally observed in large feeding patches. These patches were unoccupied for long periods and occupied the rest of the time by flocks.

Time spent in the 1 ha patches was related to flock size, the largest flocks spending most time over the patches (Figure 281).

Feeding territories

Lack & Owen (1955) have suggested that Swifts in England feed near nests and that, as a result, colonies are evenly spaced out. At Oxford, colonies are spaced out at intervals of 0.25–0.5 miles and the spacing is not due to lack of available nest sites in between. This implies that if colonies were closer together, there would be a great deal of inter-colony competition. Aggression among Swifts close to nests is well established (Lack, 1956).

At Gibraltar, colonies are tightly packed, as close as 3 m from one another. Swifts foraged over well-defined areas above the colonies. The presence or absence of Swifts and Pallid Swifts at 50 m intervals along a transect of the town showed the presence of one or other species but rarely of the two together (Figure 282). That spacing could be due to direct aggression was supported by observations of Pallid Swifts from a specific colony being released near another colony.

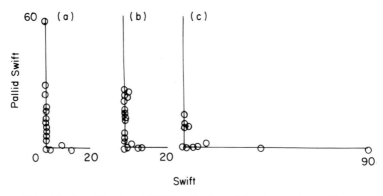

Figure 282.   Number of Swifts and Pallid Swifts observed foraging together at 50 m intervals over the town of Gibraltar (after Finlayson, 1979).

On all nine occasions in the study (Finlayson, 1979) and on all 20 subsequent occasions, Pallid Swifts and Swifts released into each others' colonies have been approached by colony members and chased off, the number of chasers varying between 2 and 10 birds. 22 of 30 Pallid Swifts ringed and released in the same colony were approached by colony members (mean number approaching = 2.57 ± 1.47) but were never chased and always rejoined the colony flock. There was no reaction on the remaining occasions.

Pallid Swifts and Swifts appear to defend foraging areas around the colony even though these areas change from one day to the next. Colonies act as discrete entities. The phenomenon is likely to be related to colonies and not species. In two mixed Swift–Pallid Swift colonies, individuals of both species foraged alongside each other and joined in screaming parties. Screaming parties of Swifts in England are observed mainly on calm mornings, and they are thought to be a form of communal activity (Lack & Lack, 1952). At Gibraltar screaming parties of swifts also occur exclusively on calm mornings and evenings. They are not confined to the immediate area of the colony, often circling high above it. It is possible that they advertise foraging areas and, as these areas change regularly, advertisement has to continue throughout the breeding season.

Foraging areas away from the colonies

Large swift flocks are regularly observed along ridges, hills, edges of woods and over fresh water in southern Spain. These are swifts from the towns of the area (including Gibraltar), roaming in search of aerial insect concentrations. There is evidence of downwind concentrations of swifts, for example at the western end of the Strait during strong easterlies (Garcia Rua, 1975). Observations of feeding movements between Gibraltar and Spain in different winds indicate clear shifts in routes to feeding areas, depending on prevailing winds.

FOOD

Analysis of food balls brought to nests by adult Pallid Swifts and Swifts indicated differences in prey, Pallid Swifts taking a wider range of prey items (including larger prey) and Swifts concentrating more on single-species swarms (Table 40), as they do elsewhere in Europe (Heyder, 1927; Lack & Owen, 1955) and in Africa (Chapin, 1939). The Swift's diet in Gibraltar was nevertheless significantly different from that in England (Lack & Owen, 1955), where Swifts are less specialized than in Gibraltar, with the main components of the diet being Hemiptera. Hemiptera were frequent in Pallid Swift samples, so the difference between England and Gibraltar cannot be related directly to non-availability of these insects. The differences were, instead, related to morphological features of the two swifts (Finlayson, 1979).

Breeding communities of aerial foragers are organized differently from other bird communities. The habitat under exploitation is structurally simpler and subject to greater environmental fluctuations than terrestrial habitats. Swifts are adapted to cope with such fluctuations in resources (e.g. Lack, 1956). The swifts of Gibraltar behave in a similar fashion to seabirds at cliff-nesting colonies, feeding ranges extending far from nest sites. In such structurally simple habitats as the air or the sea, interspecific differences are achieved by feeding in different strata or zones (distance away from colonies, altitude in the air or diving depth at sea) or by selecting different prey types. In this respect, the other swifts of the area differ in a similar manner. The large Alpine Swift ranges furthest away from the colonies and takes the largest prey (e.g. Lack 1956), the smaller White-rumped Swift does not nest colonially and is probably separated by feeding area and food and, as with the Swift, largely separated temporally, breeding after the Swifts have departed. The Little Swift on the Moroccan side is smaller and may differ in diet.

BIOLOGICAL IMPORTANCE AND CONSERVATION

The preceding chapters have analysed the migration patterns of the main species that use the Strait, the major habitats available to migrants and residents, the composition of breeding, wintering and transient bird communities. This final chapter has brought together all these elements, has examined the distribution of birds in the Strait, and has looked at three different strategies (*Sylvia* warblers, Crag Martins and swifts) and how these can influence seasonal and spatial distributions. In this concluding section the significance of the Strait is considered in the context of Palaearctic–African migration and as a reservoir of genetic diversity of southwest Palaearctic breeding species.

THE STRAIT AS A BOTTLENECK

The geographical location of the Strait at the western end of the Mediterranean makes it the key crossing point for soaring birds using the western flyway. Its

Table 40 Numbers and proportions of insects of different taxa and sizes taken by Swifts and Pallid Swifts at Gibraltar.

Size (mm)	Hymenoptera	Diptera	Hemiptera	Coleoptera	Lepidoptera	Others
Pallid Swift prey						
0–4	46	125	255	54	0	5
5–8	602	29	70	8	1	2
9–16	78	1	1	0	6	1
17–32	0	0	0	0	8	1
Swift prey						
0–4	36	97	57	30	0	0
5–8	661	6	2	2	0	0
9–16	7	0	0	0	0	0
17–32	0	0	0	0	0	0

importance is accentuated since there are no other short sea-crossings to the west; to the east the closest alternative is the Italian–Tunisian central flyway which, in any case, involves longer sea-crossings than the Strait. Soaring birds from most of western Europe and, in some cases, further north and east (e.g. Honey Buzzard) congregate at the Strait twice each year. The Strait is therefore western Europe's most important bottleneck (Bijlsma, 1987), receiving a quarter of a million raptors and up to 50 000 storks in autumn (Bernis, 1980). In numerical terms, it is most important for White Stork, Honey Buzzard, Black Kite, Egyptian Vulture, Short-toed Eagle, Montagu's Harrier and Booted Eagle. The small western European Black Stork population also crosses the Strait.

The utilization of areas within the Strait by migratory raptors and soaring birds varies according to the species. It appears that many migrating raptors fast during the journey, which in gregarious species makes sense, since the massive arrival of raptors in a bottleneck area is likely to be well in excess of the carrying capacity of the area. The storks appear to differ in this respect. They utilize traditional stopping points within the Strait and in its proximity (e.g. Marismas del Guadalquivir, Cádiz marshes, La Janda), where they actively feed. They also utilize the same roosts in successive seasons (Bernis, 1980). Specific patches of habitat are clearly of great importance to these species. Some raptors (e.g. Black Kite) also use traditional roosts on migration, whereas others (e.g. Honey Buzzard) settle to roost where the night catches them. The mass of undisturbed woodland on the eastern half of either shore of the Strait, dominated by vast tracts of cork oak woodland with many rocky areas and cliffs in particular, is of great value to migrating raptors. This becomes most conspicuous when unfavourable winds hold up migration and large numbers of raptors and storks have to await improved conditions. At such times, the density of soaring birds on either shore is very high, and the availability of large areas of undisturbed habitat on the very shores of the Strait means that they can be ready to cross as soon as conditions permit. These areas also permit opportunistic hunting by some migrants, especially Buzzards, Sparrowhawks and Booted Eagles.

The geographical position of the Strait also makes it an essential bottleneck for seabirds moving between the Atlantic and the Mediterranean (Telleria, 1981; Finlayson & Cortés, 1984). The Strait attracts seabirds from the western Mediterranean in summer and early autumn as the areas to the east become depleted of resources (see Chapter 5). These may be breeding birds that visit the Strait to collect food for the young (e.g. Cory's Shearwater) or seabirds leaving the Mediterranean at the end of the breeding season (e.g. Balearic Shearwater, Audouin's Gull). In the case of migrant seabirds, the Strait is utilized for feeding, and migrants probably remain in the area feeding for several days. Audouin's Gulls utilize traditional roosts within the Strait (e.g. Punta Secreta, Los Lances Beach) which, as the population has expanded in the past decade, have gained increasing importance. These roosts are now also used by non-breeding Audouin's Gulls during the non-migratory periods.

Later in the autumn and in spring, the Strait becomes a bottleneck for northeast Atlantic seabirds wintering in the Mediterranean (e.g. Gannet, Puffin), for seabirds migrating from the western and central Palaearctic to tropical African wintering areas (e.g. Black Tern), and for others wintering in the proximity of the Strait (e.g. Mediterranean Gull, Little Gull). The Strait has considerable seabird activity throughout the year, the quietest period being May and early June and, even then, given certain weather conditions, there can be substantial seabird concentrations.

THE STRAIT OF GIBRALTAR AS A STOP-OVER FOR NON-SOARING MIGRANTS ON PASSAGE AND IN WINTER

Although non-soaring migrants are not as restricted to narrow sea-crossings as soaring birds are, the Strait attracts unusually high concentrations of passerine and near-passerine land birds during the migratory periods (Nisbet *et al.*, 1961; Bernis, 1962; Finlayson, 1979). Non-soaring migrants travelling long distances need to make intermediate stops for refuelling. The choice of stop-over sites is determined by the position of the wintering areas in relation to the breeding areas (Moreau, 1972) and by the ecology of the areas available for stopping over (Rappole & Warner, 1976). The Strait has a particular significance in spring, when it is part of a green belt utilized by migrants after crossing the Sahara (Finlayson, 1981). At this time, trans-saharan migrants are well dispersed and conspicuous throughout the Strait, and large falls at prominent coastal headlands (e.g. Rock of Gibraltar, Cape Trafalgar) are spectacular. Trans-saharan migrants remain for several days at this time, and this permits re-fattening; in late summer, fewer migrants stay for more than a day (Finlayson, 1981).

In autumn there are also concentrations within the Strait (Bernis, 1962), in contrast with the scarcity of trans-saharan migrants in eastern Spain. The Strait is then at the eastern edge of the main areas utilized by many trans-saharan migrants in autumn, from northwest Spain, through Portugal to northwest Morocco. Specifically, the Maquis of the Rock of Gibraltar is utilized by many migrants and takes high concentrations of warblers (particularly *Sylvia* and *Phylloscopus*), while the cork oak woodland adjacent to the Strait appears to be important for Pied Flycatchers and Redstarts.

Pre-saharan migrants arrive in late autumn with the rains. The migratory movements of these birds are the most spectacular of all non-soaring birds. The Strait is within the main wintering zone of species, and the autumn passage is a combination of arrivals and continuing southward migration into more southerly areas of Morocco. Among these species the most important are the Skylark, Crag Martin, Meadow Pipit, White Wagtail, Robin, Black Redstart, Stonechat, Song Thrush, Blackcap, Chiffchaff, Chaffinch, Serin, Greenfinch, Goldfinch and Linnet. The pastures, matorral and woodland areas of the Strait receive important wintering populations of these non-soaring migrants (Arroyo & Telleria, 1984).

THE STRAIT AS AN IMPORTANT AREA FOR BREEDING BIRDS

The status and changes in status of the breeding birds of the Strait are summarized in Appendix 1. The unique range of habitats within the Strait, along with its geographical position (Chapters 6 and 7), make the area a stronghold for species which are now unique to the western Palaearctic (e.g. see Grimmett & Jones, 1989). The importance of the region for breeding species is greatest for its raptors (Chapters 6 and 7) and waterbirds (Chapter 7) and the conservation of all the remaining wetland areas is essential if some of the rarer species are to survive. The raptor populations continue to be threatened by persecution, despite increasing awareness and protection, and all breeding sites require full protection. This is especially important in cliffs where unique and highly vulnerable raptor colonies survive.

Habitat destruction continues to threaten large areas, with consequent negative effects to the rich breeding bird communities. The threat is today greatest to the areas of wetlands, which are under severe pressure from urbanization, pollution and drainage. Large areas of steppe and pasture, where bustards, harriers and other vulnerable species breed, are also coming under increasing threat from modernization of agricultural methods. The increasing numbers of summer fires, many caused deliberately by Man, are posing a serious danger to many areas of rich woodland.

The Strait has long been recognized as an outstanding area for birds. The detailed studies by ornithologists of the last century, especially Howard Irby and Willoughby Verner, enable us to establish comparisons between the avifauna of today and that of the late 19th Century. It is then that we realize how much has been lost in such a short timespan. Increasing human pressure continues to force species into smaller retreats, and despite enlightened attitudes, even natural wildernesses such as the Coto Doñana come under threat from time to time.

This book has been primarily intended as an inventory of the bird diversity of what can be considered one of the western Palaearctic's few remaining wild areas. It has attempted to describe the underlying mechanisms which cause the distributions of species in its different zones and at different times of the year, since without this knowledge a comprehensive conservation plan for the region cannot be undertaken. The protection of the Coto Doñana or of some of the vast mountain areas is not enough. Coastal garigues and beaches are also important. The availability of some of these sites for brief periods of the year can be critical for the species that need them. The nomadic movements of many wintering birds also illustrate the need to maintain large areas of habitat, parts of which may only become essential every few years. The conservation of only some lagoons, those that are considered to reach international criteria, may be misguided as others may be indispensable, albeit at irregular intervals, when the most frequently used sites become unsuitable some years.

Despite all the changes, it is still possible to experience the wild country of a century ago, so vividly described by Verner. It is still possible to see the beauty of the *vega* (grass plains), which he tells us that to see it at its best

> it should be visited in the month of May when the vivid green of the herbage is almost blotted out by the brilliancy of the masses of spring flowers. Nothing is more striking to the eye than the lavish manner in which Nature applies her colours in such districts. Riding across the vega, at one time you may traverse acres of golden marigold, perhaps half a mile to the right the land is pink for hundreds of yards with a beautiful large madder or, again, crimson with tre-foil, whilst to the left, maybe, it is as white as snow with waving camomile. As you leave the grasslands and traverse the lower spurs of the fallows, whole hillsides are covered with bright yellow mustard or big white daisies. Perhaps one of the most remarkable effects is produced by the small blue, yellow and white convolvulus (*Convolvulus tricolor*) with which the ground is carpeted so closely as to make the hillsides at a short distance appear light cobalt blue. In addition to these great masses of colour the whole plain abounds with other flowers which astonish and delight the traveller. Large purple iris and the diminutive paler-coloured one abound as does the crimson gladiolus and a hundred other brilliant blossoms of all shades and colours. Such is the country which it is my happy fate to traverse whenever I ride out from my dwelling of a spring morning.

Sadly, next to the beautiful *vega* lay the wonderful lagoon of La Janda which no longer exists. Perhaps this book will help to prevent the *vega* and other equally glorious habitats of the Strait from being lost in the next hundred years.

Cattle Egrets and Cattle. A traditional view of the countryside of the region. As modern methods of agriculture and machinery are introduced much of the open, low-lying, grassland countryside and its component species are facing increasing pressures.

Appendix 1: Systematic list of the birds of the Strait of Gibraltar

Species		Status[1]
Red-throated Diver	*Gavia stellata*	NR2/Re/2
Black-throated Diver	*Gavia arctica*	NR2/I/1
Great Northern Diver	*Gavia immer*	NR2/Re/1
Little Grebe★	*Tachybaptus ruficollis*	RNR/Re/4
Great Crested Grebe★	*Podiceps cristatus*	RNR/Re/3
Red-necked Grebe	*Podiceps grisegena*	NR/I/1
Slavonian Grebe	*Podiceps auritus*	NR2/I/1
Black-necked Grebe★	*Podiceps nigricollis*	RNR/Re/3
Cape Petrel	*Daption capense*	NR/I/1
Fulmar	*Fulmarus glacialis*	NR/I/1
Bulwer's Petrel	*Bulweria bulwerii*	NR/I/1
Cory's Shearwater	*Calonectris diomedea*	NR/Re/5
Great Shearwater	*Puffinus gravis*	NR2/Re/2
Sooty Shearwater	*Puffinus griseus*	NR1/Re/2
Balearic Shearwater	*P. puffinus mauretanicus*	NR/Re/4
Levantine Shearwater	*P. puffinus yelkouan*	NR1/Re/3
Manx Shearwater	*P. puffinus puffinus*	NR1/I/1
Little Shearwater	*Puffinus assimilis*	NR1/I/1
Wilson's Storm Petrel	*Oceanites oceanicus*	NR1/Re/2
Storm Petrel	*Hydrobates pelagicus*	NR1/Re/3
Leach's Storm Petrel	*Oceanodroma leucorhoa*	NR2/Re/3
Madeiran Petrel	*Oceanodroma castro*	NR/I/1
Red-billed Tropicbird	*Phaeton aetherens*	NR/I/1
Gannet	*Sula bassana*	NR23/Re/5
Cormorant	*Phalacrocorax carbo*	NR2/Re/3
Shag★	*Phalacrocorax aristotelis*	R/Re/2
Bittern	*Botaurus stellaris*	NR/I/1
Little Bittern★	*Ixobrychus minutus*	NR13/Re/3
Night Heron★	*Nycticorax nycticorax*	NR13/Re/3
Squacco Heron★	*Ardeola ralloides*	NR13/Re/2
Cattle Egret★	*Bubulcus ibis*	RNR/Re/5
Little Egret★	*Egretta garzetta*	RNR/Re/4
Great White Egret	*Egretta alba*	NR/I/1
Grey Heron★	*Ardea cinerea*	RNR2/Re/4
Purple Heron★	*Ardea purpurea*	NR13/Re/3
Black Stork	*Ciconia nigra*	NR/Re/3
White Stork★	*Ciconia ciconia*	NR/Re/5
Glossy Ibis⁽★⁾	*Plegadis falcinellus*	NR/I/1
Bald Ibis	*Geronticus eremita*	NR/I/1
Spoonbill★	*Platalea leucorodia*	NR/Re/3
Greater Flamingo★	*Phoenicopterus ruber*	RNR/Re/5

Species		Status[1]
Lesser Flamingo	*Phoenicopterus minor*	NR/I/1
Whooper Swan	*Cygnus cygnus*	NR/I/1
Bean Goose	*Anser fabalis*	NR/I/1
Pink-footed Goose	*Anser brachyrhynchus*	NR/I/1
White-fronted Goose	*Anser albifrons*	NR/I/1
Lesser White-fronted Goose	*Anser erythropus*	NR/I/1
Greylag Goose	*Anser anser*	NR23/Re/5
Bar-headed Goose	*Anser indicus*	NR/I/1
Barnacle Goose	*Branta leucopsis*	NR/I/1
Canada Goose	*Branta canadensis*	NR/I/1
Red-breasted Goose	*Branta ruficollis*	NR/I/1
Ruddy Shelduck	*Tadorna ferruginea*	NR/I/1
Shelduck	*Tadorna tadorna*	NR2/Re/3
Wigeon	*Anas penelope*	MR23/Re/5
American Wigeon	*Anas americana*	NR/I/1
Gadwall★	*Anas strepera*	RNR23/Re/3
Teal(★)	*Anas crecca*	NR23/Re/5
Mallard★	*Anas platyrhynchos*	RNR/Re/5
Pintail(★)	*Anas acuta*	NR23/Re/3
Garganey	*Anas querquedula*	NR13/Re/3
Blue-winged Teal	*Anas discors*	NR/I/1
Shoveler(★)	*Anas clypeata*	NR23/Re/5
Marbled Duck★	*Marmaronetta angustirostris*	RNR/Re/2
Red-crested Pochard★	*Netta rufina*	RNR23/Re/3
Pochard★	*Aythya ferina*	RNR23/Re/4
Ferruginous Duck	*Aythya nyroca*	NR/I/1
Tufted Duck	*Aythya fuligula*	NR2/Re/3
Scaup	*Aythya marila*	NR2/I/1
Long-tailed Duck	*Clangula hyemalis*	NR2/I/1
Common Scoter	*Melanitta nigra*	NR23/Re/4
Goldeneye	*Bucephala clangula*	NR/I/1
Smew	*Mergus albellus*	NR2/I/1
Red-breasted Merganser	*Mergus serrator*	NR23/Re/2
Goosander	*Mergus merganser*	NR/I/1
White-headed Duck★	*Oxyura leucocephala*	R/Re/3
Honey Buzzard	*Pernis apivorus*	NR13/Re/5
Black-shouldered Kite★	*Elanus caeruleus*	RNR/Re/2
Black Kite★	*Milvus migrans*	NR13/Re/5
Red Kite★	*Milvus milvus*	RNR/Re/3
White-tailed Eagle	*Haliaeetus albicilla*	NR/I/1
Lammergeier	*Gypaetus barbatus*	NR/I/1
Egyptian Vulture★	*Neophron percnopterus*	NR13/Re/4
Griffon Vulture★	*Gyps fulvus*	RNR/Re/5
Black Vulture	*Aegypius monachus*	NR23/I/2
Short-toed Eagle★	*Circaetus gallicus*	NR13/Re/5
Marsh Harrier★	*Circus aeruginosus*	RNR/Re/4
Hen Harrier	*Circus cyaneus*	NR23/Re/3

Species		Status[1]
Pallid Harrier	*Circus macrourus*	NR/I/2
Montagu's Harrier★	*Circus pygargus*	NR13/Re/4
Dark Chanting Goshawk	*Melierax metabates*	NR/I/1
Goshawk★	*Accipiter gentilis*	RNR/Re/3
Sparrowhawk★	*Accipiter nisus*	RNR/Re/4
Buzzard★	*Buteo buteo*	RNR/Re/4
Long-legged Buzzard★	*Buteo rufinus*	RNR/Re/2
Rough-legged Buzzard	*Buteo lagopus*	NR/I/1
Spotted Eagle	*Aquila clanga*	NR/I/1
Tawny Eagle	*Aquila rapax*	NR/I/2
Imperial Eagle	*Aquila heliaca*	RNR/Re/2
Golden Eagle★	*Aquila chrysaetos*	RNR/Re/3
Booted Eagle★	*Hieraaëtus pennatus*	NR13/Re/4
Bonelli's Eagle★	*Hieraaëtus fasciatus*	RNR/Re/3
Osprey	*Pandion haliaetus*	NR/Re/3
Lesser Kestrel★	*Falco naumanni*	NR/Re/4
Kestrel★	*Falco tinnunculus*	RNR/Re/5
Red-footed Falcon	*Falco vespertinus*	NR/I/1
Merlin	*Falco columbarius*	NR/I/2
Hobby★	*Falco subbuteo*	NR13/Re/3
Eleonora's Falcon	*Falco eleonorae*	NR/Re/2
Lanner Falcon★	*Falco biarmicus*	R/Re/2
Peregrine★	*Falco peregrinus*	RNR/Re/3
Red-legged Partridge★	*Alectoris rufa*	R/Re/5
Barbary Partridge★	*Alectoris barbara*	R/Re/3
Quail★	*Coturnix coturnix*	NR/Re/3
Pheasant★	*Phasianus colchicus*	R/Re/3
Andalucian Hemipode★	*Turnix sylvatica*	R/I/1
Water Rail★	*Rallus aquaticus*	RNR/Re/3
Spotted Crake	*Porzana porzana*	NR/I/2
Little Crake	*Porzana parva*	NR/I/2
Baillon's Crake★	*Porzana pusilla*	NR/Re/2
Corncrake	*Crex crex*	NR/Re/2
Moorhen★	*Gallinula chloropus*	RNR/Re/4
Allen's Gallinule	*Porphyrula alleni*	NR/I/1
Purple Gallinule★	*Porphyrio porphyrio*	R/Re/3
Coot★	*Fulica atra*	RNR/Re/5
Crested Coot★	*Fulica cristata*	R/Re/1
Crane	*Grus grus*	NR23/Re/3
Demoiselle Crane	*Anthropoides virgo*	NR/I/1
Little Bustard★	*Tetrax tetrax*	R/Re/3
Great Bustard★	*Otis tarda*	R/Re/2
Houbara	*Chlamydotis undulata*	NR/I/1
Oystercatcher	*Haematopus ostralegus*	NR/Re/3
Black-winged Stilt★	*Himantopus himantopus*	NR13/Re/5
Avocet★	*Recurvirostra avosetta*	RNR/Re/4
Stone Curlew★	*Burhinus oedicnemus*	RNR/Re/3

Species		Status[1]
Cream-coloured Courser	*Cursorius cursor*	NR/I/1
Collared Pratincole★	*Glareola pratincola*	NR13/Re/4
Little Ringed Plover★	*Charadrius dubius*	NR13/Re/3
Ringed Plover	*Charadrius hiaticula*	NR/Re/4
Kentish Plover★	*Charadrius alexandrinus*	RNR/Re/4
Dotterel	*Charadrius morinellus*	NR/I/2
Lesser Golden Plover	*Pluvialis dominica*	NR/I/1
Golden Plover	*Pluvialis apricaria*	NR23/Re/5
Grey Plover	*Pluvialis squatarola*	NR/Re/4
Spur-winged Plover	*Hoplopterus spinosus*	NR/I/1
Sociable Plover	*Chettusia gregaria*	NR/I/1
Lapwing★	*Vanellus vanellus*	RNR23/Re/5
Knot	*Calidris canutus*	NR/Re/3
Sanderling	*Calidris alba*	NR23/Re/4
Little Stint	*Calidris minuta*	NR/Re/3
Temminck's Stint	*Calidris temminckii*	NR/Re/2
Pectoral Sandpiper	*Calidris melanotos*	NR/I/1
Curlew Sandpiper	*Calidris ferruginea*	NR13/Re/4
Purple Sandpiper	*Calidris maritima*	NR23/Re/2
Dunlin	*Calidris alpina*	NR/Re/5
Broad-billed Sandpiper	*Limicola falcinellus*	NR/I/1
Ruff	*Philomachus pugnax*	NR/Re/4
Jack Snipe	*Lymnocryptes minimus*	NR/Re/2
Snipe	*Gallinago gallinago*	NR23/Re/4
Great Snipe	*Gallinago media*	NR/I/1
Short-billed Dowitcher	*Limnodromus griseus*	NR/I/1
Woodcock	*Scolopax rusticola*	NR23/Re/3
Black-tailed Godwit	*Limosa limosa*	NR/Re/5
Bar-tailed Godwit	*Limosa lapponica*	NR/Re/3
Whimbrel	*Numenius phaeopus*	NR1/Re/3
Slender-billed Curlew	*Numenius tenuirostris*	NR23/Re/1
Curlew	*Numenius arquata*	NR23/Re/4
Spotted Redshank	*Tringa erythropus*	NR/Re/4
Redshank★	*Tringa totanus*	RNR/Re/5
Marsh Sandpiper	*Tringa stagnatilis*	NR/I/2
Greenshank	*Tringa nebularia*	NR/Re/3
Lesser Yellowlegs	*Tringa flavipes*	NR/I/1
Green Sandpiper	*Tringa ochropus*	NR/Re/4
Wood Sandpiper	*Tringa glareola*	NR/Re/3
Common Sandpiper	*Actitis hypoleucos*	NR/Re/4
Terek Sandpiper	*Xenus cinereus*	NR/I/1
Turnstone	*Arenaria interpres*	NR23/Re/3
Wilson's Phalarope	*Phalaropus tricolor*	NR/I/1
Red-necked Phalarope	*Phalaropus lobatus*	NR/Re/2
Grey Phalarope	*Phalaropus fulicarius*	NR2/Re/3
Pomarine Skua	*Stercorarius pomarinus*	NR13/Re/3
Arctic Skua	*Stercorarius parasiticus*	NR/Re/3

Species		Status[1]
Long-tailed Skua	*Stercorarius longicaudus*	NR/I/1
Great Skua	*Stercorarius skua*	NR23/Re/4
Mediterranean Gull	*Larus melanocephalus*	NR23/Re/4
Laughing Gull	*Larus atricilla*	NR/I/1
Little Gull	*Larus minutus*	NR23/Re/3
Sabine's Gull	*Larus sabini*	NR/Re/2
Black-headed Gull★	*Larus ridibundus*	NR23/Re/5
Grey-headed Gull	*Larus cirrocephalus*	NR/I/1
Slender-billed Gull★	*Larus genei*	NR13/Re/2
Audouin's Gull	*Larus audouinii*	NR1/Re/4
Ring-billed Gull	*Larus delawarensis*	NR/I/1
Common Gull	*Larus canus*	NR23/I/2
Lesser Black-backed Gull	*Larus fuscus*	NR23/Re/5
Herring Gull	*Larus argentatus*	NR23/Re/2
Yellow-legged Gull★	*Larus cachinaans*	R/Re/5
Glaucous Gull	*Larus hyperboreus*	NR/I/1
Iceland Gull	*Larus glaucoides*	NR/I/1
Great Black-backed Gull	*Larus marinus*	NR23/I/2
Kittiwake	*Rissa tridactyla*	NR23/Re/4
Gull-billed Tern★	*Gelochelidon nilotica*	NR13/Re/3
Caspian Tern	*Sterna caspia*	NR/Re/3
Royal Tern	*Sterna maxima*	NR/Re/3
Lesser Crested Tern	*Sterna bengalensis*	NR/I/3
Sandwich Tern	*Sterna sandvicensis*	NR23/Re/4
Forster's Tern	*Sterna forsteri*	NR/I/1
Roseate Tern	*Sterna dougallii*	NR/I/1
Common Tern	*Sterna hirundo*	NR/Re/4
Arctic Tern	*Sterna paradisea*	NR/I/1
Little Tern★	*Sterna albifrons*	NR/Re/4
Whiskered Tern★	*Chlidonias hybridus*	NR13/Re/4
Black Tern★	*Chlidonias niger*	NR13/Re/5
White-winged Black Tern	*Chlidonias leucopterus*	NR/I/2
Guillemot	*Uria aalge*	NR/I/2
Razorbill	*Alca torda*	NR23/Re/4
Little Auk	*Alle alle*	NR2/I/1
Puffin	*Fratercula arctica*	NR23/Re/5
Black-bellied Sandgrouse	*Pterocles orientalis*	NR/I/1
Pin-tailed Sandgrouse★	*Pterocles alchata*	R/Re/3
Rock Dove★	*Columba livia*	R/Re/3
Stock Dove	*Columba oenas*	NR/Re/3
Woodpigeon★	*Columba palumbus*	RNR/Re/4
Turtle Dove★	*Streptopelia turtur*	NR13/Re/4
Collared Dove	*Streptopelia decaocto*	NR/I/2
Great Spotted Cuckoo★	*Clamator glandarius*	NR23/Re/3
Cuckoo★	*Cuculus canorus*	NR3/Re/4
Barn Owl★	*Tyto alba*	RNR/Re/3
Scops Owl★	*Otus scops*	NR13/Re/3

Species		Status[1]
Eagle Owl★	*Bubo bubo*	R/Re/3
Little Owl★	*Athene noctua*	RNR/Re/4
Tawny Owl★	*Strix aluco*	R/Re/4
Long-eared Owl★	*Asio otus*	RNR/Re/2
Short-eared Owl	*Asio flammeus*	NR23/Re/3
Marsh Owl★	*Asio capensis*	R/Re/2
Nightjar★	*Caprimulgus europaeus*	NR13/Re/3
Red-necked Nightjar★	*Caprimulgus ruficollis*	NR13/Re/4
Swift★	*Apus apus*	NR13/Re/5
Pallid Swift★	*Apus pallidus*	NR13/Re/5
Alpine Swift★	*Apus melba*	NR13/Re/4
White-rumped Swift★	*Apus caffer*	NR1/Re/3
Little Swift★	*Apus affinis*	R/Re/3
Kingfisher★	*Alcedo atthis*	RNR/Re/3
Blue-cheeked Bee-eater	*Merops superciliosus*	NR/I/1
Bee-eater★	*Merops apiaster*	NR13/Re/5
Roller	*Coracias garrulus*	NR13/Re/3
Hoopoe★	*Upupa epops*	NR13/Re/4
Wryneck	*Jynx torquilla*	NR23/Re/3
Green Woodpecker★	*Picus viridis*	R/Re/3
Levaillant's Green Woodpecker★	*Picus vaillantii*	R/Re/2
Great Spotted Woodpecker★	*Dendrocopos major*	R/Re/4
Lesser Spotted Woodpecker★	*Dendrocopos minor*	R/Re/2
Calandra Lark★	*Melanocorypha calandra*	R/Re/4
Short-toed Lark★	*Calandrella brachydactyla*	NR13/Re/4
Lesser Short-toed Lark★	*Calandrella rufescens*	R/Re/3
Crested Lark★	*Galerida cristata*	RNR/Re/4
Thekla Lark★	*Galerida theklae*	RNR/Re/4
Woodlark★	*Lullula arborea*	RNR/Re/4
Skylark★	*Alauda arvensis*	RNR23/Re/5
Shore Lark	*Eremophila alpestris*	NR/I/1
Brown-throated Sand Martin	*Riparia paludicola*	NR/I/2
Sand Martin★	*Riparia riparia*	NR13/Re/3
Crag Martin★	*Hirundo rupestris*	RNR23/Re/4
Swallow★	*Hirundo rustica*	NR/Re/5
Red-rumped Swallow★	*Hirundo daurica*	NR/Re/3
House Martin★	*Delichon urbica*	NR/Re/5
Richard's Pipit	*Anthus novaeseelandiae*	NR/I/1
Tawny Pipit★	*Anthus campestris*	NR13/Re/3
Tree Pipit	*Anthus trivialis*	NR/Re/4
Meadow Pipit	*Anthus pratensis*	NR23/Re/5
Red-throated Pipit	*Anthus cervinus*	NR/Re/2
Rock Pipit	*Anthus petrosus*	NR/Re/2
Water Pipit	*Anthus spinoletta*	NR23/Re/3
Yellow Wagtail★	*Motacilla flava*	NR13/Re/4
Grey Wagtail★	*Motacilla cinerea*	RNR/Re/3
White Wagtail★	*Motacilla alba*	RNR23/Re/4

Species		Status[1]
Common Bulbul★	*Pycnonotus barbatus*	R/Re/3
Dipper★	*Cinclus cinclus*	R/Re/2
Wren★	*Troglodytes troglodytes*	R/Re/4
Dunnock	*Prunella modularis*	NR23/Re/3
Alpine Accentor	*Prunella collaris*	NR23/Re/3
Rufous Bush Chat★	*Cercotrichas galactotes*	NR13/Re/2
Robin★	*Erithacus rubecula*	RNR23/Re/4
Nightingale★	*Luscinia megarhynchos*	NR13/Re/4
Bluethroat	*Luscinia svecica*	NR23/Re/3
Black Redstart★	*Phoenicurus ochruros*	RNR23/Re/4
Redstart★	*Phoenicurus phoenicurus*	NR13/Re/4
Moussier's Redstart★	*Phoenicurus moussieri*	R/Re/3
Whinchat	*Saxicola rubetra*	NR13/Re/4
Stonechat★	*Saxicola torquata*	RNR23/Re/5
Wheatear★	*Oenanthe oenanthe*	NR13/Re/4
Black-eared Wheatear★	*Oenanthe hispanica*	NR13/Re/4
Desert Wheatear	*Oenanthe deserti*	NR/I/1
White-crowned Black Wheatear	*Oenanthe leucopyga*	NR/I/1
Black Wheatear★	*Oenanthe leucura*	R/Re/3
Rock Thrush★	*Monticola saxatilis*	NR13/Re/3
Blue Rock Thrush★	*Monticola solitarius*	RNR/Re/3
Ring Ouzel	*Turdus torquatus*	NR23/Re/3
Blackbird★	*Turdus merula*	RNR/Re/4
Fieldfare	*Turdus pilaris*	NR23/I/2
Song Thrush	*Turdus philomelos*	NR23/Re/4
Redwing	*Turdus iliacus*	NR23/Re/3
Mistle Thrush★	*Turdus viscivorus*	RNR/Re/3
Cetti's Warbler★	*Cettia cetti*	RNR/Re/4
Fan-tailed Warbler★	*Cisticola juncidis*	RNR/Re/4
Grasshopper Warbler	*Locustella naevia*	NR/Re/2
Savi's Warbler★	*Locustella luscinioides*	NR13/Re/2
Moustached Warbler★	*Acrocephalus melanopogon*	NR/Re/1
Aquatic Warbler	*Acrocephalus paludicola*	NR/I/1
Sedge Warbler	*Acrocephalus schoenobaenus*	NR3/Re/2
Blyth's Reed Warbler	*Acrocephalus dumetorum*	NR/I/1
Marsh Warbler	*Acrocephalus palustris*	NR/I/1
Reed Warbler★	*Acrocephalus scirpaceus*	NR13/Re/4
Great Reed Warbler★	*Acrocephalus arundinaceus*	NR13/Re/4
Olivaceous Warbler★	*Hippolais pallida*	NR13/Re/3
Icterine Warbler	*Hippolais icterina*	NR/I/1
Melodious Warbler★	*Hippolais polyglotta*	NR13/Re/4
Marmora's Warbler	*Sylvia sarda*	NR/I/1
Dartford Warbler★	*Sylvia undata*	RNR2/Re/4
Tristram's Warbler	*Sylvia deserticola*	NR/I/1
Spectacled Warbler★	*Sylvia conspicillata*	NR13/Re/3
Subalpine Warbler★	*Sylvia cantillans*	NR13/Re/4
Sardinian Warbler★	*Sylvia melanocephala*	RNR/Re/5

Species		Status[1]
Orphean Warbler★	*Sylvia hortensis*	NR13/Re/3
Lesser Whitethroat	*Sylvia curruca*	NR/I/1
Whitethroat★	*Sylvia communis*	NR13/Re/4
Garden Warbler	*Sylvia borin*	NR13/Re/4
Blackcap★	*Sylvia atricapilla*	RNR23/Re/5
Arctic Warbler	*Phylloscopus borealis*	NR/I/1
Yellow-browed Warbler	*Phylloscopus inornatus*	NR/I/1
Radde's Warbler	*Phylloscopus schwarzi*	NR/I/1
Dusky Warbler	*Phylloscopus fuscatus*	NR/I/1
Bonelli's Warbler★	*Phylloscopus bonelli*	NR13/Re/4
Wood Warbler	*Phylloscopus sibilatrix*	NR3/Re/2
Chiffchaff★	*Phylloscopus collybita*	RNR23/Re/5
Willow Warbler	*Phylloscopus trochilus*	NR13/Re/5
Goldcrest	*Regulus regulus*	NR/I/2
Firecrest★	*Regulus ignicapillus*	RNR23/Re/3
Spotted Flycatcher★	*Muscicapa striata*	NR13/Re/4
Red-breasted Flycatcher	*Ficedula parva*	NR/I/1
Collared Flycatcher	*Ficedula albicollis*	NR/I/1
Pied Flycatcher	*Ficedula hypoleuca*	NR13/Re/4
Long-tailed Tit★	*Aegithalos caudatus*	R/Re/2
Crested Tit★	*Parus cristatus*	R/Re/3
Coal Tit★	*Parus ater*	R/Re/2
Blue Tit★	*Parus caeruleus*	RNR/Re/5
Great Tit★	*Parus major*	R/Re/4
Nuthatch★	*Sitta europaea*	R/Re/2
Wallcreeper	*Tichodroma muraria*	NR/I/1
Short-toed Tree Creeper★	*Certhia brachydactyla*	R/Re/4
Penduline Tit	*Remiz pendulinus*	NR23/Re/3
Golden Oriole★	*Oriolus oriolus*	NR13/Re/3
Black-headed Bush Shrike★	*Tchagra senegala*	R/Re/3
Red-backed Shrike	*Lanius collurio*	NR/I/1
Great Grey Shrike★	*Lanius excubitor*	RNR/Re/3
Woodchat Shrike★	*Lanius senator*	NR13/Re/4
Masked Shrike	*Lanius nubicus*	NR/I/1
Jay★	*Garrulus glandarius*	R/Re/3
Azure-winged Magpie★	*Cyanopica cyana*	R/Re/3
Magpie★	*Pica pica*	R/Re/3
Alpine Chough	*Pyrrhocorax graculus*	NR/I/1
Chough★	*Pyrrhocorax pyrrhocorax*	R/Re/4
Jackdaw★	*Corvus monedula*	R/Re/5
Rook	*Corvus frugilegus*	NR/I/1
Carrion Crow	*Corvus corone*	NR/1/2
Raven★	*Corvus corax*	R/Re/3
Starling	*Sturnus vulgaris*	NR23/Re/5
Spotless Starling★	*Sturnus unicolor*	R/Re/5
House Sparrow★	*Passer domesticus*	RNR/Re/5
Spanish Sparrow★	*Passer hispaniolensis*	RNR/I/2

Species		Status[1]
Tree Sparrow★	*Passer montanus*	RNR/Re/3
Rock Sparrow★	*Petronia petronia*	R/Re/3
Common Waxbill	*Estrilda astrild*	NR/Re/2
Red Bishop	*Euplectes orix*	NR/I/1
Chaffinch★	*Fringilla coelebs*	RNR23/Re/5
Brambling	*Fringilla montifringilla*	NR23/Re/2
Serin★	*Serinus serinus*	RNR23/Re/5
Greenfinch★	*Carduelis chloris*	RNR23/Re/5
Goldfinch★	*Carduelis carduelis*	RNR23/Re/5
Siskin	*Carduelis spinus*	NR23/Re/4
Linnet★	*Carduelis cannabina*	RNR23/Re/5
Redpoll	*Carduelis flammea*	NR/I/2
Crossbill★	*Loxia curvirostra*	RNR/Re/3
Trumpeter Finch	*Bucanetes githagineus*	NR/I/2
Bullfinch	*Pyrrhula pyrrhula*	NR/I/2
Hawfinch★	*Coccothraustes coccothraustes*	RNR/Re/3
White-throated Sparrow	*Zonotrichia albicollis*	NR/I/1
Slate-coloured Junco	*Junco hyemalis*	NR/I/1
Snow Bunting	*Plectrophenax nivalis*	NR/I/1
Pine Bunting	*Emberiza leucocephalos*	NR/I/1
Yellowhammer	*Emberiza citrinella*	NR/I/2
Cirl Bunting★	*Emberiza cirlus*	R/Re/3
Rock Bunting★	*Emberiza cia*	R/Re/3
House Bunting	*Emberiza striolata*	NR/I/2
Ortolan Bunting★	*Emberiza hortulana*	NR13/Re/3
Little Bunting	*Emberiza pusilla*	NR/I/1
Reed Bunting	*Emberiza schoeniclus*	NR23/Re/3
Yellow-breasted Bunting	*Emberiza aureola*	NR/I/1
Red-headed Bunting	*Emberiza bruniceps*	NR/I/1
Black-headed Bunting	*Emberiza melanocephala*	NR/I/1
Corn Bunting★	*Miliaria calandra*	RNR/Re/5
Bobolink	*Dolichonyx oryzivorus*	NR/I/1

[1] *Key*

1st item: R, resident; NR, non-resident; RNR, resident and migratory populations. 1, Principal period of occurrence June–September; 2, principal period of occurrence October–January; 3, principal period of occurrence February–May.

2nd item: Re, regular; I, irregular.

3rd item: 1, rare; 2, scarce; 3, common; 4, abundant; 5, numerous.

★Breeding species.

Appendix 2: Dominant plant species in some habitats of the Strait of Gibraltar

Species	Habitat			Species	Habitat		
	1	2	3		1	2	3
Olea europaea	+	+		*Euphorbia characias*	+		
Osyris quadripartita	+	+		*Asphodelus ramosus*		+	
Rhamnus alaternus	+	+		*Laurus nobilis*		+	
Rhamnus frangula	+	+		*Ilex aquifolium*		+	
Pistacia lentiscus	+	+		*Chamaespartium tridentatum*	+	+	
Pistacia terebinthus	+			*Quercus fruticosa*	+	+	
Clematis cirrhosa	+	+		*Cistus populifolius*	+	+	
Simlax aspera	+	+		*Cistus salvifolius*		+	
Aristolochia baetica	+			*Cistus ladanifer*	+		
Callicotome villosa	+	+		*Cistus albidus*	+		
Teline linifolia	+	+		*Dittrichia viscosa*	+		
Chamaerops humilis	+			*Rosmarinus officinalis*	+		
Phlomis purpurea	+			*Asparagus albus*	+		
Ruscus hypophyllum	+	+		*Jasminum fruticans*	+		
Ruscus aculeatus		+		*Coronilla valentina*	+		
Quercus suber		+		*Halimium atriplicifolium*		+	
Quercus canariensis		+		*Teucrium fruticans*	+	+	
Pinus pinaster		+		*Lavandula stoechas*	+	+	
Pinus pinea		+		*Lavandula multifida*	+		
Pinus halepensis		+		*Lavandula dentata*	+		
Abies pinsapo		+		*Daphne gnidium*		+	
Juniperus oxycedrus		+		*Calluna vulgaris*	+	+	
Phillyrea latifolia	+	+		*Lithodora prostrata*	+		
Phillyrea angustifolia	+	+		*Arbutus unedo*	+	+	
Lonicera implexa	+	+		*Viburnum tinus*	+	+	
Ulex parviflorus	+	+		*Genista tridens*		+	
Stauracanthus bovinii	+			*Rhododendron ponticum*		+	
Quercus coccifera	+	+		*Digitalis purpurea*		+	
Myrtus communis	+	+		*Alnus glutinosa*		+	
Crataegus monogyna		+		*Fraxinus angustifolia*		+	
Pteridum aquilinum		+		*Populus albus*		+	
Davillia canariensis		+		*Ulmus minor*		+	
Hedera helix		+		*Arundo donax*	+		
Erica arborea	+	+		*Nerium oleander*	+	+	
Erica australis	+	+		*Acanthus mollis*	+	+	
Erica scoparia	+			*Dactylis glomerata*			+
Erica umbellata	+			*Aegylops geniculata*			+
Erica erigena	+			*Poa annua*			+
Erica ciliaris	+			*Cynodon dactylon*			+
Rubus ulmifolius		+		*Anthoxanthum ovatum*			+

Species	Habitat 1	2	3	Species	Habitat 1	2	3
Lolium perenne			+	*Chamaemellum fuscatum*			+
Lolium multiflorum			+	*Chamaemellum mixtum*			+
Agrostis pouretti			+	*Bellis annua*			+
Agrostis castellana			+	*Leonthodon taraxacoides*			+
Briza maxima			+	*Tolpis barbata*			+
Vulpia bromoides			+	*Calendula arvensis*	+		+
Vulpia geniculata			+	*Crepis capillaris*			+
Bromus rubens			+	*Silene colorata*			+
Bromus hordaceus			+	*Silene gallica*			+
Bromus madritensis			+	*Spergula arvensis*			+
Hedysarum coronarium			+	*Diplotaxis siifolia*			+
Tetranoglobulus purpureus			+	*Capsella rubella*			+
Lotus subbiflorus			+	*Raphanus raphanistrum*			+
Ornithopus compressus			+	*Erodium cicutarium*			+
Lathyrus angulatus			+	*Geranium molle*			+
Medicago polimphora			+	*Plantago lagopus*			+
Medicago trunculata			+	*Plantago lanceolata*			+
Trifolium campestre			+	*Plantago coronopus*			+
Trifolium baeticum			+	*Scilla peruviana*	+		+
Trifolium stellatum			+	*Asphodellus albus*	+		+
Trifolium subterraneum			+	*Asphodellus fistulosus*	+		+
Trifolium resupinatum			+	*Narcisus papyraceus*	+		+
Trifolium repens			+	*Iris filifolia*	+		+
Carlina corymbosa			+	*Gynadiris sisyrinchium*	+		+
Carlina racemosa			+	*Gladiolus illyricus*			+
Scolymus hispanicus	+		+	*Gladiolus communis*	+		
Scolymus maculatus			+	*Urginea maritima*			+
Cynara humilis			+	*Scilla autumnalis*	+		+
Galactytes tomentosa	+		+	*Leucojum tricophyllum*			+
Xanthium stumanium			+				

Key: 1, matorral; 2, woodland; 3, pastures.
Based on Fernandez-Pasquier (1982), Finlayson and Cortes (1987), Fernandez-Palacios *et al.* (1988).

Appendix 3: Mean densities of breeding birds in sites described in Chapter 6

	Density (birds/10 ha)			
Species	Zahara	Trebujena	Janda	Ojén
Little Bittern	—	—	0.7	—
Cattle Egret	33.3	5.4	14.3	—
Little Egret	—	9.2	2.9	—
Grey Heron	—	0.8	—	—
Purple Heron	—	1.5	—	—
White Stork	—	—	7.1	—
Spoonbill	—	6.2	—	—
Mallard	—	3.1	35.0	—
Black Kite	—	31.5	4.3	—
Red Kite	—	1.5	—	—
Griffon Vulture	—	—	5.7	9.2
Short-toed Eagle	2.5	—	0.7	0.8
Marsh Harrier	—	0.8	0.7	—
Montagu's Harrier	1.7	—	2.1	—
Sparrowhawk	—	—	—	—
Goshawk	—	—	—	—
Buzzard	—	—	—	—
Golden Eagle	—	—	—	—
Booted Eagle	—	—	—	2.5
Kestrel	2.5	0.8	1.4	1.7
Hobby	—	—	—	—
Peregrine	—	—	—	—
Red-legged Partridge	—	—	2.9	—
Barbary Partridge	—	—	—	—
Quail	—	—	—	—
Moorhen	—	10.8	4.3	—
Little Bustard	—	—	—	—
Black-winged Stilt	—	7.7	—	—
Collared Pratincole	—	11.5	1.4	—
Lapwing	—	11.5	—	—
Redshank	—	7.7	—	—
Yellow-legged Gull	—	—	—	—
Whiskered Tern	—	27.7	—	—
Pin-tailed Sandgrouse	—	1.5	—	—
Rock Dove	—	—	—	—
Woodpigeon	—	—	—	—
Turtle Dove	—	0.8	4.3	—
Cuckoo	1.7	—	2.9	15.0
Barn Owl	—	—	0.7	—
Little Owl	—	—	—	—

	Density (birds/10 ha)			
Species	Zahara	Trebujena	Janda	Ojén
Swift	1.5	3.6	197.5	
Pallid Swift	—	—	—	—
Bee-eater	—	—	1.4	0.8
Hoopoe	—	—	0.7	—
Wryneck	—	—	—	—
Green Woodpecker	—	—	—	—
Great Spotted Woodpecker	—	—	—	—
Calandra Lark	22.5	14.6	10.7	—
Short-toed Lark	1.7	3.1	3.6	—
Lesser Short-toed Lark	—	1.5	—	—
Crested Lark	11.7	15.4	5.0	—
Thekla Lark	—	—	—	3.3
Woodlark	—	—	—	5.0
Skylark	—	—	—	—
Crag Martin	—	—	—	—
Swallow	—	20.8	2.1	5.8
Red-rumped Swallow	—	—	—	—
House Martin	—	—	71.4	—
Tawny Pipit	0.8	—	—	4.2
Yellow Wagtail	—	19.2	8.6	—
Grey Wagtail	—	—	—	—
Wren	—	—	—	—
Rufous Bush Chat	—	—	—	—
Robin	—	—	—	—
Nightingale	—	—	2.1	6.7
Black Redstart	—	—	—	—
Redstart	—	—	—	—
Stonechat	11.7	—	8.6	15.8
Wheatear	—	—	—	—
Black-eared Wheatear	—	—	0.7	0.8
Black Wheatear	—	—	—	—
Rock Thrush	—	—	—	—
Blue Rock Thrush	—	—	—	—
Blackbird	—	—	—	0.8
Mistle Thrush	—	—	—	—
Cetti's Warbler	—	—	4.3	—
Fan-tailed Warbler	9.2	8.5	14.3	5.0
Great Reed Warbler	—	10.8	6.4	—
Olivaceous Warbler	—	—	—	1.7
Melodious Warbler	—	—	—	—
Dartford Warbler	—	—	—	—
Spectacled Warbler	—	—	—	—
Subalpine Warbler	—	—	—	—
Sardinian Warbler	0.8	—	1.4	3.3
Orphean Warbler	—	—	—	—
Whitethroat	—	—	1.4	—

Continued.

Species	Density (birds/10 ha)			
	Zahara	Trebujena	Janda	Ojén
Blackcap	—	—	—	—
Bonelli's Warbler	—	—	—	—
Chiffchaff	—	—	—	—
Firecrest	—	—	—	—
Spotted Flycatcher	—	—	—	—
Crested Tit	—	—	—	—
Coal Tit	—	—	—	—
Blue Tit	—	—	—	1.7
Great Tit	—	—	—	—
Nuthatch	—	—	—	—
Short-toed Tree Creeper	—	—	—	—
Golden Oriole	—	—	—	0.8
Great Grey Shrike	—	—	—	—
Woodchat Shrike	—	—	—	6.7
Jay	—	—	—	0.8
Azure-winged Magpie	—	—	—	—
Magpie	—	—	—	—
Chough	—	—	—	—
Jackdaw	—	3.9	5.7	—
Raven	—	1.5	0.7	0.8
Spotless Starling	21.7	—	2.9	8.3
House Sparrow	—	—	2.1	0.8
Spanish Sparrow	—	—	—	—
Tree Sparrow	—	—	2.1	—
Rock Sparrow	—	—	—	—
Chaffinch	—	—	—	0.8
Serin	—	—	1.4	3.3
Greenfinch	—	—	5.0	—
Goldfinch	15.0	3.9	20.7	20.0
Linnet	—	11.5	5.7	4.2
Crossbill	—	—	—	—
Hawfinch	—	—	—	—
Cirl Bunting	—	—	—	—
Rock Bunting	—	—	—	0.8
Corn Bunting	48.3	—	13.6	23.3

Species	Density (birds/10 ha)				
	Manilva	Carnero	Gibmaq	Jara	Jimena
Little Bittern	—	—	—	—	—
Cattle Egret	—	—	—	—	—
Little Egret	—	—	—	—	—
Grey Heron	—	—	—	—	—
Purple Heron	—	—	—	—	—
White Stork	—	—	—	—	—
Spoonbill	—	—	—	—	—

Species	Density (birds/10 ha)				
	Manilva	Carnero	Gibmaq	Jara	Jimena
Mallard	—	—	—	—	—
Black Kite	—	—	—	—	—
Red Kite	—	—	—	—	—
Griffon Vulture	—	6.0	—	—	3.0
Short-toed Eagle	—	—	—	—	—
Marsh Harrier	—	—	—	—	—
Montagu's Harrier	—	—	—	—	—
Sparrowhawk	—	—	—	—	—
Goshawk	—	—	—	—	1.0
Buzzard	0.8	—	—	—	—
Golden Eagle	—	—	—	—	—
Booted Eagle	—	—	—	—	1.0
Kestrel	6.9	4.7	1.0	1.0	—
Hobby	—	—	—	—	—
Peregrine	—	—	2.0	—	—
Red-legged Partridge	—	0.7	—	—	—
Barbary Partridge	—	—	—	—	—
Quail	—	—	—	—	—
Moorhen	—	—	—	—	—
Little Bustard	—	—	—	—	—
Black-winged Stilt	—	—	—	—	—
Collared Pratincole	—	—	—	—	—
Lapwing	—	—	—	—	—
Redshank	—	—	—	—	—
Yellow-legged Gull	—	—	—	—	—
Whiskered Tern	—	—	—	—	—
Pin-tailed Sandgrouse	—	—	—	—	—
Rock Dove	—	—	—	—	—
Woodpigeon	—	—	—	—	—
Turtle Dove	—	—	—	2.0	—
Cuckoo	—	—	—	4.0	7.0
Barn Owl	—	—	—	—	—
Little Owl	—	0.7	—	—	—
Swift	7.7	—	—	—	—
Pallid Swift	—	—	—	—	—
Bee-eater	—	—	—	—	—
Hoopoe	—	—	—	—	—
Wryneck	—	—	—	—	—
Green Woodpecker	—	—	—	—	—
Great Spotted Woodpecker	—	—	—	—	—
Calandra Lark	—	—	—	—	—
Short-toed Lark	—	—	—	—	—
Lesser Short-toed Lark	—	—	—	—	—
Crested Lark	20.8	—	—	1.0	—
Thekla Lark	—	—	—	—	—
Woodlark	—	—	—	—	3.0

Continued.

| | Density (birds/10 ha) | | | | |
Species	Manilva	Carnero	Gibmaq	Jara	Jimena
Skylark	—	—	—	—	—
Crag Martin	—	—	—	—	4.0
Swallow	2.3	4.0	—	9.0	—
Red-rumped Swallow	—	—	—	—	—
House Martin	3.1	3.3	—	—	—
Tawny Pipit	—	—	—	—	—
Yellow Wagtail	—	—	—	—	—
Grey Wagtail	—	—	—	—	—
Wren	—	4.7	7.0	—	6.0
Rufous Bush Chat	—	—	—	1.0	—
Robin	—	—	—	—	—
Nightingale	—	7.3	—	28.0	—
Black Redstart	—	—	—	—	—
Redstart	—	—	—	—	—
Stonechat	9.2	20.7	—	14.0	9.0
Wheatear	—	—	—	—	—
Black-eared Wheatear	0.8	—	—	—	3.0
Black Wheatear	—	—	—	—	—
Rock Thrush	—	—	—	—	—
Blue Rock Thrush	—	—	—	—	—
Blackbird	1.5	10.0	18.0	4.0	1.0
Mistle Thrush	—	—	—	—	—
Cetti's Warbler	—	—	—	3.0	—
Fan-tailed Warbler	13.1	—	—	6.0	—
Great Reed Warbler	—	—	—	—	—
Olivaceous Warbler	—	—	—	2.0	—
Melodious Warbler	—	1.3	—	4.0	—
Dartford Warbler	8.5	—	—	—	16.0
Spectacled Warbler	5.4	—	—	—	—
Subalpine Warbler	—	—	—	—	—
Sardinian Warbler	16.2	32.0	25.0	24.0	20.0
Orphean Warbler	—	—	—	1.0	—
Whitethroat	—	—	—	—	—
Blackcap	—	—	27.0	6.0	—
Bonelli's Warbler	—	—	—	—	—
Chiffchaff	—	—	—	—	—
Firecrest	—	—	—	—	—
Spotted Flycatcher	—	—	—	—	—
Crested Tit	—	—	—	—	—
Coal Tit	—	—	—	—	—
Blue Tit	—	—	4.0	—	1.0
Great Tit	—	0.7	1.0	—	—
Nuthatch	—	—	—	—	—
Short-toed Tree Creeper	—	—	—	—	—
Golden Oriole	—	—	—	—	—
Great Grey Shrike	—	—	—	—	—

Species	Density (birds/10 ha)				
	Manilva	Carnero	Gibmaq	Jara	Jimena
Woodchat Shrike	0.8	0.7	—	5.0	—
Jay	—	—	—	—	—
Azure-winged Magpie	—	—	—	—	—
Magpie	—	—	—	—	—
Chough	—	—	—	—	—
Jackdaw	—	—	—	—	—
Raven	—	—	—	—	—
Spotless Starling	—	—	—	1.0	—
House Sparrow	0.8	—	—	1.0	—
Spanish Sparrow	—	—	—	—	—
Tree Sparrow	—	—	—	—	—
Rock Sparrow	—	—	—	—	—
Chaffinch	—	—	—	1.0	—
Serin	1.5	0.7	2.0	2.0	—
Greenfinch	—	0.7	—	1.0	—
Goldfinch	10.0	11.3	—	10.0	—
Linnet	8.5	2.0	—	—	2.0
Crossbill	—	—	—	—	—
Hawfinch	—	—	—	—	—
Cirl Bunting	—	2.0	—	—	—
Rock Bunting	—	—	—	—	5.0
Corn Bunting	11.5	—	—	24.0	—

Species	Density (birds/10 ha)				
	Blsc	Nvsc	Gbmsc	Grsc	Nvclf
Little Bittern	—	—	—	—	—
Cattle Egret	—	—	—	—	—
Little Egret	—	—	—	—	—
Grey Heron	—	—	—	—	—
Purple Heron	—	—	—	—	—
White Stork	—	—	—	—	—
Spoonbill	—	—	—	—	—
Mallard	—	—	—	—	—
Black Kite	—	—	—	—	—
Red Kite	—	—	—	—	—
Griffon Vulture	—	—	—	2.0	—
Short-toed Eagle	—	—	—	—	1.0
Marsh Harrier	—	—	—	—	—
Montagu's Harrier	—	—	—	—	—
Sparrowhawk	—	—	—	—	—
Goshawk	—	—	—	—	—
Buzzard	—	—	—	—	—
Golden Eagle	0.9	—	—	0.7	—
Booted Eagle	—	1.1	—	—	—
Kestrel	—	—	—	2.7	2.0

Continued.

Species	Density (birds/10 ha)				
	Blsc	Nvsc	Gbmsc	Grsc	Nvclf
Hobby	—	—	—	—	—
Peregrine	—	—	1.0	—	—
Red-legged Partridge	—	—	—	2.7	2.0
Barbary Partridge	—	—	6.0	—	—
Quail	—	—	—	—	—
Moorhen	—	—	—	—	—
Little Bustard	—	—	—	—	—
Black-winged Stilt	—	—	—	—	—
Collared Pratincole	—	—	—	—	—
Lapwing	—	—	—	—	—
Redshank	—	—	—	—	—
Yellow-legged Gull	—	—	399.0	—	—
Whiskered Tern	—	—	—	—	—
Pin-tailed Sandgrouse	—	—	—	—	—
Rock Dove	—	—	—	2.7	—
Woodpigeon	—	2.5	—	—	—
Turtle Dove	—	—	—	—	—
Cuckoo	—	1.1	—	3.3	—
Barn Owl	—	—	—	—	—
Little Owl	—	—	—	—	—
Swift	—	—	—	2.7	—
Pallid Swift	—	—	94.0	0.7	—
Bee-eater	—	4.4	—	1.3	—
Hoopoe	—	—	—	—	—
Wryneck	—	—	—	—	—
Green Woodpecker	—	—	—	2.0	—
Great Spotted Woodpecker	—	—	—	—	—
Calandra Lark	—	—	—	—	—
Short-toed Lark	—	—	—	—	—
Lesser Short-toed Lark	—	—	—	—	—
Crested Lark	—	—	—	—	—
Thekla Lark	—	—	—	—	2.0
Woodlark	—	4.4	—	1.3	1.0
Skylark	—	—	—	—	5.0
Crag Martin	—	1.1	—	4.0	—
Swallow	—	—	—	—	—
Red-rumped Swallow	—	—	—	—	—
House Martin	—	—	—	2.0	—
Tawny Pipit	—	—	—	—	2.0
Yellow Wagtail	—	—	—	—	—
Grey Wagtail	—	—	—	0.7	—
Wren	2.7	—	3.0	1.3	2.0
Rufous Bush Chat	—	—	—	—	—
Robin	—	—	—	—	—
Nightingale	2.7	5.6	—	1.3	—
Black Redstart	—	—	—	2.0	13.0

Species	Density (birds/10 ha)				
	Blsc	Nvsc	Gbmsc	Grsc	Nvclf
Redstart	—	—	—	—	—
Stonechat	0.9	2.2	—	4.7	5.0
Wheatear	—	—	—	—	13.0
Black-eared Wheatear	—	—	—	6.7	7.0
Black Wheatear	—	2.2	—	4.7	—
Rock Thrush	—	—	—	—	6.0
Blue Rock Thrush	—	1.1	12.0	9.3	4.0
Blackbird	0.9	6.7	3.0	2.0	2.0
Mistle Thrush	—	2.2	—	—	4.0
Cetti's Warbler	—	—	—	—	—
Fan-tailed Warbler	—	—	—	—	—
Great Reed Warbler	—	—	—	—	—
Olivaceous Warbler	—	—	—	—	—
Melodious Warbler	0.9	—	—	2.0	—
Dartford Warbler	19.1	1.1	—	0.7	1.0
Spectacled Warbler	—	—	—	—	—
Subalpine Warbler	0.9	7.8	—	1.3	8.0
Sardinian Warbler	4.6	1.1	10.0	3.3	—
Orphean Warbler	—	2.2	—	—	—
Whitethroat	—	—	—	—	—
Blackcap	—	—	1.0	—	—
Bonelli's Warbler	—	8.9	—	1.3	1.0
Chiffchaff	—	—	—	—	—
Firecrest	—	1.1	—	—	—
Spotted Flycatcher	—	1.1	—	—	—
Crested Tit	—	—	—	—	—
Coal Tit	—	—	—	—	4.0
Blue Tit	0.9	3.3	—	0.7	—
Great Tit	—	4.4	—	2.0	—
Nuthatch	—	—	—	—	—
Short-toed Tree Creeper	—	—	—	—	—
Golden Oriole	—	—	—	—	—
Great Grey Shrike	—	—	—	—	2.0
Woodchat Shrike	—	—	—	—	—
Jay	—	1.1	—	—	—
Azure-winged Magpie	—	—	—	—	—
Magpie	—	—	—	—	—
Chough	2.7	4.4	—	48.0	12.0
Jackdaw	—	2.2	—	17.3	—
Raven	—	—	—	—	—
Spotless Starling	—	—	1.0	—	—
House Sparrow	—	—	9.0	—	—
Spanish Sparrow	—	—	—	—	—
Tree Sparrow	—	—	—	—	—
Rock Sparrow	—	—	—	2.0	—
Chaffinch	—	5.6	—	—	8.0

Continued.

Species	Density (birds/10 ha)				
	Blsc	Nvsc	Gbmsc	Grsc	Nvclf
Serin	1.8	2.2	—	5.3	5.0
Greenfinch	—	—	—	2.0	—
Goldfinch	—	15.6	—	9.3	7.0
Linnet	5.5	1.1	—	9.3	5.0
Crossbill	—	—	—	—	2.0
Hawfinch	—	—	—	—	—
Cirl Bunting	—	2.2	—	—	—
Rock Bunting	1.8	1.1	1.0	2.7	15.0
Corn Bunting	—	6.7	—	1.3	—

Species	Density (birds/10 ha)				
	Prey	Alg	Blanca	Bermeja	Nieves
Little Bittern	—	—	—	—	—
Cattle Egret	—	—	—	—	—
Little Egret	—	—	—	—	—
Grey Heron	—	—	—	—	—
Purple Heron	—	—	—	—	—
White Stork	—	—	—	—	—
Spoonbill	—	—	—	—	—
Mallard	—	—	—	—	—
Black Kite	0.9	43.8	—	—	—
Red Kite	—	—	—	—	—
Griffon Vulture	—	—	—	—	—
Short-toed Eagle	—	—	—	—	1.3
Marsh Harrier	—	—	—	—	—
Montagu's Harrier	—	—	—	—	—
Sparrowhawk	—	—	—	1.0	—
Goshawk	—	—	—	—	—
Buzzard	—	—	—	—	—
Golden Eagle	—	—	—	—	—
Booted Eagle	0.9	—	—	1.0	—
Kestrel	—	—	0.6	—	2.5
Hobby	—	1.3	—	—	—
Peregrine	—	—	—	—	—
Red-legged Partridge	—	—	—	—	1.3
Barbary Partridge	—	—	—	—	—
Quail	—	—	—	—	3.8
Moorhen	—	—	—	—	—
Little Bustard	—	—	—	—	—
Black-winged Stilt	—	—	—	—	—
Collared Pratincole	—	—	—	—	—
Lapwing	—	—	—	—	—
Redshank	—	—	—	—	—
Yellow-legged Gull	—	—	—	—	—
Whiskered Tern	—	—	—	—	—

Species	Density (birds/10 ha)				
	Prey	Alg	Blanca	Bermeja	Nieves
Pin-tailed Sandgrouse	—	—	—	—	—
Rock Dove	—	—	—	—	—
Woodpigeon	2.7	1.3	2.5	1.0	3.8
Turtle Dove	2.7	2.5	—	—	—
Cuckoo	6.4	—	—	—	1.3
Barn Owl	—	—	—	—	—
Little Owl	—	—	—	—	—
Swift	9.1	—	—	—	—
Pallid Swift	—	—	—	—	—
Bee-eater	7.3	—	—	—	—
Hoopoe	—	1.3	—	—	—
Wryneck	1.8	—	—	1.0	—
Green Woodpecker	—	—	4.4	—	6.3
Great Spotted Woodpecker	—	—	0.6	—	—
Calandra Lark	—	—	—	—	—
Short-toed Lark	—	—	—	—	—
Lesser Short-toed Lark	—	—	—	—	—
Crested Lark	—	—	—	—	—
Thekla Lark	—	—	—	—	1.3
Woodlark	5.5	—	—	—	6.3
Skylark	—	—	—	—	—
Crag Martin	—	—	—	—	—
Swallow	2.7	—	—	—	—
Red-rumped Swallow	—	—	—	—	—
House Martin	0.9	—	—	—	—
Tawny Pipit	—	—	—	—	—
Yellow Wagtail	—	—	—	—	—
Grey Wagtail	—	—	—	—	—
Wren	0.9	—	8.1	6.0	—
Rufous Bush Chat	—	—	—	—	—
Robin	—	—	1.9	—	—
Nightingale	9.1	1.3	4.4	—	—
Black Redstart	—	—	—	—	—
Redstart	—	—	—	—	1.3
Stonechat	1.8	—	—	—	5.0
Wheatear	—	—	—	—	—
Black-eared Wheatear	—	—	—	—	3.8
Black Wheatear	—	—	—	—	—
Rock Thrush	—	—	—	—	—
Blue Rock Thrush	—	—	—	—	1.3
Blackbird	10.0	—	5.6	3.0	3.8
Mistle Thrush	—	—	—	—	—
Cetti's Warbler	—	—	—	—	—
Fan-tailed Warbler	—	—	—	—	—
Great Reed Warbler	—	—	—	—	—
Olivaceous Warbler	—	—	—	—	1.3

Continued.

Species	Density (birds/10 ha)				
	Prey	Alg	Blanca	Bermeja	Nieves
Melodious Warbler	—	—	—	—	7.5
Dartford Warbler	—	—	3.1	14.0	—
Spectacled Warbler	—	—	—	—	—
Subalpine Warbler	—	—	2.5	—	12.5
Sardinian Warbler	4.6	21.3	1.9	—	—
Orphean Warbler	0.9	—	—	—	2.5
Whitethroat	—	—	—	—	—
Blackcap	0.9	—	3.8	1.0	—
Bonelli's Warbler	1.8	—	—	—	2.5
Chiffchaff	—	—	—	—	—
Firecrest	1.8	—	0.6	2.0	—
Spotted Flycatcher	—	—	3.1	—	—
Crested Tit	—	—	1.9	3.0	5.0
Coal Tit	—	—	2.5	—	2.5
Blue Tit	3.6	1.3	1.3	—	2.5
Great Tit	2.7	15.0	1.9	5.0	1.3
Nuthatch	—	—	—	—	—
Short-toed Tree Creeper	—	3.8	1.3	6.0	—
Golden Oriole	2.7	—	—	—	—
Great Grey Shrike	—	—	—	—	1.3
Woodchat Shrike	13.6	—	—	—	1.3
Jay	1.8	—	—	2.0	1.3
Azure-winged Magpie	—	35.0	—	—	—
Magpie	—	1.3	—	—	—
Chough	—	—	1.3	—	8.8
Jackdaw	—	—	—	—	—
Raven	—	2.5	—	—	—
Spotless Starling	—	1.3	—	—	—
House Sparrow	—	—	—	—	—
Spanish Sparrow	—	—	—	—	10.0
Tree Sparrow	—	15.0	—	—	—
Rock Sparrow	—	—	—	—	—
Chaffinch	9.1	2.5	9.4	7.0	10.0
Serin	—	—	13.1	1.0	2.5
Greenfinch	11.8	—	0.6	—	1.3
Goldfinch	7.3	—	0.6	—	5.0
Linnet	—	—	—	2.0	3.8
Crossbill	—	—	0.6	—	3.8
Hawfinch	1.8	—	—	—	—
Cirl Bunting	4.6	—	—	—	—
Rock Bunting	—	—	—	6.0	6.3
Corn Bunting	7.3	—	—	—	3.8

Species	Density (birds/10 ha)			
	Benalup	Almoraima	Valdeinfierno	Grazalema
Little Bittern	—	—	—	—
Cattle Egret	15.0	—	—	—
Little Egret	—	—	—	—
Grey Heron	—	—	—	—
Purple Heron	—	—	—	—
White Stork	—	—	—	—
Spoonbill	—	—	—	—
Mallard	—	—	—	—
Black Kite	3.6	—	—	—
Red Kite	—	—	—	—
Griffon Vulture	0.7	—	—	—
Short-toed Eagle	—	—	—	—
Marsh Harrier	—	—	—	—
Montagu's Harrier	—	—	—	—
Sparrowhawk	—	—	—	—
Goshawk	—	—	—	—
Buzzard	3.6	1.3	—	—
Golden Eagle	—	—	—	—
Booted Eagle	5.0	0.7	—	—
Kestrel	0.7	—	—	—
Hobby	—	—	—	—
Peregrine	—	—	—	—
Red-legged Partridge	2.1	—	—	—
Barbary Partridge	—	—	—	—
Quail	—	—	—	—
Moorhen	—	—	—	—
Little Bustard	—	—	—	—
Black-winged Stilt	—	—	—	—
Collared Pratincole	—	—	—	—
Lapwing	—	—	—	—
Redshank	—	—	—	—
Yellow-legged Gull	—	—	—	—
Whiskered Tern	—	—	—	—
Pin-tailed Sandgrouse	—	—	—	—
Rock Dove	—	—	—	—
Woodpigeon	1.4	5.3	8.3	0.5
Turtle Dove	7.1	2.0	—	—
Cuckoo	12.1	4.0	9.2	4.2
Barn Owl	—	—	—	—
Little Owl	—	—	—	—
Swift	—	—	—	—
Pallid Swift	0.7	—	—	—
Bee-eater	7.9	10.0	—	4.2
Hoopoe	8.6	—	—	—
Wryneck	—	—	—	—
Green Woodpecker	—	—	—	0.8

Continued.

Species	Density (birds/10 ha)			
	Benalup	Almoraima	Valdeinfierno	Grazalema
Great Spotted Woodpecker	1.4	—	2.5	4.2
Calandra Lark	—	—	—	—
Short-toed Lark	—	—	—	—
Lesser Short-toed Lark	—	—	—	—
Crested Lark	1.4	—	—	—
Thekla Lark	—	—	—	—
Woodlark	2.1	0.7	—	0.8
Skylark	—	—	—	—
Crag Martin	—	1.3	—	—
Swallow	5.0	0.7	1.7	—
Red-rumped Swallow	7.1	2.0	—	0.8
House Martin	—	—	—	—
Tawny Pipit	—	—	—	—
Yellow Wagtail	—	—	—	—
Grey Wagtail	—	—	—	—
Wren	1.4	4.0	3.3	5.8
Rufous Bush Chat	—	—	—	—
Robin	—	0.7	2.5	7.5
Nightingale	10.7	10.7	0.8	10.8
Black Redstart	—	—	—	—
Redstart	—	—	—	—
Stonechat	5.7	0.7	—	1.7
Wheatear	—	—	—	—
Black-eared Wheatear	0.7	—	—	—
Black Wheatear	—	—	—	—
Rock Thrush	—	—	—	—
Blue Rock Thrush	—	—	—	—
Blackbird	—	1.3	1.7	3.3
Mistle Thrush	—	2.7	5.8	2.5
Cetti's Warbler	—	—	—	—
Fan-tailed Warbler	—	—	—	—
Great Reed Warbler	—	—	—	—
Olivaceous Warbler	—	1.3	—	—
Melodious Warbler	1.4	—	—	2.5
Dartford Warbler	—	—	—	1.7
Spectacled Warbler	—	—	—	—
Subalpine Warbler	—	—	—	11.7
Sardinian Warbler	12.9	7.3	—	4.2
Orphean Warbler	—	—	—	—
Whitethroat	—	—	—	—
Blackcap	0.7	4.7	9.2	2.5
Bonelli's Warbler	0.7	2.7	16.7	10.0
Chiffchaff	—	—	5.0	0.8
Firecrest	—	—	3.3	3.3
Spotted Flycatcher	4.3	1.3	0.8	0.8
Crested Tit	—	—	5.0	2.5

Species	Density (birds/10 ha)			
	Benalup	Almoraima	Valdeinfierno	Grazalema
Coal Tit	—	—	—	—
Blue Tit	13.6	8.7	9.2	8.3
Great Tit	4.3	2.7	5.8	1.7
Nuthatch	—	—	—	0.8
Short-toed Tree Creeper	4.3	—	7.5	3.3
Golden Oriole	—	—	5.8	2.5
Great Grey Shrike	—	—	—	—
Woodchat Shrike	6.4	—	—	—
Jay	—	2.7	3.3	1.7
Azure-winged Magpie	—	—	—	—
Magpie	—	—	—	—
Chough	—	—	—	—
Jackdaw	7.9	—	—	—
Raven	—	—	—	—
Spotless Starling	1.4	3.3	1.7	
House Sparrow	9.3	—	—	—
Spanish Sparrow	—	—	—	—
Tree Sparrow	—	—	—	—
Rock Sparrow	—	—	—	—
Chaffinch	3.6	3.3	28.3	8.3
Serin	10.7	6.7	—	5.8
Greenfinch	9.3	2.0	—	0.8
Goldfinch	20.0	7.3	—	8.3
Linnet	—	—	—	—
Crossbill	—	—	—	—
Hawfinch	5.0	0.7	5.0	—
Cirl Bunting	—	2.7	—	0.8
Rock Bunting	—	0.7	—	—
Corn Bunting	4.3	—	—	—

Key: Gibmaq, Gibraltar maquis; Blsc, Blauca scrub; Nvsc, Nieves scrub; Gbmsc, Gibraltar cliff scrub; Grsc, Grazalema scrub; Nvclf, Nieves low scrub; Prey, Pinar del Rey; Alg, Algaida.

Appendix 4: Methods used in some of the studies described in the text

CHAPTER 2

The soaring bird figures were derived as follows. Spring data were compiled from the Rock of Gibraltar alone from days when westerly winds directed passage over this peninsula. The data used spanned the period 1971–87 (not all years), and there were therefore sufficient days of suitable winds in each time-period. This allowed mean counts per day with appropriate confidence limits to be established for each species. The autumn data were derived from Bernis's (1980) counts across the width of the Strait in 1976 and 1977.

CHAPTER 3

The passerine data used in the figures were based on data gathered from Windmill Hill, Gibraltar, over a period of years from 1970 to 1989. The site censused was a standard 13 ha. In certain specific instances, data from 1987 and from a detailed study conducted at this site by the author in the spring of 1984 have been used. In the latter case, this site was censused daily from February to May.

CHAPTER 4

Waterfowl and wader counts used in this chapter are maximum recorded counts for each month in the published records of the Strait of Gibraltar Bird Observatory or obtained by the author for the period 1985–89 in the main wetlands censused regularly (i.e. Bonanza saltpans, Laguna de Medina, Los Lances Beach).

CHAPTER 5

Data used are derived from the author's extensive observations off Europa Point (and other sites where specified) from 1971 to 1989. In the case of the figures, these cover the period July 1982 to June 1983, when observations at Europa Point were made almost daily. Other years have also been used (e.g. for Audouin's Gulls or Kittiwakes).

CHAPTER 6

The data presented on breeding and wintering bird counts were derived from spot censusing studies carried out by the author in the sites described in 1987–89. The method involved stopping at specified sites within the habitat and recording all birds seen or heard within a radius of 50 m of the observer within 10 min. Additional birds seen outside this radius were recorded separately and were used in the information presented for other species (e.g. non-passerines). Within-habitat dispersion is measured using the Simpson index for individual plots in each habitat and between-habitat dispersion using the same index from global habitat data. Within-habitat abundance similarly measures abundance per plot and between-habitat abundance, per habitat.

Further information on methods is available in published papers or those which are in the process of publication at present.

Note. In all figures, confidence limits are 95% confidence limits of the mean.

Appendix 5: Abbreviations used in Chapters 6 and 7

GROUP CODES USED IN CHAPTER 6

BUN	Buntings	PIP	Pipits and Wagtails
CHA	Chats and Thrushes	SHR	Shrikes
COR	Corvids	SPA	Sparrows
FIN	Finches	STA	Starlings
HIR	Hirundines	STT	Short-toed Tree Creeper
LAR	Larks	TIT	Tits
ORI	Golden Oriole	WAR	Warblers
PEN	Penduline Tit	WRE	Wren

SEASON CODES USED IN CHAPTER 6

After the species code, BR refers to the breeding season and WN to the winter.

HABITAT CODES USED IN CHAPTER 6

B	Broad-leaved woodland	O	Open ground
M	Mattoral	P	Pine Woodland

Numbers after letters refer to sites named in the text. In figures, sites are arranged in approximate order of decreasing vegetation height and density.

SPECIES CODES USED IN CHAPTER 7

AVOC	Avocet	GRHE	Grey Heron
BLHG	Black-headed Gull	GRSA	Green Sandpiper
BLTG	Black-tailed Godwit	GRSK	Greenshank
BNGR	Black-necked Grebe	KENT	Kentish Plover
BWST	Black-winged Stilt	KNOT	Knot
COOT	Coot	LAPW	Lapwing
COSA	Common Sandpiper	LBIT	Little Bittern
CURS	Curlew Sandpiper	LEGR	Little Egret
DUNL	Dunlin	LGRE	Little Grebe
GADW	Gadwall	LIRP	Little Ringed Plover
GARG	Garganey	LITT	Little Tern
GBTE	Gull-billed Tern	LSTI	Little Stint
GCGR	Great Crested Grebe	MALL	Mallard
GFLA	Greater Flamingo	MARB	Marbled Duck
GREY	Grey Plover	MOOR	Moorhen

PINT	Pintail	RUFF	Ruff
POCH	Pochard	SHOV	Shoveler
PRAT	Collared Pratincole	SNIP	Snipe
PUGA	Purple Gallinule	SPRD	Spotted Redshank
PURH	Purple Heron	TEAL	Teal
RCPO	Red-crested Pochard	WHDU	White-headed Duck
REDS	Redshank	WOOD	Wood Sandpiper
RINP	Ringed Plover	WSTO	White Stork

SPECIES CODES USED IN FIGURE 37, PAGE 78

TD	Turtle Dove	WW	Willow Warbler
HP	Hoopoe	CC	Chiffchaff
SK	Skylark	MW	Melodious Warbler
ST	Short-toed Lark	FW	Fan-tailed Warbler
CL	Crested Lark	RB	Robin
WD	Woodlark	NG	Nightingale
MP	Meadow Pipit	BR	Black Redstart
TP	Tree Pipit	RD	Redstart
TW	Tawny Pipit	WN	Whinchat
YW	Yellow Wagtail	ST	Stonechat
WW	White Wagtail	WR	Wheatear
GW	Grey Wagtail	BW	Black-eared Wheatear
WH	Whitethroat	ST	Song Thrush
BC	Blackcap	PF	Pied Flycatcher
GW	Garden Warbler	SF	Spotted Flycatcher
SB	Subalpine Warbler	GF	Goldfinch
SP	Spectacled Warbler	GR	Greenfinch
OP	Orphean Warbler	CH	Chaffinch
DF	Dartford Warbler	SR	Serin

References

Able, K.D. and Noon, B.R. (1976) Avian community structure along elevational gradients in the Northeastern United States. *Oecologia* **26**: 275–294.

Abramsky, Z. and Safriel, U. (1980) Seasonal patterns in a Mediterranean bird community composed of transient, wintering and resident passerines. *Ornis. Scand.* **11**: 201–216.

Acosta Bono, G. (1984) *Plan espacial de proteccion del medio fisico y catalogo de espacios y bienes protegidos de la provincia de Cádiz.* AMA: Junta de Andalucia.

Affre, G. and Affre, L. (1967) Observations automnales sur une colonie de Martinets pales *Apus pallidus* a Toulouse. *Alauda* **35**(2): 108–117.

Aidley, D.J. and Wilkinson, R. (1987) Moult of some Palaearctic warblers in northern Nigeria. *Bird Study* **34**(3): 219–225.

Alba, E. (1981) Nota sobre *Sterna bengalensis. Ardeola* **28**: 159.

Alba, E. (1982) Nota sobre *Sterna maxima. Ardeola* **29**: 186.

Alba Padilla, E. and Garrido Sanchez, M. (1983) Observaciones invernales de aves en la desembocadura del Rio Guadalhorce (Málaga). Años 1977–1981. *Alytes* **1**: 225–244.

Alberto, L.J. and Velasco, I. (1988) Limicolas invernantes en España. In *Invernada de Aves en la Peninsula Iberica*, J.L. Tellería (ed): 71–78, SEO Monografias, 1. Madrid: SEO.

Alerstam, T. and Enckell, P.H. (1979) Unpredictable habitats and evolution of bird migration. *Oikos* **33**: 228–232.

Allen, F.G.H. (1971) Observacion de *Egretta alba* en Cádiz. *Ardeola* **15**: 103.

Allen, F.G.H. (1973) Royal and Lesser Crested Terns in Cádiz Province. *Seabird Report* **3**: 36.

Allen, F.G.H., Hoogerheide, J. and Loterijman, J. A. (1971) Observaciones de *Sterna maxima* en Cádiz. *Ardeola* **24**: 144.

Alonso, J.A. (1983) Propuesta de proteccion para la pajarera de Garcillas Bueyeras del Tajo de Barbate (Cádiz. *Alytes* **1**: 139–150.

Alonso, J.A. and Alonso, J.C. (1988) Invernada de la Grulla Comun (*Grus grus*) en la Peninsula Iberica. In *Invernada de Aves en la Peninsula Iberica*, J.L. Tellería (ed): 123–136, SEO, Monografias, 1. Madrid: SEO.

Alonso, J.A. and del Junco, O. (1981) Primer censo de buitreras (1979). Informe sobre el sur y oeste del sistema betico. *Ardeola* **26–27**: 290–309.

Amat, J. (1981) Descripcion de la comunidad de patos del Parque Nacional de Doñana. *Doñana Acta Vert.* **8**: 125–158.

Amat, J. (1982) The nesting biology of ducks in the Marismas of the Guadalquivir, southwestern Spain. *Wildfowl* **33**: 94–104.

Amat, J. (1984) Las poblaciones de aves acuaticas en las Lagunas Andaluzas: composicion y diversidad durante un ciclo anual. *Ardeola* **31**: 61–79.

Amat, J. (1986) Numerical trends, habitat use, and activity of Greylag Geese wintering in southwestern Spain. *Wildfowl* **37**: 35–45.

Amat, J., Diaz Paniagua, C., Herrera, C.M., Jordano, P., Obeso, J.R. and Soriguer, R.C. (1985) Criterios de valoracion de zonas humedas de importancia nacional y regional en funcion de las aves acuaticas. *ICONA Monografias 35.* ICONA.

Amat, J.A. and Ferrer, X. (1988) Respuestas de los patos invernantes en España a diferentes condiciones ambientales. *Ardeola* **35**(1): 59–70.

Amat, J.A. and Raya, C. (1989) Aves en la lista roja—La Malvasía. *La Garcilla* **75**: 8–11.

Andrada, J. and Franco, A. (1975) Sobre el area de invernada de *Falco naumanni* en España. *Ardeola*, **21**(especial): 321–324.

Andrews, J., Beaman, M., Fisher, P., Hereward, T., Heubeck, M., Morton, M., Porter, R. and Round, P. (1977) A 'new' raptor migration route through NE Turkey. *Bull. Ornithol. Soc. Turkey* **14**: 2–5.

Arn, H. (1945) Zur biologie des Alpenseglers *Micropus melba melba. Schweizerisches Archiv. für Ornithol.* **45**(2): 137–184.

Arroyo, B. and Telleria, J.L. (1984) La invernada de las aves en el area de Gibraltar. *Ardeola* **30**: 23–31.

Asensio, B. (1984) Sobre los origenes de los fringilidos migrantes en el extremo sur de España. *Ardeola* **31**: 128–134.

Asensio, B. (1985a) Migracion e invernada en España de *Fringilla coelebs* de origen europeo. *Ardeola* **32**(1): 49–56.

Asensio, B. (1985b) Migracion en España del Verdecillo (*Serinus serinus*), segun los resultados del anillamiento. *Ardeola* **32**(2): 173–178.

Asensio, B. (1985c) Migracion e invernada en España de luganos (*Carduelis spinus*) de origen europeo. *Ardeola* **32**(2): 179–186.

Asensio, B. (1986) La migracion en España del Jilguero (*Carduelis carduelis*, L.) segun los resultados de anillamiento. *Ardeola* **33**(1–2): 176–183.

Ash, J.S. (1969) Spring weights of trans-Saharan migrants in Morocco. *Ibis* **111**: 1–10.

Atkinson-Willes, G.L. (1976) The numerical distribution of ducks, swans and coots as a guide in assessing the importance of wetlands. *Proc. Int. Conf. Wetlands and Waterfowl, Heiligenhafen, 1974*: 199–254.

Atkinson-Willes, G.L. (1978) The numbers and distribution of sea-ducks in north-west Europe, January 1967–1973. *Proc. IWRB/NSEPB Symp. on Sea Ducks, Stockholm 1975*: 28–67.

Baggott, G.K. (1975) Moult, flight muscle "hypertrophy" and premigratory lipid deposition of the juvenile Willow Warbler (*Phylloscopus trochilus*). *J. Zool. Lond.* **175**: 299–314.

Baillon, F. (1989) Nouvelles données sur l'hivernage du Goeland d'Audouin (*Larus audouinii*, Payr.) en Senegambie. *L'Oiseau et RFO* **59**: 296–304.

Bainbridge, I.P. and Minton, C.D.T. (1978) The migration and mortality of the Curlew in Britain and Ireland. *Bird Study* **25**(1): 39–50.

Bairlein, F. (1983) Habitat selection and association of species in European Passerine birds during southward, post-breeding migrations. *Ornis. Scand.* **14**: 239–245.

Bairlein, F. (1985) Body weights and fat deposition of palaearctic passerine migrants in the central Sahara. *Oecologia* **66**: 141–146.

Bairlein, F. (1987) The migratory strategy of the Garden Warbler: a survey of field and laboratory data. *Ringing & Migration* **8**: 59–72.

Bairlein, F. (in press) Migratory strategies of songbirds across the Sahara. *Proc. 7th Pan African Ornithol. Congress. Nairobi, 1988.*

Bairlein, F., Beck, P., Feiler, W. and Querner, U. (1983) Autumn weights of some Palaearctic passerine migrants in the Sahara. *Ibis* **125** 404–407.

Baker, R.R. (1978a) *The Evolutionary Ecology of Animal Migration.* London: Hodder and Stoughton.

Baker, R.R. (1978b) The significance of the Lesser black-backed Gull to models of bird migration. *Bird Study* **27**(1): 41–50.

Bannerman, D.A. (1963) *The Birds of the Atlantic Islands*, vol. 1. Edinburgh: Oliver and Boyd.

Barcena, F., Texeira, A.M. and Bermejo, A. (1984) Breeding seabird populations in the Atlantic sector of the Iberian Peninsula. *ICBP Technical Publication* **2**: 335–345.

Bartels, M. (1931) Beobachtungen an Brutplatzen des Alpenseglers. *Micropus melba melba* (L.). *J. Ornithol.* **79**(1): 1–28.

Beaman, M. (1973) Bosphorus migration, Autumn 1971. *Bull. Ornithol. Soc. Turkey* **8**: 3–4.

Beaman, M. (1977) Further news on raptor migration in the north east. *Bull. Ornithol. Soc. Turkey* **15**: 9.

Beaman, M. and Galea, C. (1974) The visible migration of raptors over the Maltese Islands. *Ibis* **116**: 419–431.

Beaman, M. and Jacobsen, F. (1973) Bosphorus migration, Autumn 1972. *Bull. Ornithol. Soc. Turkey* **10**: 10–11.

Beaubrun, P. (1981) Le Goeland d'Audouin sur les côtes nord–Marocaines en 1980–1981. *Rapport Final. Projet 1413.* IUCN/WWF.

Beaubrun, P. (1983) Le Goeland d'Audouin (*Larus audouinii* Payr.) sur les côtes du Maroc. *L'Oiseau et RFO* **53**: 209–226.

Beaubrun, P. (1985a) Recensement hivernal d'oiseaux marins au Maroc, Janvier 1984. *Documents de l'Institut Scientifique, Rabat,* **9**: 1–19.

Beaubrun, P. (1985b) Arrivée massive et mortalité de Mouettes Tridactyles (*Rissa tridactyla*) en Janvier 1984 le long des côtes du Maroc. *Documents de l'Institut Scientifique, Rabat,* **9**: 21–26.

Beaubrun, P. and Thevenot, M. (1983) Recensement hivernal d'oiseaux d'eau au Maroc—Janvier 1983. Rabat: Direction des Eaux et Forets/Institut Scientifique.

Benvenutti, S. and Ioale, P. (1983) Site attachment and homing ability in passerine birds. *Monitore Zool. Ital.* **17**: 279–294.

Bergier, P. (1987) Les rapaces diurnes du Maroc. Statut. repartition et ecologie. *Annales du CEEP No. 3.* Aix-en-Provence : CEEP.

Bermejo, A., Carrera, E., de Juana, E. and Texeira, A.M. (1986) Primer censo general de gaviotas y charranes (Laridae) invernantes en la Peninsula Iberica (enero de 1984). *Ardeola* **33**: 47–68.

Bernis, F. (1962) Sobre migracion de nuestros passeriformes transaharianos. *Ardeola* **8**: 41–119.

Bernis, F. (1963) La invernada y migracion de nuestros ansares (*Anser anser* y *Anser fabalis*). *Ardeola* **9**: 76–109.

Bernis, F. (1966a) *Aves Migradoras Ibericas*, vol. 1: 1–164. Madrid: SEO.

Bernis, F. (1966b) *Aves Migradoras Ibericas*, vol. 2: 165–318. Madrid: SEO.

Bernis, F. (1966c) *Aves Migradoras Ibericas*, vol. 3: 319–502. Madrid: SEO.

Bernis, F. (1966d) *Aves Migradoras Ibericas*, vol. 4: 503–706. Madrid: SEO.

Bernis, F. (1967) *Aves Migradoras Ibericas*, vol. 5: 707–968. Madrid: SEO.

Bernis, F. (1970) *Aves Migradoras Ibericas*, vol. 6: 1–170. Madrid: SEO.

Bernis, F. (1971) *Aves Migradoras Ibericas*, vols. 7–8: 171–493. Madrid: SEO.

Bernis, F. (1980) *La Migracion de las Aves en el Estrecho de Gibraltar*, vol. 1, *Catedra de Zoologica de Vertebrados*. Madrid: Universidad Complutense.

Berthold, P. (1975) Migration control and metabolic physiology. In *Avian Biology*, vol. V: Farner, D.S. and King, J.R. (eds): 77–128, New York: Academic Press.

Berthold, P. (1976) The control and significance of animal and vegetable nutrition in omnivorous songbirds. *Ardea* **64**: 140–154.

Berthold, P. (1984) The endogenous control of bird migration: a survey of experimental evidence. *Bird Study* **31**(1): 19–27.

Berthold, P. and Querner, U. (1981) Genetic basis of migratory behaviour in European warblers. *Science* **212**: 77–79.

Berthold, P. and Terrill, S.B. (1988) Migratory behaviour and population growth of Blackcaps wintering in Britain and Ireland: some hypotheses. *Ringing & Migration* **9**,(3): 153–159.

Berthon, D. and Berthon, S. (1984) Compte rendu de l'expedition Balbuzard sur les côtes mediterraneennes du Maroc. *L'Oiseau et RFO* **54**: 201–213.

Bibby, C. (1979) Breeding biology on the Dartford Warbler *Sylvia undata* in England. *Ibis* **121**(1): 41–52.

Bibby, C. and Green, R. (1980) Foraging behaviour of migrant Pied Flycatchers *Ficedula hypoleuca* on temporary territories. *J. Anim. Ecol.* **49**: 507–521.

Bibby, C.J. and Green, R. (1983) Food and fattening of migrating warblers in some French marshlands. *Ringing & Migration* **4**(3): 175–184.

Biebach, H. (1983) Genetic determination of partial migration in the European Robin (*Erithacus rubecula*). *Auk* **100**: 601–606.

Biebach, H., Freidrich, W. and Heine, G. (1986) Interaction of bodymass, fat, foraging and stopover period in trans-Saharan migrating passerine birds. *Oecologia* **69**: 370–379.

Bijlsma, R. (1983) The migration of raptors near Suez, Egypt, Autumn 1981. *Sandgrouse* **5**: 19–44.

Bijlsma, R.G. (1987) Bottleneck areas for migratory birds in the Mediterranean Region. An assessment of the problems and recommendations for action. *ICBP Study Report No. 18*.

Blomqvist, S. and Peterz, M. (1984) Cyclones and pelagic seabird movements. *Mar. Ecol. Prog. Ser.* **20**: 85–92.

Blondel, J. (1969) *Synecologie des Passeraux residents et Migrateurs dans le Midi Mediterranéene Français*. Marseille: Cent. Reg. Ped.

Blondel, J. (1970) Biogeographie des oiseaux nicheurs en provence Occidentale, du Mont-Ventoux à la mer Mediterranée. *L'Oiseau et RFO* **40**: 1–47.

Blondel, J. (1978) L'avifaune du Mont-Ventoux, essai de Synthese Biogeographique et Ecologique. *Terre et Vie*, suppl. 1978: 111–145.

Blondel, J. and Blondel, C. (1964) Remarques sur l'hivernage des limicoles et autres oiseaux aquatiques en Maroc. *Alauda* **32**: 250–279.

Bourne, W.R.P. (1955) The birds of the Cape Verde Islands. *Ibis* **97**: 508–556.

Bourne, W.R.P. (1963) A Review of Oceanic Studies of the Biology of Seabirds. *Proc. XIII Int. Ornithol. Congress*: 831–854.

Bourne, W.R.P. and Norris, A.Y. (1966) Observaciones durante una travesía marina de ida y vuelta entre Gran Bretaña y Gibraltar, Septiembre 1964. *Ardeola* **11**: 57–63.

Bourne, W.R.P., Mackrill, E.J., Paterson, A.M. and Yesou, P. (1988) The Yelkouan Shearwater *Puffinus* (*puffinus?*) *yelkouan*. *Brit. Birds* **81**: 306–319.

Branson, N.J.B.A., Ponting, E.D. and Minton, C.D.T. (1978) Turnstone migration in Britain and Europe. *Bird Study* **25**: 181–187.

Breuil, l'Abbé H. (1922) Palaeolithic Man at Gibraltar: new and old facts. *J. Roy. Anthrop. Inst* **LII**: 46–54.

Brickenstein-Stockhammer, C. and Drost, R. (1956) Uber den Zug der europaischen Grasmuchen *Sylvia a. atricapilla, borin, c. communis* und *c. curruca* nach Beringungsergebnissen. *Die Vogelwarte* **18**: 197–210.

Brizhetti, P. (1980) Distribuzione geografica degli uccelli nidificanti in Italia, Corsica e Isole Maltesi. I. Parte introduttiva, famiglie Podicipedidae, Procellariidae, Hydrobatidae. Natura Bresciana, *Ann. Mus. Civ. Sci. Nat. Brescia* **16**: 82–158.

Brooke, R.K. (1975) Seasonal distribution of the migratory European Swift *Apus apus* (Linnaeus) (Aves: Apodidae) in the Ethiopian Region. *Durban Mus. Novit.* **10**: 239–249.

Brown, R.G.B. (1979) Seabirds of the Senegal upwelling and adjacent waters. *Ibis* **121**: 283–292.

Brudenell-Bruce, P.G.C. (1969) White-rumped Swift in southern Spain. *Brit. Birds* **62**: 122–123.

Bruhn, J.F.W. and Jeffrey, B. (1958) Notas sobre aves de Murcia y Cádiz. Observaciones de fin de verano. *Ardeola* **4**: 107–117.

Burgis, M.J. and Morris, P. (1987) *The Natural History of Lakes*. Cambridge: Cambridge University Press.

Callebaut, E. and Snyders, A. (1981) Note on *Sterna bengalensis*. *Ardeola* **28**: 159.

Cameron, R.A.D. Cornwallis, L., Percival, M.L.J. and Sinclair, A.R.E. (1967) The migration of raptors and storks through the Near East in autumn. *Ibis* **109**: 489–501.

Cano, F.H. and Ybarra, L. (1973) Primera observacion en España de *Anas americana*. *Ardeola* **15**: 15–16.

Carboneras, C. (1988) The auks in the western Mediterranean. *Ringing & Migration* **9**(1): 18–26.

Carrera, E. (1988) Invernada de gaviotas y charranes en la Peninsula Iberica. In *Invernada de Aves en la Peninsula Iberica*. J.L. Tellería (ed): 79–95. SEO Monografias, 1. Madrid: SEO.

Carrera, E., Ferrer, X., Martinez-Vilalta, A. and Muntaner, J. (1981) Invernada de Laridos en el Litoral Mediterraneo Catalan y Levantino. *Ardeola* **28**: 35–50.

Carrera, E., Monbailliu, X. and Torre, A. (in press) Ringing recoveries of Yellow-legged Gulls in northern Europe. In *Status and Conservation of Seabirds: Ecogeography and Mediterranean Action Plan*, Medmaravis (ed).

Casement, M.B. (1966) Migration across the Mediterranean observed by radar. *Ibis* **108**: 461–491.

Castan, R. (1955) Le Martinet Pale a Gabes *Apus pallidus brehmorum*. *L'Oiseau et RFO* **25**(3): 172–178.

Castroviejo, J. (1971) Primeras capturas de Ansar Indico (*Anser indicus*) y de Barnacla Cuellirroja (*Branta ruficollis*) en España. *Alauda* **29**: 74–77.

Chapin, J.P. (1939) The birds of the Belgian Congo. Part II. *Bull. Amer. Mus. Nat. Hist.* **75**: 1–632.

Chapman, A. and Buck, W. (1910) *Unexplored Spain*. London.

Chokomian, M. (1981) Nota sobre *Sterna bengalensis*. *Ardeola* **28**: 159.

Christensen, S., Lou, O., Muller., M. and Wohlmuth, H. (1981) The spring migration of raptors in southern Israel and Sinai. *Sandgrouse* **3**: 1–42.

Cody, M.L. (1974) *Competition and the Structure of Bird Communities. Monogr. Pop. Biol.*, vol. 7. Princeton: Princeton University Press.

Cody, M.L. (1978) Habitat selection and interspecific territoriality among the sylvid warblers of England and Sweden. *Ecol. Monogr.* **48**(4): 351–396.

Cody, M.L. (1985) Habitat selection in the sylviine warblers of western Europe and North Africa. In *Habitat Selection in Birds*, M.L. Cody (ed): pp. 86–129. London: Academic Press.

Cody, M.L. and Walter, H. (1976) Habitat selection and interspecific interactions among Mediterranean sylviid warblers. *Oikos* **27**: 210–238.

Collman, J.R. and Croxall, J.P. (1967) Spring migration at the Bosphorus. *Ibis* **109**: 359–372.

Cortés, J.E. (1990) Comments on altitudinal changes in birds in southern Spain. *Alectoris* **7**: 83–85.

Cortés, J.E., Finlayson, J.C., Garcia, E.F.J. and Mosquera, M.A.J. (1980) *The Birds of Gibraltar*. Gibraltar: Gibraltar Bookshop.

Costa, L. (1985) La reproduccion de la gaviota picofina (*Larus genei*) en las Marismas del Guadalquivir (sur de España). *Ardeola* **32**(1): 115–136.

Cox, G.W. (1968) The role of competition in the evolution of migration. *Evolution* **22**: 180–192.

Cramp, S. (1980) *Handbook of the Birds of Europe, the Middle East and North Africa. The Birds of the Western Palaearctic*, vol. II: *Hawks to Bustards*. Oxford University Press.

Cramp, S. (1985) *Handbook of the Birds of Europe, the Middle East and North Africa. The Birds of the Western Palaearctic*, vol. IV: *Terns to Woodpeckers*. Oxford University Press.

Cramp, S. and Simmons, K.E.L. (1977) *Handbook of the Birds of Europe, the Middle East and North Africa. The Birds of the Western Palaearctic*, vol. I. Oxford University Press.

Cramp, S., Bourne, W.R.P. and Saunders, D. (1974) *The Seabirds of Britain and Ireland*. London: Collins.

Creutz, G. (1941) Vom zug des grauen Fliegenschnappers. *Vogelzug* **12**: 1–14.

Curry, P.J. and Sayer, J.A. (1979) The inundation zone of the Niger as an environment for Palaearctic migrants. *Ibis* **121** : 20–40.

Cushing, D.H. (1971) Upwelling and the production of fish. *Adv. Mar. Biol.* **9**: 255–334.

Debussche, M. and Isenmann, P. (1983) La consommation des fruits chez quelques fauvettes mediterrannéenes (*Sylvia melanocephala, S. cantillans, S. hortensis* et *S. undata*), dans la region de Montpellier (France). *Alauda* **51**: 302–308.

Debussche, M. and Isenmann, P. (1984) Origine et nomadisme des Fauvettes à tête noire (*Sylvia atricapilla*) hivernant en zone mediterrannéene française. *L'Oiseau et RFO* **54**: 101–107.

Debussche, M. and Isenmann, P. (1986) L'Ornithochorie dans les garrigues languedociennes: les petits passeraux disseminateurs d'importance secondaire. *L'Oiseau et RFO* **56**: 71–76.

Dejonghe, J.F. (1980) Analyse de la migration prenuptiale des rapaces et des cigognes au Cap Bon (Tunisie). *L'Oiseau et RFO* **50**: 125–147.

Dhont, A.A. (1983) Variations in the number of overwintering Stonechats possibly caused by natural selection. *Ringing & Migration* **4**(3): 155–158.

Diamond, J.M. (1973) Distributional Ecology of New Guinea Birds. *Science* **179**: 759–769.

Dick, W.J.A. and Pienkowski, M.W. (1979) Autumn and early winter weights of waders in north-west Africa. *Ornis Scand.* **10**: 117–123.

Dick, W.J.A., Pienkowski, M.W., Walther, M. and Minton, C.D.T. (1976) Distribution and geographical origins of Knot *Calidris canutus* wintering in Europe and Africa. *Ardea* **64**: 22–47.

Diesselhorst, G. (1973) Zur oekologie von *Sylvia melanocephala* und *S. sarda* auf Sardinien in der endphase der brutzeit. *Op. Zool.* **124**.

Dimarca, A. and Iapichino, C. (1984) *La Migrazione del Falconiformi sullo Stretto di Messina: Primi Dati e Problemi di Conservazione*. Parma: LIPU.

Dolz, J.C. and Gomez, J.A. (1988) Las anatidas y fochas invernantes en España. In *Invernada de Aves en la Peninsula Iberica*. Tellería, J.L. (ed): 55–69. SEO, Monografias, 1. Madrid: SEO.

Dominguez, J.M. (1971) Captura de *Branta canadensis* en Cádiz. *Ardeola* **15**: 125.

Dovrat,, E. (1982) Summary of 5 years' observations of fall raptor migration at Kaffer Kassem. *Torgos* **2**(1): 63–116.

Dowsett, R.J. and Fry, C.H. (1971) Weight loss of trans-Saharan migrants. *Ibis* **113**: 531–533.

Drake, C.F.T. (1867) Notes on the birds of Tangier and Eastern Morocco. *Ibis* **1867**: 421–430.

Dubois, P. and Duhautois, L. (1977) Notes dur l'ornithologie Marocaine. *Alauda* **45**(4): 285–291.

Duckworth, W.L.H. (1911) Cave exploration at Gibraltar in September, 1910. *J. Roy. Anthrop. Inst.* **XLI**: 350–380.

Duckworth, W.L.H. (1912) Cave exploration at Gibraltar in 1911. *J. Roy. Anthrop. Inst.* **XLII**: 515–526.

Duclos, C. (1955) Captura de un *Branta leucopsis* anillado, *Ardeola* **2**: 181.

Durman, F. (1976) Ring Ousel Migration. *Bird Study* **23**(3): 197–205.

Eastham, A. (1968) The avifauna of Gorham's Cave, Gibraltar. *Bull. Inst. Arch.* **7**: 37–42.

Elgood, J.H., Sharland, R.E. and Ward, P. (1966) Palaearctic migrants in Nigeria. *Ibis* **108**: 84–116.

Elkins, N. (1976) Passage of Fan-tailed Warblers (*Cisticola juncidis*) through Gibraltar. *Ibis* **118**: 251–254.

Elkins, N. (1988) Can high-altitude migrants recognize optimum flight levels? *Ibis* **130**(4): 562–563.

Elkins, N. and Etheridge, B. (1974) The Crag Martin in winter quarters at Gibraltar. *Brit. Birds* **67**: 376–387.

Elkins, N. and Etheridge, B. (1977) Further studies of wintering Crag Martins. *Ringing & Migration* **1**(3): 158–165.

Elosegui, J. and Elosegui R. (1977) Desplazamientos de buitres comunes (*Gyps fulvus*) pirenaicos. *Munibe* **29**(1–2): 97–104.

Ena, V. and Purroy, F.J. (1982) *Censos Invernales de Aves Acuaticas en España (enero 1978, 79 y 80)*. Min. Agric., Pesca y Alim.

Engelmoer, M., Piersma, T., Altenburg, W. and Mes. R. (1984) The Banc d'Arguin (Mauritania). In *Coastal Waders and Wildfowl in Winter*, P.R. Evans, J.D. Goss-Custard and W.G. Hale (eds): 293–310. BOU/Cambridge.

Erard, C. (1958) Sur les zones de reproduction et d'hivernage et les migrations du Goeland Railleur *Larus genei*. Brehme. *Alauda* **26**: 86–104.

Erard, C. (1960) Sur l'aire de reproduction, les zones d'hivernage et les migrations de la Mouette Pygmee, *Larus minutus*, Palla. *Alauda* **28**: 196–228.

Erard, C. (1964) Complements a l'etude de l'aire de reproduction et des migrations de Goeland railleur *Larus genei*. *Alauda* **32**: 283–296.

Erard, C. and Vielliard, J. (1966) Comentarios sobre avifauna invernal en el Oriente Español. *Ardeola* **11**: 95–100.

Erard, C. and Yeatman, L. (1966) Coup d'oeil sur les migrations des sylvides d'apres les resultats du baguage en France et au Maghreb. *Alauda* **34**: 1–38.

Escardo, A.L. (1970) The climate of the Iberian Peninsula. In *World Survey of Climatology*, vol. 5. H. Flohn (ed). Amsterdam: Elsevier.

Estrada, M., Vives, P. and Alcaraz, M. (1985) Life and the productivity of the Open Sea. In *Western Mediterranean: Key Environments*, R. Margalef (ed): 148–197. Oxford: Pergamon.

Evans, P.R. (1969) Winter fat deposits and overnight survival of yellow buntings. *J. Anim. Ecol.* **38**: 415–423.

Feare, C.J. (1983) Mass spring migration of European Rollers *Coracias garrulus* in eastern Tanzania. *Bull. Brit. Ornithol. Cl.* **103**(2): 39–40.

Fernandez-Cruz, M. (1975) Revision de las actuales colonias de ardeidas de España. *Ardeola* **21**(especial): 65–126.

Fernandez-Cruz, M. (1981) La migracion e invernada de la Grulla comun (*Grus grus*) en España. Resultados del proyecto Grus (Crane Project). *Ardeola* **26–27**: 1–164.

Fernandez-Cruz, M. (1982) Capturas de aves anilladas en España: informes nos 17–22 (años 1973–1978). *Ardeola* **29**: 33–175.

Fernandez-Cruz, M., Martin-Novella, C., Paris, M., Izquierdo, E., Camacho, M., Rendon, M. and Rubio, J.C. (1988) Revision y puesta al dia de la invernada del Flamenco (*Phoenicopterus ruber roseus*) en la Peninsula Iberica. In *Invernada de Aves en la Peninsula Iberica*, J.L. Tellería (ed): 23–53. SEO, Monografias, 1. Madrid: SEO.

Fernandez Palacios, J. and Figueroa Clemente, E. (1987) Le vegetacion de las Marismas Gaditanas del entorno del Estrecho. *Congr. Int. Estrecho de Gibraltar*: 407–424.

Fernandez-Palacios, A., Fernandez-Palacios, J. and Gil Gomez, B. (1988) Guias naturalistas de la Provincia de Cádiz. I. El litoral. Diputacion de Cádiz.

Fernandez Pasquier, V. (1982) Relaciones entre la estructura de la vegetacion y las comunidades de pajaros en las sierras de Algeciras. Tesis Licenc., Universidad de Sevilla.

Ferns, P.N. (1975) Feeding behaviour of autumn passage migrants in north-east Portugal. *Ringing & Migration* **1**(1): 3–11.

Ferrer, X. and Martinez Vilalta, A. (1986) Fluctuations of the Gull and Tern populations in the Ebro Delta, NE Spain, 1960–85. In *Mediterranean Marine Avifauna*, Medmaravis and Manbailliu, X. (eds), NATO ASI Series G, vol. 12: 273–284. Berlin: Springer-Verlag.

Figueroa, E., Fernandez-Palacios, J. and Castellanos, E. (1987) Estuarios y marismas del litoral de Huelva (SO, España). *Actas VII Reunion sobre el Cuaternario, Santander*: 211–214.

Finlayson, J.C. (1977) Wintering Chiffchaffs. *Bull. Gib. Ornithol. Group* **1**(2): 8–9.

Finlayson, J.C. (1978a) Roosting behaviour of the Crag Martin *Hirundo rupestris* in its winter quarters at Gibraltar. *Alectoris* **1**(1): 23–29.

Finlayson, J.C. (1978b) Irruptive behaviour in the Dartford Warbler *Sylvia undata dartfordiensis*, Latham, in Gibraltar. *Alectoris* **1**(1): 47.

Finlayson, J.C. (1979a) The ecology and behaviour of closely related species at Gibraltar (with special reference to swifts and warblers). D.Phil. Thesis, University of Oxford.

Finlayson, J.C. (1979b) Movements of the Fan-tailed Warbler *Cisticola juncidis* at Gibraltar. *Ibis* **121**: 487–489.

Finlayson, J.C. (1980) The recurrence in winter quarters at Gibraltar of some scrub passerines. *Ringing & Migration* **3**: 32–34.

Finlayson, J.C. (1981) Seasonal distribution, weights and fat of passerine migrants at Gibraltar. *Ibis* **123**: 88–95.

Finlayson, J.C. (1983) Recent trends and changes in the status of the birds of Gibraltar. *Alectoris* **5**: 2–9.

Finlayson, J.C. (1990) The distribution of the Coal Tit *Parus ater* in southern Spain. *Alectoris* **7**: 86–87.

Finlayson, J.C. and Cortés, J.E. (1984) The migration of Gannets *Sula bassana* past Gibraltar in spring. *Seabird* **7**: 19–22.

Finlayson, J.C. and Cortés, J.E. (1987) The birds of the Strait of Gibraltar. Its waters and northern shore. *Alectoris* **6**: 1–74.

Finlayson, J.C. and Holliday, S. (1990) The Eleonora's Falcon *Falco eleonorae* at Gibraltar. *Alectoris* **7**: 88–89.

Finlayson, J.C., Garcia, E.F.J., Mosquera, M.A. and Bourne, W.R.P. (1976) Raptor migration across the Strait of Gibraltar. *Brit. Birds* **69**: 77–87.

Fisher, R. (1930) *The Genetical Theory of Natural Selection.* Oxford: Oxford University Press.

Flos, J. (1985) The Driving Machine. In *Western Mediterranean: Key Environments*, Margalef, R. (ed): 60–99. Oxford: Pergamon.

Fogden, M.P.L. (1972) Premigratory dehydration in the Reed Warbler (*Acrocephalus scirpaceus*) and water as a factor limiting migratory range. *Ibis* **114**: 548–552.

Franco, A., Garcia Rua. A. and de Juana, E. (1973) Observacion de un posible *Pluvialis dominica* en Cádiz. *Ardeola* **19**: 19–20.

Frochot, B. (1971) L'evolution saisonniere de l'avifaune dans une futaie de chenes en Bourgogne. *Terre et Vie* **25**: 145–182.

Fry, C.H., Ash, J.S. and Ferguson-Lees, I.J. (1970) Spring weights of some Palaearctic migrants at Lake Chad. *Ibis* **112**: 58–82.

Fry, C.H., Britton, P.L. and Horne, J.F.H. (1974) Lake Rudolf and the Palaearctic exodus from East Africa. *Ibis* **116**: 44–51.

Furness, R.W. (1978) Movements and mortality rates of Great Skuas ringed in Scotland. *Bird Study* **25**(4): 229–238.

Furness, R.W. (1987) *The Skuas.* Calton: T. and A.D. Poyser.

Garcia, E.F.J. (1973) Seabird activity in the Strait of Gibraltar: a progress report. *Seabird Report* **1971**: 30–36.

Garcia, E.F.J. (1977) The systematic list 1 July–31 December 1976. *Bull. Gib. Ornithol. Group* **1**(2): 11–19.

Garcia, E.F.J. (1983) An experimental test of competition for space between Blackcaps *Sylvia atricapilla* and Garden Warblers *Sylvia borin* in the breeding season. *J. Anim. Ecol.* **52**: 795–805.

Garcia Rua, A.E. (1975) Migrantes y migracion visible en la zona del Estrecho de Gibraltar (años 1972–1974). *Ardeola* **21**: 627–655.

Garrod, D.A.E., Buxton, L.H.D., Eliot Smith, G. and Bate, D.M.A. (1928) Excavation of a Mousterian rock-shelter at Devil's Tower, Gibraltar. *J. Roy. Anthrop. Inst.* **LVIII**: 33–115.

Gathreaux, S.A. Jnr (1978) The ecological significance of behavioural dominance. In *Perspectives in Ethology*. P.P.G. Bateson and P.H. Klopfer (eds): 17–54. New York: Plenum.

Gathreaux, S.A. Jnr (1982) The ecology and evolution of avian migration systems. In *Avian Biology*, vol. 6, D.S. Farner, J.R. King and K.C. Parkes (eds): 93–168. New York: Academic Press.

Gauci, C. and Sultana, J. (1979) Evidence of spring passage of Sardinian Warblers in Malta. *Il-Merill* **19**: 18–19.

Gehu, J.M. and Rivas Martinez, S. (1984) Classification des communautes halophiles europeenes. In *La Vegetation Halophile en Europe. Collection Sauvegarde de la Nature N° 20*: 34–40. Strasbourg: Conseil de l'Europe.

Geyr von Schweppenberg, H. (1963) Zur Terminologie und Theorie der Leitlinie. *J. Ornithol.* **104**: 191–204.

Giraud-Audine, M. and Pineau, J. (1973) *Emberiza striolata* and *Vanellus gregarius* dans le Tangerois. *Alauda* **41**: 317.

Gomez, J.A., Garcia, R.D., Franco, A.M. and Matheu, V.N. (1983) Memoria de la estacion ornitologica Albufera. *La Ciutat* (supp. especial).

Gonzalez, B. and del Junco, O. (1968) Notas sobre aves de la Provincia de Cádiz. *Ardeola* **12**: 214–217.

Gonzalez Diez, M. (1965) Nueva observacion de *Egretta alba* en España. *Arrdeola* **10**: 60.

Greenberg, R.S. (1980) Demographic aspects of long-distance migration. In *Migrant Birds in the Neotropics*, Keast, A. and Morton, E. (eds): 493–504. Washington D.C.: Smithsonian Institute Press.

Greenwood, P.J. (1980) Mating systems, philopatry and dispersal in birds and mammals. *Anim. Behav.* **28**: 1140–1168.

Greenwood, P.J. and Harvey, P.H. (1976) The adaptive significance of variation in breeding area fidelity of the Blackbird (*Turdus merula* L.). *J. Anim. Ecol.* **45**: 887–898.

Grimes, L.G. (1969) The Spotted Redshank *Tringa erythropus* in Ghana. *Ibis* **111**: 246–251.

Grimmett, R.F.A. and Jones, T.A, (1989) Important Bird Areas in Europe. *ICBP Technical Publication No. 9*. Cambridge.

Groebbels, F. (1928) Zur physiologie des vogelzuges. *Verh. Ornithol. Ges. Bayern* **18**: 44–74.

Grupo Ornitologico del Estrecho (1987) Proyecto de proteccion del Estuario del Rio Guadiaro. San Roque, Cádiz.

Gwinner, E. and Wiltschko, W. (1978) Endogenously controlled changes in migratory direction of Garden Warbler, *Sylvia borin*. *J. Comp. Physiol.* **125**: 267–273.

Haartman, L. von (1968) The evolution of resident versus migratory habit in birds. Some considerations. *Ornis Fennica* **45**: 1–7.

Haila, Y., Tiainen, J. and Vepsalainen, K. (1986) Delayed autumn migration as an adaptive strategy of birds in northern Europe: evidence from Finland. *Ornis Fennica* **63**: 1–9.

Hale, W.G. (1971) A revision of the taxonomy of the Redshank. *Zool. J. Linn. Soc.* **50**: 199–268.

Hale, W.G. (1973) The distribution of the Redshank, *Tringa totanus*, in the winter range. *Zool. J. Linn. Soc.* **53**: 177–236.

Hale, W.G. (1980) *Waders*. London: Collins.

Hartley, P.H.T. (1949) The biology of the Mourning Chat in winter quarters. *Ibis* **91**: 393–413.

Heim de Balsac, H. (1951) Les dates de migration et de reproduction du Martinet Pale en Afrique du Nord. Tests ethologiques de differentiation specifique. *Alauda* **17–18**: 108–112.

Heim de Balsac, H. and Mayaud N. (1962) Les Oiseaux du Nord-Ouest de l'Afrique. Paris: Lechevalier.

Henty, C.J. (1961) Further observations on migrants in south-west Iberia. *Ibis* **103**: 28–36.

Herrera, C.M. (1974) Paso otonal de *Sylvia borin* y *S. communis* en la Reserva de Doñana. *Doñana Acta Vert.* **1**: 83–119.

Herrera, C.M. (1977) Ecologia alimenticia del petirrojo (*Erithacus rubecula*) durante su invernada en encinares del sur de España. *Doñana Acta Vert.* **4**: 35–59.

Herrera, C.M. (1978a) On the breeding distribution pattern of European migrant birds: MacArthur's theme reexamined. *Auk* **95**: 496–509.

Herrera, C.M. (1978b) Ecological correlates of residence and non-residence in a Mediterranean passerine bird community. *J. Anim. Ecol.* **47**: 871–890.

Herrera, C.M. (1981a) Fruit variation and competition for dispersers in natural populations of *Smilax aspera*. *Oikos* **36**: 51–58.

Herrera, C.M. (1981b) Are tropical fruits more rewarding to dispersers than temperate ones? *Amer. Nat.* **188**: 896–907.

Herrera, C.M. (1981c) *Prunus mahaleb* and birds: the high-efficiency seed dispersal system of a temperate fruiting tree, *Ecol. Monogr.* **51**(2): 203–218.

Herrera, C.M. (1984a) Adaptation to frugivory of Mediterranean Avian seed dispersers. *Ecology* **65**(2): 609–617.

Herrera, C.M. (1984b) A study of avian frugivores, bird-dispersed plants, and their interaction in Mediterranean scrublands. *Ecol. Monogr.* **54**(1): 1–23.

Herrera, C.M. and Hidalgo, J. (1974) Sobre la presencia invernal de *Clamator glandarius* en Andalucia. *Areola* **20**: 307–311.

Herroelen, P. (1953) Het gedrag van de gierzwaluw *Apus apus* L. in Belgisch Kongo. *Gerf.* **43**: 161–164.

Heyder, R. (1927) Merkwurdiges Verweilen von Seglern, *Ornithol. Mber.* **33**: 178–179.

Hidalgo, J. (1971) Captura de *Emberiza aureola* en Cádiz. *Ardeola* **15**: 155–156.

Hidalgo, J. (1989) Sobre el Tarro Canelo en las Marismas del Guadalquivir. *Ardeola* **36**(2): 237.

Hidalgo, J. and Rodriguez, P. (1972) Captura de *Anser erythropus* en las Marismas del Guadalquivir. *Ardeola* **16**: 254–255.

Hidalgo, J. and Rubio, J.M. (1974) Sobre *Anser indicus* en las Marismas del Guadalquivir. *Ardeola* **20**: 332–333.

Hilgerloh, G. (1988) Radar observations of passerine trans-saharan migrants in Southern Portugal. *Ardeola* **35**(2): 221–232.

Hiraldo, F. (1971) Observaciones de *Tringa stagnatilis* en las Marismas del Guadalquivir. Ardeola **15**: 136–138.

Hoffmann, L., Hue, F., Schwarz, M. and Wackernagel, H. (1951) Nouvelles observations sur les Martinets Pales. *L'Oiseau et RFO* **21**(4): 304–309.

Hogg, P., Dare, P.J. and Rintoul, J.V. (1984) Palaearctic migrants in the central Sudan. *Ibis* **126**: 307–331.

Holliday, S. (1990a) Report on the birds of the Strait of Gibraltar: 1987. *Alectoris* **7**: 3–48.

Holliday, S. (1990b) List of unpublished records of significance for Gibraltar to 31 December 1986. *Alecctoris* **7**: 49–57.

Hoogendoorn, W. and Mackrill, E.J. (1987) Audouin's Gull in southwestern palaearctic. *Dutch Birding* **9**: 99–107.

Hope Jones, P. (1975) The migration of Redstarts through and from Britain. *Ringing & Migration* **1**(1): 12–17.

Hope Jones, P., Mead, C.J. and Durham, R.F. (1977) The migration of the Pied Flycatcher from and through Britain. *Bird Study* **24**(1): 2–14.

Hopkins, T.S. (1985) Physics of the Sea. In *Western Mediterranean: Key Environments*, Margalef, R. (ed): 100–125. Oxford: Pergamon.

Horin, D. and Dovrat, E. (1983) Autumn migration in Kaffer Kassem, Autumn 1982. *Torgos* **3**(1): 60–85.

Houghton, E.W. (1973) *Highlights of the NATO–Gibraltar Bird Migration Radar Study*. Supplement to the proceedings of the Bird Strike Committee Europe, Paris Conference. May 1973.

Hovette, C. (1972) Nouvelles acquisitions avifaunistiques de la Camargue. *Alauda* **40**: 343–352.

Hsu. K. (1983) *The Mediterranean was a Desert*. Princeton: Princeton University Press.

Hue, F. (1951) Le Martinet Pale nidificateur en France continentale. *L'Oiseau et RFO* **21**(3): 217–221.

Iapichino, C. (1984a) *Sula bassana*, Stercorariidae e *Larus melanocephalus* nella Sicillia Orientale. *Riv. Ital., Ornnithol. Milano* **54**(1–2): 38–44.

Iapichino, C. (1984b) Rondine di mare del ruppell, *Sterna bengalensis*, in Sicilia. *Riv. Ital., Ornithol. Milano* **54**(1–2): 96–97.

Ingram, C. (1960) Lavendera Blanca Enlutada en Andalucia. *Ardeola* **6**: 392.

Irby, L.H. (1875) *The Ornithology of the Straits of Gibraltar*. London: Taylor and Francis.

Irby, L.H. (1895) *The Ornithology of the Straits of Gibraltar*, 2nd edn, revised and enlarged. London: Taylor and Francis.

Isenmann, P. (1972) Notas sobre algunas especies de aves acuaticas en las costas Mediterraneas españolas (enero 1972). *Ardeola* **16**: 242–245.

Isenmann, P. (1973) Le passage de la Sterne Caspienne *Hydroprogne caspia* en 1971 et 1972 en Camargue. *Alauda* **49**(4): 365–370.

Isenmann, P. (1975) Le passage prenuptial de la Guifette Leucoptere (*Chlidonias leucopterus*) en Camargue. *Bull. Mus. Hist. Nat. Marseille* **35**: 149–151.

Isenmann, P. (1976) Note sur le stationnement hivernal des larides sur la côte Mediterranéenne d'Espagne. *L'Oiseau et RFO* **46**: 135–142.

Isenmann, P. (1978) Note sur les stationnements de larides sur la côte Atlantique du Maroc. *Bull. Inst. Scientifique* **2**: 77–86.

Isenmann, P. and Czajkowski, M.A. (1978) Note sur un recensement de Larides entre Nice et Naples en decembre 1977. *Riv. Ital. Ornithol.* **48**(2): 143–148.

Jacob, J.P. and Courbet, B. (1980) Oiseaux de mer nicheurs sur la côte algerienne. *Gerfaut* **70**: 385–401.

Johnston, D.W. (1958) Sex and age characters and salivary glands of the Chimney Swift. *Condor* **60**: 73–84.

Jones, P.J. and Ward, P. (1976) The level of reserve protein as the proximate factor controlling the timing of breeding and clutch-size in the Red-billed Quelea *Quelea quelea*. *Ibis* **118**: 547–574.

de Jong, A. (1974) *Raptor Migration over Cap Bon, Spring 1974*. Report, Wageningen.

Jordano, P. (1981) Alimentación y relaciones troficas entre los passeriformes en paso otonal por una localidad de Andalucía central. *Doñana Acta Vert.* **8**: 103–124.

Jordano, P. (1982) Migrant birds are the main seed dispersers of blackberries in southern Spain. *Oikos* **38**: 183–193.

Jordano, P. (1983) Fig seed predation and dispersal by birds. *Biotropica* **15**: 38–41.

Jordano, P. (1985) El ciclo anual de los paseriformes frugivoros en el matorral Mediterraneo del sur de España: importancia de su invernada y variaciones interanuales. *Ardeola* **32**: 69–94.

Jordano, P. (1987) Frugivory, external morphology and digestive system in Mediterranean sylviid warblers. *Sylvia* species. *Ibis* **129**(2): 175–189.

Jorgensen, O.H. (1976) Migration and aspects of population dynamics in the Grey Wagtail *Motacilla cinerea*. *Ornis Scand.* **7**: 13–20.

Jourdain, F.C.R. (1936) The birds of Southern Spain. Part I. Passeres (pt.). *Ibis* 725–763.

Jourdain, F.C.R. (1937) The birds of Southern Spain. Part II. Passeres (concluded). *Ibis*: 110–152.

de Juana, E. 1976 (1977). Nuevos datos de invierno sobre aves de Marruecos. *Ardeola* **23**: 49–62.

de Juana, E. (1982) Noticiario ornitologico. *Ardeola* **29**: 177–193.

de Juana, E. (1984a) The status and conservation of seabirds in the Spanish Mediterranean. *ICBP Technical Publication No. 2*: 347–361. Cambridge: Cambridge University Press.

de Juana, E. (1984b) Noticiario ornitologico. *Ardeola* **30**: 115–121.

de Juana, E. (1985) Noticiario ornitologico. *Ardeola* **32**: 409–424.

de Juana, E. (1987) Noticiario ornitologico. *Ardeola* **34**: 123–133.

de Juana, E. (1988a) Noticiario ornitologico. *Ardeola* **35**: 167–174.

de Juana, E. (1988b) Noticiario ornitologico. *Ardeola* **35**: 297–316.

de Juana, E. (1989) Noticiario ornitologico. *Ardeola* **36**: 231–264.

de Juana, E. and Paterson, A.M. (1986) The status of the seabirds in the extreme western Mediterranean. In *Mediterranean Marine Avifauna*, Medmaravis and X. Monbailliu (eds), NATO ASI, series G, vol. 12: 39–106. Berlin: Springer Verlag.

de Juana, E. and Varela, J.M. (1980) La conservacion de las Islas Chafarinas y de su gran colonia de cria de la Gaviota de Audouin. *SEO Bull.* **60**: 28–31.

de Juana, E., de Juana, F. and Galvo, S. (1988) La invernada de las aves de presa [O. Falconiformes] en la Peninsula Iberica. In *Invernada de Aves en la Peninsula Iberica*, J.L. Tellería (ed): 97–122. SEO Monografias, 1. Madrid: SEO.

del Junco, O. (1966) Nota sobre migracion de avefrais (*V. vanellus*). *Ardeola* **11**: 148–149.

del Junco, O. and Dominguez, J.M. (1975) Ardeidas: Nueva colonia en Andalucía. *Ardeola* **22**: 103.

Kalela, O. (1954) Populationsokologische Gesichtspunke zur Entstehung des Vogelzuges. *Ann. Zool. Soc. Vanamo (Helsinki)* **16**: 1–30.

Karlsson, L., Persson, K., Petterson, J. and Walinder, G. (1988) Fat–weight relationships and migratory strategies in the Robin *Erithacus rubecula* at two stop-over sites in south Sweden. *Ringing & Migration* **9**(3): 160–168.

Karr, J.R. (1976) Seasonality, resource availability and community diversity in tropical bird communities. *Amer. Nat.* **110**: 973–994.

Kerlinger, P. (1989) *Flight Strategies of Migrating Hawks*. Chicago: University of Chicago Press.

Kersten, M. and Smit, C.J. (1984) The Atlantic coast of Morocco. In *Coastal Waders and Wildfowl in Winter*, P.R. Evans, J.D. Goss-Custard and W.G. Hale (eds): 276–292. Cambridge: BOU/Cambridge University Press.

King, J.R. (1972) Adaptive periodic fat storage by birds. *Proc. XV Int. Orn. Congress*: 200–217.

Kluyver. H.N. (1966) Regulation of a bird population. *Ostrich* **6** (suppl.): 389–396.

Knight, P.J. and Dick, W.J.A. (1975) Recensement de Limicoles au Banc d'Arguin (Mauretanie). *Alauda* **43**: 363–385.

Koskimies, J. (1950) The life of the Swift, *Micropus apus* (L.), in relation to the weather. *Ann. Acad. Sci. Fenn. A IV Biol.*: 1–151.

Lack, D. (1943) The problem of partial migration. *Brit. Birds* **37**: 122–130.

Lack, D. (1944) The problem of partial migration. *Brit. Birds* **37**: 143–150.

Lack, D. (1954) *The Natural Regulation of Animal Numbers*. Oxford: Oxford University Press.

Lack, D. (1956) *Swifts in a Tower*. London: Methuen,

Lack, D. *Apus pallidus* in Northern Rhodesia. *Ostrich* **29**(2): 86.

Lack, D. (1966) *Population Studies of Birds*. Oxford: Oxford University Press.

Lack, D. (1968) Bird migration and natural selection. *Oikos* **19**: 1–9.

Lack, D. (1971) *Ecological Isolation in Birds*. Oxford: Blackwell.

Lack, D. and Lack, E. (1951) Decouverte de la reproduction d'*Apus pallidus* en France. *Alauda* **19**: 49.

Lack, D. and Lack, E. (1952) The breeding behaviour of the Swift. *Brit. Birds* **45**: 186–215.

Lack, D. and Owen, D.F. (1955) The food of the Swift. *J. Anim. Ecol.* **24**(1): 120–136.

Lacombe, H. and Richez, C. (1982) *The Regime of the Strait of Gibraltar*. Elsevier.

Laferrere, M. (1972) Sur le mode de nidification d'*Apus pallidus* (Shelley) et d'*Apus affinis* (Gray). *Alauda* **40**: 290–292.

Langslow, D.R. (1976) Weights of Blackcaps on migration. *Ringing & Migration* **1**(2): 78–91.

Langslow, D. (1977) Movements of Black Redstarts between Britain and Europe as related to occurrences at observatories. *Bird Study* **24**(3): 169–178.

Lathbury, G. (1970) A review of the birds of Gibraltar and its surrounding waters. *Ibis* **112**: 25–43.

Lawn, M.R. (1982) Pairing systems and site tenacity of the Willow Warbler *Phylloscopus trochilus* in southern England. *Ornis Scand.* **13**: 193–199.

Leach, I.H. (1981) Wintering Blackcaps in Britain and Ireland. *Bird Study* **28**(1): 5–14.

Leck, C.F. (1972) The impact of some North American migrants at fruiting trees in Panama. *Auk* **89**: 842–850.

Le Mao, P. and Yesou, P. (in press) The annual cycle of Balearic Shearwaters and west Mediterranean yellow-legged Gullls: an ecological approach. In *Status and Conservation of Seabirds: Ecogeography and Mediterranean Action Plan*, Medmaravis (ed).

Lloyd, C. (1974) Movement and survival of British Razorbills. *Bird Study* **21**: 102–116.

Lope, F. de, Guerrero, J., Garcia, M.E., Cruz, C. de la, Carretero, J.J., Navarro, J.A., Silva, E., Otano, J. (1983) Masiva afluencia de pinzones reales (*Fringilla montifringilla*) en la baja extremadura. *Alytes* **1**: 393–400.

Lopez Gordo, J.L. (1975) Sobre la migracion posnupcial del Abejaruco (*Merops apiaster*) en el Estrecho de Gibraltar. *Ardeola* **21**: 615–625.

Lundberg, P. (1987) Partial Bird Migration and Evolutionarily Stable Strategies. *J. Theor. Biol.* **125**: 351–360.

MacArthur, R.H. and Wilson, E.O. (1967) *The Theory of Island Biogeography*. Princeton: Princeton University Press.

MacArthur, R.H., Diamond, J.M. and Karr, J.R. (1972) Density compensation in Island Faunas. *Ecology* **53**: 330–342.

Mackrill, E.J. (1989) Audouin's Gulls in Senegal in January 1989. *Dutch Birding* **11**(3): 122–123.

Magnin, G. (1986) Assessment of illegal shooting and catching of birds in Malta. *ICBP Study Report No. 13*. Cambridge.

Mainwood, A.R. (1976) The movements of Storm Petrels as shown by ringing. *Ringing & Migration* **1**(2): 98–104.

Margalef, R. and Castelvi, J. (1967) Fitoplancton y produccion primaria de la costa catalana, de julio de 1966 a julio de 1967. *Inv. Pesq.* **31**(3): 491–502.

Martin, J.A. (1977) Nota sobre Cerceta aliazul (*Anas discors*). *Ardeola* **22**: 108.

Martin, J.A. (1981) Nota sobre *Sterna maxima*. *Ardeola* **28**: 159.

Martinez A. and Motis, A. (1982) Quelques observations sur la presence du Goeland d'Audouin (*Larus audouinii*) pendant le periode postnuptial au Delta de l'Ebre. *Misc. Zool.* **6**: 158–161.

Martinez Vilalta, A. (1988) Espectacular aumento de Gaviotas y Charranes en el Delta del Ebro. *GIAM Bol.* **3**: 3.

Martinez Vilalta, A., Ferrer, X. and Carboneras, C. (1984) Situacion de los pagalos (*Stercorarius* spp.) en el litoral catalan (NE de la Peninsula Iberica). *Misc. Zool.* **8**: 217–223.

Mason. C.F. (1976) Breeding biology of the *Sylvia* warblers. *Bird Study* **23**: 213–232.

May, R. (1975) Patterns of species abundance and diversity. In *Ecology and Evolution of Communities*, M.L. Cody and J.M. Diamond (eds): 81–120. Cambridge: Belknap.

Mayaud, N. (1982a) Les oiseaux du nord-ouest de l'Afrique: Notes complementaires. *Alauda* **50**(1): 45–67.

Mayaud, N. (1982b) Les oiseaux du nord-ouest de l'Afrique: Notes complementaires. *Alauda* **50**(2): 114–145.

Mayaud, N. (1982c) Les oiseaux du nord-ouest de l'Afrique: Notes complementaires. *Alauda* **50**(4): 286–309.

Mayaud, N. (1983) Les oiseaux du nord-ouest de l'Afrique: Notes complementaires. *Alauda* **51**(4): 271–301.

Mayaud, N. (1984) Les oiseaux du nord-ouest de l'Afrique: Notes complementaires. *Alauda* **52**(4): 266–284.

Maynard Smith, J. (1974) The theory of games and the evolution of animal conflicts. *J. Theor. Biol.* **47**: 209–221.

McNaughton, S.J. and Wolf, L.L. (1970) Dominance and the niche in ecological systems. *Science* **167**: 131–139.

Mead, C.J. (1968) BOU supported expedition to north-west Iberia, autumn, 1967. *Ibis* **110**: 235–236.

Mead, C.J. (1974) The results of ringing auks in Britain and Ireland. *Bird Study* **21**: 45–86.

Mead, C.J. (1979) Mortality and causes of death in British Sand Martins. *Bird Study* **26**(2): 107–112.

Mead, C.J. (1983) *Bird Migration*. Country Life.

Mead, C.J. and Harrison, J.D. (1979) Overseas movements of British and Irish Sand Martins. *Bird Study* **26**: 87–98.

Medway, Lord G. (1962) The relation between the reproductive cycle, moult and changes in the sublingual salivary glands of the Swiftlet *Collocalia maxima* Hume. *Proc. Zool. Soc. Lond.* **138**: 305–315.

Mehlum, F. (1983a) Weight changes in migrating Robins *Erithacus rubecula* during stop-over at the island of Store Faerdar. Outer Oslofjord, Norway. *Fauna Norv. Ser. C, Cinclus* **6**: 57–61.

Mehlum. F. (1983b) Resting time in migrating Robins *Erithacus rubecula* at Store Faerder, Outer Oslofjord, Norway. *Fauna Norv. Ser. C, Cinclus* **6**: 62–72.

Melcher, R. (1977) Observacion de Andarrios de Terek en las Marismas de Hinojos. *Ardeola* **22**: 134–135.

Michelot, J.L. and Laurent, L. (1988) Observations estivales d'oiseaux marins en mer Mediterranée occidentale. *L'Oiseau et RFO* **58**: 18–27.

Mikkola, H. (1983) *Owls of Europe*. Calton: T. and A.D. Poyser.

Minas, H.J., Coste, B., Gascard, J.C., Le Corre, P. and Richez, C. (1982) Proprietes chimiques et circulation des masses d'eau dans le detroit de Gibraltar et en mer d'Alboran (Campagne MEDIPROD IV du N.O.JK. Charcot, Oct.–Nov.1981). *Rapp. Proc. Verg. Reun. Comm. Int. Mer Medit.* **28**(2): 129–130.

Mooney, H.A. (1981) Primary production in the Mediterranean region. In *Ecosystems of the World II. Mediterranean-type Shrublands*, F. di Castri, D.W. Goodall and R.L. Specht (eds): 249–255. Amsterdam: Elsevier.

Mooney, H.A. and Kummerow, J. (1981) Phenological development of plants in Mediterranean-climate regions. In *Ecosystems of the World II*, F. di Castri, D.W. Goodall and R.L. Specht (eds): 303–307. Amsterdam: Elsevier.

Mooney, H.A., Parsons, D.J. and Kummerow, J. (1974) Plant development in Mediterranean climates. *Ecological Studies No. 8*, Leith, H. (ed): 255–268. New York: Springer-Verlag.

Moreau, R.E. (1961) Problems of Mediterranean-Saharan migration. *Ibis* **103**: 373–427, 580–623.

Moreau, R.E. (1967) Water-birds over the Sahara. *Ibis* **109**: 232–259.

Moreau, R.E. (1969) Comparative weights of some trans-Saharan migrants at intermediate points. *Ibis* **111**: 621–624.

Moreau, R.E. (1972) *The Palaearctic–African Bird Migration Systems*. London: Academic Press.

Moreau. R.E. and Dolp, R.M. (1970) Fat, water, weights and wing-lengths of autumn migrants in transit on the north-west coast of Egypt. *Ibis* **112**: 209–228.

Morel, G. (1968) Contribution a la synecologie des oiseaux du Sahel senegalais. Paris Mem. O.R.S.T.O.M. 29.

Morel, G. (1973) The Sahel Zone as an environment for Palaearctic migrants. *Ibis* **115**: 413–417.

Morel, G. and Roux, F. (1966) Les migrateurs palaearctiques au Senegal. *Terre Vie* **113**: 19–72, 143–176.

Morgan, R. and Glue, D. (1977) Breeding, mortality and movements of Kingfishers. *Bird Study* **24**(1): 15–24.

Morse, D.H. (1971) The insectivorous bird as an adaptive strategy. *Ann. Rev. Ecol. Syst.* **2**: 177–200.

Morse, D.H. (1974) Niche breadth as a function of social dominance. *Amer. Nat.* **108**: 818–830.

Mosquera, M.A.J. (1978) Plumage variation in raptors as observed at Gibraltar. *Alectoris* **1**(1): 35–42.

Mosquera, M.A.J. and Cortés, J.E. (1978) The systematic list: July–December. *Alectoris* **1**(1): 59–69.

Mougin, J.L., Jouanin, C. and Roux, F. (1987) Les annees sabbatiques des Puffins cendres *Calonectris diomedea* borealis de l'ile Selvagem Grande (30°09'N, 15°52'W). Influence dusexe et de l'age. *L'Oiseau et RFO* **57**: 368–381.

Mountfort, G. and Ferguson-Lees, I.J. (1961) The Birds of the Coto Doñana. *Ibis* **103**: 86–109.

Muntaner, J. and Ferrer, X. (1981) Invernada del Porron Bastardo *Aythya marila* en España. *Misc. Zool.* **VII**: 139–144.

Murton, R.K., Westwood, N.J. and Isaacson, A.J. (1974) Factors affecting egg-weight, body weight and moult of the Woodpigeon *Columba palumbus*. *Ibis* **116**: 52–73.

Muselet, D. (1982) Les quartiers d'hivernage des Sternes pieregarins (*Sterna hirundo*) europeennes. *L'Oiseau et RFO* **52**: 219–235.

Muselet, D. (1985) Les quartiers d'hivernage des Sternes naines europeennes *Sterna albifrons albifrons*. *L'Oiseau et RFO* **55**: 183–193.

Naik, R.M. and Naik, S. (1965) Studies on the House Swift *Apus affinis* (J.E. Gray) 5. Moult Cycle in the adults. *Pavo* **3**: 96–120.

Nelson, B. (1978) *The Gannet*. Calton: T. and A.D. Poyser.

Nelson, B. (1980) *Seabirds: their Biology and Ecology*. Hamlyn.

Newton, I. (1968) The temperature, weights and body compositions of moulting Bullfinches. *Condor* **70**: 323–332.

Newton, I. (1969) Winter fattening in the Bullfinch. *Physiol. Zool.* **42**: 96–107.

Newton, I. and Evans, P.R. (1966) Weights of birds in winter. *Bird Study* **13**: 96–98.

Niethammer, G. (1938) *Handbuch der Deutschen Vogellumde*. Band II. Leipzig.

Nisbet, I.C.T. (1960) El Bisbita de Richard en Cádiz. *Ardeola* **6**: 391–392.

Nisbet, I.C.T., Evans, P.R. and Feeny, P.P. (1961) Migration from Morocco into south-west Spain in relation to weather. *Ibis* **103a**: 349–372.

Norman, S.C. and Norman, W. (1985) Autumn movements of Willow Warblers ringed in the British Isles. *Ringing & Migration* **6**(1): 7–18.

Norman, S.C. and Norman W. (1986) Spring movements of Willow Warblers ringed in the British Isles. *Ringing & Migration* **7**(2): 75–84.

O'Connor, R. (1985) Behaviour regulation of bird populations; a review of habitat use in relation to migration and residency. In *Behavioural Ecology: Ecological Consequences of Adaptive Behaviour*, R.M. Sibly and R.H. Smith (eds): 105–142. Oxford: Blackwell.

Osterlof, S. (1977) Migration, wintering areas and site tenacity of the European Osprey *Pandion h. haliaetus. Ornis. Scan.* **8**: 61–78.

Paterson, A.M. (1987) A study of seabirds in Malaga Bay, Spain. *Ardeola* **34**(2): 167–192.

Paterson, A.M. (1990) *Aves Marinas de Malaga y Mar de Alborán*. Agencia de medio Ambiente.

Peach, W. and Baillie, S. (1990) Population changes on constant effort sites. 1988–1989. *BTO News* **167**: 6–7.

Pearson, D.J. (1972) The wintering and migration of Palaearctic passerines at Kampala, southern Uganda. *Ibis* **114**: 43–60.

Pennycuick, C.J. (1969) The mechanics of migration. *Ibis* **111**: 525–556.

Petterson, J. and Hasselquist, D. (1985) Fat deposition and migration capacity of Robins *Erithacus rubecula* and Goldcrests *Regulus regulus* at Ottenby, Sweden. *Ringing & Migration* **6**: 66–76.

Pettitt, R.G. (1972) A comparison of auk movements in spring in north-west Spain and western Ireland. *Seabird Report* **1970**: 9–15.

Pienkowski, M.W. (1975) Studies on coastal birds and wetlands in Morocco 1972. Joint report of the University of East Anglia expedition to Tarfaya Province, Morocco 1972, and the Cambridge Sidi Moussa expedition 1972. Norwich: University of East Anglia.

Pienkowski, M.W. and Evans, P.R. (1985) The role of migration in the population dynamics of birds. In *Behavioural Ecology: Ecological Consequences of Adaptive Behaviour*, R.M. Sibly and R.H. Smith (eds): 331–352. Oxford: Blackwell.

Pienkowski, M.W. and Knight, P.J. (1977) La migration post-nuptiale des limicoles sur la côte atlantique au Maroc. *Alauda* **45**: 165–190.

Pienkowski, M.W., Knight, P.J., Staynard, D.J. and Argyle, F.B. (1976) Primary moult of waders on the Atlantic coast of Morocco. *Ibis* **118**: 347–365.

Pienkowski, M.W., Lloyd, C.S. and Minton, C.D.T. (1979) Seasonal and migrational weight changes in Dunlins. *Bird Study* **26**: 134–148.

Pineau, J. and Giraud-Audine, M. (1974) Notes sur les migrateurs traversant l'extrème nord-ouest du Maroc. *Alauda* **42**: 159–188.

Pineau, J. and Giraud-Audine, M. (1976) Notes sur les oiseaux hivernant dans l'extreme nord-ouest du Maroc. *Alauda* **44**: 47–75.

Pineau, J. and Giraud-Audine, M. (1977) Notes sur les oiseaux nicheurs de l'extreme nord-ouest du Maroc. *Alauda* **45**: 75–104.

Pineau, J. and Giraud-Audine, M. (1979) *Les Oiseaux de la Peninsule Tingitane*. Rabat: Institut Scientifique.

Polunin, O. and Walters, M. (1985) *A Guide to the Vegetation of Britain and Europe*. Oxford: Oxford University Press.

Porter, R.F. and Beaman, M.A.S. (1985) A resumé of raptor migration in Europe and the Middle East. In *Conservation Studies of Raptors*. ICBP Technical Publication No. 5.

Porter, R.F. and Willis, I. (1968) The autumn migration of soaring birds at the Bosphorus. *Ibis* **110**: 520–537.

Prater, A.J. (1975) The wintering population of the Black-tailed Godwit. *Bird Study* **22**: 169–176.

Prater, A.J. (1976) The distribution of coastal waders in Europe and North Africa. *Proc. Int. Conf. on Conservation of Wetlands and Waterfowl, Heiligenhafen 1974*: 255–271.

Prater, A.J. (1981) *Estuary Birds of Britain and Ireland*. Calton: T. and A.D. Poyser.

da Prato, S.R.D. and da Prato, E.S. (1983) Movements of Whitethroats *Sylvia communis* ringed in the British Isles. *Ringing & Migration* **4**(4): 193–210.

Purroy, A.J. (1988) Sobre la invernada de la Paloma Torcaz (*Clumba palumbus*) en Iberia. In *Invernada de Aves en la Peninsula Iberica*, J.L. Tellería (ed): 137–151. SEO, Monografias, 1. Madrid: SEO.

Quiros, J.L. de (1920) Excursion ornitologica a La Janda (Marzo-Abril de 1920). *Bol. Real. Soc. Esp.* **XX**: 236–248.

Rait-Kerr, H. (1934–35) The birds of Gibraltar. Articles in the *Gibraltar Chronicle*.

Rappole, J.H. and Warner, D.W. (1976) Relationships between behaviour, physiology and weather in avian transients at a migration stopover site. *Oecologia (Berlin)* **26**: 193–212.

Ree, V. (1973) Birds of the delta of the River Guadalquivir, S. Spain. *Sterna* **12**: 225–268.

Reid, S.G.W. (1885) Winter notes from Morocco. *Ibis*: 241–255.

Ritzel, L. (1980) Der Durchzug von Greifvogeln und Storchen uber den Bosporus im Fruhjahr 1978. *Vogelwarte* **30**: 149–162.

Rivas Goday, S. (1968) Algunas novedades fitosociologicas de España meridional. *E. Collectania Botanica* **7**: 1015–1023.

Rivas Martinez, S. (1975) La vegetacion de la clase Quercetea ilicis en España y Portugal. *Anal. Inst. Bot. Cavanilles* **31**: 205–259.

Roo, A. de (1966) Age characteristics in adult and subadult swifts *Apus apus apus* (L.) based on interrupted and delayed wing-moult. *Gerfaut* **56**: 113–134.

Rooth, J. (1971) The occurrence of the Greylag Goose *Anser anser* in the western part of its distribution area. *Ardea* **59**: 17–27.

de la Rosa, D. and Moreira, J.M. (1987) *Evaluacion Ecologica de Recursos Naturales de Andalucía*. Sevilla: Agencia del Medio Ambiente, Junta de Andalucía.

Roux, F. (1973) Censuses of Anatidae in the central delta of the Niger and the Senegal delta—January 1972. *Wildfowl* **24**: 63–80.

Rowan, M. and Bernis, F. (1956) Barbate (Cádiz) y su colonia de garzas. *Ardeola* **3**: 71–81.

Rubio Garcia, J.C. (1986) Estudio de la Comunidad de Limicolos de las Marismas del Odiel (Huelva). *Oxyura* **3**(1): 97–132.

Ruiz Martinez, F.J., Almorza Gomar, D. and Fernandez Zapata, J.M. (1990) The salt-pans of the Bahía de Cádiz as a new and unique nesting habitat for Herring Gulls *Larus argentatus*. *Alectoris* **7**: 70–76.

Safriel, U.N. and Lavee, D. (1988) Weight changes of cross-desert migrants at an oasis— do energetic considerations alone determine the length of stopover? *Oecologia* **76**: 611–619.

Sagot, F. and Tanguy le Gac, J. (1984) *Orgambideska Col Loibre, Pertuis Pyreneens. Fasc. 1: Rapaces & Cigognes 1979–1983.* Editions d'Utovie, Lys.

Salomonsen, F. (1955) The evolutionary significance of bird migration. *Dan. Bio. Medd.* **22**: 1–62.

Salt, G.W. (1957) An analysis of avifauna in the Teton Mountains and Jackson Hole. Wyoming. *Condor* **59**: 373–393.

Santos, T. and Tellería, J.L. (1985) Patrones generales de la distribucion invernal de passeriformes en la peninsula Iberica. *Ardeola* **32**(1): 17–30.

Santos, T., Suarez, F. and Telleria, J.L. (1981) The bird communities of Iberian Juniper woodlands (*Juniperus thurifera*) L.). In *Censos de Aves en el Mediterraneo*, F.J. Purroy (ed): 79–88. Leon: University of Leon.

Saunders, H. (1871) A List of the Birds of Southern Spain. *Ibis* **1871**: 54–68, 205–225, 384–402.

Schuster, L. (1930) Über die Beerennahrung der Vogel. *J. für Orn.* **78**: 273–301.

Schwabl, H., Wingfield, J.C. and Farner, D.S. (1984) Endocrine correlates of autumnal behavior in sedentary and migratory individuals of a partially migratory population of the European Blackbird (*Turdus merula*). *Auk* **101**: 499–507.

Scott, D.A. (1982) Problems in the management of waterfowl populations. *Proc. 2nd Tech. Meeting Western Migratory Bird Management, Paris 1979*,: 89–106. Slimbridge: IWRB.

Seel, D.C. (1977) Migration of the northwestern European population of the Cuckoo *Cuculus canorus*, as shown by ringing. *Ibis* **119**(3): 309–322.

Serle, W., Morel, G.J. and Hartwig, W. (1977) *A Field Guide to the Birds of West Africa.* London: Collins.

Sharrock, J.T.R. (1967) The sea-watching at Cape Clear Bird Observatory. *Seabird Bull.* **3**: 21–26.

Simmons, K.E.L. (1951) Interspecific territorialism. *Ibis* **93**: 407–413.

Smith, G.A. (1979) Spring weights of selected trans-Saharan migrants in north-west Morocco. *Ringing & Migration* **2**(3): 151–155.

Smith, K.D. (1965) On the birds of Morocco. *Ibis* **107**: 493–526.

Smith, K.D. (1968) Spring migration through southeast Morocco. *Ibis* **110**(4): 452–492.

Smith, K.D. (1972) The winter distribution of *Larus audouinii*. *Bull. BOC* **92**: 34–37.

Snow, D.W. (1967) *A Guide to Moult in British Birds.* BTO Field Guide 11.

Snow, D.W. (1978) Relationships between the European and African Avifaunas. *Bird Study* **25**(3): 134–148.

Solis, F. (1977) Note on *Calidris maritima*. *Ardeola* **24**: 259.

Somsag, S. (1981) Autumn migration over the Bosphorus. *Bull. Orn. Soc. Middle East* **6**: 6.

Soriguer, R.C. (1978) Primera cita de Collalba Yebelica (*Oenanthe leucopyga* Brehm.) en la Peninsula Iberica. *Doñana Acta Vert.* **5**: 109–110.

Spaans, A.L. (1977) Are Starlings faithful to their individual winter quarters? *Ardea* **65**: 83–87.

Spaepen, J. (1953) De terk van de Boompieper, *Anthus trivialis* (L.), in Europa en Afrika. *Gerfaut* **43**: 178–230.

Spaepen, J. (1957) De trek van kleine gele kwikstaart *Motacilla flava*. *Gerfaut* **47**: 17–43.

Staav, R. (1977) Etude du passage de la Sterne Caspienne *Hydroprogne caspia* en Mediterrannée a partir des reprises d'oiseaux bagues en Suede. *Alauda* **45**: 265–270.

Stanford, W.P. (1953) Winter distribution of the Grey Phalarope *Phalaropus fulicarius*. *Ibis* **95**: 483–491.

Steinfatt, O. (1932) Der Bosporus als Landbrucke fur den Vogelzug zwischen Europa und Kleinasien. *J. Ornithol.* **80**: 354–383.

Stresemann, E. (1948) Die Wanderungen des Pirols (*Oriolus o. oriolus*). *Orn. Ber.* **1**: 126–142.

Sutherland, W.J. and Brooks, D.J. (1981) The autumn migration of raptors, storks, pelicans and Spoonbills at the Belen Pass, southern Turkey. *Sandgrouse* **2**: 1–21.

Swanquist, R. (1981) Raptor migration summary, Eilat, spring 1978–1979. *Torgos* **1**(2): 14–16.

Taning, A.V. (1933) The winter quarters of the phalaropes. *Ibis* **13**: 132–133.

Taylor, L.R. (1963) Analysis of the effect of temperature on insects in flight. *J. Anim. Ecol.* **32**: 99–117.

Tejero, E., Camacho, I. and Soler, M. (1983) La alimentacion de la curruca cabecinegra (*Sylvia melanocephala*, Gmelin 1788) en olivares de la provincia de Jaén (otono–invierno). *Doñana Acta Vert.* **10**(1): 133–153.

Tellería, J.L. (1979) La migracion postnuptiale du Guepier d'Europe *Merops apiaster* L. au detroit de Gibraltar en 1977. *Alauda* **47**: 139–150.

Tellería, J.L. (1981) *La Migracion de las Aves en el Estrecho de Gibraltar. Volumen II: Aves no Planeadoras.* Madrid: Universidad Complutense.

Tellería, J.L. (1987) Biogeografia de la avifauna nidificante en España central. *Ardeola* **34**(2): 145–166.

Tellería, J.L. and Potti, J. (1984a) La segregacion espacial de los Turdidos (Turdidae) en el sistema central. *Ardeola* **31**: 103–113.

Tellería, J.L. and Potti, J. (1984b) La distribucion de las currucas (G. Sylvia Cl. Aves) en el sistema central (España). *Doñana Acta Vert.* **11**(1): 93–103.

Tellería, J.L., Santos, T. and Carrascal, L.M. (1988) La invernada de los paseriformes (O. Passeriformes) en la Peninsula Iberica. In *Invernada de Aves en la Peninsula Iberica*, J.L. Tellería (ed): 153–166. SEO, Monografias, 1. Madrid: SEO.

Terborgh, J. (1971) Distribution on environmental gradients: Theory and a preliminary interpretation of distributional patterns in the Avifauna of the Cordillera Vilcabamba, Peru. *Ecology* **52**: 23–40.

Terborgh, J. (1977) Bird species diversity on an Andean elevation gradient. *Ecology* **58**: 1007–1019.

Terborgh, J. and Weske, J.S. (1975) The role of competition in the distribution of Andean Birds. *Ecology* **56**: 562–576.

Thake, M.A. (1980) Gregarious behaviour, among migrating Honey Buzzards (*Pernis apivorus*). *Ibis* **122**: 500–505.

Thevenot, M. (1973) Compte-rendu d'activite de la station de baguage du Maroc 1971. *Bull. Soc. Nat. Phys. Maroc* **53**: 199–245.

Thevenot, M. (1982) Contribution a l'etude ecologique des Passeraux forestiers du Plateau Central et de la corniche du Moyen Atlas (Maroc). *L'Oiseau et RFO* **52**: 96–152.

Thevenot, M. and Thuoy, P. (1974) Nidificacion ou hivernage d'especes peu connues ou nouvelles pour le Maroc. *Alauda* **42**: 51–56.

Thevenot, M., Bergier, R. and Beaubrun, P. (1981) Compte-Rendu d'ornithologie Marocaine. Annee 1980. *Documents de l'Institut Scientifique No. 6.* Rabat: Institut Scientifique.

Thevenot, M., Beaubrun, P., Baouab, R.E. and Bergier, P. (1982) Compte Rendu d'ornithologie Marocaine. Annee 1981. *Documents de l'Institut Scientifique No. 7.* Rabat: Institut Scientifique.

Thiollay, J.M. (1974) Nidification du Martinet Pale *Apus pallidus* et du Martinet alpin *Apus melba* en Afrique occidentale. *Alauda* **42**: 223–225.

Thiollay, J.M. (1975) Migration de printemps au Cap Bon (Tunisie). *Nos Oiseaux* **33**: 109–121.

Thiollay, J.M. (1977) Importance des populations de rapaces migrateurs au Mediterranée occidentale. *Alauda* **45**: 115–121.

Thiollay, J.M. and Perthius, A. (1975) La migration d'automne a Gibraltar (1–20 Octobre 1974): Analyse et interpretation. *Ardeola* **21**: 595–614.

Thomas, D.K. (1979) Figs as a food source of migrating Garden Warblers in southern Portugal. *Bird Study* **26**: 187–191.

Thomson, A.L. (1939) The migration of the Gannet: result of marking in the British Isles. *Brit. Birds* **32**: 282–289.

Thuoy, P. (1976) Variations saisonnieres de l'avifaune d'une localite du Maroc Atlantique. *Alauda* **44**(2): 135–151.

Torre, J. (1955) El matorral en Yebala (Marruecos Español). Madrid: CSIC.

Torres Esquivias, J.A. and Claveria, A. (1985) Estudio de la comunidad de paseriformes del bosque mixto mediterraneo de la Sierra de Hornachuelos. (Cordoba–España). Córdoba: Univ. de Córdoba.

Tramer, E.J. (1974) Proportion of wintering North American birds in disturbed and undisturbed dry tropical habitats. *Condor* **76**: 460–464.

Trigo de Yarto, E. (1960) Notas sobre capturas de aves raras e interesantes. *Ardeola* **6**: 367–369.

Tuck, L.M. (1971) The occurrence of Greenland and European birds in Newfoundland. *Bird Banding* **42**: 184–209.

Tuke, A.J.S. (1953) *An Introduction to the Birds of Southern Spain and Gibraltar*. Gibraltar: Gibraltar Chronicle.

Turcek, F.J. (1961) *Oekologische Beziehungen der Vogel und Geholze*. Bratislava: Slovak Academy of Sciences.

Tye, A. (1984) Attacks by shrikes *Lanius* spp. on wheatears *Oenanthe* spp.: competition. kleptoparasitism, or predation? *Ibis* **126**(1): 95–102.

Vagliano, C. (1985) The continental and island migration route of the southeast Mediterranean problems and propositions. In: *Conservation Studies on Raptors*, I. Newton and R.D. Chancellor (eds): *ICBP Technical Publication No. 5*: 263–269.

Valverde, J.A. (1955–56) Aves de Marruecos Español en Julio. *Ardeola* **2**: 87–114, 213–240.

Valverde, J.A. (1957) *Aves del Sahara Espanol*. Madrid.

Valverde, J.A. (1959) Cuatro interesantes especies en Andalucía. *Ardeola* **5**: 143–148.

Valverde, J.A. (1960) Vertebrados de las Marismas del Guadalquivir. *Arch. Inst. Aclimatacion* **19**: 1–168.

Van den Berg, A.B. (1990) Habitat of Slender-billed Curlews in Morocco. *Brit. Birds* **83**(1): 1–7.

Vargas, J.M., Antunez, A. and Blasco, M. (1978) Comportamiento reproductivo y alimentario de la Pagaza Piconegra (*Gelochelidon nilotica*) en la laguna de Fuente de Piedra, Malaga. *Ardeola* **24**: 227–231.

Vaughan, R. (1961) *Falco eleonorae*. *Ibis* **103a**: 114–128.

Vega, A. (1988) *Report on the Palmones Marsh*. GOES.

Verheyen, R.F. (1970) Resultats de l'oeuvre Belge de baguement. 1969. *Gerfaut* **60**: 327–401.

Verner, W. (1890) Shooting expeditions in the neighbourhood. *The Gibraltar Directory*: 103–108.

Verner, W. (1910) *My Life among the Wild Birds in Spain*. London: John Bale, Sons and Danielsson, Ltd.

Verner, W. (1911) Shooting. *The Gibraltar Directory*: 73–81.

Vilalta, I. and Carrera i Gallissa, E. (1983) Nova colonia de Gavina Corsa (*Larus audouinii* Payr.) a l'Estat Espanyol. *Bull. Inst. Cat. Hist. Nat.* **49** (Sec. Zool., **5**): 159–161.

Voous, K.H. (1960) *Atlas of European Birds*. London: Nelson.

Waechter, J. d'A. (1964) The excavation of Gorham's Cave Gibraltar. *Inst. Archaeol. Bull.* **4**: 189–221.

Walter, H. (1979) *Eleanora's Falcon. Adaptations to Prey and Habitat in a Social Raptor.* Chicago: University of Chicago Press.

Ward, P. (1963) Lipid levels in birds preparing to cross the Sahara. *Ibis* **105**: 109–111.

Ward, P. (1969) The annual cycle of the Yellow-vented Bulbul *Pycnonotus goiavier* in a humid equatorial environment. *J. Zool. Lond.* **157**: 25–45.

Weickert, P. (1960) Nidificacion de Gaviota Picofina en Doñana (Huelva). *Ardeola* **6**: 383.

Weitnauer, E. (1947) Am Neste des Mauerseglers, *Apus apus apus* (L.). *Orn. Beob.* **44**: 133–182.

Welch, G. and Welch, H. (1988) The autumn migration of raptors and other soaring birds across the Bab-el-Mandeb Straits. *Sandgrouse* **10**: 26–50.

White, G. (1789) *The Natural History of Selborne*. London: Penguin.

Wiens, J.A. (1989a) *The Ecology of Bird Communities*. Volume 1: *Foundations and Patterns, Cambridge Studies in Ecology*. Cambridge: Cambridge University Press.

Wiens, J.A. (1989b) *The Ecology of Bird Communities*. Volume 2: *Processes and Variations. Cambridge Studies in Ecology*. Cambridge: Cambridge University Press.

Williamson, K. (1960) *Identification for Ringers. The Genera* Cettia, Locustella, Acrocephalus *and* Hippolais. BTO Field Guide No. 7. Tring: BTO.

Williamson, K. (1962) *Identification for Ringers. The Genus* Phylloscopus. BTO Field Guide No. 9. Tring: BTO.

Williamson, K. (1964) *Identification for Ringers. The Genus* Sylvia. BTO Field Guide No. 9. Tring: BTO.

Willis, E.O. (1966) The role of migrant birds at swarms of Army Ants. *Living Bird* **5**: 187–231.

Wimpfheimer, D., Bruun, B., Baha el Din, S.M. and Jennings, M.C. (1983) *The Migration of Birds of Prey in the Northern Red Sea Area*. New York: Holy Land Conservation Fund.

Winstanley, D., Spencer, R. and Williamson, K. (1974) Where have all the Whitethroats gone? *Bird Study* **21**: 1–16.

Witt, H.-H. (1976) *Zur Biologie der Koralenmowe*, Larus audouinii. Bonn.

Witt, H.-H. (1984) Dichte, Diversitat und Aquitat von Seevogelge-meinschaften im Mittelmeeraum und die sie beeinflussenden Faktoren. *Okol. Vogel.* **6**: 131–139.

Witt, H.-H., de Juana, E. and Varela, J.M. (1984) Seevogel (Procellariiformes, Pelecaniformes, Lariformes) der marokkanischen Nordkuste. *Beitr. Vogelkd., Jena* **30**(2): 81–89.

Wood, B. (1978) Weights of Yellow Wagtails wintering in Nigeria. *Ringing & Migration* **2**(1): 20–26.

Wood, B. (1982) The trans-Saharan spring migration of Yellow Wagtails (*Motacilla flava*). *J. Zool. Lond.* **197**: 267–283.

Wood, B. (1989) Comments on Bairlein's hypothesis of trans-Saharan migration by short stages with stopovers. *Ringing & Migration* **10**(1): 48–52.

Ybarra, L. (1966) Captura de un *Anser indicus* en Hinojos. *Ardeola* **11**: 145–156.

Yeates, G.K. (1945) *Bird Life in Two Deltas*. London: Faber and Faber.

Yesou, P. (1982) A propos de la presence remarquable du Puffin cendre *Calonectris diomedea* pres des côtes du golfe de Gascogne et de la mer Celtique en 1980. *L'Oiseau et RFO* **52**(3): 197–217.

Yesou, P. (1985a) Nouvelles donnees sur la mue de *Puffinus p. mauretanicus*. *L'Oiseau et RFO* **55**: 177–182.

Yesou, P. (1985b) Le cycle de presence du Goeland leucophee *Larus cachinnans michahellis* sur le littoral Atlantique français: l'exemple des marais d'Olonne. *L'Oiseau et RFO* **55**: 93–105.

Yesou, P. (1986) Balearic Shearwaters summering in France. In *Mediterranean Marine Avifauna*, Medmaravis and X. Monbailliu (eds): NATO ASI Series G vol. 12: 39–106. Berlin: Springer-Verlag.

Yom-Tov, Y. (1984) On the difference between the spring and autumn migrations in Eilat, southern Israel. *Ringing & Migration* **5**: 141–144.

Yunick, R.P. (1983) Winter site fidelity of some northern finches (Fringillidae). *J. Field Ornithol.* **54**(3): 254–258.

Zamora, R. (1987) Variaciones altitudinales en la composicion de las comunidades nidificantes de aves de Sierra Nevada (Sur de España). *Doñana Acta Vert.* **14**: 83–106.

Zamora, R. (1988) Composicion y estructura de las comunidades de paseriformes de alta montana de Sierra Nevada (SE de España). *Ardeola* **35**(2): 197–220.

Zamora, R. and Camacho, I. (1984a) Evolucion estacional de la comunidad de aves en un encinar de Sierra Nevada. *Doñana Acta Vert.* **11**(1): 25–44.

Zamora, R. and Camacho, I. (1984b) Evolucion anual de la avifauna en un robledal en Sierra Nevada. *Doñana Acta Vert.* **11**(2): 129–150.

Zink, G. (1973) *Der zug Europaischer Singvogel: ein Atlas der Weider funde Beringter Vogel*, vol. 1. Vogelwarte, Radolfzell.

Zink, G. (1975) *Der zug Europaischer Singvogel: ein Atlas der Weider funde Beringter Vogel*, vol. 2. Vogelwarte, Radolfzell.

Zwarts, L. (1972) Bird counts in Merja Zerga, Morocco, December 1970. *Ardea* **60**: 120–123.

Index